U0572897

"中国法治论坛"编辑委员会

主　任：李　林

副主任：冯　军　张明杰

委　员（以姓氏笔画为序）：

王晓晔　王敏远　刘作翔

刘俊海　孙宪忠　杨一凡

李明德　吴玉章　张广兴

陈泽宪　陈　甦　邹海林

周汉华　陶正华

学术秘书：胡微波

中国法治论坛

CHINA FORUM ON THE RULE OF LAW

中国法治论坛
CHINA FORUM ON THE RULE OF LAW

法治发展与法治模式：
中国与芬兰的比较

Rule of Law in China and Finland：
Comparative Studies of their Development
History and Model

主　编　李　林

副主编　谢增毅

社会科学文献出版社
SOCIAL SCIENCES ACADEMIC PRESS (CHINA)

总　序

　　故宫北侧，景山东麓，一座静谧的院落。蕴藉当年新文化运动的历史辉煌与典雅的土地上，流淌着中国法律理论的潺潺清泉，燃烧着法治思想的不息火焰。多年来，尤其是 1978 年中国改革开放以来，一代代法律学者在这里辛勤劳作，各领风骚，用他们的心血和智慧，谱写了许多可以载入史册的不朽篇章。

　　为了记载和激扬法治学问，推动法治，继往开来，中国社会科学院法学研究所设立"中国法治论坛"系列丛书。一方面，重新出版最近 20 余年来有重要文献价值的论文集，如始于 20 世纪 70 年代末的关于人治与法治、法律面前人人平等、起草新宪法以及法律阶级性等问题的专项讨论，90 年代初以来关于人权、市场经济法律体系、依法治国、司法改革、WTO 与中国法、环境保护、反酷刑、死刑存废等问题的专项讨论；另一方面，陆续编辑出版今后有足够学术含量和价值、比较成熟的国际国内相关研究项目和会议的论文集。

　　法律乃人类秩序规则。法治乃当世共通理念。"中国法治论坛"不限于讨论中国的法律问题,也并非由中国社会科学院的学者独自担当。我们期望,这个论坛能够成为海内外学者、专家和广大读者、听众共同拥有的一个阐解法意、砥砺学问的场所,一片芳草茵茵、百花盛开的园地。

夏　勇

2003 年 6 月 6 日

Preface to China Forum
on the Rule of Law

To the north of the Forbidden City and east of Jingshan Hill lays a peaceful courtyard. It is the seat of the Institute of Law of Chinese Academy of Social Sciences, the most prestigious national institute in China devoted to legal research and legal education. On this small piece of land, rich in historical splendor and elegance of the New Culture Movement of 1919, flows an inexhaustible spring of Chinese legal theory and rages an inextinguishable flame of the ideal of the rule of law. Since several decades ago, especially since the "reform and opening up" in 1978, generations of Chinese legal scholars have been working diligently on this small piece of land and, with their wisdom and painstaking efforts, composed many immortal masterpieces of law that will go down in history.

China Forum on the Rule of Law is a series of books published by the Institute of Law with a view to carrying on the past and opening a new way for the future in the research of the rule of law and promoting the development of the rule of law in China. In this series, we will, on the one hand, republish papers published in China in the past 20 years which are of great historical significance, such as those relating to the discussions since late 1970s on the rule of man and the rule of law, the equality of everyone before the law, the drafting of the new Constitution, and the class nature of thelaw and those relating to debates since early 1990s on human rights, the legal system under the market economy, ruling the country in accordance with the law, judicial reform, WTO and China, environmental protection, eradication of torture, and abolition of the death penalty. On the other hand, we will edit and publish papers from future research projects and academic seminars, both in China and abroad, which are relatively mature and of sufficiently high academic value.

The law is the norms of order for all mankind and the rule of law a universal ideal of all peoples in the contemporary world. China Forum on the Rule of Law is not limited to the discussion of the legal issues in China, nor will it be monopolized by scholars of the Institute of Law. We sincerely hope that it will be able to provide an opportunity for scholars, experts, as well as readers to freely express their ideas and exchange their views on legal issues, a forum for a hundred schools of thoughts to contend, and a garden for a hundred flowers to bloom.

Xia Yong

6 June 2003

目　录

第二部分　宪法实施与行政法治

第三部分　刑事法治与经济社会管理法治

CONTENTS

Part Two: Implementation of the Constitution and Administrative Law

Part Three: Criminal Law and Economic and Social Management

Preface

In the Analects of Confucius we find some interesting remarks about law and governance. In Book 2 the master says: 'He who exercises government by means of his virtue may be compared to the north polar star, which keeps its place and all the stars turn towards it.' Pole Star is characterized by its stability, which gives it a special significance among the stars.

Rule of law and good governance certainly are of equal importance for all people, for all states and nations, irrespective of their particular histories and traditions. Just like the Pole Star, they cannot be really reached, but rather always remain ideals and aspirations. In the folk narratives the Pole Star often also guides people seeking the way either forward or home.

The Finnish national poem, Kalevala, has been collected on the basis of very old oral tradition. A particular magical artifact, Sampo, which is a source of wealth and happiness figures prominently in Kalevala. It is not quite clear what Sampo actually was. It may have been some kind of a mill. Sampo has been connected with the world order so that it may have got its name from the name of the pillar that was thought to keep the firmament standing. On top of the pillar was the pole-star, like a needle stitch in the firmament. In the mindset of the northern people, the pole-star and the firmament seem to have played an important role. It is highly inspiring to think that the cosmological views also may have had an impact of thinking about law and governance.

It has been a very wise and foresighted decision of the Academy of Finland and the Chinese Academy of Social Sciences to start cooperation in the field of legal science and to focus especially on issues of rule of law, comparative law, and governance. I was lucky to be able to participate already in the first Sino-Finnish seminar held in Beijing in 2009. Delegates from three Finnish universities had been invited to participate. The outcome of that meeting has been published.

This volume presents the outcomes of the two bilateral colloquia that followed. The 2010 colloquium was held in Helsinki, focusing on a comparison of the models of rule of law between Finland and China. In 2011, we again convened in Beijing, discussing this time matters of rule of law and social governance.

I am very happy that also this time the fruits of the bilateral meeting can be published and that in this way our contributions may reach the broader academic audiences of our respective countries, and even internationally. In spite of our different legal, historical, and political traditions, we have a lot to learn from each other. Personally I believe that imagination is an important aspect of legal thinking. Our imagination is always limited. We need to test our ideas against a variety of models, and experience is a very important aspect of law. Law is also a public good and must be cherished and cultivated as such. Law also must always be practiced in the service of the people.

In the Nordic legal tradition the Instructions that the Christian theologian and lawyer Olaus Petri, a pupil of the famous Martin Luther, formulated almost 500 years ago have served the function of formulating a certain ethos of law. Also they tell about rule of law and good governance in terms of ethics and virtues. He instructs, e. a.:

> *All the laws have been enacted for the sake of justice and equity and not for fines. For a fine is to punish those who break the law; but the law prefers not to be broken and would willingly go without fines.*

Today, law is increasingly looked at in terms of its instrumental values, as means to ends. No doubt that is part of the truth as we increasingly need to regulate the lives in our societies for various purposes. As scholars we always need to remember that underneath the fast-moving surface of law there are deeper levels which actually strongly contribute to the success also of the instrumental functions of law. Rule of law, democracy, human rights, fundamental rights, good governance, legal and ethical traditions, they all become relevant when we wish to reach a deeper-level understanding of law.

We are very grateful to our Chinese partners for an intensive cooperation with us over the last years. We have seen a rapidly growing interest in this activity on the Finnish side, the last sign of it being that seven Finnish universities and one research institute have in January 2013 jointly established a National Center of Chinese Law and Chinese Legal Culture, coordinated by the University of Helsinki. We wish to provide, for example, for all law students basic knowledge about Chinese law.

The ties between various Finnish and Chinese academic institutions have also been strengthened by way of establishing bilateral cooperation agreement. On the Chinese side, the director of Institute of Law of the Chinese Academy of Social Sciences, professor Li Lin, has been a determined promoter of the Sino-Finnish cooperation. A good start is half way to success. We certainly have had a good start. I would, on behalf of the Finnish legal academia, wish to thank our Chinese partners for the cooperation so far.

Kimmo Nuotio

Dean

Faculty of Law

University of Helsinki

序　言

在孔子的《论语》中我们发现了一些有关法律和治理方面的令人颇感兴趣的言论。例如在该书第二篇中，这位大师说道："为政以德，譬如北辰，居其所而众星共之。"北辰即北极星，因其稳定而在众星中被赋予了特殊的地位。

法治和良政对于所有人、所有国家和所有民族来说，无论具体的历史和传统如何，无疑都具有同等的重要性。就像北极星永远无法触及一样，法治和良政也永远不可能真正实现，而只是人们的一种理想和渴望。在民间传说中，北极星往往还为人们指引前进或回家的方向。

在基于古老口头传说的芬兰民族史诗《卡莱瓦拉》中，一种名叫"三宝"（sampo）、被认为是财富和幸福之源泉的魔法神器占据了显著的地位。我们不知道"三宝"究竟为何物，但是它可能是某种神磨。"三宝"被与世界秩序联系在了一起，因此其名称可能来自一根被认为支撑着苍穹的擎天柱。在这根柱子的顶端就是像缝合苍穹的一个针脚一样的北极星。北极星和苍穹在北欧人的思维模式中扮演着重要的角色。宇宙观也可能影响人们有关法律和治理的思想，这是一个非常发人深省的现象。

芬兰科学院和中国社会科学院所做出的在法律领域开展合作并将合作重点放在法治、比较法和治理等问题上的决定是非常明智和富有远见的。我有幸参加了 2009 年在北京召开的第一次中芬研讨会。这次研讨会有 3 个芬兰大学的代表团应邀参加，其成果已经出版。

本书收录了在此之后召开的两次中芬研讨会的成果：2010 年研讨会在赫尔辛基召开，其主题是中芬法治模式的比较；2011 年研讨会在北京召开，其主题是法治与社会治理。

我很高兴我们这次研讨会的论文集也将出版，从而使我们两国甚至全世界的读者都能够分享我们的学术成果。尽管中国和芬兰有着不同的法律、历史和政治传统，但是我们仍然可以从对方学到很多东西。我个人认为，想象力是法律思想的一个重要方面。但是我们的想象力总是受到限制。我们的思想需要接受各种模式的检验，并且经验也是法律的一个重要方面。法律是一种公共利益，并且因此而应该受到珍爱和培养。法律还必须服务于人民。

在北欧法律传统中，著名的基督教神学家兼律师马丁·路德的学生奥劳斯·彼得里（Olaus Petri）在将近500年前所作出的教导对于我们法律精神的形成起到了重要的作用。他也是从道德伦理的角度论述法律和良政的：

> 所有的法律都是出于公正和平等的目的，而非出于罚款的目的而制定的。罚款是为了惩罚那些违反法律的人，而法律不希望自己被违反，因此它也不希望看到任何人被罚款。

如今人们越来越从工具价值观的角度将法律看作实现某种目的的工具，这无疑是正确的，因为我们为了达到各种目的而越来越需要对社会生活进行规制。作为学者，我们应该时刻牢记，在瞬息万变的法律表象之下的一些更为深层的东西对于法律的工具性功能的成功实现也是至关重要的。当我们希望在更深层次上理解法律的时候，法治、民主、人权、基本权利、良政以及法律和道德传统就都具有了相关性。

我们非常感谢我们的中国伙伴们在过去几年中与我们的密切合作。我们看到，芬兰国内对于这一合作的兴趣正在迅速增长，在这方面的一个最新迹象就是：芬兰的7个大学和一个研究所在赫尔辛基大学的协调下于2013年1月共同成立了一个国家级的"中国法律和中国法律文化中心"。该中心的目的之一就是为所有法律专业的学生提供有关中国法律的基本知识。

芬兰和中国的各学术机构还通过达成双边合作协议来加强其相互关系。在中国方面，中国社会科学院法学研究所所长李林教授就是中芬合作的一位坚定的推动者。良好的开端就是成功的一半。毫无疑问，我们的合作已经有了一个良好的开端。对此我要代表芬兰法学界向我们的中国合作伙伴们表示衷心的感谢。

基默·诺迪欧（Kimmo Nuotio）

赫尔辛基大学法学院院长

第一部分

法治模式与法治变迁

中国法治的现状、 挑战与未来发展

李　林[*]

【摘要】中国法治建设取得了有目共睹的辉煌成就，但离人民群众的期待还有一定差距。中国共产党的十八大报告高屋建瓴、言简意赅地对过去五年民主法治建设成就做出了评价，并提出了到 2020 年全面建成小康社会的民主法治建设目标。未来中国法治发展的总体思路，应当努力实现四个基本转变，即从法治到社会主义宪政的转变，从法律体系到法治体系的转变，从注重立法到加强宪法和法律实施的转变，从法治的表面"维稳"向深层次解决社会公平正义和权力腐败问题的转变。全社会应当尽快把对中国法治状况的认识和评价统一到全面推进依法治国、加快建设社会主义法治国家的战略部署上来，在新的历史起点上为中国民主法治建设事业做出新贡献。

【关键词】法治　现状　发展趋势　社会主义宪政

一　中国法治现状的评价

（一）法学界、法律界对于中国法治状况的评价

近年来，中国法学界、法律界以及社会其他各界人士，在谈到法治问题时，往往有不同的评价。综合起来看，目前国内主流媒体和法学界、法律界对于中国法治状况的评价，大致有如下四种观点：

一是认为近年来法治建设取得了巨大成就，法治状况好得很。官方媒体、领导人讲话和部分专家学者持这种观点。

二是认为近年来法治建设是"进一步、退两步"，与改革开放前 20 年

＊　中国社会科学院法学研究所研究员。

法治建设"进两步、退一步"的状况相比，形成明显反差。持这种观点的学者，人数不多，但影响较大。

三是认为近年来法治建设明显倒退，主要表现是司法改革倒退和某些领域人治现象回潮，法治状况令人担忧。司法界的某些法官、检察官和律师持此种观点，法学院的部分师生也很认同。

四是认为目前中国法治建设处在一个十字路口，何去何从，思路不清，目标不明，需要尽快研究定夺。专家学者中持此种观点者较多。

（二）民间对于中国法治状况的评价

在民间，前一阵有关"段子"对中国法治现状做出了以下调侃式的描述：

三大基本法——领导的看法、领导的想法、领导的说法；

三个诉讼规则——大案讲政治、中案讲影响、小案讲法律；

三个法律效力原则——宪法服从国外看法、法律服从内部规定、内部规定服从领导决定；

法治基本状况——严格立法、普遍违法、选择执法；

执法依据原则——百分之十人大通过、百分之九十高院释法。

尽管民间"段子"对于中国法治状况的上述评价，颇为直观、夸张、片面、消极，甚至捕风捉影、以偏概全。但是，为什么会出现此种评价，是否也在一定程度上反映了民意对于中国法治状况的某些感受和期待，需要我们正面理解和认真对待。

（三）地方法治指数的评价

在地方法治建设层面，近年来，一些地方借鉴国际和香港法治建设经验，试行用"法治指数"来进行法治的量化评价。这些地方主要有杭州市余杭区、昆明市、江苏省的南京和无锡、四川省成都市等。它们采用量化分析方法，评价以百分制为计量单位，近几年各地的得分基本上都在 70 ~ 80 之间，而且总体上是小步上升的。例如，2008 年杭州市余杭区在全国率先发布 2007 年度"余杭法治指数（满意度）"为 71.6 分，2008 年度为 71.84 分，2009 年度为 72.12 分，2010 年度为 72.48 分，2011 年度为 72.56 分，每年分值都微幅上升①。地方法治指数评价出台后，对地方法治建设起到了积极推动作用，但也受到两方面的批评：一是中国是一个单一制国家，

① "法治指数　余杭一年一度的体检"，http：//hznews. hangzhou. com. cn/chengshi/content/ 2012 - 09/04/content_ 4367406. htm，最后访问日期：2012 年 12 月 10 日。

在全国法治建设"不景气"的大环境下，地方法治建设的空间是十分有限的，不可能取得实质性突破；二是即使有些地方法治建设在"法治指数"评价中得了高分，也没有实际意义，因为它在方法和坐标体系上没有可以比较的参照系，在实践上与人们的真实感觉出入较大。

如何评价当下中国的法治状况，需要实事求是的态度和科学精神、科学方法。例如，从时间跨度来看，评价中国法治状况的时间起点是 1949 年、1978 年、1997 年还是 2002 年、2007 年？多数认为中国法治建设倒退的，主要是指近几年，但是对之前的法制改革、司法改革和法治建设，总体上还是比较肯定的。依法治国基本方略是中国法治建设的里程碑，而 2012 年是依法治国基本方略正式确立的第 15 年，因此应当以 1997 年以来的 15 年作为评价中国法治状况的时段。

从法治建设的宏观内容来看，根据党的十五大、十六大和十七大三个政治报告对依法治国和法治建设战略目标做出的规定或描述，可以将其中的"依法治国、政治体制改革、执政党依法执政、形成法律体系、加强宪法和法律实施、建设法治政府、推进司法改革、保障民主权利、反腐倡廉、法制宣传教育、维稳"等 11 项重大任务作为主要评价对象（参见下表）。通过分析可以看出，除"中国特色社会主义法律体系如期形成"和法制宣传教育完成任务外，其他方面都很难说达成目标。

依法治国基本方略确立十五年来任务完成情况

任务	十五大报告	十六大报告	十七大报告	完成情况
依法治国	依法治国，就是广大人民群众依照宪法和法律规定，通过各种途径和形式管理国家和社会事务……保证国家各项工作都依法进行，逐步实现社会主义民主的制度化、法律化。	发展社会主义民主政治，最根本的是要把坚持党的领导、人民当家作主和依法治国有机统一起来。	全面落实依法治国基本方略，加快建设社会主义法治国家。	有所进步，但各种评价均有
政体改革	政治体制改革的主要任务是：发展民主，加强法制，实行政企分开、精简机构，完善民主监督制度，维护安定团结。	继续积极稳妥地推进政治体制改革，扩大社会主义民主，健全社会主义法制，建设社会主义法治国家。	深化政治体制改革，必须……扩大社会主义民主，建设社会主义法治国家，发展社会主义政治文明。	进展不明显

任务	十五大报告	十六大报告	十七大报告	完成情况
依法执政	党在宪法和法律范围内活动。从制度和法律上保证党的基本路线和基本方针的贯彻实施,保证党始终发挥总揽全局、协调各方的领导核心作用。	党的领导主要是政治、思想和组织领导,通过制定大政方针,提出立法建议,推荐重要干部,进行思想宣传,发挥党组织和党员的作用,坚持依法执政,实施党对国家和社会的领导。	坚持党总揽全局、协调各方的领导核心作用,提高党科学执政、民主执政、依法执政水平,保证党领导人民有效治理国家。	进展不明显
立法	到2010年形成有中国特色社会主义法律体系。	到2010年形成中国特色社会主义法律体系。	坚持科学立法、民主立法,完善中国特色社会主义法律体系。	如期完成
法律实施	维护宪法和法律的尊严,坚持法律面前人人平等,加强对宪法和法律实施的监督,维护国家法制统一。	坚持法律面前人人平等,确保法律的严格实施。	加强宪法和法律实施,坚持公民在法律面前一律平等,维护社会公平正义,维护社会主义法制的统一、尊严、权威	进展和效果不尽如人意
政府法治	一切政府机关都必须依法行政,实行执法责任制和评议考核制。实现国家机构组织、职能、编制、工作程序的法定化。	加强对执法活动的监督,推进依法行政,提高执法水平。	推进依法行政。加快行政管理体制改革,建设服务型政府。	进展明显,效果尚可
司法改革	推进司法改革,从制度上保证司法机关依法独立公正地行使审判权和检察权。	推进司法体制改革,从制度上保证审判机关和检察机关依法独立公正地行使审判权和检察权。	深化司法体制改革,保证审判机关、检察机关依法独立公正地行使审判权、检察权。	进展明显,效果待观察
民主权利	实行民主选举、民主决策、民主管理和民主监督,保证人民依法享有广泛的权利和自由,尊重和保障人权。	扩大公民有序的政治参与,保证人民依法实行民主选举、民主决策、民主管理和民主监督,享有广泛的权利和自由,尊重和保障人权。	从各个层次、各个领域扩大公民有序政治参与。保障人民的知情权、参与权、表达权、监督权。尊重和保障人权,依法保证全体社会成员平等参与、平等发展的权利。	有所进展,但还需努力

续表

任务	十五大报告	十六大报告	十七大报告	完成情况
反腐倡廉	加强对各级干部特别是领导干部的监督，防止滥用权力，严惩执法犯法、贪赃枉法。	加强对权力的制约和监督。建立结构合理、配置科学、程序严密、制约有效的权力运行机制。	完善制约和监督机制，保证人民赋予的权力始终用来为人民谋利益。	力度加大，但成效不明显
法制宣传教育	深入开展普法教育，增强全民的法律意识，着重提高领导干部的法制观念和依法办事能力。	加强法制宣传教育，提高全民法律素质，尤其要增强公职人员的法制观念和依法办事能力。	加强公民意识教育，树立社会主义民主法治、自由平等、公平正义理念，树立社会主义法治理念。深入开展法制宣传教育，弘扬法治精神，形成自觉学法守法用法的社会氛围。	持续开展了25年，按规划完成了任务，成效有待观察
维稳	维护安定团结，对人民内部矛盾，要……正确运用经济、行政和法律等手段加以处理，防止矛盾激化。	维护社会稳定，正确运用经济、行政和法律等手段，妥善处理人民内部矛盾特别是涉及群众切身利益的矛盾。	推进社会主义民主政治制度化、规范化、程序化，为党和国家长治久安提供政治和法律制度保障。维护群众合法权益。发挥社会组织在扩大群众参与、反映群众诉求方面的积极作用，增强社会自治功能。	力度越来越大，矛盾越来越多，任务越来越重

党的十八大报告从党和国家工作的大局和全局着眼，高屋建瓴、言简意赅地对过去五年的民主法治建设成就做出了评价——"民主法制建设迈出新步伐。中国特色社会主义法律体系形成，社会主义法治国家建设成绩显著……司法体制和工作机制改革取得新进展。"

法学界、法律界和全社会应当尽快把对中国法治状况的认识和评价统一到党的十八大报告上来，统一到中央关于全面推进依法治国、加快建设社会主义法治国家的战略部署上来，在新的历史起点上为中国民主法治建设事业作出新贡献。

二 中国法治面临的主要挑战

中国法治建设15年来尽管取得了有目共睹的辉煌成绩，但离人民群众的期待还有差距；依法治国基本方略虽然得到实施，但发展还不平衡；法律体系尽管已然形成，但还需进一步完善和发展；立法尽管成就斐然，但执法、司法、守法和法律监督还不尽如人意；法制宣传教育尽管 25 年来成绩巨大，但法治环境并未根本改善……正如 2012 年 12 月 4 日习近平总书记在纪念现行宪法颁行 30 周年大会上的讲话中所指出的，"在充分肯定成绩的同时，我们也要看到存在的不足……保证宪法实施的监督机制和具体制度还不健全，有法不依、执法不严、违法不究现象在一些地方和部门依然存在；关系人民群众切身利益的执法司法问题还比较突出；一些公职人员滥用职权、失职渎职、执法犯法甚至徇私枉法严重损害国家法制权威；公民包括一些领导干部的宪法意识还有待进一步提高。"具体来讲，中国法治建设和依法治国事业还面临以下主要问题和挑战。

一是社会主义民主法治建设与经济社会文化发展的要求还不完全适应，领导干部中的人治现象、公民中的非法治现象、社会上轻视和无视法治的现象，在有些地方、部门、领域和群体中有所抬头和蔓延。

二是坚持党的领导、人民当家作主和依法治国的有机统一，是社会主义政治文明的本质要求，但在一些地方和部门实际上被统一于党委的"一把手"，法治被"人治"所弱化，依法治国从党领导人民实行的"治国基本方略"，演变为某些地方和部门"维稳"以及发展经济①的工具。

三是中国特色社会主义法律体系有待不断完善，立法质量需要不断提高。立法中存在的部门利益、特殊群体利益问题，部门立法争权夺利问题依然存在。国家立法部门化、"部门权力利益化、部门利益合法化"的现象仍未消除，一些明显带有部门或集团利益痕迹的立法，把畸形的利益格局或权力关系合法化，行政部门借立法扩权卸责、立法不公等从制度设计的基础上影响了社会主义法治的权威和法律的实施。

四是中国特色社会主义法律体系形成后，中国法治建设的主要矛盾是宪法和法律实施的问题，② 主要表现为普遍存在的有法不依、执法不严、违法不究，许多法律形同虚设（参见下表）。地方保护主义、部门保护主义和执行难的问题时有发生；法治缺乏权威，司法缺乏公信力；公民"信权不

---

① 马怀德教授指出："但是经济 GDP 往往是通过不遵守法治甚至破坏法治的方式获得的。"参见马怀德等《中国法治愿景》，《中国改革》2010 年第 6 期。

② 江平先生认为："我们现在法治的状况，离遵守宪法、贯彻宪法的目标还太远。"例如"宪法里面明确讲，法院依法独立审判，不受行政机关、社会团体和个人的干涉。但是，现在居然有说法提出，不要提司法独立。司法机关能否做到真正独立，能否做到按照自己的意志来判决，这是对我们宪法原则很重要的考验。现在很多说法，严格说来是违反宪法的。"参见"十二位法学家谈中国法治愿景"，《中国改革》2010 年第 6 期。

信法"，"信访不信法"，"信关系不信法"，"小闹小解决，大闹大解决，不闹不解决"等问题。加强法治教育，提高全社会的法律意识和法治观念，仍是一项艰巨任务。

经过 30 多年的努力，中国特色社会主义法律体系已经形成，无法可依的问题基本解决，法律实施成为法治建设的重点。您认为当前我国法律实施的状况（以法律得到实施的百分比来表示）是：

投票项（%）	百分比（%）	得票
很好（90）	3	772
较好（70）	4	1027
一般（50）	14	3780
较差（30）	20	5443
很差（10）	59	15609
总投票人数	100	26631

注：中国法学网截至 2013 年 3 月 12 日的统计。

五是政府多头执法、多层执法和不执法、乱执法问题；有令不行、有禁不止、行政不作为、失职渎职、违法行政等行为；少数执法人员知法犯法、执法寻租、贪赃枉法甚至充当"黑恶势力"的保护伞；出现了一些不正确的执法倾向，如钓鱼执法、寻租性执法、非文明执法、限制性执法、选择性执法、运动式执法、疲软式执法、滞后性执法等；粗暴执法激发冲突，甚至引发群体性事件或极端恶性事件，突出表现在征地拆迁领域。

六是司法改革轰轰烈烈，解决了办公条件、经费、人员编制以及一些长期制约法院、检察院建设和发展的体制机制等老大难问题，基本上实现了各个阶段司法改革方案预设的目标，但司法独立、司法公正、司法权威、司法效率、司法公信力和干预法院、检察院依法独立行使职权等深层次问题依然存在。[①]

---

① 例如陈卫东教授指出，"在充分肯定前些年司法改革工作取得的重大成绩的同时，我们也不得不承认，许多更深层的问题并没有彻底解决，并且面临更大的困难。司法改革本是一项涉及机制设置、权力机关协调等多方位的全面改革，需要一种宏观的、战略性的规划。然而，目前的司法改革措施大多停留在工作机制层面上，深层次的体制改革尚未展开。"参见陈卫东《未来五年我国司法体制改革的若干建议》，《河南社会科学》2012 年第 2 期。

七是"消极腐败现象仍然比较严重"，一些领域腐败现象仍然易发多发；公职人员贪赃枉法、权钱交易、执法犯法、以言代法、以权压法，对法治造成损害；执法不公、行政不作为乱作为等问题比较突出。如何用法治思维和法治方式应对和解决腐败问题，是对党领导的中国法治建设事业的极大挑战。

三　中国法治的未来发展

根据国家"十二五"规划提出的民主法治建设任务和党的十八大提出的到 2020 年全面建成小康社会的民主法治建设目标——"人民民主不断扩大。民主制度更加完善，民主形式更加丰富，依法治国基本方略全面落实，法治政府基本建成，司法公信力不断提高，人权得到切实尊重和保障"，从我国政治、经济、社会、文化未来改革发展的实际需要出发，积极稳妥推进政治体制改革，全面推进依法治国，加快建设法治国家，"更加注重发挥法治在国家和社会治理中的重要作用，维护国家法治的统一、尊严、权威，保障社会公平正义，保证人民依法享有广泛权利和自由"，是未来中国法治发展的大方向和大趋势。

在实施"十二五"规划和贯彻落实十八大精神的过程中，未来中国法治发展的总体思路，应当努力实现四个基本转变：

一是坚持党的领导、人民民主和依法治国有机统一，在依法治国实践进程中和社会主义法治轨道上积极稳妥地推进政治体制改革，更加注重发挥法治在国家治理和社会管理中的重要作用，实现从法治到社会主义宪政的转变，从制度上和程序上实现"三者有机统一"。

二是在我国法律体系如期形成的基础上，进一步强化民主法治建设，全面推进依法治国，加快建设法治国家，实现从法律体系构建到法治体系建设的转变，尽快从法律大国走向法治强国。[①]

三是在有法可依的目标基本达成后，中国法治建设的重心实现从注重立法到加强宪法和法律实施的转变，从纸面的法律向生活中法律的转变，确保有法必依、执法必严、违法必究，真正实现严格执法、公正司法、全民守法和党在宪法和法律范围内活动。

四是用法治思维和法治方式服务党和国家工作大局，更加注重发挥法

---

① "法治立国、法治稳国、法治救国、法治强国，是人类文明发展的经验总结。"参见胡建淼《走向法治强国》，《国家行政学院学报》2012 年第 1 期。

治在维护党权、建设政权和保障民权中的重要作用，实现从法治的表面"维稳"向深层次解决社会公平正义和权力腐败问题转变，用法治更好地巩固和发展党和国家政权的合法性权威，更加夯实党领导人民治国理政的政治基础、社会基础、民意基础和法律基础，为国家长治久安和中华民族的伟大复兴提供强有力的法治保障。

您认为未来我国法治建设的重点应当是

投票项	百分比（%）	得票
全面落实依法治国基本方略	10	1213
树立法治理念	6	666
推进依法执政	9	1040
完善法律体系	5	604
建设法治政府	10	1139
深化司法改革	11	1288
加强宪法法律实施	26	3129
深化法制宣传教育	2	224
尊重和保障人权	22	2594
总投票人数	100	11897

注：中国法学网截至 2013 年 3 月 12 日的统计。

具体来讲，应当从以下主要方面着力加强法治建设，全面推进依法治国。

1. 高度重视法治建设，全面推进依法治国

党的领导是人民民主和依法治国的根本保证。贯彻落实十八大精神，全面推进依法治国，加快建设社会主义法治国家，必须进一步加强执政党对法治建设的重视、领导和支持。一是执政党进一步高度重视依法治国和法治建设事业，自觉坚持依宪执政、依法执政、依法行政和依法办事，切实把依法治国作为治国理政的基本治国方略来加以落实，切实在宪法和法律范围内活动。二是在推进依法治国和依法执政的实践过程中，执政党的各级领导干部和所有公职人员要以身作则、率先垂范，执政党要领导立法，带头守法，保证执法；任何组织或者个人都不得有超越宪法和法律的特权，绝不允许以言代法、以权压法、徇私枉法。三是党中央着力研究解决以下推进依法治国的重大问题：召开一次依法治国（或者社会主义民主法治建设）的中央全会，对中国民主法治建设和依法治国做出专门决议，中央成立依法治国的专门领导机构,制定依法治国发展战略和实施规划。四是在党的领导下,通过全面落实依法治国基本方略,积极稳妥地推进政治体制改革和法治发展。

2. 充分发挥法治在社会主义现代化建设和全面建成小康社会中的重要作用

法治是人类文明进步的重要标志,是实现十八大战略部署、全面建成小康社会的重要保障。应当努力做到:一是按照社会主义市场经济是法治经济的要求,继续完善市场经济法律体系,充分发挥法治在配置市场资源、调控市场秩序和保障市场主体权利中的作用。二是按照社会主义民主政治是法治政治的要求,完善宪法和公法体系,依法调整政治关系,规范政治行为,制约公权力,保障民主自由和其他基本人权,充分发挥法治在政治文明建设和治理国家中的作用。三是按照社会主义和谐社会和全面小康社会是民主法治社会的要求,加强和完善社会法体系,充分发挥法治在创新社会管理和治理社会中的作用。四是按照加强社会主义文化建设的整体部署,弘扬法治精神,树立法治理念,培养法治思维,全面推进法治文化建设,充分发挥法治在精神文明建设和以德治国中的作用。五是按照人与自然协调发展的要求,完善和加强环境生态保护、能源资源利用、污染防治等方面的法治体系,充分发挥法治在生态文明建设中的作用。六是根据中华民族伟大复兴和"一国两制"原则的要求,更加重视国际法与国内法、港澳台法与内地法的协调发展,更加重视依法治港、依法治澳,充分发挥法治在维护国家主权、保障国家利益、实现国家统一和中国和平发展中的重要作用。

3. 继续推进民主立法、科学立法,不断完善法律体系

按照十八大报告对立法工作的要求,"推进科学立法——完善中国特色社会主义法律体系,加强重点领域立法,拓展人民有序参与立法途径",应当努力做到:一是进一步完善立法体制和立法机制,统筹立法资源,提高立法质量,防止"立法腐败"。二是积极推进民主立法、科学立法,保障公众的立法参与,使立法更充分地体现人民的意志和党的主张,实现立法的"分配正义"。三是进一步加强社会立法、文化立法和权利保障立法,使中国特色社会主义法律体系的内容更加丰富、布局更加合理、体系更加完整。四是按照"一国、两制、三法系、四法域"的国情和实际,积极谋划构建"中国特色法律体系",为中华民族的统一、强盛和伟大复兴提供坚实的法律基础。五是进一步加强和创新立法理论,推进法典化立法,统筹制定法律与修改法律，全面推行立法后评估，保证立法与政治经济社会文化的发展相适应、相协调。

4. 切实加强宪法和法律实施

"天下之事，不难于立法，而难于法之必行。"宪法和法律的生命在于实施。我国法律体系的形成，在从总体上解决了有法可依问题的同时，也对"有法必依、执法必严、违法必究"等法律实施提出了更为突出、更加紧迫的要求。① 根据十八大精神，应当努力做到：一是根据加快建设社会主义法治国家的总体目标要求，把法治建设和依法治国的重点转向宪法和法律实施，使宪法和法律在我国改革开放和现代化建设中发挥更大的作用。二是可以考虑在全国人大中设立与其他专门委员会平行的宪法委员会，专门负责对法律、行政法规和地方性法规的合法性与合宪性审查。三是根据宪法、立法法的规定，全面启动违宪审查机制，强化法规备案审查，使合法性与合宪性审查制度化、常态化。四是根据十八大精神积极稳妥地修改宪法，充分行使宪法解释权，通过宪法解释保证宪法的稳定性和适应性。五是把法律实施状况作为评价立法、执法和司法工作的主要依据，作为考核司法人员和领导干部政绩的重要内容。六是继续加强对公民尤其是领导干部的法制宣传教育，增强法治观念，提高法治意识，养成法治习惯，努力"提高领导干部运用法治思维和法治方式深化改革、推动发展、化解矛盾、维护稳定能力。"

5. 全面推进依法行政，加快建设法治政府

依法行政是全面推进依法治国的中心环节，是深化政治体制改革的重要方面。十八大报告明确指出，要"推进依法行政，切实做到严格规范公正文明执法"，到2020年基本建成法治政府。全面推进依法行政，加快建设法治政府，应当做到：一是不断提高各级公务员依法行政的意识和能力，提高各级领导干部运用法治思维和法治方式深化改革、推动发展、化解矛盾、维护稳定、建设法治政府的能力，在法治轨道上深化行政体制改革。二是进一步健全行政决策制度，完善科学民主依法决策程序，建立重大决策跟踪反馈和评估制度。三是进一步加强和改进制度建设，完善政府立法工作，消除部门立法色彩，健全规范性文件制定和发布程序，建立规章和

---

① "全国人大通过的法律在实践中应得到有效实施，可事实不是如此。比如《破产法》的实施，从2007年6月1日到现在，全国的破产案件不到1万件。2009年全国的破产案件才3120件，而全年有接近80万家的企业在工商监管部门以注销或吊销方式退出市场。也就是说，绝大多数企业退出市场并不是通过法治的途径，而是通过行政注销和吊销的方式。"参见"十二位法学家谈中国法治愿景"，《中国改革》2010年第6期。

规范性文件评估和清理制度,强化法规规章和规范性文件备案审查。四是进一步加强行政执法队伍建设,保证严格、公正、文明执法,完善行政执法体制和机制,健全行政执法程序,规范行政执法行为。五是坚决预防和惩治行政腐败,不断强化行政监督和问责,切实增强行政监督效能,大力推进政府信息公开。六是坚持依法化解社会矛盾纠纷,健全社会矛盾纠纷调解裁决制度,完善行政复议制度,认真做好行政应诉工作。

6. 继续深化司法体制改革,保证司法独立,实现公正司法

司法体制改革是中国政治体制改革的重要组成部分,是全面推进依法治国的重大举措,是全面实施宪法和法律的重要基础。深化司法体制改革,应当努力做到:一是在深入调查研究的基础上,对前15年司法改革成效进行深刻反思和全面评估,总结经验,修正错误,矫正偏差,调整思路,为深化司法体制改革提供实践依据。二是立足国情,借鉴国外先进经验,深入研究和确立中国特色的司法理论,为中国新一轮司法体制改革提供科学理论指导。三是根据十八大的战略部署,结合政治体制改革和全面推进依法治国的新形势和新要求,做好新一轮司法体制改革的顶层设计和科学规划。四是根据宪法的政治架构和法治原则,依法处理好人大与司法、政法委与司法、媒体与司法、公众与司法以及公、检、法之间的关系,确保审判机关、检察机关依法独立公正行使审判权、检察权。五是高度重视发挥司法作为解决矛盾纠纷最后一道防线的功能,重建司法终结社会矛盾纠纷的良性循环机制,不断强化司法公信力和权威性。① 六是进一步增强司法的透明度和公开性,强化司法的民主性和专业化,消除司法的行政化、地方化、官僚化倾向,充分发挥司法在国家和社会治理中的救济作用。

7. 进一步加强人权的法治保障

十八大报告明确提出,到2020年全面建成小康社会时,要实现"人权得到切实尊重和保障"的目标。这是一个要求很高、难度很大但意义非凡的奋斗目标和战略任务。应当努力做到:一是全面落实《宪法》和《党章》规定的"尊重和保障人权"的基本原则,保证公民依法享有广泛权利和自由,全面完善中国人权保障的各项法律规定和法律制度。二是继续推进宪法基本权利的法律化,研究制定新闻法、结社法、宗教信仰自由法、国家

---

① "'大调解'和'能动司法'的最大流弊恰恰是导致责任和'问责(accountability)'无从谈起,甚至还会以表面上各人负责的民主政治的名义,诱发某种最终无人负责的事态。"参见季卫东《大变局下中国法治的顶层设计》,《财经》2012年第5期。

补偿法、公职人员财产申报法、个人信息保护法等法律，废除《劳动教养条例》等法律法规。三是进一步修改《刑法》，大幅度减少死刑的刑种，同时更加严格审慎地适用死刑。四是进一步加强对公民的经济、社会和文化权利保障，着力解决"上学难"、"看病难"、"住房难"、"两极分化"、"贫富不均"等老大难问题，着力保障弱势群体的权利，努力通过法治实现社会公平正义和共同富裕。五是认真实施新一轮的《国家人权行动计划（2012－2015年）》，加强对联合国《公民权利和政治权利国际公约》的研究，适时审议批准这个国际人权公约。

8. 用法治思维和法治方式"反腐治权"

腐败是民主法治的死敌。全面推进依法治国，必须竭尽全力地反腐治权。法治思维和法治方式是反腐治权的基本要义：一是要承认公权力面前的"人性恶"，即面对公权力的巨大诱惑，任何人都不是圣人，都有弱点、缺点和局限，都可能犯错误、滥用权力。"即使像毛泽东那样伟大的革命家、伟大的马克思主义者也会犯错误，也犯过错误"。承认"人性恶"，就不能信任或者放任任何公权力主体，而要建立有效的法律制度和法治机制，把一切公权力放到法律和制度打造的"法网恢恢，疏而不漏"的笼子里，监督制约所有公权力和每一个公权力行使者。二是要以法律控制权力、以制度规范权力、以民主监督权力、以权力和权利制约权力、以道德约束权力，最大限度地减少公权力腐败的机会，最大限度地增加公权力腐败的成本。法治思维下反腐治权的当务之急，就是要尽快从制度和法律上切实解决"谁来监督监督者"、"谁来监督'一把手'"、"谁来监督掌握人财物实权者"的问题。为此，应当认真研究国际上广泛认同的"立法、行政、司法三权分立，相互制衡"机制的合理性，积极引入连中外小朋友都熟悉的"锤子、剪刀、布"游戏的循坏制约机制。三是不仅要注重反腐治权的"顶层设计"和宪政制度安排，也要注重从具体的制度、环节、程序和机制入手；不仅要注重对公权力主体的教育、防范和惩治，也要注重对侵蚀公权力的市场行为、经济行为、社会行为等腐败渠道和腐败条件的防范与整治，从各个层面、各个环节、各个领域、各个方面切实堵住产生腐败的制度性、体制性和机制性漏洞，真正从产生腐败的"土壤和温床"上解决问题。四是充分发挥司法在反腐治权中的作用，排除各种干预和干扰，切实保证司法机关依法独立行使职权，把判决执行权归还行政机关，把审判权和矛盾纠纷解决的终结权回归人民法院。尽可能地剥离或者减少司法权的经济、民事、行政和社会活动，避免司法机关自己成为被告，从制度设计和程序安排上最大限度地减少司法腐败的可能。另一方面，司法机关要以事实为根据，以法律为准绳，秉公司法，依法严惩各种腐败犯罪。尤其要坚持法律面前人人平等，切实做到"不管涉及什么人，不论权力大小、职位高低，只要触犯党纪国法，都要严惩不贷"。

Current Situation，Challenges and Development Trend of the Rule of Law in China

Li Lin

【**Abstract**】Although China has already made remarkable achievements in the construction of the rule of law, there is still certain gap between the current situation of the rule of law in China and the expectations of the Chinese people. In the Report to the Eighteenth National Congress of the Communist Party of China, President Hu Jintao gave a concise and comprehensive evaluation of the achievements made by China in the construction of democracy and the rule of law in the past five years and set the goal of building China into a comprehensively well-off society by the year 2020. In the future development of the rule of law, China should strive to realize four basic transformations, namely transformations from the rule of law to the socialist constitutionalism, from the system of law to the system of the rule of law, from focusing on legislative work to focusing on strengthening the implementation of the Constitution and laws, and from maintaining stability and superficial rule of law to eliminating the root causes of social injustice and the corruption of power. Chinese people should reach as soon as possible a unified understanding and assessment of the current situation of the rule of law in line with the strategic plan of promoting overall implementation of the policy of ruling the country by law and speeding up the construction of a socialist state under the rule of law, so as to make new contributions to the construction of democracy and the rule of law in China at a new historical starting point.

【**Key words**】Rule of Law, Current Situation, Trend of Development, Socialist Constitutionalism

Rule of Law: One of the Core Principles of the Finnish Constitution[*]

Pekka Länsineva[**]

【Abstract】 The purpose of this paper is to study the changing Finnish concept of rule of law in its current constitutional context. Traditionally, the Finnish doctrine of rule of law was based on the nineteenth century idea of *Rechtsstaat* (*legal state*) strongly emphasizing the requirement of legality of public administration. My main thesis is that within the current constitutional framework, strict obedience to black letter law is not enough but the rule of law requires much more. This proposition is based on the fact that the Constitution Act of Finland including its core principles has been recently reformed. Along with the reform, the traditional list of core constitutional principles was supplemented with new principles of inviolability of human dignity, guarantee of freedom and rights of the individual, the promotion of justice in society, right of an individual to participate and influence in democratic decision making as well as Finland's participation in international co-operation and membership in the European Union. One of the main ideas of the reform was to bring individual human beings into the heart of constitutional focus. In other words, the constitution was not intended to operate only on the top level of state institutions

* The article is part of the research project "How to Rule the Economy" funded by the Academy of Finland, Which based on a presentation in 2nd Sino-Finnish International Seminar on Comparative Law, Helsinki, September 28th, 2010.

** Pekka Länsineva, Professor of Public Law, University of Helsinki.

but the treatment of individuals was raised as primary constitutional interest too.

Nowadays, the principle of rule of law shall be interpreted as part of the system of core constitutional principles. Consequently, only such laws rule that do not contradict with human dignity, fundamental rights, social justice or any other of the core constitutional principles. Reconstructed in the light of the core constitutional principles the contemporary Finnish understanding of the rule of law (*constitutional rechsstaat*) could be described at least with adjectives of democratic, participatory, transparent, egalitarian, just and social. Respecting human dignity, individual self-determination, social responsibility as well as environmental sustainability belong to the fundamental values of it.

I. Legalist Tradition of Rechsstaat

Rule of law has been one of the traditional cornerstones of the Finnish legal system. However, the traditional Finnish conception of rule of law is not necessarily equivalent with current constitutional understanding of the same notion. Historically, the Finnish doctrine of rule of law resembles the continental European and especially German nineteenth century idea of *Rechtsstaat* (legal state). Instead of rule of law, this doctrine could be described with words of rule by law. A strict commitment to the idea of legality is the most characteristic feature of this traditional understanding. In Finland, the widespread respect and obedience to the letter of the law dates back to times when the country was a part of the Russian empire and tried to defend her autonomous status against Russian oppression by steadfastly relying on the statutes inherited from the earlier period under the Swedish crown.

Hence, the principle of legality is a key element within the Finnish concept of rechsstaat. In the Constitution of 1919, this principle was manifested by stating that "under threat of a legal sanction, in all official functioning the law shall be strictly observed" (Section 92. 1). In other words, the principle of legality required that all activities of public authorities had to meet the requirement of conformity to law. According to the current Constitution of 2000 "the exercise of public power shall be based on law and in all public activity, the law shall be strictly observed" (Section 2. 3). This provision requires that all exercise of public power shall be based on legal norms enacted by the parliament, and the public authorities have a duty to strictly obey the provisions of parliamentary acts as well as statutes of lower degree if they are based on appropriate delegation in an act of parliament. In addition to the requirement of conformity to law, the new constitution more clearly emphasizes that the use of executive and administrative powers shall have an express basis in statutory law.

In the Finnish context, the principle of legality is not understood only as law in books but, above all, law in action. According to a widespread understanding, a legalistic approach is deep-rooted in Finnish legal culture and civil servants are considered as strictly law-abiding actors. Reading and obeying law very literally has been and still is an integral element of the self-image of Finnish officials on all levels of public administration.

At least to certain limit, the strong commitment to the principle of legality sketched above offers a solid foundation for the development of the system of government based on the idea of rechtsstaat/rule of law also in the future. Firstly, the adherence to the basic premises that the use of executive power is subjected to the control of law and no one is above law is widespread and well-established. Secondly, the steadfast respect of legality safeguards that legal decision making is rather predictable and reliable with respect to citizens' expectations. Moreover, it guarantees that people are treated equally before the law and no privileges are for sale. And finally, it underscores the idea that democratically elected parliament representing the will of people is the supreme body of the state and the administrative authorities have a duty to enforce its will, and not of their own.

However, under current social and legal circumstances there are well-founded reasons to reassess the doctrine and analyse what are the main weaknesses of it and how it should be updated. From a critical point of view, it could be argued that most of the difficulties in this respect are connected with the fact that the principle of rechsstaat is typically interpreted in rather formalistic, narrow and inflexible manner within Finnish legalistic tradition. In practice, the principle of legality has been understood more from administrative than from constitutional point of view. Among other things, there has been no established tradition to challenge the legitimacy of parliamentary acts. The traditional starting point has been that any provision of statutory law has to be observed in very literal meaning irrespective of what it may stipulate or how it relates to other relevant legal norms. Moreover, there has been a tendency to interpret specific laws and their single sections in rather separate and isolated manner. To some extent, this formalistic and literal method of interpretation may produce predictability and legal certainty but at least in some cases, it may result in somewhat arbitrary outcomes as well. If single provisions of law are interpreted and enforced in too narrow and inflexible manner, it might ensue that both contextual considerations of equity as well as more comprehensive perspectives of justice and fairness are ignored.

In this paper, my intention is to outline the changing role and function of the principle of rule of law in its current Finnish constitutional context. The principle is understood and approached as one of the core constitutional principles. At first, a brief comparative introduction to Nordic constitutionalism and recent constitutional developments in Finland will be presented.

II. Constitutional Developments in Brief

Quite recently, the Constitution of Finland was reformed in two stages. The first part of the reform took place in 1995 when the fundamental rights chapter of the Constitution was amended in its entirety, and the reform process was finalized in 2000, when the whole new Constitution Act came into force. In addition, some minor constitutional amendments were made in 2011.

However, the revision of the Finnish Constitution was not an all-embracing reform of the constitutional system but a significant amendment nevertheless. In many respects, the new Constitution was built on the idea of continuity of Finnish constitutional tradition. The manifested intention of the reformers was to codify and update the text of the constitution to match with the customs and practices developed since the enactment the old constitution of 1919, but without altering its most fundamental principles. Professor *Jaakko Nousiainen* has characterized the aim of the reform process as a synchronisation and modernisation of the normative structures of the constitution-a sort of periodic maintenance project. ①

On the other hand, afterwards, it has become obvious that at least in some

---

① Jaakko Nousiainen, "The Finnish System of Government: From a Mixed Constitution to Parliamentarism", p. 9 (http: //www. om. fi/21910. htm).

respects the constitutional reform-in tandem with Finland's membership in the European Council (1990) and European Union (1995) -started a new era in the Finnish constitutional history. Especially in the context of constitutional rights and human rights the paradigm shift was significant. Unlike in the era of the old Constitution, nowadays, the fundamental rights guaranteed in the constitution as well as human rights obligations based on international treaties are understood as legally binding and applicable norms belonging to the effective Finnish legal order. According to Section 22 of the new Constitution all public actors shall guarantee the observance of constitutional and human rights. Consequently, the legislator, the courts of law as well as all public authorities have a legal duty to take these norms seriously in all of their activities. According to Section 106 of the Constitution the courts of law shall give primacy to the Constitution if an application of a parliamentary act will be in evident conflict with the Constitution. From a point of the rule of law this signifies that constitutional and human rights norms are an essential part of the main body of the law that rules. Ordinary laws shall not be interpreted in a manner that will contradict with the norms of the Constitution.

III. Nordic Comparisons

Compared with the other Nordic countries, and especially with Norway and Denmark, the new Finnish Constitution clearly represents a younger generation of writing constitutions. The constitution of Norway dates back to 1814 and the Danish constitution were enacted in 1953. On the other hand, the Swedish constitution (*Regeringsform*) from 1974 was recently (2010: 1408) amended. However, the basic structure of the Swedish constitutional document was left unchanged.

Still, it could be argued that there exists a certain kind of common Nordic understanding of constitutionalism, and in many respects, the Finnish constitutional doctrine still reflects this common conception. [1] However, at least to certain

---

[1]   See e. g. Jaakko Husa, "Nordic reflections on Constitutional Law, A Comparative Nordic Perspective," Peter Lang 2002, pp. 155 – 166, 172 – 180, Jaakko Husa, "Nordic Constitutionalism and European Human Rights-Mixing Oil and Water?", *Scandinavian Studies in Law* Vol. 55, pp. 101 – 124, Stockholm 2010, pp. 106 – 111 and Juha Lavapuro, Tuomas Ojanen and Martin Scheinin, "Rights-based constitutionalism in Finland and the development of pluralist constitutional review", *International Journal on Constitutional Law* 2011, Vol. 9 No. 2, pp. 505 – 531.

extent, Finland has grown apart from the Nordic constitutional tradition. ①

From a traditional point of view, the Nordic conception of constitutionalism has been built on at least the following common assumptions and commitments:

* There exists an established tradition of giving strong emphasis on the idea of legislative supremacy. Laws (parliamentary acts) are understood as paramount legal sources. The democratic legitimacy of legislation is high ranked since the Parliament represents the people and the laws enacted by it are understood as primary means of carrying out the will of the people. Also in other respects the legislation enjoys appreciation among citizenry. Rather than a threat to individual liberty the legislation is understood as an instrument for implementing and guaranteeing individual rights, social security, equality and other widely shared goals and values of the welfare state.

* The normative role of the constitution and constitutionally guaranteed rights has been relatively weak within the Nordic legal systems. According to the Nordic understanding, the idea of the constitution is not to set strict normative limits on the will of the majority of the democratically elected Parliament.

* The courts of law are not considered as focal constitutional bodies. There are no constitutional courts and the scope and relevance of judicial review has traditionally been rather limited in the Nordic constitutional systems. Moreover, there is certain inborn distrust and reluctance to take advice from domestic or international courts. In addition, the courts of law seem to be rather loyal towards the legislature and more inclined to judicial self-restraint than judicial activism.

* If problems concerning fundamental rights would occur, they were approached rather from legislative than adjudicative point of view. The duty to guarantee fundamental rights and solve conflicts between them falls mainly to the legislature. Legal claims and arguments based on fundamental rights have not been typical in Nordic judicial practices.

* All in all, the Nordic model of constitutionalism rests heavily on the ideas of

---

① Of course, there are many differences between the Nordic countries (see Husa 2010, pp. 110 – 111) and the tradition is evolving in all of them.

parliamentary system and majoritarian democracy. According to a recent analysis "rights and judiciaries have had rather marginal legal roles on the Nordic Scene of constitutionalism" . [1]

The idea of the Finnish constitutional reform was not to make a clear break away from this Nordic tradition but nevertheless to take some steps towards stronger constitutionalism and more effective protection of individual rights. The Finnish accession to the European Convention of Human Rights (1990) and the membership in the European Union (1995) were the main factors behind this doctrinal change. One of the main objectives of the reformers of the constitution was to update the system of constitutionally protected fundamental rights to be compatible with international human rights obligations of Finland and try to assure that, in most cases, the human rights issues and conflicts could be solved on the domestic level. Consequently, the drafters of the new constitution recommended that the domestic courts of law should be ready to apply the fundamental rights provisions of the constitution as well as binding human rights treaties as the normatively effective and valid law of the land, and not regard them only as ceremonious proclamations as had been the case earlier. The courts of law were instructed to interpret ordinary laws in the light of domestic constitutional rights and international human rights; and in utmost cases the new Constitution (Section 106) gave the courts the authority to give primacy to the constitution, if the application of an ordinary act would be in evident conflict with a constitutional norm.

To sum up recent developments, Finland has taken at least some distance from the traditional Nordic weak constitutional tradition but still our legal system is far from German type of strict constitutional culture with a strong constitutional court having the last word on multiple legal and political issues. However, application of constitutional and human rights norms in the Finnish courts of law has become much more common than was the case in the 1990s. At least in some cases parliamentary acts have been subordinated to judicial review on the basis of fundamental rights guaranteed in the Constitution. And more generally, constitutional arguments have gained more weight in the Finnish legal discussion. However, as the new Finnish Constitution has just celebrated its first decade it is

---

[1]   See Lavapuro, Ojanen and Scheinin, p. 505.

still too early to predict how far the process of constitutionalization and the system of judicial review will develop in years to come.

IV. Core Principles of the Finnish Constitution

1. General Remarks

As described above, commitment to the idea of rule of law is an integral part of Finnish legal culture and currently, it is acknowledged as one of the core constitutional principles. Before the constitutional reform, the principle of rechsstaat was declared in Section 92 of the Constitution while some other basic principles were listed down in the first sections of the same document. [1] In the new Constitution, all of the most fundamental constitutional principles-including the principle of rule of law-are codified in the first three provisions of it. [2]

"Section 1   *The Constitution*

Finland is a sovereign republic.

The constitution of Finland is established in this constitutional act. The constitution shall guarantee the inviolability of human dignity and the freedom and rights of the individual and promote justice in society.

Finland participates in international co-operation for the protection of peace and human rights and for the development of society. Finland is a Member State of the European Union (1112/2011, entry into force 1. 3. 2012).

Section 2   *Democracy and the rule of law*

The powers of the State in Finland are vested in the people, who are represented by the Parliament.

Democracy entails the right of the individual to participate in and influence the development of society and his or her living conditions.

The exercise of public powers shall be based on an Act. In all public activity, the law shall be strictly observed.

---

[1]   Moreover, some of the constitutional principles were more indirectly derived from the text of the constitution (see Kaarlo Tuori.)

[2]   As the Constitution of Finland has no preamble the fundamental principles are an organic part of the Constitution itself.

Section 3   *Parliamentarism and the separation of powers*

The legislative powers are exercised by the Parliament, which shall also decide on State finances.

The governmental powers are exercised by the President of the Republic and the Government, the members of which shall have the confidence of the Parliament.

The judicial powers are exercised by independent courts of law, with the Supreme Court and the Supreme Administrative Court as the highest instances. "

At least the following constitutional principles are manifested in these three provisions:

Section 1:

-sovereignty of republic

-inviolability of human dignity

-guarantee of freedom and rights of the individual

-promotion of justice in society

-participation in international co-operation and membership of the EU

Section 2:

-sovereignty of the people

-the parliament representing the people (representative democracy)

-participatory democracy

-rule of law

Section 3:

-separation of legislative, executive and judicial powers

Some of these principles were already recognized in the old Constitution, namely the sovereignty of republic, the sovereignty of the people represented by the parliament, the rule of law and separation of powers. Along with the constitutional reform, the traditional list was supplemented with the principles of inviolability of human dignity, guarantee of freedom and rights of the individual, the promotion of justice in society, right of an individual to participate and influence in democratic decision making as well as Finland's participation in international co-operation.

Even if the significance of this amendment is not crystal clear yet it might be justified to argue that the introduction of several new principles as well as the modifications concerning traditional principles signals a considerable change in

Finnish constitutional understanding. ① As the old set of principles reflected more or less state-centred constitutional approach the current one clearly brings individual human beings into the heart of constitutional focus. In other words, the idea of the reform was to emphasize that the constitution does not operate only on the top level of state institutions but the treatment of individuals is of primary constitutional interest, too. Traditional top-down approach was replaced or at least supplemented with a firm bottom-up and rights based perspective. To sum up, the prime normative message was that every individual count and shall be treated with equal concern and respect. People are not subservient of the state and its government but vice versa. This foundational shift in the constitutional paradigm should not be ignored when interpreting constitutional principles or any other constitutional norms.

The list of the core constitutional principles was reconstructed and codified with the view to consolidate and give people an updated and transparent image of the fundamental constitutional values and ideological commitments which the constitution-and the whole legal order is currently built on. Moreover, the normative function of the fundamental constitutional principles is not only to serve as an ideological declaration of certain democratic ideals and respect for individuals behind the constitution, but to serve more practical legal functions as well. The principles are supposed to give normative guidance and reason when interpreting other constitutional norms and balancing conflicts between them. Some of the principles may even have more direct legal effect. Naturally, most of the core principles are not precise legal norms, but more or less relative principles leaving considerable amount of space for interpretation.

Furthermore, the principles may easily fall in conflict with each other and striking a proper balance between them becomes the most crucial issue. In certain contexts, e. g. the protection of individual freedoms and promotion of justice in society may point out opposite directions. Similarly, balancing is needed in the reconciliation of the principles of the sovereignty of the people and representative

① However, at least some academic commentators seem to hold the view that the transformation has not been so remarkable and they still tend to emphasize the primacy of traditional principles such as representative democracy and separation of powers (see etc. Antero Jyränki 2002).

democracy vis-à-vis the fundamental rights of individuals.

The list of the core constitutional principles should not be read as a hierarchical or priority list but it is important to acknowledge that all of the principles play an important role from a point of view of the total system of principles. Therefore, it would be problematic to claim that for instance democracy or separation of powers should be understood as the supreme principles of the system. [1] Moreover, the systemic approach requires that the core principles should not be interpreted as isolated but in light of each other. Consequently, the rule of law as well as the other constitutional principles shall be read in the context of the other core constitutional principles.

Still, a closer examination of constitutional principles is justified to start from the principles of human dignity, individual rights and social justice since they are new principles in the Constitution and may therefore modify the context and influence the substance how the more traditional principles shall be interpreted. In addition, starting from the first section of the Constitution seems to be natural as this provision aims to manifest the most fundamental values of the whole constitutional order.

2. Core Principles

Inviolability of human dignity

The respect of human dignity is a fundamental background value and presumption of any legitimate and workable system of human and constitutional rights. As the Universal Declaration of Human Rights pronounces the predominant conception of human rights is built on a basic premise that "all human beings are born free and equal in dignity and rights". Consequently, the dignity of every individual shall be equally respected and protected irrespective of any distinctions such as ethnic or social origin, sex, age, nationality, religion or belief, opinions, wealth, disability, birth or other status. In the Finnish constitutional reform, the fundamental principle of inviolability of human dignity was recognized as a basic premise of the Finnish constitutional order as well. Thereby, it is worthwhile of discussing what the normative relevance of this amendment is.

---

[1] Cf. e. g. Antero Jyränki, Valta ja vapaus, Talentum 2003, pp. 33 – 39.

Read as itself, the principle of inviolability of human dignity seems to be a fairly open and indefinite legal norm-just like many other constitutional norms. Moreover, it is a new principle in the Finnish Constitution and there is not yet well-established doctrine about the exact meaning of it and how it should be interpreted and applied in different contexts. On the other hand, the principle is not totally unknown within Finnish legal order. Namely, in addition to the Universal Declaration of Human Rights the principle of inviolability of human dignity is recognized and guaranteed in the preamble of the UN Covenant on Civil and Political Rights and in a number of other international human rights instruments binding Finland. ① Moreover, the European Court of Human Rights has often stated that "the very essence of the Convention is respect for human dignity and human freedom" although this principle was not written down in the original text of the European Convention on Human Rights. According to the European Court on Human Rights notions of self-determination and personal autonomy are important principles underlying the interpretation of its guarantees. ② Currently, the inviolability of human dignity is guaranteed in the EU Charter of Fundamental Rights too. Thus, the case law of several international human rights bodies as well as international human rights literature are available and giving guidance on the aim of concretizing the meaning and applicability of the principle of human dignity.

According to the preparatory legislative materials concerning the Finnish constitutional reform, the principle of inviolability of human dignity refers-in the spirit of Universal Declaration-to the recognition of the inherent dignity and equal worth of all human beings. Moreover, human dignity and the most fundamental rights innately belong to every individual irrespective of the prevailing will of state or positive law. ③

Section 1 of the Constitution is not the only point of reference relating with the inviolability of human dignity but this concept is confirmed in several other articles

---

① See e. g. Liisa Nieminen, "Ihmisarvon loukkaamattomuus perus-ja ihmisoikeussuojan lähtökohtana", in Lakimies 2005, pp. 49 – 78.

② See e. g. Christine Goodwin v. United Kingdom, 11 July 2002, para. 90 and Jehovah's Witnesses of Moscow v. Russia, 10 June 2010, para. 135.

③ Government Bill (GB) 309/1993, p. 42.

of the Constitution too. Section 7 concerning the right to life, personal liberty and integrity stipulates that no one shall be sentenced to death, tortured or otherwise treated in a manner violating human dignity. Moreover, according to Section 9. 4 no one shall be deported, extradited or returned to another country, if in consequence he or she is in danger of a death sentence, torture or other treatment violating human dignity. And finally Section 19. 1 concerning the right to social security states that those who cannot obtain the means necessary for a life of dignity have the right to receive indispensable subsistence and care. At least to some extent, these provisions fortify the status of inviolability of human dignity as a basic value of the constitution, and clarify its content too. Among other things, these provisions indicate that in addition to death sentence and torture human dignity can be violated in many other ways by grievously hurting, injuring or otherwise mistreating or humiliating a person. ① Not only public actors but private actors, too, are capable of committing offences constituting violations against human dignity. ② In addition, it seems possible that human dignity can be violated by gross discriminatory actions. ③

So far, the principle of respect for human dignity has influenced more on legislative procedures than judicial practices. Especially in fields such as health care and medical research this principle has had strong impact on legislation. One reason is that the scope of application of human dignity is somewhat wider than is the case with constitutional rights. According to the prevailing doctrine, constitutional rights are only guaranteed to living human beings (from the moment of birth to death) but the principle of human dignity may apply to unborn and deceased persons as well. Therefore, it has to be taken into account when regulating issues

---

① E. g. the Finnish Parliamentary Ombudsman stated in his decision (28. 1. 2011) that such a procedure in hospital was humiliating and offensive from a point of view of patient's human dignity in which he had to relieve himself on the floor of the isolation room and had to wait even for a long time before the secretions were cleaned away. Moreover, offending words spoken on the telephone by the emergency exchange officer have been regarded as offences against human dignity (Parliamentary Ombudsman 10. 5. 2010).

② See Finnish Supreme Court, decisions 2009: 46 and 2009: 82 in which gross private assaults were regarded as violations of human dignity and constituting liability for damages.

③ This kind of possibility was considered in decisions 2011: 22 of Supreme Administrative Court and 2010: 74 of the Supreme Court.

such as fertilization treatment, abortion, medical experimentation or funerary functioning. Moreover, the principle of inviolability of human dignity has been given normative effect in other types of legislative issues too. For instance, in the field of insolvency and debt adjustment legislation the Constitutional Law Committee of the Parliament approved an argument that long-lasting and excessive indebtedness may result in a serious threat to the individual survival and the life of dignity as protected by the Constitution. Therefore, it was justified to intervene by retroactive legislation into the property rights of the creditors in order to relieve the situation of the debtors. ①

Freedom and rights of the individual

By declaring freedom and rights of the individual as a fundamental value and general constitutional principle, the reformers of the constitution intended to manifest that constitutional rights and human rights shall play a significant role within the Finnish constitutional and legal system. The intention was to deviate from the traditional doctrine which largely had denied the normative effect of these rights. Formerly, fundamental rights were regarded as some kind of upper level ceremonial principles which predominantly guided the legislature but were not applicable norms on the level of judicial practices. Individuals were not able to institute proceedings claiming that their constitutional rights had been violated.

Now, the objective of elevating the freedom and rights of the individual on the level of core constitutional principles was to underline that fundamental rights shall be taken seriously as binding legal norms in all kinds of legal activities. Moreover, the idea was boosted by Section 22 of the Constitution which stipulates that all public authorities have a constitutional obligation to guarantee the observance of constitutional rights and international human rights. Read in conjunction with the-rather comprehensive-catalogue of fundamental rights defined in the second chapter of the Constitution these two provisions require that all public authorities shall respect, protect and ensure the rights of individuals guaranteed both in the domestic constitution as well as in binding international human rights treaties. In other words, not only individual autonomy and civil liberties but also economic, social and cultural rights as well as rights connected to equality, due process and

---

① See opinions of the Constitutional Law Committee of the Parliament 33/2002 and 42/2006.

environmental issues shall be observed in all public activities. Furthermore, the duty to observe constitutional and human rights does not limit itself only to vertical relations between the state and individuals but reaches horizontal relations between private actors as well.

Promotion of justice in society

Undoubtedly, justice in society is one of the most open and intangible constitutional concepts to define. According to the *travaux preparatoires* of the constitutional reform, the main function of this principle was to accompany the previous principle concerning freedom and rights by emphasizing the importance of equality rights as well as economic, social and cultural rights. In other words, with this principle the drafters aimed to make sure that not only traditional civil liberties but also ESC-rights and equality rights are of primary constitutional interest.

Moreover, it might be suggested that the principle of social justice confirms and constitutionalizes some of the core ideas and achievements of the Nordic model of welfare state with its egalitarian tenets. The Constitution does not only protect prevailing rights and liberties but it also requires the government to take positive measures in order to promote actual equality and social security within society.

According to *Antero Jyränki*, the principles of individual rights and social justice manifest two conflicting in-built aspects of Finnish constitutional ideology, namely the liberal and social side of it. [1] It is a duty of all public authorities to strike a balance between these competing constitutional ideals of liberal and welfare states. In order to fulfil its dual constitutional obligations the state shall not only refrain from interfering in individual rights and liberties but in addition it has to take care of social welfare and promotion of equality in society. Thereby, issues concerning social and egalitarian programs do not completely fall in the domain of political choice but have a constitutionally defined normative dimension as well.

State Sovereignty, participation in international co-operation and EU-membership

The principle of state sovereignty is declared in the first sentence of Section 1 of the Constitution. Actually, this provision manifests two different constitutional principles, namely that Finland is a sovereign state and it has a republic form of government. Although the formulation of this provision corresponds with the old

---

[1]   Antero Jyränki, Uusi perustuslakimme, Turku 2000, p. 61.

constitution its context of interpretation was significantly changed by the constitutional reform. Traditionally, the concept of state sovereignty was interpreted in a rather strict manner, and even minor transfers of powers to international organizations or foreign states were regarded as unconstitutional actions. Thereby, it is needless to say that the 1994 treaty concerning the accession of Finland to the EU was regarded to be in conflict with the sovereignty of state, and consequently the treaty had to be approved by a two-thirds majority in the Parliament. The accession treaty was incorporated into Finnish law through a so called exceptive enactment which at that time was a standard procedure to promulgate acts conflicting with the constitution.

The aim of the constitutional reform was to introduce an updated and more internationally oriented constitutional concept of state sovereignty which would be compatible with the EU-membership and other recent developments concerning the international relations of Finland. In this purpose, the first section of the Constitution was supplemented with a new provision according to which Finland participates in international co-operation for the protection of peace and human rights and for the development of society. According to the travaux preparatoires, the list of acceptable purposes of international co-operation was not intended to set strict or exhaustive limits on international interaction but on the contrary, it was meant to cover most forms of such international co-operation which could be deemed as ordinary under prevailing circumstances. ① According to Section 94. 3 of the Constitution only such international obligations are completely precluded that would endanger the democratic foundations of the Constitution. Still, it is relevant to note that fight for peace, protection of human rights and development of society are declared as the most essential constitutional functions of international co-operation. At least to some extent, this provision seems to support the importance of the above mentioned principles concerning the rights of individuals and promotion of justice in society as principal constitutional objectives.

After the amendment, the paradigm of interpreting the constitutional concept of state sovereignty has shifted from nationally oriented and narrow reading to more international construction of the same concept. Currently, most of the

---

① Government Bill 1/1998 concerning the new Constitution, p. 73.

conventional forms of international co-operation are regarded as unproblematic from a point of view of state sovereignty. [1] Moreover, the first section of the Constitution was recently[2] amended with an express clause stating that Finland is a member of the EU.

People's sovereignty and democracy

The ideas of people's sovereignty and democratic form of government belong to the traditional hard-core of Finnish constitutional ideology. The ideological starting point has been that the powers of the state emanate from the people and people are represented by the parliament. However, in this context "people" have typically been understood as an abstract and collective subjectivity rather than a particular group composed of individuals. Moreover, the idea of people's sovereignty has primarily been utilized as an underlying theoretical principle without extensive or direct normative implications. Probably the main function of this principle has been to serve as a justification for claiming that the parliament shall be the supreme organ of the state as a representative of the sovereign people. For this reason it is justified to require, inter alia, that the highest legislative power shall belong to the parliament, and all exercise of public powers shall be based on acts enacted by the Parliament. All in all, the idea of democracy and especially the representative tenets of it have played the predominant role within Finnish constitutional ideology.

During the constitutional reform, it was emphasized that representative democracy based on (nationwide and local) elections is still an essential element of democracy, i. e. self-government by the people. On the other hand, it was acknowledged that a true democracy is and should be much more than simply a possibility to vote in periodical elections. According to the drafters, democracy also presupposes safeguards for open and well-functioning civil society as well as wide-ranging possibilities for the people to participate in opinion-and will-formation processes concerning various spheres of social and political life. [3] In order to highlight the importance of this kind of participatory elements of democracy the

---

[1] See Tuomas Ojanen, *The Europeanisation of Finnish Law*, in Paul Luif (Hg.), Österreich, Schweden, Finnland. Zehn Jahre Mitgliedschaft in der Europäischen Union, Böhlau Verlag 2007, pp. 150 – 155.

[2] The amendment came into force in the beginning of March 2012.

[3] See GB 1/1998, pp. 73 – 74.

second section of the Constitution was supplemented with a general statement that democracy entails the right of the individual to participate in and influence on the development of society and his or her living conditions. In addition to this general clause some of the fundamental rights provisions in the second chapter of the Constitution were supplemented with statements concerning the opportunities of people to participate and influence in public decision making relating to themselves as well as to more general societal matters. The Section 14 concerning electoral and participatory rights was amended with a clause obligating "the public authorities to promote the opportunities for the individual to participate in societal activity and to influence the decisions concerning him or her". According to Section 20. 2 concerning the responsibility for the environment "the public authorities shall endeavour to guarantee for everyone the right to a healthy environment and for everyone the possibility to influence the decisions that concern their own living environment".

As a whole, the reformers of the Constitution wanted to send a clear message that the role of participatory forms of democracy should be strengthen and lifted from the periphery to the centre of the Finnish constitutional paradigm. However, due to a strong tradition the doctrine of representative democracy still seems to dominate the constitutional understanding and the emancipatory potentials of more direct forms of democracy have not been taken as seriously as the Constitution seems to require, at least so far. Obviously, it takes some time before the political and academic elite will realise that developing new forms and methods for extending the possibilities of people to participate in decision making is not an issue of political good-will but a normative obligation based on the Constitution.

However, a recent constitutional amendment concerning the citizens' initiative might signify at least a modest step towards participatory democracy. According to the new[①] Section 53. 3 of the Constitution at least fifty thousand Finnish citizens have a right to make a legislative initiative to the parliament.

Separation of powers and parliamentarism

Read together, Sections 2 and 3 of the Constitution declare that the Parliament is

---

① Came into force Jan. 3 2012.

the supreme body of the state. The Parliament[1] exercises legislative powers as well as decides of state finances. To some extent the Parliament may delegate its legislative powers to the President, the Government and the Ministries but at least the basic rules and principles governing the rights and obligations of private individuals as well as other matters of a legislative nature shall be governed by the acts of Parliament. The executive bodies may issue decrees only on the basis of an express authorisation given to them by the Constitution or by an Act of Parliament.

In the Finnish constitutional system, the governmental/highest executive powers are vested in both the President of the Republic and the Government. One of the main objectives of the constitutional reform was to develop the parliamentary features of the Finnish system of government by slightly diminishing the presidential powers and reasserting the status of Government respectively. In other words, the idea was to strengthen the status of the Parliament by shifting the balance of executive powers from the President towards the Government the members of which are required have the confidence of the Parliament. However, the President still has some relevant competences especially in the fields of foreign policy and international relations.

The judicial powers are exercised by independent courts of law. By emphasizing the *independence of the judiciary* the drafters of the constitution wanted to express that no external actors are allowed to influence the judicial decision-making of the courts. When deciding individual cases the independent courts and their impartial judges shall only apply law and they shall not take orders or advice from the representatives of the government or any other political or administrative actors-or even from the other judicial bodies. Still there seems to be some challenges concerning the Finnish political and legal culture in this respect. At least occasionally there have been allegations about inappropriate interventions by the political elite into the field of judicial discretion.

During the constitutional reform, the scope and acceptability of *judicial review* was another disputed issue relating to the role of the courts and division of powers between the legislature and the judiciary. According to the traditional doctrine, the

---

[1]　The Parliament is a unicameral body consisting of 200 members elected for a term of four years.

courts of law had no authority to review the constitutionality of parliamentary acts and consequently, individuals had no effective means to bring suits based on the claim that their constitutionally protected rights had been violated. Due to the strong commitment to the idea of legislative supremacy the courts were prohibited to judge whether the ordinary laws passed by the Parliament were in conflict with the constitution or not. Under the system of the old Constitution, the constitutionality of parliamentary acts was supervised only by the Parliament itself and especially by the Constitutional Law Committee of it. [1]

In practice, the prohibition of judicial review resulted to a situation in which the courts almost never applied the norms of the constitution. As one of the main objectives of the constitutional reform was to change the state of affairs and reconstruct constitutional rights as applicable legal norms the role of the prohibition of judicial review had to be reconsidered. Moreover, alongside with the EU-membership the Finnish courts of law had already been empowered to review whether domestic legislation was compatible with the EU-legislation and in negative cases give primacy to EU-law. Thus, the door for judicial review had already been opened and it would have been inconsistent if this option would not have been available in the context of the domestic Constitution.

The main problem of the reformers was how to empower and encourage the courts of law to apply constitutional rights and simultaneously hold onto the idea of legislative supremacy. In other words, they puzzled about the proper scope of judicial review. In the new Constitution this dilemma was attempted to be solved with the Section 106 which stipulates that the courts of law shall give primacy to the Constitution "if in a matter being tried by a court of law the application of an Act would be in *manifest conflict* with the Constitution". In other words, the intention of the drafters was to introduce a rather limited model of ex post judicial review and maintain the dominant role of the traditional ex ante control carried on by the Constitutional Law Committee of the Parliament. The main idea was that the courts of law would use their option of bypassing norms of parliamentary acts on constitutional basis in exceptional cases only. In more typical cases, the

---

[1] See Tuomas Ojanen, "From Constitutional Periphery toward the Centre-Transformations of Judicial Review in Finland," *Nordic Journal of Human Rights* Vol 27, 2009. pp. 194 – 207, p. 195.

normative standards set by the constitution were meant to be reached by the method of constitution-oriented interpretation of statutes. [1]

In many respects the reform was successful. Nowadays, the application of constitutional and human rights norms in judicial practices has become a rather common phenomenon and on the other hand, manifest conflicts between ordinary laws and the Constitution are found very seldom as was the intention of the reformers. This development seems to suggest that the reconciliation of *prima facie* contradicting ideas of protecting individual rights and respecting legislative supremacy is not a mission impossible. Moreover, not only the courts of law but e. g. the Parliamentary Ombudsman and different administrative authorities have adjusted their practises to better correspond with the requirements constitutional and human rights. All in all, in recent years, the Finnish system of judicial review has developed towards a more plural model in which several institutions take part into a mission of making fundamental rights real. In addition, this kind of weak model of judicial review does not seem to extinguish the idea of legislative supremacy.

At the moment, there is going on a discussion whether the model of judicial review adopted in Finland is still too weak and placing too much emphasis on respect for parliamentary sovereignty. Some constitutional scholars have suggested that the courts of law are too cautious in applying fundamental rights and some additional steps towards stronger judicial review should be taken before the proper balance between the protection of individual rights and respect of the legislature would be reached. However, the proposition of removing the requirement of "manifest" conflict from the text of the Constitution was rejected during the preparation of the latest constitutional amendment. Even so, there still seems to be a plenty of potential to make the enforcement of constitutional and human rights more extensive and intensive by the judiciary without jeopardizing the democratic foundations of the society. In this respect, it is worthwhile remembering that human rights are newcomers within Finnish legal culture and the learning-process concerning the application of them will take some time.

---

[1] See Ojanen 2009, pp. 204 – 207.

3. Conclusion

The short presentation of the core principles of the Finnish Constitution above exposes that the constitutional system-just like in any other modern constitutional polity-consists of several diverging ideas and values. Picking up only one or few favourites among these principles would be nonchalant from a point of view of the comprehensive constitutional perception pronounced during the constitutional reform. Thereby, the only legitimate option is balancing and reconciliation between these in-built polarities and tensions of the system. Among other things, it means that the ideas of sovereignty of the people and representative democracy have to be balanced with the demands of respecting human dignity and freedom and rights of the individual. And in order to guarantee equal opportunities for weak and poor or to promote justice in society the powerful majority has to be ready to give up maximizing their rights. The image of a person behind the Constitution is not an isolated and atomistic free-rider only striving for his/hers self-interest but a responsible member of the society having inalienable human dignity, right to self-determination and several other freedoms and rights but some liabilities and social responsibilities towards co-citizens and environment at the same time.

Thereby, balancing is the key element of understanding and interpreting the Finnish Constitution and the core principles of it. Finland is a sovereign republic but participation in international co-operation relativizes the concept of national sovereignty. The parliament representing the sovereign people is a supreme body of the state but still the courts of law have at least a limited authority to review whether legislative power has been exercised within the limits set by the constitution. And if domestic courts fail with this task, the European Court of Human Rights and European Court of Justice may have a last word about the issue in question. Moreover, the self-government of the people is built on a model of representative democracy, but it has to balanced by leaving enough room and creating possibilities for direct participation of individuals and free interest groups.

V. Rule of Law in Current Constitutional Context

When the rule of law is regarded as one of the core constitutional principles it appears to be self-evident that the traditional formalist and thin concept of legality is insufficient from a point of view of understanding the overall normative relevance of this principle. Naturally, this traditional concept is tailored to serve certain constitutional values and principles including legislative supremacy and representative democracy as well as legal certainty, predictability and formal equality before the law. On the other hand, it may be rather ill-equipped in assuring that the principles of inviolability of human dignity, freedom and rights of the individual and justice in society will not be disregarded. Consequently, the traditional formalistic starting point according to which "whatever law accepted by the Parliament has to be strictly observed" needs to be updated and supplemented with certain new substantial and procedural requirements. Under current constitutional regime, the laws have to be interpreted and applied in a manner guaranteeing that no exceptions from the respect human dignity and fundamental rights will be made. Moreover, the demands for promotion of justice in society and empowering people to participate should govern both legislative and adjudicative decision making.

All in all, the narrow or blind reading and obeying of the black letter law is not enough but the current constitutional concept of rule of law requires much more. [1] Without going into details, individuals shall be treated with dignity and as equals, their voice shall be heard and their rights shall be respected. The requirement of equal treatment does not refer only to formal equality but it also covers measures promoting substantive equality. For example, favouring disadvantaged groups is unproblematic from a point of view of rule of law in cases where the intention of the special treatment is to create equal opportunities for all and thereby promote justice in society. Furthermore, access to justice and right to fair trial as well as many other procedural requirements are essential elements of the rule of law.

Reconstructed in the light of the core constitutional principles the current Finnish understanding of rule of law (constitutional *rechsstaat*) could be described at least with adjectives democratic, participatory, transparent, egalitarian, just and social. Respecting human dignity, individual self-determination, social

---

[1]   See Tom Bingham, "The Rule of Law", *Penguin Books* 2011, p. 8 and p. 37 and *Report on the Rule of Law of the European Commission for Democracy Through Law* (Venice Commission), 28 March 2011, Strasbourg.

responsibility as well as environmental sustainability belong to the basic values of it. Nowadays，only such laws rule that do not contradict with human dignity，fundamental rights，social justice or any other of the core constitutional principles.

法　治

——芬兰宪法的核心原则之一

佩卡·兰斯尼瓦

【摘要】本文的目的是在现行宪法框架下探讨变化着的芬兰法治理念。传统意义上，芬兰的法治学说是基于 19 世纪的法治国观念建立的，大力强调公共行政的合法性要求。我的主要论点是：在现行宪法框架之下，严格遵守法律的白纸黑字是不够的，法治要求得更多。这一主张是建立在最近芬兰宪法法案及其核心原则已经被改革的这个事实上。在改革的同时，传统的核心宪法原则被以下新原则所补充：人格尊严不受侵犯、保障个人自由和权利、促进社会正义、个人参与和影响民主决策和芬兰参与国际合作和作为欧盟成员国的权利。改革的一个主要观念是把个人变成宪法关注的核心。换句话说，宪法并不仅仅意图在国家机构的高层运作中发挥作用，个人的待遇被提升为宪法的首要兴趣。

如今，法治原则应被解读为宪法核心原则体系中的一部分。因此，只有采用这样的法律，才不违反人类尊严、基本权利、社会正义或任何其他的核心的宪法原则。鉴于对宪法核心原则的重构，当代芬兰对法治的理解至少可以用以下形容词描述：民主的、参与的、透明的、平等的、公正的和社会的。尊重人的尊严、个人的自主决定、社会责任以及环境的可持续性都属于其根本价值。

芬兰法治模式的特点和新发展

——中国社会科学院访问芬兰法学代表团的报告

柳华文[*]

【摘要】 在中国和芬兰两国友好关系不断加强的背景下，中苏法律界的交流与合作获得新的更大的推动和发展。2010 年 9 月底至 10 月初，中国社会科学院法学代表团访问芬兰，既增强了两国法律领域的相互了解和共识，又开启了未来两国法律界相互学习和借鉴的新路径。代表团参加了中苏法治模式研讨会，访问了芬兰国会宪法委员会、最高法院、最高行政法院、最高检察院、司法部、国会监察官办公室、赫尔辛基大学，既介绍了中国法治建设的成就和发展趋势，又学习了荷兰法治模式的特点、宪法改革的新进展、国会宪法委员会的独特性、最高行政法院的特点、最高法院的特色、检察官制度和国会监察官制度的特色，以及芬兰法治建设中人权法地位上升的趋势和轻刑化政策的实践经验。

【关键词】 芬兰　北欧　法治模式

2010 年 9 月 27 日至 10 月 1 日，根据中国社会科学院与芬兰科学院的合作协议，在 2009 年中苏比较法国际研讨会成功举办的基础上，由法学研究所李林所长率领的我院代表团访问芬兰。期间，代表团在赫尔辛基参加了中苏法治模式研讨会，并根据合作方赫尔辛基科学院和赫尔辛基大学法学院的安排，访问了芬兰国会宪法委员会、最高法院、最高行政法院、最高检察院、司法部、国会监察官办公室、赫尔辛基大学。代表团的访问受到芬兰最高司法部门和法学界的高度重视，获得较高规格的接待。代表团从

---

* 中国社会科学院国际法研究所研究员。

研讨会和访谈中了解到芬兰法治模式的若干特点和新发展。

一　中芬关系及法律领域的交流概述

芬兰是一个人口只有 530 万的北欧小国，却拥有 "森林王国"、"欧洲绿色之肺" 和 "圣诞老人故乡" 等诸多美称。芬兰连续多年被评为世界上腐败程度最低、廉洁程度最高的国家。在世界经济论坛公布的全球竞争力报告中，芬兰几度蝉联榜首。

2010 年是中芬建交 60 周年，胡锦涛总书记在 10 月 28 日致芬兰总统塔里娅·哈洛宁的贺电中说："建交 60 年来，中芬关系健康稳定发展。进入新世纪，两国领导人互访不断，政治关系更加成熟，经贸合作务实开展，各领域合作成果显著。双方在重大国际和地区问题上密切沟通和协调。中国高度重视对芬关系，希望双方以建交 60 年为新的起点，增进政治互信，扩大互利合作，丰富合作内涵，共同应对全球性挑战，使中芬关系成为不同社会制度、不同文化传统国家关系的典范。"同样值得关注的是，哈洛宁总统在贺电中提到："两国在科技、教育和法制等领域的交流与合作顺利，文化交流与民间往来日益多元化并富有活力。"

同日，国务院总理温家宝与芬兰总理基维涅米互致贺电。温总理在贺电中说："建交以来，中芬关系得到全面发展。双方人员往来密切，各领域合作成果丰硕，两国在国际事务中保持密切沟通与协调。进一步发展中芬友好互利合作关系已成为双方共识。在新的历史阶段，中方愿与芬方共同努力，推动中芬关系不断向前发展。"基维涅米在贺电中表示："芬中关系稳步发展，两国在经贸、科技、教育、文化、司法和国际事务等领域的合作不断深入，芬兰对这些成就倍感骄傲，愿以此为契机，进一步深入发展对华关系。"

赫尔辛基大学校长、商法学家 Thomas Wilhelmsson 告诉代表团，哈洛宁总统知晓并非常重视和鼓励他们与我院开展的法学交流活动。

二　芬兰法治模式的特点和新发展

访问期间，芬兰科学院 Markku Mattila 院长，最高法院 Pauliine Koskelo 院长，最高行政法院 Pekka Hallberg 院长，芬兰国会宪法委员会 Kimmo Sasi 主席，国家检察官办公室 Jukka Rappe 检察官，司法部 Tiina Astola 常务秘书长，芬兰赫尔辛基大学 Thomas Wilhelmsson 校长，国会监察官办公室 Maija Sakslin 副专员等分别热情接待了代表团，还与代表团进行了专题座谈。

中芬法治模式研讨会于 9 月 28 日至 29 日在赫尔辛基举行。会议围绕"中芬法治的核心价值比较"、"中芬法律史比较"、"当代中芬法治模式比较"、"当代中芬法治模式的挑战与未来"四个大的主题展开研讨。中国社会科学院的参会人员包括：法学所所长李林教授，副所长冯军教授，《环球法律评论》主编徐炳教授，法制史研究室高旭晨教授、高汉成副教授，法理学研究室胡水君教授、贺海仁副教授，国际法研究所所长助理柳华文副教授，国际合作局施雪华女士。芬兰与会者包括了芬兰国内法学界和司法界的权威学者近三十人。双方通过会议更深刻地了解到两国历史、传统和文化对现今法治工作的影响，两国法治模式的发展脉络，遇到的挑战、机遇和未来的发展趋势。与会者认为两国法治事业的发展有许多共通之处，可以互相切磋和借鉴，有必要开展密切、长期的联系与交流。

（一）北欧法治模式具有自身特点

在 9 月 27 日芬兰科学院 Markku Mattila 院长举办的招待宴会、9 月 28 日研讨会开幕式和芬兰司法部举行的招待会上，司法部 Tiina Astola 常务秘书长强调，北欧国家的法律体系有自身的独特性，与其他国家，包括欧洲大陆国家有所不同。她强调，英语反映不了北欧国家的法律概念。

以宪法为例，根据图尔库大学 Pekka Länsineva 教授等的介绍，与其他许多欧洲国家如德国相比，传统上，北欧国家的宪法有以下特征：①强调立法主权（与英国的议会至上类似）；②法律主要被视为政治和国家的工具（是在积极意义上的观点，将法律视为人民意志的反映，并通过民主和合法程序制定法律），是实现福利国家、社会改革、收入分配等目标的主要手段；③特别强调法治的理念，由此重视国会立法者的意志。

（二）芬兰宪法改革的新进展

芬兰现行宪法是经过 1995 年和 2000 年两次修订的结果。两次改革总的目标是延续芬兰既有的宪法传统，巩固法治经验，因应社会和时代发展的新需要。欧洲一体化进程产生了直接的影响。芬兰 1990 年批准了《欧洲人权公约》、1995 年加入了欧洲联盟。1995 年芬兰对有关基本权利的宪法内容进行了修订，2000 年则全面完成了宪法修订。

芬兰宪法在北欧属于年青一代的宪法，因为现行挪威宪法颁布于 1814 年，丹麦宪法颁布于 1953 年，瑞典宪法颁布于 1974 年。不过，瑞典和挪威都正在进行修订宪法的工作。芬兰宪法中当然存在一些北欧宪政主义的特殊理解或特定概念，反映了北欧的宪法文化，并且是最新的北欧宪法文化的体现。

芬兰宪法改革的目标不是摆脱北欧的传统，而是要谨慎地加强宪政，更有效地保护个人权利，并从欧洲大陆其他宪法制度中借鉴经验。为了与加入欧盟后其承担的国际法义务相符合，芬兰宪法的起草者们强调，法院要重新理解宪法中关于基本权利的规定，将其视为法律上可操作和有效的法律规则，而不是仅仅起一种宣示的作用。而且，解释普通法律，也要在宪法规定的指导下进行，当法律规定发生矛盾时，宪法规范应当优先。芬兰宪法改革的结果虽然在某种程度上克服了北欧国家较弱的宪法传统，但是与拥有宪法法院的德国相比，还是有很大的不同。

现行芬兰宪法的核心原则规定在该宪法的第一章当中，分别是：①国家主权（单一制共和国）；②人的尊严不可侵犯；③个人自由与权利（保护基本权利）；④社会公正；⑤法治；⑥人民主权和民主（国会作为国家的最高权力机关）；⑦立法、行政和司法的权力分立。

法律对于法治原则做出明确规定：公共权力必须根据法律行使；在所有的公共活动中，法律应该被严格遵守。传统上，在芬兰有一种强烈的法律崇拜；阅读和遵守法律是在严格的字面上进行的；对成文法有一种盲目和形式上的信仰；制定法在法律渊源中具有至高的地位。宪法改革以后，法治原则强调实质意义上的法治，一方面，要求法律的产生必须符合所有民主标准——包括法律草案的公开透明，广泛的社会参与；另一方面，所有法律不仅要严格进行字面上的解读，更要符合宪法的标准，特别是宪法的核心原则。

芬兰宪法的特点是：①强调宪法是法治核心，立国之本；②除了反映国家的政治结构和社会制度之外，特别强调加强对基本权利的保护；③关注宪法的可操作性、可执行性，使宪法在法律和社会实践中发挥效用。芬兰宪法改革反映的宪法发展趋势具有一定的普遍性，而它的经验又表明，加强宪政并不一定要开展激进的政治和法律改革，比如以成立宪法法院的形式实现基于宪法的司法审查，现有法律体系的革新同样是一条值得重视的途径。

（三）芬兰国会宪法委员会制度独树一帜

赫尔辛基大学 Kaarlo Tuori 教授认为，虽然宪法审查司法化似乎是一个全球化趋势，但是他认为这也不无问题。特别是以司法审查的方式解决问题并不民主，并且可能侵犯了某些团体的利益。

在芬兰，国会地位高于最高法院。2000 年前，国会不允许最高法院插手宪法审查，而由国会宪法委员会负责宪法审查。现在，最高法院的合宪性审查可以对宪法委员会工作予以补充。如果政府认为合宪，而法院认为违宪，则司法部会把争议提交宪法委员会解决。

芬兰国会成立于1806年，自始即设有法律委员会。芬兰独立后，在国会中成立了宪法委员会，负责审查法律的合宪性。其成员均为国会议员（现共有17名委员），而多数成员既不是法学专家，也可能根本就不是法律界人士，但是委员会并不基于政党政治做出决定。

宪法委员会Kimmo Sasi主席介绍说，他们很尊重宪法学专家的意见，在具体工作中经常邀请宪法专家出具专家意见。芬兰最高行政法院等也在具体领域负责维护宪法的权威，但不同的是，国会宪法委员会实施的是事前审查，保证国会通过的法律的合宪性。其第二个优点是，宪法问题涉及根本性的大问题，必须考虑不同的社会价值和利益，在这方面，议员比法官或者法学教授更了解社会和政治的发展变化。他认为，芬兰并不需要像德国等国家那样设立宪法法院。

芬兰的宪政实践对我国宪法实施机制的研究，包括进一步完善全国人民代表大会制度的研究具有一定借鉴意义。

（四）芬兰最高行政法院的特色

9月30日，代表团访问了芬兰最高行政法院。院长Pekka Hallberg先生热情接待了代表团一行，还特别向代表团成员赠送了他2009年用中文出版的专著《法治国家的建设》。院长访问中国十余次，对中国非常有感情。

他强调，关于法治，就像房子一样，要有四个支柱：第一，合法性；第二，权力分立和司法独立；第三，公民的权利和义务；第四，功能性及透明性。

芬兰的法院分为普通法院和行政法院。行政法院的机制在欧洲大陆国家很普遍，欧盟国家均有这种建制，在全世界有七十个国家设立了行政法院。在亚洲，只有泰国建有严格意义上的行政法院。芬兰有八个大区设立了行政法院，即八个平行的行政法庭，有同样的可上诉的权力。这些法院均具有监督政府的权力和功能，但是政治层面的决策问题不在管辖范围之内。

最高行政法院规模不大，共100多人，其中有20多名法官，每年受理4000多个案件，涉及税务、福利、环境、竞争、移民等方面。每个案件由5名法官组成合议庭，但是税务案件由3个人组成合议庭。另外，这个法院每年要做出2000万个决定。

最高行政法院的法官是由总统任命的，他不向国会负责，而向人民负责。国会监察官由国会提名，虽然没有裁决权，但是可以监督法官，比如某个法官不正当，专员可以提出建议和指导意见。

一审行政诉讼案件中，公民的胜诉率为 15%。如果包括上诉到最高法院的行政诉讼案件，公民胜诉率可达 50%。院长强调，行政法院的原则是保证政府决策的合法性，视公民起诉政府为公民积极参与公共管理的表现，实践中倾向于原告而不是被告。

芬兰的透明度非常之高，老百姓对于政府每一个部门的官方文件都有权查看。院长认为这是打击腐败的最重要的因素。

（五）芬兰最高法院的特色

9 月 30 日，代表团访问了芬兰最高法院。Pauliine Koskelo 院长是芬兰享有盛誉的女法官。她热情接待了代表团，并亲自介绍了芬兰最高法院的情况。

李林所长介绍了我国首位女司法部长史良和现任女司法部长吴爱英，以及我国妇女权益保障的成就。Koskelo 院长说，芬兰法律专门规定了男女平等的法律原则，禁止歧视，但并未规定司法机关中司法人员的性别比例。但是，在最高法院，包括院长在内的 19 名法官中，有 5 名是女性。最高法院还有约 80 人的法律秘书队伍，女性占到一半。在最高法院之下，设有 6 个上诉法院和 27 个地区法院。在地方法院中，女性法官的数量日益增加，在未来有超过男性的可能。

她着重介绍了芬兰最高法院在实施宪法方面与国会宪法委员会的关系。她说，宪法委员会有权就任何事项宣布违宪，而法院只可以在个案中提出国会的某项法律是不可行的，从而决定不予适用，但并不意味着相关的法律条文是无效的。在国会修改法律之前，在理论上相关法律仍然有效。因此，与美国不同，芬兰最高法院不是宪法法院，不承担违宪审查之责。

实践中极少涉及违宪的情况。这主要是因为宪法委员会在法案公布前就已经做了合宪性审查，同时法院对法律条文有解释的权力，多数情况下能够通过法律解释化解法律冲突或者法律中与事实不符的问题。在过去的 10 年中只出现过一次不能通过解释解决问题的情况。

Koskelo 院长还着重介绍了适用欧洲理事会法律，特别是《欧洲人权公约》与适用欧盟法的不同及其对国内司法的影响。随着欧洲一体化进程的加强，对人权保护的强调，国内司法的国际性特征非常明显。

关于国际法与国内法的冲突问题。因为欧洲理事会的《欧洲人权公约》已经纳入芬兰国内法律了，所以不存在它高于国内法的问题；一般认为，公约并不享有优先于国内法的地位，遇有冲突时法院努力予以协调。但是值得注意的是，适用该公约的欧洲人权法院的判决现在已经成为芬兰国内解释法律的重要依据。与此不同，欧盟法是有等级的，具有直接的效力，高于国内法；与国内法冲突时，法院主要通过法律解释处理，如果仍然不能解决问题，则欧盟法优先。不过，欧盟法一般只是阻止某些国内法的适用，它本身不能脱离国内法解决问题。因为欧盟法的解释最终是由欧洲法院负责的，所以芬兰最高法院也时时关注欧洲法院的案例。实践中遇到不清楚的问题，也可以向欧洲法院请求解释，后者会给一个初步裁决。她认为，这种司法活动的结果是有益于欧洲法律体系的统一性。

（六）芬兰检察官制度的特色

10月1日，代表团访问了芬兰总检察长办公室。起诉处处长、国家检察官 Jukka Rappe 先生接待了代表团一行。

据介绍，芬兰共有15个检察办公室，主要集中在南部，北部较少；从2011年开始要合并两个，变成13个。每个地方办公室有15名至18名检察官。

欧盟国家的检察体系基本相似，功能也是一样的，都是追诉犯罪。但芬兰也有自己独特的地方，比如在芬兰，检察机构享有相当高的独立地位。事实上，检察官独立于警察、法院和司法部。司法部不是检察机构的上级机关，也无权命令检察长起诉案件。

在芬兰，警察隶属于内政部。检察官可以告诉警察，他想做什么。总体而言，警察局和检察机关保持了良好的合作关系。当然，例外的情况是，罪犯为警察，调查者是检察官时，调查要由专门的人员负责。在总检察长办公室，起诉处中有一个专门小组负责此类案件。在地方检察部门中，也有专人负责。

芬兰的检察官分为总检察长、副总检察长、国家检察官，以及实习检察官。总检察长下设有行政处、起诉处、规划与发展处和国际处。其中起诉处的人员是最多的。国家总检察长办公室的职责是：处理犯罪行为、指导与监督地方检察官、起诉最严重的刑事案件。

在芬兰的检察体系中，检察官独立办案。检察官对所有审级的案件都要负责，不分层级。总检察长也没有权力指导下级检察官业务，如对下级检察官所办案件不满意，可以转移此案给其他检察官办理，或自行办理。

就反腐败而言，检察机关的任务并不多。由于行政的透明度高，加之教育程度比较高，芬兰的腐败现象不多。

（七）国会监察官制度的特色

监察官制度起源于北欧,现在已经以不同形式存在世界许多国家中。10月1日,在芬兰国会监察官办公室,副专员 Maija Sakslin 女士接待了代表团一行。她介绍说,该制度对芬兰的民主制度具有重要意义,它要维护宪法的权威,监督所有的公共权力机构,确保国会立法被认真贯彻。

从理论上说,监察官可以监督、调查任何人。任何人只要行使公权力,都要受其监督,甚至包括国防力量（包括海外国防力量）。

监察官的具体工作包括调查任何人（包括外国人）的申诉。这种申诉每年大概有4000多件,一般1/6的案件可获得结果。申诉需要以书面形式进行。一般而言,申诉所涉及的行为,时限是5年。对于公民申诉,监察官要进行审查,判断是否有违法行为后决定是否立案。对于报假案、提供假证据、诬告行为的,如果涉及违法犯罪,将追究刑事法律责任。但其申诉标准很宽泛,一般而言,不会轻易对恶意行政投诉的进行惩罚。

监察官可以基于自己的意愿,主动调查。如在全国范围内追踪新闻事件、影响较大的案件。有权从相关方面获取有关信息和文件。

在芬兰,国会监察官的权力很大,具有某种意义上的特权地位。区别于许多国家的监察官机制,它甚至可以提起刑事诉讼,还可以通过发出谴责、发表意见、提供建议等方式促进更好的行政。但是,在涉及司法时,它并不能干预司法独立,仅可以就法官的不当行为进行监察,如言辞、态度等。

通过办案,监察官办公室将调查公权力机关是否有滥用行政权、自由裁量权的情况发生,督促行政官员履行良好行政的义务。他们特别注意那些封闭性机构,如警察局、监狱、精神病院、移民中心等。通常会采取私下、秘密对话的调查方式,以保证调查内容的真实、可靠。

国会的监察官也以法律专家的身份工作。监察官可以参与立法活动,以专家的身份提供立法意见。在工作中,该办公室经常与非政府组织合作,掌握信息来源;并与媒体合作,将有关监察事件的进展情况及时披露。

国会是其行为的最终监督者。同时,监察官机制倡导公开性,媒体也会对其行为进行必要的监督。

（八）人权法地位上升

赫尔辛基大学权威学者 Tuomas Ojanen 教授等介绍了近年来人权法对于芬兰法治的影响。

芬兰批准了联合国和欧洲理事会的全部人权公约、国际劳工组织除第

169 号公约（关于土著人，涉及土地权利）以外的全部公约。芬兰有一种双重模式。宪法第 94 条明确规定了接受国际义务的问题。但是在直接实施国际公约的同时，也应该以国会通过法案或者政府颁布法令的形式进行。

现行的芬兰宪法面面俱到，包括公民和政治权利，经济、社会和文化权利，还有环境权等。除了自由迁徙权和选举权之外，所有这些权利是面向所有人的，既包括芬兰公民，也包括在其管辖下的外国人。芬兰国内的案例也努力靠近国际人权条约。芬兰的主张是，参照国际人权文件，使内法律体现国际人权法的精髓。1990 年中期国会就开始这样做了。下一届国会也会将人权提到更高的层面。在出现冲突时，既要适用国内法，也要适用国际法，甚至后者更高。

芬兰还强调基于人权基准的法律解释方法，使所有法律、国会行为贴近芬兰必须遵守的国际人权法。法院和国会都不能在执行国内法中挑战国际人权法，而是遵循。

（九）芬兰轻刑化政策取得成功

芬兰法律政策国家研究院 Tapio Lappi-Seppälä 主任应邀专门为代表团介绍了芬兰刑事司法的总体发展趋势。

在 20 世纪 50 年代，芬兰监狱中羁押的犯人人数是北欧邻国的三到四倍。在过去几十年中，芬兰在建设福利国家的同时，逐渐采取了轻刑化政策，减少监狱服刑，加强社区矫正，特别是在少年司法中引入专门政策和措施。统计表明，刑罚的减轻与犯罪率的降低成正相关关系。

现在，芬兰只有约 3350 名罪犯正在监狱服刑，与北欧的挪威、瑞典、丹麦在人数上基本持平。无期徒刑在芬兰只适用于谋杀犯罪且实际上服刑时间为 12 年至 14 年，社区服务替代了 35% 的有期徒刑的适用。

北欧国家还独创了日罚金制度。最早是 1921 年芬兰使用的，现在已为世界上很多国家使用。该制度也减少了羁押刑的适用。在芬兰，罚金总额等于处以日罚金的天数乘以日罚金数额。一方面，它在确定罚金时做到了根据不同犯罪人的财产状况确定不同的数额，使得刑罚针对财产状况不同的犯罪人起到了同样的威慑作用；另一方面，正常日罚金的数额相当于犯罪人平均日收入的一半，同时根据犯罪人的具体财产状况不同又可以适当变化，兼具合理性与科学性。

传统上，我国社会中存在一种重刑思想，而且是"治乱世用重典"。但是，应对社会治安问题和犯罪问题的根本还是社会建设，对刑罚本身的局限性要有清醒的认识。芬兰在这方面的实践经验值得借鉴。

三 双方表达了加强中芬包括法学在内的社会科学交流的真诚意愿

芬兰科学院院长 Markku Mattila 强调，过去十年，中国经济与社会发展迅速，中国在科学研究方面的投入在国际社会排名第四。芬兰是研究型国家，研究实力雄厚。目前芬兰研究人员占工作人口的比例在欧洲经济合作组织国家中名列第一。芬兰的成功，也主要是基于教育水平的提高，科研能力的推动以及社会和谐发展。芬兰科学院对与中国社会科学院的合作非常满意。双方的合作历时已久，成果丰硕，前景看好。

赫尔辛基大学校长、商法学家 Thomas Wilhelmsson 专门为代表团举办招待晚宴，高度评价中芬法学领域的合作前景。赫尔辛基大学法学院专门为中方代表团准备了一次专题演讲会，由芬兰各法学院院长介绍他们法学院的情况，宾主双方热情探讨了下一步合作的方式。芬兰一共有三所法学院，除赫尔辛基大学法学院外，还有图尔库大学法学院和拉普兰大学法学院。此次交流非常深入，表达了诸多合作意向。

李林所长转达了我院领导向芬兰科学院院长的问候，并向芬兰朋友介绍了中国法治发展和法学教育的新成就。他在访问期间的不同场合指出，中芬两国有各自有特色的文化、传统和法治模式，均面临机遇与挑战。我国在全面学习海洋法系、大陆法系，挖掘西方法律文化资源的同时，还要向更多的国家学习有益的法治经验，尤其是要向北欧斯堪的那维亚国家学习。目前，我们对北欧斯堪的那维法系中的法学理论、司法制度和法治实践的了解还非常不足，更谈不上系统研究。北欧国家特别坚持的"solidarity"（译为团结、稳定）理念，以及根据这种理念构建的社会体制和法律制度，尤其值得我们在构建社会主义和谐社会和中国特色法治体系过程中加以关注和研究。

代表团深切感受到，芬兰司法界和法学界对发展中芬合作的高度重视，对开展平等对话和交流的真诚态度。在全方位开展对外交流的战略格局中，北欧国家特别是芬兰应当占有一席之地，并予以加强。我国与芬兰包括法学在内的社会科学交流还有巨大潜力。

（代表团包括李林、冯军、徐炳、柳华文、高旭晨、高汉成、施雪华，本文由柳华文执笔）

Characteristics and New Development of the Finnish Model of the Rule of Law: Report on a Study Visit to Finland by CASS Delegation

Liu Huawen

【**Abstract**】 Against the general background of continuous strengthening of friendly relationship between China and Finland, the exchange and cooperation between the law circles of the two countries has gained new momentum. In late September and early October of 2010, a delegation from the Institute of Law, CASS paid a study visit to Finland, which increased the mutual understanding and consensus between the Chinese and Finnish law circles and opened up new channels for them to learn from each other's experiences. During the study visit, the delegation participated in the Seminar on the Chinese and Finnish Modes of the Rule of Law and visited various Finnish government and academic institutions, including the Constitutional Law Committee of the Parliament, the Supreme Court, the Office of the Prosecutor General, the Supreme Administrative Court, the Ministry of Justice, the Office of Parliamentary Ombudsman, and the University of Helsinki. Through these activities, the members of the delegation introduced to their Finnish colleagues the achievements made in and the trend of development of the construction of the rule of law in China, and learned a lot from their Finnish colleagues about the characteristics of the Finnish mode of the rule of law, the new development of the constitutional reform, the unique features of the Parliamentary Constitutional Law Committee, the Supreme Court, the Supreme Administrative Court, the Prosecution System, and the Parliamentary Ombudsman system, the increasingly important role of human rights in the construction of the rule of law, and the policy of lenient criminal punishment in Finland.

【**Key words**】 Finland, Nordic countries, Mode of the Rule of Law

中国法治的人文道路

胡水君[*]

【摘要】 文化与政治是影响法治发展道路的两个重要因素。就现实处境而言，中国法治的构建在这两方面还面临着一些需要跨越的障碍。现时代需要一种融合中西人文主义之精髓、兼济人的认知理性与道德理性的新人文主义。从人文主义的视角看，道德人文维度与民主政治维度是构建中国法治需要着力加强的两个方面。在法治发展道路上，中国需要协调好法治的道德、功利、政治与行政四个层面，沿着自身的文化传统，打造政治和社会的理性与道德基础，开拓一种具有厚重人文底蕴的"道德的民主法治"，实现仁义道德与自然权利、民主法治在现代的历史衔接。

【关键词】 法治　人文主义　民主

文化与政治是影响法治发展道路的两个重要因素。就现实处境而言，中国法治的构建在这两方面还面临着一些需要跨越的障碍。在文化层面，尽管自 20 世纪 90 年代以来中国传统文化在持续平稳的社会环境中得到更大生发，但百年现代"新文化"与千年文化传统之间仍有待深入协调，而且，在商品化浪潮和理性化进程中，道德也继续遭受着巨大冲击，因此，会通作为传统之道出发点的仁义道德与作为现代之道出发点的自然权利，在理论和实践上都需要长期努力。在政治层面，法治的构建仍受制于形成门户稳固的现代国家或海洋国家这一近代历史任务，在此条件下，稳固国家秩序和实现国家富强的现实政治目标，容易对民主化进程构成挤压，由此使得法治可能停滞于乃至滑向更有行政效率的法家法治路径，阻塞法治的现代民主维度和道德人文维度的充分展开。鉴于此，本文拟从西方和中国的

两种不同人文主义切入，分析梳理历史上法家、儒家与西方的三种典型法治模式，探究法治的认知理性基础和道德理性基础，以此开拓中国法治乃至现代法治的道德人文维度。这也可以说是在"古今中外"的时空背景下对古今法治所作的一种总体文化审视，有助于理清现代法治之文化缘起、发育过程、历史特性和时空方位，进而展示出中国法治构建需要着力维护的发展方向。本文认为，现时代需要一种融合中西人文主义之精髓的"新人文主义"，以实现自然权利与天然明德、权利主体与道德主体、自由意志与自然道义、民主法治与仁义道德的统合，最终形成一种"道德的民主法治"，而深厚的传统人文底蕴以及近一百多年间西方人文主义的浸染，为中国在 21 世纪迈向这样一种重开"内圣外王"的道德和政治理想提供了现实可能。本文首先分析中西两种人文主义，接着比较法家、儒家与西方的三种典型法治模式，最后讨论立足人的认知理性和道德理性构建"道德的民主法治"的必要性和可能性。

一　两种人文主义：西方与中国

本文将中西人文主义视为人类文明史上历时长久的文化和思想系统，同时侧重于在"现代性"语境下对它们作出分析和考量。鉴于西学大肆进入中国后中国人文主义受到冲击和削弱的历史现实，本文关于中国人文主义的论述主要循着中国文化传统的内在理路展开。因而，文中关于两种人文主义的比较分析，在一定程度上也映衬出中国传统文化与"新文化"的对照。还要指出的是，本文关于中西人文主义的对比主要建立在中西各自文化传统的主体或主流基础之上。从普适的立场看，每一人文主义的特质在另外一种文化中其实也多少有所显现，即使它们在一定历史时期受到抑制排挤而未能发展成为主流。尽管如此，就文化所偏向的不同认知路径，以及由此所表现出的基本特质乃至身处其中的人群所长期养成的生活态度和习惯思维而言，将中西人文主义作为两个适成对照的系统看待仍是大致成立的。以下先分析西方人文主义。

凡文化，无论是关于物的、神的或人的，都可以因为由人化成或通过人之一中介，而被认为是"人文"的，但人文主义作为一种在"现代"产生深远影响的特定历史现象，通常被认为萌发于欧洲的"文艺复兴"时期。循着西方文化系统从希腊文化到希伯来宗教文化再到人文主义的发展脉络看，"文艺复兴"在文化上对于"现代"具有历史开端意义，可谓西方文化在经历上千年的希伯来宗教文化对希腊文化的否定之后，对宗教文化实现

"否定之否定"的重要转折点。"文艺复兴"时期的人文思潮,开启了神本主义的宗教文化走向衰落、人和自然的世界得以迅速发展的历史进程。一如学者所指出的,"如果说人文主义真的重新发现了对人、对人的能力和人对各种事物的理解力的信念,那么科学试验的新方式、革新了的世界观、企图征服和利用自然的新努力也应当归功于人文主义的影响。"① 到 20 世纪,人文主义发展成为拒斥宗教信仰、只关心人类福祉的西方主体文化。② 甚至可以说,西方近代以来的经验主义、包括理性至上在内的理性主义、功利主义、人道主义、自由主义等,无不处在人文主义的大脉络中。有学者指出,"人文主义文化于过去五百年间在西方占据着主流地位……在现代工业化经济的发展过程中,特别是在我们称之为'现代化'的重大社会转型中,人文主义文化扮演了一个主要角色。人文主义同时还是渐次成长起来的自由民主的西方政治模式的重要推手。"③ 照此看,西方人文主义其实也是近一个半世纪以来对中国社会转型产生重要影响的文化形态。

大体上,从人出发,以人间世相为中心,以人的能力、尊严和自由发展为价值准轴,重人事而轻宗教,是人文主义的基本特质。在这些方面,现代人文主义有别于宗教和纯粹的自然科学。尽管如此,人文主义与科学、宗教并非完全不相容。④ 事实上,纵向地看,希腊文明、希伯来宗教、"文艺复兴"以来的人文主义以及 17 世纪以来的自然科学,都共同表现出西方文化系统的某些特性,从而看上去与中国文化传统显出差异。例如,古希腊关于"德性就是知识"⑤ 的看法,突显了一种依循知识途径追寻美德的倾向,这与中国文化传统中沿着德性路径"明明德"、"致良知"的观念存在很大不同,而现代西方主要在经验和知识领域考虑道德和公正问题,其实正承接了古希腊的智识路径。再如,西方宗教中"第一主宰"、人神两分的显著特点,与中国文化传统中"天人合一"、"本性具足"观念也有着重要差异。这些表明,在一定程度上,西方人文主义也多为科学思维所渗透,

① 〔意〕加林:《意大利人文主义》,李玉成译,三联书店,1998,第 215 页。
② Antony Flew and Stephen Priest, eds., *A Dictionary of Philosophy* (London: Pan Books, 2002), p. 175; Gordon Marshall, eds., *A Dictionary of Sociology* (Oxford: Oxford University Press, 1998), pp. 289 – 290.
③ 〔美〕卡洛尔:《西方文化的衰落:人文主义复探》,叶安宁译,新星出版社,2007,中文版序。
④ 关于人文主义与宗教、科学的辨别,参见〔英〕布洛克《西方人文主义传统》,董乐山译,三联书店,1997,第 12 ~ 13 页。
⑤ 苗力田主编《古希腊哲学》,中国人民大学出版社,1989,第 222 ~ 223 页。

类似于宗教中"天人两分"、"第一主宰"的主客两分思维亦绵延其间，它们共同受制于西方整个文化道路。也可以说，西方人文主义在很大程度上蕴含着对在不同历史时期持续存在的西方文化系统基本特性的深化和铺展。就此而言，把握西方人文主义，有时也不能脱离西方宗教和科学而作孤立分析，透过西方人文主义发现西方主体文化与众不同的特质或根本才是重要的。

归纳起来，以"文艺复兴"为正式开端的西方人文主义，在过去五百年间的主要历史特质可大致概括为这样一些方面：

1. 摆脱宗教和神的束缚，从人出发并以人为中心来观察和思考世界

西方人文主义有时被追溯到普罗塔哥拉那里，因为他提出"人是万物的尺度"。[①] 在"文艺复兴"时期，这一观念得以复活。人进而处在了认识的主体地位，并被确定为世界的中心。米兰多拉就认为，"人是万物的核心"，"人是自己的主人，人的唯一限制就是要消除限制，就是要获得自由，人奋斗的目标就是要使自己成为自由人，自己能选择自己的命运，用自己的双手编织光荣的桂冠或是耻辱的锁链。"[②] 而且，神或上帝与人被严格隔开，人的注意力、希望和归宿转向尘世。被称为"人文主义之父"的彼特拉克认为，"上帝的世界是经过七层铅封的世界，非凡人的智力所能理解"，"我是凡人，只要凡人的幸福"。[③] 这样一种"人化"的过程，在后世蔓延到世俗社会的经济、政治、法律、文化等各个领域，直至形成"祛魅"的"人的王国"。

2. 意志自由，充分认可人的能力和尊严

意志自由是人文主义的核心特征。宗教的衰微以及对"上帝之死"的宣告，都直接源于意志自由。在伊拉斯谟与路德关于意志自由的著名争论之后，历经宗教改革和"启蒙"运动，人成为独立的精神个体，人的意志自由得以最终确立。这可以说是影响近代西方政治经济发展特别是民主化和市场化的一个关键点。而且，人的潜在能力得到充分肯定和信任，甚至被无限放大。米兰多拉讲的"我们愿意是什么，我们就能成为什么"，[④] 以

---

① 苗力田主编《古希腊哲学》，中国人民大学出版社，1989，第 183～186 页。

② 〔意〕加林：《意大利人文主义》，李玉成译，三联书店，1998，第 59、102 页。

③ 〔意〕加林：《意大利人文主义》，第 23 页及译序。

④ 〔美〕卡洛尔：《西方文化的衰落：人文主义复探》，叶安宁译，新星出版社，2007，第 3 页。

及阿尔伯蒂讲的"人们能够完成他们想做的一切事情"，① 都是关于人的潜能的典型话语。因为意志自由和人的潜能，人被视为有价值和有尊严的主体，所以应受到平等尊重。西方近代以来的权利、民主以及自由主义政治，在很大程度上正以这种意志自由和人的尊严为基础。② 一如学者所指出的，"代表选举是人文主义的派生事物，因为它赋予公民群体中的每一个我一份特别权力。"③

3. 立足自然世界和人的自然本性

从宗教文化到人文主义的转变，经历了一个"世界的发现和人的发现"④ 过程。一旦对世界的宗教解释被舍弃，对自然世界的客观把握和审美观察就成为可能并得到发展。"人化"的过程由此也成为世界自然化的过程，世界获得了一种基于自然科学的人文解释，以致人本身也被自然化，成为物种进化过程中有血有肉、具有理性的自然生物。禁欲主义因此被解除，人的身体特别是生理本性受到重视并被重新认识。拉伊蒙迪在15世纪重述伊壁鸠鲁的观点说，"我们既然是大自然的产儿，就应当竭尽全力保持我们肢体的健美和完好，使我们的心灵和身体免遭来自任何方面的伤害。"⑤ 菲莱尔福也质问："自从弄清楚人不仅仅是灵魂的时候开始，人们怎么可以忘记人的身体呢？"⑥ 而且，人的快乐成为价值评判的基本标准，以至于"追求幸福"连同生命、自由一起，在政治和法律文献被确定为基本人权。与此相应，历史上以宗教的、道德的或自然的义务为基点的伦理政治或道德政治，转变为从"自然权利"出发的自然政治。⑦

4. 在认知上，以人的经验和理性为判断根据

无论是笛卡尔讲"我思故我在"，洛克讲心灵犹如一张"白纸"，还是

---

① 〔瑞士〕布克哈特：《意大利文艺复兴时期的文化》，何新译，商务印书馆，1979，第135页。

② Ian Shapiro, eds., *The Rule of Law* (New York: New York University Press, 1994), pp. 13 – 19.

③ 〔美〕卡洛尔：《西方文化的衰落：人文主义复探》，叶安宁译，新星出版社，2007，第140页。

④ 〔瑞士〕布克哈特：《意大利文艺复兴时期的文化》，何新译，商务印书馆，1979，第143、280、302页。

⑤ 〔意〕加林：《意大利人文主义》，李玉成译，三联书店，1998，第47页。

⑥ 〔意〕加林：《意大利人文主义》，第46页。

⑦ 〔美〕列奥·施特劳斯：《霍布斯的政治哲学》，申彤译，译林出版社，2001；〔美〕列奥·施特劳斯：《自然权利与历史》，彭刚译，三联书店，2003。

贝克莱讲"存在就是被感知"，① 都将知识的来源归结于经验和理性。无论是诉诸感官的经验主义、诉诸利害的功利主义，还是诉诸理智的理性主义、诉诸情感的浪漫主义，都抛弃了天赋或先验的道德原则，消解了宗教和传统的权威，而将是非对错、善恶标准、社会交往以及政治法律制度安排，建立在经验和理性的基础上。"敢于认知"② 并由此将人的经验和理性作为认知基础，是西方人文主义的基本特点。有学者指出，人文主义"重视理性，不是因为理性建立体系的能力，而是为了理性在具体人生经验中所遇到的问题——道德的、心理的、社会的、政治的问题——上的批判性和实用性的应用。"③ 理性，在此更多地指人的认知理性，它受到激情、欲望、利益的支使，意味着合乎逻辑的思考、计算、推理和判断能力，其功能在于计算欲望和利益如何得到满足，不同欲望和利益如何相互协调。④ 道德、经济、政治、法律、社会各领域的现象都从经验和理性获得合理解释，其问题也都在经验和理性范围内形成合理的解决方案，而超出经验和理性之外则通常被认为是不可理解的或"不合理的"。

总的说来，"文艺复兴"以来的西方人文主义，既与西方整个文化系统有着难以分割的内在联系，又是一种不同以往、有新特点的文化形态。与古希腊文化相比，它不再赋予善、德性或某些形而上的先验原则以天然的基础地位，而是在人的经验和理性的基础上讨论善、德性以及正当问题。与中世纪的宗教文化相比，它不再以神或人的宗教义务为中心，而是围绕人的自然本性，基于经验和理性来解释和构造外在世界。可以说，西方人文主义开出的是一个以人的经验和认知理性为基础的人的世界，其价值体系主要是围绕人的身体以及生理本性构建起来的，人的自由特别是意志自由构成了其基本原则。尽管从中国法家那里，也能看到一种基于人的生理本性的知识拓展，但在价值诉求上，西方人文主义又表现出很强的现代意义。在西方人文主义的视野下，人因其自然本性、潜在能力和意志自由而被认为享有尊严、平等价值和自然权利；权力分立和制衡、宪政、人民主权、法治则是从人的自然生理本性出发，基于人的经验和认知理性构建起

① 参见北京大学哲学系外国哲学史教研室编译《西方哲学原著选读》（上卷），商务印书馆，1981，第 369、450、503 页。

② 〔德〕康德：《历史理性批判文集》，何兆武译，商务印书馆，1990，第 22 页。

③ 〔英〕布洛克：《西方人文主义传统》，董乐山译，三联书店，1997，第 235 页。

④ 参见〔英〕阿巴拉斯特《西方自由主义的兴衰》，曹海军等译，吉林人民出版社，2004，第 42 页。

来用以保障人的自然权利、维护正常社会交往的外在制度形式。用历史比较的眼光看，在西方文化系统中，人文主义与中世纪以前的古代文化存在着明显的断裂。这集中表现在："自然权利"取代"自然法"、"神法"而成为现代政治、道德、法律领域的基本出发点，"意志自由"取代"自然道义"、宗教义务而成为现代社会的基本处事原则。与此相应，人在作为权利主体与作为德性主体之间发生分裂，道德精神与自然权利、民主政治、自由法治之间也出现缝隙。质言之，西方人文主义在将现代人文世界的基础奠定在人的认知理性之上的同时，其实也划出了现代人文世界的范围和边界。在很大程度上，西方人文主义因此弱化或忽略了人的道德理性，享有"自由意志"的个人可能享有"做错事的权利"，有些基于民主投票机制产生的政治和法律决议可能偏离"道义"，而"自由国家"也可能因为缺乏必要的道德原则限制而沦为政治、经济乃至文化势力的功利手段，乃至滑向"自由国家主义"以及具有侵略性的"自由帝国主义"。如果说，西方人文主义在为现代民主政治和法治铺设文化底垫的重要历史过程中，一定程度上也附带有道德和政治上的"现代性"问题，那么，与之相比，近一百多年间，中国文化传统中的人文主义则因为其对道德理性的偏重而既受到西方人文主义的猛烈冲击，也在重构"外王"的过程中遭遇到重重困境。

　　中国文化传统因为其所包含的人文主义而与西方文化以及世界其他文化传统相比表现出较大的独特性，也因为此种人文主义的普适因素而透显出一种至今仍得以生发延展的普遍性。因为历史流变中某些未尽合理的历史现象而彻底否定中国文化，或者只从历史文化形态上把握中国传统文化，视之为比西方文化或其他现代文化更为落后的文化形态，而不从根本道理上作去粗取精、去伪存真的辨别，就不可避免地会忽视乃至损害中国文化中的普遍人文要素，而这些要素恰是中国文化历经大浪淘沙式的千年流转而仍得以延绵不断的根源所在。基于人文主义的角度审视，中国文化传统并不能被仅仅视为一种与君主政制不可分割的独特历史文化形态，它在道理层面实际蕴涵有某些足以穿越"古今中外"的人文精神或要素，并因此对于现代世界以及未来具有重要历史意义，也有着在摆脱君主政制的支配或影响后与现代生活相适应或融合的可能性。可以说，人文主义或人文精神构成了中国传统文化以及整个中国文化不可或缺的基本内容和独特维度，以致有人认为，"中国文化乃是一在本源上即是人文中心的文化。"① 在此意

---

① 唐君毅：《中国人文精神之发展》，广西师范大学出版社，2005，第6页。

义上，理解中国文化，甄别和准确把握其中的人文要素是必不可少的。而就此人文主义或人文精神相对西方以及其他文化系统的独特性和普遍性而言，这样一种把握也显得尤为重要。在更多地立足经验、理性乃至功利来构建民主法治的现时代，对中国法治以及现代法治作适当人文审视的必要性和重要性也正发源于此。

一般认为，中国人文主义大致形成于周代，但从古文《尚书》等文献看，它至少还可上溯至尧舜。这集中体现在"天命"与"人力"的关系上。无论中西，命运与人的自由意志之间的关系都构成人文主义的一个关键。在很大程度上，西方自"文艺复兴"以来的人文运动，可谓一个建立在经验和理智基础上的人的自由意志的扩展过程。与此形成对照的是，中国人文主义从其产生之初就具有明显而深厚的道德取向。在中国人文主义中，始终存在一种人通过自己的努力可以达至或超越"天命"的道德认知。人文主义的开始大致是以"天命"与"人力"发生一定分化、肯定"人力"的实际效果为前提的。在从夏到商、从商到周的王朝更替过程中，"受命于天"的观念不断遭受冲击，"人力"特别是人的道德努力对于维持天命甚至改变命运的重要作用，基于一种充满危机感的政治实践被提炼出来并受到高度重视。天命靡常，惟人力或人德可恃，因之作为道德和政治原则得以确立。与此相关的话语在古代有很多，例如，"天命靡常……聿修厥德……自求多福"，① "惟克天德，自作元命。"② 在认识到"天命"不再可以永久依赖之后，人从"天命"转向"人力"，"自"、"我"的道德努力作为人始终可以把持的基本方面得到了充分展现。此种"自求多福"、"自造元命"的生命态度也深入到政治领域，从而形成了中国政治文化传统中根深蒂固的"德治"和"民本"观念。提升统治者自身的德行，成为维护巩固政权、赢得上天眷顾的重要方式。而且，基于现实政治经验的总结，上天眷顾的标准最终被归结为获得人民支持，由此，"德"成为沟通"天"与"民"的通道，"德"与"民"也成为政治领域两个至为基本而又相互联系的方面。"天"、"德"、"民"这些因素融合在一起，既为中国传统政治设置了超验维度，也为其开展造就了现实途径。

不难发现，中国人文主义透显着厚重的道德意蕴，因此，一些学者也以"道德人文精神"来表述它。这是一种与西方的理性人文主义存在差异

---

① 《诗·大雅·文王》。
② 《尚书·吕刑》。类似的话语在《尚书》中比比皆是。

的人文主义。大体而言,肯定一个虽然难以通过经验认知但客观上存在并对人产生实效的道德系统,构成了中国人文主义的基本特质。就西方人文主义对人的经验、理智的侧重而言,中国人文主义表现为一种明显的道德人文主义。这样一种人文主义在中国后世得到了延续传承和进一步发展,一直是中国传统道德哲学和政治哲学的根基所在。依循根本道理和历史脉络看,中国的道德人文主义可说是始终围绕人的道德主体精神展开的。这主要表现在以下四个方面:

(1)人的道德本性。认可人的道德本性或人性善,构成了包括儒、释、道在内的中国文化主流的一个必需要素,正所谓"天地间,至尊者道,至贵者德而已矣。至难得者人,人而至难得者,道德有于身而已矣。"① 中国文化路径得以展开的基点正在于人生而皆具有的善性、"明德"、"恻隐之心"、"良知"。换言之,从人的道德本性出发,是中国人文主义的一个重要特质。传统中国对"德治"的高度重视,与这种对人的道德本性的充分认可和侧重密切相关。如果说西方近代以来日渐形成了一个立足自然本性的物理世界观,那么,中国文化则一直贯穿着一种立足道德本性的道德世界观。宇宙与人由此被认为是同构的,这设定了人生以及政治的道德进路,中国传统政治因而更多地表现为一种道德政治。所谓"内圣外王",由于始终需要基于"内圣"开"外王",这样的"外王"也呈现出鲜明的道德本色,显然有别于立足人的生理或自然本性的自然政治。如果说,自然政治遵循的是在世俗的政治、经济、社会等领域通行的自然律,那么,道德政治则遵循的是同样对人产生实际效果的道德律。对人道德本性的侧重和对道德律的遵循,决定了中国传统政治和法律实践的道德路向。

(2)人的道德能力。不仅西方人文主义强调意志自由,中国人文主义也同样强调人的意志自由。有所不同的是,中国文化里的意志自由具有深厚的道德意义,这主要表现在对人的道德能力和内在尊严的充分认可上。在人的能力方面,所谓"万物皆备于我"②、"天地之道备于人,万物之道备于身"③、"吾性自足"④ 等话语,强烈突显出人无所不备的道德潜质。如果说,在西方人文语境中,自由意志多表现为是非善恶的标准完全取决于个人自己,而这并不以一种客观存在的超验法则为准绳和必要限制,那么,

---

① 周敦颐:《周敦颐集》,中华书局,1990,第33页。

② 《孟子·尽心上》。

③ 邵雍:《邵雍集》,中华书局,2010,第554页。

④ 王守仁:《王阳明全集》,上海古籍出版社,1992,第1228页。

在中国文化中，人的自由意志则始终处于道德指引或道德律的主导下，有着明确的道德方向，是一种与"自然正当"紧密结合在一起的自由意志。人之为人的尊严，也恰源于人的自由意志对此道德路向的不懈坚持。而且，在中国文化语境中，人的这种道德能力具有极强的能动性和创造性，以至于在"天人合一"之外还存在着天人并立的观念。"我命在我不在天"①、"不能自强，则听天所命；修德行仁，则天命在我"② 等话语，表明了这一点。无论是"天人合一"还是天人并立，与西方的"天人两分"以及"第一主宰"观念都有着重要不同。在中国文化中，人的道德努力在终极意义上其实是以超越天人的"道"、"理"、"法"为依归。在很大程度上，这样一种对"道"、"德"、"理"、"法"的终极和超越追求，抑制了以人的生理本性为基础的自然政治的发展。

（3）人的道德责任。道德责任规制和引导着中国人文主义的目的和方向。在自由主义理论中，个人在无涉他人的领域是完全自治的，只要"无害他人"就有权利做任何事。③ 这种理论虽然为个人的道德选择留有空间，但由于它并不以"自然正当"或确定的是非善恶体系为圭臬，个人的道德责任事实上并不明确。而沿着中国文化理路看，出于"天地万物为一体"④、"民吾同胞，物吾与也"⑤ 之类的观念，人对他人乃至所有人负有一种普遍的道德责任。从人的道德本性和道德能力，不仅可以推导出人对他人的道德责任，也可推导出人对自己的道德责任。在传统政治下，此种道德责任也得以向政治、法律和社会领域普遍扩展。如果说，统治者基于对政权稳固的担忧而注重自身道德更多地表现为一种消极意义上的"德治"，那么，建基于"万物一体"观念之上的人的道德责任，则深化了一种更为积极的、旨在从终极意义上提升所有人的道德觉悟的"德治"。这在很大程度上加固了"民本"政治的道德根基，使之不致深陷于单纯的关于政权兴替的功利考量之中，而使政治和行政领域的"若保赤子"⑥ 态度具有更为实在的道德意义，也使道德意识广泛扩及于社会和每个人。而且，在

① 参见《抱朴子内篇·黄白卷》。
② 朱熹：《四书章句集注》，中华书局，1983，第280页。
③ 参见〔英〕密尔《论自由》，程崇华译，商务印书馆，1959，第10、104页。
④ 程颢、程颐：《二程集》，中华书局，1981，第15页；王守仁：《王阳明全集》，上海古籍出版社，1992，第54页。
⑤ 张载：《张载集》，中华书局，1978，第62页。
⑥ 《尚书·康诰》。

中国文化中，此种公共道德责任并非建基于个人权利，而渊源于他人乃至万物与自己不可分割的同一性或相关性。因此，人对自己的道德责任与人对他人的道德责任其实是融合在一起的，道德行为所体现的并非仅仅是一种利他或兼顾他人的心态，而是一种与道德主体自身休戚相关的道德责任。

（4）人的道德认知。在人的感官或物理认知之外，中国人文主义一直保持和发展着一种独特的道德认知方式。此种认知方式构成了人的道德本性、道德能力以及道德责任的认识论前提，也制约着中国学术的发展方向，道德知识体系因此在中国传统学术中长期处于主导地位。所谓"德性之知"，在孟子那里主要表现为"不学而能……不虑而知……达之天下"① 的良知良能。良知良能或"德性之知"，并不依赖于人的经验感知或"闻见之知"，一如宋儒所言："世人之心，止于闻见之狭。圣人尽性，不以见闻梏其心，其视天下无一物非我，孟子谓尽心则知性知天以此。……见闻之知，乃物交而知，非德性所知；德性所知，不萌于见闻"；② "闻见之知，非德性之知。……德性之知，不假闻见。"③ 在中国文化传统中，"德性之知"的开通，有其独特的门径和方法。一般认为，"德性之知"不是通过感官而是通过心思，通过内心虚静诚明从而达致"天人合一"来实现的。④ 此种道德认知路径，显出浓厚的人文意蕴。

总之，就文化主流而言，人的道德精神、主体精神和责任精神构成了中国人文主义的精神实质。与此适成对照的是，近代以来的西方人文主义主要立足于人的身体和生理本性来构建作为主体的人及其责任。虽然中西人文主义都表现出人的理性精神，都力图使人成为有尊严的"主体"，但它们所据以立足的理性基础其实有差异。大体上，中国人文主义建基于人的道德理性，西方人文主义则建基于人的认知理性。同样，虽然中西人文主义都表现出从人天然具备的本性出发，但它们对人的本性的不同方面实际上有所侧重。如果说，中国人文主义从人的道德本性出发最终成就的是道德主体，那么，西方人文主义从人的生理本性出发最终成就的则是权利主

---

① 《孟子·尽心上》。

② 张载：《张载集》，中华书局，1978，第 24 页。

③ 程颢、程颐：《二程集》，中华书局，1981，第 317 页。

④ 参见《孟子·告子上》，《孟子·离娄上》，《礼记·中庸》，《荀子·解蔽篇》。还可参见张载《张载集》，中华书局，1978，第 20 页；程颢、程颐：《二程集》，中华书局，1981，第 178 页。

体。由于中西人文主义在基点和路向上的差异，中西政治和法律发展道路在很多方面也有所不同。鉴于此，本文接下来在中西人文背景下，进一步对比分析中西法治模式。

二　法治的三种模式：法家、儒家与西方

法治主张和实践的一个前提是关于人的理论。侧重于人的不同方面，或者，立足于对人的性质的不同判断，法治主张和实践通常有与之相应的不同朝向。这从法家、儒家以及西方近代以来关于法治的看法可以明显看到。法治主张和实践与人的理论之间的这种紧密联系，使得将法治与人文主义结合起来讨论成为可能，也显得必要。本文关于法治与人文主义的讨论着重沿着中国历史发展线索，开掘蕴藏在各种主张和实践之中的学理。历史地看，可大致发现三种法治的历史和理论形态：法家法治、儒家法治以及源自西方的民主法治。上升到理论层面，可将其分别表述为"作为武功的法治"、"作为文德的法治"和"作为宪政的法治"。①

在方法上，对三种法治模式的区分和把握，有必要兼顾事实与学理。首先，此种区分并不排斥各种法治类型的历史性。在很大程度上，法家法治以春秋战国以及秦朝奉行法治的意识形态和社会实践为事实基础；儒家法治以周代礼制以及汉代至清代受儒学深层影响的法律实践为事实基础；民主法治则以近代以来围绕民主和民权展开的法治实践为事实基础。其次，此种区分也不否认作为理论形态的各种法治类型对历史的相对独立性。三种法治类型，虽然与中国从封建贵族政治向君主郡县政治再向现代民主政治发展，以及从礼制向法制再向宪制发展的历史进程，大体可以对应起来，但本文并不将它们只视为与一定历史时期或条件不可分割的历史形态，而是将它们视为各具学理基础、可以跨越古今的理论类型。从学理看，三种模式各有所本，并且在与人文主义的关系上表现出明显差异。大体上，法家法治立足人的趋利避害本性，侧重于武功，旨在富国强兵，无论是人的道德还是人的权利，都不属政治考虑的重点；儒家法治立足人的道德本性，侧重于道德，倡导德主刑辅，力图唤起人的道德本性；民主法治虽然也立足人的经验和理性，但侧重在政制，着意于权力制约的外在形式和民主的法律构造，以及对以身体和生命为核心的人权和公民权利的保障。鉴于各

---

① 参见胡水君主编《法理学的新发展：探寻中国的政道法理》，中国社会科学出版社，2009，导论。

自的学理根据,本文并不认为,在从传统向现代转型的现代化进程中,法家法治、儒家法治乃至民主法治,终究会成为历史陈迹而不再起作用,而是力图辨明分清这些源于历史实践的理论类型在新的历史条件下可能起作用的具体层面或领域。三种法治模式内在的学理根据,是它们突破特定历史时空的局限而在现代仍得以发挥作用的基本条件。

在学理上,本文倾向于同时从文化与政治或道德哲学与政治哲学双重维度展开对三种法治模式的理论分析。以道德哲学和政治哲学为横纵两轴,并且进一步将其各自区分出道德与功利、政治与行政四个考量层面,就可较为清楚地辨明三种法治模式的理论位置。结合实际历史来看,大体可说,法家法治主要是行政和功利层面的法治,儒家法治主要是行政和道德层面的法治,民主法治主要是政治和功利层面的法治。显然,政治与道德层面的法治至今尚无对应的历史形态,而这尤其值得引起现时代人的关注。这里,对于道德、功利、政治与行政四个考量标准,需要做必要的阐释和限定。“道德”,重在人的仁德或人的道德能力和努力,它与前述人的道德本性、道德能力、道德责任和德性认知密不可分;“功利”,则与世俗事功、权利、经验和理性相通,它主要立足人的生理本性或自然物欲。两者共同实存于古今社会之中,大致相对于中国传统学术中的“义”、“利”范畴,有时也被表述为“德”与“道”①、“道德”与“自然”、“道德”与“理性”②的差异,其区分的基础在于“道德理性”与“认知理性”的不同。无可否认,在客观上,法家法治与民主法治都可能,也需要表现出一定的道德实效。例如,法家讲“心无结怨”③,“德生于刑”④,而现代理论中亦流行着以个人的自私、自爱、欲望甚至恶质能够成就社会公益和经济繁荣之类的看法。尽管如此,无论是法家还是宪政主义,都缺乏一种以道德来统合法治的理想。而儒家法治虽然也包含一个“外王”层面,但其所充分表现出的道德人文维度,如对客观道德系统或道德律的认可、对人的道德能力的高度肯定、对美德和贤人的依赖和重视、对超验道德认知形式的诉

---

① “道者,人之所共由;德者,己之所独得”;“道是天地间本然之道,不是因人做工夫处论。德便是就人做工夫处论。德是行是道而实有得于吾心者,故谓之德。”陈淳:《北溪字义》,中华书局,1983,第42页。

② 道德理论中作为“君子”、“大人”、“圣贤”的“道德人”,不同于经济理论和民法理论里在市场或市民社会中精于计算、精心看护自我利益的“理性人”。前者是道德的,后者是理性的。

③ 《韩非子·大体》。

④ 《商君书·说民》。

求等，是法家法治与民主法治所不具备的。正是在此意义上，道德与功利可以用来作为相对比较的考量标准，而政治和社会的理性基础与政治和社会的道德基础也因此而显出差异。"行政"，重在管理或治理，基本上存在于各类社会；"政治"，在此则主要指民主或民权政治，也就是一些学者所认定的中国古代有道无"政"、有治道无"政道"之类判断中的"政"。历史地看，通过诸如游行、示威、集会、结社，特别是"一人一票"的选举等公开有序的"政治活动"乃至民权运动来达致政治和法律诉求，这在中国传统社会是缺乏的。就此而言，无论是封建贵族政制，还是君主政制，在治理上采用的都是自上而下的管制，而不具备规范的自下而上的"政治活动"形式。鉴于此，民主法治或"作为宪政的法治"若仅从行政或治理层面去理解是不合适的。这同时意味着，虽然法家法治与儒家法治在历史上是在君主政制下展开的，但在现代，它们作为行政层面的法治形态，未必不能涵容于民主政制之下。

法治的历史和理论形态

	道德	功利（理性/自然）
政治	道德的民主法治	作为宪政的法治 （民主法治）
行政	作为文德的法治 （儒家法治）	作为武功的法治 （法家法治）

从道德、功利、政治与行政四个层面对法治所作的这种审视，不仅兼及历史与学理，也有利于引出并拓展中国法治的道德和政治维度，从而突显现代法治的人文处境或困境。在此审视中，纵向的政治与横向的道德之间所形成的空格，在一定程度上昭示出现有法治形态的某些不足，同时也为法治的进一步发展和开拓留出了可能空间和方向。一如法家法治与民主法治在功利层面的融通，历史上主要在行政层面起作用的儒家法治是否可能以及如何提升到政治层面，从而实现道德与政治在现代条件下的新的重构，亦值得深思。对于近一百多年一直处于文化"低谷"的中国来说，融会"古今中外"的文明成果，来做这样一种前所未有的发展、开拓和重构，无疑具有重要历史意义。接下来，本文在前文所述的人文主义背景下，从道德、功利、政治、行政不同层面，尝试着对三种法治模式作一分析和考量。

大体而言，法家法治与儒家法治可谓中国自古以来的两种基本治道或治国方式。古中国的治道源远流长，而其间总可见到这两种基本形式。从地理和文化源起看，与长江和黄河两大流域相应，中国文化在远古即有一种南北分化的格局，并在后世大致呈现出南道北德、南法北礼的面貌，以致南北差异随着文化的交流融合逐渐被冲淡后，在儒学长期居于主导的时期，仍可发现儒法合流或"阳儒阴法"、"儒表法里"的特点。对此，梁启超、刘师培、谢无量、蔡元培等人均有阐述。① 南北文化差异也表现为尚自然与崇仁道、行法术与尽人力、重智识与讲仁爱、常冷漠与多温情、遵循客观规律与开拓主观的或主体的能动性和创造性等分别。这既可说是"道"（自然之道）与"德"（人之仁德）的差异，也可说是两种"道"（自然律与道德律）的差异。就周公和孔子对礼义的重视，以及法家刑名之学"本于黄老"② 而言，法家与儒家的分野在很大程度上正表现为南北文化差异的自然延伸。当然，在先秦历史上，此种地域差别并不是固定的，法治改革主要发生在齐、晋、秦这样地处北方的诸侯国。这正表明，由地理影响而形成的分别，亦各有其学理根据，因而在地域界限被突破后仍得以并行或融会。由于立足于不同的学理根据，南学北学以及儒法文化呈现出不同的人文特征。就此，有学者明确提到，"北派的政见，多依据德性上的感情；南派的政见，多依据利害上的需要"；"北学是人文主义，南学是自然主义"。③

古中国的治道，既可从地理和文化的角度审视，也可从学理和历史的角度分析。实际上，基于学理和历史来把握中国治道，是古人更为经常的思路。典型的是，鉴于秦以前的历史，古中国的治道被区分为"皇帝王霸强"五种，有时也被区分为"皇帝王霸"四种或"王霸强"三种。其中，"皇"指三皇的无为之治，"帝"指五帝的德教，"王"指三王的仁政，"霸"亦称"伯"，指五霸的法治，"强"指秦专任刑杀。关于治道的此类划分广泛流行于后世。④ 这些不同的治道，既以历史上的道德和政治实践为事实基础，也在学理上各自表现出侧重自然、礼让、德政、利争、兵战，

---

① 参见梁启超《论中国学术思想变迁之大势》，《饮冰室合集》文集之七；刘师培：《南北学派不同论》，载劳舒编《刘师培学术论著》，浙江人民出版社，1998，第 133～167 页；谢无量：《古代政治思想研究》，商务印书馆，1923；蔡元培：《中国伦理学史》，商务印书馆，1937，第 30 页。

② 《史记·老子韩非列传》。

③ 谢无量：《古代政治思想研究》，商务印书馆，1923，第 3、4、27、29 页。

④ 参见《说苑·政理》，《文中子·问易》；邵雍：《邵雍集》，中华书局，2010，第 13～16、547、556 页。

或者侧重无为、德、义、智、兵的特征。在从"皇"到"帝"到"王"到"霸"再到"强"的历史演化过程中，可明显看到从德教、仁政向法治、刑杀的转变。因此，"德"与"刑"还被更为概括地提炼出来，成为判定和区分"皇帝王霸强"这些不同治道的两个基本考量标准。一如古人所说，"治国有二机，刑、德是也。王者尚其德而布其刑，霸者刑德并凑，强国先其刑而后德。夫刑德者，化之所由兴也。德者，养善而进阙者也；刑者，惩恶而禁后者也"①；"夫治国之本有二，刑也，德也。二者相须而行，相待而成也。……故任德多、用刑少者，五帝也；刑德相半者，三王也；杖刑多、任德少者，五霸也；纯用刑、强而亡者，秦也。"② 这种以德与刑之间的主次、先后、多少关系来分析判断不同的治道，是中国传统政治哲学的主要特点。无论是先秦儒家和法家，还是古中国后来的各种政治和法律理论，其实无不是围绕"德"、"刑"及其相互关系来展开的。从秦之后历朝的实践看，朴素无为的"皇道"与专任刑罚的"强道"，都只作为理想的或需要避免的极端形式存在，刑与德始终是治理实践不可或缺的两个要素，实际的治道通常沿着"王道"上下漂移，时而推崇"帝道"，时而偏向"霸道"。就此而论，尽管"德"一直是儒学中最重要的主体内容，但"刑"或法制远不是对传统社会长期起主导作用的儒学所忽略的要素。在古中国，"德"与"刑"，就如同"阳"与"阴"一样，是并立于中国传统政治及其哲学中的两对基本范畴，是古中国文治武功的两个基本方面，正所谓"刑德皇皇，日月相望，以明其当。"③

　　从"德"与"刑"在古代治理中的这种基础地位来看，"德"与"刑"正表现为道德和治理实践中"文德"与"武功"两个方面；刑或法律，不仅是法家法治主张的核心范畴，也是儒学的基本概念。在儒法争论中，否弃仁德而专任刑法的观点在法家那里甚为常见，而儒家虽然力主道德教化，对刑法有一定贬抑，并期望"刑措"、"无讼"的理想状态，但很少有在现实中完全否定、摒弃刑或法律的想法。事实上，在儒学成为主导的意识形态之后，一直流行着"虽圣帝明王，不能去刑法以为治"④ 之类的话语。孔

---

① 《说苑·政理》。

② 《全三国文》卷三十七。

③ 《黄帝四经·十大经·姓争》。另可参见《管子·四时》，《申鉴·政体》，《礼记·乐记》等。

④ 《元史·刑法一》。另可参见《抱朴子·用刑》，《日知录·法制》，《论衡·非韩》，《唐律疏议》卷一，《四库全书总目提要·政书类》按语等。

子讲"道之以政，齐之以刑，民免而无耻；道之以德，齐之以礼，有耻且格"，① "礼乐不兴，则刑罚不中。刑罚不中，则民无所措手足"，② 在很大程度上也表明了一种德举刑备的态度。凡此皆为开掘儒学中的法治因素提供了可能。如果将法家一任于法的主张视为一种典型的法治理论，那么，在儒学所支持的"王道"和"帝道"中，其实也包含有一种始终不脱离刑或法的法治理论，只不过，它是一种受制于道德的法治理论，或者，相对于法家的纯粹法治而言，是一种复合的法治理论，其间不仅有法律因素，更包含有仁德礼义等因素。大体而言，立足人的仁德来开展政治和法律实践是儒家法治的基本特征，其特质可归结为"德主刑辅"或"德本刑末"。这主要有三点具体表现：其一，以仁德为根本，而以法律为不得已也不可废的治世工具，强调"先德而后刑"。③ 例如，"德礼为政教之本，刑罚为政教之用，犹昏晓阳秋，相须而成者也"；④ "法令者，治之具，而非制治清浊之源也"；⑤ "仁义礼制者，治之本也；法令刑罚者，治之末。无本者不立，无末者不成。……先仁而后法，先教而后刑，是治之先后者也"⑥；"明其刑不如厚其德也。"⑦ 其二，明刑弼教，以"德"主导法律实践，以"刑"维护德教。例如，"刑者，德之辅"；⑧ "刑以弼教"。⑨ 其三，"德"与"刑"具有不同功效，适用于不同时期或领域。例如，"刑罚者，治乱之药石也；德政者，兴平之粱肉也。夫以德教除残，是以粱肉理疾也；以刑罚理平，是以药石供养也"；⑩ "本之以仁，成之以法，使两通而无偏重，则治之至也。夫仁义虽弱而持久，刑杀虽强而速亡，自然之治也。"⑪ 从这三点看，尽管"德主刑辅"、"德本刑末"突出了"德"的基础或核心地位，从而使儒家因此有别于法家，但"刑"实际上也构成儒家政治理论不可脱离的基本方面。

---

① 《论语·为政》。

② 《论语·子路》。

③ 参见《黄帝四经·十大经·观》，《盐铁论·论灾》，《说苑·政理》，《文中子·事君》，《大学衍义》卷二十五等。

④ 《唐律疏议》卷一。

⑤ 《汉书·酷吏传》。

⑥ 《群书治要·袁子正书·礼政》。

⑦ 《群书治要·袁子正书·厚德》。

⑧ 《春秋繁露·天辨在人》。

⑨ 《宋史·刑法一》。

⑩ 《后汉书·崔骃列传》。

⑪ 《群书治要·袁子正书·礼政》。

　　总之，无论是就南北地理文化差异而言，还是就"皇帝王霸强"五种治道形态以及"德""刑"两种基本考量标准而言，侧重于"德"的儒家法治与侧重于"刑"的法家法治，正可谓绵延长久的中国传统治道的两种基本样式。而在儒学作为主导意识形态的两千多年时间里，中国法律实践一直受到"德"的影响或支配，以致形成了一种融合道德与法律、以德刑为本末、先后、文武、内外次第的立体复合法治结构，与西方近代以来所形成的形式法治适成对照。对此，钱穆曾指出，"中国自秦以下之政治，本为儒、吏分行之政治，亦即法、教分行之政治"，"凡使中国传统政治之不陷于偏霸功利，而有长治久安之局者，厥惟儒家之功。"① 这样一种独到的儒家法治，亦可谓"内圣外王"在法律领域的具体表现，它呈现出这样一些特性，这些特性使得它与法家法治以及现代西方法治显出差别：

　　第一，它是道德的。儒学以具有客观价值的人生道德意义为理论前提，但它并不完全否定人性的卑微方面。只是，儒学并不以人性的卑微或生理方面作为道德和政治的基点，相反，它始终不离人的道德善性，坚持人性善论，而将利欲视为需要提防、克服或节制的。无论是"德"还是"刑"，都紧紧围绕人的德性和善性展开，以极力保存、维护和张扬人的德性和善性为目的。对于人的道德本性，法家既不承认也不信任。在现代西方法治理论中，人的善性同样不被认为是可依靠的，法治因此主要建立在人的生理本性以及对人性的不信任基础上。无论是法家的还是现代西方的法治理论，都与一种通过内心调节来达致中正仁和的道德理论严格区分开。在这两种法治理论中，人欲是明显开张的，人的生理和自然本性亦得到充分认可，并被用来作为治理的基点。第二，它是综合的。这主要表现在儒家主张以"德"为本，以"刑"为末，"德""刑"并用，正所谓"政刑所以禁民之身……德礼所以善民之心。"② 而且，儒家在不舍弃"刑"的同时，高度重视道德和贤人对治理的积极功效。一种融合道德、贤人、礼乐、刑政的复合格局，构成了儒家政治和法治的主要特点。而法家法治与现代西方法治通常都坚持法律与道德、法治与贤人相分离的立场，在治理形式上强调只诉诸并依靠法律。在现代西方法治理论中，人与人之间也主要不是表现为道德关系，而是更多地表现为权利关系，这种受到法律明确保护的权利关系甚至可以是某种对立关系。至于道德和贤人，无论是法家法治还是

---

① 钱穆：《政学私言》，九州出版社，2010，第79页。
② 《大学衍义》卷二十五。

现代西方法治都不寄厚望,它们对于法治甚至被认为是不利的。第三,它是超越的。从"内圣外王"来看,可以说,法家法治和现代西方法治更多地侧重于或流于"外王"层面,着力沿着社会、经济、政治体制平铺展开,而未涉"内圣"层面,难以触及形而上的超验或超越领域。与此不同的是,儒家法治受着一种人的道德完善理论的支配。在人的道德完善与国家治理之间,呈现出相互影响的立体复合结构。在自然法与西方法治之间,本也存在这种立体复合结构,不过,自从更具道德意蕴的自然法在近代落实为自然权利后,西方法治所受的道德张力实际受到削弱,抑或转变为权利张力,一幅流于功利、经验和理性层面的日趋平面化的现代法律图景因此也更渐明显。在很大程度上,立体复合结构在现代社会的平面化,与"德性之知"路径的堵塞有着重要关联。就此而言,儒家法治的道德超越维度在现代能否得以进一步生发,有赖于中国文化传统中"德性之知"渠道的重新开通。

　　总体来看,上述"道德的"、"综合的"和"超越的"特性是法家法治和西方宪政所缺乏的。在儒家法治与法家法治、西方宪政之间,明显呈现出"道德"与"自然"的差异。结合前述人文主义而言,儒家法治的铺展始终不离人的道德本性、道德能力、道德责任和道德认知,而法家法治和西方宪政则主要以人的生理或自然本性为根基,在经验和理性范围内思考和处理政治、法律和国家问题,弱化或避开了人的道德责任,也隔断了人的道德认知维度。由于着眼于自然世界并建基于人的自然本性,法家法治和民主法治看上去表现为更为纯粹、也更为客观的政治和法治。这样一种非人格化的治理,为社会的客观发展造就了较为确定的规范形式和制度依托,使得个人和社会得以摆脱道德伦理的束缚而获得自由发展,也在很大程度上消解了治理者和被治理者的道德责任。在法家法治下,作为统治者的君主对被治理者不仅不负有道德责任,而且力图"戒民"、"备民"、"御民"、"制民"、"胜民"。在宪政体制下,非人格化的治理机制,以及治理者的政治和法律责任取代其道德责任,同样是明显的。宪政或现代法治的重要特征在于,它不再沿仁义道德的路向发展,而是以自然权利为出发点,一些学者将其归结为"建立在人的意志基础之上的治理"或"受意志指导的人的治理"①。立足人的生理或自然本性并循着经验和理性的认知路径而生发的自然权利和自由意志,淡化了现代政治和法治的道德浓度。个人因

---

　　① Ian Shapiro, eds. , *The Rule of Law* (New York: New York University Press, 1994) , pp. 13 – 19.

此一方面由其意志行为而对其自主选择各自承担责任，另一方面亦可在法律不禁止的范围内按其自由意志放任发展。这也最终形成了一套客观的、非人格化的社会、经济、政治和法律体制，个人、社会、国家因之得以共同发展。合起来看，治理的非人格化，政治的客观化、形式化和法律化，以及由此所致的个人"疾功利于业"① 与国家和社会客观发展之间的一致性，构成了法家法治与西方宪政的共同特征。法家法治与民主法治因此既切合人的功利需求和生理本性，也在国家强盛、社会发展等方面时而表现出较为明显的实际效果和外在优势。这使得儒家法治及其道德取向面临一定质疑和挑战，以致在国家间竞争加剧的情况下遭受冷遇乃至批判。

尽管法家法治在外在形式和功用上与现代民主法治颇为近似，但它在政治领域并未确立起宪政体制下的人权和公民权利取向。此种个人权利或"自然权利"取向，是民主法治与法家法治乃至儒家法治形成对照的独到之处。从合法性的角度看，如果说儒家法治旨在使统治或治理获得一种道德正当性，那么，法家法治与民主法治则更加侧重于赋予统治或治理以纯粹的法律正当性。而且，在通过法律的形式合法性之外，民主法治比历史上的儒家法治和法家法治实际多出一条通过维护个人权利来获致政治正当性的渠道。这是法治在现代开出的新的人文维度，也可以说是现代语境下"外王"在政治层面的重要表现。如前所述，无论是法家法治还是儒家法治，在历史上都主要表现为自上而下的治理，而缺少自下而上兴起的民权或民主政治。明显的是，在中国传统社会，没有人民通过常规政治活动而展开的权利诉求和法律体制，也没有对君权的宪法制约以及人民对政府的政治和法律制约。在人民与政府之间构建合理的政治和法律关系，使政府和国家受制于宪法以及人民意志和权益，这是民主法治所要达到的基本政治目标。一如有学者所指出的，"法治……在更一般的意义上，包含着政府与被治理者之间的关系必须正义和公平的理念"。② 如果说历史上与自上而下的治理相联系的儒家法治和法家法治，成就了一种主要流于行政层面的、国民之间的治理——这种治理可针对官吏和国民而不能从根木上针对君权或皇权，那么，民主法治所要成就的则是政制层面的、旨在通过法律约束和规范君主权力、政府权力、政治权力以及国家权力的治理。这是现代法

---

① 《韩非子·难三》。

② T. R. S. Allan, *Law, Liberty and Justice: The Legal Foundations of British Constitutionalism* (Oxford: Clarendon Press, 1993), p. 21.

治在政制层面的重要特征，也可谓现代法治的精义之所在。虽然民主法治与法家法治相比多了人权和公民权利价值体系，而且这一体系如同凌驾于实在法之上的自然法一样，看上去也处在指引乃至约束实在法律的历史地位，但从人的自然本性以及自然权利这一基点看，法律、权利、民主在"作为宪政的法治"下仍处于沿着身体和生命展开的生理乃至物欲功利层面，人的德性认知和道德本性在其中依然是空缺或不明确的。因此，一些学者将现代政治归结为旨在保护身体和保全生命的"身体政治"（the politics of body）和"生命政治"（bio-politics）[1]。就对人的身体和生命的尊重和爱护恰是德性的重要外在表现而言，虽然民主法治并不以儒家所维护的那样一套被认为是客观有效的道德系统为依托和前提，但其基于人的认知理性而生发的、用以有效保障人权和公民权利的那样一套政治和法律体制，亦显出相当的人道功效。

三　迈向道德的民主法治

就中国的和西方的两种人文主义而言，现时代需要一种会通中西人文主义精髓、兼济人的认知理性和道德理性的新人文主义。这对于中国是如此，对于世界也是如此。从道德、功利、政治、行政四个层面看，融合"古今中外"的实践智慧和经验，开拓"道德的民主法治"，重新实现道德哲学与政治哲学的统合，在现时代既是历史需要，也是历史契机。中国的法治发展目前仍处在形成过程中，鉴于中国文化传统的衰败与民主政治尚有提升空间，中国法治的道德维度和政治维度，是尤其需要加强的两个基本方面。这两个维度，与中西两种人文主义有着重要的知识联系。尽管道德与功利以及中西人文主义所各自侧重的道德理性与认知理性，在历史上表现出较大张力，但就学理而言，融会中西人文主义，同时打造政治和社会的理性和道德基础，构建"道德的民主法治"，在现时代仍是存在历史可能的。

总体上，与其说现代政治或民主法治是道德的，毋宁说它是理性的。如果说法家法治与民主法治旨在构建政治和社会的经验或理性基础，为政治设置法律正当性或权利正当性，那么，儒家法治则旨在构建政治和社会

---

[1]　Cf. Michel Foucault, "The Birth of Biopolitics", in Michel Foucault, *The Essential Foucault: Selections from the Essential Works of Foucault*, 1954－1984（New York: New Press, 2003）, pp. 202－207.

的道德基础，力图为政治设置道德正当性。作为现代政治基始点的人的自然权利、自然本性和认知理性，决定了现代政治和法治的理性的——而非道德的——发展路向。就其治理逻辑而言，在认知理性而非道德理性的主导下，虽然最终不排除能够达致某种结束或中止争斗的默契或协定，但在平等博弈的过程中，亦可能如同军备竞赛一般，彼此以一种时刻提防、共损同毁的方式来保护和发展自己。在国际政治和经济中相互角逐的"自由国家"，至今远未突破现代发展的这一瓶颈。如果说，"启蒙"运动开启了人依凭自己的经验和理性"勇于认知"的大门，那么，现代社会的这样一种强劲的认知理性路向则使得人们越来越担忧理性的过度使用。经历了"启蒙"的世界，在外在方面可能处处看上去是理性的、光明的，但这并不足以保证人的道德世界是同样明白而确定的。在"启蒙"之下，光明与阴影可以同在共生。与中国文化传统的道德人文维度对照来看，沿着人的认知理性和自然本性而展开的现代人文主义，其道德界限不容忽视。例如，权利路向虽然看上去维护了社会公德底线，但它与道德却也有着很大的张力——人权或权利通常并不以人是道德的以及促进人的道德完善为条件，事实上，人在现代被认为有权利做并不总是最好的事，甚至"有权利做错事"或道德败坏的事。由于人的道德善性不被广泛认可，道德律的作用空间受到限制，而建立在"人是人"这一自然事实基础上的人权论和死刑废除论，亦将因为缺乏根本的道德理据而面临挑战。又如，权利自近代以来的发展史显示出，"自由国家"的奴隶贸易、种族歧视、侵略战争等与人权的提出适相伴随，人权在国内政治和国际政治中所处的地位和作用并不完全一致，国际人权保护机制中的人道主义干预时常与人权侵犯纠缠在一起。由此看，权利政治与仁义道德在现代社会也未必总是正相关的。凡此都反映出从人的自然权利、认知理性和生理本性出发的现代道路的倾向、侧重和缺失，也衬托出延续和重新开掘人的德性认知和道德善性的历史必要。

　　综合起来，从普适的立场看，中西古今历史上的法治大致突显出人文的两条路向：一是理性的，以人的生理本性为起点；二是道德的，以人的道德本性为起点。尽管法家法治与现代西方法治在权利价值取向上存在差异，但就其对德性认知的阻隔、对生理本性的侧重以及某些客观的人道效果来说，二者可同归于功利或理性一路。结合前述中西两种人文主义，从这两条路向可简约地提炼出理性人文维度和道德人文维度。由于理性人文维度终究要落实到人的生理欲望和世俗功利层面，它也可说是功利的，从而在学理上与不计利害得失的道德人文维度形成对照。在道德人文维度上，人欲通常受到克制，但这一维度并不完全排斥人的生理本性和世俗生活，而是秉持一种适当的中正仁和态度。可以说，道德人文维度经过但并不停留于人的生理和世俗层面；基于德性认知以及"天人合一"乃至天人并立，人在这一维度上还有高于世俗功利的道德追求。在理性人文维度上，虽然人在"人是目的"这一人文要求下力图被塑造成有尊严的权利主体，人们客观上也可能达致人在道德人文维度上所能取得的某些实际效果，但由于受"闻见之知"的支配以及"闻见之知"对"德行之知"的制约，人在这一维度对于超验或超越层面的认知总体是隔断的。就学理而言，理性人文维度并不以德性认知和德行生活为必需，但也未必与德性认知和德行生活完全不相容。这为权利与德性的现代结合提供了理据支持和实现途径。理性人文维度和道德人文维度，在现代构成为重开"内圣外王"的两个立足点。在历史上，这两个维度长期呈现出紧张乃至对立。犹如在传统社会仁义道德对人的生理本性、"义"对"利"、"天理"对"人欲"的一定抑制那样，认知理性对于道德理性的挤压和张力在现代社会也是明显的。在基于人的自然或生理本性而扩展的现代体制下，人的德性认知渠道可能受到蒙蔽而不得开通，甚至为科学认知所拒绝和堵塞，进而也阻碍人的道德本性和道德能力的生发。这是现代进程中能否实现道德与政治、"内圣"与"外王"新的统合的一个关键问题。重开德性之知，疏解德性认知与物理认知之间的隔阂，使人的德性之知与闻见之知、道德本性与生理本性相容并行，可谓现代中国开"新外王"并将"内圣"与"新外王"重新衔接起来的认识论前提。确立这一认知前提，才足以打开法治的道德之维，进而使得将道德与政治重新结合起来、构建"道德的民主法治"成为可能。在现代语境下，道德与政治的融通不必是美德的法律强制以及纲常伦理、等级秩序的重构，而在于使人的德性认知在现代经济、政治、法律、社会和文化体制下仍得开通和生发，由此为道德人文要素渗溶于现代体制创造历史可能，从而弥补"现代性"之不足，达致仁义道德、道德本性、自然正当与民主法治、生理本性、自然权利相互融合的"仁内义外"、"内圣外王"状态。相对中国上千年的古代史和一百多年的近代史而言，实现"内圣"与"新外王"的衔接，或者，实现仁义道德与民主法治以及现代经济和社会体制的融合，当代中国有必要尽可能避免理性人文主义与道德人文主义的直接对立。换言之，中国的道德和政治发展道路，当兼顾理性人文主义和道德人文主义，不以仁义道德强行地抑制人的生理本性的伸展，也不以物理认知一意地扼杀人的德性认知和道德本性的生发空间。唯有立基认知理性造就民主法治以及现代经济和社会体制，同时立基德性之知培育道德主体，并由此赋予现代经济、政治、法律、社会和文化体制以道德态度和导向，现代法治才足以既从理性人文主义那里获得民权民主维度，也从道德人文主义那里获得仁义道德维度。

（一）沿着个人权利和社会秩序，从外在客观方面打造民主法治的理性基础

在道德律以及人的道德本性上，儒法两家表现出极大分歧，但在法律与外在而客观的社会体制的联系上，儒家法治与法家法治、民主法治却也表现出较大的一致性。儒家的"外王"，终究要落实到一套政治、经济、社会和制度体系之中。所不同的是，物欲或人的自然本性在法家以及现代经验、情感、功利和理性主义者那里是开张甚至放纵的，并被用来作为治理的起点，而儒家则始终基于德性之知而对"人欲"保持着适当节制。由于坚持人的道德善性，在守法或预防违法上，儒家也积极倡导道德教化的社会作用，注重通过提升人的道德觉悟来避免违法犯罪，这也是法家法治和现代政治有所弱化的方面。在很大程度上，基于人性恶或"原罪"观念而展开的非人格化治理，忽视或遮蔽了更为主观的道德进路，法家法治与西方宪政因此表现为一种鲜明的摆脱德性约束的自然政治。此种政治的"自然"特征主要体现于两点：一是以人的自然本性为出发点，二是建立在由此所形成的近乎自然演化的社会体系及其客观规律基础之上。法家以及现代理性人文主义大多从自然的眼光、自然律的角度看待这一近乎自然的体系，并任其客观扩展；而儒家则以"皇天无亲，惟德是辅"[①]、"大德必得其位"[②] 之类的看法，赋予这一体系以道德意义，并表现出以仁义道德或道德律来涵容这一"自然"体系的倾向。这里，如果将"道"理解为客观的自然过程，而将"德"更多地理解为人心向善的主观努力，那么，法家法治以及现代政治与儒家法治或"仁政"之间大体可以说存在"道"与"德"的区分。就道德律而言，"道"与"德"实难分开，而仅就自然律而言，在以"人"为自然生物乃至"机器"的近代潮流中，关于"德"的客观作用的认识明显淡化乃至被切断了。相对来说，中国文化传统高度重视人的仁德，但也从不忽视客观的"道"。古人以"阴""阳"、"春""秋"来比照

① 《尚书·蔡仲之命》，《左传·僖公五年》。
② 《礼记·中庸》。

"德"、"刑",在一定程度上显示出传统道德政治中的自然或客观要素。而法家以及现代政治对客观自然之"道"的因循,弱化甚至排除了仁德在社会治理中的作用空间。就此而论,关于法家"源于道德之意"①、"有见于国,无见于人;有见于群,无见于孑"②的判断,可谓深切之见。经历了"启蒙"之后的理性人文路向,以人权和公民权利弥补了法家"无见于人"、无见于个体的不足,但在对客观之"道"或自然过程的推崇上,仍与法家的法治道路表现出高度一致。无论是围绕个人权利而展开的现代法治,还是围绕社会秩序和国家富强而建立的法家法治,都具有明显的自然政治特征。这样一种沿着自然之"道"向前发展的路向,虽然可能蒙蔽人的仁德,但相对传统社会中宗教和道德的形式化、外在化、强制化实践来说,它在现代对于仁德的自由开展仍具有别样的历史意义。

从近代以来自然政治的崛兴看,人们社会交往的相互性和公共性、基于人的生理本性而展开的经济和社会体制以及政治权力运行的客观规律,更适合用来作为构建民主法治的着力点。在中国文化语境下,立足人性恶或"原罪"观念来建立法治将始终面临道德质问和文化隔阂,而完全从道德观念出发、抛开外在社会体制而在"大社会"构设法治也是不现实的,历史事实上并不是如此发生的。一些法律史学者将法律的现代发展视为一个摆脱宗教和道德束缚的历史过程,随着这一历史进程的加深,法律以及相关的法律知识体系在现代社会越来越成为与经济、政治、社会和文化体制相互联系的并立体系。对此,有学者指出,"在现代条件下,作为话语的法律应该只标出那些对'对'与'错'从技术上作了明确界定的领域。我们只应期待法律从其自身的标准得出是或不是的结论——决定一件事情要么合法,要么不合法。就此而论,努力从道德体验中找寻当前规则的基础是天真的。法律成了一个自我参照的交流系统:一种应对社会复杂性并为之提供便利的必不可少的特定工具。"③还有法社会学者从行为预期和规范的角度,将法律视为社会系统的一种内生的、必不可少的机制和结构,并由此认为,在现代社会,"法律改变了它的特性。我们对法律的界定可以不再从本体论上,而是从功能上去构思……法律不再只是那些应该成就的东西。这是自然法的失败之处。……作为伦理原则的'正义'现在被放在了

---

① 《史记·老子韩非列传》。也有学者认为法家渊源于儒家。不过,就学理,特别是就人际冷漠这一点而言,法家与道家更趋一致,而与儒家则存在难以消除的理论分歧。

② 《国故论衡·原道》。

③ Roger Cotterrell, *Law's Community* (New York: Oxford University Press, 1995), pp. 289 – 290.

法律之外。"① 从这些关于法律的现代处境的描述，不难洞察一种脱离宗教和道德而客观发展的现代世俗法律体制乃至现代经济、政治、社会和知识体制。由意志自由或道德留给个人自由决定这一点看，在形式法律、自由政治以及经济、社会和学术体制的此种现代发展过程中，人的仁"德"与自然之"道"的分化是明显的。尽管如此，只要将科学认知与德性认知的人为对立扭转过来，疏通德性认知途径，并由此达致对道德本性的自觉，自然之"道"与人的仁"德"在现代的重新结合仍是存在现实可能的。质言之，道德可能也需要融入基于人的自然本性而客观延展的现代政治、经济、法律和社会体制。而且，这样一种现代融合，比之于传统的"由仁入礼"的道德强制路径，更有利于突显道德的主体性和能动性。甚至可以说，沿着人的自然本性，围绕个人权利和社会秩序，着眼于现代经济、社会和权力体制及其运行规律，造就民主法治国家，构成在现代重启德性之门的客观、历史和理性条件。

（二）存留德性认知的生发空间，实现自然权利与仁义道德的历史衔接

基于道德的角度审视，法家法治和民主法治都主要表现为循着经济和社会体制展开的自然政治，而对人的道德本性或置之不顾或有所淡化。相比受制于一套天人体系和道德观念的道德政治而言，此种自然政治虽具有外在而客观的特点，与人的意志却也密不可分，明显受到人的理智和自由意志的主导。一个立足于人的生理本性而拓展出的，完全由人自主判断、自主建构、自主支配的知识和社会领域，构成了自然政治的认知前提和物质基础。在这一点上，即使带有宗教背景的洛克的自然权利理论也表现得尤为充分。按照洛克的看法，自然法本质上是上帝对其创造物的自然权利，而在自然法所限定的范围内，人如同上帝一样具有创造能力，并对其创造物了如指掌、享有支配的自然权利。② 由此，不难洞察一个完全受人的理性掌控的世界，在其中，依凭经验、情感和理性，人可自主立法、自由创造乃至人为虚构。"启蒙"之后的现代进程，在很大程度上可被认为是这一受人的理性掌控的世界的成长和膨胀过程。此种理性的人文世界，为实证主义、功利主义、理性主义、情感主义开辟了知识道路，也在很大程度上隔

---

① Niklas Luhmann, *A Sociological Theory of Law* （London： Routledge & Kegan Paul, 1985）, pp. 77, 82, 105, 174.

② 参见〔美〕伊安·夏皮罗《政治的道德基础》，姚建华、宋国友译，上海三联书店，2006，第 13 - 15、18 - 21、143、174 页。

断了德性认知途径，生理因素因而成为政治、法律乃至道德、宗教的基础。① 然而，如果将人的仁义道德与自然权利，或者道德理性与认知理性，视为古今之"道"以及现代条件下"内圣"与"新外王"的基点，那么，在理性化进程中涵容古今，培育道德价值，由此构建作为道德责任的人权，融通自然权利与仁义道德，可谓21世纪需要开拓提升的一个重要发展路向。

　　无论是从历史上的"义"与"利"、"天理"与"人欲"之间的关系看，还是从现代"启蒙"运动基于经验、理性和情感而对超越或超验维度的隔断或挤压看，自然权利与仁义道德在现代的协调都存在一定困难。特别是，在物理认知的主导下，由于德性认知"不萌于见闻"、"不假闻见"，"内圣"在现代理性化进程中很容易被舍弃。尽管经验、理性、情感乃至功利也能带来一些道德效果，但它们终究受限于一个立足人的生理本性、受人的理性支配的平面世界，在此世界中，德性认知蒙蔽于经验、理性、情感乃至功利之下，人的道德善性、超越性以及相应的道德律因而难有广阔的生发和作用空间。在认知理性盛行的现代潮流下，立足"内圣"开"外王"、以仁义道德抑制自然权利的传统道路亦难再畅通无碍。尽管如此，就中国文化理路而言，实现自然权利与仁义道德的历史衔接，达致"内圣"与"外王"新的统合，不仅成为一种历史需要，而且也存在现实可能。鉴于道德责任在现代的一定衰败以及"由仁入礼"在古代所致的某些道德缺失，在现代语境下协调融合仁义道德与自然权利，需要重新摆正"内圣"与"外王"的分合关系。这既不是舍弃"内圣"，也不是像传统道路那样完全从仁义道德而不从自然权利出发来开"外王"。融通"内圣"与"新外王"的关键在于，在物理认知、经验认知或科学认知之外存容德性认知渠道，由此为人的道德本性和道德律产生社会功效造就作用空间。德性之知与闻见之知、道德理性与认知理性、仁义道德与自然权利，在现代适合作为两个共立并行的系统对待，不以物理认知堵塞替代德性认知，也不以人的道德本性压制扼杀人的生理本性。由于德性认知的开通，这两个看上去分立的系统亦得以发生联系并最终统合起来。中国古人所讲的"果无功利之心，虽钱谷兵甲，搬柴运水，何往而非实学？何事而非天理？"②"果能于此处调停得心体无累，虽终日做买卖，不害其为圣为贤。何妨于学？学何

---

① 参见〔美〕伊安·夏皮罗《政治的道德基础》，第26页。
② 王守仁：《王阳明全集》，上海古籍出版社，1992，第166页。

二于治生？"① 最足以来说明功利系统与道德系统、自然权利与仁义道德的现代统合。以高尚美德而论，务农、经商、从政等世俗事业，皆可怀抱济世之心而为。以基本义务而论，德性认知的开张亦得为功利行为设置必要的道德限制。"明于庶物，察于人伦，由仁义行，非行仁义"②，体现出世俗生活与道德心态的分立统合。"有德司契"、"执左契，不责于人"③，则体现出内在道德系统与外在法律或规范系统的分立统合。中国文化传统中的这些智慧都适于在现代继续生发传承。从中国文化的这种世俗与道德的融合视角审视，基于人的生理本性而展开的自然权利体系，亦可能被容纳统合于仁义道德体系。人权，从主体自身眼光看是以死相争的"自然权利"，而从主体之外的其他人的眼光看，则是需要尊重和保护的人之基本要素，而此种对人权的尊重和保护正可谓人之德性、道德责任的外在彰显。就此而言，人权理论在中国文化语境下更适合沿着"民胞物与"、"万物一体"的理路展开，由此使作为自然权利的人权得以转变为作为道德责任的人权。按照中国文化传统中的"天地万物为一体"观念，此种道德责任并非源于权利与义务或权利与权利之间的交换或相互性，而是源于他人与自己的道德一体性、相关性或共通性，因此权利主体的人权才可能成为权利主体之外的人发自内心的道德责任。④ 自然权利与仁义道德的这样一种现代融通，终将使现代权利政治和法治获得必要的道德维度和限度。

（三）构建道德的民主法治，开拓民主政治下的为民之道

历史地看，作为一种现代文明，民主法治构成了现代中国在政治层面需要着力达到的主要目标。尽管不能说中国文化中完全缺乏民主的精神要素，但民主作为一种政制在中国传统社会是长期缺乏的。未获充分发展的民权宪法、民主政治以及独立司法，在古中国看上去并不是必需的，只是在"一离一合，一治一乱"⑤ 的王朝翻覆运动中才衬出其历史意义。治乱相循、兴亡相仍的历史现象，很大程度上显出传统治理在政治维度上的不足以及由此向民主法治方向拓展提升的历史必要。从政权角度看，"天下为公"的道德理想与"天下为家"、"天下为私"的政治现实之间的持久矛盾，为近代中国实现向民主法治的转变造就了历史动力。如果说，在传统治理

---

① 王守仁：《王阳明全集》，第 1171 页。
② 《孟子·离娄下》。
③ 《道德经》。
④ 参见胡水君《法律与社会权力》，中国政法大学出版社，2011，第 249～254 页。
⑤ 《读通鉴论》卷十六。

方式下，围绕政权而展开的政治活动在体制上受到抑制，而不得不只以革命起义的方式时不时地大规模爆发，那么，使社会中因为各种利益和价值分歧而产生的政治冲突，通过一定的法律渠道或制度形式得到合理疏通，从而不至于发生国家和法律损毁于反复的政治动荡或者政治势力长期逾越凌驾于国家或法律之上的政治局面，则是民主法治所要获致的政治功效。结合 20 世纪"大民主"实践所致的深重灾难而言，使政治活动在国家和宪法体制下依循权利形式和法律轨道得以合理展开，实现政治与国家或民主与法治的良性互动，避免上层之间以及上层与底层之间的政治斗争带给整个国家和民族以大的动乱，仍是现代中国构建政制层面的民主法治的一个关键。

在中国文化语境下，现代中国从政治层面完成构建民主法治的历史任务，仍需要达至与传统仁义道德的融通，进而最终迈向一种"道德的民主法治"。此种道德向度的现代延展，主要不在于对民族历史上所形成的独特文化的刻意固守，而在于使现代政治获得普适法理的支撑，因此不仅在外在方面具有权利正当性和法律正当性，同时也在内在方面具有道德正当性。"人文"，不只意味着隔断"天人"而将生存和关注领域限定于人的经验、理性、情感和意志，它还必须内在地包含诸如"人是目的"、"民胞物与"、"万物一体"这样的价值和道德要求。总体上，立足人的生理本性展开，只将政治关注集中于君权的维护和国家的富强，而置人的道德善性、"生活世界"和精神努力于不顾——法家法治的这些特征，虽然看上去与人文主义着眼于人和现世的特点存在一致，但在人文价值和道德根基上却显得很不完备。相比而言，民主法治通过将政治权力与人的权利和自由糅合在一起，旨在使国家权力依循一定的程序法则而屈从于人的自由生活这一政治目标，由此从权利和法律方面为政治权力的存续谋得了更大的正当性，也提升了政治的理性价值和人文素养。尽管如此，沿着人的自然本性以及"自然权利"而展开的民主法治，在很大程度上仍具有脱离仁义道德的特点，甚至与人的道德善性、德性认知、道德能力保持着较大的张力。就此而言，现代民主法治的人文侧重也是明显的，它更加偏向于理性人文主义而于道德人文主义有所弱化。"道德的民主法治"旨在兼顾理性人文主义与道德人文主义、权利正当性与道德正当性，使外在权利政治与内在道德精神在现代条件下各自沿着人的生理本性和道德本性并行不悖，并最终通过人的德性之知实现道德系统对民主政治的涵容。在此现代建构中，外在层面的民主政治、市场经济、公民社会与内在层面的仁义道德，须以圆融的观点而不是对立的观点看待。尽管"道德的民主法治"最终并不仅仅停留于人的生理本性，但它也不排斥人的世俗功利。事实上，任何伦理教义，在倡导人成为道德主体的同时，也都必然要对他人或社会成员的物质生活需要给予合理承认或高度重视，这甚至是道德行为的主要目标。"道德的民主法治"所要达到的理想状态在于：无论是政治、法律和社会精英，还是普通民众，对于世俗功利事业最终皆得以秉持道德心而为，以他人的权利为自己的道德责任，以政治、经济和社会事功为完善个人道德的载体和形式。

从道德与政治、天理与民意、"内圣"与"外王"相统合的角度看，中国法治既需要培植政治领袖和行政精英的人文素养、道德认知和政治伦理，也需要疏通和扩展德性之知在民众中的普遍生发渠道，发挥作为道德主体的人在民主法治实践中的积极作用。从自然权利与仁义道德相融合的角度看，德性之知在政治精英与社会民众的普遍延展，将为民主法治开通贯注道德人文精神的途径，传统的民本治理因此在民主政治下仍通过政治领袖和行政官员的道德责任形式得以存续，而民众在权利生活、政治生活、经济生活以及社会生活的行为亦因此呈现更加深厚的道德自觉，从而使法治获得良好的人文底垫和道德环境。总之，中国的法治道路更适合吸收历史上法家法治、儒家法治和民主法治三种法治形态的优长，并在学理上融通自然权利与仁义道德，由此形成兼具理性人文和道德人文向度的"道德的民主法治"。也就是，在"外王"方面，基于人的自然本性，沿着公民权利保障和社会秩序维护两条线索，拓展中国法治的政治和行政层面，并将法家法治置于权利取向和宪政体制之下，达致民主与民本的衔接；在"内圣"方面，立基人的道德善性，疏通物理认知与道德认知的人为对立，提升人的"德性之知"，从而将法家法治、民主法治涵容于道德系统，最终成就一种民主政治下的为民治道。这可谓现代语境中的"内圣外王"，也是契合中国文化传统的政治理想。

The Humanistic Path for the Rule of Law in China

Hu Shuijun

【 **Abstract** 】 Culture and politics are two important factors affecting the development of the rule of law. As far as the realistic situation is concerned, the construction of the rule of law in China is faced with some obstacles in the above mentioned two aspects. In contemporary times, China needs a new form of humanism that can integrate the essence of both Chinese and western humanisms and take into consideration both the cognitive and moral rationalities. From the perspective of humanism, moral humanism and democratic politics are the two dimensions of the construction of the rule of law in China that need to be strengthened. In the process of the development of the rule of law, China needs to coordinate moral, utility, political and administrative aspects of the rule of law, adhere to its own cultural tradition, create rational and moral bases of politics and society, develop a "moral and democratic rule of law" with rich humanistic content, and realize the historical connection between Chinese virtue and morality on the one hand and natural rights, democracy and the rule of law on the other hand.

【**Key words**】Humanism, the Rule of Law, Culture, Politics

On the Sources of Law

Aulis Aarnio [*]

【**Abstract**】 The doctrine of sources of law is a cornerstone of argumentation as it draws the boundary between what is law and what is not. Knowledge of valid law is acquired through analysis of sources of law. Theory of legal argumentation has been one of the focal areas in Finnish and European legal theory since the 1970s. In this article professor Aulis Aarnio, one of the developers of that theory, presents his latest views on the classifications and structures of legal argumentation especially with regards the doctrines about the sources of law. The article is significant as it seeks to adapt the doctrines of the sources of law to the increasingly important phenomenon of law beyond the state. Finnish law adopts basically the dualistic view that international law needs to be transposed to domestic law for it to become applicable in the domestic courts. EU law, for instance, increasingly gets importance directly, which renders it necessary to take such phenomena into account in the doctrines of sources of law themselves. The doctrine on the sources of law also still enables legal theorists to express and present the view about law in a specific country, such as Finland.

The doctrine of sources of law is a cornerstone of argumentation. It *draws a boundary between what is legal and what is not*. The matter concerns the foundations and justification used when making a statement concerning a legal question *de lege lata*. There is no other way to define what is "legal" and to separate it from "non-legal" in the adjudications or in legal research.

It is exactly the doctrine of sources of law that gives the lawyers, judges and

---

[*] Professor Emeritus, University of Tampere.

researchers of any given age the pieces of the interpretative game, forming their constitutive rules and creating a foundation for deliberation. Knowledge of valid law-inasmuch as the received certainty can be called knowledge-is acquired through analysis of sources of law. In this sense, the doctrine of sources of law mirrors the conception of law prevalent in given time in a given society.

For above reasons, the doctrine of sources of law has been an essential part of the theory of legal reasoning. In Nordic thinking, *Aleksander Peczenik was* the first who made a distinction between three different categories of binding force, dividing the sources in terms of the degree of being binding into the categories "ought to be", "should" and "permitted". Since then, the development of the doctrine of sources of law has in Nordic countries gone side by side with the development of the theory of argumentation, being a part of the theory.

Preliminarily, a legal source could be described as any argument, in the support of which a decision or a interpretative proposition is either *found* (context of discovery) or *justified* (context of justification) as a valid legal decision or an interpretative proposition. Still, this characterisation does not draw attention to which individual arguments are held as sources of law in a given period of time and in a given legal order.

One must also make a distinction between the concept of a legal source and its *weight*. A legal source can have a *positive or negative* weight, or it may be *indifferent* as regards the interpretative procedure. A source of law has a positive weight if it strengthens the justification. In the theory of argumentation, the term "pro-argument" is used to describe this. A negative weight reduces the credibility of the decision or interpretative proposition. It is a contra-argument. Sometimes a source of law has neither positive nor negative weight. For example, the decision or statement can be derived directly from the legal text, even though a "clarifying" precedent has been given.

The *doctrine* of the sources of law can be understood in a *wide* or a *narrow* sense. In the first case, the doctrine deals with the foundation of the doctrinal study of law and the adjudication. When interpreted as such, the doctrine contains besides the sources of law also *the rules of their use* as well as *the other norms of legal discursion*.

In a narrow sense, the doctrine of the sources law is a doctrine on the arguments used in legal justification. According to this view, only so-called official sources, for instance, the statutes, the intention of the legislator and precedents are accepted as proper sources of law. Usually, the definition is, however, more liberal. In this case, the doctrine of the sources of law covers all the arguments that are relevant in legal justification, either in the adjudication or in the doctrinal study of law.

In practice, the *content* of the doctrine of sources of law has varied depending on the time and place. In Napoleon's France, in the time of the legal codifications, there were only two valid sources of law: the statues and the intention of the legislator. As far as the foundation of law is concerned, the width of the list of sources of law is not essential, nor is the "distribution of degrees" by which they are binding. What is essential in this very respect, is only the requirement set for the doctrine, according to which the *legal* argumentation can be separated from the from non-legal one.

A distinction should also be made between a *legal* source and an *informational* source. As was stated above, the first category consists of the authoritative or material grounds by which the legal decision is either justified or made. Informational sources give, literally, information concerning sources of law. The intention of the law giver is a source of law, while the draft of law gives information about the intention. The same holds true as far as the precedents are concerned. A precedent is a source of law whereas all kind literal or computerized material is the basis of information about the precedent.

The next distinction concerns *actual* and *ideal* sources of law. Actual sources consist of the arguments *de facto* used by the judge (or researcher) in making or justifying the decision. Ideal sources of law are a group of arguments used in a *model* of legal reasoning. Therefore, ideal sources of law are a part of the theory of argumentation if and when the theory is understood as *an ideal model of legal discursion.*

In the American doctrine has been separated *sources of law* and *materials.* This distinction is important, because *other materials* than the proper sources of law may also be used in legal discursion. Examples of such are the analogy and the e contrario arguments. It is not natural to say that analogy between A and B is a *legal source.* Despite of this, analogy is a an accepted as well as common *argument* used to justify a given interpretation. Actually, it is one of the most common arguments, because human thought is to a large degree built on repetitive similarity inferences and expectations of invariance.

On the other hand, analogy and the e contrario argument have a special *dual role* in legal argumentation. The analogy principle is one of the *rules of reasoning* directing legal deliberation, as are the e contrario and the argumentum a fortiori principles. Similarity and deviance, in their turn, are arguments. The same goes for the reference to e contrario, or the relation a fortiori. Both can either mean an argument or a way of reasoning.

Besides the above distinction, also another concept-pair of great importance has been introduced, that is, a separation between *goal reasons and rightness reasons*. The first looks " forward " in argumentation, into the consequences of a given interpretation. This way of thinking is analysed in more detail below, in connection with consequence deliberation. Rightness reason refers to action that is, for example, morally right. As such it looks " backward ", and takes into account grounds and criteria that have already been accepted. In this sense, most of the material (substantial) arguments are rightness reasons.

As an ideal model, the doctrine of sources of law is weakly normative, which means that the doctrine gives the criteria for (a) what is *law* and (b) what is *good* (correct) law. In this regard, the degree to which the sources of law are binding, is of importance. Aleksander Peczenik was the first who classified the sources of law by their weight as legal arguments. Here, Peczenik's classification is introduced with some minor specifications:

I. Strongly Binding Sources of Law

1. Norms external to national law
* The binding parts of European law
* Norms of the European Convention on Human Rights
* Certain precedents of the European Court of Justice
* Certain precedents of the European Court of Human Rights
2. Norms of national law
* Fundamental rights of the Finnish constitution
* Statutes and lower-level norms given by virtue of laws (etc.)
* International treaties incorporated into national law
* System arguments

3. National custom

II. Weakly Binding Sources of Law

1. The intention of the legislator

2. Precedents

III. Permitted Sources of Law

1. Practical arguments (economical, historical, social, etc.)

2. Ethical and moral arguments

3. General legal principles

4. Standpoints presented by the doctrinal study of law (prevailing opinion)

5. Comparative arguments

6. Others

IV. Forbidden Sources of Law

Sources of law that can be held as forbidden are only arguments that are against the law or good practice and ones that are openly political.

The concept of binding legal source has above been characterised as having two meanings. A legal source can be either strongly or weakly binding. As regards the strongly binding degree, and especially the way in which precedents are binding, In this very context, the term *formally binding* has often been used. The sub-categories of "formally binding" are:

(a) *Strongly formally binding*: Ignoring the legal source as an argument makes the decision illegal, and it should thus be overruled in appeal.

In some cases the fact that the source is strongly formally binding can be bypassed. These situations are left outside this contribution. They do not concern the Nordic doctrine of the sources of law, which is the basis and framework of my analysis.

The constitution, and in the countries belonging to the European Union, certain norms external to national law are strictly binding ones. Other strictly binding sources of law, like the statutes and national custom, can be overruled in terms of their binding force. They can be bypassed if there are special grounds for doing so. This is the case, for instance, as far as *contra legem* decisions are concerned.

(b) A legal source is not formally binding in the sense of being strongly binding, but it has *significance in argumentation.*

(c) Sources of law that are not formally binding and have no binding force in the sense of point (b) but have a *significance that strengthens the argumentation.* All sources of law that are permitted belong to this category.

The binding force of the decisions of the European Court of Human Rights (ECHR) and the European Court of Justice (ECJ) does not depend on the loyalty of Finnish instances in following them. Examples can be sought from the principle of primacy of EU law and the minimum requirements of a fair trial. The decisions of the ECJ and the Court of First Instance are thus strongly binding *in principle.* They have a so-called *erga omnes* effect. In summation, a source-related "metanorm" concerning this legal source would be written as follows: The norm N that is external to national law should be unconditionally followed in all circumstances.

However, one reservation concerns all legal norms, even ones that are strongly binding. The norm is binding, assuming *that it can be applied in the first place* to the case at hand. Applicability can be excluded primarily by stating that there is no sufficient analogy between the decided case and the case being decided. This fact does not prevent saying that the source is strongly binding in the aforementioned sense.

The EU dimension includes problems of another type. The ECJ has no means of executing its decisions in the Member States. This is the responsibility of national authorities, and because of this, the decisions of the ECJ have to be accepted by the national courts in order to be effective. Sometimes this succeeds and sometimes it does not.

In any case, sources external to national law demand that the aforementioned category of sources of law that are strongly binding is augmented. In this contribution, the EU law and the human rights commitments has been placed at the top of the scale of binding force.

There is no special difficulty in placing new sources to the three categories of binding force. The matter concerns, as was mentioned above, sources of law that are *problem-and situation-specific*. When categorizing the binding force in a Peczenikian way, the *weight* given to a specific source, like a precedent of the ECJ, is in an individual decision-making situation not essential.

The starting point of the interpretation is always the text of the statute. The setting is the same as in the interpretation of a will, in which the text is similarly in a key position. In legal theory, a noteworthy distinction has been presented as regards the literal interpretation. The literal meaning may mean following qualities:

(1) *Clear or plain meaning*. Here the matter is not actually about interpretation but more on the redundancy of interpretation.

(2) *Lexical meaning*. It is the meaning found in *the* general semantics of language. This meaning becomes evident in the normal linguistic practice, or it can be found in dictionaries.

(3) *Grammatical meaning*. It concerns the syntax of the language at issue.

The power of the linguistic argument is also in that the citizens of a constitutional state should, at least in principle, be capable of reading their rights and obligations from the law. They should become evident to the people directly from the legal texts. Even though this demand is impossible in practice, it expresses an important democratic principle. The wording of the statute as a starting point thus receives support from the founding values of democracy and the constitutional state.

The linguistic argument is necessary already due to language itself. We understand language through its ordinary meanings, as part of the ordinary circumstances in which we have learned to play language-games and still play them. Therefore, language-games of ordinary language are a natural starting point for us, and the game that contests them resides on meta-level. It is not a game played *in* (ordinary) language. In cases, where the statute is one way or another unclear, the reference to the wording of the statute is an *argumentum absurdum*.

The statutes provide information of the *legal order*, that is, of the mass of legal norms, whether the norms are, for instance, regulative or constitutive. As was stated above, law is always a *system*. It is a general whole formed by means of conceptual commitments, easy to use and efficient in terms of intellectual economy. The system locks down the structures that define the decision-related possibilities that can be used in different situations. If the boundaries of the system are breached, the decision does not correspond to valid law.

The intention of the legislator has traditionally been connected to the category of weakly binding sources. This is, however, the case only as far as the so-called *historical* (subjective) intention concerns. It can be used as a second-level argument lending support to a certain interpretation of a statute. On the other hand, the *ratio of the law*, is an objective intention given to the statute all things considered. The ratio of law is thus a *result* of an interpretative procedure, not an argument. The *hypothetical* intention, for its part, refers to the idea the legislator would have presumably had if given circumstances were known when passing the law, or if they would have been of relevance in terms of the regulation's content.

The second category of weakly binding sources are *precedents*. Before going further, a conceptual specification is important. Sometimes, the notion of precedent refers to the *facts* (case) to which the decision has to be given. In this contribution, the term "precedent" means the *decision* made by the highest court. This conceptual choice makes it clear, that the precedent is a *norm* to be followed in identical or similar (analogous) constellation of facts.

According to the Nordic legal systems, precedents in the narrow sense (sensu stricto) consist of all the substantial and public decisions of the Supreme Court. They have the weakly binding normative force. Precedents in the wide sense (sensu largo) consist, in their turn, of every decision that *may have* precedential value in the future court practice. In the Finnish system, these include cases which have not received appeal permission, and the decisions of Appellate Courts to which appeal has not or could not be sought.

Precedents in the proper sense of the term can only be discussed *inside the judiciary*. The reason for this is simple. A precedent has value as regulative information only in terms of the highest instance itself or in relation to lower instances. A precedent regulates only the future the administration of justice. Of course, precedents have value outside the judiciary as well. The doctrinal study of law uses precedents as "weakly binding" arguments when providing reasons for an interpretation that is expected to be accepted by the judiciary. Attorneys use precedents as "predictions" of how a given matter will be solved or in deciding whether an action should be filed in the matter.

The Finnish system of precedent is based on an idea about *prospective* regulative information. The highest instance aims to (consciously) affect the future administration of justice. *Retrospective* dimension in the American style, in which the deciding instance always tries to find legal instructions from earlier decisions, is foreign to the Finnish doctrine of precedent.

The fact that precedents are weakly binding is based on the following technical norm: If you wish to produce a decision that is unlikely to change in a higher instance, give the precedent the weight of a legal source. The efficiency of the technical norm (the binding force of the legal source) is reduced in cases, where there are more than two conflicting decisions, and the precedent is old or was given in different circumstances than those in which the case is now to be decided.

On the other hand, being weakly binding also means that the precedent is not legally binding toward another court. Such an effect has not been given to the decisions of the highest instance in Finland, which is also illuminated by the fact that a decision that only refers to precedent is not justified enough as a valid *legal* decision. An exception to this can be found in Section 21 of the standing order of the Finnish Supreme Court. Pursuant to the provision, the Supreme Court itself is bound to a decision it has given in a similar matter. If it is wished to deviate from the line, the decision has to be made in a strengthened division or in plenum. Thus, it could be said that the decisions are horizontally legally binding for the part of the Supreme Court.

Permitted sources of law include, for instance, different type of practical arguments as well as legal principles. Historical arguments can either function as a part of the consequential reasoning explained below, or as a source of information concerning the background of the statute (legislative history), or the development of the statute itself. A historical argument can also refer to the history of institutions. The goal may be to make a specific institution, like the rights of the spouses in the case of divorce, understandable by describing the development from the previous matrimonial property system to the current one. Similar distinctions can also be made with social and legal-comparative arguments.

The *consequential deliberation* is a pattern of legal thought used both in the adjudication and in the doctrinal study of law. Actually, it the model of thought in all such cases where the other sources of law does not give a sufficient justificatory support to the decision. A typical subgroup of this model is the *teleological reasoning*:

The decision D is justified, because it ensures the furthering of the state of affairs S, and this state of affairs is the best, or at least acceptable goal to be reached.

The key of consequential deliberation is in the comparison of more than one consequence with each other. The final choice between the consequences is on the value based order of preference as regards the "goodness" of the consequences. In this sense, the consequential deliberation is nothing more that a special type of weighing and balancing. Now concerning the *weighing of interests*.

Law is a teleological phenomenon as regards its foundations. According to this, the statutes as well as precedents are instruments for the furthering of a given configuration of states of affairs which is valuable from the point of view of legal order as whole. The consequential deliberation is a natural part of this dimension of law and legal reasoning. From a more practical perspective, the consequential deliberation tells what is meant by practical reasons as arguments for legal interpretation. They are quite simply the consequences that the interpreter holds as ones worth pursuing.

The consequential deliberation concerns always interpretation in a relatively *open situation*. The interpreter has, for instance, two interpretative alternatives (T1 and T2) for a statute S, The alternatives are results from the prevuous use of the sources of law. These sources have fixed the framework of legally possible interpretations as far as S is concerned. The primacy of T1 and T2 can no longer be derived from the doctrine of sources of law, for example, due to the fact that there are two contradictory precedents, and no other even weakly binding source of law. In this situation, one might invoke the consequences of the interpretations, C1 and C2.

The consequences can be *general* or *individual*, and are usually based on social or economical interests. In this sense, the process could be characterised as the weighing of interests. However, the consequences can also be systemic, in which case they concern contradictions caused by a specific interpretation elsewhere in the same system. Here, the consequential deliberation leads to the evaluation of the legal system in the given area, and thus returns to the so-called systemic reasoning.

Sometimes the consequences are *ethico-moral*, and in this way it is possible that the deliberation has to lean on general legal principles or fundamental or human rights. Therefore, practical argumentation connects the decision with *the society*, *the system and morality*, and also with fundamental rights.

If there are enough justificatory reasons for C1 and C2 to be consequences of T1 and T2, then C1 and C2 have to be compared with each other and one of them has to be positioned as primary. This is where the weighing of interest appears in practice, for example concerning the interests of the buyer and seller or the individual and the general government. As was mentioned above, the comparison cannot be value-neutral, why the practical argument is a good example of value-based legal reasoning as is analogy and reasoning e contrario as well. Fundamental and human rights have also deliberative effects in the weighing, being either direct or indirect depending on the circumstances.

Let us assume that the consequence C2 gains primacy in comparison to C1. In this case, the reasoning proceeds as "feedback": Due to the consequence C2, the interpretation T2 should be defended with better reasons than T1. The chain of arguments has thus become to the end point, and the reasoning is concluded. However, let us still recall some general views.

In modern law, the problem no longer lies in whether the doctrine of sources of law is relevant or not but in the *strength of reasoning* (degree of being binding). In general terms, the question concerns the boundary between what is law and what is not. This borderline has turned to be especially important due to the role which *different kinds of principles* have nowadays in the legal reasoning. The strengthening role of principles is partly caused by the fact that legislation in different countries leaned more and more on *open and elastic norms*. Simultaneously some classical principles rose to the centre of discussion, as an examples pacta sunt servanda, the loyalty principle and the principle of equal division. First this and later on the fundamental and human rights made it necessary to draw demarcation line *between different rules and principles*.

A specific general principle (at least) in Finland rarely if ever receives the status of a legal source *solely* in support of communal acceptance, especially as the area of application of all kind of customary law has become the more unusual the more the area of statutes has grown. When a principle has the value of a legal source, its *position* is in the category of *permitted* sources of law.

Interpretation and decision-making can only function within the legal system. Flexibility that crosses the boundaries of the system breaks the spine of law. This breaking, in turn, is a threat to the democratic constitutional state, the core of which remains the *guarantee of maximum legal certainty*. It is, for its part, in modern law built on *predictability*, which is supported by systematisation and stability, among others. Actually, legal protection is often thought to consist only of predictability.

This is the way of thought in Anglo-American systems especially. Predictability is seen to guarantee the well-functioning of the social system, whereas the lacking of predictability makes law arbitrary "non-law" that changes from case to case. Regardless of whether the matter is understood in such a narrow way, it is obvious that no democratic *constitutional* (rule of law) state can sacrifice predictability on the altar of flexibility and case-based reasonability. Flexible regulations, their large-scale application and "soft" interpretation jeopardise predictability. Law stops being law and becomes primarily the delivery of "reasonability".

BIBLIOGRAPHY

Contains only texts in English. See in more detail in *Aarnio*, Essays on the Doctrinal Study of Law (below).

Aarnio, *Aulis*, Essays on the Doctrinal Study of Law. 2011.

Eckhoff, *Torstein*, Rettskildelaere. 2nd ed. 1987.

Peczenik, *Aleksander*, Juridisk argumentation. En lärobok i allmän rättslära (Legal Argumentation. A Textbook in Jurisprudence). In co-operation of Aulis Aarnio and Gunnar Bergholtz. 1990.

Doctrinal Study of Law and Science. In: Österreichise Zeitschrift für öffentliches Recht 1. 1967 p. 80.

Ross, *Alf*, Om ret og retfaerdighed (On Law and Justice). 1953.

Strömholm, *Stig*, Rätt, rättskällor och rättstillämpning (Law, Sources of Law and Application of Law). 3rd ed. 1988.

Summers, *Robert*. S. , The Tyes of Substantive Reasons: The Case of the Theory of Common Law Justification. In: Cornell Law Review 63. 1978 p. 724.

论法律的渊源

奥利斯·阿尔尼奥

【摘要】法律渊源学说在法律和非法律之间作出区分，因而是法律论证的一个基础。有关有效的法律的知识是通过对法律渊源的分析获得的。自20世纪70年代以来，法律论证理论就一直是芬兰和欧洲法律理论界关注的一个焦点。在本文中，法律论证理论的创建者之一的奥利斯·阿尔尼奥教授介绍了有关法律论证的分类和结构，特别是有关法律渊源学说的最新观点。本文寻求使法律渊源学说适应超国家法律这一日益重要的现象，因而具有重大意义。芬兰法律制度对国际法基本上采取了"二元主义"的态度，即国际法只有在被转化为国内法后才能为国内法院所适用。但是欧盟法等国际法日益通过直接的方式获得重要性，有必要在法律渊源学说中考虑这一现象。根据法律渊源学说，法学理论家们仍然能够就诸如芬兰等特定国家的法律来表达和介绍其观点。

社会管理创新的法制化路径

冀祥德[*]

【摘要】 司法权的优化配置问题始终是国内外理论界和实务界共同关注的热点与焦点问题。然而在此问题的研究上，研究者似乎更多的关注司法权力之间的分工、配合与制约，而忽略了公民权利，尤其是被追诉人权利对于司法权力的制衡。本文中，笔者试图以刑事司法过程中强调被追诉人权利保障的控辩平等原则为核心，探讨司法权的配置问题。

【关键词】 司法权配置　配合　制约

随着司法理念的不断更新和司法实践的变化发展，刑事诉讼的价值追求也在发生显著变化。一般认为，现代意义上刑事诉讼追求表现为保障人权与控制犯罪的二元价值。从对被害人权利的重视与对被追认人权利的漠视，到对被追诉人人权的保障，再到对被追诉人与被害人权利的共同保护，代表着国家对人权的不同认识，体现出人权保障的不断进步。从打击犯罪，到惩罚犯罪，再到控制犯罪，代表着国家对犯罪的不同态度，体现出打击犯罪立场与方法的变革。刑事诉讼价值追求一次又一次的更迭中，司法权配置是实现这一目标的关键性因素。

一　人类诉讼文明发展与司法权配置优化

司法作为一种行为的存在不是天然的，它是建立在国家职能权力分化基础之上的。在我国，"司法"的概念是一个舶来品，系清朝末年从西方引进而来。我国有学者认为，"司法"之"司"乃动词，有"掌管"、"操纵"之意，如司机、司仪、司令等，即指操纵机动车者、掌管仪式者、发布命

---

*　中国社会科学院法学研究所研究员。

令者，司法即掌管或者操纵法律，对法律和事实进行裁判。① 研究认为，资产阶级启蒙思想家孟德斯鸠第一次论述了司法的概念，认为在国家的立法权力和关于国际事项的行政权力以及有关民政法规事项的行政权力中，将第二种简称为行政权力，而将后者称为司法权力。孟德斯鸠提出，司法权就是惩罚犯罪和裁决私人讼争的权力，司法权应当与立法权和行政权分离，否则，"自由就不存在了"，"法官将拥有压迫者的力量"。② 可见，就刑事司法而言，国家追诉犯罪的行为具有权威性，不能随意而为之，因此国家将追诉犯罪的职能设定为国家的一项权力，最初附属于国家行政权之下，随着西方的分权思想而逐渐成为国家的一项独立的权力之一。因此说司法权的产生是建立在人类诉讼产生与发展的基础之上的。基于此，探讨司法权配置的问题，就必须考察人类诉讼的产生与历史。笔者研究认为，在人类刑事诉讼发展的历史上，至少经历了三次重大革命：第一次革命是司法权和行政权的分离——司法权摆脱行政权的束缚，独立主导于纠纷裁判场域；第二次革命是裁判权与控诉权的分离——裁判权趋于中立，控诉权受到制约；第三次革命是辩护权与控诉权的平衡——控辩双方平等武装、平等对抗。可以说，刑事诉讼三次革命的过程，实质上是司法权配置不断变化的过程。

二　司法权配置的要素

《辞海》中将配置解释为"配备、安排"之义，③ 即配置是建立在分工负责的前提之下的。司法权的配置体现了配合与制约两方面的要素。这就需要，一方面，要考量司法权配置中的配合要素，提高司法的效率；另一方面，要设置司法权配置中的制约要素，来实现对司法权的制衡，实现司法的公正。

（一）司法权配合要素

根据我国《宪法》第135条以及《刑事诉讼法》第5条、第7条和第8条等相关规定，可以看到我国立法司法都十分重视司法权力运作机关分工负责以及相互配合的职能优化配置关系。我国《宪法》第135条规定："人民法院、人民检察院和公安机关办理刑事案件，应当分工负责，互相配合，

① 孙笑侠：《司法权的性质是判断权》，《法学》1998年第8期。
② 〔法〕孟德斯鸠：《论法的精神》（上册），商务印书馆，1982，第154～156页。
③ 参见《辞海》，商务印书馆，1979，第1958页。

互相制约，以保证准确有效地执行法律。"《刑事诉讼法》第 5 条规定："人民法院依照法律规定独立行使审判权，人民检察院依照法律规定独立行使检察权，不受行政机关、社会团体和个人的干涉。"第 7 条规定："人民法院、人民检察院和公安机关进行刑事诉讼，应当分工负责，互相配合，互相制约，以保证准确有效地执行法律。"第 8 条规定了人民检察院依法对刑事诉讼实行法律监督。这些立法条文以基本原则的方式规定了公、检、法三机关分工负责、相互配合的职权配置；相互配合是建立在分工负责基础上的配合，规定公检法三机关相互配合的原则的初衷是基于三机关同为追诉犯罪的国家权力机关，并在刑事诉讼任务中具有同向性；体现在制度设计上，公检法三机关的相互配合主要涵盖了"公、检配合"与"检、法配合"两个方面，即公安机关的立案、侦查为检察院的批准逮捕、审查起诉做好准备，检察院的审查起诉为法院的审理裁判做好准备。[①] 通过观察研究实践经验，应该说，我国公安司法机关对于这些原则规定的落实已十分积极稳妥，以至于当前公安司法机关之间配合的问题已经达到了一个相当默契的程度。我们不得不承认，公检法三机关适当地配合对于提高司法效率、节约诉讼成本和司法资源具有显著的成效。

　　然而，当我们用更加审慎的眼光来看待我国司法权的相互配合问题，可以客观地说，目前我国整个司法行为的运作，却是"配合有余、制约不足"。1979 年修改《刑事诉讼法》时规定"分工负责、相互配合、相互制约"原则，有其特定的历史背景和时代意义，当时公、检、法三机关刚刚分离开来，为了矫正"下去一把抓、回来再分家"的司法状况而作此规定，有着十分重要的意义。然而经过了二十余年的沧桑变化，该条规定在实践中贯彻的状况似乎已经早已实现其目的、完成其历史使命。在已有的分工、配合效果显著的今天，再不停地强调"分工负责"，便意味着三机关在刑事诉讼程序的"流水线"上存在"各管一段"的嫌疑；而一再强调"相互配合"，只能将众人的目光更多地引向一种"法外的配合"——政法委协调意见，法院参与、提前介入等"配合司法"的形式在实践中，尤其在基层公安司法机关处理重大、疑难案件时屡见不鲜，佘祥林案、赵作海案甚至其他那些被告人已被枪毙的冤假错案就是这种分工不明、配合失度、制约缺失的司法行为所留下的惨痛教训。另一方面，过分强调公安机关、人民检察院、人民法院三机关之间的"相互配合"，那么无论是在人们对于刑事诉

---

① 谢佑平、万毅：《分工负责互相配合互相制约另论》，《法学论坛》2002 年第 4 期。

讼程序参与者的认识当中，还是权力主体在刑事司法职权的行使过程中，都有可能潜移默化地将"辩护"一方排除在刑事诉讼主体之外，从而迫使被追诉人及其辩护律师对于自己一方的权利保障丧失了发言权；这就严重违反了司法公正和人权保障的现代刑事诉讼基本理念。因此，在优化司法权的配置中，如何实现对于司法权力的制衡或者制约，就成为我们应当深度重视的一个问题。

（二）司法权制约要素

在西方，权力制衡理论有着深厚的产生基础与深刻内涵。权力之所以需要制衡，笔者概括为两方面的原因：一方面取决于权力的性质；另一方面取决于权力与权利的关系。首先，从权力的性质来看，权力需要制衡。孟德斯鸠认为：自由只存在于权力不被滥用的国家，但是拥有权力的人都容易滥用权力是一条亘古不变的经验；"有权力的人们使用权力一直到遇有界限的地方才休止"；"从事物的性质来说，要想防止滥用权力，就必须做到以权力来约束权力"。① 可见，任何权力在其行使者的手中都如同一把"双刃剑"，掌权者常常希望手中的权力能够得到无限的延伸，所以从这个意义上来说，权力如果没有制约，掌权者人性中恶的一面——贪婪、任性、懒惰等便会发生作用。因此美国麦迪逊宣称："立法、行政和司法权置于同一人手中，不论是一个人、少数人或许多人，不论是世袭的、自己任命的或选举的，均可公正地断定是虐政。"② 另一方面，从权力与权利的关系来看，权力需要制衡。如前所述，司法是在国家产生以后才有的，进一步说是国家权力分化之后才产生了司法权。关于国家权力的来源，历来有着很多说法。无论是中国夏商周时代的"天赐王权"，还是西方早期的"君权神授"，都代表了一种国家至上、王权至上的观点，意味着人民只能承担国家的义务，是统治者治理、奴役的对象，毫无权利可言。英国经验主义哲学开创者洛克推翻这种观点并认为，人类享有天赋自由和平等；为了确保正常的社会秩序，人们定下契约结合成为一个政治团体——国家，脱离所谓的自然状态，保护自己的生命、自由和财产；同时放弃自我保护和复仇的权利，将这种权利交给国家，然后设置专门的裁判者，裁决争端、修复被破坏的社会秩序。在洛克的社会契约理论下，产生国家权力的初衷是保护

① 〔法〕孟德斯鸠：《论法的精神》（上册），张雁深译，商务印书馆，1985，第154页。
② 〔美〕汉密尔顿等：《联邦党人文集》，人民出版社，1995，第246页。转引自董超《司法独立在中国》，《政法论坛》2005年第1期。

公民的各种权利，国家权力由公民交出的一部分权利形成，权利是权力的源泉，对国家权力予以制衡的目的是更好的保护公民权利。

由此，对于刑事司法权力的制衡，至少可以从两个方面得以实现：一个是通过司法权来制衡司法权，即所谓的以 power 来制衡 power；第二个是通过私权利的保障或者行使，以制衡或者制约公权力，即以 right 来制衡 power。

1. 以 power 制衡 power

如笔者前文所述，西方国家倡导三权分立的宪政原则，分权制衡是权力制衡理论不可或缺的内容并与其相伴而生，权力的分立是为了对权力行使者有所限制；而在我国这种权力配置形式则表现为权力的分离与权力主体之间的相互制约。《刑事诉讼法》第 7 条规定，公安机关、检察院、法院三机关在刑事诉讼活动中的互相制约。例如，公安机关对人民检察院不批准逮捕的决定认为有错误的，有权要求复议；又如，人民法院对于决定开庭审理的案件应当通知人民检察院派员出庭支持公诉，而人民检察院应当派员出庭支持公诉；人民法院经过审理认为检察院指控的案件应当认定被告人无罪的，驳回起诉并作出无罪判决；反过来，人民检察院认为法院的裁判确有错误的，有权依第二审程序或审判监督程序提起抗诉，等等。尤其是检察机关作为宪法赋予法律监督权的权力主体，对于刑事诉讼活动中的侦查机关的侦查职能、法院的审判职能以及对于法院裁决的执行职能进行法律监督，充分体现出中国特色的侦、检、审三机关通过权力来制约权力的司法职权配置方式。

然而倘若仔细分析我国司法权力的相互制约，我们又会发现存在着许多弊端。首先，检察院作为国家的法律监督机关，对于侦查阶段的监督主要是建立在侦查机关对案件进行处置的基础之上的——审查起诉职权是在侦查机关侦查终结移送案件材料的基础上发挥职能作用，其中侦查机关所起到的导引性作用不可忽略；行使批准逮捕的权力仅限于一种书面形式的监督，未涉及对于案件具体事实情况的介入，对于被追诉人第一时间的权利是否受侵犯便无法起到应有的屏障作用；而对于审判结果以及对于监所超期羁押等的监督更是基于一种事后救济的途径，对于被追诉人合法权利的现实保障显得十分滞后。这种被人戏称为"公安机关做菜、检察院端菜、法院吃菜"的流水线式的刑事诉讼程序，三机关司法权的优化配置亟待加强：在从侦查中心主义向审判中心主义转变的过程中，检、法相互配合并不符合刑事诉讼控审分离的基本原则，而检、法相互制约也不符合审判中心主义原则；另外，公、法关系的缺失在我国司法权配置方面问题突出，公安机关的强制侦查措施缺乏法院的司法审查制度加以规制，而强制措施当中除逮捕权外公安机关都可以自行决定，制约其逮捕权却是检察院这样一个行使控诉职能的权利主体，从而导致"侦审阻隔"、"条块分割"的局面，这就大大削弱了司法的公正性和对被追诉者人权的保障力度。另一方面，检察机关作为国家的公诉机关，无论是庭前准备还是在庭审阶段，作为国家的追诉机关拥有强大的控诉权力以及较高的取证能力和技术手段，司法权的制约正是为了维护司法的公正与权威，应当如何对控诉权加以配置才能保护被追诉人诉讼权利的有效行使，这就必须端赖于以 right 来制衡 power 的方式，即通过私权利的保障或者行使，以制衡或制约公权力，来弥补我国在短期内以 power 来制衡 power 方式所无法解决的问题。

2. 以 right 制衡 power

从洛克的观点我们可以推导出，权力是由权利转化而来，权力与权利的关系处于一种此消彼长、此长彼消的状态：权力膨胀，则权利缩小；权力规制，则权利扩张。由此可见，权利最大的威胁来自于权力，权力需要权利的制衡不言而喻。因此说，公民的权利就是国家的义务，公民的义务即是国家的权力，确立公民权利的范围、制定保障公民权利的措施可以制约国家权力，也是衡量国家权力是否被滥用的标准。《圣经》云："既听其隆著者，亦听其卑微者。"在刑事诉讼当中，控辩双方平等对抗与法官居中裁判是司法权配置的优化格局。美国学者威廉姆斯·道格拉斯指出，权利法案的大多数条款都是程序性条款，这一事实确实非常有意义，程序决定了法治和恣意的人治之间的基本区别。因此，只有在实质上保证控辩双方力量均衡的"平等武装"和在形式上保证控辩双方机会对等的"平等保护"的前提下，才能实现控辩双方的"平等对抗"，进而才有可能实现双方的"平等合作"；也只有实现了控辩平等，才能实现法官中立，才能最大程度地实现公平正义这一司法职权优化配置的最终价值目标。因此，为了保障人权，实现司法公正，除了构建国家诉讼权力之间的制衡关系外，还必须构建以被追诉人权利制约国家诉讼权力的机制。在笔者看来，就是以"无罪推定原则"为基准，通过赋予被追诉人特定的程序保障和相应的特权，如建立刑事正当程序，赋予被追诉人沉默权，强化被追诉人的辩护权等，使被追诉人在诉讼地位和参与能力上能够与控方形成平等对抗。

意大利法学家贝卡利亚于 1764 年在其名著《论犯罪与刑罚》中提出了刑事法的两大基石原则——罪刑法定原则和无罪推定原则。其中无罪推定原则被认为是"刑事诉讼程序正义的基石"。此后，在 1789 年该原则首次被法国《人权宣言》第 9 条以法律的形式被表达；1947 年首次在《意大利宪法》第 27 条以宪法的形式确立下来；1949 年首次在联合国文件中得以确立；而 1976 年《公民权利和政治权利国际公约》第 14 条第 2 项弘扬了这一原则。[①] 无罪推定原则的内涵至少包括如下几个方面：首先，无罪推定原则的前提是"罪从判定"原则，即非法官依法定程序作出的判决、裁定不得认定为有罪的原则；第二，无罪推定奉行"谁主张、谁举证"原则，即国家的控诉机关负有提出证据并证明被追诉人有罪的责任，这在控辩双方的力量对比上为实现"平等武装"奠定了基础；第三，被追诉人在没有被作出有罪判决之前，应当被认为是无罪的人；既然如此，其在刑事诉讼程序中，不能因被追诉人被逮捕、被起诉、被审判而认为其有罪，其享有作为一个无罪的人应有的权利保障，比如不被羁押的权利等。要对无罪推定原则进行正确的理解，我们必须注意到无罪推定是刑事诉讼程序的起点，而非终点；它是一种假定，是可以被推翻的，而能够推翻这种假定的唯有合法的证据，因此无罪推定强调证据裁判主义，而不是罪行擅断；而其追求的是刑事案件的实质真实，而不是形式真实。[②] 因此，无罪推定原则是一项程序法原则，而不是实体法原则。它所反映的是被追诉人在刑事诉讼中的法律地位。如上文所述，从某种意义上说，对于公民权利最大的威胁莫过于国家权力，国家权力应该时刻保持一种理性，避免权力滥用而侵犯公民权利。无罪推定原则的逻辑起点和价值基础，正是保护公民权利——无罪推定原则的受益者，不仅仅是被追诉人，而是全体公民，因为任何一个公民都是刑事诉讼的潜在主体，都有可能由于某种原因进入刑事诉讼程序。从这个角度上说，无罪推定原则推导出了两个极为重要的刑事诉讼原则——一个是辩护原则，另一个便是控辩平等原则。

在关于以私权利对公权力制衡或者制约的发展历程中，显然，辩护权作为被追诉人的一种天然权利，不仅具有存在的正当性，而且还具有理论基础和生存的基本根源。第一，辩是诉的本能反应，作为一种事实现象，它普遍存在于各个历史时期以及现代三大诉讼程序之中。在人权之生命权、健康权、自由权等诸多内容中，被追诉人的辩护权是存在于其中的一项特殊权利，它是被追诉人作为人的一项天然权利。第二，辩护权作为一项基本人权，古已有之，这从人类刑事辩护的发展史中可清晰辨明。刑事辩护

---

① 参见冀祥德《控辩平等论》，法律出版社，2008，第 121～122 页。
② 陈卫东主编《刑事诉讼法》，中国人民大学出版社，2004，第 92 页。

的历史经历了萌芽、形成、断层和繁荣几个阶段，这是一个从无到有、从强调被追诉人权利到兼顾被害人权利的过程，被追诉人的权利保护也不断地强化和完善；这是一项伴随着控辩平等理念产生而产生、发展而发展的权利，因此说"刑事诉讼的历史就是扩大辩护权的历史"。同时，辩护权也是一项被普遍承认的权利。尽管世界各国的政治体制、社会制度、意识形态、文化传统不同，但被指控人有权获得辩护却是各国公认的法律原则，并且得到国际社会的高度认同。第三，在固属自然权利的辩护权之中，律师辩护权是一项能将被指控人的辩护权利真正还原为一种现实权利的派生权利。基于辩护律师的有效帮助而使被追诉人获得一种相对独立的地位，便为被追诉人被无罪推定的实现创造了条件，由此，被追诉人成为一个自主的、与控诉方平等的诉讼主体，为控辩双方的平等对话创造了条件，因此，辩护权的存在与律师辩护权的派生和延伸，是现代宪政制度中以权利制约权力的人民主权思想在司法权优化配置当中的重要体现。

无罪推定原则及其推导出的辩护原则，皆注重的是公民权利，保护的是被告人的利益，体现的是对国家权力的限制和对人权的尊重——因为人权保障的起源便是建立在"每一个人都有可能成为被追诉人"的假设之下，保障被告人的合法权利；而被告人的权利保障直到诉讼被提起之时，实际上一直在运行当中。因此说，无罪推定原则的确立奠定了控辩平等的基础，使刑事诉讼结构更富有理性，使司法公正成为可能与现实。第一，无罪推定的确立可以有效防止侦控机关对案件产生片面性的主观认识。第二，无罪推定赋予被追诉人处于无罪的诉讼地位，是为了确保其在侦查、起诉和审判阶段得到公正的待遇，维护其作为人的尊严，防止国家司法权力对个人权利的侵犯，可见无罪推定原则保障了诉讼程序的公正，使控辩平等原则有了用武之地。第二，无罪推定最大的贡献在于通过推定被追诉人在有罪判决之前仍是无罪之人，仍然具有宪法规定的各种公民权利，比如对于羁押的正当性、证据的合法性等予以质疑的权利和赋予其有效的辩护帮助等一套完整的防御性权利，使得被追诉人具有了对抗控诉权的资格，为控辩平等原则在刑事诉讼中驻足奠定了有效的制度基础。第四，由无罪推定原则所确立的证明责任催生了被追诉人的沉默权，使辩护方拥有了一项重要的防御特权，从而实现与控方侦查取证权的攻击与对抗的平等。

综上所述，我们在研究司法权优化配置的过程当中，不仅要研究司法权力之间如何配置的问题，还要特别重视被追诉者一方的权利，尤其是保障其对控方权力制衡的辩护权利，以促进司法公正，增强人权保障。

除此之外，在司法权配置问题的研究中，要应当考虑司法权的优化问题。在笔者看来，司法权的优化，就是要在现有的司法权的职能配合与职权制约的基础上，通过对司法权要素及司法权运行环境以及司法权要素和司法权运行环境关系的改变，实现司法权最大的目标追求。

Allocation of Judicial Power under
the Rule of Law

Ji Xiangde

【Abstract】 The optimal allocation of judicial power has always been a focus of attention of researchers of legal theory and practice, both in China and abroad. However, researchers seem to focus more attention on the division of labor, cooperation and check and balance between judicial powers than on civil rights, especially on the balance between rights of the accused and judicial power. This article explores the allocation of judicial power from the perspective of emphasizing the principle of equality between the prosecution and the defense and the protection of the rights of the accused in the criminal proceedings.

【Key words】 Allocation of Judicial Power, Cooperation, Check and Balance

熟悉与陌生之间： 中国法治的
自我建构和方向性选择

【摘要】在走向现代化过程中，中国的法治建设吸收或移植了大量源于西方的法治要素，具有标识性的社会主义成文法体系的形成以及案例指导制度的推行都是百年来西学中用的产物，它们服务于建构民族国家这一现代性总体任务。然而，即使运用相同或相似的法律原理和学说，中国的法治建设在实践运行中产生了不同的效果，例如接受权利观念却拒绝认同个人主义，倡导国家责任但不必以国家主义为前提，这既反映了当代中国法制与法治的家族相似性，也与中国传统文化产生了内在的亲和力。本文对权利与调解、"孝"与国家责任等关系范畴的分析展示了合法与合理、西方与中国、传统与现代之间的冲突和纠结。作者认为，不是现代性本身出了问题，否弃的不是现代化的走向，而是对现代性本身的性质和面向做出新的解释，它取决于对现代性的判断是建立在对陌生人社会还是新熟人社会的方向性判断上，对后者的坚持和把握有助于从中国内在视角和理路建构具有中国特色却不失普遍性的法学理论。

【关键词】法治　权利　国家责任　新熟人社会

> 在西方成长起来的思想和知识近百年来深刻改变了当代世界，但是我们很难把它看作是一种纯而又纯的西方孕育的产物。
>
> ——〔印度〕阿马蒂亚·森（《身份与暴力》）

---

* 中国社会科学院法学研究所副研究员。

在走向现代化过程中，我国的法治建设吸收或移植了大量源于西方的法治要素，总体上服务于建构民族国家的现代性任务。然而，即使运用相同的法律原理和学说，我国的法治建设在中国化过程中产生了不同的效果。例如，接受权利观念与拒绝认同个人主义并重，倡导国家责任却不必以国家主义为前提等，这既反映了当代中国法律制度与法治原理的家族相似性，也与中国传统文化产生了内在亲和力。本文对权利与调解、"孝"与国家责任等关系范畴的分析展示了合法与合理、西方与中国、传统与现代之间的冲突和纠结，均关涉中国法治的现代化走向。不是现代性本身出了问题，需要否弃的不是现代化的走向，而是对现代性的性质和面向做出新的解释，这取决于对现代性的判断建立在陌生人社会还是新熟人社会的基础上，对此所做得取舍和把握有助于从我国的内在视角建构具有中国特色却不失普遍性的法学理论。

一

法律制度和法律文化是考察一个国家属性的基本标准。2001年4月当代法哲学家哈贝马斯第一次访问中国。在中国社会科学院学术报告厅所作的题为"论人权的文化间性——假想的问题与现实的问题"的首场演讲中，哈贝马斯依据交往行为原理讨论了人权的普遍性和特殊性。2002年5月美国法学家德沃金对中国进行首次学术访问，在清华大学作了"认真对待人权"的演讲。同关心中国问题的其他外国学者相比，哈贝马斯和德沃金的论域及其对中国问题的关注并没有超出理论想象的范围。哈贝马斯和德沃金的学术进路和理论出发点或有不同，但在演讲宗旨上均捍卫了以个人主义为中心的宪政国家基石，这种观念成为西方思想家认识和判断中国社会的前提和预设。哈贝马斯在中国社会科学院演讲后，当天下午参加了《读书》编辑部的小范围讨论会。① 开会伊始，他提出了想要着重了解和讨论的三个问题：第一，中国当代的法律制度与西方法律制度以及与中国传统法律制度之间的关系；第二，中国的宗教和法轮功问题；第三，中国当代"自由派"和"新左派"的争论问题，这三个问题可以分别概括为"法律"、"宗教"和"学术"三个方面。

---

① 《读书》是当代中国最有影响力的公共知识分子话语平台，是有所谓"自由派"和"新左派"之争的主战场。数十年来，它在介绍和评议国内外的经典文本的同时，开辟和发展出体现自己风格的公共领域。

来自中国社会科学院法学研究所的信春鹰研究员对哈贝马斯的提问做出了简明却不乏深度的回答。她认为可从三个方面概括中国传统法：第一，没有权利和分权概念；第二，没有公共领域和市民社会的分化；第三，不鼓励个人去伸张权利，主张无讼的社会和谐观。中国当代的法律制度从渊源上讲是 19 世纪末从德国经日本移植过来的"大陆法系"，但移植运动没有把它的理论和哲学一起引进来。1949 年以后，中国的法哲学有了一些新的特点，受前苏联的法哲学的影响，强调法律工具论。改革开放后西方经典的自由主义法学思想在中国的法律哲学和法律制度中有了表达和表现。在哈贝马斯的追问下，信春鹰谈到了普通法系传统对中国的影响，开始强调法律职业、法官队伍建设等。当信春鹰提到法律制度改革是政治体制改革的一部分的时候，哈贝马斯插话说法律制度的改革基础应当是彻底民主化的社会，如果没有基本的自由、平等以及政治参与的权利，就没有基本的社会公正，现代法律制度就无从谈起。哈贝马斯的这一评判为理想的而不是现实的当代中国法律制度提出了标准，再现了一个西方学者心目中的法治国家标准。[①]

本文关于中国当代法律制度的解释从信春鹰与哈贝马斯对话中的部分内容为基本线索，我愿意相信这些内容是当代乃至未来中国法治建设和对外学术对话绕不过去的主题。在第一部分，我从当代中国的国家制度而不是党政实践惯例讨论国家制度设计问题，重在说明和阐释；第二部分从权利话语和调解制度这两个维度讨论当代中国法律制度的悖论，调解的本质在于妥协和让步，这与争取权利的思维形成了内在的紧张关系；第三、四部分则从中国文化角度讨论现代性面向问题，指出中国法律制度为什么具有中国性，本部分将从讨论"孝与国家责任"开始，揭示中国传统文化与现代性的冲突，认为不是现代性在中国水土不服的适应性出了问题，而是现代性理论对人与人关系的定位和属性出现了方向性误判。

二

（一）"统"与"治"的辩证历史

中国是一个历史悠久、统一的多民族国家，在公元前 221 年形成了以皇权为中心的郡县制，这种政治制度有别于此前"三代"的统治模式，它以高扬"国法"而不是"家法"具有划时代的历史意义。作为家法的"礼"

[①] http://www.cc.org.cn/，2001 年 5 月 25 日，曹卫东根据录音资料整理。

是"治家"而不是"治国"的规则体系，体现了伦理政治和家庭成员之间的权利义务关系。经由商鞅变法，秦国率先瓦解了家国体制的政治、经济和文化基础，采纳了迎合世事的法家主张和学说，开创了"废井田、开阡陌，废封建，立郡县"的崭新格局，成就了帕森斯所称的"哲学上的突破"。哲学上的突破是指某一民族在文化发展到一定的阶段时对自身在宇宙中的位置与历史上的处境经历了一种系统性、超越性和批判性的反省；通过反省，新的思想和话语表达方式得以确立，整个文化或制度进入了一个崭新的、更高的境地。在公元前一千年之内，希腊、以色列、印度、中国等古老民族先后方式各异地经历了这种"突破"。① 郡县制在西汉有过短暂的"分封"复辟，但未从根本上影响延续了中国两千多年的政治法律制度。②

从统与治的辩证关系看，"统而不治"和"治而不统"将导致不同的政体模式，形成各自不同的治理策略。秦朝采取了"既统又治"的统治模式，国家的政治权力高度统一，形成了世界上最早的政治官僚组织架构。③ 带有"秦记"的郡县制度有两个重要的特征：一是治理的范围"止于县"，县以下的乡、村则实施自治，这是国家和社会分离的最显著的标志。通过这个分离，政治权力被限定在"国"的范围内，政治权力以外的权力则由以家族为代表的社会组织享有；二是"官"和"吏"的分野。"官"是经过科举选拔程序进入到统治阶层的"政治人"，"吏"则是服务于"官"的"事务人"，日常的政治事务的运行往往要借助吏的力量。④ 这个统治模式形成了中国两千年的"超稳定的系统结构"。要认识中国的传统制度以及它的连

---

① 关于中国式的"哲学上的突破"，参见余英时《士与中国文化》，上海人民出版社，2003，第83页。

② 封建制和郡县制的主要区别在哪里呢？我们用历史学家唐德刚的一段话作为解答："在封建制下，那统治中国各地区的统治者（多时多达1800个）都是世袭的封建主（分公、侯、伯、子、男五级）。他们属下的土地，大致都属国有。但是在郡县制之下，这些封建公侯被取消掉了，代替他们的则是一些省级和县级，有一定任期的官吏（政治学上叫'文官制'，civilservice）。同时全国的土地，也化公有为私有，人民可以自由买卖，也就是搞农村市场经济，不搞'公社'了。"参见唐德刚《晚清七十年》，岳麓书社，2006，第6页。

③ 在秦帝国立朝之初，在国体问题上采"分封制"还是"郡县制"曾有过激烈的讨论，见《史记·本纪第六》卷六。此外，官僚法是昂格尔讨论中国法律特点的核心词，以区别现代国家的法律制度，参见〔美〕昂格尔《现代社会中的法律》，吴玉章、周汉华译，译林出版社，2001。

④ 事君之人为官，官皆命于王，这成为官与吏、役的重要区别。吏、役是官的派生物，从属于官。《周礼·天官》："云凡府史皆其长官自辟除者，明府史即庶人在官者，不命于王也。"

续性进程，就应当处理好皇帝、官、吏和普通民众之间的权利和义务关系，正确统合"家"、"国"、"天下"的三元场域结构，从规则的角度看，传统社会形成了"齐家以礼"、"治国以法"、"平天下以德"等相关却不同的规范体系，这与西方社会关于"市民社会"和"国家"的二元统治观形成了鲜明的对比。

20世纪初中国率先在亚洲成立了第一个共和国，确立了主权在民的现代型国家，建立了以民族国家为目标的共和体制。在中华民国时期，以现代性为标识的宪政模型在文本意义上基本得以确立，六法全书的制定和颁行进一步强化了现代国家的形式合法性。不过，宪政制度、现代国家以及其他现代性制度的元素是被"嵌入"到中国社会结构中的，原有的"家"和"天下"的观念和制度并没有因此而消亡，它们只是被扑面而来的现代制度遮蔽了，这或许是当代复古主义者的主张和思想仍具有一定市场的重要原因。[①] 正如下面所分析的，无论宪政的实践如何展开以及实施的效果如何，由民族国家作为单一的力量解释中国问题的努力仍然存在观念和文化上的障碍。

（二）作为自治体系的国家制度

阐释中国当代的国家制度，就不能忽视法律制度设计及其结构的规范性存在。在现代社会的顶层设计中，法律制度都是顶层设计中最为重要的方面或组成部分。新中国成立后，在指导思想上采纳了人民民主专政的学说和理论，接受了前苏联的苏维埃代表制的政体形态。然而，无论马克思学说还是前苏联的社会主义体制，都不是本源于中国传统社会的文化和政治资源，它们仍然是近代以来的移植法运动在新的历史时期的延续。民族国家、宪政、共和等国家治理方式是西方社会的产物，无产阶级专政、马克思主义、一党政治、人民代表大会制度等同样是西方社会的产物。"五四宪法"综合体现了上述不同的西方理论和制度，被中国法学界寄予厚望的1982年新宪法承继了"五四宪法"相当多的原则和内容。不过，即使从民族国家的角度看，中华人民共和国的国家结构既不是纯粹的单一制国家，也不是纯粹的联邦制国家，而是统一、多民族的自治国家，在这一点上中国传统治理实践的惯性发挥了不可替代的作用。

第一，地方国家权力的固有性。国家权力属于人民，这是共和体制与

---

① 从中国文化的起源和内在发展视角讨论现代性问题显示了当代中国学人的志气和抱负，以史学方法论证中国治理秩序原理强调了历史观念和制度的连续性，也兼容了现代性的某些因子，参见秋风《华夏治理秩序史》，海南出版社，2011。

郡县制的重大区别之一，也是中华人民共和国通过法律构建民族国家的重要表征。今天讨论中国的"大一统"问题，强调的是国家权力源于人民权力这一终极性渊源，而与传统社会描述"大一统"概念所使用的"天"或"皇权"具有本质上的区分。然而，人民的权力不能等同于国家权力，国家权力也不等同于中央权力。依托于人民权力的国家权力被有效地分为"中央国家权力"和"地方国家权力"，[①] 后者作为一个专有术语意味着人民权力被平行地分配给中央和地方，由中央和地方两级治理主体共同分享。地方享有了固有的自治权力，它与中央权力一样，来自于通过宪法性文件的人民授权，而不是中央的授权。地方固有的自治权力是国家权力的组成部分，通过法律规定的权限和运行方式体现人民的意志。当然，地方在享有其固有权力的同时不排除中央通过授权的方式将其权力赋予地方代为行使。[②]

第二，地方自治的多样性。中国是世界上人口最多的国家，从权利角度看，由一个个具体公民构成，但这一个个公民不是孤立的个体，他们分别或共同属于省、市、县、乡镇、村等组织机构中。[③] 在制度设计上，每一个省、市、县、乡或镇都是一个完整的区域自治单位，有权在不与宪法、法律和行政法规相抵触的前提下在本区域自治单位范围实施自我治理。各区域自治单位的最高权力机关（各级人民代表大会）和最高行政长官（如省长、市长、县长、镇长等）都是选举产生的，有的是直接选举，有的是间接选举。根据自治程度的高低，各区域自治单位享有不同自治权限，具体分为普通地方区域自治、少数民族区域地方自治和香港、澳门特别行政区地方自治三种类型。此外，农民则在自然村或行政村的范围内享有与城市居民自治性质相同的基层群众自治，乡村自治和居民自治成为基层群众自治的核心。

第三，国家最高权力机构的依附性。每一个地方区域自治单位在本区

---

① 《宪法》第 2 条规定，中华人民共和国的一切权力属于人民。人民行使国家权力的机关是全国人民代表大会和地方各级人民代表大会。

② 关于中央和地方的关系，毛泽东在《论十大关系》中指出，"处理好中央和地方的关系，这对于我们这样的大国大党是一个十分重要的问题。这个问题，有些资本主义国家也是很注意的。它们的制度和我们的制度根本不同，但是它们发展的经验，还是值得我们研究。"在这篇经典性文章中，毛泽东多处在正面意义上多处使用了地方"独立性"的概念，它的基本含义应当理解为地方所享有的"正当的权利"，为此，他号召地方在中央统一领导下有权"争取"权利，而不被视为"闹独立"。

③ 据不完全统计，全国有省级城市 34 个，地级城市 333 个，县级城市 2862 个。另外，有 11 个区公所，19522 个镇，14677 个乡，181 个苏木，1092 个民族乡，1 个民族苏木，6152 个街道，乡镇级合计 41636 个。

域范围内，就制度设计意义上而言，都存在一个最高的权力机构，即各级人民代表大会及其常设机构，它们有权根据宪法性文件的授权决定本区域自治范围内所有事项，有权决定由己出的人民政府、人民法院和人民检察院的工作和行动的合法性，这种设计体现了具有中国特色的"议会至上"制度，这种制度源于马克思"巴黎公社"的设想和前苏联的苏维埃组织形式并融合了自由主义民主的部分内容。单独考察每一个具体的地方自治单位，在性质上与联邦制国家下的各州地位相似，都拥有较为独立的立法机构、行政机构和司法机构。虽然还没有划分中央和地方权限的专门法律，但宪法、组织法和立法法都从不同角度划分了中央和地方的权限。全国人大拥有法定的最高权限，有权决定一切在全国范围内的重大事项以及国家主席、副主席、总理、中央军事委员会主席、最高人民法院长和最高人民检察院长的人选。这是大一统的体现，也是最高权威的体现，但还不是大一统本身。就法律的结构看，如果有一个"中央权威"的存在，在法律意义上就只能是指全国人大，其他中央机构的权力均来自于这个最高权力机关，也受制于最高权力机关。最高权力不意味着它是绝对的权力或无限的权力。作为最高国家权力机构的全国人大的权力是后定的，它受制于地方各级人大的功能性结构安排。① 没有县级人民代表，就不会产生省级人民代表，没有省级人民代表就不会产生全国人民代表，而没有全国人民代表，就不会组成国家最高权力机构。设想一个或几个省没有或没有及时选出全国人大代表，或者县级人大没有及时选举出省级人大代表，就会发生中国式的宪法危机。

（三）民主"四化"建设：有待完成的国家制度任务

以上我们提纲挈领地描述了当代中国法律制度的规范性特征，还没有触及这样一种法律规范的实效问题以及它需要进一步改进的走向。② 在现代化、城市化和全球化思潮的推动下，对国家制度的各种改制主张和学说层出不穷，其中不乏截然对立的思想和政策导向上的争锋，而思想界的"左"、"右"之争有相当多的内容都会涉及这个话题。不过，大多数讨论都避不开对党与国家关系的论证（政府与市场关系的问题群中也隐含着党与市场的关系问题），这个主题乃是当代中国政治实践中最为重要也最具特色

---

① 《宪法》第 59 条规定："全国人民代表大会由省、自治区、直辖市、特别行政区和军队选出的代表组成。各少数民族都应当有适当名额的代表。"

② 法律效力和法律实效是不同的两个问题，法律效力体现了法律的权威，它往往与法律实效有一定的距离，但不因此否认法律效力对法律体系的价值，有关的讨论详见〔奥〕凯尔森《法与国家的一般理论》，沈宗灵译，中国大百科全书出版社，1996。

的方面。在改革开放之初，邓小平就敏锐地看到了党的改革对整个国家制度建设的极端重要性，提出了只要有政治改革就不能回避党的改革这一尖锐提问或经典难题。只有改革和完善党和国家的领导制度，才能"从制度上保证党与国家政治生活的民主化、经济管理的民主化、整个社会生活的民主化，促进现代化建设事业的顺利发展。"① 民主的"四化"问题将长期主导中国政治体制改革的性质和方向。在后邓小平时代，党的领导、依法治国和人民代表大会制度三统一论是对中国政治实践的表达，演绎了党、法律和人民之间的逻辑关系，即使官方也反复强调当前的政治实践仍需要不断地完善和发展。在法律和政治关系如此紧密，而政治实践对法律还具有相当影响力甚至支配力的时候，从法律改革的角度推进政治体制改革，对那些遵循了邓小平路线的改革者而言就属于题中应有之意。事实上，邓小平变法在方法上遵循了实验主义的渐进路线，这个路线在维护人民权利、自由和幸福的原则下，倡导个案或局部实验，成熟之后在全国范围内推广适用。正因为承认个案和局部领域的可实验性与先行性，就允许出现"差别对待"的问题，这是大一统下多元化和多样性的体现，在这方面的一个例子就是在香港和澳门实施的"一国两制"实践，很难相信在毛泽东时代或冷战时期，以实现共产主义为己任的社会主义中国在自己的领土内允许资本主义制度的存在和成长。

　　哈贝马斯或许不太了解中国实际运作的政治实践及其方法，对信春鹰提出把"法律改革作为政治体制改革的方法"没有给予应有的重视甚至不以为然，但是，对于政治民主，如果不是作为具体的改革方案，而是一种基于构建民族国家的原则和方向，哈贝马斯无疑是正确的，它也是中国作为民族国家正在努力实现的原则和方向，人们看到，"依法治国"和"国家尊重和保障人权"相继入宪都是朝着现代性方案前进的具体例证。

三

（一）私权观念的兴起

　　1978 年党的十一届三中全会开启了中国改革开放的序幕，逐步确立了社会主义市场经济的大方向和大原则。不论社会主义市场经济如何具有特殊性，但按照市场经济规律办事，遵循市场经济的法则是不可动摇的原则。在三十年间，中国就建立起一套较为完善的市场经济体制。土地、人力、资本、技

---

① 《邓小平文选》第 2 卷，人民出版社，1994，第 336 页。

术等相继进入市场，并且以惊人的发展速度不断创造出经济奇迹；证券市场、期货市场、房地产市场乃至人才市场——这些前所未闻的具有典型市场经济特征的元素在摸索和争论中建构起来。市场经济向越来越多的非公有制经济主体开放，以致非公有制经济在重大经济指标上都超过或远远超过了公有制经济。① 随着深化改革步伐的加快，向非公有制经济主体开放市场的程度也在向更高、更广和更深的方面发展，被视为禁区和由国家垄断经营的市场领地越来越受到置疑，一种市场经济的大格局和大发展正在生成和发展。

以市场经济导向为中心的改革开放运动重新肯定了私益以及相应的观念、规则和制度设计。私权、私人财产不仅不是被限制或消灭的对象，而且成为要着力扶植和保护的对象。肯定私有财产的价值趋向首先是通过"让一部分人富起来"的国家鼓励政策而进行的，尽管这项政策由于贫富加剧后果的产生受到批评，但批评的重点已经不是致富和私有财产本身，而是公平获取财富的方法、手段及其分配机制。因此，获取财富、维持财富，然后再获取更大的财富成为主流价值观，以致是否拥有财富和拥有多少财富成为衡量人的价值的重要标准之一，而这是市场经济发展的必然结果。

1989 年到 1992 年是中国改革开放史上的重要年份，包含了更多的疑惑、冲突、悖论和艰难，这一特殊时期日后被证明成为一系列有关进一步改革开放及其方案的重要转折点。1991 年 11 月国务院首次发表了《中国人权状况》白皮书，称人权是"一个伟大的名词"，号召所有仁人志士要矢志不渝地为"充分的人权"努力奋斗。几个月后，邓小平南行并发表了具有历史意义的讲话，果断提出了发展市场经济"不争论"，"发展才是硬道理"的实用主义改革主张和路线。这两个事件的内在关联性尚不能确定，但是它们巩固了从 1978 年到 1992 年之间改革开放的初步成果，明确了改革开放的信心、方向和路线。从那时起到现在，新一轮对财富追求的运动更加积极、热烈乃至狂热，而对私人利益的认可度也在进一步提升和发展。

权利的观念和理论为私人利益的价值趋向提供了合法性的背景和方向。

---

① 据统计，非国有企业（国有及国有控股之外的企业，如工商个体户、个人独资企业、私营公司、外商投资企业以及它们相互之间形成的股份合作企业）2005 年占所有企业数量的比重为 89.89%，2008 年提升至 95%，产值比重由 2005 年的 66.72% 上升到 2008 年的 71.66%，资产比重由 2005 年的 51.95% 升到 2008 年的 56.62%，利润总额比重由 2005 年的 55.96% 升至 2008 年的 70.34%，就业人数比重由 2005 年的 72.81% 升到 2008 年的 79.70%。2009 年国家统计局局长马建堂用数字反驳了国进民退的说法，新华网：http://news.xinhuanet.com/fortune/2009 – 11/24/content_ 12527933.htm。

权利概念表达了私人主体的意志、愿望和利益，言说了私人主体追求财富的合理性以及保持财富可能带来的一系列个人价值。中国法学界对改革开放的过程和方向给予了充分的肯定，及时提出了权利本位说，指明了这个时代也是"走向权利的时代"。权利方法继承了早期马克思主义关于人的解放的哲学方法，借鉴了自由主义哲学的核心内容。这种渊源和方法论上的判别固然重要，但更为迫切的是在改革开放过程中要用一种正当性话语表达私人主体的私人利益。权利是一个指涉性概念，它肯定了私性的合理性，表达了私性的过程和结果，打破了"大公无私"的观念，颠覆了"君子喻义，小人喻利"的古训，推动了人人可以言利的社会氛围和局面。在权利话语之下，权利的内涵和意义不断得到挖掘和张扬，从权利的利益说很快就走向了权利的资格说、自由说、主张说和权能说，从不同的侧面深化了对权利本质的认识，为契约自由、平等对待和社会正义的命题提供概念性工具和理论解说的资源。因此，对权利概念内涵的扩大化解释解放了被压抑已久的人性的某些方面，激发了利己的本能冲动，指认了人们在新的时代的位置和方向，确立了人在经济、社会和政治上的主体性属性。①

（二）妥协的权利

对权利乃至人权的探讨和接受虽然可以用来表达私人意志、愿望和利益等，却鲜有把权利与个人主义——这个自由主义哲学思想的基石连接起来。对权利的提倡与对个人主义有意或无意的排斥形成了令人惊异的反差，这种反差很难用"权利观念还不够发达"做出解释。权利主体可以利己，但不能自私；可以独立，但不能孤立；可以保护自己的权利及其财富，但不能"争权夺利"。例如，通过诉讼手段争取权利至今也未能随着权利观念普及而成为被社会广泛接受的事物。②

---

① 有关权利价值的判断，参见夏勇主编《走向权利的时代——中国公民权利发展研究》，中国政法大学出版社，2000。

② 1993 年由著名导演张艺谋执导的电影《秋菊打官司》风靡全国，其影响力至今不衰。影片讲述的是邻居打官司的故事。农村妇女秋菊因其丈夫被村长踢伤"私部"要求村长道歉，村长碍于面子宁可赔钱也不道歉，引发了秋菊打官司的一系列故事。故事的结局展示了秋菊的困惑和不解：村长被查明犯有故意伤害罪而被拘留。这是一个关于人格权的案例，在中国具有代表性。秋菊为了"讨要一个说法"动用了律师、法院等公力救济手段，然而对于秋菊而言，这些方法和手段都是为了让村长说一声"我错了"，以此达到和解的真正目的。村长是秋菊家的邻居，他们需要维系未来的多维度社会关系，而司法手段不仅未能也背离了当事人的愿望。秋菊的困惑也是当代中国人对法律和权利的困惑。对《秋菊打官司》中法律与习惯的冲突分析，参见苏力《秋菊的困惑与山杠爷的悲剧》，载苏力《法治及其本土资源》（修订版），中国政法大学出版社，2004，第 24～39 页。

与权利的宗旨不同，调解体现了让步、妥协和中庸等传统价值。权利是对抗性的、调解是非对抗性；调解要求当事人放弃权利，而不是锱铢必较。调解之后，双方当事人"案结事了"，皆大欢喜，均有"面子"，而面子是中国人表达尊严的文化概念。比较德国法学家耶林对维护"面子"的方法，就有了"妥协的权利"和"对抗的权利"两种权利发展的路径。①妥协的权利观并不排斥权利本身，但它着重强调"争取权利"的方法，它糅合了"息事宁人"和"权利主张"的两个方面，成为和谐社会的主要方法论基础。妥协的权利实践不仅表现在人与人之间、人与集体之间，也表现在人与政府和国家之间。在行政诉讼法中，"不得调解"是一项重要原则，是依法行政原理的重要体现，但正是在依法治国方略不断深化的时候，无论是法学界还是司法界，对"有条件调解"的认识正在达成共识，这种变化很难用纯粹的依法行政的原理加以解说。既主张权利又不放弃调解构成了当代中国法律实践的特色。

（三）调解与律师的职业伦理

调解制度已成为中国法律制度最为耀眼的"品牌"，在某种程度上，它也是传统法律与当代中国法律保持连续性的最主要的因素。调解是中国人处理日常纠纷的重要方式，但何尝又不是一种国家的统治策略和方案呢？这种源于民间被国家借用过来的纠纷解决机制浓缩了中国社会的文化性格——有缺陷却长久存在。被官方推崇的大调解制度显示了调解的民间性和文化性，被用来作为判断司法和政治正当性的标准，进一步表明调解开始从过去的非制度纠纷解决机制向制度性纠纷解决机制转化，提高了调解在制度建设中的地位和作用。然而，在大调解制度之下，强制调解的情况不可避免，为了追求"高调解率"，作为"调解人"的社会组织、法院或政府以违背当事人的愿望强行推行调解的事情时有发生，"各打五十大板"漠视了当事人的应有权利，"和稀泥"式调解反而成为"案结事未了"的原因。对于大调解制度本身的效果有待于进一步观察。

权利话语和大调解构成了相互作用但又矛盾的组合体。一方面，鼓励和支持人民维护自己的合法权益，这是时代的要求也是宪法的制度性安排；另一方面应妥善处理好权利人与其他人和组织的和谐关系，绝不因为"打

---

① 德国法学家耶林强调"斗争是法的生命"，斗争的主要方法就是诉讼，放弃斗争或诉讼不仅是弃权的问题，而是放弃做人的义务，参见〔德〕耶林《为权利而斗争》，载梁慧星主编《为权利而斗争》，中国法制出版社，2000，第1~52页。

官司"而发生"一年官司十年仇"的局面。不可否认的是，调解本身所具有的基础是文化性的，而不是制度性的，是内生性的，而不是嵌入性的，它源于中国古老文化中对"和为贵"、"中庸"等儒家理念的自觉信奉和遵从。因此，权利观念虽然日益深入人心并正在作为衡量行为正当性的主要标准，但在通过诉讼的方式维权方面仍然受制于传统文化的制约。

诉讼被认为是一场民事战争，是在法庭上的硬对硬的较量，是针锋相对的利害计较，是"你死我活"的最后博弈，而这些情况对那些想要继续维持未来社会关系的当事人而言往往具有杀伤力，他们不愿意因为一场诉讼而"伤了和气"。正如观察日本社会纠纷解决机制的棚濑孝雄指出的那样，即使在资本主义高度发达的现代日本，当一个人说"这是我的权利"或"咱们法庭上见"的时候，无意间就给人威胁或强硬的味道，成为"宣战"的信号。权利确立了衡量个人利益及其界限的现代性是非标准，但它与传统文化中的"人际和谐"发生了冲突，后者强调忍让、妥协甚至迁就。在纠纷解决过程中，恰当的调解往往带来"四两拨千斤"的效果，在一场激烈的利益冲突中，调解显示了"以柔克刚"的功效，而这是"争权夺利"的权利方法不能比拟的。

受现代化大潮的影响，在权利和调解之间，前者的分量和比重都在增强，虽然这并不导致人们放弃对调解的信念。我们从中国律师制度的迅猛发展中可以看到这一点。20 世纪 90 年代，中国的律师制度率先从司法制度的大板块中脱离出来，在制度上成为实实在在的"社会工作者"，律师既不是公务员或司法人员，也不是任何意义上的干部，只是依法为当事人提供法律帮助的法律职业人员。修改后的律师法明确了当代中国律师的使命，[①]认可了律师作为"民权标识"的崇高地位。[②] 虽然律师的社会地位仍有待于进一步提高——这取决于律师的职业伦理、政策导向和民间社会认可度等综合因素，但把律师称为"调词架讼"的"讼棍"时代一去不复返了。律师依赖法律服务于市场，是"靠法律生存"的一批人，这个特征决定了只有不遗余力地为委托人利益"斤斤计较"才能体现出他们应有的价值，这无疑增加了律师"为权利而斗争"的权重，除非调解对律师的获利性具有激励价值，偏重于诉讼而不是调解将成为律师工作的重点。为此，如何在

---

① 《中华人民共和国律师法》第 2 条规定："律师应当维护当事人合法权益，维护法律正确实施，维护社会公平和正义。"

② 参见张志铭《当代中国的律师业：以民权为基本尺度》，载夏勇编《走向权利的时代：中国公民权利发展研究》（修订版），中国政法大学出版社，2000。

"忍气吞声"与"为权利而斗争"之间开辟出一条中间道路就成为社会建设和国家建设的共同任务。

四

（一）无赖与父母官

自由主义哲学在方法论上划分了市民社会和国家的二元领域，成为理解现代国家性质的重要视角。在这种视角之下，国家的目的是保护私人权利，但如果没有一套分权制衡的制度，像所有其他权力一样，权力会越过应有的界限走向设立权力目的的反面，从而限制或剥夺私人权利，因此，时刻对国家权力保持警惕并将其限制在一定范围内是现代法治国家的任务。分权制衡的原则建立在人性恶的基础上，根据这种人性观假定，组成政府的成员被看作一个个具体的无赖，但政府并不因此就一定具有无赖性。大卫·休谟说："在设计任何政府体制和确定该体制中的若干制约、监督机构时，必须把每个成员都设想为无赖之徒，并设想他的一切作为都是为了谋求私利，别无其他目标。"[1] 罗素·哈丁对此做了深刻地解读："自由主义的核心含义是公民不应该信任政府，并且要提防政府。大卫·休谟提出，我们应该设计一系列政府制度，以便即使流氓占据政府职务时，也将为我们的利益服务。詹姆斯·麦迪逊及其他一些联邦主义者试图在美国宪法中构筑休谟所设想的制度。麦迪逊的看法实质上是，任何拥有权力的人至少部分地怀有为他们自身利益而滥用权力的动机。这也就是说，政府官员会有不为公民利益服务的动机。"[2] 不信任政府并且把政府的存在看作"不得不存在的恶"的观点强化了公民和政府之间的紧张关系。

中国社会受"家国同构"传统文化的影响，臣民和国家之间是"家长和家子"的关系，政府作为家长虽然专制却不失温情，这种观念不因封建制度的瓦解而消失。尽管在现实政治中圣人往往不在天子位，但这不妨碍政府和国家具有善的正当性，无赖无论如何都不应占据政府要位，哪怕无赖可以为民众带来利益。正如家不是坏的事物，国也不能被视为一种"最低限度的恶"，如果有问题也是它的执行者而不是政府。与休谟的无赖假定所适用的效果相反，无赖政治在现实中是"真理"，在观念上则是"谬误"，

---

[1] 〔英〕大卫·休谟：《休谟政治论文选》，张若衡译，商务印书馆，2010，第27页。

[2] 罗素·哈丁：《我们要信任政府吗？》，载〔美〕马克·E. 沃伦编《民主与信任》，吴辉译，华夏出版社，2004，第20页。

在两千多年的王朝更替中，发生变化的不是中国国家本身，而是具体的统治者。郝大伟、安乐哲指出："中国人对个人与权威的关系明显是非对抗性的，就如同个人与家庭的关系是非对抗性一样。"① 个人与国家之间不存在根本性的对立和冲突，也无需对有"父母官"之称的政府采取像无赖那样的防范和制约措施，因为父母官本应该按照儒家教义履行保护和抚恤子民的责任。此外，政府权力的界限"止于县"，在县以下的地方实行由家族负责的地方自治制度，子民的生老病死等社会保障工作完全由家族或家庭负责，国家只在重大的自然灾害发生时提供有限的慈善性救助。一个人既有受家庭或家族及其成员护佑的权利，也有为其他家族或家庭成员负责的义务，责任的大小取决于人与人关系的远近和亲疏程度。因此，政治责任和日常伦理之间具有明显的差异，子民的具体生活不属于政治的范围，子民之间通过血缘关系的纽带相互负责，产生了弥散性的社会连带责任机制。

（二）"养"与"敬"的背离

在家族连带责任关系中，孝是最高和最大的责任。对于成年的晚辈子女而言，以合乎礼的方式赡养父母乃是"天职"。② 孝的地位之高以致成为修身、齐家、治国、平天下的工具之首。孝的本质是"无违"，它贯穿于成年子女对父母生老病死全过程，正所谓"生，事之以礼；死，葬之以礼，祭之以礼。"子女给父母提供生存所需的物质条件只是孝的一部分，而且是其中很小的部分，纯粹的物质赡养恐怕还会走向孝的反面。子曰："今之孝者，是谓能养。至于犬马，皆能有养。不敬，何以别之？"重要的是用心尊重父母，做到精神上的愉悦和享受，而这只有在家这个温情脉脉的共同体中通过履行敬的义务才能实现。成年子女既是父母物质生活的义务主体，也是父母精神生活的义务主体，他要在"养"和"敬"两个方面完成对父母的人生义务。

近现代社会以来，随着民族国家的兴起和发展，一种新型的人际关系被逐渐建构出来。国家与个人发生了直接的关系，它不再需要中间组织（如家族）作为缓冲地带，国家第一次有了自己的人——公民。如同新教改革，教民不再通过教会这个中间机构直接就可以与上帝对话了，上帝才拥

---

① 〔美〕郝大伟、安乐哲：《先贤的民主：杜威、孔子与中国民主之希望》，何刚强译，江苏人民出版社，2004，第117页。
② 子曰："夫孝，天之经也，地之义也，民之行也。"又曰："五刑之属三千，而罪莫大于不孝。"

有了自己的"子民"。有了自己人的国家开始逐渐替代家庭的部分或大多数职能。过去，一个人的生、老、病、死、教育等都由家庭承担和完成，家庭成员相互之间组成了抵御或减轻人生风险的"保险公司"，如今，家庭的职能开始由国家负责，这种情况在福利国家尤为明显和突出。[①] 因此，个人主义只在公民和民族国家关系的意义上才能成立和得到认可。

从家庭或家族走出来的个体人为此进入到一个更大的家庭——国家，他对这个大家庭直接负责和承担义务，也享受由国家提供的一系列福利和社会保障，在这个意义上，难道不应该说人们仍然生活于"国家家庭主义"的氛围和环境之中吗？当然，这个问题还没有引起世人的重视。在现代社会生活中，"自己人"和"邻人"的关系扩大了，"在国家范围内建立社会福利，那是把邻人群体的大门向任何愿意加入的人们敞开。"[②] 然而，家还不是国，国家虽然肩负起照管公民的基本教育和生活的任务，但在"敬"的方面却爱莫能助。孝发生了内涵上的分裂，产生了物质意义上的孝（"养"）和精神意义上的孝（"敬"）之间的冲突。随着民族国家社会保障制度的建立和完善，这两种意义上的孝的冲突情况日益激烈，出现了物质赡养充沛而精神赡养空缺的现代性现象。精神赡养需要解决的是老人们的"色难"问题，即要消除他们的精神世界的孤独感。保有家庭才能提供的温馨和情感，但这似乎越来越成为难以完成的现代性任务。对标榜价值中立的现代国家而言，一系列体现人的温情和道德价值的规范早已从自己的领地被清除出去，那些为了寻求家园的人，都成了无家可归的人。

（三）伦理义务与法律责任

就制度设计而言，我国法律制度既规定了国家对老人的"物质帮助义务"，也明确了成年子女对父母的"赡养扶助义务"。[③]《宪法》第49条规定："父母有抚养教育未成年子女的义务，成年子女有赡养扶助父母的义务。"该条前款的规定乃是父母的自然义务，在古今中外趋同，没有例外，但在由成年子女赡养父母的问题上却缺乏统一性。例如，联邦德国基本法规定了父母抚养与教育子女"至高义务"（第6条），而无赡养父母的内容。不过，我国宪法虽然确立了国家和成年子女帮助或赡养老人的共同义务，

---

① 关于家庭职能的转变，参见〔美〕加里·斯坦利·贝克尔《家庭论》，商务印书馆，1998。

② Michael Walzer, *The Spheres of Justice* (New York: BasicBooks, 1993), p. 39.

③ 《宪法》第45条规定："中华人民共和国公民在年老、疾病或者丧失劳动能力的情况下，有从国家和社会获得物质帮助的权利。国家发展为公民享受这些权利所需要的社会保险、社会救济和医疗卫生事业。"

但《中华人民共和国老年人权益保障法》则把这种共同义务做了主次之分，规定家庭成员（主要指成年子女、配偶）是第一责任人，要承担赡养或抚养老人的主要义务，而国家的义务是次要和补充性质的。该法第 10 条规定："老年人养老主要依靠家庭，家庭成员应当关心和照料老年人。"在赡养的内容方面，赡养义务人应当提供力所能及的物质保障，包括但不限于生活费用、住房、医疗费用等，同时该法也规定了对老年人的精神赡养义务。该法第 11 条规定："赡养人应当履行对老年人经济上供养、生活上照料和精神上慰藉的义务，照顾老年人的特殊需要。"家庭成员的这些义务是绝对的、无条件的，除非赡养义务人丧失了赡养的能力。相比之下，对国家的义务则用了较多的较为含糊的道德话语，如"有关组织"或"有关部门"要负责老年人的基本生活；在赡养义务人无能力赡养的情况下，"当地人民政府根据情况要给予适当帮助"或"给予救济"。即便如此，该法在国家义务方面也没有忘记将它的模糊的次要义务尽量转嫁给"社会"，号召"提倡社会救助"（第 26 条）、"鼓励公民或者组织与老年人签订扶养协议或者其他扶助协议"（第 24 条）、"国家鼓励、扶持社会组织或者个人兴办老年福利院、敬老院、老年公寓、老年医疗康复中心和老年文化体育活动场所等设施"（第 33 条）。"因此，从法律的现有规定来看，孝的义务仍然保有了传统社会的观念和履行方式，它并未因老年人早已是中华人民共和国的公民这一基本事实以及《宪法》第 45 条的原则规定而改变国家免于或象征性地承担义务的事实。

究其原因，人们或许可以说国家忘记了自己的义务，为此应当加重国家的责任；或者说国家能力问题还不足以建立覆盖全社会的社会保障制度。前者关涉国家和公民的法律上的权利和义务关系，这恰恰是民族国家需要首先解决的问题，中国是否以及如何进一步推进民族国家的建设是一个重大的、基础性的工作，后者则涉及国力问题。这是两个具有相关因素的问题，在改革开放 30 年后的今天，国家正在着力打造具有中国特色的社会保障制度，已经颁布实施的《社会保险法》试图为具有中国特色的社会保障制度提供基础性的法律规范。在一个人口大国难以建立像欧洲国家那样的高福利的社会保障制度，建立与经济发展相适应的城乡一体化的社会保障制度却是可能的，但国家为其公民提供平等的福利不应当因其国力问题而免除，除非国家已经破产，国家为其公民提供与其国力相适应的社会保障制度都是第一和无条件的义务。

无论国家推行的社会保障制度的水平是高是低，都不能解决传统文化中"孝"的本质要求，尤其难以解决父母或老年人的"色难"即"精神赡养"的问题。在社会保障制度下，国家可以有计划地解决全体公民在其年老时的"物质赡养"问题，逐步实现"老有所养、老有所医、老有所为、老有所学"的小康社会任务，但国家难以做到"老有所乐"的精神赡养问题，并将这一问题提升到国家义务的高度。在基本的生活有保障的前提下，老年人渴望来自子女和社会其他人的精神抚慰。当代中国的一些关于"不孝"的司法案例中，老年人状告其子女的诉求开始从过去的"物质赡养"向"精神赡养"发展，一些"空巢老人"（即长期孤独生活的老人）借助公力救济的目的只是为了让子女"常回家看看"或可以多陪老人吃吃饭。①在现代性话语支配下，权利观念、个性自由越来越发达，家庭观念却越来越淡薄，这些都对精神赡养问题构成了威胁，提出了挑战。

中国传统孝文化正在衰落，但还没有到真正死亡的地步。因为绝大多数人（包括那些被现代性启蒙的社会、文化或政治精英）在观念上并没有放弃自己对父母尽孝的义务，尽管在实践效果上已大不如从前。中国社会对那些放弃或疏于尽孝的人总是给予有力的道义谴责，即使国家在物质赡养方面要负更大的责任。为了挽救孝心、孝行，不断有人提议在刑法中增加"不孝罪"，惩罚针对父母不孝的行为，如虐待、遗弃老人，不尊重老人的隐私权、婚姻权、财产权等，引发了社会的广泛关注和讨论。② 这些情况显示了孝道在中国人观念的重要性，反映了道德和法律以及传统与现代之间的内在紧张关系。

五

（一）民族国家与文明国家

文明国家的概念由美国著名政治学家白鲁恂首创而被雅克着重发挥。在雅克看来，中国构建现代民族国家为形，打造文明国家是实，而这是由中国两千多年的文化传统决定的，它不因中国是社会主义国家或信奉马克思主义思想而有所改变，也不因近代以来中国着力构建民族国家的努力而

---

① 2012 年 12 月《中华人民共和国老年人权益保障法》作出修订，其第 18 条增加的条款规定："与老年人分开居住的家庭成员，应当经常看望或者问候老年人。"

② 2003 年 7 月，由四川省老龄工作委员会办公室、省委宣传部、省委组织部、省人事厅联合下发《关于共产党员和国家干部带头敬老养老助老的意见》，该意见要求各级组织、人事部门要把尊老敬老作为考核党员、干部的内容，对党员、干部中不履行赡养义务，甚至虐待、遗弃父母、长辈的，社会舆论要严厉谴责，同时一律不予提拔任用……

有所偏离。将中国独自称为文明国家首先意味着中国不是也很难成为西方式的民族国家。民族国家兴起以来，威斯特伐利亚体系不仅支配着国家关系，也主导着国内政治形态和走向。在近代民族国家建立之前的近两千年前，中国就以一种明确的国家形式屹立于世界，它不同于民族国家的特性在于："统一具有至高无上的重要性，国家机器的权力和作用，内部凝聚力的特性，大中华理念，中心王国的思想，族群观念，家族和祖训，甚至还包括中医。"① "文明国家"元素重家庭轻国家，重道德轻法治，重多样性统一轻单一民族认同。

中国人追求统一的力量，与其说是迷恋于中央集权的前现代心理需要，不如说是一种源远流长的习惯或生活方式，由此积淀的惯性力量压过了任何外来的学说、主张和思想，后者如果想要有所作为，要么以温和的方式改头换面以"旧貌"体现自己，要么通过强制的力量使劲"嵌入"到这个大一统的共同体中，因此所导致的后果要么是无可奈何的"被同化"，要么往往造成历史进程的"巨大断裂"。不过，大一统自身不同于现代官僚制度所塑造的铁板一块的僵化、刻板和一致，毋宁说治理这个国家的是"统而不治"的形态，这种统治形态有别于体现中央集权的"既统又治"的形态，也与"治而不统"的地方割据或无政府主义拉开了距离。马丁·雅克观察到："我们不应当将中国看作一个通常意义上的民族国家，而应当将它理解成由许多拥有极大自治权的省份所组成的大陆体系国家。……我们可以将每个省都看作类似于一个民族国家，具有相应的人口规模和独特的文化。中国各省之间的差异比欧洲各民族间的还要大得多，甚至超过了东欧和巴尔干地区的那些国家。……尽管中国有着中央集权式的政府结构，但其实际运作方式却更像联邦制，比如某些经济政策的实施方面就是这样。"② 支持"统而不治"统治形式的文化理念是"和而不同"的多元一体的儒家思想，开出了"天下"这个高于国家共同体的概念。

民族国家意味着一个民族就是一个国家，一个国家就是民族。民族虽然不是指向"一个纯粹的民族"，但要成为民族就需要具备一系列"共同"的因素：文化、历史、语言、习俗、记忆等。中华民族作为一个民族却很难说有一个单一纯粹民族，也缺乏统一的语言、习俗或文化，用民族国家统摄中国社会无异于"削足适履"，更有可能出现"邯郸学步"的尴尬局

---

① 〔英〕马丁·雅克：《当中国统治世界》，张莉等译，中信出版社，2010，第 296 页。
② 〔英〕马丁·雅克：《当中国统治世界》，张莉等译，中信出版社，2010，第 166 页。

面。在长期的历史发展中，典型的"中原人"或"华夏"人早已和被称为"蛮夷"的众多少数民族通过通婚、杂居等方式融为一体，占据人口多数的汉民族是一个"杂种"的民族，汉人之不纯早已是不争的事实。天下的概念既然高于国家，它就要担负起统领和包容众多不同民族的任务。在历史上，"国将不国"的局面时有发生，典型的如元、清两朝，这些王朝由"异族"统治，但这并不妨碍"天下"的存在。顾炎武说："有亡国，有亡天下。亡国与亡天下奚辨？曰：异姓改号，谓之亡国；仁义充塞，而至于率兽食人，人将相食，谓之亡天下。……是故知保天下，然后知保其国。保国者，其君其臣肉食者谋之；保天下者，匹夫之贱与有责焉耳矣。"政权更迭，国家亡与不亡，那是统治者的事情，与没有参与权的老百姓关系不大，但是人欲横流、人性泯灭、人道尽失则是亡天下的征兆，关乎所有的人，对此人人都有担负中兴天下的责任和义务。如果中国作为文明国家的存在是一个历史事实，那么也只有在天下的理念下而不是民族国家的学说中才可以得到理解。

（二）国家主义意识的缺乏

按照凯尔森的理解，国家是法律体系的非人格体现，法律代表和体现了现代国家的存在和成就。现代社会的法律是以宪法作为基础规范的具有等级秩序的强制规范体系，任何不能进入这个规范体系的规则或规范（如习俗、惯例、道德、伦理等）都不是法，也不应当把它们称为法律。民族国家是法制国家，它消解了一切包含在习俗、惯例和道德规范中的传统权威，确立了至高无上的法律权威。然而，不同于民族国家的这种统治原理，中国传统社会没有把国家立为最高的组织单位，也没有用单一的类似公民的概念把所有社会成员统一到国家这个政治单元中，社会成员分属于不同的组织，它从基本的家庭组织开始直到作为人的天下的精神世界。

如果用民族国家的单一视角改造中国传统社会就需要承认作为主权单位的国家的最高性和唯一性，随之要求提高法律在所有治理结构中的首要地位。事实上，正如梁启超指出："中国人则有文化以来，始终未尝认国家为人类最高团体。其政治论常以全人类为其对象，故目的在平天下，而国家不过与家族同为组成'天下'之一阶段。政治之为物，绝不认为专为全人类中某一区域某一部分人之利益而存在。其向外对抗之观念甚微薄，故向内之特别团结，亦不甚感其必要。就此点论，谓中国人不好组织国家也可，谓其不能组织国家也亦可。无论为不好或不能，要之国家主义与吾人夙不相习，则甚章章也。"① 一种西方式的民粹主义至少在中国民间缺乏观念上的支持，如果产生也是"一个巨大而空洞的符号"（许纪霖语）或阿Q式的精神胜利法。不过，建立一套像样的天下体系是十分困难的，这样的体系从未在古老的中华大地上产生过，但是，天下无外的原则始终支配着中国人对自己、家庭和国家的看法，时至今日，这种观念也被用来与国际社会的"世界"、"全球"等概念相提并论，试图在全球一体化的当下提供重构世界政治秩序的文化和理论资源。② 当天下理念再次出炉并与现代性理论遭遇后，它就开出了关于现代性面向的问题。

（三）　去熟人化：对抗的现代性问题

现代性理论是欧洲启蒙思想的重要产物，它提供了影响人类社会的一系列相互关联的观念、方法和制度体系，例如社会契约、人权、民主、法治、自由、科学、工业化、城市化、共和、权力制衡、多党制等，揭示出人类生活和组织方式的重大变化和成就。没有工业文明的有力推进，缺乏对市场经济的精心呵护，特别对传统权威和宗教的无情抛弃，要取得这样一些成果是难以想象的。在标准的现代性叙事中，有两种意义上的现代性：一是从封建社会脱胎而来并与之正面交锋的工业社会，它瓦解了等级制世界观和宗教世界，消解了封建社会的结构。工业社会也被称为早期资本主义社会，它因其科学技术的发达、契约自由、稳定的经济增长等著称。二是立足于工业社会但对其给予理想批判的反思性现代性，它强调在职业和技术的系统性推动下所产生的对未来的不确定性，这种不确定性导致了地区、国家或全球意义上的"风险社会"。如果说早期现代性的成就还在或多或少地为未来许愿，或者像有人宣称找到了一劳永逸关于"历史终结"的预言，那么，反思现代性则看到了转瞬即逝的"当下"的"去未来化"，看到了现代性本身作为一个危险来源的实质。③

无论早期现代性还是反思性的现代性都是启蒙哲学在不同阶段的体现，它们之间的关联性要大于或多于其中的断裂。启蒙哲学在成功瓦解了一切束缚人的传统权威或"祛魅"之后，也削弱了人与人之间的自然的纽带关系，打造出一切以自我为中心的契约关系。对非自然关系的描述有时也被

---

① 梁启超：《先秦政治思想史》，浙江人民出版社，1998，第5页。
② 对天下无外原则的阐述，参见赵汀阳《天下体系——世界制度哲学导论》，江苏教育出版社，2005。
③ 关于反思性现代性的讨论，参见〔英〕吉登斯《现代性与自我认同》，赵旭东译，三联书店，1998。

称为理性人的关系或非人格关系，这种关系本质上是对抗性关系，它表现为市场领域中的竞争和政治领域中的斗争，冲突而非和谐占据了社会关系的主要方面。在这个意义上，现代性产生了它自身无法克服的弊端，它在造就了人的自由和解放的同时，也在无意之间开创了人与人疏远、隔阂和机械性属性，导致了人"自由但孤独"的"非自然人"状态，这也是韦伯精辟提炼出的"铁笼"状态，呈现出后现代主义的"现代性碎片"。个体的人获得了前所未有的解放，但它是以社会总体性解体为代价的，这个代价昂贵而且过于昂贵了。

（四）自由建构新熟人社会

对现代性的描述是一个方面，对现代性的定性与解决方案是另外一方面，后者作为一种理论体系总结了启蒙运动的实践，也系统地提出和强化了陌生人理论。对社会关系的描述宁可选择陌生人而不选择朋友，宁可选择敌人也不选陌生人。陌生人是一个令人始终不能放心的角色，它无法承担分崩离析的社会再次统一的社会功能。对"经济人"、"理性人"、"自由人"、"真的人"等人的属性判断和解说充斥在几乎所有的社会科学领域，都是陌生人在不同领域（经济的、哲学的、政治的或社会的）再现。这是陌生人理论的自我决定和自我合法性，也是具有"地方性经验"的西方历史进程中的典型现象，还不具有理论上的规范性和经验层面的普遍性。

现代性瓦解了传统社会的熟人关系，但它没有也无力消灭熟人关系本身，只要人还是生活于现实当中，就不能摆脱天然或拟制的熟人关系。在日常生活的层面上，我们所处的依然不是陌生人社会，也不是传统的熟人社会，而是不断扩展的新熟人社会。大学、公司、俱乐部、社团、协会等扩展了熟人关系，为我们自由建立熟悉关系提供了基础，搭建了更多、更新的桥梁。如果说传统熟人社会更多地以血缘或地缘构建熟人关系，现代社会则借用了自由这一手段能动地建构或解构熟人关系，其适用范围超出了血缘、地缘等领域。① 不可思议的是，陌生人理论否认了自由建构熟人关系的现代性本质属性，任凭从传统中解放出来的个休以原子式的生存方式自生自灭。陌生人理论看到了传统熟人社会不断瓦解的事实，却没有看到新的熟人关系借助于自由这一手段被建构起来的图景，对后者的忽视使现

---

① 传统熟人社会的论述，参见费孝通《乡土中国生育制度》，北京大学出版社，1998。新熟人社会理论的详细讨论，参见贺海仁《无讼的世界——和解理性与新熟人社会》，北京大学出版社，2009。

代性往往处于"未完成"的停滞状态，人为地割裂了"历史的连续性"。陌生人被赋予了越来越多的"危险"品行，随着利益冲突的加剧，不是拉一把让陌生人回到熟人行列，而是让其进入敌人的阵营似乎成为趋势，以致出现熟人陌生化、陌生人敌对化的"两化"运动，它的极端化表现就是"杀熟"和"敌我政治观"在现实生活中的反复演练。

对现代性的误判加剧了现代社会的冲突，对现代性病理的分析是康复现代性的智识性努力。新熟人社会理论不是一种元理论，只是为现代性找到重生的新理由。需要承认的是，新熟人社会一方面迅速地自由建构熟人关系，另一方面也在用同样快的速度解构熟人关系，"自由建构熟人关系"和"自由解构熟人关系"可能同时发生，发生的次数和频率也在加快，这个特征形成了新熟人社会的一个急需要克服的难点。对向现代化急行军的当代中国而言，新熟人社会命题既可以让传统暂时有了保存的空间，争取片刻的话语合法性，更为重要的是，它依然是在现代性叙事中的现代化表达，而不是回归传统的复辟主义路线。只有建构成立，解构才有价值，哈贝马斯说："解构劳动一泻千里，但只有当一个具有认知能力和行为能力的孤立主体的自我意识范式、自我关涉范式被另一个范式，即被理解范式（交往社会化和相互承认的个体之间的主体间关系范式）取代时，解构才会产生明显的效果。"① 在历史上，任何一次看上去是复辟的行动都是为向前迈出一大步的前提做准备，托古改制如此，文艺复兴也是如此。在这个意义上，权利与调解、孝与国家等关系命题的内在冲突就是可以理解的。在一个不断扩展的熟人社会中，面向未来的不再是"焦虑的社会"（贝克语），也不是你死我活的"阶级社会"，而是体现了自由和温情双重性格的现代社会。

六

熟悉和陌生具有哲学上的辩证法关系，从不熟悉的事物走向熟悉的事物是一个人和民族成熟的标准。站在现代性法律和传统文化十字路口的当代中国社会正面临着艰难的抉择。2008 年 2 月国务院首次向海内外发布了《中国的法治建设》白皮书。它从立法、行政、司法、普法教育、国际法律合作等方面较为全面地阐释了当代中国的法律制度，宣称："法治是政治文明发展到一定历史阶段的标志，凝结着人类智慧，为各国人民所向往和追

---

① 〔德〕哈贝马斯：《现代性的哲学话语》，曹卫东译，译林出版社，2004，第362页。

求。中国人民为争取民主、自由、平等，建设法治国家，进行了长期不懈的奋斗，深知法治的意义与价值，倍加珍惜自己的法治建设成果。"这段话表达了中国社会当下对法治的基本态度和信念。在哈贝马斯首次访问中国十年后，社会主义法律体系也宣告形成，如何看待、解释和评判改革开放三十年的法治建设、成果及其特征将是后小康社会法理学的重要使命。

Between Familiarity and Strangeness: Self-Construction and Directional Choice for the Rule of Law in China

He Hairen

【**Abstract**】In the process of modernization and construction of the rule of law, China has absorbed and transplanted many western elements of the rule of law. The formation of the landmark system of socialist statutory law and the implementation of the case-guidance system are the products of application of western learning in China—both of them serve the general modernity purpose of constructing a nation state. However, the application of the same western legal principles and doctrines has produced different effects in China on the practice and operation of the rule of law. For example, China has accepted the concept of rights, but not that of individualism and it has advocated state responsibility, but not necessarily based on nationalism. This reflects both the family resemblance of the rule of law in contemporary China to that in western countries and its the inherent affinity to the traditional Chinese culture. This article, through the analysis of such relationships as those between rights and mediation and between filial piety and state responsibility, reveals the conflicts and entanglements between legality and reasonableness, between the West and China, and between tradition and modernity. The author of this article holds that what is wrong in contemporary China is not modernity itself and what China has negated and abandoned is not the trend of development towards modernization, but the new interpretation of the nature of modernity, which depends on whether the judgment of modernity is based on directional judgment of the strangers' society or on that of the new acquaintance society. Adhering and mastering the latter is crucial to the construction from the inherent Chinese perspective of a legal theory with Chinese characteristics but without losing universality.

【**Key words**】 the Rule of Law, Rights, State Responsibility, New Acquaintance Society

法治与宽容原则

陈根发[*]

【摘要】古代中国的伦理思想曾经包含有丰富的类似于今天的法治宽容原则。在孔子和儒家的学说中，宽容是"仁"的具体做法。但是我国传统的宽容思想从近代以来并没有得到很好的传承和发展，与"严刑峻法"、"严惩"或"严打"的法律思想相比，法治宽容的市场和声音要小得多。今天，宽容不仅是一种超法律价值，还是一种超伦理价值，在一定程度上已经成了一个关乎人类命运的问题。如果要在自由和平等的市民中建立一种公平的合作体系，那么该社会就必须建立在政治和法治宽容的原则之上。近年来，宽容原则不仅在我国的治安、刑事法治领域，而且在民事、行政法治等领域也达成了不少共识，得到了某些有效的运用。

【关键词】法治　宽容原则　宽猛相济　法哲学　真理原则

法治社会同时也应该是一个和谐社会，和谐社会允许在一定程度上的多元价值并存和相互包容。从宗教宽容到政治宽容、法律宽容和法治宽容，是社会文明发展的必经之路。[①] 在当今世界的法治社会中，宽容原则越来越发挥着积极的和其他法治原则所不可替代的和谐作用。

一　法治与宽容原则

在古代中国的伦理思想中，曾经包含有丰富的类似于现代法治宽容原则的思想。《周易》的"丰卦"篇中就有："天地盈虚，与时消息，而况于人乎……雷电皆至，丰，君子以折狱致刑。"意思是人如天地之变化，不可

---

*　中国社会科学院法学研究所副研究员。

①　陈根发：《论宗教宽容的政治化和法律化》，《环球法律评论》2007 年第 2 期。

能什么人什么时候都明智,因此执法者要把握违法犯罪的相对性,要像宽容亲人一样宽容他人,既要惩罚违法犯罪者,也要挽救帮助他们。[1] 春秋战国时期的"百家争鸣"不仅是古代中国宽容思想的一次伟大实践,而且在各家学派的讨论和争鸣中形成的政治、道德和法律理论也包含丰富的宽容思想。如儒家以"仁爱"为本,墨家以"兼爱"为行动指针,道家提倡"慈爱",尽管三家在各自理念的实践和实施方法上存在不同见解,但三家的学说却包含有共同点的"爱",都包含"宽容"的成分。

"宽容"一词最早出自《庄子·天下》的记载:"常宽容于物,不削于人,可谓至极。关尹、老聃乎! 古之博大真人哉!"[2] 孔子也曾用宽宏大量的龙来比喻老子。《庄子·天运篇》中说:"孔子见老聃归,三日不谈。弟子问曰:'夫子见老聃,亦将何归哉?'孔子曰:'吾乃今于是乎见龙。龙,合而成体,散而成章,乘云气而养乎阴阳。予口张而不能嗋,予又何归老聃哉!'"[3] 《荀子·非十二子篇》则对"宽容"有精辟的解释。荀子说:"遇君则修臣下之义,遇乡则修子弟之义,遇友则修礼节辞让之义,遇贱而少者,则修告导宽容之义。无不爱也,无不敬也,无与人争也,恢然如天地之苞万物。"[4] 另外,《宋书·郑鲜之传》中有:"我本无术学,言义尤浅,比时言论,诸贤多见宽容。"[5]

我国的宽容思想从其产生一开始就是与法治宽容联系在一起的。孔子曾对仁与宽容的关系有专门的论述:"夫温良者,仁之本也;慎敬者,仁之地也;宽裕者,仁之作也。"即孔子认为,温和善良是仁的根本,谨慎恭敬是仁的基础,宽容则是仁的具体做法。[6] 在孔子看来,"仁"实际上是关于人与人之间的关系准则,其出发点应该是承认他人与自己一样也是人。孔子曾说:"性相近也,习相远也。"(《论语·阳货》)所以应该"能近取譬"

---

[1] 也有学者把"雷电皆至,丰,君子以折狱致刑"直译为:隆隆的雷电和闪闪的电光一齐大作,声威与光明俱备,象征丰厚盛大;君子观此,效法雷之威和电之明审断狱讼,动用刑罚。参见《四书五经大系》第2卷,天津古籍出版社,1998,第147页。

[2] 郭庆藩撰《庄子集释》(下),王孝鱼点校,中华书局,2004,第1095页。

[3] 刘志雄、杨静荣:《龙与中国文化》,人民出版社,1992,第10页。

[4] 意即:"面对君王就奉行臣之道,面对同乡就讲求长幼之道,面对长辈就遵行子弟之道,面对朋友就实行礼节之道,面对卑贱而年纪又小的人就实行劝导宽容之道。对人没有不爱护的,没有不尊敬的,从不与人争执,心胸开阔如同天地包容万物那样。"参见潘嘉卓等译注《荀子》,广州出版社,2004,第21页。

[5] 李伟民主编《法学辞海》第3卷,蓝天出版社,1998,第2395页。

[6] 《孔子家语》,中国文史出版社,2003,第31页。

即推己及人，承认别人。孔子还说："三军可夺帅也，匹夫不可夺志也。"（《论语·子罕》）即我们应该承认别人也有独立的意志，肯定人人都有独立的人格，对人要宽容，这就是"仁"的核心。当然，孔子的"仁爱"或"宽容"是有界限的，孔子用"是可忍，孰不可忍也"（《论语·八佾》）表达了他的主张。据春秋《左传·昭公二十九年》记载，孔子在批评晋国铸造刑鼎、铸刻范宣子所著的刑书时说："贵贱不愆，所谓度也……贵贱无序，何以立国？"即强调"仁爱"必须以"贵贱"秩序为界限。从总体上讲，孔子赞同和提倡的治国方略是曾为春秋时代的郑国政治家子产及其子太叔所实践的"宽猛相济"的政策。根据春秋《左传·昭公二十年》的记载，春秋时，郑国著名的政治家子产，治国有方，郑国一度兴旺发达。公元前522年，子产病重，嘱咐其子太叔曰：你当政后注意，唯有有德的人才能用宽大政策使百姓服从，其次就莫如严厉措施。子产死后，其子太叔继任执政。他不忍心严厉而务行宽大政策。结果郑国盗贼猖獗一时，为害甚烈。于是太叔立即调整政策，严厉打击不法之徒。孔子对这件事很赞赏。他说：好啊！政宽则百姓不受约束，不受约束则以猛来整治；过猛则百姓要受到伤害，受到伤害就再实行宽的政策。宽以济猛，猛以济宽，政事因此和平。东汉"建安七子"之一的王粲在《儒吏论》中说："吏服雅训，儒通文法，故能宽猛相济，刚柔自克也。"① 孟子在孔子学说的基础上，则更是将"仁爱"的界限明确为："或劳心，或劳力。劳心者治人，劳力者治于人；治于人者食人，治人者食于人，天下之通义也。"（《孟子·滕文公（上）》）

由于儒家面对现实，有一套政治、伦理和道德修养的理论可讲，子不语："怪，力，乱，神"，而是主张"三人行，必有我师焉。"（《论语·述而》）的宽容哲学，加上历代儒学大师又极力向人们宣传正心修身齐家治国平天下的道理，自汉武帝以后，几乎浸浸上升为国教，备受封建统治阶级的推崇。德国的马克斯·韦伯在《儒教与道教》一书中也指出："祖先崇拜和作为世袭制臣民心态基础的世俗的孝之基本意义，也正是儒教国家的实际宽容的最重要的绝对界限。这种宽容，一方面表现出同西方古代态度的亲缘关系，另一方面，也表现出同这种态度的本质区别。国家祭祀的对象是那些官方承认的大神。但是，皇帝偶尔也参拜道教与佛教的圣迹，不过，不必磕头——甚至在孔圣人面前倒也要磕头的——只要有礼貌地鞠个躬就

---

① 杨五湖总主编《案件学大辞典——办案大全》，人民出版社，1990，第645页。

够了……不过，政治观点总是要求相当残酷的迫害。皇帝的谕诏，甚至孟子这样的著作家，都以迫害异端为己任。"① 可见，我国古代的法治宽容实际上就是一种治国理论和方略，与西方从宗教宽容发展到法治宽容的进程是有区别的。美国的郝大维教授等曾指出："在传统中国，如同在其他亚洲社会一样，存在着一种活力，它促使儒教、道教和佛教和谐相融，形成一种丰富的传统，而这种传统最后都不破坏其任何的构建部分。这种'价值观的综合'（values synthesis）为容忍与服从的发展模式提供了基础，因为这一模式不要求政治与精神文化作彻底的分离。"② 可惜的是，这种传统的宗教宽容和法治宽容思想从近代以来并没有得到很好的传承和发展，与"严刑峻法"、"严惩"或"严打"的法律思想相比，法治宽容的市场和声音要小得多，这与古代中国法律思想中的"宽猛相济"方略正好走了一个次序颠倒。

宽容原则在我国法治建设中遭受冷遇和不畅有其自身解释方面的原因，但更为直接的是法哲学与实定法之间的对话不足所造成的格局。要尽快地消除人们对宽容原则的误解，最好的办法莫过于在法哲学上阐明法治宽容概念的起源和价值，并在法律的制定和实施中有效地借鉴域外的经验。有学者在研究"司法对传媒的宽容"时指出："强调以宽容的态度对待传媒，可以在域外的经验中找到理由。英美法的藐视法庭罪前紧后松的适用即明显证明了这一点……美国司法对传媒的宽容，是因为他们相信只有经历了舆论的风雨，法官才能变得更为强大与坚韧，才能更独立、更公正，以此赢得人民的信任、尊敬与服从，树立司法真正的权威。"③ 今天，人类正面临人口爆炸，所以宽容原则越来越迫切。在 1996 年底，世界上已经有 24 个城市的人口超过了一千五百万。在这种城市和人口日益膨胀的情况下，秩序应该如何运作，特别是随着人口密集地区的暴增，暴力与犯罪亦随之增加。这个世界若没有宽容，必然成为地狱。德国的法哲学家考夫曼曾发出这样的感慨："的确如此。在面对当今复杂、充满风险的情况时，我们所能提供的，不能再是如结构单纯、数量较小的中世纪社会所能提供者：一个封闭、静态、当权、不宽容的世界。这并不夸张：宽容在今日世界，乃至

---

① 〔德〕马克斯·韦伯：《儒教与道教》，王容芬译，商务印书馆，1999，第 264～265 页。
② 〔美〕郝大维、安乐哲：《先贤的民主：杜威、孔子与中国民主之希望》，何钢强译，江苏人民出版社，2004，第 99 页。
③ 康为民主编《传媒与司法》，人民法院出版社，2004，第 277～279 页。

于明日世界是一个人类的命运问题——Dürrenmatt 甚至称此为一个存活的问题。"① 从法治的层面而言，正如有学者指出的那样，宽容应该成为"宪政生态主义的价值取向"② 之一。现代宪法之所以不同于历史上的一切权力分配方式就在于不同的政治势力之间能够达成妥协，容许不同的政治集团和合理主张在法律范围内存在，体现出宪政的宽容与民主精神。

二　法哲学上的宽容原则

在西方宪法史上有所谓的宽容条款，它在集权主义猖獗的 16 世纪和 17 世纪中被解释为赦免性的容忍、宗教禁令的宽免、移居国外的许可等，在性质上都是国家（强者）对人民（弱者）的一种恩赐，或被认为是一种"政治上的睿智"。但是在现代宪法中却并未见到"宽容"或"容忍"的用语，③"宽容"似乎尚未完全被确定为是人民的具体权利或义务。如在德国联邦基本法及各邦的宪法中，也没有直接出现"宽容"（Toleranz）的字眼，而仅仅出现了"忍耐"（Duldsamkeit）、"尊重"（Achtung）和"顾虑"（Rücksichtnahme）等几个与"宽容"接近的用语，但是上述这些类似规定在司法实务中和法学教学领域则一般被解释为宽容原则。

德国的拉德布鲁赫在他的《法哲学》中把宽容看成是与赦免相关的一个法律概念。他认为，赦免"不仅是一种和善的法律形式，而且是完全与法律无关的领域中映射进法律领域的，并使冷漠昏暗的法律世界真正得以可见的耀眼光芒……赦免使与法律无关的价值领域兀立于法律世界的中央，比如宗教的慈悲价值、伦理的宽恕价值。"④ 法国的保罗·利科与拉德布鲁赫一样，认为宽容原本"不属于法律秩序"，"甚至也不属于法的层面"，但是由于"宽容源于一种天赋的理由"，因此它"不仅仅是一种超法律价值，还是一种超伦理价值。"并且，"从其目的而论，宽容还是规避不了法的领域……宽恕的'目的'不是消除记忆，不是忘却；相反，宽恕的'目标'是消除债务，而这与消除忘却的'目标'是不可调和的。"⑤ 按照拉德布鲁赫和利科的理论，我们可以把法治宽容理解为是从

① 〔德〕考夫曼：《法律哲学》，刘幸义等译，法律出版社，2004，第 475 页。
② 魏健馨：《和谐与宽容——宪法学视野下的公民精神》，法律出版社，2006，第 68 页。
③ 李震山：《论宽容与宪法》，载刘幸义编《多元价值、宽容与法律》，五南图书出版股份有限公司，2004，第 412 页。
④ 〔德〕G. 拉德布鲁赫：《法哲学》，王朴译，法律出版社，2005，第 176 页。
⑤ 〔法〕保罗·利科：《论公正》，程春明译，法律出版社，2007，第 165 页。

"完全与法律无关的领域"或法律秩序以外的领域中映射进法治领域的超法律价值。

考夫曼在他的《法律哲学》中指出：宗教宽容学说原则上并没有错误，错误的只是，这些原则直接从道德领域被转移到了法律领域。"法律与道德尽管有许多接触点，但是并不相同。因此，对于法学上涉及宽容的问题——学校祷告、宗教学校、学校及法庭中的十字架、婚姻问题、吸烟者与非吸烟者的争议、将道路命名为 Rosa Luxemburg 或将大学命名为 Karl von Ossietzky、外国人问题、战争役的拒绝、堕胎、自愿结扎、依请求而同情杀人等，均不能单纯以宗教或世界观团体的教条——道德见解予以解决。的确如此，但是法律领域的宽容问题并未因此而穷尽。特别有一个刚好是法律上的问题会出现，即法律的真实性或正确性如何？以及对于正确法的认识又如何？于此宽容是否有其适用或支配，因为是涉及真理、教条论上不宽容的原则？"① 人们或许可以从宽容原则具有何种法律意义的观点来做出不同的论述，但是应该能够比较顺利地达成如下共识：由于宽容确保多种价值观的并存，因此展现出一项重要的秩序要素，并将一种有趣的思想带进了法律讨论当中。②

当然，真正的宽容并不意味着容忍一切，而是意味着容忍那些应该容忍的事物。这一原则在早期的宗教宽容中就有所实验了。如法国的伏尔泰在他的《论宽容》中指出："虽然在《旧约》中有许多表示宽容的例子，但是也有严厉的事例和律法。"③ 可以说，宽容与严厉是对立统一的关系，两者并行不悖、相辅相成才是法治宽容的理想状态。而区分应该容忍的和不应该容忍的事物，这要求我们对人类生活中的重要事实有全面的理解。在规则的意义上，对这些事物的促进和保护是由适当的规则和适当的限制两个方面所预先假定的，因此，一部有关这些事物的禁止性宪法，与允许有关它们的错误方法的宪法一样，将同样对真正的宽容起到损害作用。美国宪法的构造和批准方式似乎对这一问题有比较好的理解。一方面，它们献身于联邦和州政府对各种各样的事物的促进和保护，另一方面，通过权利的保证——禁止那些最终会暗中破坏它们的方法，其构造和批准方式将更好地促进和保护这些事物。可以说，宪法本身的前景应该与真正的宽容广

---

① 〔德〕考夫曼：《法律哲学》，刘幸义等译，法律出版社，2004，第460页。
② 陈根发：《宽容的法理》，载《2007年中国法律年鉴》，中国法律年鉴出版社，2007，第727页。
③ 〔法〕伏尔泰：《论宽容》，蔡鸿滨译，花城出版社，2007，第136页。

泛地保持一致。但不幸的是，某些宪法解释的方法并非如此。①

三　宽容原则的价值

在现代多样性的社会中，宽容已经成为一个不可或缺的生活原则。多样性社会中的独立生存力要求生活其中的个人知道如何去应付不可避免的差异性和冲突。因此，从结论上说，宽容是当代社会的一个基本价值，而宽容原则也因此成为法治社会的基本原则之一。我们不需要同意密尔所主张的个人的差异性，即使这些令人不快的差异是丰富我们所有人的生活中的实验。我们也不必同意某些哲学家所提出的冲突的超价值是"迎接我们走上右倾路线的标志"②。宽容原则的重要性仰赖于下列这些朴素的主张：首先，差异性和冲突是不可避免的；其次，宽容原则为处理那些并不违反其他诸如正义、民主、自由和平等的基本价值的差异性和冲突提供了程序上的最低限度。无论你对差异性和冲突欢迎与否，或顺从，或痛恨，它们都是生活的事实。人们在许多问题上经常会出现一些喜欢或不喜欢、违法或不构成违法、违反现行法律但不违反自然法或正义的意见。如堕胎曾经是一个世界性的争论点，而宽容原则通常是处理这些争论的一个程序价值。尽管在最初的步骤上宽容原则并不是一个实质性的价值，但它却是在意见和价值发生分歧的情况下，和平地处理诸如有关堕胎那样的争论点的先决条件。美国的怀特教授曾指出："当我们不再用我们与我们对上帝的信仰、与自然或者进步的关系来作为界定自身的主要参照时，差异的存在便具有了一种非常不同的价值。它们不再是某种一上来就需要被说明、被规范化、被无可奈何地宽容的东西，而是一个该被赞扬的东西……对差异的注意成为了对有限性的确认。"③

宽容在一定程度上允许一个社会的价值和平地或和谐地演进。在不存在宽容的地方，就会发现众所周知的诸如大屠杀、私刑、恐怖主义、暗杀和种族清洗等恐惧。如果对手们不同意容忍另一方以寻找共同基础为目的的长期争论，那么其主要选择只能是一种形式或另一种形式的斗争和战争，

---

① J. Budziszewski, *True Tolerance: Liberalism and the Necessity of Judgment* (New Brunswick and London: Transaction Publishers, 1992), p. 44.

② W. Paul Vogt, *Tolerance & Education: Learning to Live With Diversity and Difference* (Thousand Oaks and London: Sage Publications, 1997), p. 24.

③ 〔美〕斯蒂芬·K. 怀特：《政治理论与后现代主义》，孙曙光译，辽宁教育出版社，2004，第 150 页。

或怀有敌意的"冷漠"。当然，有时对手们宁肯选择斗争和战争，有些斗争和战争也似乎是"正义"的，值得人们为之去战斗。但是，在许多情况下，解决冲突的其他方法如和解、宽容等则是更可取的。宽容原则也许听起来是非常消极的、有限的甚至与法治国家的其他原则难以相融。有人也许会问，与宽容他人的责任和罪行相比，我们难道不能有更高的目标了吗？是的，我们能够有，并且也应该有。但是，如果我们拥护多元主义，如果人们及其行为上的不同之处和法律上的不同认识是有意义的话，那么我们就需要有一个法治的宽容原则。美国实用主义的创始人之一威廉·詹姆士在《多元的宇宙》中这样表达宽容乃至法治宽容的价值："生命总是从它的全部资源里立即找到了同时满足许多对立面的方法。这正是我们的文明所呈现的相反相成的方面。我们用武装来保障和平，我们用法律和制度来保障自由……我们容忍无政府主义的和革命的言论才是减少这些危险的唯一办法；我们的慈善事业不施惠于乞丐才能完成这个事业想要达到的目的；真正的享乐主义者需要极大的节制；通过极端的怀疑，才能导向确实；节操不意味着无知，而意味着知道罪恶，而且克服罪恶；服从自然，我们才能征服自然……"①

约翰·罗尔斯在被广泛议论的政治自由主义中也采取了类似的立场。罗尔斯认为，如果要在自由和平等的市民中建立一种公平的合作体系，那么该社会就必须建立在政治和法治宽容的原则之上。这是因为，在一个自由社会中，合理的人类活动的自然结果更具有多样性，而不是变少了。甚至在田园诗般的条件中——一个没有偏见、愚昧或利己主义倾向的社会——通情达理的人们仍然会经常对基本价值、生活哲学、政治和法律规则表示不同意见。这一认识的性质和限度，罗尔斯称之为"判断的负担"，在通情达理的人们之间制造出分歧。在一个自由社会中，可能没有一个真正的普适的教义，因此通情达理的人们必须学习与不同的人一起生活，该社会的政治和法律规则必须包含宽容的核心。宽容，首先可以作为"权宜之计"——例如，结束宗教战争的一个办法——但是，罗尔斯断言，在社会、政治和法律的演进过程中，宽容最终将凭借自己的魅力变成一种价值。② 这是因为，政治和法律可以与有关最重要问题的信仰相分离。这就是说，公民在这类问题上的共同信仰并不构成一个民主社会的必要条件，对于公民美德来说，只要有一种为典型的有神论者和典型的无神论者所共有

---

① 〔美〕威廉·詹姆士：《多元的宇宙》，吴棠译，商务印书馆，2002，第 54~55 页。
② Jhon Rowls, *Political Liberalism* (New York: Columbia University Press, 1993), pp. 54-58.

的道德官能就足够了。罗蒂曾指出："罗尔斯所提倡的哲学宽容，实乃是对杰弗逊所提倡的宗教宽容的一种可能的扩展。'宗教'和'哲学'都是模糊的词语，总是可以作出说服性的重新定义的。当这些词的定义足够宽泛时，每一个人，甚至是无神论者，都可以说具有一种宗教信仰（在蒂利希'终极关怀的象征'意义上）。"①

　　例如，关于对表达的宽容，其中的一个主要论证是基于"真理原则"给予表达与行动不一致的豁免。发现真理的经验表明，既然一个可能性中存在着错误，因此我们就不能仅仅依靠那些出现在我们眼前的所谓正确的东西作出判断。这就是说，即使在已经确定的情况下，我们也必须保持一些不确定的因素，而容忍是与意愿和领会那些远离我们的不同认识方式的能力相连接的。我们也许能够很快地发现，真理的特征已经出现在我们的视野中，但它却仍然是不完全的，只有通过其他不完全的真理的补充才能得到完善。即使我们相信已经知道了真理是什么，那么我们也不能停下来休息，而应该继续把我们的真理付诸于试错法以证明我们并没有犯错。此外，我们应该保证每个人和各种意见都能够得到被听取的机会，否则我们就会在发现真理的道路上设置障碍。这一假定是，尽管我自己并不相信，但是承认他人的想法也许是正确的这一可能性，就是承认我的想法也许是错误的可能性。这一假定也有足够的空间适用于那些完全持不同意见的团体和个人。一个观点之所以应受到怀疑，简单地说是因为它为少数人所掌握，并也许阻碍真理的发现。尽管许多新的思想和创新开始于少数人的想法，但是我们在头脑中必须注意到上述负面影响的存在。这一"真理原则"指示我们对那些强烈地和认真地被相信是正确的意见提出质疑，以探索一些更加深远的真理和揭露它们的错误方面。这一论证的方法事实上已经为美国的最高法院在一些判决中所利用。②

四　结语

　　近年来，宽容原则不仅在治安、刑事法治领域，而且在民事、行政法治等领域也达成了不少共识，得到了某些有效的运用。如有学者在探讨我国"宽严相济"的刑事政策时指出："宽严相济的'宽'，是指宽大、宽缓

---

① 〔美〕理查德·罗蒂：《后哲学文化》，黄勇编译，上海译文出版社，2004，第166页。

② Raphael Cohen-Almagor, *The Boundaries of Liberty and Tolerance* (Gainesville: University Press of Florida, 1994), pp. 106 – 107.

和宽容，表现为以下三种情形：一是非犯罪化；二是非监禁化；三是非司法化。宽严相济的'严'，是指严格、严厉和严肃。"① 在建设社会主义和谐社会的时代背景下开始尝试的"刑事和解"制度，实际上也是一个"宽严相济"刑事政策的体现，对被告人而言无疑是一种宽大或宽容。"刑事和解"的理论基础并不是一定的具体方法、对策和程序，而是一系列的原则和价值，主要体现的是宽恕或法律宽容的原则。可以说，无论是中国古代的和合文化，还是西方宗教中的宽恕、博爱理念，都十分推崇和缓、宽容的纠纷解决方式，倡导人们化解冲突，和睦友爱相处。② 在现实的法院审理中，法官事实上也经常可以围绕法律——比法律更为宽容，透过法律的解释做出判决，以实现个案正义。可以说，这种在宽容原则指引下的法律解释正是一种普遍的现实的法治宽容。2007 年修订的我国《科学技术进步法》第一次将"宽容"一词写进了法律，该法第 56 条规定："国家鼓励科学技术人员自由探索、勇于承担风险。原始记录能够证明承担探索性强、风险高的科学技术研究开发项目的科学技术人员已经履行了勤勉尽责义务仍不能完成该项目的，给予宽容。"从此，在我国，法治宽容原则也有了一定的法律依据。

　　那么，当宽容原则通过规避法律秩序而使自己置于法律秩序之上时，这种状态对法律秩序本身而言是否就是某种副作用呢？如果我们从法哲学的角度来审视司法的话，下面的结论也许更能为人们所接受：司法虽然是人类的正义，但它绝不能将自己设想为最终的裁判。司法的远大目标是不仅要使自己与野蛮的复仇、酷刑相分离，而且也要与宗教式的复仇和不宽容相分离，这就需要一种神圣的宽容原则。

Rule of Law and the Principles of Tolerance

Chen Genfa

【**Abstract**】 Traditional Chinese ethics contains rich content similar to modern

---

① 陈剑虹主编《宽严相济刑事政策在检察工作中的运用》，中国检察出版社，2007，第 5 页。
② 陈光中、葛琳：《刑事和解的理论依据与适用构想》，载黄京平、甄贞主编《和谐社会语境下的刑事和解》，清华大学出版社，2007，第 16 页。

principles of the rule of law and tolerance. According to the Confucian doctrine, tolerance is a concrete manifestation of benevolence (ren). However, this traditional Chinese doctrine of tolerance has not been adhered to or developed since modern times. Compared to the legal ideas of " severe penal codes ", "inflexible administration of justice" and "strike hard", the voice of the advocators of legal tolerance is much weaker. Today, tolerance is a value that transcends not only law, but also ethics, and has, to a certain extent, become an issue that affects the fate of mankind. In order to establish a fair system of cooperation among free and equal citizens, the society must be based on the principle of political and legal tolerance. In recent years, many consensuses have been reached on, and effective applications made of, the principle of tolerance in China, not only in the fields of public security and criminal law, but also in the fields of civil, administrative and other laws.

【Key words】 the Rule of Law, the Principle of Tolerance, Tempering Justice with Mercy, Philosophy of Law, the Principle of Truth

社会转型背景下的中国近代法律变迁

高汉成[*]

【摘要】 1840 年后西方国家强加给中国的不平等条约制度对中国社会的转型起了两方面复杂而巨大的影响。在中国社会转型的大背景下，中国传统法律的变革随之展开，其直接动因就是领事裁判权问题。清朝末年清政府全面推行法制改革，传统法律体系解体，中国法律开始了近代化进程。1927 年南京政府建立后，加快了法律近代化步伐，六法体系的形成，标志着中国法律近代化进程得以初步完成。就中国法律变迁而言，中国法律近现代化的成功依赖于法哲学的逻辑和法历史学的逻辑的有机统一。

【关键词】 社会转型　近代法律　法律变迁

一　条约制度与近代中国社会的转型

一般的看法，中国近代史开始于 1840 年中英鸦片战争的爆发，结束于 1949 年新中国成立，涵盖了清朝晚期和中华民国两个时期。

中国踏入近代比西方国家要晚二百到三百年。从世界范围看，近代史就是一部资本主义在西方产生、发展并向全世界扩张并随之在全世界产生巨大影响的历史。中国从 1840 年起被英国用枪炮打开大门以后，西方列强以军事侵略为手段，大肆进行商品输出和资本输出，使中国从一个以皇权为中心、闭关自守的封建帝国一步步变成了半封建半殖民地社会，于是中国社会第一次面临着转型问题。鸦片战争是中国近代史的开端，也是中国现代化的起点。世界走向中国、中国被迫走向世界，这个过程是艰难的。其中，西方国家强加给中国的不平等条约对中国社会的转型起了巨大影响。

---

*　中国社会科学院法学研究所副研究员。

不平等条约制度形成于 19 世纪 40 年代至 60 年代，第一次鸦片战争中签订的《南京条约》等一批不平等条约，确定了整个条约制度的基本内容：割地、赔款、通商、关税协定、领事裁判权、租地造屋、五口通商地传教等。第二次鸦片战争后，通过《天津条约》、《北京条约》的签订，列强的特权得到扩大，并增加新的特权：外国人管理中国的海关权、内河航运权、鸦片贸易权、苦力贸易权、内地传教权等。有学者统计，中国近代历届政府签订的中外条约超过了一千个，其中与 22 个国家签订的 745 个条约为不平等条约。从内容实质来看，"条约制度"是列强对中国行使"准统治权"，使中国成了列强共管的国际化半殖民地。

"条约制度"在近代中国产生了复杂的影响，马克思在《不列颠在印度统治的未来结果》中阐述了这样一种观点：西方列强要求亚洲社会完成双重使命，即破坏性使命和建设性使命。侵略战争给了中国以致命的打击，"迫使它们在自己那里推行所谓的文明"和"采用资产阶级的生产方式"。可以说，中国近代史上的所有重大改变，无一不是在"条约制度"所带来的西方文明的影响下发生的。比如，19 世纪 60 年代至 90 年代的洋务运动，就是在经济、军事领域向西方学习，由此，中国诞生了第一批近代军工企业和民用企业，出现了新的社会力量（早期民族资本家和从农民转化而来的近代工人）。1901 年至 1911 年的清末"新政"，是清王朝在其统治的最后十年中试图挽救其衰亡命运而在政治制度领域所进行的改良努力，产生了中国第一部宪法和准议会性质的咨询机构——中央的资政院和省一级的咨议局。特别是 1905 年清廷废除科举制度，转向追求实用科技的现代教育制度，此举彻底动摇了中国前现代社会政治结构的基础。1911 年爆发的辛亥革命中清王朝被推翻，亚洲第一个以美国制度为样板的共和国——中华民国创立。帝制的瓦解和王权的崩溃，极大地动摇了传统社会生活的各个方面。1919 年前后的"五四"新文化运动中包括马克思主义、自由主义在内的西方各种社会新思潮竞相引入中国，以陈独秀、胡适为代表的中国知识分子用西方文化和精神对以儒家文化为代表的传统思想进行了全面批判，这是"重估一切价值"的思想革命，有点类似于西方的文艺复兴时代。① 根据衡量一个社会现代性的强弱的具体指标，即工业化、都市化、识字率、现代契约关系、社会流动性和政治制度化，来分析 1840 年后的中国社会变

---

①　有趣的是，五四时期由北京大学学生出版的一本著名杂志《新潮》，其封面上英文名字就是"The Renaissance"。

迁，我们可以看到中国前现代社会的政治、经济、意识形态结构在大约一百年的时间内都发生了急剧的变化。

但同时，在西方因素影响下的中国社会转型并不顺利，甚至不能称得上成功。从一个封建落后的农业国家转变为一个先进的近代工业国家，从一个封建专制的国家转变为一个具有现代意义上的民主法治的国家，从一个有着几千年"尊尊、亲亲"封建传统的大国转变为一个尊重人权、人人平等的新型国家，这些任务在中国近代史上都没有完成。其中的原因可能是多方面的，比如，西方国家通过条约制度在中国攫取的特权严重损害了中国的主权和领土完整，破坏了推动现代化中枢的中国政府的权威；频繁的外敌入侵不时地中断了中国现代化的进程；长时间、巨额的战争赔款使得中国的发展始终处于失血状态；清王朝崩溃和袁世凯复辟帝制失败使中国大一统的中央集权制度急速衰微，地方军阀趁机崛起，国内政治出现了长期动荡；改革仅集中于上层结构，很少波及下层社会，而农村传统的社会结构根深蒂固，没有受到重大冲击，少数沿海、沿江城市的繁荣并不能从根本上改变中国社会的整个面貌。直到 20 世纪 40 年代，承载着近代工商业的城市，仍然像一个个小岛，掩映在传统乡村的汪洋大海之中。以毛泽东为首的中国共产党之所以能以"农村包围城市"的战略取得革命的成功，原因就在这里。这件事所反映的，实际上是中国近代社会转型在某种意义上的失败。

二 领事裁判权制度与晚清法律改革

在中国社会转型的大背景下，中国传统法律的变革随之展开，其直接动因就是领事裁判权问题。

领事裁判权是指一国通过其驻外领事等对在另一国领土之内的本国公民按照本国法律行使司法管辖权的制度。英国通过发动鸦片战争，在 1843 年强迫清政府签订的《中英五口通商章程》中首先取得了这项特权。之后，美国、法国、俄国、德国、日本、意大利等国相继在中国取得领事裁判权。列强在华实施的领事裁判权制度既有损一个国家司法主权的尊严，也在实践中折射出了中国传统法律制度落后和不文明的一面。在 1901 年清朝最高统治者明确向西方学习、肯定西方文化的价值后，为了鼓励、推动新政的展开，西方列强和国内的改革派迅速就废除领事裁判权问题达成了共识。1902 年 9 月清政府与英国在上海签订了《续议通商行船条约》，该约第 12 款规定："中国深欲整顿本国律例，以期与各西国律例改同一律，英国允愿尽力协助，以成此举。一俟查悉中国律例情形及其审断办法，及一切相关事宜皆臻妥善，英国即允弃其治外法权。"① 这是西方列强第一次承诺有条件地放弃领事裁判权，随后美国、日本等国家在与中国签订的条约中都承诺了这一条款。这大大激发了中国人的民族自尊，"修律以收回领事裁判权"成了法律改革的旗帜。为此清政府成立专门的法律修订机构，派沈家本、伍廷芳为修律大臣修订现行律例，以求中外通行。1906 年清政府决定以九年为期"预备立宪"，政治制度和政治理念的重大变革，使得法律改革大大加速。

晚清十年法律改革，在立法方面，包括宪法、行政法、刑法、民法、商法、诉讼法在内的部门法体系初步建立。为了"以商兴国"，鼓励商业发展，首先制定商事法律，1903 年至 1907 年包括《公司律》、《破产律》在内的商事法律颁布，并制定了一批鼓励投资实业、建立工厂的实业奖励法规和促进行业发展的行会组织法规。1908 年《钦定宪法大纲》颁布，这是中国第一部宪法。1908 年《钦定行政纲目》颁布，明确规定了君主立宪政体的行政原则，随之颁布了一批调整行政法律关系、规范行政行为的法律、法规。1911 年《钦定大清刑律》颁布，《大清民律》也完成起草工作。新刑律彻底废弃了《大清律例》的体例和内容，基本以日本、德国的刑法为模本，分总则、分则两编，共 36 章 411 条，确定了感化教育、量刑从刑、罪刑法定等一系列刑法制度和刑法精神。② 民律草案包括总则、债权、物权、亲属、继承五编，共 36 章 1596 条，在内容上，总则、债权、物权三编以西方通行的民法理论和原则为依据，亲属、继承两编则更多地考虑了中国的传统习惯。

在司法改革方面，新的诉讼制度和司法机构建立。通过《大理院审判编制法》（1906）、《各级审判厅试办章程》（1909）、《法院编制法》（1910），司法机构改革改变了司法与行政合一、司法不独立的传统，出现了司法机构和审判机构的分立。原中央六部之一、主掌审判的刑部改为法部，为中央司法行政机关。原掌复核的大理寺改为大理院，为中央最高审判机构。地方设立初级审判厅、地方审判厅和高等审判厅，实行四级三审制。1910 年完成的《刑事诉讼律草案》和《民事诉讼律草案》，改变了民、刑不分的传

---

① 朱寿朋：《光绪朝东华录》（第五册），中华书局，1958，第 103 页。领事裁判权在当时被称为治外法权。

② 如感化教育和轻刑原则的确立，使旧刑法典有 840 余条死刑条款变为新刑法典只有 36 条死刑。

统，区分了民事案件与刑事案件，确立了平等、公开、公正审判原则以及律师辩护、陪审制度。新建立的司法机构，按照新的司法原则，包括审判独立、审判与检察职能划分、民刑案件分别审理、适用新的诉讼程序等，传统司法体制开始向近代转型。

在短短十年时间里，晚清法律改革以日本、德国为榜样，对传统法律制度进行了颠覆性的变革，传统的中华法系被废弃，一个包括宪法、行政法、刑法、民法、诉讼法、法院编制法在内的全新部门法律体系及一个标榜"司法独立"、"平等、公开、公正审判"原则的司法系统已经初步建立。"自由"、"平等"、"博爱"、"人权"等西方法律精神、法律理念开始为中国人所接受，这毫无疑问大大推动了中国立法和司法过程的民主化和现代化的进程。也确定了此后三十年中国法律变迁的基本方向和内容。

但同时，急剧的变革在偌大的中国也产生了很多问题和矛盾，引起了很多人的质疑和批评。1907 年至 1911 年，围绕着刑法典的制定，发生了一场较大规模的激烈论争——"礼法之争"。[①] 传统法律是需要用西方法律精神进行修改的，双方对此没有异议。问题在于，用西法修订中律到底以谁为主？新修法律的灵魂是中国的还是外国的？礼教派所允许的底线是对旧律"大修大补"，而法理派主张要"推倒重来"，这是双方争执的焦点。这一争论实质上反映了双方在确立新的法律体系时如何对待西方近代法律精神与中国传统法律原则的分歧。众所周知，中国传统法律中最为成熟和发达的就是刑法，无论是法典的编纂体例，还是刑法理念和原则，二千多年的中国传统刑法都积累了丰富的经验。按照常理，清朝官方和主持修律的沈家本如均以中西融合为宗旨，则制定刑律时，传统法律资源中可供汲取者很多，又何必舍近求远，假手洋人呢？洋务运动的领导人之一、1902 年成功说服英国人承诺有条件放弃领事裁判权的张之洞对基本移植和照搬西方法律的 1907 年大清刑律草案进行了激烈的批评。这一方面展示了他对中国传统刑法文化的自信，希望借此能有和西方法律文化平等对话的机会；另一方面他也担心，如果连这"最拿手"的东西都没有和西方平等对话的资格和机会，那中国传统法律文化还有何存在的价值。斟酌、融合中西岂不成了一句空话。即使今天看来，这的确也是个问题。1907 年大清刑律草

---

① 礼教派和法理派之间的争论：礼教派维护传统礼教精神，主张法律应与礼教结合，以张之洞、劳乃宣为代表；法理派拥护近代法制精神，主张法律应与传统的礼教相分离，以沈家本、杨度为代表。

案对于中国传统刑法典中有价值的规定，并没有能够很好地予以消化吸收而留存于新刑法典之中，而是"把孩子连同洗澡水一并泼掉了"。法律文本的"先进性"与社会现实的"落后性"形成了强烈反差，立法精神与文化背景和民众观念大大相悖，因而难以发生实际效力。

三　中华民国的法律变迁

按照 1908 年《筹备（宪政）事宜清单》确定的九年预备立宪，1916 年清政府将正式实施宪政，清末修律中制定的很多法律（草案），实际上是为宪政后的中国准备的。1911 年辛亥革命虽然推翻了清王朝的统治，建立了中国民国，但晚清法律改革的成果却被基本继承了下来并在深度和广度上继续向前发展。

1. 北京政府时期的法律制度

1911 年 10 月 10 日，辛亥革命在武昌爆发后，全国不少省区纷纷宣布独立，脱离清政府。11 月，已宣布独立的 17 个省代表集会，制定了《中华民国临时政府组织大纲》，决定采用美国总统制共和政体组织新政府，1912 年 1 月 1 日，以孙中山为临时大总统的南京临时政府成立。随后南北议和，在袁世凯逼清帝退位后，他于 3 月 10 日在北京被推举为中华民国临时大总统。

自 1912 年至 1927 年，中华民国北京中央政府为具有不同派系的军阀集团所把持。他们为了获取在北京的中央统治权，一方面镇压政治上的反对派，逼迫其他军阀就范，并以军事实力作为保持政权的最终手段。所以这一时期的宪法性立法和作为立法机构的国会更迭特别频繁。南京临时政府解散前夕，公布了内阁制政体的《临时约法》以对袁世凯的大总统权力进行约束。1914 年袁世凯解散国会，另组约法会议制定《约法》代替了《临时约法》，恢复了总统制。1916 年袁世凯复辟帝制失败后，军阀混战加剧，国会时断时续，直到 1923 年才正式制定了第一部《中华民国宪法》。这部宪法共 13 章 141 条，包括：国体、主权、国土、国民、国权、国会、大总统、国务院、法律、会计、地方制度、宪法之修正解释及效力，它确立了"统一、民主"的国体、责任内阁制的中央政府、司法独立和最高法院的违宪审查权、地方自治。这部宪法本身很好，但因为这届国会部分议员接受了选举曹锟为总统的金钱贿赂而蒙上了"贿选宪法"的阴影而受到各种非议。另一方面，为了争取有利的社会舆论，也需要借助近代民主共和政体的运作模式来表明自己中央统治权的合法性，为此也进行了法律创制和司法制度建设活动。其表现是：清朝末年制定颁布的一系列法律、法规，被继续援用，如《大清刑律》易名为《中华民国暂行新刑律》，民法则沿用1910年颁布的《大清现行刑律》中的民事部分；清末一些法律草案经过简单修改，完成立法程序，颁布生效；根据实际情况，补充、完善清末立法或在清末修律未涉及的领域继续新的立法活动；落实清末司法改革中的四级三审制，将检察机构独立于审判机构，设立平政院主管行政诉讼和对官吏的弹劾权。

值得一提的是，军阀混战以及与孙中山为首的革命党南方政权的对立，可能使得掌握中央统治权的军阀无暇他顾，从而放松了思想控制和司法干涉。因此这一时期在言论思想自由、舆论监督和司法独立方面都是中国近代史上最好的时期，如规定司法人员不得加入政治组织的规定就体现了司法独立于政党政治的强烈意愿，几乎是空前绝后的。

2. 南京国民政府时期的法律制度

通过北伐，1927年4月18日，以蒋介石为首的国民党在南京建立了国民政府。南京国民政府遵奉孙中山提出的民族、民权、民生的"三民主义"，其宪政法律思想包括：权能分治（政权属于人民，治权属于政府，人民拥有选举权、罢免权、创制权、复决权）、五权宪法（政府的治权分为立法权、司法权、行政权、监察权和考试权。对于人民权力的保护及对政府权力的限制，最终都要靠宪法）、建国三时期理论（出于对民众素质水平的考虑，民国的最终建立要经过军政、训政、宪政三个时期）。南京国民政府建立后，宣布进入训政时期，实行党治原则（以中国国民党主持政权、掌握国家权力，以"政治保姆"的身份训练国民行使政权的能力）。1931年6月1日颁布的《训政时期约法》将"以党治国"原则以法律形式予以确认。1947年1月1日，《中华民国宪法》颁布，宣布结束训政时期，实行宪政。但此时，中国已经陷入了国共两党全面内战时期，"还政于民"已经没有多少实质意义了。

南京国民政府时期在立法方面的主要成就，就是以制定各项法典为主要任务，逐步形成以宪法、民法、刑法、民事诉讼法、刑事诉讼法、行政法六大类法律为主体的"六法体系"。民法典的制定，采取了分编起草、分别通过的形式，1928年至1931年，民法典的总则编、债编、物权编、亲属编、继承编相继获得颁布。从内容上看，下列原则被确认：民商合一、人格平等与男女平等、社会本位与相对所有权原则、契约自由、过失责任原则、废除传统宗法原则（对亲属、继承的影响）、保留传统典权、家庭制度和家长权。刑事法律方面先后有两部刑法典，即1928年颁布的刑法和1935

年制定的刑法，其中 1935 年刑法是中国近代史上的最后一部刑法、也是生效时间最长的刑法。[①] 该刑法分总则、分则两编，共 47 章 357 条，全面继承了清末法制改革以来在刑事立法方面向西方学习的成果，如罪刑法定原则、罪刑等价主义、刑罚人道主义等，同时吸收西方最新立法经验，设立"保安处分"专章，采取正式的刑罚和行政处罚手段以外的手段，加强对特定犯罪和特定人群的特别预防。在刑法典以外，国民政府又先后制定了一大批刑事特别法和相应的特别诉讼程序，按照特别法优于普通法的原则，这些特别法往往与国民党的政策紧急相连，扩大了刑事管辖的范围，加重了刑罚，破坏了法制的统一和尊严。

司法制度建设方面，值得一提的是法定调解程序和三级三审制。1930 年 1 月 20 日颁布的《民事调解法》规定民事案件不经调解程序，不得提起诉讼，这显然将中国传统重道德教化、慎诉讼的精神入法了。1932 年《法院组织法》改变了清末法律改革以来确立的四级三审制，取消初级法院的建制，县市设地方法院，省设高等法院，首都设最高法院，[②] 实行三级三审制。

自清朝末年清政府全面推行法制改革，传统法律体系解体，中国法律开始了近代化进程。中华民国北京政府时期，中央政权更迭频繁，法律近代化进程时断时续。1927 年南京政府建立后，加快了法律近代化步伐，立法者总结前人的经验教训，吸收西方各国的法律精神和制度，同时继承和保留中国传统法律中的一些原则，以期建立一个既符合法律发展的内在一般规律，又适应中国社会国情民风的法律体系。以宪法、民法、刑法、民事诉讼法、刑事诉讼法、行政法为主干的六法体系的形成，标志着以近代法律理念为指导、具有近代法律特征的法律制度在中国最终确立，中国法律近代化进程得以初步完成。但很快，1949 年 2 月，即将取得政权的中国共产党发出声明，宣布全面废除南京国民政府确立的六法体系法律制度。1949 年 10 月 1 日，新中国成立后，中国近代法律变迁随之转向。

四　小结

就中国社会转型而言，中国向现代社会的转变是被动的。在救亡图存的紧急历史使命下，中国人没有能够从容地、自信地、理性地判断西方文明和传统文化的优缺点，妄自菲薄和盲目自信同在。而中国传统文化"以

---

① 目前 1935 年刑法在台湾地区继续有效。
② 改变了北京政府时期设立最高法院分院的做法，确立了最高法院的唯一性。

不变应万变"的强大整合能力，常常能够借助西方文化的外壳而自存。因此，如何做到既不保守排外，又不全盘西化，而是根据中国社会的现实和实践，在价值判断上将中西文化因素一视同仁，才能真正将中西文化融为一炉，从而诞生一种全新的东方文化。这既是中国近代社会转型的历史教训，也是未来中国社会成功转型的关键。

就中国法律变迁而言，中国法律现代化的成功依赖于法哲学的逻辑和法历史学的逻辑的有机统一。中国近代以来的法律变革中，呈现的是法律传统的失落和外国法律在中国的水土不服。在显性的法律形式层面，传统法律基本被抛弃殆尽，政治家和法律家们更倾向于全盘接受西方法律；而在隐性的实质层面，继受而来的西方法律在很多方面难以适应中国的社会现实，传统的价值观和调控方式仍然在社会生活中发挥着主导作用。在一百多年的法律变革进程中，有两个根本性的问题一直困扰着我国的法律现代化事业：一是如何实现"传统法律文化的创造性转化"，把数千年积淀下来的法律经验转变为现代法治的资源；二是在继受外国法律的过程中，如何避免简单地拿来，真正实现"西方现代法律文化的本土化"。其中的经验教训是：①从国家的最高统治者到一般的平民百姓，全社会必须有对法律的信仰。法律必须得到遵守，违法必须得到追究，这是一个"法治国家"的基础免疫力，也是一个"法治社会"的底线；②法律不能成为政治的工具。作为一个后发的现代化国家，法律的制定既不能为了对外宣传的粉饰，也不能成为对内政治斗争的工具，法治中国本身就是目的；③区分理想与现实。面对着复杂的社会现实，我们当然必须有法治的理想和系统解决问题的方案，但同时必须根据问题的轻重缓急设计解决问题的步骤。避免法治建设中"单兵突进"和"四面出击"。既"仰望星空"又"脚踏实地"，一步一个脚印，才能实现法治的最终目标。

Evolution of Chinese Laws in Modern Times against the Background of Social Transition

Gao Hancheng

【**Abstract**】 The unequal treaties imposed on China by western powers after 1840 had two huge and complicated impacts on the social transition in China. The reform of the traditional Chinese law was carried out against the general background of social transition and directly motivated by the issue of consular jurisdiction. In late Qing Dynasty, the government carried out an all-round legal reform, marking the disintegration of the traditional Chinese legal system and the beginning of the modernization of the Chinese law. After the establishment of the Nanjing Government in 1927, the pace of legal modernization quickened. The establishment of the "Six-Law System" marked the preliminary completion of the modernization of Chinese law. The success of the modernization of the Chinese law depended on the organic unification of the logic of the philosophy of law with the logic of history.

【**Key words**】Evolution, Legal System, Social Transition, Modern History

中国古代法律发展的基本进程与模式

高旭晨*

【摘要】中国古代法律发展基本进程，简略而言，可以分成三个阶段：中国古代法律的起源与初建阶段、法家思想主导阶段、儒家化法律阶段。秦朝的"二世而亡"对中国历史的发展影响深远，秦朝以后的历朝历代都以秦朝覆灭作为前车之鉴，由此对法治主义加以深刻的怀疑，在客观上阻碍了中国法律与时俱进的脚步。中国古代法律制度有两种基本模式特别应该注意，其一是礼法体系，其二是律例体系。所谓礼法体系，即中国古代法律制度由法制与礼制共同建构，两者在很大程度上达到合二为一的程度。礼法体系是中国古代法律最为重要的标志，在中国法律近代化过程中，打破礼法体系成为最艰难的工作。认识律例体系，对于理解中国古代法律的实际运行是一个关键所在。所谓律例体系，就是在法律适用过程中，法典与成例成为共同的法律根据。在很大程度上，中国古代法律制度有判例法的因素，这种情况主要是明清时期形成的。

【关键词】古代法律　礼法体系　律例体系

中国古代法律发展的基本进程，简略而言，可以分成三个阶段：中国古代法律的起源与初建阶段、法家思想主导阶段、儒家化法律阶段。

一　中国法律的起源与初建——夏商周法律

近八十年前，近代中国法律史学的创立者杨鸿烈先生曾言道："中国的信史，自殷商以前犹是漆黑一团。经过千余年学者的辨伪功夫，直到如今，都还没有拨云雾见青天的志愿。所以，要说中国的法律起源于何时代，真

---

*　中国社会科学院法学研究所副研究员。

是难于置答。"① 在此后的八十年间，中国的考古学取得了重大进展，许多重要的考古挖掘取得了难以想象的成果。但应该说，这些对于中国古代法律起源的认识与理解并没有太多助益。我们对于商周时期以前的法律的基本状况，还是处于一种模糊的认识之中。但通过不懈的努力，我们已经基本上可以认定，中国的历史，从国家形态完全形成来说，应该是从夏朝开始的。

据史料记载，远在夏商以前，中国历史有所谓三皇五帝的时代，在那个时候，法律已经开始萌芽了。这一时期的有关法律的记载，我们完全依靠后人带有传说性质的描述。皋陶也被认定为刑狱之祖。所谓"皋陶造狱，法律存也。"② 中国上古有关法律的记载，多假皋陶之名以传世。皋陶是中国历史上有史记载的最早掌管法律的官员。也就是说，此时已有主管法律的官员，也有以之适用的法律和适用法律的原则。

如前所述，上古之事多为后人补述，虽有重要参考价值，但不能作为确切史证。根据我国古代文献和地下发掘的考古成果可以推定，夏初已具备了国家的基本特征。但应该说，此时的法律还没有达到完备的程度。后人虽有"禹刑"③ 的称谓，但具体内容已难复原。大约公元前16世纪，商族首领汤灭了夏，建立了商王朝，商代的法律制度，因为有了传统史料的比较完整的记载和甲骨文等出土文物的佐证，而被比较完整地加以学术意义上的复原。据文献记载，夏朝的法律颇具神权法特点。

商代的法律虽然比较完备，但也必然不能尽脱原始野蛮的痕迹，肉刑似乎是刑罚的主要手段。韩非也称："殷之法，弃灰于公道者断其手"，可见其刑罚相当严酷。"神判"与"天罚"是商朝司法审判的一大特点。卜者参与司法，伪托神意断罪，实行所谓神判乃是常例，有不少卜辞为证。一般说来，神权法思想包括如下几个方面的内容：其一，宣扬王权来源于神权，王是按照神意进行统治的。其二，王的法律和命令是神意的体现，任何违法犯罪行为都被视为对神意的亵渎而要受到制裁。其三，立法活动的支配者是神祇，法律的制订、修改和废止，须经过神祇的决定，而这一过程又是通过特殊的求神仪式来完成的。其四，司法审判也要通过特定的求神仪式祈求神助。

周朝是中国古代法律真正开始发展的阶段。金文中已有"法"字出现。

---

① 杨鸿烈：《中国法律发达史》，中国政法大学出版社，2009，第1页。

② 史游：《急就篇》。

③ 所谓"夏有乱政，而作禹刑，商有乱政，而作汤刑，周有乱政，而作九刑"。

由此可见，周朝的法律制度已经从社会存在的层面上升到社会意识的层面。周朝的法律制度与礼治和德治密不可分，它们不但是周朝法制的基本特征，也深刻影响了中国古代法制发展，甚至可以说决定了中国古代法律传统的形成和发展。

周朝对于中国古代政治体制构成的最大贡献是制定了周礼，并以此作为治理国家的基本方式。等级制度成为礼制的核心内容。这种封建的形式，要以什么基本原则来维系呢？周朝的统治者创造了一套在当时社会条件下极其完美的社会规范，以此作为政治统治的基础，这套社会规范就是周礼。在周礼的规范下，宗法制和等级制结合起来，形成了一套完整而严格的君臣、上下、父子、兄弟、亲疏、尊卑、贵贱的礼制。各级贵族的衣、食、住、行和婚姻、丧葬、祭祀、会盟等都要严格遵守礼制的规定。违犯者受到处罚。周礼所确立的全部规范和制度，始终贯穿着"亲亲"、"尊尊"、"长长"、"男女有别"四个原则。

"礼治"的基本特征是"礼不下庶人，刑不上大夫"。"礼不下庶人"是指"礼"所赋予各级贵族的世袭特权，平民和奴隶一律不得享受；"刑不上大夫"是指刑罚的主要锋芒不是针对大夫等贵族，而是指向广大平民。"礼不下庶人，刑不上大夫"，不仅是西周"礼治"的特点，也是西周指导立法、司法的重要原则。

西周初期，周代统治者提出以"德"济"天命之穷"，于是"德"作为一个政治概念出现了。在西周的青铜器铭文中，有很多关于"德"的记载。"德"的思想基本贯穿于整个西周时期，是周人所独有的思想。在西周"德"有多重含义，但大致可以理解为"敬天"和"保民"。所谓"以德配天"是主张"天"或"上帝"并非归哪一族群所独有，而是天下各族所共有的神；至于"天命"属于谁，就看谁有能使人民归顺的"德"。"以德配天"思想的提出，在中国思想史上具有重大的意义。礼治与"德"思想的结合反映到法制方面就是要求"明德慎罚"。西周统治者主张德刑并用，反对专任刑罚。周朝的慎刑是为了明德，而明德是为了配天，无德就无以配天，也就失去了统治者的资格。明德慎刑思想的提出，在当时和后世都具有很大的意义，对儒家思想的形成有直接的影响。

应该指出，周朝的礼治和德治并不是单纯以礼仪与道德手段进行社会控制，而是以礼治和德治为主要统治方式。礼治和德治在许多层面上与法律手段相结合，甚至是相融合，成为一种特殊形态的法律。"礼"不断被国家上升为法律，从而获得更高的权威。礼的这种作用，虽然起到了法律难以达到的广泛的社会控制作用，但从另一方面来说，它也决定了中国古代法律的内容和形式与现代意义上的法律产生了重要差别。

二　法家思想主导阶段

春秋战国时期是中国法律制度建立的关键时期，在此期间，中国法传统意义上的法律理念和法律制度开始建立。中国传统法律制度与法律文化的基本内容都在这一时期出现。

春秋以降，诸侯争霸，周王室的地位虚悬，中国社会进入一个制度转型时期，有推崇周礼，意图维持宗主体制者；也有视周礼为过时的制度模式，而思以另外的方式为治国手段者。前者坚持礼治，而后者倡言法治，形成了礼治与法治的分野。与此同时，还有其他许多思想体系纷纷建立，中国进入所谓百家争鸣时期。在这一时期，学术思想大兴，形成了诸多流派。其中最为关注国家政治发展的是儒家和法家。而在诸子百家中，真正对中国社会体制有根本性影响的也的确是儒家和法家。① 儒家的代表人物有孔子、孟子和荀子。儒家坚持礼治理想，认为社会秩序应该是由社会等级的确立而获取的。而法家虽然也认可君臣上下之分，但他们坚持这种区分应该是在法律的统治下获得的。法家的代表人物有李悝、商鞅和韩非。礼治与法治，在春秋时期开始成为两种对立的思想主张，这种对立对中国古代的法律制度的构建和发展影响巨大而且深远。可以说，中国古代法律制度的特点，就是被这种对立所决定的。最终，这一时期，法家在社会中占据了统治地位，法治成为社会控制的主要选择。

在中国古代社会，在很长的时间中，法律并没有作为最重要的统治工具。周朝最主要的社会规范不是法，而是礼。也就是说，礼治是最主要的社会控制手段。春秋以降，周王室的控制力大为减弱，形成了天下诸侯争霸的局面。在这种形势下，周朝所倡导的礼治秩序开始崩塌，也就是史籍所言的"礼崩乐坏"。在这种情况下，必然需要一种新型的社会规范来代替礼的社会作用。随着法家思想占据主导地位，法律成为治国的主要手段。这时，在一些国家开始逐渐以法律替代礼乐而成为主要的社会规范，其标志就是公布成文法。在这场成文法运动中，最彻底、最全面，也是影响最为深远的立法活动是魏国的李悝所制定的《法经》。

---

① 其余诸家对中国社会的影响也是很大的，如道家对汉初社会政策的决定起了极大作用，而阴阳家的阴阳五行说更被儒家所改造，成为儒家思想的重要内容。

如前所述，夏商周的法律制度，虽然可以称日近完善，但基本上没有一部现代意义上的在社会上公布的法典。中国古代最早的成文法典，一般认为是《法经》。《法经》已经开始使用中国古代修律的基本分类方法和基本的立法技术，对后代法律影响深远。秦国所实施的法律，不过是照搬了《法经》，而秦国的法律也在很大程度上为汉代所继承。

应该指出，《法经》并非春秋战国时期法制建设的终极产物，而只是一个开端。当时的许多诸侯国都开始推行法治，而且都根据不同的社会条件和自然条件而具有自己的特色。特别是秦国，在商鞅携《法经》入秦以后，坚决推行法治，虽然商鞅功成身死，但其开创的以法治国的方针得到了长期而有效的贯彻和执行。秦国法制的完备，我们可以从秦朝的法制状况而推想出来。但由于秦朝二世而亡，为天下多不齿。故后世立国者都避之唯恐不及，不愿意充当秦朝法律的继承者，故都声称其法制出自《法经》，这也使得后人误以为《法经》代表了春秋战国时期法制的最高水平。实际上，从现在已经掌握的情况看，秦国的法制已经远远高于《法经》的水平了。

秦朝（公元前221—前207年）的建立，标志着中国封建统一专制国家的确立。相应地，封建法律制度也开始确立。秦朝的法律是秦国多年推行法治的成果，它在各个方面都堪称完备。或因为年代久远，或因为后世王朝对其的否定，秦朝法律的内容在历史文献中并没有留下许多记载。但幸运的是出土文物大大地弥补了这一缺失。1975年，在湖北省云梦县出土了大批秦代的竹简，由于其发掘于睡虎地11号秦墓中，故定名为"睡虎地秦墓竹简"。经过考古工作者的整理，这批竹简相当完整地被保留下来，供学者们进行研究。在1155支竹简中，大部分是有关秦律的内容。根据内容，可以分为《编年纪》、《语书》、《秦律十八种》、《效律》、《秦律杂抄》、《法律答问》、《封诊式》、《为吏之道》等。从制度建构的角度上而言，秦朝的法律制度已相当完备，这从其关于定罪量刑的原则上也可以得到证明。秦朝的刑罚原则有以下几方面内容：①刑事责任年龄。秦以身高确定责任年龄，这大概与当时的人体发育基本情况相适应。②以有无犯罪意识作为认定是否构成犯罪的标准。③区分故意和过失。④确定免予追究刑事责任的条件。⑤累犯加重。⑥数罪并罚原则。⑦共同犯罪要加重刑罚。⑧自首减刑。⑨诬告反坐。⑩教唆犯与现行犯同罪。秦律的内容十分丰富，除以上所介绍的刑事法律制度以外，秦律在经济法律、行政法律和民事法律方面也相当完备。

应该说，秦朝的法律制度总体上来说在当时的社会条件下是相当发达的。它主要体现在以下几个方面：第一，秦律调整的范围相当广泛。秦朝在法治的前提下，要求一切"皆有法式"，社会关系中的方方面面都被法律所规范，不但刑法发达，而且在民事、经济、行政等各个方面都有比较完备的法律予以调整。第二，秦律的内容详细具体。我们在秦律中可以看到，其法律规定的内容非常细致，这就减少了法律操作时的误差。第三，秦律语言精确，通俗易懂。这也是秦律立法的原则之一。第四，秦朝创造了多种的法律形式。秦朝法律有许多形式，这些法律形式互相补充，形成了比较完整的法律体系，同时也为后世的立法提供了样板，成为中国封建社会立法的一个特色。

秦朝的"二世而亡"对中国历史的发展影响深远，秦朝以后的历朝历代都以秦朝覆灭作为前车之鉴，由此对法治主义加以深刻的怀疑。虽然在实际的政治实践中不能废弃法律的作用，即所谓"阳儒阴法"；但在思想理念上对法律的作用自觉或不自觉地加以回避或掩盖，这不能不在客观上阻碍了中国法律与时俱进的脚步。

三　儒家化法律的形成与发展

由于秦朝法制的声名扫地，汉朝西汉建立后，起码在表面上对秦法采取了彻底废除的做法。汉代最早的法律《九章律》是在《法经》六篇"盗、贼、囚、捕、杂、具"的基础上增加了《户律》、《兴律》、《厩律》三章，合为九章。此外，在高祖与惠第年间还制定了《傍章》十八篇，它是参照先秦和秦代的礼仪而制定的礼仪制度。此外，汉武帝时期还制定了两部法律：《越宫律》和《朝律》，[①]《越宫律》是有关宫廷警卫的法律；而《朝律》是有关朝贺制度的法律。这四部法律，共六十篇，合称为"汉律六十篇。"

经过西汉前期的基本稳定的发展，社会经济得到极大的恢复，包括法律制度在内的各种政治制度也确立起来。到汉武帝时，社会思想逐渐统一到儒家思想上。通过"春秋决狱"这种司法手段，儒家的思想被融入封建法制的具体活动中，并形成了封建正统法律思想。

"春秋决狱"是董仲舒根据当时的社会条件与法制状况而倡立的一种审判方式。汉武帝时，开始推崇儒家的思想主张，但当时的法律与儒家的思想有相当多的不协调之处。虽然汉代初期采取更秦之法、约法省禁的种种

---

① 《晋书·刑法志》称："张汤越宫律二十七篇，赵禹朝律六篇。"

对法律的修正，汉文帝更废除肉刑，使汉代的法律比秦律要轻简得多，但他们的改革并没有从根本上对秦法加以改造，而实际上继承了秦法的基本内容。这就使法律的存在与法律的实施之间出现了矛盾，而春秋决狱在很大程度上解决了这一矛盾，使儒家的思想渗透于法律中。即在法无明文规定，或原有法律不符合儒家的思想主张时，运用儒家经典，特别是《春秋》这部儒家典籍中的事例和原则来指导案件的审判。春秋决狱的基本精神是"原心定罪"，即不仅要考虑犯罪行为人的客观行为，还要注意行为人的心理状态，即要考虑他的行为时的动机和目的。春秋决狱是儒家思想染指和支配司法的开端，使中国法律开始了它的儒家化进程。此后，历经魏晋南北朝数代法律的"以礼入律"的漫长过程，"礼"的内容通过立法的确定，正式成为法律的内容。概括而言，魏晋南北朝的法律有以下重要变化：①八议、官当入律。魏律以周礼之"八辟"为据，规定了"八议制度"，即议亲、议故、议贤、议能、议功、议贵、议勤、议宾，这八类人犯罪依法享有免刑或减刑的特权。北魏和南陈还创立了官当制度，即允许以官品或爵位抵罪。②确立"重罪十条"。始于北齐律，它将危及国家根本利益的十条最严重的罪名，置于律首，以强调主要打击。这十条重罪不在八议和论赎之列。③刑罚制度有所改革，表现在免除宫刑，进一步废除肉刑，改革妇女从坐制度，定流刑为减死之刑，作为死刑与徒刑的中间刑。这一时期是中国封建法律制度和律学长足发展时期，在中国法制史上有重要地位。魏晋南北朝时期是中国古代律学发展的重要阶段。在这一时期，正值中国的法律制度面临重大变革，中国法律的儒家化进程在这一期间走向完善，同时许多朝代兴灭踵续，立法频繁也是顺理成章的事情。可以说，这种历史背景造就了许许多多的立法家，也造就了许许多多的律学家。

　　"以礼入律"的法律儒家化进程直至发展到"一准乎礼"的《唐律疏议》出现而完成其历史使命。隋唐时期的法律虽然渊源于魏晋南北朝时期，但它们并没有限于简单的继承，而是在此基础上进行了彻底的变革，完成了中国法律的儒家化，使中国古代法律体系最终形成。《唐律疏议》是一部完备的具有代表性的封建法典，它以封建正统法律思想为指导而修定完成。其规范详备、科条简要；采取中典治国的立法原则，用刑持平，不畸轻畸重；依礼制刑，礼法合一，处处体现礼的精神。可以说，《唐律疏议》在中国封建法制发展史中处于承前启后的重要历史地位。同时，唐律也对东亚许多国家的立法产生过深刻的影响。

　　唐朝以后的法律，基本上不脱离唐律儒家化的精神实质。宋朝法制的基本精神与唐朝完全一致，其主要法典《宋刑统》的内容源于《唐律疏议》。《宋刑统》的篇目、条数与唐律完全相同，内容的差异也极为有限。宋朝在历史上是军事柔弱、经济和文化比较发达的王朝。与此相适应，民事法律相对比较发达。宋代从法律上确认不动产所有权和动产所有权，法制上对这些所有权加以保护。宋代民事法律发达最突出的标志是契约制度有了重大的发展。两宋时期，人们在买卖、租赁、借贷、典卖、抵押、雇佣等民事活动中，普遍订立契约，表明这一时期民事法律关系有了广泛的发展。宋朝法医学有重大发展。宋慈（1186—1249 年）编著了世界上第一部比较系统的法医学专著《洗冤集录》，获准颁行全国。该书选定官府历年颁定的条例格目，吸取民间医药学知识，编成检复总说、验尸、四季尸体变化、自缢、溺死、杀伤、服毒等 53 项内容。明朝以后，它还被译成朝鲜、日本、法、英、德、荷兰等国文字出版。

　　明清两朝法制在继承唐、宋法制基础上，因时变革，不断完善，在法制建设的多个方面有所创新和发展。《大明律》基本上沿袭了唐律，但较之唐律又有创新和发展。它总结了唐、宋以来，特别是明初三十年封建统治与司法镇压的经验，增加和充实了加强专制主义中央集权制度的内容，是一部比唐律有所发展的封建法典。明律的最大特色是实现了篇目和体例的革新，它以六部分目体例取代唐律的十二篇体例，是中国法典编纂史上的重大变化。按照学者们的概括：这种新体例的优点体现在两个方面，一是包罗广泛，繁简得当。唐律为 502 条，明律缩减到 460 条，但包含的内容并不少于唐律；二是既方便了官员执法，又便于民众守法。清代法制也达到了比较完善的程度，比较前代，它也确实有其进步的一面。田涛先生称："清朝的法律制度，在继承了中国传统的法律制度的基础上，进一步得到了发展，形成了在中国古代历史上最为系统和完善的法律制度。"不但法律体系比较完备，律例关系也渐趋和谐。同时，司法和执法的水平也达到了一定的高度，社会的法律意识也在不断提升。其"在编纂过程中，继承了汉、唐以来形成的中华法系的大量传统，并且成为中国历朝法典发展最高阶段的标志。"如果我们不以固有的观念去看问题，不以"西方论"的标准去衡量，不以"革命性"作为历史评价的标准，只从制度层面而言，就会看到以上论点是有其合理性的。

　　明清两代进一步健全了司法制度，其中较之前代有了新发展的制度是：在采取多管齐下的做法，加强对地方司法监督的同时，完善了中央的会审制度，凡遇重大案件，由三法司的正官刑部尚书、大理寺卿和都察院左都御史会审，称为"三司会审"。如三司会审意见不一，则奏请皇帝裁决。遇到特别重大的案件，要由六部尚书的大理寺卿、左都御史、通政司通政使会审，称为九卿会审。较之前代，明清律学无论是数量还是研究的深度都有新的发展。"明清两代律注文献及律学著作就达数百种。这两朝学者不断开拓了律学研究的领域，在应用律学、比较律学、律学史、古律辑佚和考证诸方面，取得了令人瞩目的成就，把古代律学向前推进了一大步"。

中国古代法律制度有两种基本模式特别应该加以注意，其一是礼法体系，其二是律例体系。这是中国古代法律史中最为重要的两个基本课题。由于篇幅关系，难于展开论述，以下用比较少的篇幅简略谈一下其基本内容。

所谓礼法体系，即中国古代法律制度由法制与礼制共同建构，二者在很大程度上达到合二为一的程度。礼法合一这种局面是中国法律儒家化的必然结果。如前所述，儒家是对中国古代法律制度、法律思想影响最大的一个学派，由春秋时期的孔子所创立。"儒"者，在西周时期是指掌握一定文化知识，懂得周礼，并提倡以"礼"为治理国家的基本社会规范。儒家法律思想主张主要有以下内容：①人性善的礼治出发点；②坚持礼治为主要社会规范；③德刑并用的法律观。体现在法律制度上，就是不但法典中包含有大量的礼的内容。同时，在法律适用过程中也以礼的原则、礼的方法来处理法律案件和法律纠纷。瞿同祖先生在其卓越的著作《中国法律与中国社会》中断言：中国古代法律传统是儒家化的法律占据主导地位，其主要特征是家族制度和等级制度。① 而家族制度和等级制度恰恰就是礼制也极力维持的社会秩序。在礼法体系中，礼的内容成为法制的基本准则和内容。《唐律》所谓的"一准乎礼"，实际上就是要把法律规范统筹于礼的范围之中。最能体现礼法体系内涵的就是所谓"以服制定罪"的规定。也就是说，按照亲属的亲等来处理家庭成员之间的侵害和其他法律纠纷。在《唐律》以后的历代法典中，都把《服制图》列于法典之前，为定罪量刑提供法定依据。实际上，它也是法典的有机组成部分。在处理案件时，当事人身份的认定是很重要的。当事人的身份和相互关系是决定刑罚的前提条件。比如，同一类案件的处罚差别很大，尊长侵犯卑幼，可以比照一般人降低两档治罪；而卑幼侵犯尊长，则要比照一般人加重两档治罪。同时，在适用法律时，情理的成分是要被充分考虑的，所谓"情法适得其平"。礼

---

① 参见瞿同祖《中国法律与中国社会》。

法体系是中国古代法律最为重要的标志，在中国法律近代化过程中，打破礼法体系成为最艰难的工作。

所谓律例体系，就是在法律适用过程中，法典与成例成为共同的法律根据。也可以说，在很大程度上，中国古代法律制度有着判例法的因素。这种情况主要是明清时期形成的。明清两代注重制例、修例，以例补律，以例辅律，使法制更加完善，这是明清法制较之前代的一个重大发展。明清两代，修例构成了国家立法活动的主体部分。明清的修例不仅是创制新的条例，也包括修改、补充、废止条例以及对条例作一些编纂技术上的处理。在现代法学家看来，这都属于立法活动。明代经过近百年的探讨，逐步形成了一套比较完整的律例关系理论。"律例关系理论的基本观点是：既重律，又重例，二者是相得益彰的主辅关系，这种关系具体表现在两个方面，一是例以辅律，一是律例并行。"清代的修例基本仿效明朝，并有了进一步的发展。清代修例制度的经常化、规范化便于现实统治者根据社会状况的变化随时对法律、政策进行调整，加强立法的协调性和统一性，减少不同法源之间的矛盾和冲突，这是其积极的一面。但是由于政治日趋腐败，加之官僚体制的惰性，越往后期，修例便越流于形式。认识律例体系，对于理解中国古代法律的实际运行是一个关键所在。

Basic Trajectory and Model of
Legal Development in Ancient China

Gao Xuchen

【**Abstract**】 Briefly speaking, the development of law in ancient China can be divided into three stages, namely the stage of emergence and initial development, the stage of domination by legalism, and the stage of Confucianization of law. The collapse of Qin Dynasty, the first feudal dynasty in China which lasted for only 15 years, had a profound impact on the development of Chinese history. The failure of the Qin Dynasty served as a warning to the rulers of all the succeeding dynasties, thereby increasing the skepticism towards the idea of the rule of law and obstructing the development of law in China. In ancient China, there existed mainly two modes of legal system: the system of rite-law (lifa) and the system of codes and precedents (lǜlì). The former, which was the combination and unity of the system of law and the system of rites, had been the most important symbol of the legal system in ancient China and the abolition of the rite-law system was proved to be the most difficult task in the modernization of Chinese law. The lǜlì system, which was formed mainly in the Ming and Qing dynasties, is the key to the understanding of the actual operation of law in ancient China. Under this system, both codes and precedents were taken as legal bases for adjudication of cases. Therefore, it can be said that the legal system in ancient China contained to a large extent the element of the case law system.

【**Key words**】 Ancient Chinese Law, Mode of Development, Rite-law, Codes and Precedents

Harmonization of Law: From European to Global Approach

Pia Letto-Vanamo *

【 Abstract 】 In the paper questions related to legal harmonization are discussed. The starting point lies mainly in debates on harmonization of legal norms and institutions in Europe, but also topics relevant for a more global approach are discussed. The perspective is dominated by the author's interest in legal history. The focus of the paper is on official harmonization projects, mainly within the European Union (EU), but ideas and proposals of unofficial academic projects (such as Lando Commission drafting Principles of European Contract Law, Principles of European Contract Law) are analyzed as well.

The author argues that EU Law has questioned the foundations of national state doctrines of legal sources and current legal argumentation as well. This is also true when the competence of the European Court of Human Rights is concerned. In Finland, entry to the EU (in 1995) was no legal revolution, but ratification of the European Convention on Human Rights (1990) was-at least-a small one. Article 6 of the Convention was the main reason for a deep-going reform of the Finnish court system and legal procedure.

It can be seen that Europeanization and globalisation have tended to weaken, fragment and sometimes even to restructure the state, but they have not destroyed or replaced it. For instance, public law vocabulary based on the idea of the modern nation state is still required, but needs to become more nuanced. Hence,

* Professor, Faculty of Law, University of Helsinki.

a new and more global approach could be based on the comparative method, and on understanding foreign, including non-European, legal cultures. But this would require not only conceptual studies but also a concrete analysis of the role and functions, of various legal actors. Special focus should be placed on discussing the role of legal scholarship. Comparative analysis combined with a global standpoint also enlightens the relativity and limits of legal regulation, and legal argumentation as well. From comparative analysis it is possible to learn that there have been, and still are, different ways to understand the boundaries and interplay between law and politics, or law and morality.

I. Harmonization of European Legal Systems

In the following I will discuss questions related to legal harmonization. My starting point lies mainly in debates on possibilities and challenges of harmonization of legal norms and institutions in Europe, but I will also come to topics relevant for a more global approach. The focus will be on what we call official (mainly within the EU) and unofficial (academic) projects for harmonization of law, and the perspective is dominated by my interest in legal history.

Today, the most powerful actor for legal harmonization in Europe is the European Union (the EU). We see that the EU is not only furthering economic and political integration. It is furthering legal integration by using legal instruments (e. g. EU legislation) for the purposes of economic integration. And the law is also present as a criterion for membership of the Union: According to the so-called Copenhagen criteria, only states respecting the principle of the rule of law can become members of the EU. Thus, the law is important for European and international economic relations, for a well-functioning market economy, and for co-operation between state authorities.

At the same time, it also appears that European integration-the founding of the European Community in the 1950s-would not have been possible without countries with similar legal orders: sharing the same basic ideas concerning, for example, contract law and issues of liability. Similarities between European legal systems were / are based on common legal history, and on regional (e. g. between the Nordic Countries) or international or supranational co-operation between countries.

Today, it can be said that EU Law has questioned the foundations of national state doctrines of legal sources and current legal argumentation as well. This is also true when the competence of the European Court of Human Rights is concerned. Thus, it is not the European Union that has been the agent of legal harmonization in Europe. The Council of Europe, the European Convention on Human Rights (1950) and the European Court of Human Rights ought to be mentioned here, as well. And in Finland, entry to the European Union (in 1995) was no legal revolution, but ratification of the European Convention on Human Rights (1990) was-at least-a small one. Article 6 of the Convention on the right to a fair trial was the main reason for a deep-going reform of the Finnish court system and legal procedure in the 1990s. Indeed, several cases against Finland in the Strasbourg Court have dealt with the requirement of Article 6 that a decision must be made within a reasonable time.

Further, many other EU countries-not only new Member States-have been on the receiving end of judgments from the Court of Human Rights based on Article 6 concerning, for example, access to justice, independence of the judiciary, and parties' right to be heard. In addition, ratification of the European Convention of Human Rights has brought into arenas of law discussions of values as well as weighing between different values-generally expressed in different rights of individuals.

Several academic expert groups are working for European legal harmonization, too. An idea of so called bottom-up-harmonization-partly based on examples taken from the European legal history has inspired most of these academic groups, such as the Lando Commission drafting Principles of European Contract Law (PECL), or the Acquis Group (European Research Group on Existing EC Private Law), or the group of professors that recently drafted and published (in cooperation with the European Commission) a Draft Common Frame of Reference (DCFR; Principles, Definitions and Model Rules of European Private Law). Members of the groups argue for common European legal thinking and for common concepts and principles based on comparative analysis of national legal systems. These principles could then be referred to by contracting parties, and used as a model by the EU legislative organs or national legislators for drafting new, more coherent, legislation.

The academic working groups have so to say an opposite agenda to that of the EU legislator with "sending" often quite fragmented competition law, consumer law, and other norms (regulations and directives) to Member States, where national state authors with the help of legal professionals try to place them into the national legal order and implant them into the national legal doctrinal system. This can be called a top-down-approach to European harmonization. However, also the bottom-up model has been criticized-and quite often by legal scholars. Similarly with the top-down-model, its is based on idealistic expectations for a "convergence" of European legal systems, neglecting fundamental differences between the English common law system (based on case law) on one hand, and the Continental-European so called civil law systems (with codifications of law) on other hand. ①

Of course, also other (official) approaches exist to European legal co-operation, even within the European Union. Especially international private law, its system based on complicated choice of law rules and the principle of *ordre public* protecting basic values of the national legal order/ society concerned ought to be mentioned. Also quite a new EU Regulation called the Rome I Regulation (EC 593/2008) on the law applicable to contractual obligations (based on the Rome Convention, 1980) is interesting. The regulation includes, for example, rules on freedom of choice and on the applicable law in the absence of choice. However, this contains no references to the Principles of European Contact Law (PECL) or to the (global) International Institute for the Unification of Private Law Principles of International Commercial Contracts (2004). It was the will of the EU Member States not to open up the use of bottom-up-drafted principles-because these were "made by law professors-not through the democratic legislative procedure of the European Union".

Apart from law professors, national states, the European Parliament, and the European Commission, at least one other actor interested in development of European (Union) law has to be mentioned. This is the EU judiciary. Today, the European Union Court is-perhaps not "running wild", but playing a crucial role by widening the scope of European Union Law. This can especially be seen when human rights and other basic rights are concerned. ② At the same time, the

---

① Pierre Legrand, "European Legal Systems are not Converging", *International Comparative Law Quarterly* (1996): 57.

② At least one ECJ case ought to be mentioned. This is the so called *Kadi* case (*Yassin Abdulla Kadi and Al Barakaat International Foundation against the Council and Commission*; *Joined Cases C-402/05 P and C-415/05 P*). Through this case, the European Court of Justice is re-defining the relationship between international law and EU law-by annulling a Council Regulation based on a Resolution of the Security Council of the United Nations, because it infringes Kadis and Al Barakaats fundamental rights under European Community Law.

Court is also contributing in development of new doctrines of the EU law.

II. Historical Dimensions of Harmonization

Quite often, a historical dimension seems to be present when European legal harmonization is discussed. It can also be said that ideas for furthering harmonization reflect the histories or narratives that legal historians use to tell when discussing the "roots" or the historical background of contemporary law (s) and legal systems. In the Nordic Countries, where the number of legal scholars and legal historians is small, it is easy to find two main-and in a way competing-narratives. This is true at least when doctoral theses and textbooks on legal history are concerned.

The first-partly inspired by the ideas of Max Weber-is that of so-called "modern law" -situated between pre-modern and late or post-modern law. This is referred to especially in discussions of the rationale but also of the legitimacy of legal order (s), and in discussions on the hierarchy of legal sources, too. This is the law of the modern nation state systematized with the help of the doctrine of legal sources, where parliamentary legislation stands at the top of the hierarchy of sources. At the same time, the idea of positive law (and legal positivism) is important, and a quite clear division of labour is drawn between various legal actors (the legislator, the judiciary, and legal scholarship). The legislator is the most important and legitimated actor of the modern law era, and the legitimacy of a legal order is based above all on democratic participation.

It is quite easy to agree with this narrative, especially concerning the European continent and the era after the French Revolution-that of modern civil law codifications such as the *Code civil*, the *Bürgerliches Gesetzbuch* and the first *Codice civile italiano*. During this period, judges (who became state servants) have been obligated or assumed to "follow" the law, while the university education of legal professionals has focused on training to interpret and apply national, positive law.

This narrative is also a foundation narrative for "no longer modern" law (late modern or post-modern law), discussed by many scholars today. Thus, we seem to be facing the "weakening power of nation states", the "diminishing role of national, ordinary legislation", tendencies "towards privatized legal regulation", "towards judge-made law" and towards various alternatives to ordinary dispute resolution.

Again, legal historians are interested in the characteristics of "not yet modern" law. Legal historians seem to agree at least that this period was long but included many local and regional variations. In every case, during the pre-modern law period, characterized by a plurality of legal orders, the main arenas for discussions on law-non law (in German: *Recht-Unrecht*), i. e. law applicable in a certain case, were court sessions, also in terms of commonplaces of legal communication.

Hence, one meets early courts or judiciary obtaining their authority from various sources of domination (according to Max Weber, *Herrschaft*), but also those with a communitarian nature of conflict resolution. Concerning the latter, the most crucial questions-having parallels with the late modern law period and the weak (ening) power of the sovereign state-are those of legitimacy and acceptance of conflict resolution and of law "made by the courts". Indeed, it is not difficult to draw parallels with late modern mediation systems or the various ADR-models: the legitimacy and acceptance of conflict resolution seem to be based on the active participation of the parties themselves and of other members of the (interest) community, as well as on court procedures (e. g. certain rituals or forms) as such.

The narrative of the emergence and development of modern law reflects quite accurately an understanding of the foundations of national legal orders-and division of labour between legal actors "producing" those orders-in the European Continent as well as contemporary doctrine of legal sources with legislation at the top of the hierarchy of sources. But it can also be criticised. Founded on a certain democratic romanticism, it underestimates the role of legal actors other than the legislator.

In particular, it neglects legal scholarship and substantial continuities in legal systems based on impacts of former legal doctrine: The European private law codifications of the 19th and 20th centuries were to a great extent based on legal concepts, classifications and ideas of previous centuries. They were-like laws today-drafted by a trained elite, by working groups of legal specialists, and in spite of brand new laws the problems of real life also challenged the idea of a "passive" judge. For instance, continuity is discernible in applying the Roman Law clause *clausula* rebus sic *stantibus*: German judgments of the 1920s were based on the clause, but before the idea of the clause could be implemented it was to be transferred into the sphere of application of the BGB § 242. [1]

Criticism does not mean that the democratic element of the idea of modern law would be meaningless, but in discussions on contemporary legal problems more nuanced histories would be needed. For instance, when discussing legal pluralism, it cannot be enough to point out only that a plurality of legal orders also existed before the modern era. At the same time, in "post-modern" discussions of freedom of choice and of various (legal) identities of an individual it would be useful to remember the egalitarian element of modern law. Since the French Revolution (1789) the idea of status-based law-and judiciary-has been superseded by the idea of equality before the law, one of the most revolutionary ideas in the legal history of mankind.

The other main narrative of European legal historians with reflections on current legal debates is that of law without or beyond the state. This very well reflects hopes embedded in current academic bottom-up proposals for harmonisation of European (private) law. [2] This narrative, popular among many younger Nordic legal historians, is about the emergence of the universities and of so-called "learned law", and of the influence or reception of Roman Canon law, as *ius commune*, in European legal systems.

This, too, has some problems. For instance, one has to remember that in spite of the emergence of quite homogenous academic training in law and the foundation of new types of legal institutions (high courts) applying the *ius commune* in medieval Europe-and even later-several legal orders were based on several centres of power: strong cities with their privileges and their own judiciary, or feudal law and *lex mercatoria*, with an active interplay taking place between different legal orders. Additionally, there were several variations of the *ius commune*, and several ways and grades of its influence in existing legal orders or in judicial argumentation, also geographically.

---

[1]   Klaus Luig, Die Kontinuität allgemeiner Rechtsgrundsätze. Das Beispiel der clausula rebus sic stantibus. Rechtsgeshichte und Privatrechtsdogmatik, Reinhard Zimmermannn etc. (eds.). Müller Verlag 1999, pp. 171 – 186.

[2]   See an interesting contribution to the discussion: Nils Jansen, *The Making of Legal Authority: Non-legislative Codifications in Historical and Comparative Perspective*, (Oxford University Press, 2010)
.

Actually, this history is especially problematic when studying the early development of law in the Nordic Countries. Influences of Canon law can be seen in Sections on family and inheritance of Nordic medieval laws (e. g. the Swedish *landskapslagar*), and the few scholars were well informed on Roman law literature as well, but the main forum for legal communication until the 17th century was the local court (*ting*), usually without trained lawyers, and for resolution of local, minor conflicts. And like today, early legal scholarship had "dual citizenship": the problems and the working environment of scholars were (usually) local, but legal ideas, concepts, or even individual rules were often common (pan-European, international).

In an interesting way, this can be seen in Rules for Judges (1530s) by Olaus Petri, a Swedish theologian and reformer who studied in Rostock and Wittenberg and who drafted the rules (e. g. "The good judge knows to decide according to the circumstances"; and "The law is that which is best for humanity, even when the written statute provides otherwise") as criticism against disadvantages in Swedish legal administration and court procedure of the beginning of the 16th Century. In the Rules, continuously published in the first pages of Codes of Law in Sweden and Finland, one can see that Olaus was well informed in ideas of Roman-Canon law, for instance those in the law of evidence,[1] but his proposals were wisely modified to fit into the current social environment, into a court system without an academically trained judiciary.

In every case, the early wave of Roman law influence (that of the *ius commune*) is missing in the Nordic Countries where the first universities were founded in the 17th century, while legal science is mainly a phenomenon of the 19th century. However, it would be impossible to think, for example, of early Danish, Swedish, or Finnish legal literature without German influence. When national legal science emerged in the Nordic countries during the 19th century, it happened mostly by adapting German legal ideas, quite often also by translating texts from

---

[1] further Heikki Pihlajamäki, Gründer, Bewahrer oder Vermittler? Die nationalen und internationalen Elemente im Rechtsdenken des Olaus Petri. Juristische Fakultäten und Juristenausbildung im Ostseeraum, Jörn Eckert & Kjell Å. Modéer (eds.), Stockholm: Institutet för rättshistorisk forskning, 2004, pp. 29 – 38.

German legal authors[1]-which then also became channels for the influence of Roman Law-based terminology and systematization.

The most influential German "school" in the Nordic Countries was *Begriffsjurisprudenz* (Conceptual Jurisprudence). This dominated in Finland until the 1950s, but was superseded by the ideas of Scandinavian Realism-with the idea of law as an instrument of social engineering and pointing out the role of the judiciary and so called "real considerations" in judicial argumentation-in Denmark and Sweden from the beginning of the 20th century.

In Finland, which had an autonomous position within the Russian Empire in 1809 −1917, the role of the Parliament (Estates) was either non-existent (1809 − 1863) or weak. Thus, many legal reforms necessary for industrialization were realized by the judiciary, through the legal practice of the high courts (courts of appeal). And because of lack of democracy and constitutional guarantees, legalistic thinking and constitutional doctrine became important, too. The first professorship in the Nordic countries solely for administrative law was founded at the University of Helsinki in 1907. Central topics of the discipline were, and still are, the principle of the rule of law and its interpretations. An important model for Finnish doctrine was German literature discussing the concept of the *Rechtsstaat* and the principle of legality.

In other fields of law, too, an orientation towards Germany was common. However, interest in German legal science was not only a Finnish or Nordic phenomenon. It is well known that German legal literature inspired legal professionals in many other European countries, too. A Finnish phenomenon, however, is that this influence was both long lasting and quite one dimensional. According to Lars Björne, Conceptual Jurisprudence with its "apolitical" nature and its self-referential notion of legal science fitted very well with the political and social climate in Finland-first with the Era of Autonomy's orientation towards legalistic thinking, and then with the politically sensitive circumstances after the Civil War of 1918. [2]

---

[1]   For instance Robert Montgomery's book Handbok i Finlands allmänna privaträtt I, Helsinki 1889, was based on Bernhard Windscheid: Lehrbuch des Pandektenrechts I, Düsseldorf 1862.

[2]   Lars Björne: Den konstruktiva riktningen. Den nordiska rättsvetenskapens historia III, Stockholm: Institutet för rättshistorisk forskning 2002, p. 169.

The domination of Conceptual Jurisprudence diminished in Finland-not through Legal Realism as in other Nordic Countries but above all through influences from the Analytic School of law. Analytic criticism focussed mainly against "conclusions from concepts". But concepts were not neglected. They played a heuristic role-they were necessary for clarifying and classifying legal problems. Additionally, it was important to identify those concepts that connected better than the old ones with the legal reality. Generally speaking, the analytic turn after World War II can be seen as a reflection of social changes, but also of efforts by legal scholars towards concepts, which could serve the interests of trade and business better than the old ones.

Still, it is possible to assert that, in Finnish legal life, legal science (scholarship) holds an exceptionally strong position and, moreover, is dominated by a quite heavy theoretical dimension. ①In legal doctrine, principles have become important as part of a general doctrine of law but concepts are still in use: they prepare the way for principles-based legal argumentation.

III. Towards a Global Perspective

Europeanization of law is no longer discussed as actively as a couple of decades ago. Instead, current debate and study focus on influences and challenges of globalisation. Again, we are witnessing two conflicting tendencies. On the one hand, a particularistic tendency exists that emphasises differences, the uniqueness of (legal) history, culture and identity. On the other hand, awareness of globalisation points to the changing, even diminishing, significance of national boundaries.

Still, quite few legal historians are interested in telling other than these two narratives. An exception could be Danish legal historian Ditlev Tamm, who in the latest textbook on global legal culture② advocates a "global approach". According to the words of the author, the book has been written to help law students to better understand the world, but also to demonstrate that national or local law still

---

① The basic idea is that legal discourse has three equally strong actors: (1) legislator (s), (2) the judiciary, (3) legal scholars. The law will be improved and reformed through communication between these three parties.

② Ditlev Tamm, Global retskultur. En indforing i komparativ ret på historisk grundlag, Samfunds Litteratur 2009.

matters, in spite of the globalization of legal culture, that of legal ideas. Law is still discussed, drafted and applied mainly by national organs.

Viewing globalization from a political and economic-but also from a legal-standpoint enables one to recognize the rise of new actors such as multinational firms, non-governmental organisations and social movements. Globalisation has also blurred and splintered the boundaries between the domestic and external spheres of nation states and of regional integration organisations such as the EU. At the same time, new terms, such as (European or global) governance, have found their way from the political arena into legal vocabulary and into legal practice as well.

As a cultural phenomenon, globalisation implies the emergence of a new (global) culture. To some extent, this is shared by many elite groups, including many legal professionals. At the same time, this has contributed to the transformation of many local cultures. In legal practice, for instance, judicial comparisons are becoming more widespread. To illustrate, it is quite usual for constitutional courts to refer to foreign law. They do so for many reasons. Among other things, national legal orders are increasingly bound together in supra-national and global regulatory regimes, which facilitate the opening up of national legal systems towards each other. It has been said that judges of the constitutional courts of the world, coming together regularly, form an "epistemic community" when discussions on fundamental and human rights are concerned. [1]

The rise of new (regulatory) actors and the changing role of old ones have also challenged legal scholarship: i. e. the traditional, nation state and Eurocentric doctrine of legal sources requires re-thinking. Generally speaking, new academic approaches are needed to take account of multiple levels of legal ordering. Then-according to William Twining, interested mostly in a universalistic approach-one of the central questions is, how far is it possible and desirable to generalise about legal phenomena (e. g. conceptually, normatively, empirically) as part of understanding law. Twining, who is a legal theorist, points out above all the importance of analysis of concepts. A "cosmopolitan" discipline of law needs a vocabulary and conceptual apparatus that can be used across jurisdictions and cultures: "If jurispru-dence is to be general, its vocabulary and concepts need to

---

[1] Sabino Cassese: Il Diritto Globale. Giustizia e democrazia oltre lo stato. Einaudi 2009.

travel well". ①

For legal history, however, a general or universalistic approach is quite problematic. This is also true when legal concepts and their travel are concerned. On the one hand, we know that ideas and concepts have always been travelling: voluntarily, mandatorily, successfully, or "irritatingly". On the other hand, we know that concepts-as well as legal language more generally-are historically (and locally) determined.

Additionally, it should be pointed out that globalisation has tended to weaken, fragment and sometimes even to restructure the state, but it has not destroyed or replaced it. Public law vocabulary based on the idea of the modern nation state is still required, but needs to become more nuanced: Its dominance, and its use in supranational contexts, for instance for naming or labelling EU institutions, are problematic. There are, e. g. , the European Council and European Parliament, and there were-mostly for political reasons-plans and hopes for a European constitution.

Concepts and their analysis are also important for future studies in law. Language is a means of legal communication, while concepts are-even today-central instruments of legal scholarship. And as German legal historian and public law scholar Michael Stolleis has written,② with linguistic analysis legal historians do "translations" when trying to understand how certain legal terms have been used in a foreign context: At the same time, when we explain the meaning of an expression we translate it. However, operating with concepts can also lead to misunderstandings, to assume that above legal sources there is a supra-historical level to which linguistic findings belong. This is a danger especially when studying legal phenomena. Legal language is bound by tradition; it is changing slowly, and is even resistant to changes. Too easily legal historians, who are usually educated in law or legal dogmatics, are led to believe that in old texts they can find phenomena with which they have become familiar within the current legal system. Too quickly (meanings of) past circumstances are changed into current ones and (seemingly) similar legal problems are defined with the same concepts.

---

① William Twining, Reviving general jurisprudence. Globalisation and Power Disparities. Governing globalization in Transnational Legal Processes, M. Likosky (ed.), Butterworths 2002, pp. 3 – 22.

② Michael Stolleis, Rechtsgecshichte als Kunstprodukt. Zur Entbehrlichkeit von Begriff und Tatsache. Nomos 1997.

Problems of linguistic and conceptual analysis do not exist only when temporally analyzing foreign legal cultures. Similar problems arise when studying today's legal systems. Still, a new and more global approach could be based on the comparative method, and on understanding foreign, including non-European, legal cultures. But this would require not only conceptual studies but also a concrete analysis of the role, functions, and even instruments of various (legal) actors. Special focus should be placed on discussing the role of legal scholarship-in maintaining legal reforms by its classic means: conceptualising and systematising.

Interesting ideas can be found in Amartya Sen, who writes much in his book "The Idea of Justice"[1] of the importance of comparisons, and of the history of other than Western European societies. Sen's contribution is a theory of justice in a very broad sense, where analysis of the concept of democracy plays an important role. Thus, discussion of global justice calls for us to examine whether the tradition of democracy is essentially a Western phenomenon, either in its broadly legal-organizational interpretation in terms of ballots and elections, or more generally as government by discussion.

Comparative analysis combined with a global standpoint also enlightens the relativity and limits of legal regulation, and legal argumentation as well. From comparative analysis it is possible to learn that there have been, and still are, different ways to understand the boundaries and interplay between law and politics, or law and morality.

Historical and regional variations also exist between legal orders in their sensitivity to political and social changes, and to values, as well. This is important to notice, especially when discussing justice (in German *Gerechtigkeit*), and the relationship between law and justice. I would like to suggest that different "techniques" are available for bringing idea (s) of justice within the modern application of law. These techniques are historically determined, and the "technical" dimension-the means and style of argumentation of various legal actors-cannot be neglected when analyzing the role or challenges of legal scholarship. These techniques are historically determined, while local variations exist in their use, even within the "Nordic legal family". For instance,

---

[1]   Allen Lane 2009.

constructivist traditions, i. e. *Begriffsjurisprudenz* with its self-referential notion of legal science, Legal Realism with an approach of social engineering, and Analytic Jurisprudence interested in linguistic aspects-all have different reflections on judicial argumentation and legal reasoning.

Thus, I would like to advocate a non-Eurocentric approach based on comparative analysis for re-thinking the legal vocabulary, especially that of public law. For that analysis, an actor perspective is also needed for enlightening the role and the critical potential of legal scholarship for further development of law.

法律的统一化： 从欧洲到全球的方法

皮亚·勒特·瓦纳莫

【摘要】本文讨论了有关法律协调的问题，其出发点主要是欧洲关于统一法律规范和机构的争论，也涉及与全球主义方法有关的议题。上述视角是基于作者对法律史的兴趣产生的。本文的重点是欧洲联盟的官方统一项目，但也分析了非官方学术项目的想法和建议（如兰多委员会起草的欧洲合同法原则等）。

欧盟的法律对法律渊源的民族国家学说以及现行法律论辩的基础提出了质疑。欧洲人权法院的管辖权问题就是一个例子。芬兰 1995 年加入欧盟并没有带来法律革命，但是 1990 年批准《欧洲人权公约》却带来了一个法律革命——至少是一次小的革命。《欧洲人权公约》第 6 条是芬兰法院系统和法律程序进行深度改革的主要原因。

可以看到，欧洲化和全球化已经趋于弱化，分裂有时甚至重新建构国家，但它们尚未摧毁或取代国家。例如，以现代民族国家观念为基础的公法词汇仍然是需要的，但要更为细致。因此，一个全新的、更为全球主义的方法是基于比较和对外国（包括非欧洲）法律文化的理解而产生的。但是，这不仅要求概念性的研究，还要对概念的角色和功能，以及所有的法律行为者进行具体分析。应当重点探讨法律学说的作用。结合全球化观点来进行比较分析，有助于说明法律规制和法律论辩的相对性及其限制。比较分析还可以发现法律和政治或是法律和道德之间的界限及其相互作用的不同理解方式。

论国际法上对非强迫性干涉之禁止

——理论思考和中国实践

陈一峰*

【摘要】 本文主要批判和反思了西方主流国际法学说将国际法禁止之干涉限于强迫性干涉的观点。通过分析国际法上非强迫性干涉的国家实践和学者学说，并结合对有关国际法文本的解读，本文提出了国际法一般性的禁止非强迫性干涉的法律公式：对有着根本重要性的主权事务，例如国家人格等主权要素，进行任何形式的干预均属国际法禁止的干涉行为。在此基础上，本文进一步阐明了国际法禁止强迫性干涉和非强迫性干涉在结构上的内在统一性。中国近年来提出的有关核心利益的国际法主张和外交实践，可以认为属于对国际法禁止非强迫性干涉的国家实践。

【关键词】 不干涉原则　强迫　非强迫性干涉　核心利益

一　引言

　　不干涉内政是国际社会普遍承认的当代国际法基本原则之一。国际法禁止国家或者国家集团以强迫手段干涉其他国家的内政，在学说和实践中均不存在疑义。其中，武力干涉不仅违反不干涉原则，同时也违反《联合国宪章》所宣示之禁止使用武力原则。然则，在强迫性干涉之外，不干涉原则是否包含对非强迫性干涉的禁止，学说上颇具争议。对此问题，西方学者总体上持消极态度，一般认为强迫是不法干涉的充分及必要条件，即强迫是识别不法干涉的法律标准，同时国际法对不法干涉的禁止也止于强

---

　　* 法学博士，芬兰赫尔辛基大学法学院博士后，埃里克·卡斯特伦国际法与人权研究所研究人员。

迫性干涉。依此种见解，不能被定性为强迫性干涉的行为就排除在了不干涉原则的管辖之外。但是，大量国际实践表明，在武力干涉等强迫性干涉之外，存在着相当数量的非强迫性质的干涉行为，例如对外国的竞选资助、对一国分裂势力的政治和经济支持等。这些干涉行为虽然在手段上不具强迫性质，在性质上同样构成对一国主权的严重危害，破坏国家间友好及和平关系，有必要在法律上予以禁止。因此，有必要在国际法上厘清不干涉原则的适用范围，其核心问题是不干涉原则是否禁止非强迫性干涉行为。这既涉及在理论上如何理解和认识不干涉原则，同时也决定着在实践中对不法干涉的识别方法和禁止之范围，有重要的理论意义和实践相关性。

　　还要指出的是，对这个问题的理论解答在国际法学说上还具有更一般性的方法论意义。当前国际法上大量的干涉学说和不干涉原则的研究，主要是由欧美学者在探讨，论述的基本社会背景都是西方国家从事的干涉实践，因此干涉学说主要是为本国的干涉实践提供正当理由，使得国家权力趋于理性化运作。将非强迫性干涉纳入国际法学研究的视野，是尝试将被干涉国的经验作为国际法研究内容和基本出发点，并以此拓展国际法视野和深度、强化国际体系中边缘或半边缘国家的国际法话语的学术努力。

二　西方主流意见：强迫和干涉的同构性

　　干涉被公认为国际法学上最复杂的问题之一，原因就在于界定干涉所存在的困难。"在国际法通常使用的所有术语当中，没有什么比'干涉'一词更具有挑战性了。"① 在日常用语中，干涉可能指国家或国家集团单方面采取的非法军事行动，也可能是联合国依据宪章采取的合法行动，还可能是一种政治要求，或是一份官方报告，等等。但是，国际法上禁止的干涉，有别于日常用语中的干涉，是具有特定法律意义的术语。定义"干涉"，是为了明确不干涉原则的适用范围，在法律技术上区分合法的国家间相互影响和国际法禁止的干涉行为，这也是落实不干涉原则的关键。

　　西方学者的主流意见对于干涉的解释，限定于强迫性干涉。干涉被认为是否定被干涉国主权的强迫性行为。从 20 世纪初开始，学者开始从行为本身的性质来限定国际法所禁止之干涉，在此过程中，强迫成为一个重要概念。1905 年，英国学者奥本海在《奥本海国际法》中强调说："干涉毫无

---

① Charles G. Fenwick, "Intervention: Individual and Collective", 39 *American Journal of International Law* (1945): 645.

例外地是专横的干预，而非纯粹的干预"。① 因此，斡旋、调停都不构成专横的干涉。劳特派特进一步界定了干涉"是指专横的干预，是否认国家独立的行为。它暗含了一种强制性的作为或不作为的要求，这种要求如果不被服从，就会引起某种形式的强制威胁或诉诸强制。"② 第 9 版《奥本海国际法》进一步发挥了这个见解，"虽然国家经常泛泛的用干涉这个术语来涵盖批评另一个国家的行为这样的事情，在国际法上干涉有着较为严格的意义，国际法上的干涉是指对另一个国家事务的武力的或者专横的干预，向该另一国强加某种行为或结果。"③ "必须强调的是，构成干涉的干预必须是武力的、专横的、或者是强迫的，实际上剥夺了被干涉国对有关事项的控制。纯粹的干预不是干涉。"④

与此同时，西方学者主流意见认为当今国际法仅仅禁止强迫性干涉。意大利学者阿兰焦·鲁伊斯就认为，"国际法禁止的干涉是对他国的内外事务的专横的干预"，包含两个要素，一是"行为的强迫性质"，二是"试图侵犯受害国的领土完整或政治独立（这种行为不可避免地与使用武力或武力威胁有关），或试图通过强迫受害国的意愿来获取某种不正当利益，或者两者兼具"。⑤ 因此他不承认存在非强迫性质的干涉行为。另有甚者，如英国学者布赖尔利⑥和美国学者亨金⑦，认为国际法只禁止使用武力或武力威胁的干涉行为。

学者们还经常援引国际法院 1986 年在"尼加拉瓜案"的判决来支持上述观点。国际法院在该案中说："一项禁止的干涉必须是针对一个国家依据国家主权原则被允许自由决定的事项的行为。这些事项之一就是政治、经济、社会和文化制度的选择和外交政策的制定。就上述仍然属于自由事项

---

① L. Oppenheim, *International Law: A Treatise*, 1ˢᵗ ed., 1905, Volume 1, p. 182.

② H. Lauterpacht, "The International Protection of Human Rights", 70 *Recueil des cours* (1949) 1 – 108: 19.

③ Robert Jennings & Arthur Watts, *Oppenheim's International law*, 9th ed. (London: Longmans, 1992), Volume 1, p. 430.

④ Ibid., p. 432.

⑤ Gaetano Arangio-Ruiz, "Human Rights and Non-Intervention in the Helsinki Final Act", 157 *Recueil des Cours* (1977): 264.

⑥ 参见英国学者布赖尔利在 1949 年国际法委员会第十二次全体会议上的发言，United Nations, *Yearbook of the International Law Commission* (1949): 90.

⑦ Louis Henkin, "Human Rights and 'Domestic Jurisdiction'", in Thomas Buergenthal, ed., *Human Rights, International Law and the Helsinki Accord* (Montclair, N. J.: Allanheld Osmun, 1977), p. 22.

的方面，使用强迫的方法（methods of coercion），干涉是不法的。强迫的要素界定了禁止性干涉，并且是构成了禁止性干涉的实质。使用武力干涉的情况下，不论是军事行动的形式或者是间接的支持另一个国家内部的颠覆或者恐怖主义军事行动，强迫的要素尤其明显。"①

总结来说，强迫决定了一个行为的干涉性质，同时国际法禁止的不法干涉也是以强迫性手段的行为为限，强迫和干涉具有同构性。正如德国学者库尼奇认为的，强迫这个要素不仅定义了国际法禁止之干涉行为，并且构成了其本质。② 英国外交部原法律顾问伍德在 2009 年发表的一篇《不干涉原则》的论文中也说，"干涉的本质是强迫"，并且进一步评论说，"不干涉原则有时被批评说明显的排除了所有国家间的相互作用；而强迫这个要求恰当地界定了这个原则的范围。"③

根据上述西方主流观点，国际法上不存在或者禁止非强迫性的干涉。即便一个行为的结果在事实上构成了干涉，如果不具备强迫性，那么也不是国际法所禁止的，而是国际政治调整的范围。英国学者麦克格德里克的意见颇具代表性，"可以推定，如果有什么是干涉但不是强迫性干涉，那它也是不被禁止的。"④ 美国法官施瓦贝尔在"尼加拉瓜案"中发表不同意见认为，法院承认超出专横手段之外的干涉是错误的。⑤

三　非强迫性干涉：学者学说与实践

虽然西方学者的主流意见认为国际法仅仅禁止强迫性干涉，还是有少数西方学者注意到了非强迫性干涉的存在，承认存在极个别非强迫性干涉的例外情况。

1. 学说

比较早地注意到非强迫性干涉问题的是美国学者杰赛普，他在 1948 年

---

① Military and Paramilitary Activities in und against Nicaragua（Nicaragua v. United States of America），Merits，Judgment. *I. C. J. Reports 1986*，pp. 107 – 108，para. 205.

② See Philip Kunig，"Prohibition of Intervention"，*Encyclopedia of Public International Law*，www. mpepil. com.

③ Maziar Jamnejad and Michael Wood，"The Principle of Non-intervention"，22 *Leiden Journal of International Law*（2009）：348.

④ Dominic McGoldrick，"The Principle of Non-intervention：Human Rights"，in Vaughan Lowe and Colin Warbrick（ed.），*The United Nations and The Principles of International Law：Essays in Memory of Michael Akehurst*（London：Routledge，1994），p. 92.

⑤ *ICJ Report 1986*，p. 305.

出版的《当代国际法》一书中认为，"干涉可以也可以不涉及使用武力。……这个结果可以通过对一个准备接受干涉国来主导政治或经济的个人所领导的革命团体公开赞同或者放松武器禁运来实现。还可以通过不承认一个新政府，结合各种形式的经济和金融压力，直到强国的意愿战胜而它所不喜欢的政府辞职或倒台来实现。"①

《奥本海国际法》一方面坚持了对干涉的传统定义，"必须要强调的是，干预必须是武力的或专横的、或其他强迫性的，效果上是剥夺了被干涉国对有关事项的控制的，才构成干涉。纯粹的干预不是干涉。"② 另一方面，《奥本海国际法》在脚注中也不得不承认，1970 年《关于各国依联合国宪章建立友好关系及合作之国际法原则之宣言》（以下简称《国际法原则宣言》）规定了"武装干涉和其他所有形式的干预或试图威胁"的不法性，采用的标准没有这么严格。③

德国学者托穆沙特对强迫这个标准是否涵盖了所有的干涉情况也提出了质疑。他还特别列举了过急的承认这个例子，在一个实体分离成为新国家的过程中，过急的承认被国际法学说公认为是对母国的干涉。承认作为国家的单方面宣告行为，很难说是强迫性质的。但是，在这种特殊情况下鉴于其行为结果的严重性，导致国际实践认定它是违法的。④ 他总结说，"还存在第 2625 号决议没有充分规定的更微妙的干涉形式。"⑤ 但是，他反对无限地扩大禁止干涉的范围，他认为 1981 年联合国大会决议中的一些行为不构成干涉。他主张对非强迫性的干涉行为采取较为审慎的态度，"所有主张背离强迫标准的规则都必须特别地予以证明。国际共同同意没有超出强迫。"⑥

希腊学者阿比·萨阿卜属于西方学者中对这个问题反思较为深刻的。他敏锐地注意到了非强迫性干涉的问题，因此他认为十涉存在两种形式。第一种是行为本身构成对他国主权的否定，例如在分离的情况下急于承认一个事实上尚未独立的实体，再如一国未经许可在他国的领土范围内逮捕

---

①　Philip C. Jessup, *A Modern Law of Nations* (New York: The Macmillan Co., 1948), pp. 172 – 173.

②　Robert Jennings & Arthur Watts, *Oppenheim's International law*, 9th ed., p. 432.

③　Ibid, p. 432, footnote 10.

④　Christian Tomuschat, "International Law: Ensuring the Survival of Mankind of the Eve of a New Century", 281 *Recueil des Cours* (1999): 236.

⑤　Ibid., p. 236.

⑥　Ibid., pp. 236 – 237.

个人。第二种干涉行为是由于其行为效果在于违反他国的意愿并强迫它以一种违背自身意愿的方式从事特定行为，而这个领域依据国际法是国家有权自由决定的。这也构成对国家主权的否定。① 阿比·萨阿卜的分析比托穆沙特更进一步，托穆沙特认为非强迫干涉需要有国际法上一般或特殊的明确的禁止性规则存在，而阿比·萨阿卜通过分类提炼出一般原理和规则，而不仅仅限于一些明确的禁止性规则。

2. 非强迫性干涉的个案研究：过急的承认

对主张分离的实体的国家资格的过急的承认，是传统国际法上最确定无疑的干涉行为。美国学者霍奇斯说，在冲突结果还不能排除所有合理怀疑之前，一国承认反叛地区的独立，是对母国内政的干涉。② 赫尔希说："对一个反叛地区的独立的承认，如果是过急的，可以是一个伪装了的干涉行为。"③ 英国学者布赖尔利明确地说："过急的承认一个起义地方的独立，是对他国内部事务的毫无道理的干涉。"④ 另外，对叛乱团体、交战团体的过急的承认，也都构成对母国的主权和内政的不法干涉。"对叛乱团体、交战团体、或叛乱、分离团体的国家资格的过急的承认，毫无疑问构成外交干涉。"⑤ 2008年科索沃地方单方面宣告独立，遭到了塞尔维亚的坚决反对。在此情况下，欧美国家迫不及待地承认科索沃的独立，毫无疑问构成了对塞尔维亚主权的严重违反和对其内政的干涉。

3. 其他形式的非强迫性干涉

国际法是否还存在其他形式的非强迫性的干涉行为呢？答案是肯定的。国际实践表明，还有很多其他非强迫性的干涉行为也都是国际法所禁止的。例如，一个国家对他国的内战予以干涉，向一方提供军事顾问或者大量的贷款等，这些都是国际法所禁止的干涉性行为。又如，一个国家对另一个国家的分离或者叛乱势力的大量资金支持，属于对这个国家主权完整的

---

①　Georges Abi-Saab, "Some Thoughts on the Principle of Non-intervention", in Karel Wellens ed., *International Law: Theory and Practice, Essays in Honour of Eric Suy* (The Hague: Martinus Nijhoff, 1998), p. 228.

②　Henry G. Hodges, *The Doctrine of Intervention* (Princeton: The Banner Press, 1915), p. 108.

③　Amos S. Hershey, *The Essentials of International Public Law and Organization*, 2nd ed. (New York: The Macmillan company, 1927), p. 236, footnote.

④　J. L. Brierly, *The Law of Nations*, 6th ed., ed. by Humphrey Waldock (Oxford: The Clarendon press, 1963), p. 138.

⑤　Quincy Wright, "Domestic Jurisdiction as a Limit on National and Supra-National Action", 56 *Northwestern University Law Review* (1961 – 1962): 28.

"试图威胁"。①

再如，一个国家对他国内部竞选提供大量资金资助某个特定政党，试图影响选举结果，毫无疑问损害了他国人民享有的自决权利。从 2001 年第56 届联合国大会开始，大会的若干决议反复确认了"任何试图直接或间接干涉特别是发展中国家人民自由发展其国家选举程序的外部活动或意图操纵这些选举程序结果的外部活动，都侵犯了《联合国宪章》和《国际法原则宣言》所规定的原则的文字和精神"，并"强烈呼吁所有国家不要直接或间接地为政治党派或团体提供资金或任何其他形式的公开或秘密支持"。②

从现今国家实践来看，非强迫性的干涉实践是极其丰富的，否定非强迫性干涉的存在，会极大地抹杀不干涉原则应当具有的法律效果。

4. 小结

就法律技术而言，用"通过强迫"来定义干涉，存在严重的不足，主要表现为以下三个方面：①通过强迫来限定国际法所禁止的干涉行为，并不能涵盖所有的干涉行为，存在明显的疏漏，例如过急的承认等问题。②没有平衡好手段和目的之间的关系。一个干涉行为，包括了干涉手段和干涉对象两个方面；行为手段并非是判断干涉行为的排他性标准。仅仅通过行为的性质来界定国际法上禁止的干涉行为，忽略了干涉对象可能具有的规范性效力，以及实践中国家对于不同主权事务的不同敏感度和重视程度。过于简单化的法律逻辑没有充分涵盖国际社会生活的复杂性。③以强迫性作为干涉的标准，是站在了干涉国而不是被干涉国的立场上来研究不干涉问题，反映了大国、强国的历史法律传统和现实利益。即便并非必然是西方学者主观上之故意，也表明了西方学界在此问题上的盲点。

四　国际法上禁止非强迫性干涉的一般公式探讨

上述分析足以表明，非强迫性干涉是存在的，用强迫作为界定所有干涉行为的唯一标准并不恰当。强迫仅仅是界定了强迫性干涉，并不是国际法上干涉的唯一标准。非强迫性干涉的存在并不是像托穆沙特说的那样，仅仅是以少数个别国际法已经明确承认的特别规则为限。相反，国家实践存在大量的非强迫性干涉行为都是国际法所禁止的；有关行为的不法性并不依赖于一

---

① "试图威胁"是 1970 年《国际法原则宣言》的措辞。

② 参见 A/Res/44/147，A/Res/45/151，A/Res/46/130，A/Res/47/130，A/Res/48/124，A/Res/ 50/172，A/Res/52/129，A/Res/54/168，56/154。

个额外的、专门的国际法规则，而是直接源于国际法上的不干涉原则。

国际法学者应当致力于通过对非强迫性行为的归纳和对国际法文件的分析，抽象出关于非强迫性干涉行为的一般公式。通过适用这个一般公式，可以识别非强迫性的干涉行为。当然，在确认非强迫性干涉行为的时候，应当有一个基本的门槛，从而使干涉行为和正常的国际影响区分开来。

1. 干涉对象与干涉手段

多数西方学者在认定干涉行为时，仅仅考察了行为手段的干涉性质，而忽略了干涉行为的其他要素。不干涉原则的基本目的，就是要维护国家的主权平等与独立。一个干涉行为，总是具体的针对特定国家的主权事务的干涉，必须综合考察干涉手段以及干涉行为所针对的对象，才能判定一项行为是否构成了国际法所禁止的干涉。干涉行为和干涉对象是密不可分的。干涉的对象就是一个主权国家的内政和外交事务，简单来说，就是主权事务。国际法院也明白指出，"一项被禁止的干涉必须是针对每个国家依据国家主权原则而允许自由决定的事项。这些事项之一就是政治、经济、社会和文化制度的选择和外交政策的制定。"[①]

就不干涉原则的适用而言，不同的国家主权事务对于干涉的敏感度是不同的，因此主权事务的重要性程度的不同，可能影响有关国际法规则在干涉问题上的法律判断。例如，外交实践中，各国通过外交渠道对彼此施加适当的影响或压力，是实践中广泛接受或容忍的，只有性质比较严重的干预才构成国际法禁止的干涉行为，而在内政事项上，轻微程度的干预都可构成国际法所禁止的干涉。德国学者西蒙斯就说："任何形式的干涉，特别是对外国的国内事务的干涉，不仅一般而言是最危害和平的行为，也违反国际法的基本原则。"[②] 但是就现阶段的国际关系和国际法而言，国家的领土主权完整和不可侵犯性、国家的政府形式确实是国家最核心的要素。

例如，对一个国家内部分裂势力的鼓励、支持，毫无疑问构成对该国家内政的干涉。此支持不论是军事支持、财政资助、政治支持，或是言论煽动，都是不可接受的，都损害了一个国家的领土完整和主权独立。国家实践在这个方面是非常广泛的。例如，法国总统戴高乐在加拿大蒙特列尔发表演讲时说"魁北克万岁，魁北克自由万岁"，加拿大政府认为这是不可

---

① Military and Paramilitary Activities in und against Nicaragua (Nicaragua v. United States of America), Merits, Judgment. *I. C. J. Reports 1986*, pp. 107 – 108, para. 205.

② Walter Simons, *The Evolution of International Public Law in Europe since Grotius* (New Haven：Yale University Press, 1931) (reprinted 2004), p. 94.

接受的。①

总结的来说，国际法在识别国际法所禁止的干涉时，有必要平衡干涉行为的手段和对象，不能仅仅考虑行为手段，而不考虑干涉行为所指向的对象。对于国家的核心利益，轻微的冒犯都有可能构成国际法所禁止的干涉，而此种不法干涉并不以手段的强迫为条件。

2. 非强迫性干涉的法律基础

1970 年联合国大会通过的《国际法原则宣言》一般被认为是对不干涉原则习惯法的权威表述。为了分析的便利，不妨把《国际法原则宣言》中"依照宪章不干涉任何国家国内管辖事件之义务之原则"的全文引在这里。

> 任何国家或国家集团均无权以任何理由直接或间接干涉任何其他国家之内政或外交事务。因此，武装干涉及对国家人格或其政治、经济及文化要素之一切其他形式之干预或试图威胁，均系违反国际法。
>
> 任何国家均不得使用或鼓励使用经济、政治或任何他种措施强迫另一国家，以取得该国主权权利行使上之屈从，并自该国获取任何种类之利益。又，任何国家均不得组织、协助、煽动、资助、鼓动或容许目的在于以暴力推翻另一国政权之颠覆、恐怖或武装活动，或干预另一国之内争。
>
> 使用武力剥夺各民族之民族特性构成侵犯其不可移让之权利及不干涉原则之行为。
>
> 每一国均有选择其政治、经济、社会及文化制度之不可移让之权利，不受他国任何形式之干涉。
>
> 以上各项不得解释为对宪章内关于维持国际和平与安全之有关规定有所影响。

该条文共五段，从行文结构来看，第一段的第一句规定了不干涉的一般原则，第一段第二句规定了针对国家人格和国家政治、经济、文化要素的国际法禁止之干涉行为。第二段第一句明确规定了以强迫手段为特征的干涉行为的一般公式，第二段第二句列举了特别明显和重要的强迫性干涉行为，是对前一句话的例证，而不是限制。

---

① Maziar Jamnejad and Michael Wood, "The Principle of Non-intervention", 22 *Leiden Journal of International Law* (2009): pp. 345 – 346.

西方学者普遍基于第二段第一句来界定国际法禁止的干涉。事实上，第二段并非是对第一段禁止的干涉行为的限定，而仅仅是说明了涉及强迫行为的干涉，因为这种干涉行为最为明显。如果非要用第二段来套所有的干涉，不仅本末倒置、割裂了文本，还实质性剥夺了第一段所可能具有的任何规范性含义。另外，在短短的几句话里，《国际法原则宣言》采纳了"任何理由"、"一切其他形式之干预"、"任何他种措施"、"任何种类之利益"、"不受他国任何形式之干涉"等语气强烈的措辞，充分表明了各国试图最大程度地禁止和限制非法干涉的意图和努力。这些措辞本身虽然有一些含糊，但如果因此抛弃其法律上的意蕴和原则精神，将国际法禁止之干涉行为局限于强迫性的干涉，则背离了《国际法原则宣言》的宗旨和精神。

非强迫性的干涉可以从《国际法原则宣言》第一段中找到依据。如果不是先入为主地通过强迫来解读，可以发现，事实上，《国际法原则宣言》规定了两个关于干涉行为的一般公式：第二段第一句规定了强迫性干涉，而第一段第二句规定了非强迫性干涉。

恰恰是这句话，绝大多数西方学者都有意无意地忽略了。少数西方学者注意到了，批评"试图威胁"这样的词太过广泛缺乏法律上的意义。① 例如，麦戈德里克认为，"……提到的'形式的干预'、'试图威胁'很难在实在术语上界定。"② 卡塞斯甚至做了一个一般性的结论，认为虽然有关联大宣言表明了第三世界和东欧国家的观点占了上风，但是，"在一定程度上，这是一个付出极大代价获得的胜利（a Pyrrhic victory），两个主导的国家集团付出的代价是措辞的极端松散（looseness）。""规定非武装干涉的条款如此模糊，被证明事实上很难确定什么种类的干预是被禁止的。"③

上述学者的观点不能让人信服。理由有三：第一，上述表述不仅来源于美洲国家的实践，也是联合国大会对不干涉原则的阐述和贡献。如果仅仅因为有关措辞的抽象性而否定其法律性，显然违背了有关决议起草者的真实意图。联大决议的措施虽然抽象，但它分别经过联合国大会第 2131 号

---

① Gaetano Arangio-Ruiz, "Human Rights and Non-Intervention in the Helsinki Final Act", 157 *Recueil des Cours* (1977), p. 259.

② Dominic McGoldrick, "The Principle of Non-intervention: Human Rights", in Vaughan Lowe and Colin Warbrick (eds.), *The United Nations and The Principles of International Law: Essays in Memory of Michael Akehurst* (London: Routledge), 1994, 85 – 119, p. 90.

③ Antonio Cassese, *International Law in a Divided World* (Oxford: The Clarendon Press, 1986), p. 147.

决议和第 2625 号决议的两次文本的起草和审定，并经由联合国大会全体国家一致同意通过的，应当据此推定各国有意图要赋予该联大决议的条款以效力。这里可以类推适用条约解释的实效原则，应当遵循赋予决议中有关条款以效力的目的来加以解释，而不是通过解释来剥夺有关条款的效力。第二，虽然"试图威胁"等措辞是比较含糊，但是它在某些情况下的适用是非常恰当的。例如过急的承认，用"强迫"显然不合适，用威胁也好像太过了，但是如果说是对一个国家的国家人格的试图威胁，这样的措辞恐怕是再恰当不过了。第三，该条款指出了一个重要的要素，即国家人格，是非常有积极意义的。国家人格是传统国际法上比较确定的概念，包括了领土和主权完整、政府形式、国家的人口等要素。

因此，第一段的第二句可以通过适当的法律分析，而成为表述和涵盖非强迫性干涉行为的一般公式：对有着根本重要性的主权事务，例如国家人格等主权要素，进行任何形式的干预，均属国际法禁止的干涉行为。换言之，对非强迫性干涉，干涉对象的性质起决定性作用，干涉的手段是次要的。以国家政权和领土主权为例，任何轻微的违反、冒犯或者威胁，都归于国际法禁止之列。一个国家有义务对其本国境内的个人和组织采取措施防止破坏他国的政权或领土主权。

上述非强迫性干涉的一般公式有以下基本特点。第一，它坚持了手段和对象的两个要素构成，这和国际法院在"尼加拉瓜案"中提出两要素公式构成是一致的，但各有所侧重。第二，它把干涉对象的不同性质包括在了干涉行为构成要件里，反映了国际社会生活的复杂性，而这个问题是强迫性干涉所忽略的。第三，它和强迫性干涉有着某种内在的一致性，并不是根本对立的。强迫性干涉事实上也存在干涉对象的问题，但是由于手段的性质非常突出，使得干涉对象在认定干涉的构成中就不那么重要了。而对于非强迫性干涉，由于干涉对象所涉法律利益的极度重要性，任何手段的干涉都是法律所禁止的，因此手段在认定干涉的构成时也就不那么重要了。

3. 对国际法院论断的语境分析

不少西方学者在论证国际法仅仅禁止强迫性干涉的时候都援引了国际法院在"尼加拉瓜案"中的判决，有必要在此加以回应。法院在判决中说到，"强迫的要素界定了禁止性干涉，并且是构成了禁止性干涉的实质。"①

---

① Military and Paramilitary Activities in und against Nicaragua（Nicaragua v. United States of America），Merits，Judgment. *I. C. J. Reports 1986*，pp. 107 – 108，para. 205.

法院的论断对于理解国际法上的禁止之干涉是有积极意义的。问题不是法院自身的意见出了问题,而是学者在援引法院判决的时候把法院的这个论断抽离出了相关的语境,扩展成为一个一般性的表述。

法院的论断不是绝对的、无条件的,有着严格的上下文限定。法院明确说明了,它是在考虑尼加拉瓜案情的基础上提出上述公式的。在论证完国际社会存在关于不干涉原则的法律确信之后,法院在第201段说:"尽管存在接受不干涉原则的国家多次宣告,仍然有两个问题:第一,被接受的原则的确切内容是什么;第二,国家实践是否充分符合使之成为一项习惯国际法规则。不干涉原则的内容,法院将仅仅界定这个原则中看起来和解决争端有关的方面。"① 在作出这些限定之后,法院才紧接着提出了学者经常援引的公式。法院很明确地把自己提出的公式限定在跟案件有关的方面,法院并没有排除其他非强迫性的干涉。"强迫的要素界定了禁止性干涉,并且是构成了禁止性干涉的实质。"这句话的含义,如果联系上下文来看,是有限定条件的,即限于该案有关的强迫性干涉。法院的观点经限定之后是正确的,强迫的要素的确是强迫性干涉的实质。

从"尼加拉瓜案"的案情来看,美国的干涉行为,涉及的主要都是武力干涉的问题,例如对尼加拉瓜反对派的军事活动提供资金支持、培训等,因此法院在这个案件中提出强迫性干涉的一般公式是妥当的、充分的、合理的。但是,把法院的公式绝对化,并用法院的公式来排除非强迫性的干涉,恐怕是学者自己的臆造,而不是法院的本意。

五 强迫性和非强迫性干涉的内在统一性

事实上,《国际法原则宣言》提供了禁止干涉的两个公式,一个是强迫性干涉,另一个是非强迫性干涉;一个强调手段要素,另一个强调对象要素。这样一来,似乎国际法上的不干涉原则就被割裂成了两个不同的原则。但是,上述两个公式事实上是互通的。在构成国际法禁止的干涉行为的问题上,可以认为干涉手段的暴力程度和干涉对象的重要性这两个要素成反相关的:干涉手段的强迫性程度越高,就构成干涉行为的门槛而言,干涉对象的重要性就越可以减低,在涉及武力使用的情况下,干涉对象起的构成性作用和规范性效力是边缘性的。反之,干涉手段的强迫性越低,就构

---

① Military and Paramilitary Activities in und against Nicaragua (Nicaragua v. United States of America), Merits, Judgment. *I. C. J. Reports 1986*, pp. 107 – 108, para. 205.

成干涉行为的门槛而言，干涉对象的重要性程度就需要很高，在涉及一些有根本重要性的主权事务方面，轻微的冒犯行为都会构成干涉。干涉手段起的构成性作用和规范性效力就是边缘性的了。

上述分析可以简单地借用公式来说明。假定 X 表示主权事务的重要性等级，Y 表述干涉手段的强迫性等级，M 表示一个行为在构成干涉行为时干涉手段和干涉对象所需要达到的总量，并且假定这个总量是不变的，即国际法上干涉行为门槛是一定的。那么，干涉手段和干涉对象之间的关系可以通过下面这个公式来表达：$X * Y = M$（$X > 0$，$Y > 0$，$M > 0$）。上述公式可以用下面这个曲线来表示两者之间的互变关系。

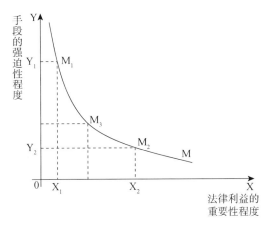

在上图中，曲线 M 事实上代表了构成干涉的门槛，在 M 曲线上方的所有的行为都构成干涉，而 M 曲线下方所有的行为都不构成干涉。X 代表了法律利益的重要性程度，Y 代表了手段的强迫性程度。M_1 比较类似于强迫性干涉，Y_1 数量级比较高，表明其手段的强迫性程度较高，而 X_1 数量级较低，表明法律利益的重要性程度相对较低。这意味着，在 M_1 这一点上，行为有着较高的强迫性，属于强迫性干涉，法律利益或干涉对象在其中的构成性作用较低。相反，M_2 属于非强迫性干涉，X_2 数量级比较高，表明其法律利益的重要性程度很高，而 Y_2 数量级比较低，表明手段的强迫性程度比较低，因此属于非强迫性干涉。

而在 M_3 的情况下，要构成干涉行为，手段的激烈程度属于中等，保护的法律利益也属于中等，在这种情况下，就很难仅仅通过一个要素如干涉手段或干涉对象来决定一个行为是否构成干涉行为，而必须同时考察干涉手段和干涉对象。一些以经济手段强迫的干涉行为就属于这个类型，它很难仅仅通过考察手段或者干涉对象来确认是否构成干涉，而必须要结合具体情况来个案考察。

在 M 曲线上方的所有的点,都是表示构成干涉行为的情况。极有可能有些行为既是用强迫性的手段,针对的又是有根本重要性的主权事务,那它就毫无疑问地构成干涉,与把它归于强迫性干涉或者非强迫性干涉是无关紧要的。

上述曲线图和解释表明,强迫性干涉和非强迫性干涉,仅仅是位于两个极端的典型情况,表面上两者之间有很大差别,但是事实上在逻辑结构上具有根本一致性。

六 不干涉原则与中国的核心利益

主权平等是国际法的根基。不干涉原则的要义在于国家间相互尊重,避免干涉他国的主权事务。中国的哲学思维是"己所不欲,勿施于人",体现在国际交往上,就是相互尊重,求同存异。新中国成立后,中国提出了"和平共处五项原则",其中一个重要的方面就是互不干涉内政。互不干涉内政不仅是中国一直以来的国际法主张,在外交实践中也得到了切实的遵守。中国始终主张通过双边对话、友好协商来解决国家间分歧,而不是通过单边的武力或者其他强硬措施来解决争端。中国不对他国的内政事务指手画脚,而是坚持尊重由一国人民自己选择其政治制度和经济社会发展道路。在国际事务上,中国积极避免非强迫性的干涉行为。

值得指出的是,中国在对外援助方面也坚持了不干涉原则。中国早在1964 年就把"不附带条件"确立为对外援助的基本原则之一,并一以贯之。"中国坚持和平共处五项原则,尊重各受援国自主选择发展道路和模式的权利,相信各国能够探索出适合本国国情的发展道路,绝不把提供援助作为干涉他国内政、谋求政治特权的手段。"[1] 作为一个发展中的大国,在涉及他国的核心利益上,不论是对大国还是小国,中国审慎行事,避免通过经济手段来不当干涉他国的主权事务。

近些年来,在和平共处五项原则的基础上,中国在其和平发展的道路上,不断与欧美国家调整权力和利益关系,反对外国干涉中国的内政,在非强迫性干涉方面对国际法作出了自己的贡献。中国的国际法实践支持了这样的观点,即在一个国家的根本利益上,非强迫性干涉也是国际法所禁止的。

---

[1] 国务院新闻办公室:《中国的对外援助》,2011 年 4 月。

第一个例子是台湾入联问题。从 1993 年第 48 届联合国大会开始，直到 2006 年第 62 届联合国大会，台湾的"邦交国"每年在联合国大会提案主张台湾加入联合国，联合国大会总务委员会连续 15 次明确拒绝将"台湾申请加入联合国"提案列入联合国大会议程。有关提案实质上否定中国对台湾的主权，构成对中国领土主权等核心利益的危害，虽然列入议程这一行为本身很难说是强迫性的，但是考虑到提案的内容和性质，一旦将有关提案列入议程，则毫无疑问会构成对中国内政的干涉。正如中国代表指出的，把有关提案列入大会议程构成对一个成员国内政的不法干涉，将严重损害中国的主权和严重干涉中国的内政。①

第二个案例是中法关于"藏独"问题的交涉。2008 年 12 月 6 日，法国总统萨科齐以法国总统和欧盟轮值主席的双重身份在波兰会见了达赖，我国政府对此作出了强烈抗议。国家元首以官方身份会见并支持一国的分裂势力，构成对他国核心利益的侵害，违反国际法上不干涉原则。会见本身很难说是强迫性的，可是在涉及一国核心利益上，不法干涉的构成不以强迫性手段为条件。2009 年 4 月 1 日，经过反复磋商，中法两国发布了《中法新闻公报》，指出"中法两国重申坚持《联合国宪章》规定的不干涉内政的原则，同意本着相互信任的精神就涉及双方根本利益的事宜加强协商。""法国充分认识到西藏问题的重要性和敏感性，重申坚持一个中国政策，坚持西藏是中国领土不可分割的一部分。这一由戴高乐将军做出的决定没有也不会改变。本着这一精神，并根据不干涉内政的原则，法国拒绝支持任何形式的'西藏独立'。"②

第三个例子是 2009 年《中美联合声明》，中美双方确认了相互尊重彼此主权和领土完整这一核心利益，并避免对分裂势力给予任何形式的支持。"双方重申，互相尊重主权和领土完整这一根本原则是指导中美关系的中美三个联合公报的核心。双方均不支持任何势力破坏这一原则的任何行动。双方一致认为，尊重彼此核心利益对确保中美关系稳定发展极端重要。"③

近期，中国政府开始系统的提出核心利益的国际法主张，进一步强化了非强迫性干涉的实践。中国政府 2011 年发布《中国的和平发展》白皮书，对核心利益进一步作了阐述："中国坚决维护国家核心利益。中国的核

---

① United Nations, *Repertory of Practice of United Nations Organs*, Volume 1, Supplement 8, pp. 14, 24.

② See http: //news. xinhuanet. com/newscenter/2009 - 04/01/content_ 11114363. htm.

③ http: //www. fmprc. gov. cn/mfa_ chn/ziliao_ 611306/1179_ 611310/t627468. shtml.

心利益包括：国家主权，国家安全，领土完整，国家统一，中国宪法确立的国家政治制度和社会大局稳定，经济社会可持续发展的基本保障。"① 显然，在上述国家核心利益问题上，中国不接受外国政府或者国际组织的干涉，不论是强迫性还是非强迫性的。中国积极强化和落实国际法上禁止非强迫性干涉的适用，既有利于维护国家利益，也为国际法上不干涉内政原则提供了有积极意义的国家实践。

Prohibition of Non-coercive Intervention in International Law: A Chinese Perspective

Chen Yifeng

【Abstract】The article makes a critical reflection on the idea of confining the prohibited intervention under international law to coercive interventions as adopted by the mainstream international legal scholarships. After an analytical exploration of the existing scholarships and state practice on non-coercive intervention, the author proposes a general formula of prohibited non-coercive intervention: Any kinds of interference or threat against fundamental interests of sovereign states, by means of coercion or not, constitutes prohibited intervention under international law. The article further illustrates the structural coherence of constituent elements of coercive and non-coercive interventions. The recent China's international law claim and diplomatic practice on core interest are relevant state practices on the international law prohibition of non-coercive intervention.

【Key words】Principle of Non-intervention, Coercion, Non-coercive Intervention, Core Interest

---

① http：//www. gov. cn/jrzg/2011 − 09/06/content_ 1941204. htm.

第二部分

宪法实施与行政法治

中国的准违宪审查研究

程　洁[*]

【摘要】本文尝试从实证的角度，对中国现行违宪审查制度以及具有违宪审查意义的活动进行研究。这一研究针对两种批评：一种批评认为中国没有违宪审查实践，另一种批评认为对中国违宪审查制度的批评是毫无根据的。本文认为，中国虽然在宪法和法律上规定了违宪审查制度，但是不存在规范意义上的违宪审查实践。另一方面，在既有的制度框架内，存在一些符合违宪审查逻辑的立法和司法活动。这些实践推而广之，假以时日，有可能为未来规范的违宪审查提供实践和制度基础。因此，可以将中国的违宪审查活动界定为准违宪审查，并在此基础上通过政治和法律实践逐步将之规范化。

【关键词】违宪审查　准违宪审查　宪法

一　为什么是准违宪审查

对中国违宪审查制度、体制和内容的讨论是持续但艰难的。[②] 以美国或德国式违宪审查为范本的研究将希望寄托在宪法司法化或宪法私法化上，[③] 他们批评中国现行的宪法实施监督机制，认为中国无违宪审查。另一方面，也有人满足于《立法法》第 90 条的规定，将之视为违宪审查的法律依据，虽然他们同样无法观察到有价值的违宪审查实践。本文认为，中国从来没

---

* 清华大学法学院副教授。

② 林来梵：《中国的"违宪审查"：特色及生成实态》，《浙江社会科学》2010 年第 5 期。莫纪宏：《中国违宪审查制度的历史演变、存在问题和发展方向》。以上两篇文章分别从语义学和制度规范两方面说明在中国界定违宪审查的困难。

③ 蔡守剑：《中国宪法实施的私法化之路》，《中国社会科学》2004 年第 2 期。

有确立规范意义上的违宪审查制度,也不存在规范意义上的违宪审查实践。但是在既有的制度框架内,存在一些符合违宪审查逻辑的司法和立法活动。这些实践推而广之,假以时日,有可能为未来规范的违宪审查提供实践和制度基础。本文统称之为准违宪审查。

称之为准违宪审查,有三方面原因。首要的原因是这些制度或实践都符合违宪审查的内在逻辑:以宪法或宪法相关法为依据,维护法律体系内在的一致性,包括形式一致性和价值一致性。从形式一致性要求看,中国《宪法》第5条和《立法法》对下位法与宪法保持一致都作出了规定。从价值一致性要求看,主要是2000年《立法法》通过之后,宪法所规定的一些基本权利保障出现分层,一些权利实际上获得了更高强度的保障,成为位阶更高的权利。根据《立法法》,这些权利主要包括《立法法》第8条所规定的人身权和政治权利。如果将立法法转换为具有违宪审查意义的表述,就成为"国务院和地方机构不得制定限制人身权和政治权利的法规和地方性法规规章⋯⋯"。由于这一原因,我们不妨将这些活动纳入违宪审查的大集合中。

然而,这些活动还有一些其他属性,使之只能以"准"称之,有别于"正统的"或"规范的"违宪审查。这两个原因是:审查过程和结果缺乏确定性、审查的对象极少针对全国性立法或中央政府的行为。就审查过程和审查依据看,这些做法的宪法根据、制度支持、实践运行的范围广度和深度方面都缺乏典型性和确定性。当然,随着法治政府和宪法权威观念的推广,类似违宪审查的经验正在不断形成,一些过去缺乏依据的实践做法正在逐渐制度化,甚至形成宪法惯例。就审查对象来看,多数审查对象是地方性法规或行政法规,显示出对违宪审查来说至关重要的"制约与平衡"理念在全国性权力机关之间还没有形成。有鉴于此,本文将这些具有违宪审查属性或某些特点的制度和实践归入"准违宪审查"范畴,认为这一概念较好地反映了中国的现实和发展阶段。

这些基于违宪审查逻辑进行的实践可以从不同角度认识,例如从审查对象的范围、审查依据等。由于宪法监督机关为全国人大及其常委会,而对违宪审查的讨论常常与以法院为主体进行的司法审查联系在一起,这就使得对中国违宪审查的讨论不能回避上述情况。有鉴于此,以下就以主体作为区分标准,将这些准违宪审查实践划分为四类:其一,由宪法监督机构全国人大及其常委会做出的合宪性决定;其二,全国人大常委会和国务院在职权范围内进行的法规规章备案审查;其三,人民法院在职权范围内进行的司法审查；其四，香港和澳门特别行政区的法院就特别行政区立法是否合乎香港，澳门的基本法进行的地区性违宪审查。鉴于港澳地区的实践有别于大陆，以下将分别就大陆地区和港澳地区的情况进行描述和分析。

二　内地准违宪审查实践

以下从审查主体、审查对象的范围、审查依据和标准、审查后果四方面对现行宪法和法律下可以纳入准违宪审查范围的制度和实践进行概述和分析，进而论证其与违宪审查逻辑的一致性或偏离。

（一）全国人大及其常委会的合宪性决定

全国人大或全国人大常委会作为宪法监督机构进行的合宪性审查是立法后审查，其宪法依据是《宪法》第63条和第67条有关宪法监督权和宪法解释权的规定，其立法依据则是《立法法》有关法律适用的规定，特别是第90条有关违宪审查程序的规定。全国人大及其常委会的宪法监督针对国务院行政法规、地方性法规的合宪性进行审查。其后全国人大常委会于2000年通过了《行政法规、地方性法规、自治条例和单行条例、经济特区法规备案审查工作程序》作为其行使监督权的程序规则。2005年，全国人大常委会又通过了《司法解释备案审查工作程序》，增加了对司法解释的监督。

宪法监督性审查的结果最重要的决定是对立法合宪性的判断。这一类的审查目前尚无先例。但是，自1982年以来，全国人大曾经做出了两次合宪性决定，分别确定1990年香港基本法和1995年澳门基本法是符合宪法的。两个决定都是在立法通过的同一天做出的，因此可以视为一种事先审查。1990年4月4日，第七届全国人民代表大会第三次会议通过了《全国人民代表大会关于〈中华人民共和国香港特别行政区基本法〉的决定》，在说明香港基本法的组成部分之后，该决定指出：

《中华人民共和国宪法》第31条规定："国家在必要时得设立特别行政区。在特别行政区内实行的制度按照具体情况由全国人民代表大会以法律规定。"《香港特别行政区基本法》是根据《中华人民共和国宪法》按照香港的具体情况制定的，是符合宪法的。香港特别行政区设立后实行的制度、政策和法律，以香港特别行政区基本法为依据。

这一决定的背景是对香港地区实行资本主义制度的质疑和讨论。《宪法》第1条规定，中国是人民民主专政的社会主义国家，而基本法则授权特区保留原有的资本主义制度不变。这两者之间是否存在冲突和抵触？虽然决定本身没有强调其对基本法合宪性的答复主要是针对上述问题，但是在提交给全国人大的说明中则不难发现，基本法规定特区实行资本主义制度是否抵触宪法，是该决定所要回答的主要问题。① 基于同样的原因，1993年澳门基本法通过的同时，全国人大通过了类似的决定，以明确澳门基本法的合宪性。

有论者认为，上述决定显示，全国人大曾经行使过违宪审查权。② 这一观点值得商榷。因为全国人大的决定和两部法律的规定同时做出，与其说是对两部法律的审查，不如说是在法律正式通过之前的确认和宣告。更为重要的是，这两个决定仅仅是对其合宪性的宣告，并没有就其合宪性进行说明。因此，即使作为公布前的审查，也是不完整的，只能纳入"准"违宪审查之列。

此后，全国人大未就法律的合宪性做出过新的决定。但是在2007年3月，部分全国人大代表在"两会"期间提出议案，要求对有关司法解释进行审查，从而再一次引发了全国人大行使宪法监督权的讨论。③

人大代表提议接受审查的司法解释被认为违反宪法平等原则，导致"同命不同价"。这一争议源于一起交通事故。2005年12月15日，刘定红驾驶铺金公司万州分公司为登记车主、刘丰云为实际车主的渝B28355号中型自卸货车在郭家沱长城公司下坡路段与何源及其同学邓莽丹、鲁静莹三人搭乘的三轮摩托车相撞，致三人当场死亡。2006年1月7日，重庆市公安局交通管理局第八支队出具《交通事故认定书》，认定刘定红承担此事故的全部责任，其余驾驶人和乘车人不承担事故责任。之后，铺金公司分别向邓、鲁两家赔偿20余万元，但以何源系农村户籍为由仅赔偿8万元。事故发生后，原告与被告达成赔偿协议，并签订了《赔偿协议书》，约定由赔偿义务人赔偿原告因何源死亡所产生的死亡赔偿金50700元、丧葬费7530元和其他一次性补偿21770元，共计8万元；并约定"此款赔付后，赔偿终止，赔偿权利人和赔偿义务人之间不再有权利义务关系"。

原告后来试图推翻协议书，认为其所获得的赔偿金远低于另外两位受害人是因为该协议的达成受到最高人民法院2004年司法解释的影响，而该解释本身对农村人口的赔偿作出了歧视性的规定，因此请求法院认定该协

① 1990年4月4日《关于〈全国人民代表大会关于中华人民共和国香港特别行政区基本法的决定（草案）〉的说明》。
② 王振民：《中国的违宪审查制度》，中国政法大学出版社，2004。
③ http://cpc.people.com.cn/GB/64093/64103/5485788.html。

议无效并要求进一步的赔偿。法院在一审判决中没有涉及法律适用的问题，而是以双方协议合法有效为由，驳回了原告的诉讼请求。① 二审法院认为，该案的交通事故发生在 2005 年 12 月 15 日，根据最高人民法院《关于审理人身损害赔偿案件适用法律若干问题的解释》第 29 条规定，死亡赔偿金按照受诉法院所在地上一年度城镇居民人均可支配收入或者农村居民人均纯收入标准，按二十年计算。但六十周岁以上的，年龄每增加一岁减少一年；七十五周岁以上的，按五年计算。由于何源发生交通事故时系农村户口，按照该规定，其赔偿金额符合法律规定。② 因此，二审判决维持了原判。

最高人民法院的司法解释引发出一系列被称为"同命不同价"的判决，并引发对该解释是否违反《宪法》第 33 条所规定的"公民在法律面前一律平等"的争议。③ 2007 年人大会议期间，当时的最高人民法院院长肖扬公开表示将重新审查该解释。④ 此后，虽然最高人民法院没有对该解释进行修改，但是对该解释的"解释"却不再限于受害人的户籍所在地。各地高级人民法院纷纷出台适用该解释的"指导意见"，⑤变通执行最高人民法院的司法解释，或者不按照受害人户籍类别为依据决定农村或城镇的赔偿标准，或者实际上采取同一标准。

倘若全国人大常委会就上述司法解释的合宪性作出决定，则会构成违宪审查第一例。不过这样的结果并未发生，虽然在制度上存在这种可能性。

(二) 立法和法规规章清理

1. 全国人大常委会的法律法规集中清理

全国人大常委会进行的法律清理工作属于立法后审查，其主要依据是《立法法》对国务院行政法规和地方性法规进行审查，其后增加对司法解释的审查，审查结果是大量修改、废止。实践中进行了四次大的法律法规清理（1954 年、1979 年、1987 年、2009 年）。

1979 年以前，全国人大及其常委会作出过两个具有法律清理性质的决议：一是，1954 年 9 月，宪法通过的同时，第一届全国人大第一次会议作

---

① （2006）江民初字第 3491 号。
② （2007）渝一中法民终字第 1083 号。
③ 更多案件及讨论参见 http://legal.people.com.cn/GB/42731/4608947.html。
④ http://politics.people.com.cn/GB/1026/5472889.html。
⑤ 例如，重庆市高级人民法院渝高法［2006］223 号文《关于审理道路交通事故损害赔偿案件适用法律若干问题的指导意见》第 27 条规定，长期在城市生活的受害人死亡赔偿金应当按照重庆市城镇居民标准计算。

出关于现行法律、法令继续有效的决议，指出《宪法》颁布以后，"所有自从一九四九年十月一日中华人民共和国建立以来，由中央人民政府制定、批准的现行法律、法令，除开同宪法相抵触的以外，一律继续有效。"这个决定明确了宪法颁布以前制定的法律、法令的效力，是一个具有法律清理性质的文件。二是，1979 年 11 月 29 日，第五届全国人大常委会第十二次会议通过关于中华人民共和国成立以来制定的法律、法令效力问题的决议，确定"从一九四九年十月一日中华人民共和国建立以来，前中央人民政府制定、批准的法律、法令；从一九五四年九月二十日第一届全国人民代表大会第一次会议制定中华人民共和国宪法以来，全国人民代表大会和全国人民代表大会常务委员会制定、批准的法律、法令，除了同第五届全国人民代表大会制定的宪法、法律和第五届全国人民代表大会常务委员会制定、批准的法令相抵触的以外，继续有效。"这是加强法律清理的一项重要措施。

1987 年，全国人大常委会对新中国成立以来至 1978 年底制定的法律、法令进行了一次全面清理。根据第五届全国人大第三次会议常委会工作报告提出清理新中国成立以来颁布的法律的要求，法工委对 1978 年底以前颁布的法律（包括有关法律问题的决定）进行了全面清理，会同有关部门对这个时期全国人大及其常委会制定或者批准的 134 件法律逐件进行了研究，并征求一些法律专家的意见，认定其中已经失效的有 111 件，继续有效或者继续有效正在研究修改的有 23 件。已经失效的 111 件法律分为以下四种情况：已由新法规定废止的 11 件；已有新法代替的 41 件；由于调整对象变化或者情况变化而不再适用或者已经停止施行的 29 件；对某一特定问题作出的具有法律效力的决定、条例已经过时的 30 件。对现已失去法律效力的 111 件法律，除已由新法规定废止的 11 件以外，对其余的 100 件，建议全国人大常委会明确这些法律已经不再适用，同时明确过去根据这些法律对有关问题做出的处理仍然是有效的。此外，在 1978 年底以前，全国人大常委会批准民族自治地方的人民代表大会和人民委员会组织条例共 48 件，因《宪法》、《地方各级人民代表大会和地方各级人民政府组织法》和《民族区域自治法》已经制定，各民族自治地方人大都已成立常委会，且都已经或正在另行制定自治条例，上述组织条例已因情况变化而不再适用。1987 年11 月，法工委向第六届全国人大常委会第二十三次会议提出了《关于对1979 年底以前颁布的法律进行清理的情况和意见的报告》，常委会通过决议批准了这个报告。

2009 年以来，按照全国人大常委会的部署，先后开展了法律、行政法规和地方性法规的集中清理工作，废止了 8 件法律和有关法律问题的决定，一揽子对 59 件法律的 141 个条文作出修改；废止行政法规 7 件，修改行政法规 107 件；废止地方性法规 455 件，修改地方性法规 1417 件，基本解决了现行法律中明显不适应经济社会发展需要、相互之间不一致或者不够衔接，以及行政法规、地方性法规与上位法明显不一致、不协调等问题，保证了法律体系内部的科学和谐统一。

可以想见，这些法规的清理工作有可能与合宪性审查结合起来。即使仅针对合法性审查，在审查逻辑上与违宪审查也十分接近。不过，这些清理往往只有结论而没有说明，缺乏规范性和说服力。

2. 国务院进行的法规规章清理

国务院法规规章清理的审查主体是国务院，审查对象是行政法规和规章，依据主要为法律和行政法规，结果是修改和废止，如对《城市流浪乞讨人员收容遣送办法》和《城市房屋拆迁管理条例》的废止。

典型案例是 2003 年孙志刚事件。孙志刚，男，汉族，27 岁，湖北省武汉市人，2001 年在武汉科技学院艺术设计专业结业。2003 年 2 月 24 日受聘于广州达奇服装有限公司。2003 年 3 月 17 日晚 22 时许，孙志刚因未携带任何证件，在天河区黄村大街被执行统一清查任务的区公安分局黄村街派出所民警带回询问，随后被错误作为"三无"人员送至天河区公安分局收容待遣所转送广州市收容遣送中转站。18 日晚，孙志刚称有病被送往广州市卫生部门负责的收容人员救治站诊治。20 日凌晨 1 时 13 分至 30 分期间，孙志刚遭同病房的 8 名被收治人员两度轮番殴打，当日上午 10 时 20 分，因大面积软组织损伤致创伤性休克死亡。案件所涉及的法律：孙志刚被强制收容的依据是国务院 1982 年通过的《城市流浪乞讨人员收容遣送办法》。根据该条例，行政机关可以未经法律程序，对无法证明身份者采取限制人身自由的强制措施。孙志刚案发生后，该办法饱受舆论批评和谴责。特别是该条例抵触《宪法》和《立法法》，被认为是违宪的条例。此后，有社会人士向全国人大常委会提起"违宪审查请求"，在全国人大常委会正式进入审查程序之前，国务院宣布废止该条例，并于 2003 年 6 月 22 日颁布《城市生活无着的流浪乞讨人员救助管理办法》。该案虽然未能启动全国人大常委会的违宪审查程序，但是国务院废止条例的理由是不言而喻的。因此，该案可以视为国务院自我审查的一起个案。

据报道，1949 年后国务院也进行过多次规章清理，如果将这些清理工作规范化，是可以和违宪审查接轨的。

3. 地方人大或常委会进行的法规规章清理

对这一类清理目前没有具体的统计，但是这一级别的清理也是经常性的。例如，2011 年 1 月 21 日，国务院总理温家宝签署国务院令公布《国有土地上房屋征收与补偿条例》，条例规定自公布之日起施行。2001 年 6 月 13 日国务院公布的《城市房屋拆迁管理条例》同时废止。与此同时，各地也纷纷开始清理与新条例不符的地方性规定。

（三） 大陆地区人民法院的司法审查

大陆地区人民法院的审理工作中和违宪审查相关的情况主要有两方面，一种是齐玉苓案件那样以宪法适用为名进行的司法审理活动。这一类司法实践实际上并不具有违宪审查的属性。另外一类则是以规范审查为基础的司法审判，其中包含了违宪审查逻辑。后者的代表性案件是 2003 年河南省种子案。

在 2003 年的河南种子案中，主审法官在判决书中认定，《河南省农作物种子管理条例》作为法律阶位较低的地方性法规，与《种子法》相冲突的条款自然无效。① 此项判决意见经洛阳市中级人民法院审判委员会讨论并形成了决议，并经主管领导签发。案件判决后，洛阳市人大常委会向河南省人大常委会就该案请示，河南省人大常委会法制办的答复要求"纠正洛阳市中级人民法院的违法行为，对直接负责人员和主管领导依法作出处理。"

主审法官认为，《河南省农作物种子管理条例》是河南省人大制定并通过的地方性法规，其法律位阶要低于全国人大及其常委会制定的法律，该地方性法规确定的种子价格条款与《种子法》、《价格法》等法律位阶较高的法律的精神相抵触；而且《种子法》、《价格法》颁布在后，《河南省农作物种子管理条例》颁布在前，依新法优于旧法之原则，关于价格问题，在本案中亦应适用《种子法》。②

但是，对于无效的法规，人民法院的法官是否有权宣告其无效呢？在中国现行法律框架内，缺乏法律依据。事实上，法官面对与上位法冲突的下位法，往往采取不予适用的方式回避对其作出进一步的判断。撤销、修

---

① （2003）洛民初第 26 号民事判决书。
② 李慧娟：《关于汝阳县种子公司诉伊川县种子公司玉米种子代繁合同纠纷一案适用法律问题的情况汇报》，未公开发布。

改或废止抵触的法律法规的权利，被置于上级人大或政府或同级人大，而非法院。例如，2001 年北京市的一起案件中，北辰出租汽车公司司机周建军（以下简称原告）于 2000 年 8 月 31 日在朝阳区北苑路口驾驶机动车遇停止信号后通过路口，北京市公安交通管理局朝阳交通支队机动队（以下简称被告）于 2001 年 3 月 12 日作出京公交（朝）行决字〔2001〕第 0551 号公安交通管理处罚决定书，认定原告以上违法事实，对其处 200 元罚款。原告不服，诉称：被告作出的处罚决定证据不足，适用法律错误，请求法院予以撤销，并判令被告赔偿其经济损失 2000 元，精神损失 1000 元，并以书面形式向其道歉。法院判决被告于 2001 年 3 月 12 日作出的京公交（朝）行决字〔2001〕第 0551 号公安交通管理行政处罚决定书违法。理由是该决定书依据的《北京市道路交通管理规定》与国务院通过的《中华人民共和国治安管理处罚条例》相抵触。与河南省种子案不同的是，该案的法官并没有进一步宣告《北京市道路交通管理规定》违法，自然无效。

此后，河南省高级人民法院在二审判决书中表示，一审判决书认定《种子条例》自然无效属于"表述不当"，但是支持了一审判决。可见，对于互相冲突的法规，法官在实践中选择适用合法之法而搁置非法之法，已经形成一种实践。2004 年最高人民法院印发《关于审理行政案件适用法律规范问题的座谈会纪要》①中也指出，"根据行政诉讼法和立法法有关规定，人民法院审理行政案件，依据法律、行政法规、地方性法规、自治条例和单行条例，参照规章。在参照规章时，应当对规章的规定是否合法有效进行判断，对于合法有效的规章应当适用。""调整同一对象的两个或者两个以上的法律规范因规定不同的法律后果而产生冲突的，一般情况下应当按照立法法规定的上位法优于下位法、后法优于前法以及特别法优于一般法等法律适用规则，判断和选择所应适用的法律规范。冲突规范所涉及的事项比较重大、有关机关对是否存在冲突有不同意见、应当优先适用的法律规范的合法有效性尚有疑问或者按照法律适用规则不能确定如何适用时，依据立法法规定的程序逐级送请有权机关裁决。"

综上所述，人民法院通过判断规范的合法性选择适用规范，已经成为法院系统内部具有共识的做法。不过，囿于我国目前的人民代表大会制，人民法院宣告法规无效或废止相关法规将受到来自其他部门的挑战。虽然实践中偶有突破，但是尚未成为一般性的做法。从宪法角度而言，人民法

---

① 法〔2004〕96 号。

院对法规、规章的违法审查与违宪审查在技术上没有实质性的差别，都需要通过法院对相关法律法规的理解来说明法规规章是否抵触更高位阶的法，而在进行此类说明时，有可能完全依据字面进行说明，也有必要参考立法原意或法律效果。如果人民法院的规范选择实践能够日渐成熟，未来向违宪审查推进时将更能够驾轻就熟。

与种子案相对，齐玉苓案可以视为人民法院试图通过适用宪法确立权威，但是误用司法审查权的典型。2001 年，该案引发了对宪法司法化的持续讨论。一部分学者认为该案是法官探索宪法司法化的技术性选择，但更多的宪法学者批评该案将违宪的概念错误地应用于个人，从而消弭了违宪审查制约政府权力的真实内涵。不过，从实践来看，人民法院援引宪法审理案件最早可以追溯到 1985 年沈涯夫、牟春霖诽谤案。在该案中，原告杜融主张自己的名誉权被侵害，而被告则认为自己在行使新闻自由权。案件上诉后，上海市中级人民法院指出，我国宪法明确规定国家保护公民的言论、出版的自由和权利。但是，新闻记者和所有公民一样，在行使宪法和法律规定的权利的时候，必须履行宪法和法律规定的义务，即"不得损害国家的、社会的、集体的利益和其他公民的合法的自由和权利"，"禁止用任何方法对公民进行侮辱、诽谤和诬告陷害"。上海市中级人民法院认为：上诉人沈涯夫、牟春霖无视杜融妻子狄振智患有精神病的客观事实，拒不接受有关组织、群众、同事和上级领导机关的忠告和规劝，故意捏造和散布虚构的事实，损害了杜融的人格和名誉，情节严重，其行为已构成诽谤罪。沈涯夫、牟春霖的上诉理由不能成立。原审法院根据沈涯夫、牟春霖的犯罪事实、情节及危害程度，依法予以处罚，均无不当。据此，依照《中华人民共和国刑事诉讼法》第 136 条第 1 项的规定，于 1988 年 4 月 11 日裁定，驳回上诉，维持原判。

综上所述，无论是全国人大及其常委会的合宪性决定，还是人民法院在种子案中基于上位法凌驾于下位法的法律适用，都体现了对法律内在一致性的追求，也就是违宪审查的基本逻辑。因此，我们可以将之纳入准违宪审查的范畴中。此外，香港和澳门特区的司法审查也具有这一特征。

三 港澳基本法下的准违宪审查

（一）香港特区的地区性违宪审查

审查主体为特区各级法院，审查对象包括特区立法和行政法规（附属立法）、政府决定等，审查的主要依据为基本法和国际人权。典型案例是

1999 年吴嘉玲案及 2011 年刚果（金）案。

1. 回归前的准违宪审查

香港特区法院的违宪审查权可以视为原有法律制度的保留。香港法院的违宪审查实践可以追溯到 1991 年。当时港英政府通过《人权法案条例》并将其地位抬高，规定其他违反该条例的香港立法无效。其结果就是在 1991~1997 年过渡时期，香港法院出现了几起违宪审查的先例。其中较为著名的有 1991 年 R V Sin Yau Ming 案、The Queen V Lum Wai-ming 案和 1994 年 R V Chan Chak Fan 案等。

2. 回归后的准违宪审查

回归后，香港法院仍然进行违宪审查，其中典型的个案包括吴嘉玲案（1999），污损国旗、区旗案（1999），庄丰源案（2001）和近期的梁国雄集会案（2005）、截取通讯命令案（2006）、刚果（金）案（2011）等。

特区法院是否拥有违宪审查权？目前主要有三种意见，第一种意见认为，全国人大常委会是基本法规定的解释机关，也是唯一的宪法监督机关，特区法院没有违宪审查权。第二种意见认为，基本法的体制是分权与制衡体制，特区法院在回归之后拥有终审权和基本法赋予的解释权，因此也拥有以往分别由英国枢密院和葡萄牙宪法法院行使的违宪审查权。第三种意见认为基本法所规定的是一种混合式的违宪审查机制，全国人大常委会和特区法院都有违宪审查权，但是两者的审查范围不同，全国人大常委会的审查具有主导性。笔者比较倾向于最后一种观点。

首先，从基本法本身来看，相关规定为违宪审查预留了空间。以香港《基本法》为例，第 8 条、第 17 条、第 19 条、第 39 条、第 158 条、第 160 条可视为特区违宪审查机制的依据。第 17 条规定了特区立法的备案发回制度，是全国人大常委会审查特区立法的合宪性基础；第 158 条规定特区法院可以对自治范围内的条款自行解释，这是主张特区法院拥有违宪审查权的重要依据。曾经有一种意见认为，《基本法》第 17 条和第 158 条应当理解为分权规定，全国人大常委会与香港法院分别审查不同事项，全国人大常委会不能审查自治范围内的立法，特区法院不能审查自治范围外的立法。不过，在香港终审法院明确承认全国人大常委会的最终解释权之后，讨论更多的是针对全国人大常委会与特区法院在行使违宪审查权之间的关系以及程序方面的问题。综上所述，特区的违宪审查权可以理解为双轨制，全国人大常委会和特区法院都有违宪审查权，其中立法审查属于主导性审查，全国人大常委会的审查是终局的审查。

第二，否定特区法院的违宪审查权在实践中难以推行，与《基本法》的规定也不完全一致。例如，按照香港特区《基本法》第 17 条，全国人大常委会发回的特区立法范围是：不符合基本法中关于中央管理的事务及中央和特区关系的条款。换言之，没有规定全国人大常委会有权发回特区自治范围内的条款。如果结合第 158 条与第 160 条，可以理解为特区立法中属于自治范围内的条款的合宪性由特区自己决定。这种分工论的理解符合基本法"高度自治"的精神，在实践中，特区法院当仁不让地承担了此项职责。

（二）澳门特区的地区性违宪审查

1. 回归前的准违宪审查

澳门特区法院的违宪审查权问题一直没有引起充分的关注，但是法院在回归前后，也曾经以相关立法不符合基本法为由拒绝适用。回归前，根据 1982 年《葡萄牙宪法》，法院可以在具体个案中审查规范的合宪性，并拒绝在个案中适用违宪的规范。例如，1993 年杨沃良案就是如此。

2. 回归后的准违宪审查

回归后，法院也曾经行使过类似的权力。例如，2004 年 2 月，澳门终审法院就一民事司法上诉作出判决，认为澳门《民法典》第 1 条第 3 款中关于赋予国际公约高于法律位阶效力的部分不具效力。因为《民法典》没有赋予国际协议等其他规范高于法律位阶的权能，只有基本法才有这种权能，应该适用《基本法》第 138 条中国际公约高于特区内部法律的规定。所以法院拒绝适用《民法典》的这一规定。从上述个案可见，在司法实践中，法院以个案审查的方式排除违宪（即违反基本法）的立法和法规已经是不争的事实。但是，法院的违宪审查权范围有多大以及法院应当如何行使违宪审查权仍然需要界定。

澳门不但存在司法实践，特区立法也对法院的规范审查权作出了专门规定。《行政诉讼法典》第 29 条第 1 款规定，即使行政行为的表现形式是法律或行政法规，也可以对其提起司法争诉，其价值是禁止逃避司法控制。该法第三章专章规定了规范异议程序，规定法院可以宣告违法的行政法规无效。不过，该法第 88 条也排除了适用规范异议程序的一些情况，包括："a）违反根本法律所载规范或从该法律所体现之原则之规范；b）违反由澳门以外有专属权限制定适用于澳门之立法文件或等同文件之机关所制定之该等立法文件或等同文件中所载规范之规范；c）违反经正式通过之与澳门以外地方订立之协议或协约所载规范之规范；d）违反以上各项所指规范或原则之由澳门以外之机关制定而适用于澳门之规范。"

既然《行政诉讼法典》限定了法院审查行政法规的范围，这是否意味着澳门的法院没有违宪审查权呢？对澳门行政法规的合宪性审查不通过诉讼法典进行规定是说得通的。因为违宪审查制度一般应当由宪法性法律进行规定。与香港类似，根据澳门《基本法》第145条、第143条与第17条，回归前全国人大常委会对全体原有法律进行审查，回归后全国人大常委会仅审查与中央政府有关的条款；自治范围内条款的审查必然涉及对《基本法》的解释，而此类条款的解释权由全国人大常委会授予了法院。

这样看来，如果不承认澳门法院的司法实践，澳门就会出现违宪审查的断层。考虑到澳门回归前的规定和实践，实际上就必须承认澳门法院可以行使如下违宪审查权：①基于对《基本法》条款的解释，宣告某一本地立法违反基本法并拒绝适用；②根据《行政诉讼法典》，审查行政法规的合宪性并予以撤销。前者与后者的区别在于前者名义上没有直接废止立法，而是停止适用，实质上也导致立法无效。

违宪审查的效果。从目前的实践来看，特区立法或其他规范被法院宣告违宪之后一般有如下后果：裁定无效并停止适用、限期停止适用、以及在个案中停止适用。

对中央和特区的审查范围界定存在分歧，未能创设有效的审查机制以适应基本法所赖以存在的中央地方框架。

综上所述，回归后特区的违宪审查机制应当理解为混合式违宪审查体制，全国人大常委会的立法审查和特区法院的司法审查并行不悖，发生冲突时以立法审查为准。在司法审查系统内部，以终审法院的审查为准。这一结论既源于《基本法》对解释权的规定，也取决于全国人大常委会与特区法院分别所代表的中央与地方的权力位阶。

四　准违宪审查的意义及展望

这些审查实践具有两方面的积极意义：一是积累了经验，为未来的违宪审查制度提供了基础。二是逐步确立了多层级的规范审查权，且基本符合中国的宪法原则（全国人大最高权保障）。作为准违宪审查，其问题也很明显：其一，审查对象的范围不够收敛，某些不成熟的案件或争议被纳入司法审查，导致法院被卷入政治争议或社会非议；其二，程序正当性及开放性不足，特别是法律法规清理过程不透明；其三，司法机构与民意机关之间的关系没有理顺。司法机构进行审查时过于强调司法机构在违宪审查中的作用，忽略立法机关和行政机构在宪法上的重要地位；而民意机构的审查由于其政治色彩而受到批评，两方面都导致特区各种权力关系紧张。

尽管如此，上述实践提高了社会对违宪审查的认识、激发了合宪性和宪法实施的讨论。此外，准违宪审查现象和中国社会和法治发展的进程是一致的：中国目前处在转型期，各种政府权力之间的关系仍然在调整期。随着法治政府观念不断深入人心，对政府的法律约束必然不断增强；与此同时，法律作为一种保护人权的机制，也逐渐冲击着法律工具主义观念。这些因素都是促成违宪审查机制发展的要素。当然，中国的国家主义理念根深蒂固。在从君主制转向共和民主制的过程中，君主主权逐渐由国家主权取代，但是集权思想却并没有真正受到冲击，只是改变了集中权力的归属。如何进一步划定国家和个人之间的界限，是有待反思的文化和学理问题。

从比较法的角度来看，一些国家和地区在正式承认违宪审查制度时，都试图从既有实践中发掘类似的制度。例如最早的美国"马伯里诉麦迪逊案"中，马歇尔大法官回顾了殖民地时期法院的司法审查权，从而为法院的违宪审查权提供了先例。英国加入《欧洲人权公约》之后，法院开始拥有类似违宪审查权的资格，实际上构成了对既有议会主权原则的挑战。而英国法院对此挑战的回应是在加入公约前，英国法院基于衡平法或普通法对议会立法的否定。

在此意义上，我们可以认为，中国目前的准违宪审查实践是严格违宪审查制度施行之前的状态，是一种"前违宪审查"状态。正如蝴蝶化蛹成蝶之前的状态一样，这个过程中的蝶蛹虽然不够美丽，却是化蝶的必经阶段。

Studies on Quasi-Constitutional Review in China

Cheng Jie

【**Abstract**】 This article is an empirical research on the current constitutional review system and other activities with the significance of constitutional review in China. The research is a response to two assertions：the first is that there is no practice of constitutional review in China; the second is that the criticism against the constitutional review system in China is groundless. This author of this article holds that, although a constitutional review system has already been provided for in the Chinese Constitution and laws, there is no constitutional review practice in the standard sense. On the other hand, there exist within the current institutional framework some legislative and judicial activities that meet with the logical criteria of constitutional review. Such practices, if give extended application, may over time provide practical and institutional bases for the establishment of a standard constitutional review system in the future. Therefore, the existing constitutional review activities in China can be defined as a kind of quasi-constitutional review, which can be gradually standardized through political and legal practice.

【**Key words**】 Constitutional Review, Quasi-constitutional Review, Constitution

论宪法审查中的合宪限定解释

翟国强*

【摘要】 通过嵌入例外规则或原则，运用合宪限定解释方法可以回避对法律法规作出违宪判断，从而避免造成政治秩序的紧张和法律体系的不安定。受正当性基础所限，在不同的宪法审查模式下这种法律解释方法也需要遵守一定的界限。中国的人民代表大会制度和司法制度同样可以提供合宪限定解释方法操作的制度空间，特别是在欠缺宪法审查实践经验的情况下，运用合宪限定解释的方法将宪法的价值秩序以水银泻地般的辐射渗透至整个法律体系，则可弥补现有制度的缺陷，实现合宪性控制的目的。

【关键词】 合宪限定解释　回避违宪判断　方法　界限

由于宪法案件本身的政治敏感性，在宪法审查程序中一旦做出违宪判断，对法律秩序的安定性，甚至于政治格局都会造成较大冲击，这也是为什么我国宪法审查制度仍然停留在法律文本层面上的主要原因。为了避免卷入政治纷争和影响既存法秩序的稳定，宪法审查机关面对宪法案件时往往首先考虑是否可以回避做出违宪的判断，以此避免导致不必要的紧张和冲突。毋庸置疑，如何回避违宪判断是需要特定的方法和技术的，其中合宪限定解释就是较为常见的一种回避违宪判断的方法。这种方法的核心是对有违宪争议的法律进行限定性的解释，使之在形式上符合宪法。通过运用这种解释技术，宪法审查机关对于一些有违宪嫌疑的法律可做出形式上合宪的判断，从而回避了违宪的判断。

这种方法一方面可以使得同为宪法之下国家机关的宪法审查机关和法律法规制定部门"化干戈为玉帛"，避免造成政治危机，同时也可以在通过

---

* 中国社会科学院法学研究所副研究员。

法律程序本身治愈有缺陷的法律，对基本权利进行切实有效的保障。在中国特色社会主义宪政体制下，承担法律法规制定功能的代议机关同时也是最高权力机关，在审查法律法规合宪性的过程中尤其需要对这种结合了政治智慧的法律技术予以高度重视。

一　概说

对于法律的合宪限定解释的方法从理论上进行系统抽象与归纳的代表学者是芦部信喜教授。根据他的归纳，合宪限定解释是指"通过对依字面意思解释有可能构成违宪的那种宽泛的法律条文含义加以限定，排除其构成违宪的可能性，从而对法令的效力加以救济的解释。"① 合宪限定解释是一种回避违宪判断的方法，对此时国康夫的定义可谓明了："如果法令的解释可有广义和狭义两种可能，如果采取广义解释则违反宪法或者违宪疑义较大，则采取狭义解释从而回避对法令本身的违宪判断。"②

作为一种回避违宪判断的方法，合宪限定解释与一般法学方法上的合宪解释具有极大的相关性。因此有必要对两者加以比较辨析。宪法审查中的法律法规是一种有待诠释的"宪法事实"，而非适用于案件的法律规范。因此与那种一般法律适用中以形成法律判断大前提为目的的法律解释大不相同，这种意义上的法律解释自然属于"作为宪法判断前提的法解释"。③因此，作为一种结果（即回避宪法判断）导向的法解释，宪法判断意义上的合宪限定解释自然不同于那种作为体系解释的一种特殊形态的合宪解释。比较而言，合宪解释的含义较"合宪限定解释"要略微广泛。

作为一般法学方法上体系解释的一种特殊形态，"合宪解释"的外延要大于合宪限定解释，合宪解释可以包含合宪限定解释，甚至回避宪法判断的法律解释也可以说是广义合宪解释的　种。根据阿部照哉教授的研究，合宪解释原则的具体含义是："法律的规定必须解释为与宪法的原则相一致，如果某一特定的法律存在复数解释的可能性，则必须选择与宪法相符

---

① 〔日〕芦部信喜：《宪法诉讼理论》，有斐阁，1973，第231页。

② 〔日〕时国康夫：《合宪解释的方法（上）》，《法学家》第326期。需要指出的是，虽然在"合宪解释"的论题之下，时国康夫主要讨论的仍是芦部信喜所指的那种"合宪限定解释"。

③ 时国康夫指出，法规在文理上存在广义和狭义两种解释的可能，如果采取狭义解释就无需对法规本身做出宪法判断，那么如果不确定采取何种解释也就无法确定是否要对法规进行宪法判断。因此理论上法解释是宪法判断的前提。参见〔日〕时国康夫《合宪解释的方法（上）》，《法学家》第326期。

合的解释。"① 由此可见，合宪解释其实不仅仅是一种回避宪法判断的方法，也可作为一种一般法学方法上的解释规则而存在。合宪解释规则可以分为如下三类②：①单纯的解释规则，即宪法相关规定应当在解释一般法律时直接发生一定影响；③ ②冲突规则，在多数可能的解释中选择与宪法相符合的解释；③保全规则，④ 即当法律有违宪疑虑而有数种解释可能，选择不违背宪法的解释。根据上述区分，所谓合宪限定解释是属于第三意义上的合宪解释，但是在现实的宪法判断中，合宪限定解释往往和第二种解释混合一起。其一般表现形态为："在不违背宪法的前提下，X 法第 x 条应当做如下解释……"（如，德国宪法法院判决 BVerfGE 49，148；50，115ff）"X 法第 x 条的含义与宪法第 y 条在下述条件下并不抵触……"（如，德国宪法法院判决 BVerfGE 69，57）

二　不同审查模式下的合宪限定解释方法比较

综观世界各国宪法审查的制度模式，大致可分为具体审查模式（如美国、日本）和抽象审查模式（如德国）。⑤ 在上述不同的模式下，宪法审查制度的功能定位不同，合宪限定解释的判例也略有不同，但是就其作为一种法律方法而言并无太大区别。

（一）具体审查模式

具体审查模式的典型代表可举推美国的司法审查制度，其合宪限定解释的方法也最有代表性，有关"合宪限定解释"的方法可以追溯至美国早期的宪法审查实践。早在 1884 年的 Grenada County Supervisors v. Brogden 案件中，美国最高法院就已经运用这种合宪限定解释方法。法院对这种方法做了如下阐释："解释法律应当尽可能与宪法一致，尽量运用法院的法律解释权，以此避免对法律作出违宪判断。如果州法有可能做出两种合理的解

---

① 〔日〕阿部照哉：《法律的合宪解释与其界限》，《法学论丛》90 卷 123 号，后收入其所著《基本人权的法理》（有斐阁，1976）。

② 此系瑞士学者 Campische 和 Muller 的分类，转自苏永钦：《合宪法律解释原则》，载《合宪性控制的理论与实践》，月旦出版公司，1999。

③ 有关的研究可参见张翔《两种宪法案件：从合宪性解释看宪法对司法的可能影响》，《中国法学》2008 年第 4 期。

④ 亦称"挽救规则"（saving rule），参见 William N. Eskridge, Jr. and Philip P. Frickey, "Quasi-Constitutional Law: Clear Statement Rules as Constitutional Lawmaking", 45 *Vand. L. Rev.* 599（1992）。

⑤ 有关的综述可参见胡锦光《中国宪法问题研究》，新华出版社，1998，第 196～198 页。

释，法院基于对州立法机关的尊重，应当推定州立法机关并未无视宪法，法院应当在不改变法条的合理含义的前提下，选择与宪法一致的解释。"①在 1936 年的 Ashwander 判例中，布兰代斯法官在补充意见中总结了最高法院以往的实践中回避宪法判断的所采纳的规则，美国宪法上称之为 "布兰代斯规则"。②布兰代斯规则共计七个规则，其中涉及合宪限定解释的规则是第七规则："法律的（合宪性）效力有争议时，即使该法律的合宪性已经有重大疑问，法院也必须首先确定是否可以适用回避宪法问题的法律解释。"③该规则其实包含了两种规则，除了此处所指 "合宪限定解释" 之外，尚包含 "回避宪法问题的解释规则"。④

继布兰代斯规则之后，当立法机关的法案产生违宪疑问时，最高法院首先确定是否可以采取合宪限定解释回避此种嫌疑。⑤法院一贯 "推定立法机关对于宪法价值的兼顾而不会通过违反宪法的法律，通过这种方式法院向立法机关表达了这种态度"。布兰代斯所确立的解释规则在后来的博格法院中期，经常被法官运用来回避违宪判断。法院通过这种方法绕开直接将法律宣告违宪的违宪判断，从而避免了直接和国会冲突。比如 NLRB v. Catholic Bishop of Chicago 案件，⑥法院首先分析指出第一修正案所蕴涵的价值，然后指出委员会是否行使权限将会引起严重的宪法疑义，为此第一修正案保障的权利有被侵犯的危险。如果对权限做广义解释则可能会侵害第一修正案保护的权利——宗教信仰自由，由此法院对法律规定的委员会的权限做出了限制解释。博格法院的其他判决也广泛采纳了合宪限定解释，在宗教自由、言论自由、正当程序和平等保护领域广泛采用。⑦时至今日，最高法院这种解释规则甚至被作为一种 "准宪法规则"（Quasi-Constitutional Law）⑧被法院系统遵守。这种最早产生于美国的合宪解释方法，后被世界

---

① Grenada County Supervisors v. Brogden, 112 U. S. 261 (1884).

② 参见芦部信喜《宪法诉讼理论》，第 231 页。

③ Ashwander et al. v. Tennessee valley authority et al., 297 U. S. 288 (1936).

④ 参见芦部信喜《宪法诉讼理论》，第 143～145 页。

⑤ Leading cases see Eastern R. R. Presidents Conference v. Noerr Motor Freight, Inc., 365 U. S. 127, 135 – 136 (1961); NLRB v. Fruit & Vegetable Packers, 377 U. S. 58, 63 (1964); Communications Workers of Am. v. Beck, 108 S. Ct. 2641 (1988).

⑥ NLRB v. Catholic Bishop of Chicago. 440 U. S. 490 (1979).

⑦ William N. Eskridge, Jr. and Philip P. Frickey, "Quasi-Constitutional Law: Clear Statement Rules as Constitutional Lawmaking", 45 *Vand. L. Rev.* 599 (1992).

⑧ William N. Eskridge, Jr. and Philip P. Frickey, "Quasi-Constitutional Law: Clear Statement Rules as Constitutional Lawmaking", 45 *Vand. L. Rev.* 599 (1992).

上许多国家所采纳，甚至直接在宪法条款中加以明确规定。①

深受美国宪法审查模式影响的日本司法机关，在宪法判决中同样较多地运用合宪限定解释方法，做出回避违宪判断的合宪判决。如早期的"交通事故的报告义务和沉默权"案件，最高法院对交通"事故内容"报告义务的规定加以限定解释，断定"并无违宪问题可言"。而类似案例还有都教组事件、② 泉佐野市民会馆案、③ 全遍东京中邮案件、④ 福冈青少年保护条例案件等。⑤

（二）抽象审查模式

虽然合宪限定解释方法在美国发展的较为成熟，但采纳这种方法并非具体审查模式所独有，比如德国的抽象宪法审查实践也广泛采纳这种方法，⑥ 而且在理论学说上也十分发达。德国联邦宪法法院在早期的判决中首先运用合宪限定解释回避违宪判断的案件是关于 1950 年的《难民收留法》的合宪性问题。该法第 1 条规定：由苏俄占领区逃难到联邦德国的人，需要向当地警察局申请居留证；如果能够证明逃离的理由是为避免生命及生活遭遇危难，则不得拒发居留证。诉愿人主张该规定违反基本法所保障的迁徙自由，但联邦宪法法院对此做出合宪判决，并指出：警察局即使按照难民法拒发居留证时，也应当符合基本法关于迁徙自由的规定。且在判决主文第 4 点明确指出："如果法律可能透过解释而符合宪法，且不失其本来意义时，则不构成违宪。"⑦ 此后联邦宪法法院在众多案件中大量采纳此种解释方法回避违宪判断："如果对于法规范的解释存在多种可能，即有违宪的解释，同时也有合宪的解释，那么必须优先采取符合基本法的解释。"⑧ 据联邦宪法法院的统计数字表明：1985 年 12 月 31 日之前，法院做出违宪判断的案件共计 199 件（联邦法 182 件，州法 21 件），但采纳合宪限定解释回

① 比如，南非 1993 年过渡宪法第 35 条第 2 款和第 232 条第 3 款规定：法律不应当因为其字面上可作违宪解释而违宪，此时如果可以合理做出符合宪法的解释，则对法律必须做出限定解释（restricted interpretation）。

② 日本最高法院大法庭 1969 年 4 月 2 日判决（刑集 23 卷 5 号，第 305 页）。

③ 日本最高裁判所平成 7 年 3 月 7 日第三小法庭判决。

④ 日本最高法院昭和 41 年（1967 年）10 月 26 日大法庭判决（刑集 20 卷 8 号，第 901 页）。

⑤ 日本最高裁判所大法庭昭和 60 年 10 月 23 日判决。

⑥ 其实德国的合宪解释方法也是受到美国判例的影响极大。参见〔日〕永田秀树《适用违宪的法理》，《法学家》1994 年第 1037 期。

⑦ BverfGE2，267.

⑧ BverfGE32，373.

避违宪判断共计 1080 件（其中联邦法 845 件，州法 235 件）。[1]

作为一种特殊的抽象审查模式，法国的宪法审查制度常常被视为宪法审查制度形态的另类，法国宪法委员会于 1959 年的判决中首次采用此方法（参见表 1），随后即经常采用，日益频繁。[2] 且时常明确附带表明"任何其他解释都将违反宪法"或"惟有采取此种解释，方才合宪"。（如判决第 181、207、215、217 号）

表 1　法国宪法委员会的合宪限定解释判决统计表

期间	判决总数	合宪限定解释判决的数目	所占判决总数比例（%）
1959 - 1974.10	9	1	11
1974.10 - 1981.5	47	7	14.5
1981.5 - 1986.3	66	13	19.5
1986.3 - 1987.3	16	5	56
1959 - 1987.3	138	30	21

资料来源：Louis Favoreu，*The Constitutional Council and Parliament in France*，*Constitutional Review and Legislation*：*An International Comparison*，Christine Landfried ed.，Nomos Verlagsgesellschaft Baden-Baden（1988），p. 101。

从法律方法论的角度看，合宪限定解释作为一种回避违宪判断的法律解释方法在两种不同模式下的操作基本相同。所不同的是，在两种模式下其解释的主体可能有所区别。合宪限定解释首先是作为回避违宪判断的方法而存在，因此宪法审查机构当然是合宪限定解释的主体。但除此之外，由于普通法院在解释法律时也需要与上位法保持一致，且合宪限定解释方法并不必然要求法官享有宪法审查权，一般法官同样可为合宪限定解释主体。[3] 在具体审查制度模式下，普通法院作为宪法审查主体自然可以作为合宪限定解释；而在德国抽象审查模式下，由专门宪法法院职司宪法判断，这种回避宪法判断的方法是否为普通法院采纳？在德国抽象审查模式下，当普通法院在审理一般案件时，发现法规确有违宪疑义，则可以申请宪法

---

[1]　Donald P. Kommers，*The Constitutional Jurisprudence of the Federal Republic of Germany*（Duke University Press，1989），p. 541.

[2]　参见欧洲宪法法院会议法国代表报告：《论宪法委员会之合宪审查权》，载《宪政时代》第 80 卷第 3 期；类似的研究也可参见〔日〕和田英夫《大陆型违宪审查制度（增补版）》，有斐阁，1994，第 408 页。

[3]　阿部照哉：《法律的合宪解释与其界限》。

法院审查。但是审查是否构成"确有违宪疑义"，是普通法院的权限范围之内。此时法院自然可以做出解释回避这种"违宪疑义"，而当案件提请宪法法院时，宪法法院亦可再就法律做出合宪限定解释，消除违宪疑虑。但问题是德国二元模式下，一般法院和宪法法院同样可以做出合宪限定解释，此时究竟由谁做出解释、解释时遵守何种界限仍是有待继续深入研究的课题。

三　合宪限定解释方法的逻辑结构

如前所述，合宪限定解释是一种通过限定性的解释来回避违宪判断的方法。作为一种特殊的法律解释方法，如果仅仅根据定义的笼统的表述，我们仍无法把握合宪限定解释方法的全貌。其实，逻辑上完整的合宪限定解释尚可包含以下步骤：①嵌入一个例外规则[①]：X 法第 x 条并非意味着……（去除违宪嫌疑的解释）；②对该法第 x 条应当做出如下解释：……;③因此，该法第 x 条与宪法第 y 条并不违背。但实践上出现的其他类型如下：仅由①、③组合而成，仅由②、③组合而成。[②] 合宪限定解释目的并非是确定作为审查对象的法规范的意义，其重心在为作为审查对象的法律规范"嵌入"一个例外规则从而回避违宪判断，[③] 至于确定法律本身的具体意义还有赖于一般法解释的方法的运用，因此很难称之为一种完整的法律解释。因为完整的法律解释尚且包括对多种合理解释做出选择。在一般法律适用时，当存在多种合理解释的情形下，据以做出选择的标准不

---

① 实践中也有嵌入例外原则的方法。比如，德国"谋杀罪无期徒刑合宪性"（BverfGE4，187）判决即是将比例原则直接嵌入限制规范中的判例。当事人认为判处死刑处罚过重，宪法法院通过对谋杀罪构成要件做合宪限定解释，回避违宪判断，判决指出："（对 221 条谋杀罪构成要件）绝对一概处以无期徒刑这样严格的刑罚，只有在如下情形下才不违宪，即当法律已经让法官能够将具体案件涵摄于抽象规范之下，而得出和宪法上比例原则相一致的刑罚时。如果能够考虑刑法总则的规定和对刑法第 221 条做出合宪解释，则可不产生宪法上的疑义。"根据上述构成要件的文意范围，应当做出更具限制性的解释，即是否"残暴"和"为掩饰另一犯罪行为"，应当解释如下：所谓残暴"需要由可责的信赖破坏"方才构成；"为掩饰另一犯罪行为"需要符合"谋杀行为已经事先计划"或寻求其他符合比例原则的解释方法。这种嵌入比例原则的方法固然可以回避违宪判断，然而这种嵌入本身使得法律规范仍然处于不确定状态，为此很难成为一种"解释"。

② 甚至可存在仅有第②步骤构成的解释，这种可谓是一种"隐蔽的合宪限定解释"。在那些宪法问题在司法程序之中仍十分敏感的时期（比如我国当下），这种解释可作为合宪限定解释的功能代替。

③ 宪法审查机关的合宪限定解释是一种否定性解释，由于仅仅嵌入例外规范，因此并未对普通法院的解释法律的权限构成侵犯。

仅仅包括宪法上的标准，还有其他标准，比如平常含义标准、融贯性标准、与特定法律原则一致的标准。[①] 而在宪法审查中，主要需考虑的是特定审查对象是否合宪，其争论焦点主要集中在宪法层次的论证。具体而言，假设 a、b、c、d 解释方法可得 4 种含义。如果 a、b、c 均符合宪法，唯 d 解释含义违反宪法。如何认定？只是排除 e 方案，还是选择最符合宪法的解释？此时应取决于判断者究竟采何种立场：合宪限定解释本身的积极立场和消极立场，如果强调宪法审查的规范控制功能，仅仅为了回避而回避，则仅仅排除 e 解释方案；如果试图通过解释积极进行合宪控制实现宪法价值，则尽量做出最符合宪法的详尽解释。

和嵌入例外规则类似，这种方法同样也可以嵌入例外原则而回避违宪判断。一般而言，法律原则是一种尽可能实现的指示规范，即所谓的最佳化或最大程度实现要求（optimization requirements）[②] 如果在不同于抽象审查的具体审查模式下这种嵌入一个例外原则的方法可能仍然无助于纠纷的彻底解决。然而如果在单纯的抽象审查程序中，该方法则既可回避直接改变法规范的内涵，同时也可避免直接和立法机关产生纠纷。可谓一种将宪法问题"留待未决"方法，法律原则的不确定性正好可以作为这种回避技术所用。[③]

与回避违宪判断的方法类似，通过限定性的法律解释同样可以直接回避合宪还是违宪的争议，从而达到回避违宪判断的目的。通过限定解释回避违宪判断的方法和通过限定解释回避宪法判断的方法在技术上并无区分，即都是通过嵌入例外规则的方法来回避特定的法律判断。其不同之处仅仅在于所嵌入例外规则不同：前者是嵌入不属于宪法判断范围的规则，如果采取 a 解释，则不涉及宪法问题，无需做出宪法判断，所以采取 a 解释。其通常表述为："如果采取……的解释，则并不涉及宪法上的争议而无需做出

---

① Lawrence M. Solan, "Private Language, Public Laws: The Central Role of Legislative Intent in Statutory Interpretation", 93 *Geo. L. J.* 427 (2005).

② Robert Alexy, *A Theory of Constitutional Right*, translated by Julian Rivers (Oxford University Press, 2002), p. 48.

③ 上述不同的方案选择其实也可佐证合宪限定解释作为一种方法并非仅仅一种宪法判断消极主义的技术，同样可能是宪法判断积极主义的一种手段。比如桑斯坦教授就曾明确指出："回避违宪判断的解释方法可能需要一个在法律解释问题上更加积极的司法角色，因为这需要将许多法律加以适度的'弯曲改变'（bending）。"同时也需要我们超越那种简单的划分积极或消极的价值立场，转向寻求宪法判断者本身的功能定位，参见 Cass R. Sunstein, "Interpreting Statutes in the Regulatory State", 103 *Harv. L. Rev.* 405 (1989)。

宪法判断。"后者是嵌入违宪解释的例外规则，即如果采取 a 种解释，则违宪，所以不得采取 a 解释方法。表述为："如果采取……的解释涵义，则并不违宪。"然而，上述两种回避方法虽然都是一种限定解释，然而其法律效果却不同。回避宪法判断则不会导致任何宪法判断，此时法律规范是否合宪仍不确定，只是回避做出是否违宪的判断而已。而回避违宪判断则会导致合宪判断，即"附条件通过"。

四　合宪限定解释方法的正当性

虽然合宪限定解释方法被各国宪法审查实践所广泛采纳，但对于合宪限定解释的正当性为何并未有一致看法。宪法学者博格斯（H. Bogs）认为合宪限定解释的正当性基础在于：[①] ①位阶较低的规范，应以位阶较高的规范为取向而解释：这是规范解释的通则，法律合宪解释也是基于同样道理。②法律受合宪有效推定：法律是代表民意的立法机关制定，应当予以尊重，为此需推定与基本法相符合。③法律体系的整体性要求。④不允许违宪的法律发现。然而也不乏有学者质疑其正当性依据，如贝特尔曼（Karl A. Bettermann）教授认为：①所谓位阶较低规范应当以位阶较高的规范为取向而解释，纯粹是为维护合宪限定解释的假定。②合宪限定解释是一种错误示范，根本不是做规范解释，而是变调的规范监督。将违宪的法律解释为合宪，名为忠于宪法，其实是放弃宪法审查的责任，而且如果直接宣告违宪，可能更是忠于宪法的表现。③合宪性解释为了避免宣告违宪，常常需要转换文本的原意，其用意是尊重代表国民意志的国会，其实是扭曲立法者的原意。④法律公布后充其量受到有效推定，决不至于受合宪推定，这项理由并不成立。[②] 与上述质疑相似，科勒（Kelley）教授也认为这种规则本身并不是对立法机关的尊重，反而更多是一种对立法权的"挤占"。[③]

在上述博格斯研究的基础之上，日本的阿部照哉教授在吸收了各方批评观点后指出合宪限定解释的正当性依据在于：遵循上位法解释的原则；合宪限定解释以合宪推定为基础；禁止违宪的法律发现原则以及基本法关

---

① H. Bogs, *Die Verfassungskonforme Auslegung von Gesetzen*, Heiddberger, Diss. 1966, S. 17 – 24, 转自吴庚《宪法的解释与适用》，三民书局，2004，第 590~591 页。

② Karl A. Bettermann, *Die verfassungskonforme Auslegung*, *Grenzen und Gefahren*, 1986, S. 191, 25. 转自吴庚《宪法的解释与适用》，三民书局，2004，第 590~591 页。

③ William K. Kelley, "Avoiding Constitutional Questions As A Three-Branch Problem", 86 *Cornell L. Rev.* 831（2001）.

于"宪法作为具有直接拘束力的法"。① 阿部照哉教授同时指出，合宪限定解释如果运用得当，则一方面可避免对法律做出违宪判断而对法律体系产生破坏性效果，从而维护法律安定性，另一方面可以实施宪法从而保障基本权利。② 由于基本权利的保障模式分为相对模式和绝对模式两种，而通过一般法律途径并非就不可进行充分保障，且通过不同位阶法律规范之间的"价值灌注"，同样可实现宪法价值，为此阿部照哉教授的观点可能较为妥当。

依照其宪法审查机关合宪限定解释空间的不同，各国合宪限定解释正当性也不同，正当性较无争议的是法国。在法国抽象审查模式下，宪法委员会积极分担着立法功能，为此其合宪限定解释正当性直接来自于宪法所设定的权限分配，因此宪法审查机关可进行较为积极的合宪限定解释。比如宪法委员会经常进行一种所谓的"取代性合宪解释"，即直接以新的法律规范代替违宪的法律规范。③ 而根据德国宪法法院的合宪解释原则，当立法者追求的主观立法目的已构成违宪时，为尽可能维持法律规范的效力，联邦宪法法院可以通过另一个立法目的来取代立法者的主观目的。当然这样一个"目的转化"（Zweckaustausch），只有当新的立法目的仍然在法律文意可能性的范围之内，而且在新的目的之下法律整体仍然构成一个合理之规定时才有可能。④ 由于采纳普通司法机关进行宪法审查的具体审查模式，较之于法国和德国的合宪限定解释方法，美国和日本的合宪限定解释正当性容易受到质疑，因为作为一般司法机关的法院对于法律解释必须遵守"适用法律"的界限，如果试图改变法律则可能欠缺其正当性，而宪法审查机关所采纳的合宪限定解释方法也较为消极，不得逾越法律目的的界限。

五　合宪限定解释方法的界限

在不同制度模式下，合宪限定解释方法的正当性依据来自于宪法审查机关的功能分配，作为一种已经被各国宪法审查机关所广为接受的解释方

---

① 阿部照哉：《法律的合宪解释与其界限》。

② 阿部照哉：《法律的合宪解释与其界限》。

③ Louis Favoreu, *The Constitutional Council and Parliament in France*, *Constitutional Review and Legislation*: *An International Comparison*, Christine Landfried, ed., Nomos Verlagsgesellschaft Baden-Baden (1988), p. 101.

④ Blackmann, Staatsrecht II, Allgemeine Grundrechtslehren, 1985, s. 289f. 转自盛子龙《比例原则作为规范违宪审查之准则：西德联邦宪法法院判决及学说研究》，台湾大学法律学研究所 1986 年硕士论文，第 38 页。

法，学说上对其正当性的争论其实可以转化为合宪限定解释方法本身应当遵守何种界限的问题。

（一）形式界限：文意的射程范围

合宪限定解释不得变更法律的实质含义，否则有侵犯立法权的嫌疑，因此法律本身的文意是合宪限定解释界限之所在。[①] 一般而言，任何法律解释自文本开始，基于对法文本（text）与法规范（norm）的区分，任何法律解释过程可以分解如下：法律文本的语义性探究和规范性探究。语义性探究是仅仅翻译文本的含义，而规范性探究是指通过具体化的过程，明确化法文本所蕴涵的规范命题。由此解释可以说从文本表述的语句开始，故在起点即已受制于文意。合宪限定解释一旦超出文意范围进行法律续造，则可谓是一种合宪性造法，这种做法也被一些国家宪法审查机关所采纳作为代位立法的一种方法（参见表2）。当然上述区分也不可以绝对化，因为二者也可以看作是连续思维的步骤，恰如拉伦茨所指出，"法律解释与法官的法的续造并非本质截然不同之事，毋宁应视其为同一思考过程的不同阶段。"[②]

表 2　合宪限定解释和合宪性造法的区别（来源：自制）

特征比较 ＼ 类别	合宪限定解释	合宪性造法
范围	文意可能含义范围	超出文意含义范围
效果	不产生新的法律规范	产生新的法律规范
立场	消极主义	积极主义
主体	一般宪法审查机关	强势审查机关

当通过各种可能的解释方法得出最终规范命题（当法律解释到达终点时）以语言形式表述之时，仍需对照反观法律文本本身的可能含义。故此，法律解释自文意开始，同时由文意终。[③] 因此，文意射程范围毋宁是划定了任何法律解释的外围界限，故此，任何解释方法所得出的结论都不可逾越文意的可能意义。如果逾越此种界限则可能有造法（改法）之嫌，而这里

①　BVerfGE 49, 148（157）；69, 1（55）；BverfGE 18, 97（111）.

②　〔德〕卡尔·拉伦茨：《法学方法论》，陈爱娥译，商务印书馆，2003，第246页。

③　William N. Eskridge, Jr., *Dynamic Statutory Interpretation*（Harvard University Press, 1994），p. 54.

的法律方法问题的实质是解释者本身的功能界限问题。对此拉伦茨指出："如果合宪性解释要维持其解释的性格，他就不可以逾越法律字义及其意义脉络所划定的界限。"[①] 如德国联邦宪法法院的实践即是谨守这种文意设定的界限。1958 年 6 月 11 日"退休金"案件判决[②]中法院在判决中指出：

> （1）法官对于一个文字及意义都十分清晰的法律，不得借合宪释方 z 式做出相反意义的解释。（2）依该法已然清晰的内容与目的，对于特定范围的退休公务员明确不予支付退休金而有违宪法平等权嫌疑时，法院不得借合宪解释，将此类公务员纳入可以支付的范围之内。（3）如果立法者偏惠某些类型的公务员而导致违反平等权时，联邦宪法法院应当宣告这些规定违宪。

该案所确定的界限被联邦宪法法院在其后的判决中广为引用，且获得学界广泛认同与肯定而成为经典判例。经由德国宪法学者阐述合宪限定解释的界限遂被框定如下：①语义明确时不得变更原意。②符合宪法的法律解释不得过度偏袒立法者，否则有违司法中立性，且破坏宪法审查制度本身。③合宪限定解释不得超越"立法者原来的判断范围"而填补法律漏洞。[③]

美国亦然，当法律文本本身明确无疑义或者不存在实质的宪法问题的场合，法院即回避采取这种合宪限定解释方法，比如 Beal v. Doe 案，[④] 法院只是阐明了《社会保障法》第 19 条的含义："州无需对贫穷者堕胎提供资助，只是重申了法律本身的明白的含义，而将可能的违宪疑义最小化。"但是美国最高法院时而基于积极的参与政策形成的取向，时常超越这种界限，对此斯卡丽亚和托马斯法官批判道："法院时而过度扭曲法律文意使其避免于违宪嫌疑，此时是改写法律而非改正其误。"[⑤] 美国法院其后的判决中，对于那些需要判断违宪的法律，如果立法本身含义

---

① 〔德〕卡尔·拉伦茨：《法学方法论》，第 217 页。
② 该案涉及 1951 年的工资法对于特定范围的退休公务员的工资的规定是否违反宪法保障的平等权，参见 BVerfGE8，28，34。
③ Erhard Denninger, "Judicial Review Revisited: The German Experience", 59 *Tul. L. Rev.* 1013 (1985).
④ Beal v. Doe, 432 U. S. 438 (1977).
⑤ X Citcment Video, 115 S. Ct. at 473 (Scalia, J., dissenting).

十分明确，则"该出手时就出手"，放弃采纳合宪限定解释方法，而是直接判断违宪。

但此处所谓"文本的可能的含义"时究竟是应以法律制定时的含义，抑或是解释者当下的意义呢？一般认为，若是涉及法律术语而且立法者显然是以制定时的意义来运用，就应以立法当时的意义作为出发点；如果立法者并未明确赋予该用语特定的意义，应以当下可能的意义作为解释的界限。① 因为，作为当下适用的法律规范，必须照顾到当事人的可预期性和法规范本身的适应性。

（二）宪法审查机关的功能界限

依一般的国家权力分工原则（功能分配），国家机关之间应彼此互相尊重，宪法审查机关仅在不侵犯立法机关权限的大前提下，才有采纳这种方法的可能。否则如果过度解释则可能会产生"代位立法"的效果，从而与合宪限定解释尊重立法机关的初衷相违背，因此合宪限定解释不得变更法律的主要目的和内容。合宪限定解释都必须遵循一般法律解释的规则和标准（包括尊重立法目的）。如果对法律做出合宪限定有违立法目的，法院就不能对法律进行合宪限定解释。然而，如果可以对法律做出多种解释，其中一种解释包括了违宪适用情形，那么法院能否排除此种解释，而认为合宪适用部分仍然有效呢？这就取决于法律的违宪部分与合宪部分是否具有可分性，也就是探究立法目的是否允许法律的合宪适用部分继续有效。

基于功能分配的不同，宪法审查机关需要避免以合宪限定解释的面具来伪装立法的政策形成而导致代位立法。如果越界过度，则可能违背了透过合宪限定解释回避违宪判断所表达的对立法机关尊重的初衷。此界限已经被各国广为接受，如德国联邦宪法法院的判决指出："合宪解释不得赋予——定义及意义上明确的——法律相反的意义、彻底重新规定其规范内容，乃至偏离立法者的主要目的。"②

需要特别交代的是，那些特定的法律制定主体与宪法审查机关有着明显功能分界的情境下，更需谨慎做出特定界限。比如美国的联邦法院对于各州的立法机关制定的法律法规不得适用合宪限定解释方法。③ 由于采取联邦制下联邦和州的权力分配不同，对于州立法机关的法律的合宪限定解释

---

① 〔德〕卡尔·拉伦茨：《法学方法论》，第228页。
② BVerfGE8，S34；BVerfGE54，S299.
③ 〔日〕时国康夫：《合宪解释的方法（上）》。

必须由州法院进行，^① 这里其实又涉及的是中央与地方的纵向分权和横向分权的交叉问题。解释州的法律是州法院的权力，州法院对于州法的解释可能约束联邦法院。州法院没有解释时，最高法院只能任其处于不确定状态。^② 其实这种问题并非美国独有，德国联邦宪法法院与州宪法法院也存在这个问题。另外，在普通法院和专门的宪法法院各司其职（比如德国模式下宪法法院与行政法院的分工）的制度模式下，其分工大致可确定为：宪法法院适用宪法做出判断，而由普通法院解释一般法律。而在宪法诉愿审查中，如果合宪限定解释过度则可能会代替一般司法机关的审判功能。所以德国宪法法院谨慎地区分宪法解释问题与法律解释问题，尽可能避免成为一个超级上诉法院（super-court of appeals），一再强调其作为宪法守护者的特殊法院地位，为此在实践中出现了所谓"赫克公式"等界限规则。^③

（三）解释学循环意义上的界限

合宪限定解释是趋向于宪法的解释，是根据宪法对法律做出解释，但问题是此处所据宪法规范的具体含义是什么？合宪限定解释是否需要首先解释宪法呢？其实合宪限定解释即使可以回避对宪法的明确界定，也无法回避对宪法的"理解"。因为涉及在二者之间的解释循环，为此，如果偏离重心所在，则可能会导致那种所谓的"符合法律的宪法解释"。在苏永钦教授看来，这种在实践中无法避免的宪法解释也有一定积极意义。^④ 但这种"符合法律的宪法解释"受到了吴庚教授的批判，他认为：

> 法律跟随宪法（Gesetz Nach Verfassung）才是常态，宪法跟随法律（Verfassung nach Gestz）毕竟是例外情形，尤其是宪法有关基本权利的规定，这时的宪法是实体权利的规范，正是用来评价相关法律是否已经建立合理的保障范围，是否已经使国家克尽其保障义务，不可认为

---

① Parson v. Bedford, 28 U. S. 433（1830）.

② Note, The Supreme Court Interpretation of Statutes to Avoid Constitutional Dicisions, 53, *Columbia L. Rev.* 633（1953）.

③ "赫克公式"是赫克法官在宪法判决中确定的原则。即，一般法律程序是否合法、事实的查明以及认定、普通法律的解释和适用都属于一般法院审判的任务，只有当"特别宪法"受到法院判决侵犯时，宪法法院方才作出宪法判断。Wolfgang Zeidler, "The Federal Constitutional Court of The Federal Republic of Germany", 62 *Notre Dame L. Rev.* 504（1987）.

④ 参见苏永钦《合宪法律解释原则》，载《合宪性控制的理论与实践》，月旦出版公司，1999。

法律规定的内容，当然就是宪法的本意。①

如果仅仅基于宪法审查控制规范的视角，吴庚教授的批判不无道理。但是如果将宪法随社会变迁的适应性考虑进来，这种符合法律的宪法解释在特定社会背景下可能也有一定的积极意义。通过宪法规范和与社会事实更接近的法律规范之间的解释循环，可以将宪法的变动置于法律体系之内进行，为此一方面可以回应社会的变动，同时又兼顾宪法规范的事实关联性造就一种动态的宪法秩序。

合宪的法律解释与合法的宪法解释由于同样涉及在宪法与法律之间的解释循环，因此在二者之间很难划定严格界限。而在宪法审查制度下，特别需要警惕的反而是那种以"合宪法律解释"之名，而行合法宪法解释之实的回避违宪判断方法。因为这种方法潜含的危险在于：如果任由宪法审查机关对宪法规范进行"揉捏塑造"可能会导致"宪法审查机关的专制"。

六　结语

作为一种回避违宪判断的方法，合宪限定解释方法在那些已有成熟的宪法审查制度作为依托的国家广为采纳。就我国当下而言，有实效性保障的宪法审查制度尚未建立，为此那种严格意义上的合宪限定解释方法可能并没有适用的制度前提。如果就一般法律适用过程中的合宪限定解释方法而言，在我国并不欠缺这种方法操作的制度空间。然而这样一种回避违宪判断的限定解释方法并未引起法律界的重视。最高人民法院关于受教育权的司法解释②和发生在洛阳的李慧娟事件说明我国的司法机关欠缺回避违宪争议的意识和方法，因此在我国人民代表大会制度背景下，合宪限定解释方法对司法机关具有举足轻重的意义。

然而在当下中国，无论是政治制度的现状还是司法的实践经验都还没有达到让法院可以做出宪法判断甚至是有关"宪法"的判断。考虑到当下中国的主流意识形态以及现有的价值权威分配格局，由法院进行宪法审查的设想是不切合实际的。为此，暂时以法律解释的方法将违宪嫌疑的宪法问题转化为一般法律解释适用问题或许是一种可行的途径。

---

① 　吴庚:《宪法的解释与适用》，三民书局，2004，第597~598页。
② 　2008年12月18日，最高人民法院发布公告废止《关于以侵犯姓名权的手段侵犯宪法保护的公民受教育的基本权利是否应承担民事责任的批复》（法释〔2001〕25号）。

　　在中国特色的社会主义宪法体制下，全国人民代表大会有"监督宪法的实施"的职权，全国人大常委会有"解释宪法，监督宪法的实施"的职权。从宪法本身的规定看，全国人民代表大会以及其常务委员会并不仅仅是立法机关，根据《宪法》第 67 条和《立法法》第 88 条的规定，权力机关也承担着对法律法规进行合宪性审查的职权。不仅如此，全国人大还有对一般法律进行解释的职权，而且实践中也不乏作出法律解释的事例。这种法律法规审查权和法律解释权的结合正好可以为合宪限定解释提供制度上的依托，通过法律解释来弥补法律文本的宪法缺陷，既可以消除法律法规违宪带来的国家行为正当性不足，同时也可以保证权力机关决定的连贯性和一致性。如果将这种方法运用在对国务院和地方人大制定法规的书面审查意见中，则可在消除法律法规违宪性的同时，避免直接将法律法规做出违宪认定造成与其他国家机关的紧张和对立。毋庸讳言，滥用这种解释方法也可能会"架空"宪法规范，使得宪法规范徒有虚名。但是在没有实效性保障宪法审查制度的情况下，这种解释方法毕竟也可有效地化解规范冲突问题。特别是，在法律实施过程中运用合宪限定解释的方法将宪法的价值秩序以水银泻地般的辐射渗透至整个法律体系，同样也可实现部分合宪性控制的功能，这个过程同时也构成了法体系的自我反思、自我创新的重要环节。

Constitutionality Restrictive Interpretation
in Constitutional Review

Zhai Guoqiang

【 **Abstract** 】 Constitutional limited interpretation can avoid unconstitutional decision by embedding an escape rule or principle in a legal norm, thereby preventing the tension in the political order and instability of the legal system. Limited by the basis of legitimacy, this method of legal interpretation must also be kept within certain boundaries under different models of constitutional review. Under the Chinese Constitution, the National People's Congress system and the judicial system can also provide some institutional space for the operation of this method. Especially under the current situation of absence of practical experience in effective constitutional review, this method can enable constitutional values to permeate the entire legal system through the radiation of the legal norm.

【**Key words**】Constitutional Limited Interpretation, Avoiding Unconstitutional Decision, Method, Limitation

法律体系中的合宪性审查机制

刘小妹[*]

【摘要】 建立有效的合宪性审查机制是保障法制统一的关键所在。基于现行的国家制度与法制传统，我国的合宪性审查采行的是复合式审查模式，即根据法律规范的效力等级不同，对法律、法规、规章分别采取不同的审查模式。本文对法律、行政法规、地方性法规、规章的合宪性审查机制进行了梳理和分析，提出了完善合宪性审查机制的具体建议。

【关键词】 法律体系　合宪性　合法性

2011 年 3 月 10 日，全国人大常委会委员长吴邦国在向十一届全国人大四次会议作的工作报告中宣布："一个立足中国国情和实际、适应改革开放和社会主义现代化建设需要、集中体现党和人民意志的，以宪法为统帅、以宪法相关法、民法商法等多个法律部门的法律为主干，由法律、行政法规、地方性法规等多个层次的法律规范构成的中国特色社会主义法律体系已经形成。"因此，在我国的法律体系中，第一是要维护宪法的统帅地位，即宪法具有最高的法律效力，是制定其他法律规范的基础和依据，一切法律、行政法规和地方性法规都不得同宪法相抵触。第二，这里的法律体系不是一个相互对等的、如同在同一平面上并立的诸规范的体系，而是一个不同级的诸规范的等级体系。这些规范的统一体是由这样的事实构成的：一个规范（低级规范）的创造为另一个规范（高级规范）所决定，后者的创造又为一个更高的规范所决定，而这一"回归"以一个最高的规范即基础规范为终点，这一规范，作为整个法律秩序的效力的最高理由，就构成

＊　中国社会科学院国际法研究所副研究员。本文系国家社会科学基金项目"社区公民参与机制及其法治保障研究（10CFX015）"的部分研究成果。

了这一法律秩序的统一体。① 第三，在法律体系中，法律规范之间的冲突是一种普遍存在的、不可避免的法律现象，而建立有效的合宪性审查机制是保障法制统一的关键所在。

根据审查主体的不同，现代世界各国的合宪性审查体制大体可分为司法机关审查、立法机关审查和专门机关审查三种模式。从审查的手段上说，合宪性审查分为事先审查和事后审查两种方式，即法律法规颁布生效之前所进行的合宪性审查和颁布实施之后进行的合宪性审查。基于我国现行的国家制度与法制传统，一方面合宪性审查注重事前审查与事后审查的结合，另一方面合宪性审查不是简单地适用某种单一的审查模式，而是复合式审查模式，即根据法律规范的效力等级不同，对法律、法规、规章分别采取不同的审查模式。

一　法律的合宪性审查

宪法的效力高于法律，因此法律与宪法不一致或抵触时应该接受合宪性审查在理论上和逻辑上是毫无疑义的，问题的关键在于合宪性判断的主体是谁，以及合宪性审查的实际运行机制如何。

（一）　法律的合宪性审查主体

我国的政体是人民代表大会制度，即国家的一切权力属于人民，人民在民主普选的基础上选派代表，组成全国人民代表大会和地方各级人民代表大会作为行使国家权力的机关，其他国家机关由人民代表大会产生，对它负责，受它监督，人大常委会向本级人民代表大会负责，人民代表大会对人民负责，受人民监督的基本政治制度。具体而言，《宪法》第 3 条第 3 款和第 128 条以前后呼应的方式规定"审判机关是由人民代表大会产生，对它负责，受它监督"；第 126 条又规定"人民法院依照法律规定独立行使审判权，不受行政机关、社会团体和个人的干涉"。可见，在人民代表大会制度下，全国人民代表大会与最高人民法院之间是前者监督后者，后者向前者负责的关系，因此最高人民法院绝无权力审查和监督全国人大及其常委会的立法权，法律的合宪性不属于司法审查的范围。

既然根据现行宪法中宪法解释权、宪法监督权、立法权和司法权的权力划分与权力结构关系，法院的司法审判权不能直接涉及法律与宪法的冲

① 参见〔奥〕凯尔森《法与国家的一般理论》，沈宗灵译，中国大百科全书出版社，1996，第 141 页。

突问题，那么合宪性审查的主体只能是全国人大及其常委会自身。

（二）法律合宪性审查运行机制

根据《宪法》第 62 条第（三）项、第 67 条第（二）项的规定，我国的法律分为由全国人大制定的基本法律和全国人大常委会制定的一般法律。无论是现行宪法还是《立法法》，都没有就全国人民代表大会制定的基本法律的合宪性审查问题作出规定。由此，涉及国家基本制度和公民基本权利的基本法律如果违宪了，只能由全国人大进行"自我监督"，换言之，全国人民代表大会制定的法律的合宪性问题游离于已有的法制规范之外，不受任何外在的监督与审查。[①] 而从现实的层面来看，全国人民代表大会曾在通过《中华人民共和国香港特别行政区基本法》和《中华人民共和国澳门特别行政区基本法》的同时，分别以决定的形式宣布这两个基本法符合宪法。[②] 全国人民代表大会的上述两个决定解释了宪法，对法律的合宪性进行了审查，因此有学者认为这两个决定以宪法惯例的形式解决了全国人民代表大会的立法有没有可能违宪，要不要接受合宪性审查，以及由哪个机构进行审查的问题。[③]

对于全国人大常委会制定的一般法律，虽然从《宪法》第 62 条第（十一）项、《立法法》第 88 条第（一）项的规定来看，全国人民代表大会有权改变或者撤销它的常务委员会制定的不适当的法律，但是迄今为止，一方面全国人大从未因为其常委会制定的一般法律违反宪法而予以改变或者撤销。也就是说，全国人大对其常委会立法的主动审查机制虽有规范依据，却无实际案例。宝剑从未出鞘，保有的仅是一种威慑和可能性。另一方面，除却全国人大的主动审查外，根据《立法法》第 90 条的规定，其他主体，即国务院、中央军事委员会、最高人民法院、最高人民检察院和各省、自治区、直辖市的人民代表大会常务委员、其他国家机关和社会团体、企业事业组织以及公民启动合宪性审查的对象仅为行政法规、地方性法规、自

---

① 胡建淼、高春燕：《法规的合宪性审查在中国——问题与对策》，《法治论丛》2005 年第 6 期。

② 1990 年 4 月 4 日，第七届全国人民代表大会通过了全国人民代表大会《关于〈中华人民共和国香港特别行政区基本法〉的决定》。该决定规定：香港特别行政区基本法是根据《中华人民共和国宪法》按照香港的具体情况制定的，是符合宪法的。1993 年 3 月 31 日，第八届全国人民代表大会通过了《全国人民代表大会关于〈中华人民共和国澳门特别行政区基本法〉的决定》。该决定规定：澳门特别行政区基本法是根据《中华人民共和国宪法》按照澳门的具体情况制定的，是符合宪法的。

③ 参见王振民《中国违宪审查制度》，中国政法大学出版社，2004，第 109～111 页。

治条例和单行条例,不包括法律。综上,对全国人大常委会制定的法律的合宪性审查只能由全国人大主动为之,不能由其他主体启动被动审查机制,而在现实层面,全国人大从未因合宪性问题改变或者撤销全国人大常委会制定的法律。

(三) 完善法律合宪性审查机制的建议

人民代表大会制度不仅是我国政权建设的经验总结,更是现行宪法规定的国家根本政治制度。在人民代表大会制度下,对于法院和法官而言,宪法和法律都具有至上性,其合宪性审查不属于司法的职权范围,而只能由全国人大自行监督和审查。在这样的制度前提下,针对全国人大制定的基本法律的合宪性审查没有宪法依据,全国人大常委会制定的一般法律的合宪性审查形同虚设,以及法律合宪性审查机制难于启动的问题,笔者提出如下两条建议:

第一,在全国人大成立一个独立的专门的宪法委员会,专司合宪性审查之职,既可主动审查,亦可依其他主体的要求或建议进行被动审查。需要说明的是,该专门委员会不同于此前全国人大常委会法律工作委员会下设的法规审查备案室。2004年5月全国人大法工委法规审查备案室的新张,曾激起了社会和学界对启动违宪审查机制的无限热情与殷切期待,然而作为法工委下设的一个工作机构,法规审查备案室一方面不具有足够的独立性,另一方面其审查范围仅限于法规,无涉法律,因此它无力担当违宪审查机制的龙头。而宪法委员会应该是一个相对独立的、专门的权力机构,其审查范围包括法律和法规,它既可以主动审查,亦可依其他主体的要求和建议启动被动审查。基于此,笔者进而建议:

第二,修改《立法法》第90条,将其他主体提请合宪性审查的范围扩展至法律,以建立法律合宪性审查的启动机制。此外,还应制定宪法委员会的工作机制和工作程序,以保障其他主体的合宪性审查要求或建议得到相应的答复和处理。

二 法规的合宪性与合法性审查

根据《宪法》和《立法法》的规定,宪法具有最高的法律效力,法律的效力高于行政法规和地方性法规,行政法规的效力高于地方性法规的效力。在这样的规范效力等级体系中,法规要同时接受合宪性与合法性审查。

(一) 法规合宪性与合法性审查主体

《宪法》第67条第(七)、(八)项分别规定,全国人民代表大会常务委员会有权撤销国务院制定的同宪法、法律相抵触的行政法规；有权撤销省、自治区、直辖市国家权力机关制定的同宪法、法律和行政法规相抵触的地方性法规。《立法法》第88条第（二）、（四）项规定，全国人民代表大会常务委员会有权撤销同宪法和法律相抵触的行政法规，有权撤销同宪法、法律和行政法规相抵触的地方性法规；省、自治区、直辖市的人民代表大会有权改变或者撤销它的常务委员会制定的和批准的不适当的地方性法规。

可见，法规分为行政法规和地方性法规，其审查主体和审查范围各不相同。第一，行政法规由全国人大常委会审查，包括对合宪性的审查（撤销同宪法相抵触的行政法规）与合法性的审查（撤销同法律相抵触的行政法规）；第二，省、自治区、直辖市人大制定的地方性法规由全国人大常委会审查，包括合宪性的审查（撤销同宪法相抵触的地方性法规）、合法性的审查（撤销同法律相抵触的地方性法规）以及对是否与行政法规相抵触的审查；第三，省、自治区、直辖市人大常委会制定的地方性法规由全国人大常委会和省、自治区、直辖市人大审查，前者的审查范围为是否同宪法、法律和行政法规相抵触，后者的审查范围为是否适当。

（二）法规合宪性与合法性审查运行机制

在如上三种类型中，本部分主要考察和分析行政法规、地方性法规的合宪性审查与合法性审查在现实层面的两种运行机制。

第一种是人大常委会的主动审查机制，即备案审查机制。根据《宪法》和《立法法》的规定，行政法规应当报全国人大常委会备案；地方性法规应当报全国人大常委会和国务院备案。备案有两种意义：一是形式上的意义，接收备案的主体需要掌握和了解国家行政机关、地方立法机关制定了哪些法规；二是实质意义，即接收备案的主体要对这些法规进行审查，审查主要包括两个方面：合法和合宪。备案审查的具体做法是：法规报全国人大常委会备案后，由办公厅秘书局分送法工委下属的专门委员会进行审查。专门委员会提出审查意见后，转送有关地方人大办理。然而这种备案审查收效甚微。据宪法学者蔡定剑统计，八届全国人大对备案法规审查了3100多件，全国共发现90多件有抵触的法规，都反馈给了地方人大。但全国人大只收到8件反馈意见；最终只有1件按全国人大内务司法委员会的意见纠正了。[1] 因此在九届全国人大期间，对备案法规事先审查这一多劳少功

---

① 《全国人大法规审查备案室新张　违宪审查还在远处》，《新闻周刊》2004年第23期。

的工作被取消了，取而代之的是 2000 年《立法法》设定的被动审查原则。

在被动审查于实际操作中遭遇尴尬后，被动审查与主动审查相结合，成为新的选择。2003 年 8 月，十届全国人大第八次委员长会议上修订的《行政法规、地方性法规、自治条例和单行条例、经济特区法规备案审查工作程序》再次确立了主动审查程序："专门委员会对备案的法规认为需要审查的，可以提出书面的报告，经常委会办公厅、法工委研究，报秘书长同意后，进行审查。"这一程序还规定，法律委员会和有关专门委员会审查认为法规同宪法或者法律相抵触而制定机关不予修改的，可向委员长会议提出书面审查意见和予以撤销的议案，由委员长会议决定是否提请常委会会议审议决定。为此，2004 年 5 月，全国人大常委会法律工作委员会新设立了法规审查备案室，专门对法规的合宪性与合法性进行主动审查，但是迄今仍未见一个法规因经审查后被认为与宪法、法律相抵触而予以撤销。

第二种是人大常委会的被动审查机制。即《立法法》第 90 条规定的两种情况：一是，国务院、中央军事委员会、最高人民法院、最高人民检察院和各省、自治区、直辖市的人民代表大会常务委员会认为行政法规、地方性法规同宪法或者法律相抵触的，可以向全国人大常委会书面提出审查要求；二是，其他国家机关和社会团体、企业事业组织以及公民认为行政法规、地方性法规同宪法或者法律相抵触的，可以向全国人大常委会书面提出审查建议。实践中，《立法法》实施以来，全国人大常委会一直没有收到国务院、中央军委、最高人民法院、最高人民检察院和各省人大常委会对哪一件法规提出进行"审查的要求"，只收到一些企事业单位和个人提出的对某些法规进行"审查的建议"，[①] 其中以《城市流浪乞讨人员收容遣送办法》（以下简称《收容遣送办法》）和《城市房屋拆迁管理条例》的废止为影响之最。

震惊全国的孙志刚案催生了民众民权意识的觉醒和对收容审查制度的反思。2003 年 5 月，俞江、腾彪、许志永以《立法法》的规定为依据，向全国人大常委会提出了"审查《城市流浪乞讨人员收容遣送办法》是否属于《中华人民共和国立法法》第 87 条第 1 款规定的'超越权限的'和第 2 款规定的'下位法违反上位法的'行政法规"的建议。

收容遣送是限制公民人身自由的一项行政强制措施。《宪法》第 37 条

---

① 全国人大常委会副秘书长刘镇在一次法制讲座上的讲话。转引自《全国人大法规审查备案室新张 违宪审查还在远处》，《新闻周刊》2004 年第 23 期。

规定：中华人民共和国公民的人身自由不受侵犯。任何公民，非经人民检察院批准或者决定或者人民法院决定，并由公安机关执行，不受逮捕。禁止非法拘禁和以其他方法非法剥夺或者限制公民的人身自由，禁止非法搜查公民的身体。《行政处罚法》第9条规定：限制人身自由的行政处罚，只能由法律设定。《立法法》第8条和第9条规定：对公民政治权利的剥夺、限制人身自由的强制措施和处罚，只能制定法律。可见，收容审查作为限制人身自由的行政强制措施只能由全国人大及其常委会制定的法律予以规定。因此，作为行政法规的国务院《收容遣送办法》规定了只能由法律规定的强制措施，即属于"超越权限的"立法，且与《宪法》、《行政处罚法》、《立法法》的规定相抵触，应该由全国人大常委会予以改变或撤销。

令人迷惑的是，三位博士究竟是建议对《收容遣送办法》进行违宪审查还是违法审查呢？违宪审查与违法审查是两个不同的概念，从逻辑上说，不可能对同一个法规既作违法审查又作违宪审查。

从建议书的"字眼"来看，无论是题目、具体的审查请求，还是理由的陈述，都将宪法和法律并举，而没有直接使用"违宪审查"或"违法审查"的表述。缘何如此？三个建议人都是法学博士，而且建议书的形成是在三位博士关注孙志刚事件后，长时间通过邮件往来探讨，最终成文。建议书全文不过几百字，以三位博士的学识和所投入的时间和精力，显然不会如此的"无知"或"疏忽"。不是因为"无知"或"疏忽"，那建议书又为何对是违宪审查还是违法审查含糊其词？其实，这是源于《立法法》的表述。

《立法法》第90条规定的审查制度有三点需要强调：一是，赋予社会组织和公民个人以审查建议权；二是，提请审查的对象只能是行政法规、地方性法规、自治条例和单行条例，不包括法律和规章；三是，提请审查的理由是认为行政法规、地方性法规、自治条例和单行条例同宪法或者法律相抵触。同时，《立法法》第56条又规定"国务院根据宪法和法律，制定行政法规"。结合本案也就是说，行政法规必须同时有宪法和法律的依据，根据法律的效力等级关系，行政法规应该是直接抵触法律，间接抵触宪法，如此在与"宪法或者法律相抵触"的选择中，应该视为行政法规违法。因此，在审查对象不包括法律，以及"和"与"或"的逻辑拼接下，立法法中所谓"行政法规、地方性法规、自治条例和单行条例同宪法或者法律相抵触"的表述中的"宪法"仅仅具有了象征的意义，体现着宪法的尊严，也将宪法的"大"与"空"表现得淋漓尽致。即《立法法》第90条建构的实质上是违法审查制度。

有趣的是，三位博士建议书中也使用了同样的"或"与"和"的文字游戏：建议书开文便截引法条"认为行政法规同宪法或法律相抵触的"，紧接着第二段认为"《城市流浪乞讨人员收容遣送办法》与我国宪法和有关法律相抵触"。同样的文字游戏，目的却大相径庭。作为对中国的宪政建设有责任心的学者，孜孜以求的是促进建立有效的违宪审查制度。然而，从前文的分析不难看出，在现行体制和法律规定下，我国违宪审查制度面临的尴尬与困境。无论是建议书暗含深意的隐微表述方法，还是之前对被誉为中国"宪法司法化第一案"的齐玉苓案的炒作，都体现了宪政人士企图建立中国违宪审查制度的"暗度陈仓"的策略与无奈。

《收容遣送办法》的废止并不是通过全国人大常委会的违宪或违法审查程序，而是国务院在认识到问题的严重性后，紧锣密鼓地于 6 月 18 日审议通过了《城市生活无着的流浪乞讨人员救助管理办法》，该办法规定："本办法自 2003 年 8 月 1 日起施行。1982 年 5 月 12 日国务院发布的《城市流浪乞讨人员收容遣送办法》同时废止。"一方面，国务院在系统内以新法自然废止了旧法。另一方面，既然《立法法》没有规定对公民建议的反馈程序和渠道，全国人大常委会对三位博士的违法审查建议书也无需作答复。如此，《收容遣送办法》与宪法、法律"相抵触"的问题也就不了了之。且不说，以违法审查"夹带"违宪审查，就是违法审查自身也夭折了。因此，有学者评述"《立法法》施行后涌现的法规合宪性审查建议案，迄今没有一例启动合宪性审查程序"。[①] 时隔六年，在强制拆迁的几个典型事件引发了社会各界广泛关注后，2009 年 12 月，北大的五位学者请求全国人大常委会对《城市房屋拆迁条例》存在的"与上位法冲突"的问题进行审查，其建议书的行文中"上位法"依然是"宪法和法律"并列，其结果亦是根据《立法法》第 91 条的规定，2011 年 1 月国务院颁行《国有土地上房屋征收与补偿条例》，该条例规定："本条例自公布之日起施行。2001 年 6 月 13 日国务院公布的《城市房屋拆迁管理条例》同时废止。"上述学者的评述依然可以作为《城市房屋拆迁管理条例》废止的脚注。

（三）完善法规合宪性与合法性审查机制的建议

如上文所述，无论是全国人大常委会对法规的备案审查，还是《立法法》确立的被动审查，甚或是主动审查与被动审查的结合，在实际操作中

---

① 胡建淼、金承东：《论法规违宪审查建议权》，《法学家》2005 年第 2 期。

都收效甚微。笔者认为，完善法规合宪性与合法性审查机制可以分两步走，第一步是完善现有的主动审查与被动审查机制，第二步是建立对法规的司法审查制度。

完善现有制度，一是要区分合宪性审查与合法性审查。一方面不能以合法性审查夹带合宪性审查，如果行政法规或地方性法规与宪法相抵触就可直接宣布无效并予以撤销，其合法性可审查亦可不审查；另一方面，可以将合法性审查作为合宪性审查的桥梁，如果行政法规或地方性法规与法律相抵触，应进一步审查其是否有宪法依据、是否与宪法相抵触，倘若在进一步审查中认为法规符合宪法，则不能草率撤销法规，而应由全国人大常委会启动相关法律的合宪性审查程序，并根据审查结果解决法规与法律之间的冲突关系。

二是要加强法规备案审查的实效性。法规审查备案室是人大法工委下面的一个工作机构，它没有撤销法律法规的权力，认为法规同宪法或者法律相抵触只能由法律委员会和/或有关的专门委员会向制定机关提出书面审查意见，由于审查意见没有法律效力，制定机关可以考虑，也可以不考虑。如果法律委员会和有关的专门委员会审查认为法规同宪法或者法律相抵触而制定机关不予修改的，可以向委员长会议提出书面审查意见和予以撤销的议案，由委员长会议决定是否提请常务委员会会议审议决定。可见，法规备案审查的工作机制和审查流程虽然明确而清晰，却刚性不足、弹性有余，在实际运行中，法规审查的决定性权力又回归到了全国人大常委会。因此，要加强法规备案审查的实效性就应当赋予法规审查备案室相对独立的地位，应当充分尊重和重视法律委员会和有关的专门委员会的审查意见。

三是要依托《立法法》第 90 条的规定，强化人民法院对法规合宪性与合法性审查的司法建议权，以充分发挥被动审查的实效性。人民法院在适用法律的过程中必定大量地涉及对法规合宪性与合法性的判断，如果整个法院系统将这些合宪性与合法性判断通过最高人民法院向全国人大常委会提出进行审查的要求或司法建议，必将为全国人大常委会对法规的审查启动一条便捷而有效的通道。

以上是对现有的全国人大常委会审查机制的完善意见，笔者认为备案审查和被动审查都是机械地字面审查，难于全面发现法规的合宪性与合法性问题，相较于法规适用过程中的合宪性与合法性判断，有着难以逾越的局限性，因此在我国的宪政体制下，建立对法规的司法审查制度是解决法规合宪性与合法性审查的有效途径。

三　司法审查的范围：从规章到法规

根据《宪法》、《人民法院组织法》的规定，法官对案件具有司法审判权，即准确认定事实和正确适用法律的权力。法律适用权是司法审判权的应有之意。法律适用权是指在与案件相关的多个法律中，法官有权力选择具体适用哪一个法律。法律适用权与司法审查权不同。司法审查权指在司法审判过程中法官对现行法律、法规本身的合宪性、合法性进行审查，并认定现行法律、法规是否违宪、违法从而宣布其是否有效的权力。

判断是一种技术性和认知性活动，而非支配性的权力活动。在涉及多个法律规定可能适用于同一案件的情形下，法官需要依次进行冲突判断、法条选择和法律适用。即法官必须首先对该多个法律规定是否存在冲突或抵触进行判断或确认，这是法官对法律适用选择的前提性作业。有"选择适用"必有"冲突判断"。① 也就是说，法官在审案过程中，对规范冲突的判断和选择适用是司法审判权的应有之义，无须法律明确赋予，法官亦当然享有对规范冲突的司法判断和选择适用权。

司法审查是西方国家解决法律冲突的最主要途径。在我国，一方面基于人民代表大会制度所构架的权力结构，司法机关不享有对法律的审查权；另一方面，1989 年《行政诉讼法》颁行时，出于对规章存在的相互冲突、质量不高等问题的担忧，没有把规章规定为法院审理行政案件的当然依据，而是规定法院审理行政案件时"参照"规章。所谓"参照"的含义，就是规章符合法律、法规规定的，法院应当作为依据；规章不符合法律、法规规定的，法院就不能作为依据，直接适用法律、法规的规定。行政诉讼法的这一规定，实际上是赋予了法院对规章的司法审查权，但法院只能决定是否适用规章，不能直接宣布规章无效。规章的撤销仍需由制定机关或者上级行政机关或者同级人大常委会决定。②

司法机关不享有对法律的审查权，因此司法审查的上限是法规；司法机关已享有对规章的部分审查权，因此司法审查的基础是规章。由此，笔者认为我国司法审查的可行范围就是从规章到规范，而实践这一范围的过程就是完善合宪性审查机制的过程。这一过程可以分为三步：

---

① 余文唐：《法律冲突：判断抑或裁决——以法官的审案遭遇为视角》，《福建法学》2008 年第 1 期。

② 刘莘主编《国内法律冲突与立法对策》，中国政法大学出版社，2003，第 173 ~ 174 页。

第一，扩大法院对规章的司法审查范围和程度。首先，将法院"参照"规章的范围从行政审判扩展到所有的司法审判活动；其次，扩大行政诉讼的受案范围，即赋予规章及其他规范性文件等抽象行政行为可诉性；最后，加大法院对规章的审查程度，即赋予法院直接宣布同宪法、法律、法规相抵触的规章无效的权力，或者要求对法院因抵触上位法而不予适用的规章，规定有权机关必须在一定的期限内予以撤销。

第二，在以《立法法》第 90 条的规定为依托，强化人民法院对法规合宪性与合法性审查的司法建议权，充分发挥全国人大常委会被动审查实效性的基础上，建立法院对法规"参照"适用的司法审查权。即在司法审判过程中，法规符合宪法、法律规定的，法院应当作为依据；法规不符合宪法、法律规定的，法院就不能作为依据，直接适用宪法和法律的规定。

第三，在法院"参照"适用法规的基础上，最高人民法院、高级人民法院可以直接宣布与宪法、法律相抵触的行政法规、地方性法规无效；或者由最高人民法院、高级人民法院就行政法规、地方性法规的合法性与合宪性判断向制定机关或有权机关提出具体的审查要求，制定机关或有权机关必须予以答复。

Constitutional Review Mechanisms in the Legal System

Liu Xiaomei

【**Abstract**】 The establishment of constitutional review mechanism is the key to ensuring the unity of the legal system. Based on the current state system and legal tradition, China has adopted a composite mode of constitutional review mechanism, namely different mechanisms are used for the review of laws, administrative regulations and ministerial rules or local regulations in light of the different levels of legal effect of legal norms. This article examines and analyzes the mechanisms for the constitutional review of laws, administrative regulations, local regulations and ministerial rules and puts forward concrete suggestions on the improvement of these mechanisms.

【**Key words**】 Legal System, Constitutionality, Legality

日本对 "平等保护" 问题的司法审查

赵立新[*]

【摘要】 日本的平等观念出现于近代以后，明治政府"四民平等"政策的推行是这一观念在法律层面的体现，但在第二次世界大战前，等级差别仍非常普遍，"人人平等"这一思想本身还没有进入大部分人的观念之中。1946 年制定的《日本国宪法》使这一状况有了很大改观，新宪法明确规定了国民在法律面前的平等并确立了美国式的司法审查制度。日本各级法院以该规定为基础，针对婚姻家庭领域和选举权等平等保护问题作出了一系列判决，同时针对"合理差别"的含义和审查标准进行了讨论，维护了《日本国宪法》的平等保护原则，同时发展了平等保护理论。

【关键词】 日本　平等保护　司法审查　法院判决

一　导论：日本平等保护原则的发展

平等权与自由权、财产权均属于法治国家所保障的三大基本人权。在西方，平等思想最早可以追溯到古希腊，当时许多哲学家都在其著作中对平等原则进行了阐述，特别是亚里士多德的正义理论（即对分配正义和矫正正义的分析）[①] 对后世产生了很大影响。现代的平等原则是 18 世纪在市民社会的基础上形成的一项政治原则。18 世纪末以后，平等原则的内涵不

---

* 河北师范大学副教授。
① 〔古希腊〕亚里士多德：《政治学》，吴寿彭译，商务印书馆，1965，第 148 页。

断扩大，从早期的否定封建制、宣告所有人在社会和身份上平等，到19世纪的政治平等，再到20世纪经济上的平等，每一次内涵的扩大都为法律上人权的发展带来一次重大的革命。

日本明治维新后，作为开放政策的一环，政府大力提倡"四民平等"，①并颁布许多消除身份差别的法令，但当时的许多措施仍然停留在法律原则阶段，离社会身份的真正解放还有很大差距。1889年制定的《明治宪法》只规定了就任公职的平等，②对作为国民的平等权以及人权一般原则的平等原则没有从正面涉及。进一步说，当时关于"人人平等"这一思想本身还没有进入大部分人的观念之中，在政治体制和社会习惯上的差别被视为当然的。以天皇制为中心的华族③和贵族院的政治特权制度自不必说，民法上的家族制度也包含了男女差别和部落差别等社会差别，在日本的外国人的人权也受到广泛制约。

1945年，日本战败投降。1946年制定的《日本国宪法》使这一状况有了很大改观。以宪法第11条"国民享有基本的人权原则"和第13条"人格权的尊重原则"为基础，宪法第14条第1款前段明确规定了："全体国民在法律面前一律平等。"该条后段则对平等权的具体内容作了列举，即"在政治、经济或社会关系中，不得以人种、信仰、性别、社会身份以及门第的不同而有所差别"。第2款宣布废除华族及其他贵族制度；第3款进一步规定了荣誉、勋章及其他荣典的授予不附带任何特权，且荣典仅限于一代有效。宪法在此后的条款中，还对家庭中的个人尊严（第24条）、教育机会均等（第26条）、平等参政权（第44条）等进行了规定，使平等原则进一步具体化。可以说，平等原则与个人尊严原则一样，都在人权体系中处于基本地位。

关于"法律面前平等"的含义，日本学术界存在一定的分歧。其主要在于：第一，宪法第14条第1款前段的一般平等条款是否含有拘束立法者

---

① 日本德川幕府时期，把除天皇和贵族以外的武士及以下的平民分为士、农、工、商四等，是一种封建的身份等级制度，明治维新后的1871年，新政府宣布"四民平等"，废除了该制度。

② 明治宪法第19条规定：日本臣民，按照法律命令所定之资格，均得充任文物官吏及就任其他公务。

③ 所谓华族，是日本在明治维新后，给予失去领主地位的诸侯和旧公卿贵族的一种称号，开始有509人，后来，伊藤博文为巩固政权的基础，又将许多维新功臣位列华族，使之与诸侯公卿出身的华族形成一体，共同作为维护皇室的屏障。

的含义;① 第二,同项后段的禁止差别条款是限定的含义还是例示的含义;第三,平等或禁止差别的条款是相对的还是绝对的。② 这些观点互相结合产生了多种解释,下面主要以日本法院的判决为中心,对相关解释进行分析。

二　日本法院对平等保护原则的运用

1947 年实施的《日本国宪法》第 81 条规定了美国式的司法审查制度,第二次世界大战后日本各级法院以该规定为基础,针对平等保护问题作出了许多判决,此处仅对代表性的判决进行分析。

日本最高法院就平等问题作出的第一个重要判决是"杀害尊属重罚规定违宪"判决(1973 年)。

该案的经过是:被告某女,14 岁时被亲生父亲强奸,此后两人同居并生有五个孩子(其中两个死亡),被告 29 岁时,和一青年相爱,当对父亲提出想和青年结婚时,遭到父亲的反对,此后,激怒之下的父亲禁止被告外出,并胁迫、虐待被告,最后,被告忍无可忍杀死了父亲。根据日本《刑法》第 200 条"杀害尊属"的规定,应对被告人加重处罚,一审法院认定该条违反《宪法》第 14 条第 1 款的规定,因此没有适用该条规定,只认定属于防卫过当,并结合实际情况免除了对被告的处罚。二审则认为刑法第 200 条的规定符合宪法,但结合实际判处被告 3 年零 6 个月徒刑。最后,最高法院推翻了二审判决,认为刑法第 200 条违反宪法、无效。

在判决中,关于平等原则,最高法院认为:"宪法第 14 条第 1 款是保障国民法律面前平等的规定,同项后段列举的事项属于对规定的例示,除非根据事情的性质以合理的规定为基础,该平等的要求宗旨应理解为禁止差别对待。"

---

① 传统的平等权更强调法律适用上的平等,它要求执行法律的机关不能因该法律规范对象的差异而有不同的规范标准。法律适用的平等应为法律适用后果的平等。随着社会的发展,该平等已不能充分表现平等权的宪法意义。因此,在 20 世纪 30 年代,要求立法者也必须遵守宪法平等权,而且在违反平等权时,法律曾因违宪而无效的思潮在德国兴起。当时,两位德国学者莱布厚兹和阿达,分别出版了同名的《法律之前的平等》论著,提出了平等权亦应该拘束立法者的新理论,他们认为:若平等权不能有效地拘束立法者,那么宪法的平等权便形同具文,为了拘束立法者违反平等权利,法院亦拥有审查法律有无违反平等原则的权限。第二次世界大战后,德国基本法接受了这一理论,明确规定了平等权可以拘束立法权。参见陈新民著《德国公法学基础理论》(下册),山东人民出版社,2004,第 674 页。

② 参见〔日〕大须贺明编《宪法》,三省堂,1981,第 104～105 页。

此后，关于平等原则的诉讼在许多领域展开。1995 年，最高法院关于"私生子继承差别"的诉讼就是一例。① 该案原告系某私生子的继承人，要求与婚生子及其继承人均分被继承人的财产，但日本《民法》第 900 条第 4 款"但书"规定，在婚生子与私生子同时作为继承人时，私生子的继承份额为婚生子的一半。因此，原告以民法的相关规定违反宪法第 14 条的平等原则为由，向法院提起诉讼，要求均分财产。一审法院没有接受原告的主张，根据民法的规定对遗产分割进行了审判。二审法院维持了一审判决，最高法院以 10 比 5 的多数意见驳回了原告的特别抗告，做出民法相关规定合宪的判决。

最高法院认为：

第一，关于继承制度应由立法机关进行合理的裁量判断。

包括本规定在内的对法定继承份额的规定，并不是规定必须按该继承份额的规定进行继承，而是在没有遗嘱继承时起补充的功能。因此，婚生子与私生子法定继承份额区别的立法理由有合理根据，并且，从该区别与上述立法理由的关联看，并非显著不合理，没有超越立法机关的合理判断范围，属于合理的差别。不违反《宪法》第 14 条第 1 款的规定。

第二，从法律婚主义与一夫一妻制出发。

民法该规定的立法理由，一方面尊重了法律上配偶所生子女（婚生子）的立场，另一方面，也充分考虑到了非婚生子（私生子）的立场，通过认可非婚生子法定继承份额是婚生子一半的规定，试图保护非婚生子的利益，以调和尊重法律婚与保护非婚生子利益的相互关系。换句话说，民法既然采用了法律婚主义，在法定继承份额方面对基于婚姻关系的配偶及其子女给予优待也是合理的，而对非婚生子给予一定的继承份额也体现了法律对其利益的保护。因此，从现行民法采用法律婚主义的原则出发，其关于法定继承份额的区别规定也不违反《宪法》第 14 条第 1 款的规定。

对于上述观点，少数法官提出了批评意见，他们认为：

尊重婚姻的立法目的本身无可厚非，但从立法目的来看，如果通过法定继承份额区别婚生子和非婚生子是合理的，就会重视非婚生子不属于婚姻家族这一属性，由此寻找区别的根据，这与《宪法》第 24 条第 2 款关于继承应以个人尊严为立法原则的规定不相容。换句话说，对出生负有责任

---

① 〔日〕最判（"最高法院判决"的简称，以下同）平成 7 年（1995）7 月 5 日，民集 49 卷 7 号，第 1789 页。

的是被继承人，非婚生子没有任何责任，其身份不因自己的意思和努力而改变，对出生不负任何责任的非婚生子基于上述理由受到法律上的差别对待，显然超出了尊重和保护婚姻的立法目的。并且，本规定正是造成社会上轻视非婚生子的原因之一。

为了尊重和保护婚姻的目的，在继承领域对非婚生子的差别对待违反了尊重个人与平等的原则，立法目的和手段之间缺乏合理的关联性。

与最高法院的判决不同，对于私生子的继承问题，地方法院的态度显然比较积极。在上述最高法院判决之前，东京高等法院曾在1993年和1994年先后两次做出民法相关规定违宪的判决。

在1993年的判决中，[①] 法院认为：毫无疑问，保护以合法婚姻为基础的家庭关系这一立法目的本身，从宪法第24条的精神来看，应予以尊重，但重要的是，非婚生子的个人尊严也必须受到同等重要的保护，应尽量回避以牺牲后者的利益来保护前者的利益。即使婚生子与非婚生子继承份额相等，对配偶的继承份额并不会产生任何影响；即使对配偶产生实质的不平等，也可以通过灵活运用寄与制度予以解决。从非婚生子方面来看，父母是否属于合法的婚姻不能根据自己的意思和努力予以改变，却要承受由此带来的不利结果。因此，该规制过于广泛，不仅缺乏正确性，也无助于抑制非婚生子的出现，与保护基于合法婚姻的家庭关系这一立法目的是否有实质上的关联性，是非常令人怀疑的。

在1994年的判决中，[②] 法院认为：如果关于继承的规定作为法律制度明显不合理时，就脱离了立法机关的裁量范围，本条款虽然在立法目的上有其合理性，但在达成鼓励法律婚的目的方面缺乏实效性，不能直接保护法律婚中妻子的利益，并且，规定的内容极其广泛。进一步说，从遗产公平适当的分配、通过遗产对未成年子女的抚养等观点来看，也难以肯定其合理性。

上述最高法院和地方法院对该条民法规定是否违宪的不同观点反映了学术界和实务界对该问题的不同认识。在日本的宪法学界和民法学界存在合宪说和违宪说的对立，宪法学界在以前对这一问题不十分关心，或者说，合宪说占主导地位，但在20世纪90年代后，持违宪说的学者逐渐增多，其

---

① 〔日〕东京高判（"高等法院判决"简称"高判"，以下同）平成5年（1993）6月23日，高民集46卷2号，第43页。

② 〔日〕东京高判平成6年（1994）11月30日，《判例时报》864号，第291页。

背景主要是趋向于婚生子与私生子平等化的国际人权条约和国外的立法动向。当然，合宪说和违宪说都有其合理的一面，其理由在上述最高法院的合宪判决和东京高等法院的违宪判决中都有充分的论述。但是，违宪说正在成为主流。① 1996 年，日本立法机关开始着手对该条进行修改，其背景正是以违宪说为前提的。

与家庭关系相关的另一判例是广岛高等法院作出的"禁止女性再婚期间法律的合理性"判决。② 根据日本《民法》第 733 条的规定，女性在离婚后 6 个月之内禁止再婚。该案原告为某女与其再婚之夫（后夫），某女在离婚后与后夫同居，并申请结婚，但婚姻登记机关以其离婚不足 6 个月违反民法规定为由不予受理。二人在禁止再婚的期间届满后迅速结婚，然后起诉，认为《民法》第 733 条违反了宪法及国际人权条约的规定，国会议员及内阁对该法的立法行为以及没有及时修改或废除该条款的行为属于《国家赔偿法》第 1 条所说的违法行为，因此，要求国家对禁止再婚期间遭受的精神痛苦给予赔偿。

二审的广岛高等法院判决认为：宪法中理想的家族关系是以个人尊严和两性本质的平等为基础，关于婚姻及家族事项的法律必须以该基础为立脚点。正是基于这一精神，民法上规定了一夫一妻制，在此基础上，可以推定妻子在婚姻存续中怀孕的子女是丈夫的子女，并且推定在婚姻成立 200 日后和婚姻解除 300 日以内所生之子女为婚姻中怀孕的子女，以明确以夫妻为中心的家庭关系，以此保护家庭生活的平稳和子女的幸福。民法只对女性规定了禁止再婚期间，其目的必须是防止父性的混同、保护出生子女的利益和婚后家庭生活的平稳，其手段必须是必要且最小限度的，否则对女子再婚期间的规定就是不合理的。而关于女性禁止再婚期间的规定难以断定属于不合理的范围。最后，法院驳回了原告的要求。

关于女性禁止再婚期间的规定，现在，学说上多持批评意见，其理由在于：为防止血统混乱的立法宗旨虽然具有正当目的，但只对女子设定 6 个月的再婚禁止期间，其手段不仅缺乏正当性，而且容易产生弊病。因为，现行制度并不能阻止事实上的再婚（同居），反而会产生私生子问题。并且，由于现代医学的发展，即使消除对再婚期间的限制，子女的归属也很

---

① 〔日〕内野正幸：《私生子相続差別と法の下の平等》，载《憲法の基本判例》（第二版），有斐阁，1996 年版，第 51 页。

② 〔日〕广岛高判平成 3 年（1991）11 月 28 日，《判例时报》1406 号，第 3 页。

容易在医学上得到证明。① 因此，该条的修改势在必然。

除婚姻家庭领域之外，在其他众多的领域也涉及法律面前平等的原则。如"议员选举定额分配不均衡"判决，该判决主要涉及选举权的平等问题。法院通过对选举权在近代以来的发展及其意义的叙述，指出了选举权内容平等性的重要意义。即："对宪法第14条第1款所规定的平等，就选举权来说，是指所有的国民在政治价值上的平等这一彻底的平等。从字面上说，宪法第15条第1款的各规定虽然只就选举人资格作了禁止差别的规定，但并不仅于此，宪法所要求的实际是选举权的内容，即各选举人投票价值的平等"。②

三　合理差别与审查标准

由于平等是一个以比较为前提的概念，因此，虽然是法律面前的平等，但也可以分为绝对平等、有限制的绝对平等和相对平等三类。③ 所谓绝对平等，即对所有人同一对待的平等，在对《宪法》第14条第1款的解释中，还没有持该观点的学说和判例。有限制的绝对平等则是在限制事实上差异的基础上，要求绝对的平等。相对平等则意味着平等前提下的平等待遇，其结果往往是具体问题具体分析，这也是目前占多数的观点。

在最高法院的判决中，对相对平等一般解释为禁止不合理的差别，换句话说，是承认合理的差别。最高法院早在违宪审查制度建立之初，在就《刑法》（修改前）第205条"伤害尊属致死重罚"的规定合宪性的判决中，就指出："在国民基本平等的原则范围内，法律会考虑到各人的年龄、自然状态、职业、人与人之间的特别关系等各方面的情况，根据道德、正义、合目的性等要求，做出具体的规定。"④ 此后，在地方公务员因高龄待岗处分事件判决中更进一步指出："对于国民来说，并不是保障其绝对的平等，应该禁止的只是没有合理理由的差别。根据事情的具体情况做出的合理的差别对待，并不是否定上述平等的条款。"⑤ 上述判决明确了宪法的平等是

---

① 〔日〕小林節：《女性の再婚禁止期間の合理性》，载《憲法判例百選》（第三版），别册ジェリスト，第130号，1994。

② 〔日〕吉田善明：《議員定数の不均衡と法の下の平等》，载《憲法の基本判例》（第二版），有斐阁，1996，第55页。

③ 参见〔日〕斎藤寿著《憲法原理の分析と展開》劲草书房，1989，第106~107页。

④ 〔日〕最判昭和25年（1950）10月11日，刑集4卷10号，第2037页。

⑤ 〔日〕最判昭和39年（1964）5月27日，民集18卷4号，第676页。

相对的平等。可以说，最高法院在其违反平等原则的判决中，基本采用了"合理性差别"的观点。

但是，关于"合理性差别"的标准一般过于抽象，因此，日本的学说和判例存在很大的争论。其中，对《宪法》第14条第1款后段所列举的事由和未列举的事由，多数主张其审查标准应有区别。第一种学说认为：对后段列举事由，鉴于平等思想的渊源和过去的经验，特别是对差别的警惕，只要不是为证明必要最小限度的特别情况，应理解为禁止差别。对该种情况应进行"严格的审查"。而对于前段含义（即包括未列举的内容），为达到法律的目的，其区别对待只需有"合理的关联"，即"合理性"。第二种学说认为：从审判规范存在的意义来看，对列举事由的差别对待应排除合宪性的推定，由主张合宪的公权力负主张和举证的责任，对差别对待的合宪性采取严格的审查标准。即"对后段的列举事由进行区别的立法，应理解为违反民主制度的基础，应推定为缺乏合理的根据，不存在给予一般立法的合宪性推定，必须由主张立法合宪的一方就其存在合理的理由，并且合宪进行论证"。关于列举事由以外的区别对待，"对于违反前段规定的法律面前平等的保障时，可以作为违反平等权的违宪，此时，对进行的区别立法可以推定合宪，在审查该种立法是否合宪时，不适用严格的标准，应广泛承认立法机关的裁量权。由主张违宪的一方就法律或行为缺乏合理性、属于恣意的产物进行论证"。① 第三种学说认为："对后段列举事由，虽然承认其差别违宪的推定，但只有在承认合宪会带来非常不利的结果时，或损害个人或社会的重大利益时，才例外地承认差别的存在。严重的差别正当化的举证责任由公权力一方负担，设定严格的审查标准，立法裁量的范围极其狭窄。"与此相对应，对其他事由下的差别，原则上采取合理性的判断标准。② 从三种观点可以看出，对后段列举事由都认为应采取严格的审查标准，其他事由则应具体分析，对涉及精神自由和其他基本人权的差别对待也应采取严格的审查标准。

对最高法院关于同样问题是合宪还是违宪的两个判决进行比较，或许有助于理解合理性与审查标准的问题。

在前述1950年"伤害尊属致死"案件的判决中，关于刑法的重罚规定

---

① 〔日〕最判昭和58年（1983）4月27日，民集37卷3号，第345页（伊藤正己法官的补充意见）。

② 〔日〕手塚和男：《平等と合理的区别》，载《憲法の争点》（第三版），ジュリスト増刊，有斐閣，1999，第81页。

是否违反宪法的争论，判决认为：刑法关于杀害尊亲属或伤害致死比一般犯罪加重处罚，显示了法律对子女亲属道德义务的重视，这不外是以道德为基础的法律的具体规定。作为支配夫妻、亲子、兄弟等关系的道德，是人伦之本，是不论古今中外都承认的人类普遍的道德准则，即属于学说上所谓的自然法。宪法根据情况予以考虑或进一步以法规的形式予以客观化都是可能的。且亲子关系不是社会身份的问题，尊亲属与卑亲属不同的待遇属于立法政策上的问题，不属于是否违反宪法的问题。

在此，法院既承认了立法目的的合理性，也承认了立法手段的合理性。法院的该种考虑在1974年的同类判决中基本上得到了继承。但是，在1973年"杀害尊属"的判决中，法院则变更了先例，做出了刑法相关条款违宪的判决。判决认为：对尊亲属的尊重报恩应该是社会生活的基本道义，维持该种自然的情爱乃至普遍的伦理是值得刑法上保护的法益，因此，把被害者是尊亲属作为犯情之一种，在具体的量刑上予以重视不仅是允许的，而且即使进一步对其类型化，并在法律上规定刑的加重条件，也难以断定该种差别对待缺乏合理的根据。但是，如果尊亲属对卑亲属做出了不道德的行为，而招致卑亲属的杀害，此时，无论对卑亲属如何酌情，其法定刑也只限于死刑或无期惩役，这显然过于严厉，[1] 在立法目的上不能得到充分的说明，不属于基于合理根据的差别对待。

本判决在立法目的合理方面没有变化，但认为达到目的的手段缺乏合理的根据，因此，违反了《宪法》第14条的平等规定。但在判决中，有6名法官认为设立该条款的目的本身也缺乏合理性。[2]

关于平等原则的另一典型判例是"议员定额分配不均衡"判决。在1964年最高法院关于"参议院议员选举诉讼"中，[3] 对前一年进行的参议院议员选举，根据"公职选举法别表"的名额分配规定，东京与鸟取两地区选举人一票的价值产生了约4∶1的差别，原告主张该"别表"违反了《宪法》第14条的规定。对此，判决认为："议员数根据各选举区人口的比例向各选举区分配，是法律面前平等的宪法原则所期望达到的目的，但根据宪法第44条的规定，议员定额、选举区等事项由法律规定，因此，该事项原则上属于立法机关裁量的范围。"

---

① 关于1995年修改前的刑法200条"杀害尊属重罚"的规定，在后来的执行中，其惩罚的下限减为惩役三年半，但不适用缓期执行。

② 参见〔日〕大须贺明编《宪法》，三省堂，1981，第111～112页。

③ 〔日〕最判昭和39年（1964）2月5日，民集18卷2号，第270页。

对于该判决，有日本学者认为：判决认可了议员定额不均衡的立法有合理性，但同时认为，以何种比例对议员数进行分配属于国会的裁量范围，这等于没有对是否有合理性进行判断。由于在极端不平等的情况下法院才进行判断，因此，司法审查几乎不可能。①

与1964年判决相对应，在1976年"众议院议员选举"诉讼判决中，对千叶一区和最小区投票价值约5∶1的差别，判决在认可了选举权的内容、即投票价值的平等是宪法要求的同时，又指出：名额与人口比例的关系也要照顾复杂微妙的政策及技术要素等非人口要素。

关于立法机关的裁量权，判决认为：对国会具体决定的问题，由是否认可其裁量权的合理行使来决定。但是，即使在该种立场来考虑，对于选举区划和名额分配造成的选举人投票价值的不平等，在考虑国会通常能够考虑的各种因素之外，也要考虑在达到了一般认为超出合理性的限度时，推定为超出了国会合理的裁量范围。只要不存在该不平等正当化的理由，就可以认为违反了宪法。

而对该件5∶1的差别，在考虑了各种因素后，认为：不仅达到了一般认为不合理的程度，甚至超过了该不合理程度。因此，判决违宪。

在该判决中，最高法院对名额分配不平等状况的违宪性判断标准有两点：① 投票价值的平等不是唯一绝对的标准，要考虑到众、参两院能够各自斟酌的事项，以公正和有效作为标准；② 强调了虽然公职选举法附属第一表规定了在合理的期间内对名额分配进行修改，但国会却不进行修改。这两项标准虽然与1964年判决相比较具体，但总体上仍然比较抽象。在此主要对第一点进行论述。关于该点，日本学术界存在两种观点，第一种认为人口比率是唯一一般的、基本的标准，属于绝对化的观点。第二种认为，人口比率始终是第一位的标准，但在不违反民主主义合理性的差别范围内，也应该考虑选举区大小的地理、历史等因素。② 最高法院的判决正是与第二种学说相同，也是日本比较流行的观点。但关键是允许度的问题。

在1976年判决中，针对选举区人口数和议员名额的不均衡，最高法院虽然认为1∶5的差别在任何地方都找不出正当化的理由，但对许可的范围却没有提及。许多学者从比较法的角度，根据国外的经验提出了自己的见解。

① 参见〔日〕大须贺明编《宪法》，三省堂，1981，第112页。
② 〔日〕吉田善明：《議員定数の不均衡と法の下の平等》，载《憲法の基本判例》（第二版），有斐阁，1996，第58页。

第一种观点认为：每一议员所代表人口的最大选举区和最小选举区的差别不应超过1:2。有学者在此基础上又提出，该标准条件过于严格，应有所缓和。即1:2的比例差别只是一个目标，超过这一比率时，被告（即选举管理委员会）方应就合理性进行论证；不超过时，原告负举证责任。第二种观点认为：应对差别进行严格解释，即一票的价值理论上应在该选举时全国平均值上下20%的范围内。① 但综合考虑，第一种观点比较适当。

Judicial Review of Issues of "Equal Protection" in Japan

Zhao Lixin

【Abstract】 The idea of equality appeared in Japan only after the country had entered into modern times and was embodied at the legal level in the abolishment of the shinoukousho system during the Meiji era. Before the Second World War, however, the hierarchical differences of social status were still very common and the idea of equality had not yet entered into the mind of the majority of Japanese people. This situation was greatly changed by the 1946 Constitution of Japan, which provided for the principle that all citizens are equal before the law and established an American-style judicial review system. Based on these constitutional provisions, Japanese courts at various levels made a series of decisions on the issue of equal protection in the fields of marriage, family, and voting rights, at the same time, carried out discussions on the meaning and criteria of "reasonable differences", thereby upholding and further developing the constitutional principle of equal protection.

【Key words】 Japan, Equal Protection, Judicial Review, Court Judgment

---

① 〔日〕吉田善明：《議員定数の不均衡と法の下の平等》，載《憲法の基本判例》（第二版），有斐閣，1996，第59页。

建立立法监督与制约相分离的
合法性审查机制

莫纪宏[*]

【摘要】本文从宪法学的基本原理出发，主张一切依据宪法和法律享有公共权力的机构所制定的针对不特定社会公众生效的规范性文件都具有法律效力，可以约束一定行政区域范围内的所有社会公众的行为，但是，一切享有规范性文件制定权的公共权力机构必须依据宪法和法律的规定制定规范性文件，必须以合宪性和合法性作为规范性文件制定的法律依据。从法理上来看，保障规范性文件具有合宪性和合法性主要有立法监督和立法制约两个途径。立法监督是基于宪法和法律所赋予的立法职权进行的，其目的是保障宪法和法律所赋予的立法职权能够得到有效的行使。立法制约是根据宪法和法律赋予的权限，对其他公共权力机构依法制定的规范性文件是否符合宪法和法律进行合宪性审查和合法性审查，从而确保规范性文件的合宪性和合法性，维护法制的统一性。

【关键词】立法监督　立法制约　合宪性　合法性

一　规范性文件的性质及法律效力

规范性文件的性质和法律效力是近年来我国宪法学界和立法学界关注的重大理论问题和实践问题。在法律实践中，规范性文件形式多样，效力不等，有自成一体、独立发展的倾向。由于规范性文件是否属于中国特色

---

* 中国社会科学院法学研究所研究员。

社会主义法律体系中的一个组成部分在学术界至今尚无定论，因此，在法律实践中，大量的没有被确认为具有法律效力的法律形式——规范性文件，实际上起到了比具有法律效力的法律形式更强的指导实践的作用。2010 年 3 月召开的十一届全国人大四次会议正式宣告中国特色社会主义法律体系如期形成，但是，从目前公认的学术观点来看，被纳入法律体系中予以考虑的法律形式只有宪法、法律、行政法规、军事法规、地方性法规、部委规章、军事规章以及地方政府规章等，而中央和地方国家机构中许多有立法权的国家机关制定和发布的决定、决议、命令、指示等，都没有被视为具有法律效力的"法律形式"。但实践中，由于不属于"法律体系"组成部分的大量规范性文件实际针对的实施对象是不特定的社会公众，故规范性文件在法律之外起到了法律自身所无法发挥的作用。例如，国务院制定的正式行政法规迄今为止只有 700 部左右，但是由国务院发布的具有规范约束力的文件却是一个非常庞大的数字。由于目前只有行政法规进入了《立法法》第 90 条和第 91 条所规定的受"合宪性和合法性"审查的法律形式之列，而大量的由国务院发布的规范性文件却"逃之夭夭"，显然是不合理的。由于造成了"依法行政"的"死角"，即既不受"具体行政行为"可以被起诉的约束，也无法进入全国人大常委会的"违宪和违法审查"的控制领域，成为真正名副其实不受监督、不受制约的"自由领地"。此种制度漏洞也导致了国务院，特别是国务院的一些部委，在日常工作中热衷于发文件，而不愿意正式制定行政法规或者是部委规章。至于说地方政府，更是通过规范性文件获得了很大的"行政自由裁量权"。出现此种现象最根本的原因在于我国目前的立法制度设计存在严重的缺陷，也就是说，没有对一切国家机关针对不特定社会公众所采取的抽象行为进行合宪性和合法性方面的总体控制。"法外"还有"法"，导致了"法"出多门，法律形式极其混乱，不仅普通民众无法有效地了解立法的真实情况，即便是训练有素的法律人在很多时候也是"丈二和尚摸不着头脑"，[①] 法治已有的"可预测性"受到

---

① 2012 年 9 月 12 日下午，美国贸易代表办公室代表团在总法律顾问蒂莫西·莱夫带领下访问中国社会科学院法学研究所。美国贸易代表办公室（USTR）隶属于总统办公厅，直接对总统和国会负责。美国贸易代表是国家的首席谈判官员，是美国在主要国际贸易组织的代表。该代表团访问法学所一个重要的讨论话题就是中国规范性文件的范围以及法律效力，说明规范性文件问题已经引起了与华交往的各国法律界的重视。参见《美国贸易代表办公室总法律顾问就政府透明度访问法学所》http://www.iolaw.org.cn/showNews.asp?id=31562，最后访问日期：2013 年 3 月 10 日。

了严重挑战。

事实上，从法治原则出发，一切国家机关，不论其主要的宪法和法律职权是什么，都必须要依法办事。只有法律授权的事项才能去做，法律没有赋予的职权，就不能随意去做，否则就构成了"超越职权"或者是"滥用职权"。但是，如果是因为贯彻宪法和法律的需要，在不与宪法和法律相抵触和违背的情况下，根据本地区的实际情况，制定和发布一些针对不特定社会公众生效的规范性文件，哪怕是仅仅具有政策指导性的文件，从法理上推导，都应当是具有法律效力的文件，当然前提是这些规范性文件应当具有合宪性和合法性，只要合宪性和合法性方面不存在问题，一切社会组织和个人就应当无条件地遵守，否则就构成了对法治原则的不尊重和破坏，法律就会缺少应有的权威。

因此，将规范性文件赋予法律上的普遍效力，通过制度机制有效地保证规范性文件的合宪性和合法性，是解决实践中规范性文件性质不清，规范性文件制定得太多、太乱的对症之药。只有首先明确和提升规范性文件的"法律地位"，才能将规范性文件有效地控制在"合宪性"和"合法性"的范围内进行有效的评价。

二　立法监督制度的基本功能在于保障立法职权的有效行使

长期以来，在我国宪法学理论研究过程中，一直没有认真研究立法监督的性质和特征，只是从简单的权威主义原则出发，将"下位法服从上位法"简单地作为保证上级机关的立法权威和效力的手段，其结果造成了立法中的"层级主义"和"官僚主义"。立法的效力不是以宪法和法治原则为依据，而只是以某种法律形式是由哪个机关制定的，这个机关本身的"行政级别"有多大为依据，行政级别高的国家机关制定的规范性文件，理所当然地具有更高的法律效力，这些就形成了一个上级立法机关可以随意监督下级立法机关的立法活动的学术观点和制度设计。

实际上这种简单化的立法监督理念，不仅没有对国家机关制定的规范性文件实行必要的合宪性和合法性控制，相反，由于立法机关，特别是最高立法机关将其他国家机关所制定和发布的所有规范性文件都视为自己的立法监督对象，导致了立法监督的范围过于宽泛，缺少工作重点，在立法监督实践中很难找到有效的突破口，来实现自身的立法监督职能。

从法理上来看，立法监督制度的基本制度功能是为了保障立法监督者自身所制定的法律规范能够得到有效的实施，监督对象应当是监督者依据宪法和法律自身有权制定的法律规范，监督的基本目的就是要保障自己的立法职权能够得到充分的实现。所以，在立法监督实践中，存在立法者对自己的立法行为进行自我监督的问题，也存在立法者通过授权方式将自身的立法职权授予特定的立法机关，为了保证被授权的立法机关能够按照授权者的意愿来立法，同时也为了防范被授权立法者所制定的法律规范背离了授权者的要求，授权者就必须要对被授权者依据授权所进行的立法的形式、内容和效果进行监督，因为不进行这样的立法监督，监督者依据宪法和法律所享有的立法职权就无法得到有效的实现。所以，立法监督最终是要使监督者自身受益，维护的是监督者自身的立法权威。在我国，全国人大及常委会曾经先后向国务院和地方人大授权制定相关法律规范，从法理上来看，根据授权而制定的法律规范毫无疑义应当接受授权者的监督。①但是，如果国务院制定行政法规不是依据全国人大及常委会的特别授权，而是基于宪法的规定直接制定，即所谓的行使"职权立法"，那么，对于国务院由此制定的行政法规，理论上讲，全国人大是无法进行监督的，因为这些行政法规与全国人大及其常委会自身的立法职权无关，是另外的国家机关独立制定的，如果全国人大及常委会要对这种方式产生的行政法规进行必要的合宪性和合法性控制，就不能采取立法监督的形式，而是要依据"立法制约"的理论，②通过违宪审查和违法审查的途径来对其他国家

---

① 十二届人大一次会议期间，针对"二手房交易差额征 20% 个税"，全国人大代表、著名编剧赵冬苓在小组发言表示，征税权力本属全国人大，但从 1985 年开始全国人大大部分授权给了国务院，至今已近 30 年，"作为最高立法机关，征税权力不能继续旁落"。这是全国人大代表要求全国人大有效行使授权监督的最好例证。参见《代表称征税权应收归全国人大：20% 售房税不能随便征》，http://news.dichan.sina.com.cn/2013/03/09/668504.html，最后访问日期：2013 年 3 月 10 日。

② 1787 年美国宪法第 1 条第 7 款规定：众议院或参议院通过的每一议案，均应在成为法律之前送交合众国总统；总统如批准该议案，即应签署；如不批准，则应附上异议书将议案退还给提出该项议案的议院，该院应将总统异议详细载入本院会议记录，并进行复议。如复议后，该院 2/3 议员同意通过，即应将该议案连同异议书送交另一院，另一院亦应加以复议，如经该院 2/3 议员认可，该项议案即成为法律。但在这种情况下，两院的表决应以投赞成票和反对票决定，投赞成票或反对票的议员的姓名应分别载入各该院的会议记录。如议案在送交总统后 10 日内（星期日除外）未经退还，即视为业经总统签署，该项议案即成为法律；但如因国会休会而阻碍该议案退还，则该项议案不能成为法律。上述规定实际上赋予了美国总统在立法方面的"口袋否决权"，这就是一种典型的"立法制约"的制度设计，即由一个国家机关来审查另一个国家机关制定的法律规范是否合宪，这种立法制约本身并不提供制约者享有立法职权，只是起到保证宪法权威和法制统一性的作用。

机关制定的法律规范进行必要的违宪和违法审查。

三　立法制约制度的基本功能旨在维护法制的统一性

在我国目前的宪法制度设计中，现行宪法只规定了全国人大及常委会行使国家立法权，并没有具体明确有没有其他国家机关可以行使"地方立法权"，也没有说明国务院有无"立法职权"，当然，像中央军事委员会制定"军事法规"，宪法文本中是只字未提，最早是由《国防法》加以确认，到 2000 年《立法法》正式加以确认。[①]　在此种情况下，国务院和中央军事委员会可以说，在理论上有一定的立法上的自主性，可以通过立法的形式来自由决定一些与国计民生相关的重大事项。全国人大及常委会不能以一个立法监督者的身份来介入国务院制定的行政法规或者是中央军事委员会制定的"军事法规"。但是，从《宪法》第 5 条所确立的法制统一原则出发，不论哪个国家机关，在制定法律规范的时候都必须服从宪法和法律的规定，因此，为了防止其他国家机关滥用立法职权，违背宪法和法律，全国人大常委会可以对行政法规、军事法规是否符合宪法和法律规定进行审查，审查后发现有违宪和违法问题的，可以及时予以纠正，当然这种纠正并不立足于维护全国人大及其常委会自身享有的立法职权，更重要的是维护宪法和法律的权威。故从尊重其他国家机关的立法职权出发，全国人大常委会对行政法规、军事法规，乃至地方性法规的合宪性和合法性控制，应当通过违宪和违法审查的途径来实现。

从违宪和违法审查的角度来看，全国人大常委会对行政法规、军事法规和地方性法规的合宪性和合法性审查并不是主动进行的，而且基于相关的审查请求进行。这是由违宪和违法审查行为的法律性质决定的。通常情况下，违宪和违法审查都由审查请求提起的，审查者本身是出于被动的地位，因而不能过于主动地去监督被审查者的立法行为。如果审查者将自己的审查地位简单地等同于监督者，那么，只要审查者态度积极，可以通过主动审查方式来事实上架空和剥夺被审查者制定相关法律规范的活动，导致通过立法监督方式产生对立法职权的实质性侵权行为。故全国人大常委会只能以立法制约者的身份来介入行政法规、军事法规和地方性法规的违

---

① 2000 年《立法法》第 93 条规定："中央军事委员会根据宪法和法律，制定军事法规。中央军事委员会各总部、军兵种、军区，可以根据法律和中央军事委员会的军事法规、决定、命令，在其权限范围内，制定军事规章。军事法规、军事规章在武装力量内部实施。军事法规、军事规章的制定、修改和废止办法，由中央军事委员会依照本法规定的原则规定。"

宪和违法审查，而不宜采取过于主动的方式，随意干预其他国家机关的立法活动，应当以维护法制统一性为目标来开展必要的违宪和违法审查工作。

四　在全国人大下设宪法委员会是解决规范性文件合宪性和合法性的唯一的制度通道

当前，不论在立法理论上，还是在立法实践中，立法监督与立法制约问题两者纠缠在一起，没有作必要的功能区分，结果导致了立法者以立法监督者身份出现在立法活动的每一个角落，而立法者本身又缺少必要的人力、物力和智力的支持来对所有的法律规范进行有效的监督。借鉴国外的经验，从宪法学的理论出发，应当明确区分立法监督与立法制约的不同制度价值，在加强立法监督工作的同时，应当将保证法律规范合宪性和合法性工作的重点转移到立法制约领域。这就要求，包括全国人大常委会在内的立法监督者，首先要真正地尊重其他国家机关在立法方面所享有的职权，只要是宪法和法律赋予某个特定国家机关的立法职权，就必须给予尊重，不能因为自身是最高立法机关就可以漠视或忽视其他国家机关在行使立法职权方面所享有的一定程度的立法自由裁量权。作为最高立法机关，也不能以立法领域的"老大"自居，认为自己什么样的法律规范都能立，什么样的法律形式或法律规范都有权监督。必须要认清立法监督和立法制约的法律性质的本质不同。立法监督主要侧重于保障监督者自身立法职权的有效行使，而立法制约是特定的国家机关依据宪法和法律的规定，对于一切依据宪法和法律规定享有立法职权的国家机关制定法律规范是否具有合宪性和合法性，通过违宪和违法审查，最终达到消除违宪和违法性，维护宪法和法律权威的目的。[①]

当下来说，要保证中国特色社会主义法律体系中的各种法律形式的法律效力的统一性和法律规范内容的一致性，最重要的制度途径就是要在全国人大下设宪法委员会，具体负责监督所有国家机关制定的规范性文件的合宪性和合法性。这样就可以尊重一切依据宪法和法律有权制定法律规范的国家机关在立法领域的一定的自由裁量权，同时也便于全国人大常委会

---

① 例如，1919 年芬兰共和国宪法第 45 条规定：国务委员会如果发现交由国务委员会执行的总统决定同法律相抵触，经咨询司法总监的意见后，应建议总统撤销或修改其决定，如果总统坚持其原决定，国务委员会应宣布该项决定不能执行。上述规定属于违法性审查的性质，如果国务委员会认为总统制定的决定与法律相抵触，可以宣布不执行，从而防止违宪和违法的法律规范的生效实施。

加强自身的立法监督职权，对于凡是宪法和法律赋予全国人大及常委会制定的法律规范，不论是自身亲自制定，还是通过授权立法方式由其他的立法机关来制定，为了保证全国人大及其常委会在立法方面的主动性和科学性，全国人大常委会可以建立更加完善的立法监督制度，① 对于各种授权立法、实施法律的条例、批准后生效的法律规范实行必要的立法监督，包括采用立法后评估机制，从而抓住工作重点，保证立法质量。与此同时，要建立正式的违宪和违法审查制度，通过违宪和违法审查来彻底解决"政出多门"、"规范性文件更多、过滥"、"宪法权威得不到有效尊重和维护"等严重影响社会主义法治建设的根本问题。

Establishing a Legality Review Mechanism with Separation of Legislative Supervision from Legislative Control

【**Abstract**】Based on the basic theory of constitutional law, this article holds that any normative document adopted by any organ holding public power in accordance with the Constitution or laws and applicable to un-specific members of the general public should have legal effect and be able to regulate the behavior of all members of the general public within the scope of specific administrative areas. However, all

---

① 事实上，2000 年《立法法》已经认识到立法监督制度的一些重要特征，例如，该法第 88 条规定："改变或者撤销法律、行政法规、地方性法规、自治条例和单行条例、规章的权限是：（一）全国人民代表大会有权改变或者撤销它的常务委员会制定的不适当的法律，有权撤销全国人民代表大会常务委员会批准的违背宪法和本法第六十六条第二款规定的自治条例和单行条例；（二）全国人民代表大会常务委员会有权撤销同宪法和法律相抵触的行政法规，有权撤销同宪法、法律和行政法规相抵触的地方性法规，有权撤销省、自治区、直辖市的人民代表大会常务委员会批准的违背宪法和本法第六十六条第二款规定的自治条例和单行条例。"上述规定的最大特点是已经将全国人大常委会批准的"自治条例"与"单行条例"在法律效力上等同于全国人大常委会制定的"法律"，接受全国人大的监督。如从法理出发，实际上对全国人大常委会批准的"自治条例"和"单行条例"的立法监督应当是全国人人常委会自身的一项重要职责。

public authorities enjoying the power of adopting normative documents must exercise such power in accordance with the Constitution and laws and on the bases of constitutionality and legality. From the jurisprudential point of view, there are mainly two methods of ensuring the constitutionality and legality of normative documents: legislative supervision and legislative control. The former is exercised on the basis legislative functions and powers provided by the Constitution and laws for the purpose of ensuring the effective exercise such functions and powers whereas the latter is the review, on the basis of the competence provided for in the Constitution and laws, by public authorities of the constitutionality and legality of the normative documents adopted by other public authorities, for the purpose of ensuring the unity of the legal system.

【 Key words 】 Legislative Supervision, Legislative Control, Constitutionality, Legality

Autonomous Areas as a Constitutional Feature in China and Finland

*Markku Suksi**

【 **Abstract** 】 A comparison between the autonomy situations in the People's Republic of China (as concerns Hong Kong and Macau) and Finland (as concerns the Åland Islands) is facilitated along several features. In both cases, international commitments exist behind the national rules. In addition, the international commitments were incorporated into national law in a somewhat similar fashion, through two separate Basic Laws in China, one for Hong Kong and one for Macau, and the Guaranty Act in Finland for the Åland Islands. In both countries, the creation of autonomies is a result of a confirmation of national sovereignty over the areas concerned, but in both countries, the creation of autonomies also resulted in the assignment of exclusive law-making powers to the legislative assemblies of the autonomous entities. Finally, the systems of competence control created with respect to the autonomies in the two countries are asymmetrical. The great difference in law is that the international commitment of China is of a temporal nature. However, the international supervision of the Finnish commitment disappeared and left the Åland Islands arrangement to depend on domestic actions of the State. The possibilities for and the forms of legal continuity of the Chinese autonomy arrangements beyond the expiry of the international commitment is therefore a challenge *de lege ferenda* in the same way it used to be for Finland. In addition to these similarities in law, some similarities in fact can also be referred to. The autonomous areas are of a similar size in the national context, around or less than 0. 5 percent of the population, which means that the national governments are

---

＊ Professor of Public Law, Åbo Akademi University.

probably not viewing these areas as primary governmental matters in the everyday politics. These autonomous areas are also relatively wealthy in comparison with the rest of the national territory.

I. Introduction

Unitary states such as the People's Republic of China (hereinafter: China) and Finland are much less monolithic in terms of institutional design than the reference to the unitary nature of the state indicates. Although this may be a surprise to the outside observer, the flexibility in the internal state structure signals an implementation of the wish in both countries to recognize the existence of different minorities and population groups inside their national territories.

In China, the recognized minority ethnic groups are altogether 55. Under the Constitution of China, two different forms of local people's congress (hereinafter: LPC) are recognized for the purposes of the minority ethnic groups. The first form of LPC is created under Art. 116 of the Constitution of China, as specified in Art. 66 of the Legislation Law and Art. 19 of the Law on Regional National Autonomy. This form of local autonomy is characterized by the possibility to exercise so-called law-varying powers, which means that national law can be modified through a decision of a LPC of this kind provided that the national authorities confirm the local variant of the law. The second form of LPC is created under Art. 100 of the Constitution of China, as specified in Art. 66 of the Legislation Law and Art. 7 and Art. 43 of the Organic Law on the Local People's Congress and Local People's Governments. This form of local autonomy is empowered to pass by-laws that implement national law. The Finnish Constitution, in addition to identifying Finnish and Swedish as national languages and establishing a linguistic and a cultural autonomy for the Sami, opens up a recognition in Art. 17 (3) of the Constitution of other minorities, too, with the Roma and those who use the sign language explicitly mentioned. [1]

While the truly autonomous nature of the two forms of the LPC maybe doub-

---

[1]　For a comprehensive outline of the Finnish system of the protection of national minorities, see Suksi 2006.

ted,① Art. 31 of the Constitution of Chian opens up for so-called Special Administrative Region as established by law. This possibility has been used in two cases, Hong Kong and Macau, after China concluded an international treaty with the United Kingdom, on the one hand, and Portugal, on the other, about granting a high degree of autonomy to each of the areas. The international treaties are entitled Joint Declaration, and they make provision about the distribution of legislative powers between Mainland China and the two areas that used to be governed by the two colonial powers. In several respects, the status of the Åland Islands in Finland was and is similar, in particular during the period of 1920 through 1994, when the formal constitutional acts of Finland did not contain any provision about the autonomy or self-government of the Åland Islands. There was constitutional silence in spite of the fact that there is an international commitment on behalf of the Åland Islands by Finland through the 1921 Åland Islands Settlement under the auspices of the League of Nations. The current Constitution of Finland establishes an autonomy arrangement for the Åland Islands with powers that are not quite as extensive as those of Hong Kong and Macau but with an entrenchment that is more elaborate.

Because the Chinese commitment with respect to Hong Kong and Macau is temporal, extending over 50 years until 2047 and 2049, the future challenge lies in the constitutional regulation of the position of the two autonomous areas after the international commitment expires. Finland has some experience from the potential of expiry of an international commitment: the international organization that undertook the supervision of the commitment concerning the Åland Islands, the League of Nations, disappeared in the wake of the Second World War. How can

---

① Territorial autonomy is here defined as a singular entity in what otherwise would be a unitary state or a federal state, so that the entity introduces an asymmetrical feature in the state through a transfer of exclusive law-making powers on the basis of provisions, which often are of a special nature and established in such a manner that the state level remains with the residual powers, while the sub-state level relies on enumerated powers, at the same time as the state level contains no institutional representation of the sub-state entity. This is a relatively stringent definition of a core understanding of territorial autonomy, where the reference to exclusive law-making powers implies the absence of a supremacy doctrine on the part of the legislation of the state, so as not to allow preemption on the part of the national level within the competences of the sub-state entity. From this perspective, territorial autonomy would be difficult to combine with the doctrine of democratic centralism. See Suksi 2011.

the disappearance of an international autonomy commitment be dealt with by a State? In which ways can open constitutional regulation of autonomous areas be positivized in the constitution of a country and how has this been done in a comparative perspective? Could the method of incorporating provisions concerning the Åland Islands in the Constitution of Finland be relevant for regulating the future position of Hong Kong and Macau in the Chinese state structure?

This comparative undertaking is facilitated by the fact that there are certain parallels between the autonomy situations in China (as concerns Hong Kong and Macau) and Finland (as concerns the Åland Islands). In both cases, an international commitment exists behind the national rules. ① In addition, the international commitments were incorporated into national law in a somewhat similar fashion, through two separate Basic Laws in China, one for Hong Kong and one for Macau, and the Guaranty Act in Finland. In both countries, the creation of autonomies was a result of a confirmation of national sovereignty over the areas concerned, but in both countries, the creation of autonomies also resulted in the assignment of exclusive law-making powers to the legislative assemblies of the autonomous entities. Finally, the systems of competence control created with respect to the autonomies in the two countries are asymmetrical in an interesting way. The great difference in law is that the international commitment of China is of a temporal nature, although it is at the same time recognized that the international supervision of the Finnish commitment disappeared and left the Åland Islands arrangement to depend on actions of the State. The possibilities for and the forms of legal continuity of the Chinese autonomy arrangements beyond the expiry of the international commitment is therefore a challenge *de lege ferenda* in the same way it used to be for Finland.

In addition to these similarities in law, some similarities in fact can also be referred to. The autonomous areas are of a similar size in the national context, around or less than 0.5 percent of the population, which means that the national governments are probably not viewing these areas as primary governmental matters in the everyday politics. As a consequence, the areas run the risk of being forgotten about in the grand

---

① It is not known that the creation of the autonomy arrangements for Hong Kong and Macau would have been inspired by the example of the Åland Islands from 1921 or by the historical example of the Memel Territory from 1924.

stream of political events that the national governments have to deal with on a continuous basis. These autonomous areas are also relatively wealthy in comparison with the rest of the national territory: the GDP per capita of Hong Kong was a few years ago US $ 44000, while that of Mainland China was US $ 3000 (and probably increasing while this article is being written), and in the Åland Islands, the same figure is in excess of US $ 50000 in comparison with US $ 28000 for the entire Finland.

II. International Commitments as a Backdrop

By the time of Finnish independence from the Russian Empire in 1917, the population of the Åland Islands started to be of the opinion that the area should secede from Finland and join the former "mother-country", Sweden. For that purpose, they petitioned the King of Sweden twice by collecting signatures, and at some point, the issue evolved into a dispute between Finland and Sweden which had the potential of threatening peace in the area. The Parliament of Finland tried to resolve the matter by adopting the first Self-Government Act in 1920 that created the autonomy arrangement, but the inhabitants of the Åland Islands did not want to recognize the arrangement. The Council of the League of Nations took up the matter in 1920 as a conflict resolution matter and concluded in its decision of 24 June 1921, against the background of the Report of a Committee of Jurists and the Memorandum of a Commission of Rapporteurs (which both investigated different aspects of the question) that sovereignty over the Åland Islands belongs to Finland, but under certain conditions that relate to the interests of the world, future cordial relations between Finland and Sweden and the prosperity and happiness of the Åland Islands themselves. At this point, the Council of the League of Nations established two different strands to achieve these aims: 1) that certain further guarantees should be given for the protection of the Islanders, and 2) that arrangements should be concluded for the non-fortification and neutralization of the Archipelago. [1]

---

[1]   As concerns the second strand, the treaty arrangement concerning the non-fortification and neutralization of the Åland Islands led in October 1921 to the adoption of the Convention on the Non-Fortification and Neutralization of the Åland Islands. In Art. 9 of the Convention, the parties to the convention, including Sweden, recognized that the Åland Islands constituted an integral part of the Republic of Finland. However, it should be noticed that this Convention does not deal with the autonomy arrangement and the internal constitutional structures concerning the Åland Islands, but is limited to international security policy.

As concerns the first strand of the decision of the Council of the League of Nations on 24 June 1921, the Council of the League of Nations established two different guarantee mechanisms:

"3. The new guarantees to be inserted in the autonomy law should specially aim at the preservation of the Swedish language in the schools, at the maintenance of the landed property in the hands of the Islanders, at the restriction, within reasonable limits, of the exercise of the franchise by new comers, and at ensuring the appointment of a Governor who will possess the confidence of the population.

4. The Council has requested that the guarantees will be more likely to achieve their purpose, if they are discussed and agreed to by the Representatives of Finland with those of Sweden, if necessary with the assistance of the Council of the League of Nations, and, in accordance with the Council's desire, the two parties have decided to seek out an agreement. Should their efforts fail, the Council would itself fix the guarantees which, in its opinion, should be inserted, by means of an amendment, in the autonomy law of 7 May 1920. In any case, the Council of the League of Nations will see to the enforcement of these guarantees."

As is clear on the basis of para. 3 of the Settlement, the Council of the League of Nations was well aware of the existence of an autonomy act, that is, of the 1920 Self-Government Act for the Åland Islands. Apparently, the arguments of Sweden and of the representatives of the inhabitants of the Åland Islands had made an impression on the Council, because some specific protection mechanisms that Finland would, after more concrete definition of the contents of these protection mechanisms, insert in the Self-Government Act concerned, *inter alia*, Swedish as the language of education, the maintenance of real property in the hands of the inhabitants of the Åland Islands, restriction of the right to vote of new inhabitants in the area and the position of the representative of the central government. ① The discussion concerning these principles between the representatives of Finland and Sweden and the agreement thereupon took place during the days immediately after 24 June 1921 so that the Council of the League of Nations could, on 27 June

---

① With a view to the position of the Chief Executive in Hong Kong and Macau, it is necessary to stress that the Governor of Åland is the head of the relatively minimal state administration present in the Åland Islands, not a part of the Government of the Åland Islands.

1921, register the more concrete guarantees in a separate text which was appended to the decision of 24 June 1921. This Åland Islands Settlement did not become a formal treaty between Finland and Sweden, but the Settlement approved under the auspices of the League of Nations nonetheless resolved the contentious issue. The legal nature of the Settlement under public international law has given rise to a certain discussion about whether the Settlement is a treaty or not, and it seems clear that the latter opinion is now commonly followed, although the Settlement is today understood by Finland as a binding international obligation in the form of customary international law.

In the Åland Islands Settlement, Finland undertook to guarantee, without undue delay, to the population of the Åland Islands the maintenance of its language, culture and local Swedish traditions through incorporation of guarantees for these matters in the Self-Government Act. What is special in this context from the point of view of international politics and public international law is that the Council of the League of Nations referred to autonomy and used the concept of autonomy when it made reference to the 1920 "Law of Autonomy of the Aaland Islands". Thus there existed a more or less established concept of autonomy under public international law and in connection to the Åland Islands by the time the status of the Memel Territory was decided in 1924. [1] The specific obligations undertaken by Finland were formulated and agreed upon by Finland and Sweden before the Council of the League of Nations. [2] The Åland Islands Settlement thus created gave the special rights granted under this autonomy arrangement a collective character, because the focal point of the special rights was the inhabitants of the Åland Islands.

As concerns Hong Kong, the international commitments concerning the autonomy of Hong Kong and Macau are clearly of a treaty-law nature under public international law, although the treaties are entitled Declarations. The reasons for the treaty-arrangements are historical. China attracted a great deal of interest

---

[1]   Convention concerning the Territory of Memel, signed at Paris, May 8, 1924, 736 *League of Nations Treaty Series* 1924, p. 87. See also *Interpretation of the Statute of Memel Territory.* Judgment of 11 August 1932, PCIJ, Series A. /B. —Fasc. No. 50.

[2]   For the text of the Åland Islands Settlement, see The Åland Islands Agreement before the Council of the League of Nations, V. Minutes of the Seventeenth Meeting of the Council, 27 June 1921. League of Nations Official Journal, September 1921, p. 701.

amongst the colonial powers during the 18th and 19th centuries, and the Empire was forced to open up for trade and other contacts with the outside world. This led to armed confrontations between China and the United Kingdom, while the co-habitation of China and Portugal was more peaceful. After being part of the Chinese Empire, the island of Hong Kong on the south-eastern coast of China was transferred to the United Kingdom under Art. III of the 1842 Treaty of Nanjing, ending the so-called Opium War of 1840. Due to further disturbances between the two empires, British possessions were enlarged on the basis of Art. VI of the 1860 Convention of Peking to the township of Kowloon, which is actually a peninsula of the Chinese mainland. Finally, British possessions on the mainland were extended to the so-called New Territories through a 99-year lease on the basis of the 1898 Convention of Peking, a period of time that would elapse in 1997. The history of Macau is longer, with Portuguese presence since the 16th century, but essentially similar with respect to treaties that placed Macau under Portuguese rule at the end of the 19th century. The Portuguese revolution in 1974, however, created momentum in Portugal for active measures to unwind the colonial possessions.

Throughout the 20th century, the Chinese governments irrespective of political orientation held these treaties to be unequal and argued for a return of the Chinese territories of Hong Kong and Macau. [1] The aggravation of the Chinese was increased by the fact that both territories could be regarded as colonies of the United Kingdom and Portugal, ruled by a Governor appointed by the colonial power. The colonial government of Hong Kong was created under the Hong Kong Letters Patent 1917 −1995 [2] and the Hong Kong Royal Instructions 1917 − 1993 (Nos. 1 and 2). [3] The system did not leave much space for the participation of the Chinese population of Hong Kong in the public affairs of the colony. Towards the end of the colonial period there were attempts to develop mechanisms to enhance political participation (*inter alia*, in 1991, the first direct elections of a portion of the Legislative Council were held). [4] These reforms were, in part, a

---

[1]   See also Leung 2006, pp. 4 f. − 16 f.

[2]   For the Letters Patent, see Leung 2006, pp. 371 − 380.

[3]   For the Royal Instructions, see Leung 2006, pp. 381 − 390.

[4]   See Leung 2006, pp. 60 − 70, 257 f.

response to criticism from the UN Human Rights Committee of Hong Kong's lack of democratic institutions. ① In principle, however, the issue of political reform was deferred to the period following the return of sovereignty over Hong Kong to China.

In the 1980s, as the UK's 99-year lease of the New Territories came closer to its end, the Chinese and the UK Governments began discussions about the future of Hong Kong. On 19 December 1984, China and the UK Government concluded the Joint Declaration on the Question of Hong Kong in which the UK Government agreed to return the entirety of Hong Kong to China on 1 July 1997 and thus end the colonial period with respect to that area. Although the agreement between China and the UK is entitled the "Joint Declaration", the document is formally to be understood as a bilateral treaty under international law, ② creating legal obligations on both of the parties after ratification. ③ In the Joint Declaration,

---

① See UN Human Rights Committee, Concluding Comments in 1995, CCPR/C/79/Add. 57, para. 19: "The Committee is aware of the reservation made by the United Kingdom that article 25 does not require establishment of an elected Executive or Legislative Council. It however takes the view that once an elected Legislative Council is established, its election must conform to article 25 of the Covenant. The Committee considers that the electoral system in Hong Kong does not meet the requirements of article 25, as well as articles 2, 3 and 26 of the Covenant. It underscores in particular that only 20 of 60 seats in the Legislative Council are subject to direct popular election and that the concept of functional constituencies, which gives undue weight to the views of the business community, discriminates among voters on the basis of property and functions. This clearly constitutes a violation of articles 2, paragraph 1, 25 (b) and 26. It is also concerned that laws depriving convicted persons of their voting rights for periods of up to 10 years may be a disproportionate restriction of the rights protected by article 25. " See also the Human Rights Committee's report to the General Assembly, A/44/40 (44th session, 1989), paras 140 – 189.

② Joint Declaration of the Government of the United Kingdom of Great Britain and Northern Ireland and the Government of the People's Republic of China on the Question of Hong Kong, 19 December 1984, 1399 UNTS 33. See also Ghai 1999, pp. 53 – 56.

③ According to Art. 8, the Joint Declaration is subject to ratification and shall enter into force on the date of the exchange of instruments of ratification, which shall take place in Beijing before 30 June 1985. The same provision says that the Joint Declaration and its Annexes shall be equally binding, which seems to imply that the entire document was intended to have normative effects between the parties. See also Xiao Weiyun 2001, p. 70. See also Mushkat 1997, p. 172, according to whom the Joint Declaration and its Annexes were not incorporated into the local law of Hong Kong. Therefore, the Joint Declaration could not, as such, give rise to justiciable claims in Hong Kong. On the treaty nature of the Joint Declaration, see also Mushkat 1997, p. 140 ff.

the UK and China also agreed to implement the separate annexes to the Joint Declaration. ① The Joint Declaration is a unique treaty about an internal governance structure because of the temporal nature of the commitments. According to Art. 3 (12) of the Joint Declaration, the autonomy arrangement concerning Hong Kong is limited in time, lasting 50 years from the Chinese resumption of sovereignty over Hong Kong on 1 July 1997. A similar Joint Declaration from 1987 exists between China and Portugal concerning Macau. ②

The temporal nature of the autonomy arrangements distinguishes Hong Kong and Macau from other autonomy arrangements in the world, but it is difficult to predict how the temporal nature of the arrangement affects its contents. ③ The question of what will happen after the fifty year period is, of course, already very topical now, in 2011, for reasons of legal certainty and legal continuity, but there have been signs that the autonomy arrangements may continue to exist after the period that guarantees autonomy for Hong Kong and Macau. ④ Autonomy could continue, in one form or another, but in such a case, the arrangement would be purely internal and solely based on the Constitution of China, without any international guarantee for its continued existence. The situation is somewhat reminiscent of the Finnish commitment concerning the Åland Islands, which may have seemed to come to an end with the demise of the League of Nations in the

---

① Annex I: Elaboration by the Government of the People's Republic of China of its basic policies regarding Hong Kong; Annex II: Sino-British Joint Liaison Group; Annex III: Land Leases.

② Joint Declaration of the Government of the Portuguese Republic and the Government of the People's Republic of China on the Question of Macao, 13 April 1987, 1498 UNTS 195. For information concerning Macau, see Jorge Oliveira & Paulo Cardinal, eds. , *One Country, Two Systems, Three Legal Orders-Perspectives of Evolution. Essays on Macau's Autonomy after the Resumption of Sovereignty by China.* Springer-Verlag: Berlin & Heidelberg, 2009.

③ As pointed out by Chan 2010, p. 129, there is "no enforcement mechanism under the Joint Declaration or at the international level" for conflict resolution by an external mechanism.

④ See Huang Jin 2009. See also Xiao Weiyun 2001, p. 112, quoting Deng Xiaoping for saying the following: "This law shall be effective for at least 50 years. I would like to add here, after 50 years, there would be less need for Hong Kong to change. Our policies regarding Hong Kong shall not change. " However, as pointed out by Ghai 1999, p. 143, the amendment restriction included in Art. 159 (3) of the Basic Law prohibiting amendments that contravene the basic principles would presumably disappear after the 50 years period. See also Chan 2010, p. 129, who concludes that it is not clear "whether the model will ultimately (or within 50 years) lead to the merger or the retention of 'two systems'" .

1940s. Although the international guarantor of the arrangement disappeared, Finland has signaled the voluntary continuance of the commitment as a unilateral commitment owed to the international community and has, as a consequence, continued to develop the autonomy arrangement, argued for particular exceptions for the arrangement in the conclusion of international treaties, such as the accession treaty to the European Union, and inserted constitutional provisions in the 1990s into the positive constitutional law of Finland.

A common feature in the international commitments of the two countries is the fact that the international commitment identified the national act by which the commitment would be implemented in the national legal order. In the case of the Åland Islands, the Settlement of 1921 identified the Autonomy Act, that is, the 1920 Self-Government Act, as the vehicle of implementation of the guarantees for the autonomy of Åland, while the Joint Declarations identify a so-called Basic Law as the vehicle of implementation for the high degree of autonomy accorded to Hong Kong and Macau.

III. Incorporation of the Commitment into National Law

A striking similarity between China and Finland is that the international commitments concerning autonomous areas have been incorporated into the national legal order in more or less the same way, namely transcription or almost exact transformation. In principle, the emergence of the international commitment was different with respect to the two States: the details of the Finnish commitment were developed by Finland and Sweden under the auspices of the Council of the League of Nations, while the details of the Chinese commitments were actually developed and proposed by the Chinese Government and appended to the general part of the two Joint Declarations. The Chinese definition of the details of the two autonomy arrangements was done in a manner that made the appendices about the contents of the two autonomy arrangements parts of the binding treaty commitments.

As established in para. 1 of the Åland Islands Settlement, "Finland, resolved to assure and to guarantee to the population of the Aaland Islands the preservation of their language, of their culture, and of their local Swedish traditions, undertakes to introduce shortly into the Law of Autonomy of the Aaland Islands of May 7th, 1920, the following guarantees: […]." These guarantees and special rights for the inhabitants of the Åland Islands were registered in 1922 in a separate Act containing Special Provisions concerning the Population of the Åland Islands, or the so-called Guaranty Act. The Parliament of Finland did not formally speaking amend the 1920 Self-Government Act, but enacted instead a separate piece of law as a complement to the Act of 1920. The Guaranty Act was enacted in the same order as the Self-Government Act, that is, in the constitutional order involving a qualified majority of two-thirds. The Guaranty Act was hence enacted with the same special and regional entrenchment stipulations as the Act of 1920. From that perspective, it is possible to say that the Guaranty Act was vested with the same elevated constitutional status as the first Self-Government Act. However, the particular legislation concerning the sale of real property in the Åland Islands, mentioned in sub-section 2 of para. 2 of the Settlement, was enacted by the Parliament of Finland only in 1938 as the Act on the Exercise of the Right of Redemption at Sale of Real Property in the Åland Islands, [①] which means that the particular protection mechanism regarding real property was inoperative during the first 15 years of the autonomy of Åland. It is possible to say against this background that immediately after the entering into force of the 1919 Form of Government (Constitution) Act, the formula of "one state" as well as the newly gained sovereignty of Finland were challenged and that Finland had to agree to and implement special measures in order to protect its territorial integrity.

In terms of the legislative strategy chosen to incorporate the Åland Islands Settlement in the legal order of Finland, it is possible to say that it was *not* incorporated in the normal way as a treaty under international law. The reason for this is that the Åland Islands Settlement is not a treaty under international law and thus there was no treaty to be incorporated under those constitutional provisions that existed in 1921 −1922. Instead, the Settlement was brought into force domestically through another procedure, namely transcription (or, in other words, reception). In this context of the Åland Islands Settlement, this method of incorporation means that the text of the Settlement, which was originally drafted in French and English,

---

① This Act was replaced in 1951 by an Act with the same title, and the current law is based on the 1975 Act on the Limitation of the Right to Acquire and Possess Real Property in the Åland Islands, also entitled the Act on the Acquisition of Real Property on the Åland Islands.

was translated in Finland *expressis verbis* into Swedish and Finnish (with the exception that the order of the sections of the Guaranty Act is different from the order of the paragraphs in the Settlement). After the translation was completed, the Government of Finland submitted the text to the Parliament of Finland in the form of a Bill, which was enacted in the Parliament pursuant to the requirements of a qualified majority and in the fast track order of constitutional amendments. ① The 1951 Self-Government Act incorporated the provisions of the Guaranty Act with some modifications, which means that the method of incorporation actually shifted over from transcription to transformation, and this latter method is also the one that applies to the incorporation of the Settlement through the 1991 Self-Government Act. ② In principle, the Self-Government Act introduces a series of exceptions to the Constitution of Finland that apply in the territory of the Åland Islands.

While regional autonomy and other forms of minority protection are regular features of the Constitution of China in relation to the 55 recognized minority ethnic groups of China, the situation with respect to Taiwan may have been the main reason for amending the Constitution in 1984 so as to allow the creation of special administrative regions. It is likely that Hong Kong and Macau were also in the picture early on. ③ The existence of a constitutional provision concerning special administrative regions was found to be a suitable normative framework for the re-incorporation of Hong Kong and for assigning the autonomy arrangement a legal basis in the constitutional fabric of the country. Article 31 of the Constitution of the People's Republic of China (PRC) grants the state the power to establish special administrative regions when necessary. In addition, the social, economic and legal systems to be instituted in special administrative regions shall be prescribed by law enacted by the National People's

---

① In the third reading on 9 December 1921, the matter was declared urgent by the votes 153 to 23 (meaning that the Bill was not left in abeyance over the next elections for a final consideration by the subsequent Parliament), after which the law was enacted on the same day by the votes 152 to 22.

② See Suksi 2008, pp. 277 – 279.

③ See Ghai 1999, p. 56 f. , Xiao Weiyun 2001, pp. 9 – 11, and Leung 2006, p. 19 as well as Chen 2009, p. 755 ff. and Chan 2010, p. 126. As pointed out by Hualing Fu et al. 2007, p. 2 f. , the concept of "one country, two systems" was by no means new in the Chinese political thinking in the beginning of the 1980s, but it has its root in the 1930s and the 1940s, first in the distinction between areas controlled by the Communists in relation to areas controlled by the Nationalist Party and later on in the relationship between China and Tibet during a short time after 1949.

Congress in light of the specific conditions. [①] The constitutional provision is open and does not say much about the powers granted to a special administrative region (hereinafter: SAR), but the reference to "administrative" indicates that the powers to be exercised could be at least regulatory in nature.

It was evidently deemed necessary to establish such SARs as a means to facilitate the transfer of sovereignty over Hong Kong and Macau from the UK and Portugal to China, as recorded in the Joint Declarations between the Governments of the three countries. For Hong Kong, the requirement of regulation through law was fulfilled by the National People's Congress (hereinafter: NPC) on 4 April 1990, when it adopted the Basic Law of the Hong Kong Special Administrative Region of the People's Republic of China. [②] A similar Basic Law for Macau was enacted on 31 March 1993. The specific condition that was taken into account was the need to return Hong Kong and Macau to China, both places with a different economic and legal system. Through the Basic Law, the capitalist system of Hong Kong with the British styled common law tradition was fitted into the overall Socialist system of

---

[①] "The state may establish special administrative regions when necessary. The systems to be instituted in special administrative regions shall be prescribed by law enacted by the National People's Congress in the light of the specific conditions." A special administrative region is apparently to be distinguished from such autonomy arrangements which are created on the basis of Art. 4 on minority rights: "Regional autonomy is practiced in areas where people of minority nationalities live in concentrated communities; in these areas organs of self-government are established to exercise the power of autonomy. All national autonomous areas are integral parts of the People's Republic of China."

[②] Adopted on 4 April 1990 by the Seventh National People's Congress (NPC) of the People's Republic of China at its Third Session. The Basic Law was promulgated on the same day by Decree No. 26 of the President of the PRC. On the same day, perhaps to dispel any doubts about the constitutionality of the Basic Law, the NPC made the Decision of the National People's Congress on the Basic Law of the Hong Kong Special Administrative Region of the People's Republic of China, according to which the Basic Law "is constitutional as it is enacted in accordance with the Constitution of the People's Republic of China and in the light of the specific conditions of Hong Kong". See Xiao Weiyun 2001, pp. 75 – 81. See also Decision of the Standing Committee of the National People's Congress on the English Text of the Basic Law of the Hong Kong Special Administrative Region of the People's Republic of China, according to which the 14th Meeting of the 7th NPCSC decided the following: "the English translation of the Basic Law of the Hong Kong Special Administrative Region of the People's Republic of China, examined and approved under the aegis of the Law Committee of the National People's Congress, shall be the official English text and shall be equally authentic as the Chinese text. In case of any discrepancy in the meaning of wording between the English text and the Chinese text, the Chinese text shall prevail." For the decision, see Leung 2006, p. 464.

China both in the area of economics and law by creating an exception to what the Constitution of China required. A similar strategy was followed concerning Macau, which follows the Portuguese civil law tradition of a continental European kind.

An explicit reference to Art. 31 of the Constitution of China was included in section 3 (1) of the Joint Declaration concerning Hong Kong [and in section 2 (12) of that of Macau], which creates an international commitment for the internal solution. The legal basis for the domestic solutions is established in the two Basic Laws which spell out in detail the contents of the arrangement under Art. 31 of the Constitution. [①] Article 3 (1) of the treaty concerning Hong Kong provides that the PRC, while upholding national unity and territorial integrity and taking account of the history of Hong Kong and its realities, has decided to establish, in accordance with the provisions of Article 31 of the Constitution, a Hong Kong Special Administrative Region upon resuming the exercise of sovereignty over Hong Kong. A provision which is to some extent similar is included in Art. 2 (1) of the treaty concerning Macau. Similarly to the regional autonomies, the Joint Declarations establish that the Governments of the two entities will be composed of local inhabitants. Finally, the two Joint Declarations provide that the basic policies established in the Declarations-and elaborated in Annex I to the treaties as declarations made by China-are to be stipulated in a Basic Law for each of the two entities, enacted by the National People's Congress, which will remain unchanged for 50 years from 1 July 1997 in the case of Hong Kong and 19 December 1999 in the case of Macau.

Pursuant to the Joint Declarations, reinforced by the two Annexes I, the National People's Congress of China was obligated, after ratification, to enact and promulgate a Basic Law of the Hong Kong Special Administrative Region of the People's Republic of China (hereinafter: the HK Basic Law) and a similar one for Macau (the Macau Basic Law) in accordance with the Constitution of the PRC.

---

① The term "Basic Law" is in this context not a reference to a special enactment and amendment formula (although the initiation of amendments from Hong Kong is a more difficult procedure), because the Basic Law does not appear to have been adopted by the National People's Congress of China by any qualified majority or special procedure. Moreover, section 159 of the Basic Law does not prescribe any more complicated amendment formula for the Basic Law than for any other act, but it does prevent such amendments to the Basic Law that are in contravention with the basic principles, found in the Joint Declaration. Therefore, the references in the Basic Law to the Joint Declaration could be interpreted as an elevation of the normative status of the Basic Law to a level above that of ordinary acts of China.

The obligation stipulates that after the establishment of the two SARs, the Socialist system and Socialist policies shall not be practiced in the SARs and that the previous capitalist systems and life-style shall remain unchanged for 50 years. Because the two social orders would normally be understood as antagonistic, the "NPC adopted a formal decision on the same day it passed the Basic Law, declaring that the Basic Law is consistent with the PRC Constitution". ① Also, the two Annexes I declare that apart from displaying the national flag and national emblem of the PRC, the two SARs may use a regional flag and emblem of their own and are in charge of the maintenance of public order in the SARs. Although military forces may sent by the central government of China to be stationed in the two SARs for the purpose of defense, they shall not interfere in the internal affairs of the SARs. ② The two Annexes I also contains a section on basic rights and freedoms according to which the Governments of the SARs shall protect the rights and freedoms of their inhabitants and other persons according to law and maintain the rights and freedoms as provided for by the laws previously in force in Hong Kong and Macau. Hence in both entities, a number of rights not available to the inhabitants of Mainland China are guaranteed to the inhabitants of the two SARs. ③

---

① See Hualing Fu et al. 2007, p. 3. This is an interesting feature from the point of view of the Finnish Constitution, which contains, in section 73, the possibility to enact limited exceptions to the Constitution.

② Expenditure for these military forces shall be borne by the Central People's Government.

③ These basic rights include, according to section XIII of Annex I, freedom of the person, of speech, of the press, of assembly, of association, to form and join trade unions, of correspondence, of travel, of movement, of strike, of demonstration, of choice of occupation, of academic research, of belief (that is, of religion, which is of importance in this context); inviolability of the home, the freedom to marry and the right to raise a family freely. Every person shall also have the right to confidential legal advice, access to the courts, representation in the courts by a lawyer of his choice, and to obtain judicial remedies, and every person shall have the right to challenge the actions of the executive in the courts. These basic rights are reinforced by the pledge that the provisions of the International Covenant on Civil and Political Rights and the International Covenant on Economic, Social and Cultural Rights as applied to Hong Kong shall remain in force. These basic rights are also reinforced by section II of Annex I which promises that the laws previously in force in Hong Kong shall be maintained, except for any that contravene the Basic Law or is amended by the HKSAR legislature. The "laws previously in force in Hong Kong" include the common law, rules of equity, ordinances, subordinate legislation and customary law, which means that the common law system is granted protection under both national constitutional law (e. g., Art. 31 of the Constitution) and international law. This is important with a view to the fact that China maintains a socialist legal system with a legal order evolving toward a civil law system. Finally, Annex I contains provisions concerning the right of abode, travel and immigration.

The fact that the two Joint Declarations are relatively faithfully reproduced in the two Basic Laws would almost indicate that a transcription of the international commitment has taken place in the national implementation. However, transformation may be the better characterization of the form of national implementation, a method towards which Finland moved already in 1951, after the transcription in the 1922 Guaranty Act. It is important to point out in the context that the texts of the international commitments concerning the Åland Islands, on the one hand, and Hong Kong and Macau, on the other, have not become parts of the national legal order through ratification. They are thus not self-executing in the event the national implementation measures would produce results that deviate from the international commitments.

IV. Entrenchment of Autonomy Arrangements

The Joint Declarations (including their Annexes), as formal treaties under international law which have been ratified by China, entrench the two autonomy arrangements in international law and provides an international legal guarantee for upholding the obligation. The guarantee is, formally speaking, bilateral and not multilateral for each of the entities, since the UK is the only other party to the international commitment concerning Hong Kong and Portugal concerning Macau. The Joint Declarations do not stipulate any supervisory mechanism, which means that China is expected to implement its obligations in good faith on the basis of the treaties[1] by means of national law explicitly mentioned in the treaty itself: Art. 3 (12) of the Joint Declaration stipulates that implementation will take place by means of a Basic Law of the HKSAR enacted by the National People's Congress, and a similar

---

[1]   In case a dispute arose between China and the UK about the implementation of the Joint Declaration, Ghai 1999, p. 72, is of the opinion that there seems to exist no basis for effective action in case of its breach. Because China has not recognized the compulsory jurisdiction of the International Court of Justice, such a dispute could be litigated before the Court only if China agrees to such litigation on a case-by-case basis. Interestingly in the context, the Sino-British Joint Liaison Group agreed, in advance of the transfer of sovereignty, that a number of international treaties, among them the Statute of the International Court of Justice, would continue to apply to the HKSAR after 1 July 1977. See Leung 2006, p. 417.

provision exists concerning Macau. In this way, China committed itself in the Joint Declarations to implementing an unusually detailed set of treaty provisions in its domestic legislation by means of a legislative decision of the highest law-making body in a piece of law which is specifically named in the treaty. ①

However, the Joint Declarations provided nothing specific about the normative level at which each of the Basic Laws should be enacted, nor were they understood by the Chinese Government so that the Declarations should be turned into national law expressis verbis: although the main bulk of the provisions in the Basic Laws, including their name, come from the Joint Declarations, they contain provisions which are not prescribed by the Joint Declarations② at the same time as some provisions of the Joint Declarations are not explicitly featured in the Basic Law, although one can always find an implicit connection. While the title of the Acts, the Basic Law, could imply that they have an elevated normative status which falls between the Constitution and ordinary legislation or as an organic law of some sort, it seems that the Basic Laws were enacted under the Constitution of China as ordinary pieces of legislation. ③ From that perspective, the Basic Laws are, in the Chinese legal order, pieces of ordinary legislation, sometimes attributed with the characteristics of a "special law" in the hierarchy of norms because the general legal principles of China imply that special laws prevail over ordinary laws: "At the national law level, laws which have the status of a special law prevail over ordinary pieces of law", and the Basic Laws are considered to be such law. ④ Hence the

---

① See also Xiao Weiyun 2001, p. 13, who concludes that the Joint Declaration is not domestic law, but that China would, after signature and ratification, start implementing it. "Naturally, it has legal status and effect." See Xiao Weiyun 2001, pp. 76, 200, 213.

② See Xiao Weiyun 2001, p. 289, Ghai 1999, pp. 67 – 70.

③ See Leung 2006, pp. 40 – 42, according to whom the norm hierarchy in China is as follows: the Constitution, the national legislation, administrative regulations and local regulations. The Basic Law is placed on the second level, among the national legislation. See also Morris 2007, p. 105, who points out that the "Basic Law is not, as many common-law commentators have declared, a constitution or 'mini-constitution' for Hong Kong. It is merely another law-a statute-enacted by the NPC. It is subordinate to the PRC Constitution and does not occupy the entire field, as much of the PRC Constitution applies in Hong Kong as well."

④ Leung 2006, p. 42. See also Leung 2006, pp. 45 – 47, 244 f.

Basic Laws seem to have some sort of elevated status. ① A more tangible entrenchment effect can be accorded to the fact that the autonomy arrangements concerning Hong Kong and Macau are based on international treaties. ② The entrenchments are of an international nature and imply that China cannot legally rid itself of the arrangements during the established period of time without the consent of the other State party to each of the two treaties. Therefore, from a holistic perspective, the two entities are entrenched on a semi-constitutional level of some sort, the exact nature of which may be difficult to determine.

The total entrenchment effect is more multifarious concerning the Åland Islands. Although not a specific treaty-based entrenchment, there is nonetheless an entrenchment under international law through the unilateral commitment of Finland to the Åland Islands Settlement even after the Second World War. Here there is an approximate correspondence between China and Finland, but the picture is different in terms of the other entrenchment forms that apply to the Åland Islands. From the very beginning, the Self-Government Act has been enacted in the order prescribed for constitutional amendments, involving a qualified majority of two-thirds when the final decision concerning the adoption or the amendment of the Self-Government Act is being made in the Parliament of Finland. Therefore, there is a special entrenchment involved, but in a manner that does not actually elevate the Self-Government Act to the rank of a formal constitutional act. Instead, the special entrenchment indicates that the Self-Government Act, which does not identify itself as a constitutional act, is a so-called Act of Exception. There also exists a so-called regional entrenchment for the autonomy arrangement of Åland by the requirement in the Self-Government Act that any amendment to it, including

---

① On the concept of basic law in China, see Ghai 1999, p. 101, making the point that it can be understood as referring to statutes, that is, ordinary national laws enacted by the NPC. As pointed out by Dowdle 2007, p. 71, "China has more than sixty 'basic laws' in force at present, of which the Basic Law of the Hong Kong SAR is simply one. Contrary to what many in Hong Kong's interpretative community presumed, at least in the 1990s, simply calling the Hong Kong Basic Law a 'Basic Law' did not endow it with some uniquely 'constitutional' essence per se." Nonetheless, according to Xiao Weiyun 2001, p. 177, "the HKSAR Basic Law is regarded as a fundamental law established by NPC; any amendment should be made by NPC", which statement of course may be limited to the amendment procedures of the Basic Law.

② For different forms of entrenchment, see Suksi 1998.

the enactment of a new Self-Government Act, has to be approved by the Legislative Assembly of the Åland Islands by a two-thirds qualified majority. What this means is that the Parliament of Finland cannot by means of a unilateral decision cause negative amendments to or rid itself of the autonomy arrangement. Instead, a high level of consensus is required, a consensus that is protective of the Åland Islands. ① Finally, through amendments in the 1990s, the Constitution of Finland was supplemented with provisions that created a so-called general entrenchment, now established in sections 75② and 120③ of the Constitution that entered into force in the year 2000.

Admittedly, and in comparison with autonomies in other countries, the autonomy arrangement of the Åland Islands is extremely well entrenched in the constitutional fabric of Finland and in the legal order. In comparison with Hong Kong, where the entrenchment is in many ways weaker, the Åland Islands seems solidly entrenched so as to give the impression of the arrangement as a permanent feature of the Finnish as well as of the European and international legal order. The one significant entrenchment type that is not present in any of the entities reviewed here is entrenchment under the principle of the self-determination of peoples. This is due to the fact that the populations of the three areas are not peoples in the meaning of Art. 1 of the CCPR and cannot therefore enjoy the protection of the argument that an autonomy arrangement accorded to a collectivity that is designated as a people should not be weakened or abolished. It can even be doubted whether any of the populations of the entities reviewed here are minorities. This is not the

---

① This is sustained by the provision in section 28 of the Self-Government Act, according to which no such amendment of the Constitution or an Act enacted by the Parliament of Finland will enter into force in the Åland Islands that deals with the principles of the right of individuals to own real estate in the Åland Islands or right to funds that belong to business activities. The provision could even imply the existence of an almost unamendable core of the Finnish Constitution, at least as concerns the Åland Islands and actions against the wishes of the inhabitants of the Åland Islands.

② "The legislative procedure for the Act on the Autonomy of the Åland Islands and the Act on the Right to Acquire Real Estate in the Åland Islands is governed by the specific provisions in those Acts. The right of the Legislative Assembly of the Åland Islands to submit proposals and the enactment of Acts passedby the Legislative Assembly of Åland are governed by the provisions in the Act on the Autonomy of the Åland Islands. "

③ "The Åland Islands have self-government in accordance with what is specifically stipulated in the Act on the Autonomy of the Åland Islands. "

case with the inhabitants of Hong Kong and Macau, and also in respect of the inhabitants of the Åland Islands, this could be the case, because they might also be understood as members of the Swedish-speaking minority in Finland.

V. Distribution of Powers by Enumeration

The essence of autonomy is constituted by the powers accorded to the sub-state entity. Section 31 of the Constitution of China makes reference to special administrative regions, which indicates that such entities could be in the possession of at least regulatory powers of an administrative nature. Section 75 (2) of the Constitution of Finland is clearer in this respect, because it goes on to hold that the enactment of Acts of Åland is determined in the Self-Government Act. Hence the Constitution of Finland makes a distinction between two different sets of Acts in Finland, one set produced by the Parliament of Finland and another set produced for the Åland Islands by another legislator. The constitutional norms (understood in the broad sense) of both countries thus delegate the determination of powers of the sub-state entities to particular legislation. In Finland, the 1991 Self-Government Act of Åland establishes the Legislative Assembly of the Åland Islands as the legislature in charge of law-making powers in Åland concerning a certain part of the legal order, while in China, the two Basic Laws identify legislative powers for the Legislative Councils of Hong Kong and Macau in a more comprehensive manner.

In China, the two Joint Declarations state that the Special Administrative Regions will each be directly under the authority of the Central People's Government of the People's Republic of China, but at the same time, they will enjoy a high degree of autonomy, except in foreign affairs and defense which are the responsibilities of the Central People's Government. This creates the impression that the two autonomous entities may exercise the residual powers, while the national government holds a minimum of enumerated powers, those central to preserving national unity and territorial integrity. However, it is clear already on the basis of the Joint Declarations that the powers of the autonomous entities are enumerated in a manner that creates exclusive law-making powers for the legislatures of Hong Kong and Macau. The debate in China is perhaps more about whether the National People's Government has enumerated powers or perhaps residual powers: the central government of China as well as Chinese doctrine seem to be strongly opposed to the characterization of the distribution of powers by reference to the fact that the central government would hold a few enumerated powers, while the residual powers, that is, the vast bulk of the legislative powers, would be vested in the SARs.

The argument put forward by the Mainland Chinese authorities and academics is that China is not a federal state in which the federation would hold enumerated powers and the states the residual powers on the basis of a distribution of powers. Instead, so the argument goes, China is a unitary state, and because the Basic Laws are pieces of ordinary legislation in the legal order of China, the residual powers are actually held by the central government, not by the SARs. Because the NPC has the plenary powers of the sovereign lawmaker, the NPC could revoke the Basic Laws. Consequently, so the argument continues, there is no distribution of powers as in a federal system, but a delegation of powers on the basis of the Basic Laws from the central government to the SARs. Moreover, the ultimate residual powers are held by the NPC. [1] In this respect, the position of the Mainland

---

[1]　See Leung 2006, pp. 34 – 36, Ghai 1999, pp. 148 – 153, and Xiao Weiyun 2001, pp. 60, 92 – 95, 98 – 101, 134 f., where the claim is repeatedly made that the HKSAR uniquely enjoys a higher degree of autonomy in many respects than a member state of a federal country. Apparently, the variant of sub-state organisation looked into in this inquiry, that of territorial autonomy, was not considered when the Joint Declaration and the Basic Law were adopted. See also Leung 2006, p. 20 f. On p. 21 f., Leung concludes against the background of a statement by Deng Xiaoping about the "one country, two systems" principle that "the special administrative regions may have a high degree of autonomy only to the extent authorized by the central government. Matters which are not within the authority of special administrative regions will be dealt with by the central government." Also Xiao Weiyun 2001, p. 134 f., concludes that because China is a unitary state, each administrative region, including the HKSAR, is only a local administrative region. However, against the background of the Joint Declaration and the granting of legislative powers to Hong Kong in the Basic Law, a reference to authorisation by the central government sounds like an understatement. See also Ghai 1999, pp. 62, 68. The aversion towards any opening towards a federal-like state organisation is generally explained by Galligan 2007, p. 304 f., by saying that "[f]ederalism requires limited government, so if the country requires strong government, either because of its poverty or fragmentation, or because the ruling party is committed to imposing a new social order, federalism is an unsuitable instrument". See also Baogang He 2007, p. 9, where the point is made that "Hong Kong's special status has weakened the traditional unitary model of China", and pp. 13 and 15, where, inter alia, China is characterised as a state that has built up hybrid federalism with the key characteristics of regional autonomy, defined as an institutional configuration that combines a unitary system with federal elements which has the capability of achieving stability and peace at the cost of inter-group equality and even democracy. See also Yongnian Zheng 2007, p. 217, in which the definition of the Chinese unitary state is brought beyond its formal boundaries and, following thebehavioural tradition,

Chinese doctrine concerning the congressional sovereignty of the NPC is akin to the concept parliamentary sovereignty in, e. g. , the United Kingdom or the concept of plenary powers of the US Congress.

From the point of view of the SARs, things can be understood differently, supported by the stipulations in the Joint Declaration and its Annex I: the international commitment signals an intention on the part of China to distribute powers between the central government and the SARs, not only to devolve powers in a manner which allows a withdrawal of those powers at the will of the central government. Therefore, while the theory of the devolution of power of the Chinese Government seems entirely plausible after the period of 50 years has lapsed, at which point the legislature of China is free to amend the autonomy arrangement as it pleases or to continue or discontinue the arrangement, China's international obligations based on the Joint Declarations to uphold the high degree of autonomy of Hong Kong and Macau with the distribution of powers established in the Joint Declarations and their Annex I points in the other direction. [①] It seems, namely, that the autonomy arrangements of Hong Kong and Macau have been created in a manner that is by and large in line with our theoretical models that juxtapose autonomy with federalism: China is not a federal state, and at the same time as the central government holds the ultimate residual competences and some of the competences of the central government are enumerated, the competences of the two autonomies remain enumerated.

Hong Kong and Macau have been granted, under the Basic Laws, complete legal powers by means of enumeration in almost all areas of the law. They have also been granted powers in the area of foreign affairs. In the area of defense, however,

---

the central-local relations are characterised as de facto or behavioural federalism. See also Cheung 2007, p. 249, where it is stated that " [t] he OCTS model has not made the PRC a federal state, because it is after all a constitutionally unitary state", although the arrangement "exhibits certain federalist characteristics". See also Chan 2010, p. 129, according to which the high degree of autonomy conferred on the HKSAR is to be exercised only in the framework of a unified country, and the central government retains all essential powers over the operation of the HKSAR".

① Interestingly, the legal effect of the reference in the Basic Law to the Joint Declaration is denied by Leung 2006, p. 31. She also states that the Joint Declaration "does not add anything to (or perhaps the correct formulation would be that it does not detract anything from-MS) the legislative power of China and, therefore, has little to do with the validity of the Basic Law".

the central government holds the entire measure of powers as laid down in art. 14 of the Basic Laws. The provision stipulates that the Central People's Government shall be responsible for the defense of the SARs. This is evidently a responsibility only in relation to defense against external aggression, because sub-section 2 of the provisions stipulate that the SARs are responsible for the internal dimension, the maintenance of public order. According to Art. 14 (3) of the HK Basic Law,[1] military forces that are stationed by the Central People's Government in the HKSAR for defense purposes shall not interfere in the local affairs of the Region. However, the Government of the HKSAR may, when necessary, ask the Central People's Government for assistance from the garrison for the maintenance of public order and disaster relief. The provision also contains some other rules that pertain to the Chinese defense forces in the HKSAR. In addition to abiding by national laws, members of the garrison shall abide by the laws of the HKSAR, which means that they are not granted immunity. Also, expenditure for the garrison is borne by the Central People's Government, which means that the Chinese defense forces do not burden the budget of the HKSAR.

As indicated above, the Joint Declarations and their Annexes I as well as the Basic Laws contain several confirmations or enumerations of the powers of Hong Kong and Macau. Much of the same substance appears in the enumerations of the two Basic Laws,[2] as faithfully established by the Chinese lawmaker against the background of the Joint Declarations and their Annexes I, but there are also a number of specifications of competences in the Basic Laws.[3] These legislative powers cover a wide range of areas and encompass most of the legal order. They are supported by appropriate criminal provisions in Hong Kong and Macau law. The Basic Law is generally silent on criminal provisions passed within the legislative powers of Hong Kong and Macau (except in Art. 23 of the Basic Law), which

---

①　There is no provision of this sort in the Macau Basic Law.

②　See Ghai 1997, p. 147, who finds information supporting the conclusion that "residual powers are indeed not with the HKSAR". This could, in turn, be supporting the conclusion that the powers of the HKSAR are of an enumerated nature, although the definition of the enumerated powers of the HKSAR is not very clear in all instances. See Ghai 1997, pp. 148 – 151.

③　Ghai 1997, p. 68, is of the opinion that there are formulations in the Basic Law which suggest a smaller area for autonomy than in the Joint Declaration. See also Ghai 1997, pp. 144 – 147.

may be interpreted as evidence of the inapplicability even in the most serious cases of Mainland Chinese criminal law in the two autonomies. According to Art. 23 of the Basic Law, the SARs shall enact laws on their own to prohibit any act of treason, secession, sedition, subversion against the Central People's Government, or theft of state secrets, to prohibit foreign political organizations or bodies from conducting political activities in the Region, and to prohibit political organizations or bodies of the Region from establishing ties with foreign political organizations or bodies. This demonstrates that the Mainland Chinese lawmakers do not have lawmaking powers with regard to the jurisdiction of the HKSAR or Macau even in this core area of provisions connected to the sovereignty of the State.

Clearly, these enumerated powers cannot be withdrawn or repealed by the Chinese central government before 2047 or 2049 without breaching the international obligations of China, in particular when considering the direct link established in the preambles of the Basic Laws to the Joint Declarations. [1] It is difficult to understand how the enumerated competences of the central government, on the one hand, and the competences of the two autonomies, on the other, would not constitute a distribution of powers on a more permanent basis than is the case with a mere administrative devolution. Certainly, in some rare instances, the competences mentioned in the Basic Laws are of a devolved nature. Provisions which grant powers to the two autonomies as authorized by the central government indicate the existence of an administrative devolution, perhaps also of a shared competence. However, for the most part, it would seem that exclusive legislative powers are established for the two autonomies by way of enumeration on the basis of Annexes I of the Joint Declarations.

In addition, the reference in the Joint Declarations to a high degree of autonomy may be contrasted with the concept of autonomy in articles 112 − 122 of the PRC Constitution. *Prima facie*, it seems that the high degree of autonomy granted to Hong Kong and Macau amounts to much more autonomy than the autonomy which has been granted to the autonomous regions elsewhere in China because the

---

[1]　The situation becomes different if a state of war or a state of emergency has to be declared under art. 18 of the Basic Law for reasons of turmoil. In such a context, the application of national legislation could be extended to the jurisdiction of the HKSAR. See Xiao Weiyun 2001, pp. 148, 165 f.

two SARs are vested with executive, legislative and independent judicial power, including that of final adjudication, and because the laws in force in the two entities at the time of the transition remained basically unchanged after the transition, as provided by the two Basic Laws. However, when considering the issue from the vantage point of the Chinese constitution, the picture may become somewhat blurred because Art. 31 of the Constitution of China does not offer any substantive protection for any arrangement created on that constitutional basis and does not even mention the concept of autonomy. The fact that Art. 31 excludes a special administrative region from the regular structures of regional autonomy, which certainly do not have any exclusive legislative powers independent of the powers of the central government, sustains the argument that the special arrangements created under Art. 31 could also be different with respect to the allocation of powers. On its face, art. 31 could be so broad as to contain not only administrative devolution of the sort regulated in articles 112 – 122 of the Constitution but also a number of other possible arrangements. In fact, the reference to "special" in Art. 31 should probably mean something besides administrative devolution, which as a maximum contains law-varying powers subject to approval by the central government.

In comparison, other autonomous areas created in Mainland China, such as Tibet, based on articles 4 and 116 of the PRC Constitution, seem to enjoy a form of autonomy which is mainly of a regulatory nature, although such autonomous entities may also have the power to modify national legislation, a power which appears to be, in practice, seldom exercised. In cases where an autonomous area in Mainland China wishes to modify national law, the modification can be approved by the authorities of the autonomous area, but there is the additional requirement that such modifications must be approved by the central government in order to take effect. Hence the effect of Art. 31 of the Constitution is to place the system of special administrative regions outside of the framework of the regular regional autonomies and to distinguish the SARs from the regular regional autonomies.

Section 75 (2) of the Constitution of Finland contains an implicit recognition of the fact that two legislatures exist in Finland, the Parliament of Finland, on the one hand, and the Legislative Assembly of the Åland Islands, on the other, because the section lays down that the enactment of acts passed by the Legislative

Assembly of the Åland Islands is governed by the provisions of the Self-Government Act. Under the 1991 Self-Government Act, this distribution of legislative competence is established by means of an enumeration of two spheres of legislative competence, one for the Legislative Assembly of the Åland Islands and another for the Parliament of Finland. Neither the constitutional recognition nor the double enumeration formed a part of the original arrangement in 1920 −1922. This means that the legal rules concerning the position of the Åland Islands have undergone a significant evolution during the past 90 years.

Originally, the distribution of powers was fashioned in a more "federal" manner in the 1920 Self-Government Act so that the legislative powers of the Parliament of Finland for the purposes of producing legal norms for the jurisdiction of Åland were enumerated, while the legislative powers of the Legislative Assembly of the Åland Islands were of a residual nature. [1] This attribution changed in the 1951 Self-Government Act so that the lawmaking powers of both legislatures were enumerated, and this is also the point of departure in the 1991 Self-Government Act. From a practical point of view, the shift in the strategy concerning the distribution of legislative powers was probably not very dramatic, but from the point of view of principle, the issue is of some importance, because the arrangement indicates that a preemption of some sort was built into the 1920 Self-Government Act. Generally speaking, therefore, it is not always beneficial to operate under the assumption that a residual competence for the sub-state entity is a better option, because such a "residual" point of departure may open up the need to recognize or accept a smaller or a greater window for national preemption through a supremacy doctrine.

The 1991 Self-Government Act followed the principle of enumeration of both spheres of competence. According to section 17, the Legislative Assembly of the Åland Islands shall enact legislation for Åland, and the actual legislative powers of the Legislative Assembly are listed in section 18 of the Self-Government Act. The conclusion that the legislative powers of the Åland Islands are exclusive in relation to the powers of the Parliament of Finland means that the Parliament of Finland cannot, by its own enactments, fill a normative void within the competence sphere

---

[1]　Suksi 2005, p. 172.

of the Legislative Assembly. Conversely, authorities of the Åland Islands cannot use legislation from the competence sphere of the Parliament of Finland to fill a void in the competence of the Åland Islands. ①

This is also established in a number of cases by the Supreme Administrative Court (hereinafter: the SAC). For instance, in SAC 2003: 1, the Court concluded that in the absence of a provision concerning the self-rectification of an administrative decision in legislation of the Åland Islands, the Government of the Åland Islands could not, by means of a decision of its own, carry out such a self-rectification, and the provision in the Administration Act applicable in mainland Finland could not be applied. In SAC 1982-A-II-1, the Court stated that provisions which in mainland Finland were included in an Act concerning the steering of agricultural production had not been enacted in the Åland Islands within the legislative competence of the Legislative Assembly. As a consequence, corresponding steering measures could not be undertaken in the Åland Islands. Therefore, in concrete instances, the parallel existence of the two legal orders is based on mutual exclusivity, which does not permit the use in one jurisdiction of such norms that belong to the other jurisdiction. The incapacity of the Parliament of Finland to enact legislation for the Åland Islands within the legislative competence of the Legislative Assembly means in effect that the national parliament cannot act on the basis of any principle of preemption in relation to the Åland Islands when enacting ordinary legislation.

Against this background, it can be concluded that the Åland Islands and the two SARs are similar in the distribution of powers because they are based on enumerations of the exclusive legislative competences for the autonomous entities. However, the rules at the level of the central state are somewhat differently fashioned in that the Chinese legislator can probably be understood as one that has kept the residual powers (and at the same time identified some enumerated powers for itself), while the Parliament of Finland functions on the basis of enumerated powers in relation to the Åland Islands. Hong Kong and Macau are therefore more typical territorial autonomies, while the Åland Islands can be termed a modified territorial autonomy.

---

① See also Palmgren 1997, p. 88.

VI. Peculiarities of Competence Control

The asymmetries introduced by the autonomous entities are underlined by the asymmetries of the mechanisms that are created for the purposes of competence control. Although the Court of Final Appeal has the final powers of adjudication of concrete cases in the jurisdiction of Hong Kong and a similar court exists in Macau, interpretations of the Basic Laws are issued by the Standing Committee of the NPC. This means that the final word about how provisions of the Basic Law should be interpreted is outside of Hong Kong and Macau. In addition, the power of interpretation is placed with a political organ. However, the Standing Committee of the NPC is assisted in its task by Basic Law Committees, one for each SAR, which contains representatives of Hong Kong and Macau and which give opinions to the Standing Committee on how the Basic Laws should be interpreted. So far, the Standing Committee of the NPC has issued three interpretations concerning Hong Kong,[1] while it seems it has not issued any concerning Macau.

In Finland, competence control is curious in that the actual legal interpretation of the compliance of the Ålandic enactments with the enumerated legislative competences of the Åland Islands in section 18 of the Self-Government Act is carried out by the Supreme Court of Finland in a particular procedure *ante legem* in a manner that is similar to that of the *Conseil Constitutionnel* of France. If the Åland Delegation, a joint committee of experts from Finland and the Åland Islands, finds that there may be a competence problem with an Ålandic enactment, the Ministry of Justice passes the Ålandic enactment to the Supreme Court that gives an opinion to the President of Finland for the purposes of using the veto (which normally is exercised in a partial manner in 2 - 4 percent of the enactments). This is the

---

[1]   *Interpretation of* 26 *June* 1999 by the Standing Committee of the National People's Congress of Articles 22 (4) and 24 (2) (3) of the Basic Law of the Hong Kong Special Administrative Region of the People's Republic of China, *Interpretation of* 6 *April* 2004 of the NPCSC of art. 7 of Annex I and art. III of Annex II to the Basic Law concerning amendments to the method of selection of the Chief Executive, *Interpretation of* 27 *April* 2005 of the NPCSC of Paragraph 2, Article 53 of the Basic Law of the Hong Kong Special Administrative Region of the People's Republic of China by the Standing Committee of the National People's Congress.

regular competence control system created by the Self-Government Act for the Ålandic competences.

However, at the same time, the Constitutional Committee of the Parliament of Finland is, under section 74 of the Constitution of Finland, the authoritative interpreter of the constitutionality of those proposals for legislative enactments that the Parliament of Finland is empowered to enact, that is, all draft laws concerning mainland Finland and a portion of the legislation that is intended to take effect in the Åland Islands. This latter portion is defined in section 27 of the Self-Government Act, that is, in the enumeration of the exclusive legislative powers of the Parliament of Finland within the territory of the Åland Islands. Hence the confusing situation exists where two provisions contained in the same Act are interpreted at the highest instance by two different bodies, one of which is a court and the other a political body. ①

So far, the system has functioned surprisingly well,② with only a few problematic situations. A major confrontation between the Constitutional Committee and the Supreme Court over the issue of who is the highest interpreter of the constitutional issues arose over the enactment of the Lotteries Act by the Parliament of Finland in 2001. Legislation of lotteries is, for the jurisdiction of the Åland Islands, within the competence of the Legislative Assembly of the Åland Islands. Therefore, an attempt by the Parliament of Finland to prevent Ålandic lotteries from being offered via the Internet for customers in mainland Finland on the basis of legislation which had been approved by the Constitutional Committee and which would have established administrative procedures, led the President of Finland to request, on the basis of section 77 of the Constitution, an Opinion from the Supreme Court. In its Opinion, the Supreme Court concluded that the provisions in the enactment of the Parliament, as formulated by the Constitutional Committee, were in breach of the distribution of competence in the Self-Government Act. As a consequence, the President exercised her right to return the

---

① For a graphic illustration of the two avenues of competence control within the Self-Government Act, see Suksi 2005, p. 537.

② A similar but a more regular and well-functioning interpretation situation arises when Finland concludes treaties that, as a consequence, have to be brought into effect also in the jurisdiction of the Åland Islands.

enactment to the Parliament of Finland, which enacted the law with the problematic provision, but which at the same time enacted a corrective amendment to the Lotteries Act that entered into force at the same time as the Act itself. [1] In the context, the question arose about which body, in fact is the highest interpreter of the Finnish Constitution or at least of the Self-Government Act, the Constitutional Committee or the Supreme Court. Another situation, although not as accentuated, arose when the Parliament of Finland in 1992 enacted the Act on Travel Tax, in which situation the Constitutional Committee concluded that because the travel tax was not such a tax on business income that the Legislative Assembly could decide about, the legislative competence was on the Parliament of Finland, which could enact the tax law with reference to the tax being a tax on consumption. [2] It is possible to conclude that this was a unilateral interpretation of the competence line.

The Chinese and Finnish forms of competence control are thus comparable from an institutional point of view: in both cases, the competences of territorial autonomies are determined by committees of the national legislatures, but obviously to different degrees. In the case of China, the Standing Committee of the NPCSC has the authority to issue interpretations regarding the entire scope of the two Basic Laws, while the Constitutional Committee of the Finnish Parliament is in principle empowered to express itself for the jurisdiction of the Åland Islands only with regard to those law-making powers that are exercised by the Parliament of Finland. In the Finnish case, however, there is the possibility that the Constitutional Committee will move the boundaries of the law-making competences of the Parliament of Finland into the competences of the Legislative Assembly of the Åland Islands, where the Supreme Court is the body issuing the judicial interpretations. At that point, two spheres of competence stand in conflict with each other, which is not a good situation in a legal order that strives towards a situation where there is no conflict between different parts of the legal order. It is also notable that for the purposes of competence control, both constitutional systems have created expert bodies, the Basic Law Committees and the Åland Delegation (although the Åland

---

[1]   See Suksi 2005, pp. 185 – 189.

[2]   See Suksi 2005, p. 216.

Delegation also has other tasks than those attached to interpretation of section 18 of the Self-Government Act and to competence control).

VII. From Comparison to Constitutional Rules: Formulating the Normative Challenge

The recognition of legislative autonomy in the constitution of a country for a territorial jurisdiction within that state is not a simple issue. The above account has indicated two dimensions along which the two countries, China and Finland, could be compared with a view to the entities that have been created as territorial autonomies.

On the one hand, there is the dimension of the normative level, which in broad terms varies between the level of the ordinary law and the level of the constitution. Autonomy arrangements that are only based on an ordinary piece of national law face the risk of being changed or even revoked by the national law-maker in a simple legislative order. If, however, the autonomy arrangement is established in the constitution of the country by means of explicit provisions, it would normally be more difficult to undertake unilateral action on the part of the central state institutions in a manner that affects the stability and continuity of the autonomy arrangement and the commitment to upholding the autonomous jurisdiction. Between the two principal extremes of the dimension, ordinary law and the constitution, it is possible to place some other normative instruments, such as organic laws of some kind and international treaty arrangements.

Evidently, the autonomy of the Åland Islands is established at the level of the Constitution of Finland, a position that is strengthened by the particular nature of the Self-Government Act and by the unilateral international commitment that Finland recognizes in relation to the Åland Islands. The situation is somewhat similar in China concerning the Local People's Congresses, for which there is an explicit constitutional recognition and an infrastructure in institutional legislation. However, the situation is different in China with respect to Hong Kong and Macau, where the Constitution does not contain any explicit recognition of the autonomous status of the two SARs, but leaves the two jurisdictions to be regulated, under the treaty commitments, on the basis of Basic Laws that are to be understood as pieces of ordinary legislation, potentially with a slightly elevated normative status. The two

SARs pose a normative problem with a view to legal certainty and legal continuity, because the arrangements may at least in theory be facing termination at the end of 2040s, when the international commitments expire. However, it should be noted that the two Basic Laws are not enacted for a limited period of application, so they could remain in force also after the expiry of the treaty commitments.

On the other hand, there is the dimension of the powers accorded to the sub-state entities. It is possible to grant exclusive law-making powers to autonomous jurisdictions, but it is also possible to grant powers of a lesser nature to sub-state entities, for instance, administrative powers of a regulatory kind. The powers of Hong Kong and Macau are very vast and contain almost every conceivable area of the law, while the powers of the Åland Islands are not as extensive and deal mainly with the area of public law, while the area of private law is with the Parliament of Finland. These three sub-state entities, Hong Kong, Macau and the Åland Islands, can be termed territorial autonomies proper. They stand in marked contrast to the two categories of Local People's Congresses in China, one category of which has, under Chinese constitutional provisions, normative powers of some sort, subject to confirmation by central authorities (LPC1 in Figure 1, below). The other category has even lesser normative powers than the power to vary national law, mainly powers to adopt secondary norms (LPC2 in Figure 1, below).

The two dimensions, that is, the normative level of the autonomy arrangement and the nature of the powers assigned to the autonomy arrangement, can be combined in a manner that illustrates the position of the different sub-state entities in relation to each other (see Figure 1, below).

When the treaty commitments of China concerning Hong Kong and Macau expire in the 2040s, the normative position of the two, entities becomes in principle weaker, provided that the two Basic Laws remain in effect. At that point, it could be possible to say that the two autonomous jurisdictions are based on pieces of ordinary legislation, which may or may not be brought to expire. However, the point has been made by significant political authorities, such as Mr. Deng Xiaoping,[1] that there is no reason to discontinue the autonomy arrangements after the expiry of the treaty commitments. Such a continuance of the two arrangements

---

[1] Deng Xiaoping 2004.

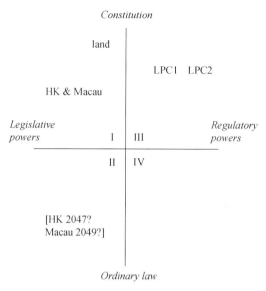

Figure 1   Various autonomy positions

would, after mid-century, place Hong Kong and Macau in section II of the figure, instead of the current section I. Arguably, it should be important at that point to avoid a situation in which Hong Kong and Macau are placed under one of the two LPC regimes, such as the one with law-varying powers in section III of the figure, or to degrade the two entities into a more provincial existence in section IV of the figure.

In case there is a wish to ensure the continuance *de lege ferenda* of the two autonomy arrangements on a stable basis in a manner that would facilitate legal continuity and, in particular, legal certainty within section I of the figure, it would not be far-fetched to seek normative solutions through amendments to the Constitution of China in a manner that identifies the autonomy arrangements of Hong Kong and Macau and describes the legislative powers of the two entities in general terms. ① The Constitution of Finland provides an interesting example of

---

① Such a solution could also be suitable for a more comprehensive regulation of the position of Tibet within the constitutional fabric of China, because a recognition of exclusive law-making powers at the level of the Constitution would suffice as the implementation of the right to self-determination of the Tibetans and against the background of the historical development of the relationship between China and Tibet. Such a solution would perhaps be more convincing also in relation to Taiwan, which at least so far has not been interested in trading in its qualified independence in exchange for a status as a Special Administrative Region under section 31 of the Constitution of China.

such constitutional regulation through sections 75 and 120 concerning the Åland Islands, but there are obviously also other alternatives for the recognition of autonomy arrangements than the one that has been used in Finland.

Another possibility could be to develop the constitutional status of the two Basic Laws by elevating their individual normative position by means of building in some qualified decision-making formulas into the amending clauses of the two laws at the level of the NPC in a manner that would strengthen the embryonic doctrinary idea that basic laws may have a particular position in relation to ordinary legislation. Such a development took place in Finland in 1920 and immediately thereafter. At that point, the Parliament of Finland enacted the first Self-Government Act of the Åland Islands in the order prescribed for constitutional enactments without, however, prescribing explicitly that the Act would be a constitutional act. In addition, the 1921 Åland Islands Settlement required that this Autonomy Act be amended according to the material prescriptions of the Settlement in the order established in the Autonomy Act, that is, in the order of constitutional amendments. Perhaps a similar internal development would be possible in China, too, in spite of the fact that the international commitments do not make reference to any such procedure that would result in an elevation of the norm-hierarchical position of the two Basic Laws.

LITERATURE

Baogang He, "Democratization and federalization in Asia", in Baogang He, Galli-gan B and Inoguchi T, eds. , *Federalism in Asia* (Edward Elgar: Cheltenham, 2007) .

Johannes Chan, "Asymmetry in the Face of Heavily Disproportionate Power Relations: Hong Kong", in: Weller M and Nobbs K, eds. *Asymmetric Autonomy and the Settlement of Ethnic Conflicts* (University of Pennsylvania Press: Philadelphia & Oxford, 2010) .

Albert H. Y. Chen, "The Theory, Constitution and Practice of Autonomy: The Case of Hong Kong", in: Costa Oliveira J and Cardinal P, eds. , *One Country, Two Systems, Three Legal Orders-Perspectives of Evolution*. Essays on Macau's Autonomy after the Resumption of Sovereignty by China (Springer Verlag: Berlin & Heidelberg, 2009) .

Peter T. Y. Cheung "Toward federalism in China? The experience of the Hong Kong Special Administrative Region", in Baogang He, Galligan B and Inoguchi T, eds, *Federalism in Asia*

（Edward Elgar：Cheltenham，2007）．

Deng Xiaoping, On "One Country, Two Systems" （Joint Publishing：Hong Kong, 2004）．

Michael W. Dowdle, "Constitutionalism in the Shadow of the Common Law-The Dys-functional Interpretive Politics of Article 8 of the Hong Kong Basic Law", in Hualing Fu, Harris L and Young SNM, eds, Interpreting Hong Kong's Basic Law-The Struggle for Coherence （Palgrave Macmillan：New York, 2007）．

Brian Galligan, "Federalism in Asia", in Baogang He, Galligan B and Inoguchi T, eds., Federalism in Asia （Edward Elgar：Cheltenham, 2007）．

Huang Jin, "Interaction and Integration Between the Legal Systems of Hong Kong, Macao and Mainland China 50 Years After Their Return to China", in Costa Oliveira J and Cardinal P, eds. One Country, Two Systems, Three Legal Orders-Perspectives of Evolution （Essays on Macau's Autonomy after the Resumption of Sovereignty by China. Springer：Berlin & Heidelberg, 2009）．

Yash Ghai, Hong Kong's New Constitutional Order：The Resumption of Chinese Sovereignty and the Basic Law （first edition） （Hong Kong University Press：Hong Kong, 1997）．

Yash Ghai, Hong Kong's New Constitutional Order：The Resumption of Chinese Sovereignty and the Basic Law （second edition） （Hong Kong University Press：Hong Kong, 1999）．

Hualing Fu, Lison Harris and Simon Young, "Introduction", in Hualing Fu, Harris L and Young SNM, eds., Interpreting Hong Kong's Basic Law-The Struggle for Coherence （Palgrave Macmillan：New York, 2007）．

Mei-fun P Leung, The Hong Kong Basic Law：Hybrid of Common Law and Chinese Law （LexisNexis：Hong Kong, Singapore, Malaysia, 2006）．

Robert J. Morris, "Forcing the Dance-Interpreting the Hong Kong Basic Law Dialectically", in Hualing Fu, Harris L and Young SNM, eds., Interpreting Hong Kong's Basic Law-The Struggle for Coherence （Palgrave Macmillan：New York, 2007）．

Roda Mushkat, One Country, Two International Legal Personalities：the Case of Hong Kong （Hong Kong University Press：Hong Kong, 1997）．

Sten Palmgren, "The Autonomy of the Åland Islands in the Constitutional Law of Finland", in Hannikainen L and Horn F, eds., Autonomy and Demilitarisation in Interna-tional Law：The Åland Islands in a Changing Europe （Kluwer Law International：the Ha-gue, London & Boston, 1997）．

Markku Suksi, "On the Entrenchment of Autonomy". In：Suksi M, ed., Autonomy：Ap-plications and Implications （Kluwer Law International：Dordrecht, 1998）．

Markku Suksi, "One (small) country, four different régimes of linguistic rights", poster for the Seminar on Minority Language Usage and Cultural Development：Chinese Theories and Practices, 19 −25 August 2006, Lhasa, China, pp. 131 −133 of the Seminar Guide （pp. 29 −31 in the

Tibetan language and pp. 82 −83 in the Chinese language）.

Markku Suksi，"Stegvisa förändringar i Ålandsöverenskommelsens innehåll?" in Aarto M and Vartiainen M，eds. *Oikeus kansainvälisessä maailmassa-Ilkka Saraviidan juhlakir-ja*（Edita：Helsinki，2008）.

Markku Suksi，*Sub-state Governance through Territorial Autonomy*（Springer-Verlag：Berlin & Heidelberg，2011）.

Markku Suksi，*Ålands konstitution*. Åbo Akademis förlag：Åbo，2005.

Xiao Weiyun，*One Country*，*Two Systems-An Account of the Drafting of the Hong Kong Basic Law*（Peking University Press：Beijing，2001）.

Yongnian Zheng，"China's de facto federalism"，in Baogang He，Galligan B and Inoguchi T，eds.，*Federalism in Asia*（Edward Elgar：Cheltenham，2007）.

中芬具有宪法特征的自治地区

马尔库·苏克西

【摘要】本文对中华人民共和国（包括香港和澳门特区）和芬兰（包括奥兰群岛）自治情况的比较研究，得益于两者具备的若干共同特点。在这两个国家中，自治制度的建立一方面确认了两个国家对有关地区的主权，然而，另一方面也授予了自治地区的相关立法机构以专属立法权。最后要指出的是，两个国家关于自治制度的权限控制机制不是等同的。对芬兰承诺的国际监督已经不复存在了，奥兰群岛的安排交由芬兰国内政治活动来决定。除了法律上的相似之处，一些事实上的相似点也值得一提。在国内层面，自治地区的规模是差不多相同的，大约是占国家总人口的0.5%左右，这也就意味着，在日常政治生活中，这些地区并不被中央政府当作是主要事务。比起国内其他地区，这些自治地区相对要富裕些。

中国行政法治的发展
历程及其主要特征

【摘要】 由法制进程的视角观之，中华人民共和国成立以后法制的产生
和发展可分为四个历史时期，即法制早期探索期、法制虚无期、工具论导
向的法制建设期以及法治导向的法制建设期。改革开放以来，行政法治的
发展阶段可以概括为四个阶段：改革开放以前行政法制的缺失、20 世纪 80
年代行政法治基本格局的奠定、90 年代行政法治的积淀与发展、21 世纪行
政法治的升级与深化。中国行政法治在逐步推进和不断成熟的过程中，形
成了自己的发展道路与特征。

【关键词】 行政　法治　行政法治　法治政府

导　　论

　　由法制进程的视角观之，中华人民共和国成立以后法制的产生和发展
可分为四个历史时期，即法制早期探索期、法制虚无期、工具论导向的法
制建设期以及法治导向的法制建设期。法制早期探索期发生于 1949 年至 20
世纪 50 年代中期。这一时期虽废除了旧法统，但法制的作用仍然受到重视，
开始了建设新的人民民主法制的实践和探索，1954 年宪法的制定是我国法
制建设早期探索所取得的最大成就。不过，这一时期还不可能提出法治的
概念。法制虚无期发生于 50 年代后期，"文化大革命"期间达到顶峰，法
制在国家治理过程中的地位和作用从根本上受到排斥和否定，法制建设的

---

　　* 中国社会科学院法学研究所研究员。

进程中断。改革开放以后我国法制建设得以恢复和发展，以 90 年代中后期"依法治国，建设社会主义法治国家"基本方略的提出为分水岭，这一时期的法制建设大致可分为工具论导向的法制建设和法治导向的法制建设两大阶段。严格说来，我国在明确的法治思想指导下建设行政法制的时间并不长，至今不过 10 年上下，① 但改革开放前 20 年的行政法制实践为后 10 年的行政法治进程做了不可或缺的准备和铺垫。我国行政法治建设是在改革开放的时代背景下孕育和逐步成长起来的，正是在这个意义上，本文将我国行政法治建设的历史起点延伸至改革开放初期。

一　改革开放以前行政法制的缺失

我国行政法制建设在新中国成立初期一度呈现出良好的发展态势。据统计，1949 年至 1952 年间，我国颁布的行政法律法规有 100 多件，1953 年至 1956 年激增至 700 多件。然而，从 20 世纪 50 年代后期开始，在"左"的思想指导以及各种封建专制残余思想的影响下，我国开展了批判资产阶级法权的运动，法律虚无主义思想兴起并盛行，这在此后颁布的行政法律法规的数量上有十分直观、明显的反映：1958 年行政法律法规的数量即由两年前的 700 多件锐减为 147 件，1960 年减至 50 件，1966 年仅为 8 件，而在 1966 年 4 月至 1976 年的十年间，除 1975 年 1 月有 1 件外，其余皆为零。② 在这种情况下，行政的依据主要是上级的政策、命令、指示和决定，③ 即便在工具论的意义上，行政对法律的需求也是低微的。行政既不以法律为依据，也不必借助法律而推行。因此，在改革开放之前，我国行政法制基本上处于严重缺失的状态，而行政法治更是无从谈起。

改革开放前我国行政法制严重缺失，主要有以下几个方面的原因：

第一，不具备形成依法行政观念和建设行政法制的经济基础。改革开放前，我国实行单一公有制基础上的计划经济体制，经济组织及其活动高

---

① "行政法治"与"法治政府"的概念相当。2004 年 3 月，时任总理温家宝在十届人大二次会议上所作的政府工作报告以及国务院《全面推进依法行政实施纲要》首次在官方重要文件中将"依法行政"与建设"法治政府"紧密联系起来，明确了依法行政的"法治"导向，倘若以此为标准，我国在明确的思想指导下开展行政法治建设不过是晚近几年的事，显然这一标准过于严格和狭义，不足以概括此前已经展开的行政法治实践。

② 张庆福主编《行政执法中的问题及对策》，中国人民公安大学出版社，1996，第 5~7 页。

③ 所谓"黑头（法律）不如红头（文件）、红头不如白头（特定范围的传阅件）、白头不如口头（领导口头指示）"，是一种在党政机关流传甚广的观念和说法，形象生动地描述了当时人治行政的主要特点。

度行政化，国家和社会高度融合，公民和社会组织均被整合到统一的国家组织体制之中，国家与公民、组织之间的关系不是实质意义上的外部关系，而是传统行政法不予调整或不加重视的内部关系，依法行政的必要性和可行性大为降低。①

第二，不具备形成依法行政观念和建设行政法制的政治环境。从20世纪50年代后期开始，我国政治运动持续不断。所谓"革命无法制"，在这样的政治环境和社会氛围下，一切问题都被高度政治化，正常的法制建设难以进行，更不用说形成法治和依法行政的观念。

第三，不具备形成依法行政观念和建设行政法制的理论基础。由于未能正确认识和把握社会主义建设时期社会的主要矛盾和国家的主要任务，党和国家错误地实行了"以阶级斗争为纲"和"无产阶级专政下继续革命"的政治指导，导致党政不分和党的绝对一元化领导，有关权力制约的理论受到彻底的批判和摒弃，显然不具备形成法治和依法行政观念的理论前提。

第四，不具备形成依法行政观念和建设行政法制的历史条件。我国是建立在革命战争取得胜利的基础之上的，因而新中国成立后各级领导干部普遍运用战争年代的观念、习惯和经验指导社会主义建设，对法治的治国方略和方式既不了解也不接受，加上我国有长达数千年的专制传统，从无实行法治的历史经验，这样的历史条件有利于人治观念的盛行而不利于包括依法行政在内的法治观念的培育和成长。

二 八十年代行政法治基本格局的奠定

（一）行政法治建设的主要成就

1. 确立法对行政的支配地位

法与行政之间相互关系的状况是衡量有无法制以及既有法制是否达到法治状态的重要标志。法与行政的关系有三种基本形态：一是行政排斥法的作用，行政的实施不以法为手段和工具，在这种情况下，行政法制难以形成和发展；二是法从属于行政，法是行政的重要手段，在这种情况下，行政法制具备产生和发展的条件，但无法形成行政法治；三是行政从属于法，法不仅仅是行政的手段，更重要的是行政必须受到法的约束，只有在

---

① 1956年完成资本主义工商业的社会主义改造之前，我国所有制结构在公有制基础上具有多元性，正是在这一时期前后立法比较活跃，此后急剧衰减，及至计划经济发展到顶峰的"文化大革命"十年，国家几乎已无立法活动。这一事实印证了计划经济对法制需求不强甚至排斥法制的理论推断。

这种情况下，行政法制与行政法治才能统一起来，行政法治才能存在并不断发展。我国行政法治建设起步于20世纪70年代末80年代初，原因就在于这一时期我国从思想上、政治上和宪法上确立了法律对行政的支配地位。

"文化大革命"的惨痛教训使新一代执政党和国家领导人认识到只有下定决心加强法制建设，切实维护宪法和法律的尊严，才能避免"文化大革命"之类的悲剧重演。邓小平在"文化大革命"结束后不久即指出："为了保障人民民主，必须加强法制。必须使民主制度化、法律化，使这种制度和法律不因领导人的改变而改变，不因领导人的看法和注意力的改变而改变"；要做到"有法可依，有法必依，执法必严，违法必究"，[①]从而将法律的地位和法制建设提升到前所未有的高度。1978年12月党的十一届三中全会指出："为了保障人民民主，必须加强社会主义法制，使民主制度化、法律化，使这种制度和法律具有稳定性、连续性和极大的权威，做到有法可依，有法必依，执法必严，违法必究。"至此，"有法可依、有法必依、执法必严、违法必究"正式成为党领导和推进我国社会主义法制建设的指导方针。这十六字方针落实到国家行政管理领域就是要求依法行政。

执政党对行政的领导如何与法律对行政的支配地位相协调，关系到法律能否真正起到支配和约束行政的作用，对于这个十分关键的问题，执政党早在改革开放初期（1982年9月）就在党章中明确规定"党必须在宪法和法律的范围内活动"，从而回答了在社会主义条件下建设行政法治必然遇到的重大理论问题，在政治上进一步巩固了法律对行政的支配关系。

1982年12月4日，第五届全国人民代表大会第五次会议通过并颁布现行宪法，虽然在当时的历史条件下宪法文本中还不可能出现"法治"的用语，但已经充分体现和确立了"法律至上"的原则和精神，而这正是法治的基本要求和前提。现行《宪法》第5条第1款明确规定："国家维护社会主义法制的统一和尊严。"同条第3款规定："一切国家机关和武装力量、各政党和各社会团体、各企业事业组织都必须遵守宪法和法律。一切违反宪法和法律的行为，必须予以追究。"此外，宪法还规定了人民对政府享有批评、建议、申诉的权利，以及国家的侵权损害赔偿责任等。法律对行政的支配地位具备了确定无疑的宪法依据，尽管当时人们对行政法的理解和行政法治建设规律的认识还不够深刻，但行政法治建设已经具备了起步和

---

① 邓小平：《解放思想，实事求是，团结一致向前看》（1978年12月13日），《邓小平文选》第2卷，人民出版社，1994，第146~147页。

发展的必要条件。

2. 形成有中国特色的司法审查体系

20 世纪 80 年代我国行政法治建设最大成就在于：全面建立了具有中国特色的司法审查（行政诉讼）体系，形成了我国行政法治的基本格局。司法审查是行政法治的核心内容之一。没有司法审查，法对行政的支配地位和作用就不可能真正落实，行政法治建设将流于形式。行政法的实质是规范和约束行政权力，而法院对行政的司法审查是确保行政法名至实归的最基础和最重要的机制，缺少这一机制，行政法治必然成为无源之水、无本之木。从世界范围内行政法产生的历史看，行政法的概念、原则和制度正是在行政诉讼的过程中孕育和发展起来的。行政法起源于法国行政法院的判例，而非立法机关制定的成文法。这就是说，一个国家如果没有关于行政的成文法规范，但只要存在司法对行政的审查机制，这个国家的行政法就能够存在并发展；反之，即使一个国家制定了很多有关行政的成文法规范，但若没有司法对行政的审查机制，这个国家也是没有行政法的。从这个意义上看，一个国家行政法以及行政法治建设的起点其实不在立法而在司法。20 世纪 80 年代我国行政法律法规规章的立法活动十分频繁，成效显著，但行政法治建设最重要的进展并不在立法上，而在于逐步形成了一套全面的行政诉讼制度。我国行政法治建设的帷幕是在改革开放初期探索和创建行政诉讼制度的过程中拉开的。

我国探索和建立行政诉讼制度，也即法院对行政的司法审查制度，是从 1982 年开始的。1982 年我国通过的《民事诉讼法》初步确立了"民告官"的制度，但其适用的条件严格，范围有限。公民能否起诉政府机关依赖于具体单行法律的规定，对行政行为没有一般的、普遍的诉权。[①] 在 1987 年以前法律允许起诉的行政案件均为经济行政案件，绝大多数为经济行政处罚案件。对于非经济性行政案件，如治安以及其他行政机关行使公权力对社会实施管理的行为，均不得起诉。1986 年的《治安管理处罚条例》在我国行政法的发展史上具有重要意义。该法突破了行政案件仅限于经济行政事务的状态，将公民的诉权扩展至治安行政案件，是促成行政诉讼普遍化、行政诉讼与民事诉讼完全分离以及制定一部独立的《行政诉讼法》的

---

① 1982 年《民事诉讼法》（试行）第 3 条第 2 款规定："法律规定由人民法院审理的行政案件，适用本法规定。"自 1982 年至 1989 年《行政诉讼法》通过之前，我国已有 130 多个法律、法规规定了法院对行政案件的审判权限。

重要因素。为审理治安行政诉讼，最高人民法院以及各地法院陆续成立了行政审判庭。至此，审理行政案件的审判机构从民事经济案件审判机构中分离出来。1989 年制定并于 1990 年施行的《行政诉讼法》是我国行政法演进过程中最为重要的里程碑。它的直接意义是建立了普遍、独立的行政诉讼制度，深远的意义是使行政法的性质和作用发生了转折性的变化。在此之前，虽然已经产生和确立了政府也应当按照"法律面前人人平等的原则"遵守法律的一般理念和原则，但基本上没有促使和保障国家行政机关守法的系统的司法机制，以及需要行政机关遵守的具体法律规则，当时国家行政领域内的法律规范主要是指向行政管理相对人的，属于"行政管理法律规范"，而缺乏严格意义上的"行政法规范"。行政诉讼制度的普遍确立从根本上改变了行政法单向约束行政管理相对人的状况，强化了的"民告官"机制，不仅使政府守法从理论变成现实，而且更为重要的是拉动了以行政机关为对象、以约束行政行为为目标的行政法规则的快速发展。在行政诉讼制度的带动下，行政复议制度和国家赔偿制度先后发展起来，有关行政机关需要遵守的实体法律规则不断增多和完善。

比较 1989 年《行政诉讼法》与 1982 年《民事诉讼法》（试行）有关行政诉讼的规定，可以发现我国现行行政诉讼制度与 20 世纪 80 年代初期建立在民事诉讼基础上的行政诉讼制度差别较大。20 世纪 80 年代初的行政诉讼制度在审判组织上与普通法系国家类似，即行政诉讼视为民事诉讼，由民事（经济）审判机构依照民事诉讼程序审理。20 世纪 80 年代中后期行政诉讼制度在发展完善的过程中，大陆法系行政法学关于行政诉讼本质上不同于民事诉讼，应当与民事诉讼分离分立的观点为我国行政法学界所接受和推崇，进而对《行政诉讼法》的制定产生重大影响。由于我国普通法院已经开展了行政案件的审判实践，故《行政诉讼法》虽贯穿了行政诉讼与民事诉讼相互独立、相互分离的精神，具有明显的大陆法系国家行政诉讼制度的特点，但却并未像大陆法系国家通行的那样在普通法院之外设立专门的行政法院，而是在普通法院内部设立专门的行政审判庭专事行政案件的审判。我国行政诉讼制度具有自己的特色，这种特色是历史形成的，尽管《行政诉讼法》实施以来一直有一些学者呼吁改革现行行政诉讼体制，设立行政法院，但是要改变现行行政诉讼体制几乎是不可能的。

3. 行政管理立法活跃、新型立法体制得到确立

改革开放前的特殊历史条件造成我国各领域普遍缺乏法制，因此，改革开放以后依法行政的首要任务是解决"无法可依"的问题，这是建立和

发展行政法治、建设法治政府的必要步骤。由于现代行政的复杂性，行政法规范的主要起草者和制定者是行政机关自身，为此，我国 1982 年制定的宪法赋予国务院以及一定范围内高级别的行政机关分别制定行政法规和规章的立法权力，这是符合世界范围内行政法发展的规律和潮流的。考察改革开放最初十年间我国依法行政的状况，其中行政立法最为活跃，取得的成绩也最为突出。1989 年《中华人民共和国法律全书》① 收录的法律、法规、规章等立法文件即已达到 1224 件，其中绝大部分是改革开放以后颁布实施的行政立法文件，而行政管理法律也几乎全部由国务院提出草案，这一时期国务院制定了《行政法规制定程序暂行条例》，这是我国第一部专门规范行政立法活动的立法文件，对于保障行政法规的立法水平，发挥行政法规对其他行政立法的示范作用，促进行政立法能力的不断提高，具有十分积极的意义。

在这一阶段，行政法法源体系与立法体制得到确立并延续至今。根据 1982 年宪法，1981 年全国人大常委会《关于加强法律解释工作的决议》以及其他有关法律，我国形成了行政法的法律渊源体系，即宪法、法律、行政法规、地方性法规（自治条例、单行条例）、规章、司法解释以及我国参加的国际条约与协定，与此同时，行政法的立法体制也得到确立。新中国第一部宪法，即 1954 年宪法最早确立了我国的法律渊源体系与立法体制，它强调全国人民代表大会是国家唯一的立法机关，规定只有全国人民代表大会才能制定法律，全国人民代表大会常务委员会只能解释法律和制定法令，而国务院只能"规定行政措施，发布决议和命令"。1975 年和 1978 年两部宪法除删去 1954 年宪法关于"全国人民代表大会是行使国家立法权的唯一机关"的明文规定外，② 承继了 1954 年宪法所确立的立法体制。1982 年宪法对前三部宪法所确立的立法体制作了较大的调整和变革，除全国人民代表大会有权制定和修改"刑事、民事、国家机构的和其他的基本法律"外，还规定全国人民代表大会常务委员会有权制定法律，一定范围内的地方人民代表大会及其常务委员会有权制定地方性法规（自治条例、单行条例），国务院有权制定行政法规，国务院部、委以及一定范围内的地方人民政府有权制定规章，从而形成了一个全国人民代表大会行使国家最高立法权、立法主体多样多级的新的立法体制以及上述行政法的法源体系。关于

---

① 吉林人民出版社，1989。

② 1954 年《宪法》第 22 条。

规章的法律地位，在 20 世纪 80 年代曾存有争议，一种观点主张规章是行政法的法律渊源之一，能够成为行政行为的法律依据；另一种观点则反对将规章视为行政法的一种表现形式，认为规章不能充当行政行为的法律依据。两种观点相持不下，故 1989 年制定的《行政诉讼法》对规章的法律地位作了折中处理，规定人民法院不是"依照"而是"参照"规章审理行政案件。但这一时期行政法学的主流理论已将规章视为行政法法源体系的组成部分，2000 年《立法法》明确将规章的制定纳入立法活动的范畴，规章的法律渊源地位至此在法律上得到完全的确立。

4. 行政复议成为与行政诉讼相辅相成的行政救济渠道

行政复议是 20 世纪 80 年代中期首先在经济行政领域出现的一个新的行政法概念与新型行政法救济制度。在此之前，行政复议的概念尚未形成，但制度雏形已开始出现。一些法律、法规规定公民、组织如对行政处罚决定不服，可向作出处罚决定的上一级行政机关提出申诉，由上一级行政机关作出裁决，[①] 这里的"申诉—裁决"制度实质上就是行政复议，只不过没有使用行政复议的法律术语而已。1988 年前后，一些经济行政法律和行政法规开始使用"行政复议"的法律术语，正式确立行政复议这样一种新型的行政救济途径。如 1988 年《中华人民共和国水法》第 48 条规定："当事人对行政处罚决定不服的，可以在接到处罚通知之日起十五日内，向作出处罚决定的机关的上一级机关申请复议；对复议决定不服的，可以在接到复议决定之日起十五日内，向人民法院起诉。"对比此前颁布的自然资源方面的法律，如 1984 年《中华人民共和国森林法》、1985 年《中华人民共和国草原法》、1986 年《中华人民共和国渔业法》，以及 1986 年《中华人民共和国矿产资源法》等均未规定行政复议的救济方式，而仅向当事人提供行政诉讼的救济途径。

行政复议是在行政诉讼之后，立法机关在行政系统内部构建的一种新型行政救济渠道，它的出现进一步加强了行政法对行政相对人合法权益的保护，是 20 世纪 80 年代中后期我国行政法制建设取得明显进展的显著标志之一。当然，这一时期的行政复议制度与行政诉讼制度一样，已在局部形成，但比较零散，尚未成为普遍、系统的法律制度。在行政复议与行政诉

---

①　例如，1985 年《中华人民共和国外国人入境出境管理法》第 29 条第 2 款规定："受公安机关罚款或者拘留处罚的外国人，对处罚不服的，在接到通知之日起十五日内，可以向上一级公安机关提出申诉，由上一级公安机关作出最后的裁决，也可以直接向当地人民法院提起诉讼。"

讼的关系上，法律和行政法规的规定没有采取统一的模式。依照行政复议与行政诉讼的关系，这一时期的行政复议主要有三种类型，即前置型行政复议（当事人提起行政诉讼之前必须先经过行政复议）、选择型行政复议（当事人可在行政复议与直接提起行政诉讼之间选择，又有两种不同情形：一是当事人在选择行政复议后还可以提起行政诉讼，二是当事人选择行政复议后就不能再提起行政诉讼），以及排他型行政复议（当事人只能选择行政复议，不能提起行政诉讼）。其中，选择型行政复议的立法例较多，排他型行政复议较少。前置型行政复议在立法上并未占据明显优势，但因尊重了行政首次判断权且有利于减轻行政诉讼负担，因而这一时期在理论上受到较多学者的推崇。

5. 行政组织法制化成绩显著

为行政组织内部活动有法可依，这一时期我国对行政组织内部活动的法制建设也十分重视。以宪法有关行政组织的规定为依据和基础，1982 年 12 月 10 日全国人民代表大会制定《国务院组织法》，1979 年 7 月 1 日全国人民代表大会制定《地方各级人民代表大会和地方各级人民政府组织法》（1982 年、1986 年、1995 年、2004 年四次修正），基本建成我国行政机关组织法体系。此外，国务院还制定了一系列行政法规，对行政机关内部事务以及行政机关工作人员的人事管理、组织纪律等作出规定，如《国家行政机关公文处理办法》（1987 年），《国家行政机关及其工作人员在国内公务活动中不得赠送和接受礼品的规定》（1988 年），《国家行政机关工作人员贪污贿赂行政处分暂行规定》（1988 年）等。

6. 政府法制工作专门化取得明显进展

依法行政必然导致政府法制工作成为国家行政活动的重要内容，有无专门的政府法制工作机构以及政府法制工作机构地位的高低，反映了依法行政受重视的程度。早在 20 世纪 80 年代初期国务院办公厅即设有法制局，作为国务院办公厅处理政府法制事务的内设机构。1986 年随着政府法制工作重要性和工作量的不断增强，国务院决定将国务院办公厅法制局和国务院经济法规研究中心两个机构合并，成立国务院法制局，负责国务院的法制工作。随后国务院各部委和直属机构以及地方各级政府及其工作部门也相继建立了自己的法制工作机构或设立专门的法制工作岗位，在全面范围内形成了专门的政府法制工作体系。政府法制工作的专门化对于推进依法行政、实现行政法治发挥着不可替代的作用，因而，20 世纪 80 年代中期我国政府法制工作体系的构建及其工作的展开，是我国改革开放最初十年间行政法治建设不断取得进展的一个重要标志。

（二）改革开放初期行政法治建设的局限性

20 世纪 70 年代末至 90 年代初，是我国改革开放的第一个阶段。这一时期我国经济模式的灵活性虽不断增强，但总体上仍属于计划经济，实行依法行政的基础总的说来比较薄弱，人治的观念、习惯、做法在行政领域还十分流行，还不可能明确提出行政法治的概念与思想。依法行政、建设行政法治的动力主要来自对改革开放前特别是"文化大革命"历史教训的反思，这一点与 20 世纪 80 年代末及其以后的依法行政有所不同。计划经济的衰微及其向市场经济快速转型的客观需要，为 20 世纪 80 年代末期以后的行政法治建设提供了坚实的基础和强大的动力。正因为改革开放初期，我国尚不完全具备深刻认识行政法治本质属性与重大意义的历史条件，因而这一时期的行政法治建设在取得显著成绩的同时，也不可避免地表现出一定的局限性。

首先，依法行政观念及其社会基础虽有明显增强，但人治的观念和习惯依旧比较浓厚，行政法治建设受到各种主客观条件的制约较大。与改革开放之前深受法律虚无主义影响的行政观相比，改革开放初期依法行政观念的产生和确立，是一次思想上的重大解放和进步，正是在这一观念的指导下，我国开始了依法行政的制度创新与实践探索，并在创新和探索的过程中丰富和深化对依法行政的认识。然而，改革开放初期的依法行政观念尚带有非常浓厚的"法律工具论"色彩，认为依法行政就是把法作为行政的主要手段和工具，因而依法行政的主要任务就是大量制定针对行政相对人的行政管理法律规范，并将其付诸实施；与此相联系，对依法行政主要规范和约束对象是"官"而非"民"的基本属性的认识不够清晰和充分，依法行政观念中还夹杂着较多的行政特权思想，行政机关特别是负责维护社会秩序、保障公共安全的行政机关以及级别较高的行政机关，对以被告身份到法院出庭应诉不适应，甚至抱有抵触情绪的情形比较突出。

其次，在立法文件"宜粗不宜细"、立法活动"宜快不宜慢"的思想指导下，行政法立法比较原则和粗糙，对行政法的确定性、约束力和权威造成较大影响。由于"文化大革命"及其之前一系列"左"的政治运动遏制了法制的成长并对新中国成立以后已经形成的法制造成全面破坏，改革开放之初的法制建设基本上是在一片废墟上进行，立法的任务非常繁重，为了在尽可能短的时间内解决"无法可依"的问题，当时确立"宜粗不宜细"、"宜快不宜慢"的立法指导思想是有积极意义的。邓小平同志早在

1978 年就明确指出:"现在立法的工作量很大,人力很不够,因此法律条文开始可以粗一点,逐步完善。有的法规地方可以先试搞,然后经过总结提高,制定全国通行的法律。修改补充法律,成熟一条就修改补充一条,不要等待'成套设备'。总之,有比没有好,快搞比慢搞好。"①为使改革开放和国家建设急需的法律、法规尽快出台,立法机关不得已进行了大量的原则性、框架性立法,制定了若干试行性的法律、法规,在法律、法规名称中标明"试行"或"暂行"等字样,是我国改革开放初期所特有的一种立法现象。正是因为采取了上述措施,我国法律制度才以超常规的速度恢复和发展起来,与此同时,也造成了立法整体上比较笼统、粗糙,法的规范性不强的问题。

再次,行政救济制度发展不平衡。行政救济特别是其中的司法救济制度是行政法特别重要的组成部分,没有针对行政活动的司法救济或司法审查,就没有行政法。改革开放最初十年我国行政法治建设最突出的成就其实并不在于制定了多少涉及国家行政管理活动的法律法规和规章,而在于孕育和发展出一套以行政诉讼为基础和主干的行政救济体系。但是,受当时历史条件的限制,当事人针对违法或不当行政行为获得行政诉讼或行政复议等法律救济的权利是通过单行法律法规②逐个规定的,凡单行法律法规没有明确授权的,当事人就不享有获得法律救济的权利,不可避免出现了行政法发展不平衡和不一致现象。即使在法律允许向法院提起行政诉讼的情况下,有关法律规定也存在较大差别,如对经济行政行为不服,法院可依当时试行的《民事诉讼法》的规定,以判决形式(包括作出确认和变更判决)结案,而对于治安行政案件,法院却只能以作出维持或撤销的裁定的方式结案。③

最后,约束行政主体的法律规范特别是程序法规范较少。这一时期的

---

① 邓小平:《解放思想,实事求是,团结一致向前看》(1978 年 12 月 13 日),《邓小平文选》第 2 卷,人民出版社,1983。

② 1987 年 10 月 9 日最高人民法院在《关于地方人民政府规定可向人民法院起诉的行政案件法院应否受理问题的批复》中把《民事诉讼法》(试行)第 3 条第 2 款有关"法律规定由人民法院审理的行政案件,适用本法规定"条文中的"法律"扩大解释为包括全国人民代表大会及其常务委员会制定的法律、国务院制定的行政法规、省和直辖市的人民代表大会及其常务委员会制定的地方性法规以及民族自治地方的人民代表大会制定的自治条例和单行条例。

③ 参见 1986 年 10 月 24 日最高人民法院关于《人民法院审理治安行政案件具体应用法律的若干问题的暂行规定》。

行政法规范主要是调整国家行政活动中行政相对人（国家行政管理所针对的公民、法人或其他组织）的行为，以规定行政相对人的权利、义务和责任为重点，对行政主体在行政管理过程中应当遵循的法律原则、法律标准以及法定程序规范较少，不少法律法规甚至完全没有这方面的规定，行政主体无论在实体上还是程序上均拥有广泛的自由裁量权，因而在很大程度上影响了行政法约束行政行为以及行政救济的力度和实效。

三　九十年代行政法治的积淀与发展

（一）市场经济为行政法治开辟广阔前景

20 世纪 90 年代是我国行政法治建设快速发展的时期，这一时期行政法治建设与 80 年代相比有两点重大区别或者说具备两个影响深远的有利条件，即从 90 年代初开始，我国明确提出发展社会主义市场经济，市场经济体制逐步占据主导地位；以及全面确立我国行政诉讼制度的《行政诉讼法》顺利实施并在实践中不断发展完善。

1982 年 3 月 8 日制定的《民事诉讼法》（试行）第 3 条第 2 款有条件地确立了我国行政诉讼制度，我国行政法治建设由此迈出历史性的一步，但这时我国的经济体制是建立在社会主义公有制基础上的计划经济，我国早期的行政法治建设其实并不具备必要的社会经济基础，更大程度上是对历史反思的产物。计划经济本身并不需要行政法治，在计划经济条件下不可能建成行政法治。

在计划经济条件下，国家与社会紧密结合，两者一体化的程度非常高，工厂、学校、医院等企事业单位以及其他社会组织实际上是国家组织的延伸，个人被整合到特定的社会组织体之中，形成个人依附于组织、组织依附于国家的格局。由于个人与组织、组织与国家之间存在一体化的组织隶属与管理关系，国家无需法律法规的特别授权，也可依照组织内部的管理关系规范个人和社会组织的行为，实现对个人和社会组织的管理。在计划经济模式下，组织和个人的职责就是执行国家计划和命令，所谓"计划就是法律"，经济发展目标不依赖于并且排斥通过组织、个人的自主行为加以实现，为此，对组织和个人行为的规范必须非常具体，这是法律法规无法做到的，只有具体的计划、指示、命令才能适应这种自上而下的经济和社会组织方式的需要。计划经济模式是权力高度集中的模式，对计划的解释只有处在权力塔形结构顶端的计划制订者才有权作出，这就排除了法院司法介入的可能。在计划经济社会，上下级之间以及个人、社会组织与政府和国家之间也会产生矛盾和利益冲突，对处于下级地位的个人、社会组织而言，唯一可行的救济方式是向上级或者上级的上级申诉，法院在处理这类矛盾和纠纷的过程中不起作用。现代法治的基本标志之一就是通过依法独立行使职权的法院处理和平衡不同法律主体之间的利益冲突，包括国家与个人、社会组织之间的冲突，而这一点在计划经济体制下是不可能实现的。计划经济的组织特点与运行模式决定了它不需要也不能容纳行政法治。

与计划经济相反，市场经济不仅能够包容而且必须依赖行政法治方能存在和发展。市场经济强调通过发挥个人、社会组织的自主性来实现国家经济和社会发展目标，而要做到这一点，就必须给予个人和组织独立、平等的市场主体地位，允许个人、组织有自己的利益追求，并在国家规定的范围内自由活动，同时对个人、组织的权利和自由给予切实有效的保障。在这种情况下，计划特别是指令性计划显然无法胜任，只有通过立法才能实现既规定一定的标准和界限，又赋予个人、组织必要自主权的使命；只有设置独立第三方担任的裁判机制，才能使个人、组织相信其权利和自由是得到切实保障的。显而易见，能够适应市场经济的国家治理机制只能是合乎民主和法治要求的机制。实行市场经济必然要求和必然导致国家与社会的分离，当个人和社会组织不再隶属和依附于国家时，国家和政府就无法依靠组织体内部的上下级关系实现对个人和社会组织的管理，而必须依据通过民主程序制定的法律规则才能对个人和社会组织发号施令。在市场经济条件下，没有法律，国家无法对社会进行管理；没有法治，个人和组织的权利和自由无法得到切实保障。法律和法治是市场经济存在和发展的基础和前提。市场经济不断发展成熟的过程同时也是它的法律、法治基础和前提不断巩固与完善的过程。

我国计划经济向市场经济的转型最早可以追溯到改革开放初期，当时在计划经济的框架内，市场经济在"发挥市场调节的辅助作用"和"有计划商品经济"的名义下萌发和生长，1992 年初邓小平南方谈话[①]为确立市场经济扫除了思想和理论障碍。1992 年 10 月党的十四大从政治上确立了市场经济的主导地位，明确阐明我国经济体制改革的目标是建立社会主义市场经济体制。[②] 1993 年宪法修正案第 7 条删去 1982 年宪法第 15 条关于"国家

---

① 邓小平：《在武昌、深圳、珠海、上海等地的谈话要点》，《邓小平文选》第 3 卷，人民出版社，1993，第 370～383 页。

② 参见江泽民《加快改革开放和现代化建设步伐，夺取有中国特色社会主义事业的更大胜利》（在中国共产党第十四次全国代表大会上的报告），1992 年 10 月 12 日。

在社会主义公有制基础上实行计划经济。国家通过经济计划的综合平衡和市场调节的辅助作用，保证国民经济按比例地协调发展"的规定，明确规定"国家实行社会主义市场经济"，确立了社会主义市场经济的宪法地位。20 世纪 90 年代初期市场经济在思想理论、政治和宪法上取代计划经济，我国进入计划经济向市场经济全面转型、市场经济快速发展的阶段，这一历史背景对我国行政法治建设产生了积极、广泛而深刻的影响。在《行政诉讼法》司法实践全方位展开的带动下，我国行政法治建设的各个方面均取得明显进步。

（二）《行政诉讼法》推动行政法全面发展

1990 年 10 月 1 日《行政诉讼法》的施行，是我国行政法治进程中具有划时代意义的一件大事，对于推动我国行政法治建设的全面发展发挥了重要作用。为适应行政审判的需要，到 1990 年底，最高人民法院、全部高级人民法院以及 90% 以上的中级人民法院和基层人民法院建立了行政审判庭。1990 年我国行政案件的数量首次突破 1 万件，同年 10 月至 12 月，《行政诉讼法》实施以后的短短两个月间行政案件数量即达 5258 件，比上一年同期上升 96.56%。[①] 1991 年行政案件的数量比上年增长 97.4%，达 25667 件，其中，治安、土地、林业、税务行政案件上升 100% 以上，许多过去没有或少有的行政案件，如水利、统计、烟草专卖、能源、劳动教养等被起诉到人民法院。[②] 此后行政案件的数量以较大的比率逐年增加，范围不断扩大，至 21 世纪初，每年行政案件的数量已达 10 万件左右，案件种类已基本覆盖行政管理领域。[③] 从案件的审判结果看，《行政诉讼法》实施之前，法院对被诉具体行政行为的维持率较高，其中，1987 年至 1988 年间达 49.9%，1989 年为 42.5%；《行政诉讼法》实施后被诉具体行政行为的维持率不断降低，1991 年降至 31.6%，1992 年为 34.1%，1993 年为 23.56%，1995 年大幅降至 17.34%。上述数据表明，法院在整体上做到了依法独立公正地审判案件，在实施《行政诉讼法》时没有走过场，对行政机关保持了应有的司法监督的力度，这就促使国家行政机关工作人员普遍认识到必须认真对待行政法、切实增强依法行政的意识和增强依法行政的水平。可以说，20

---

① 参见任建新《最高人民法院工作报告》（1991 年 4 月 3 日在第七届全国人民代表大会第四次会议上）。

② 参见任建新《最高人民法院工作报告》（1992 年 3 月 28 日在第七届全国人民代表大会第五次会议上）。

③ 参见 2002 年和 2003 年的《最高人民法院工作报告》。

世纪 90 年代以后，广泛的行政诉讼实践为我国国家行政管理由人治向法治转型、由人治不断走向法治提供了不可或缺的动力和保障。

在《行政诉讼法》实施之际，我国实体行政法和程序行政法远不够完善，如果不加快建设与《行政诉讼法》相配套的法律法规，《行政诉讼法》的实施很难取得预期的成效，甚至有落空的危险。例如，《行政诉讼法》第 54 条规定"超越职权"和"违反法定程序"是撤销被诉行政行为的法定情形，但是，在缺少规范行政职权的法律规则或者含义不清的情况下，法院很难以"超越职权"的法律手段对行政机关的越权行为进行有效的控制；同理，在法律法规几乎没有对行政机关应当遵守的程序规则作出规定的情况下，"违反法定程序"的规定很难发挥实际作用。《行政诉讼法》的实施使得全社会高度关注以行政主体为调整和规范对象的法律规范的立法工作，推动了一系列重要行政法律法规的出台。

1. 《行政复议条例》与《行政复议法》

1990 年 12 月 24 日，国务院制定《行政复议条例》，1991 年 1 月 1 日起施行。1999 年 4 月 29 日，全国人民代表大会常务委员会制定《行政复议法》，同年 10 月 1 日起施行，《行政复议条例》同时废止。1991 年的《行政复议条例》全面构建了我国的行政复议制度，确立了行政复议既审查具体行政行为合法性又审查具体行政行为适当性、书面审以及一级复议的原则以及行政复议的体制，规定了行政复议的范围、程序和法律责任。《行政复议法》将《行政复议条例》上升为法律，基本上确认了《行政复议条例》所规定的行政复议制度。《行政复议法》第 27 条规定行政复议机关具有审查具体行政行为的依据是否合法的责任，第 28 条新增了"确认具体行政行为违法"的处理方式等，是《行政复议法》对《行政复议条例》所作的较为重要的修改和补充。

2. 《国家赔偿法》

1994 年 5 月 12 日由全国人民代表大会常务委员会通过，1995 年 1 月 1 日起施行。早在 1982 年，《宪法》第 41 条第 3 款即规定"由于国家机关和国家工作人员侵犯公民权利而受到损失的人，有依照法律规定取得赔偿的权利"。1986 年《民法通则》第 121 条规定"国家机关或者国家机关工作人员在执行职务中，侵犯公民、法人的合法权益造成损害的，应当承担民事责任"。恰在这一时期，区分公法责任和私法责任的理论占据主导地位，并推动行政诉讼从民事诉讼中分离和独立出来。与此相适应，主流观点认为，国家赔偿不应当属于民事赔偿，而是一种与民事赔偿并列的公法上的赔偿责任。为此，1989 年制定的《行政诉讼法》第九章专门对行政侵权赔偿责任作了规定，但比较笼统，没有涉及赔偿的具体条件、范围和程序，特别是赔偿的方法和标准等问题，也没有涉及行政侵权以外的其他国家侵权损害行为的赔偿问题。这样的国家赔偿制度是不完整的，可操作性也不强。《国家赔偿法》则全面建立了国家行政和司法赔偿制度。当然，在当时的历史条件下，《国家赔偿法》主要解决国家赔偿制度的有无而不是水平高低的问题，因而国家赔偿的门槛相对较高、水准偏低。①

3.《行政处罚法》

1996 年 3 月 17 日，全国人民代表大会制定该法，1996 年 10 月 1 日起施行。该法是我国首部以特定具体行政行为为调整对象的单行法律，属于典型的行政法。《行政处罚法》是我国行政法治建设过程中的又一个重要里程碑，它首次引入现代行政程序规则和听证制度，第一次明确规定违反基本程序规则的行政行为不能成立，从而拉开了以公开、透明、参与为基调的我国行政程序法制建设的序幕。它还首次确立了立法机关在没有上位法规定的情况下自行"设定"某种行政权力的立法权，这是对我国立法制度进行的一次重要变革。

除上述立法成果外，在执法层面上，《行政诉讼法》使"执法"的概念在行政管理实践中得到真正的确立，并推动行政方式发生深刻的变革。在《行政诉讼法》实施之前，行政方式基本上是经验性的，不注重科学论证以及收集、保存行政活动的证据，行政的随意性较强。《行政诉讼法》第 33 条关于"在诉讼过程中，被告不得自行向原告和证人收集证据"的规定，对行政机关工作人员改变其长期形成的不良行政习惯，努力掌握与适应新的符合依法行政和科学行政要求的行政方式，具有重要的引导和促进作用。

（三）行政内部法制建设取得新的突破

以国家公务员制度和行政监察制度的法制化为标志，20 世纪 90 年代，我国行政内部法制建设取得了新的成绩和突破。

---

① 1995 年是《国家赔偿法》施行的第一年，法院全年受理国家赔偿案件仅 197 件，审结 154 件，决定赔偿 64 件。案件数量仅为当年行政诉讼案件量的 0.3%，赔偿率为 41.6%。1999 年法院审结的国家赔偿案件大幅增加为 6788 件，但也仅为当年行政诉讼案件审结量的 6.87%。根据 2003 年《最高人民法院工作报告》，1998 年至 2002 年法院平均每年审结国家赔偿案件 2264 件，赔偿率为 35%；根据 2008 年《最高人民法院工作报告》，2003 年至 2007 年，法院平均每年审结国家赔偿案件 2600 件，不到行政诉讼案件的 3%。赔偿金总额也明显偏低，年均仅为 3600 万元。

1993 年 8 月 14 日，国务院制定《国家公务员暂行条例》（以下简称《条例》），在国家行政机关工作人员人事管理现代化、法制化方面迈出历史性一步。《条例》首次引入"国家公务员"概念，确立了"公开、平等、竞争、择优"以及"分类管理"原则，特别是创立了通过公开竞争考试录用低级初任公务员的制度，这是我国行政机关人事管理制度改革的重大突破。此外，《条例》在加强对国家公务员的人事管理和纪律约束的同时，也体现了保障国家公务员合法权益的精神，设立了国家公务员权利救济渠道，尽管国家公务员与行政机关之间的人事纠纷不能通过司法途径解决，但与传统干部人事制度相比，《条例》所确立的新型人事管理制度无论在合理性、公正性还是法制化的程度上都取得了明显的进步。

行政监察是国家行政系统内部监督的重要途径，早在 1990 年国务院就制定了《行政监察条例》，以法律形式规定了行政监察的原则、行政监察机关以及行政监察人员的法律地位、职责权限、工作程序、法律责任等。该条例特别规定"监察机关依照国家法律、法规和政策独立行使职权，不受其他行政机关、社会团体和个人的干涉"。1997 年全国人民代表大会常务委员会在该条例的基础上制定《行政监察法》，将《行政监察条例》上升为法律，进一步加强了对行政监察机关的法律规范和保障。

（四）问题与不足

在行政法治意识和观念方面，依法行政的观念和原则虽已得到正式确立，但尚未明确提出法治政府的理念，并将这一理念与依法行政直接联系起来，导致依法行政在实践中仍然带有不少人治的色彩和残余。在立法方面，一些构成现代行政法基础、成为行政法产生和发展支柱的法律法规虽已制定，但受当时历史条件下法治社会基础和整体发展水平的制约，这些法律法规在构建行政法制度时，主要以解决有无的问题为立法导向，造成立法不同程度地带有试验性、过渡性、妥协性的特点和不足。以《行政诉讼法》为例，该法第 5 条规定"人民法院审理行政案件，对具体行政行为是否合法进行审查"，完全排除了法院对具体行政行为的依据进行审查的可能性，与世界其他国家的行政诉讼制度相比，在这一点上，我国《行政诉讼法》的相关规定是非常保守和落后的。又如，由于当时对行政审判的特点和规律认识不足，《行政诉讼法》没有规定法院可以通过作出确认判决的形式审结案件，导致法院在审理一些复杂的行政案件时陷入被动，无法作出适当的判决。类似的问题在《行政复议法》、《国家赔偿法》、《行政处罚法》这些重要的行政法律中均不同程度地存在。

此外，行政法立法不全面、不平衡、零散化的问题也很突出。《行政处罚法》对行政机关的行政处罚行为作了系统的法律规范，提高了对行政相对人法律保护特别是程序保护的水平，然而，与行政处罚有很多共同点的行政强制行为却不能适用《行政处罚法》的相关规定，两个相近的行为，一个受到法律较为严格的规范，当事人在其中得到较好的法律保护；另一个则缺乏法律的严格规范，当事人不能享受与行政处罚相同的法律保护，这是分散和个别立法必然带来的弊端。

四　新世纪行政法治的升级与深化

（一）　新世纪行政法治发展的机遇与挑战

1. 加入世界贸易组织是新世纪行政法治发展进步的重要外因

2001 年我国正式加入世界贸易组织（以下简称 WTO），这是我国改革开放和现代化建设历史进程中具有深远意义的重大事件。WTO 协定规定："每一成员应保证其法律、法规和行政措施与所附各协定对其规定的义务相一致"，① 而成员需要与 WTO 协定保持一致，法律、法规和行政措施都在其行政法的范围之内，确切地说，属于一国（地区）行政法之中的经贸行政法。经贸行政法是一国（地区）行政法的有机组成部分，其变化和发展不是孤立的，必然会对其他相关领域的部门行政法，以及行政法的一些基本原则和带有普遍适用性的规则产生影响。加入 WTO 加快了我国行政法制改革的进程，给我国行政法治建设带来了较为明显的变化。可以说，加入WTO 为我国行政法治建设提供了一个十分难得的外因，使我国行政法制改革经历了一次重要的提速。

行政法的实质和要旨在于保证政府守法。行政法制良性改革不断发展的过程其实就是行政法制约政府的实效性和科学性不断增强的过程。在我国加入 WTO 之前，行政法制改革和发展的动力主要来源于政府自上而下的推动，以及市场经济和民间社会的发展对政府守法产生的需求和压力，两者的结合和互动推动着行政法制改革的不断前行。由于行政法的内在精神是规范和约束政府权力的行使，这就使得政府推动型的行政法制建设有着其难以避免的弱点，即行政法制改革的动力来源于政府的政治意愿，而外在的监督和制约力量不够有力。随着市场经济的发展和公众权利意识的增强，行政法赖以存在和发展的基础日益巩固，这是不争的事实，但政府主导型的

---

① 《马拉喀什建立世界贸易组织协定》第 16 条第 4 项。

行政法制改革和发展的格局并没有改变，因而其内在弱点始终是存在的。

然而，加入 WTO 使行政法制变革增加了前所未有的新的因素。虽然加入 WTO 仍然是政府推动和主导的结果，但一经加入，就要受到这个政府之外的力量的法律约束，这种约束是一种国际约束，政府难以对其进行主导和掌控。有人批评加入 WTO 使我国丧失了经济主权，严重削弱了政府管制经贸活动的能力，对这种意见，我们当然不赞成，但它真实地反映了 WTO 所具有的从外部大范围制衡政府权力的力量。打个不一定恰当的比方，WTO 的作用，类似于在政府权力之外又形成了一个可以对政府权力进行"制约和平衡"的"权力"，构成了一种特殊形态的"权力分立"。我国行政法制改革和发展内部原有的各种因素和力量都不可能产生这种效果。如果没有加入 WTO 的因素，有些制度变革我们是不会推动的，至少不会在现阶段进行；而加入 WTO 以后，不管愿意不愿意，都必须通过改革使我国相关法律制度与 WTO 的要求一致。这样，我国行政法制改革在原有两个方面的力量之外，又增加了一个第三方面的力量，即来自国际法的推动力。这方面的力量在一定程度上弥补了我国行政法制改革和发展内驱力与外部保障机制方面的不足和弱点，三方面的因素或力量结合起来，使我国行政法制建设和改革获得了更强的动力和更加坚实的保障。WTO 直接作用于我国的经贸行政法制度，对其他方面的行政法制度没有直接影响，而当我国加入两个国际人权公约以后，外部国际法因素将对我国行政法制的变革和发展造成更加全面而直接的影响。无疑，对这个第三方面的因素，我国行政法学者应当给予高度重视，对其利弊展开研究，以趋利避害。

在加入 WTO 以后的一段时间内，我国行政法制改革，尤其是经贸行政法制改革的主要任务之一是消除原有制度与 WTO 规则之间的不一致性，以履行我国根据 WTO 协定所承担的义务，但是，我国行政法制改革显然有自己早已确立的、更为高远的目标，其改革和发展不可能停留于或满足于对 WTO 的被动适应上。这决定了受 WTO 直接推动和影响的经贸行政法制改革的经验和成果，必会产生向行政法制建设的其他方面散播的效应，WTO 有关规范和制约政府权力的精神、非歧视和透明度原则、以统一、公正、合理的方式执法的原则、设立独立复审机构和司法审查的原则等，均具有普遍的行政法意义，与我国行政法制改革和行政法治建设的大方向是契合的，将对我国行政法制改革和行政法治建设产生长远影响。

2. 法治政府理念的形成

法治政府理念的形成意味着政府守法这一行政法基本价值观的确立。

关于政府守法是否是依法行政核心价值的问题，长期以来并不明确。在 20 世纪 80 年代行政领域内的法律规范绝大多数是针对行政相对人的，规范和约束行政机关的法律规范，也即狭义上的行政法规范，十分稀少并且缺乏有效的保障机制，加上人治思想观念非常盛行，因而这一时期的依法行政观实际上是"以法行政"观。20 世纪 90 年代以后，随着行政权力制约机制的发展与完善，特别是行政诉讼制度的全面确立，狭义的行政法规范迅速成长起来，但"以法行政"的观念依旧盛行，以至出现"二元论"的依法行政观念，依法行政既针对行政机关也针对行政相对人，两者同等重要。

进入 21 世纪以后，由于市场经济对法治行政提出更高、更迫切的要求，以及实践中人治行政与市场经济和多元社会之间的不适应性日趋明显，为充分发挥依法行政观念对实践的指导作用，党和国家明确提出依法行政的核心是政府守法，在政治上确立了依法行政观念的核心价值和内容。2004 年 3 月，时任总理温家宝在十届全国人大二次会议上所作的政府工作报告中第一次明确提出了建设"法治政府"的目标，2004 年 3 月 22 日国务院发布《全面推进依法行政实施纲要》进一步强调了这个目标。2004 年 10 月 2 日第二次修订通过的《国务院工作规则》第 2 条也提出要"建设法治政府"，并将"推进依法行政"专设为一章。2004 年 10 月 2 日第二次修订通过的《国务院工作规则》提出"依法行政的核心是规范行政权力"，至此，依法行政观念的核心内涵得以明确，法治行政观念在政治上的主导地位全面确立，这与改革开放以来依法行政观念长期弱于传统人治行政观念的状况形成鲜明对比。

当然，法治行政观的政治主导地位的确立并不意味着人治行政观的影响自动消除，相反，在实践中人治行政观仍会产生相当的影响。我国现在从总体上看还不能说已经建成了法治政府，法治行政与人治行政并存的现象仍将在一定时期内存在，如何在实践中全面确立法治行政观念，积极推动人治行政观向法治行政观的转化，从而为实现《全面推进依法行政实施纲要》确立的在 10 年左右时间内基本建成法治政府的目标做好观念和思想上的准备。

3. 人权入宪的积极影响

2004 年 3 月 14 日全国人民代表大会通过《宪法修正案》，规定在《宪法》第 33 条增加一款："国家尊重和保障人权"。人权入宪将对新时期我国行政法的发展和行政法治建设的推进产生积极影响。人权保障将成为行政机关日益重要的目标和职责，行政机关不仅需要更为审慎地约束好自己的行为，以免侵犯人权，而且还需采取更加积极主动的行动，保障人权并为人权的实现创造更好的条件。人权写进宪法与社会人权意识的高涨，对行政机关而言更多是一种挑战和压力，但对行政法的发展而言却意味着更多的机遇。

（二）新时期行政法治建设取得的主要成果

1.《行政许可法》的制定与实施

《行政许可法》一定程度上可以说是我国加入 WTO 的一个重要产物，是 21 世纪我国行政法治建设取得的又一重大立法成果。

在《行政许可法》制定之前，中国有关行政许可的法律文件不在少数，广义上的行政许可法①早在《行政许可法》制定之前就有了，主要是行政机关制定的规章，部分为国务院的行政法规和地方人大制定的地方性法规，也有一些全国人大及其常委会制定的法律涉及行政许可。在《行政许可法》颁行之前，我国就已经建立了行政许可法律制度。《行政许可法》的意义不在于它创建了一种全新的行政法律制度，而在于它改造和革新了现存的制度，从整体上将行政许可纳入了法治的轨道。

从《行政许可法》的社会意义上看，该法将有力地推动行政观念的转变和行政方式的变革，对最终完成计划经济体制向市场经济体制的转型，促进市场经济体制的进一步成熟和完善，将发挥重大作用。在这个意义上，任何已经出台的其他法律，包括《行政诉讼法》、《国家赔偿法》、《行政处罚法》等法律在内，均无法和它相比。《行政许可法》立法宗旨之一是推动政府职能转变，建立适应市场经济发展要求的、权力有限的、高效的服务性政府。为此，《行政许可法》对行政许可的设定权进行了严格的规范，意在通过大幅减少行政许可和严格新设行政许可的条件，尽可能多地使政府退出经济和社会事务，尽可能多地使市场和社会发挥其自我调节的作用。权力减小了，因权力行使而产生的腐败等副作用也可随之减少，对于树立政府清廉的形象十分有利。《行政许可法》的制定和实施，将会在很大程度上改变政府机关工作人员特别是领导干部"凡事都要管、要管就要设许可"的思维习惯，使他们切实认识到在法治社会和市场经济条件下，政府权力是有限的，不能想干什么就干什么。与此同时，行政机关及其工作人员还必须学会如何在公开、透明条件下行使权力，学会适应"把方便给予群众，把麻烦留给自己"的新型行政程序。因此，可以毫不夸张地说，《行政许可法》对于建立、保持和发展政府与经济、社会之间的和谐互动关系，推动

---

① 所谓广义上的行政许可法是所有有关行政许可的法律规范和法律文件的统称，它是相对于狭义上的行政许可法而言的。狭义上的行政许可法特指一部名为《行政许可法》的法律。

政府机关及其工作人员彻底告别计划经济时期的管理理念和行政方式，将产生深远的影响。

从制度创新的角度看，《行政许可法》继承了改革开放以后，特别是《行政处罚法》、《立法法》以来我国行政法治建设的经验，如《行政处罚法》首次以法律形式确立的"行政权设定"制度、行政权的相对集中行使、行政机关作出决定之前的告知义务以及行政相对人陈述申辩权利、听证制度、"收支两条线"原则等，《立法法》所规定的行政立法的专家和公众参与机制等，都在《行政许可法》得到体现和新的发展。除此之外，《行政许可法》还在以下几个方面取得了突破：

第一，突破了行政许可的理论范畴，体现了注重权利保护的务实的行政法理念。

第二，间接确认了"信赖保护"原则。

第三，打破了一般事项立法权与特定事项设定权对等配置的格局。

第四，强化了抑制部门保护和地方保护主义的机制。

第五，确认统一、集中和联合行使权力的行政方式。

第六，在行政程序的公开性和透明度上取得较大突破。

《行政许可法》的颁布施行对于大量削减行政许可，推动政府放松和减少对市场活动不必要的干预产生了明显的效果。

2. 其他重要成果

2000 年全国人民代表大会颁布《立法法》，这部法律进一步明确了行政法的立法体制和机制，特别是系统规定了行政法规和规章的立法制度，进一步改进和完善了立法监督制度。以《立法法》为依据，国务院于 2001 年分别制定了《行政法规制定程序条例》以及《规章制定程序条例》，形成了规范我国行政法立法活动的法律体系和相对完备的法律制度，行政法立法过程的民主性、公开性、科学性、规范性以及社会参与在《立法法》及其配套法规中得到较为充分的体现和保障。

2000 年最高人民法院对《行政诉讼法》作出新的司法解释，即最高人民法院《关于执行〈中华人民共和国行政诉讼法〉若干问题的解释》，其作用和地位相当于《行政诉讼法》的实施细则。1991 年为保障《行政诉讼法》的顺利施行，最高人民法院曾经对《行政诉讼法》作出系统的司法解释，[①] 经过

---

① 最高人民法院《关于贯彻执行〈中华人民共和国行政诉讼法〉若干问题的意见（试行）》（1991 年），已废止。

将近十年的司法实践及其经验积累，一些当时没有看清或没有条件解决的问题，比较充分地暴露出来并基本具备解决的条件；随着时间的推移和客观条件的变化，原来的司法解释乃至《行政诉讼法》本身在若干方面已经不能适应21世纪经济、政治、社会和法治环境下行政诉讼实践提出的新要求。1991年的司法解释是在《行政诉讼法》施行后的很短时间内颁布的，倾向于对《行政诉讼法》作严格解释，以保证《行政诉讼法》的司法适用。2000年的司法解释则负有弥补立法缺失、通过解释技术发展行政诉讼制度的使命，故表现出很强的能动性。新的司法解释通过灵活运用扩大解释技术，拓宽了行政诉讼的范围，降低了公民、组织提起行政诉讼的条件和难度，尤其是增设了确认判决这一新的结案方式，规定人民法院应当在裁判文书中援引其适用的最高人民法院的司法解释，以及可以在裁判文书中引用合法有效的规章及其他规范性文件，从而增强了人民法院行政审判的公开性和透明度。新的司法解释不再拘泥于行政诉讼与民事诉讼的严格分野，规定人民法院审理行政案件可以参照民事诉讼的有关规定。毫无疑问，最高人民法院在世纪之交针对《行政诉讼法》作出的司法解释，体现了与时俱进的要求，是把十年前确立的行政诉讼制度带入21世纪的重要行政法文件。

政府信息公开是建设阳光政府，深入推进行政法治建设的重要条件，同时也是衡量一个国家或地区行政法治水平高低的重要指标。进入21世纪以来，一些地方和部门积极开展了政务公开的试点和实践，为在全国范围建立政府信息公开制度积累了经验。2007年4月5日，国务院颁布《中华人民共和国信息公开条例》，规定该条例自2008年5月1日起施行。这进一步完善了我国行政法体系，在我国历史上第一次全面建立了政府信息公开制度，使我国行政法治建设向前迈进了一大步。为保障信息公开的实效性，该条例不仅规定了信息公开的范围、公开方式和程序，而且还规定了较为有效的监督与救济手段，如允许法院通过行政诉讼对信息公开具体行政行为进行司法审查，行政机关须定期向社会公布信息、公开工作报告，对行政机关信息公开情况实行社会评议等。

进入21世纪以来，国务院将法治政府建设提升到前所未有的高度，2003年3月22日国务院发布《全面推进依法行政实施纲要》，提出"经过十年左右坚持不懈的努力，基本实现建设法治政府的目标"，在全国范围和政府系统内自上而下地发起了一场声势浩大而持久的全面推进依法行政、建设法治政府的行动。该纲要在多个方面对行政机关提出了高于法律标准的依法行政要求，如将"程序正当"和"诚实守信"确定为依法行政、建设法治政府的基本要求等。2008 年 6 月 18 日国务院发布《关于加强市县政府依法行政的决定》，指出 "必须把加强市县政府依法行政作为一项基础性、全局性工作，摆在更加突出的位置"，并全面提出加强市县政府依法行政的各项具体要求和举措。

2010 年 4 月全国人民代表大会常务委员会对《国家赔偿法》作出修改，这是中国行政法治建设所取得的最新立法成果。新的《国家赔偿法》进一步扩大了国家赔偿的范围，提高了国家赔偿的标准，以及简化和优化了国家赔偿的程序。

五　中国行政法治的主要特征

中国行政法治在逐步推进和不断成熟的过程中，形成了自己的发展道路与主要特征：

第一，行政法治具有社会主义属性。当代中国的行政法治建设必须与国家的根本制度相适应。

第二，行政法治采取自上而下与渐进式的发展模式。当代中国的国家治理仍然呈现 "人治" 与 "法治" 双轨并行的特征，仍处于由人治向法治、政策治理向法律治理转型的过程之中。

第三，行政立法是行政法的主要渊源。在中国，行政机关享有制定行政法规和规章的立法权力。其中，行政法规由最高国家行政机关即国务院制定，规章由国务院的部委（或相当于部委的机构），以及一定范围内的地方政府制定。行政法规和规章构成行政法规范的主要部分，并依法享有立法设定权（即在无上位法明确依据的情况下，先行立法的权力）。

第四，行政法治具有较强的行政主导特征，法院在行政法治中的地位相对较弱。

第五，中国行政法治受大陆法系法治文化的影响较大，但近年来英美法系法治文化的影响有逐步增大的趋势。

Development History and Main Characteristics of Administrative Law in China

Feng Jun

【Abstract】 The establishment and development of the Chinese legal system since the funding of the People's Republic of China can be divided into four historical stages, namely, the stage of early exploration, the stage of legal nihilism, the stage of legal construction guided by instrumentalism, and the stage of legal construction guided by the rule of law. The development of the administrative law since the "reform and opening up" can be further divided into the following four stages: the stage of absence of administrative law before the "reform and opening up", the stage of establishment of the basic framework of administrative law system during the 1980s, the stage of accumulation and development during the 1990s, and the stage of upgrading and deepening the reform of administrative law in the new century. In the process of gradual evolution and maturing, the Chinese administrative law has developed its own path of development and characteristics.

【Key words】 Administration, the Rule of Law, Administrative Law System, Government Under the Rule of Law

Rule of Law and Administrative Procedure

Matti Niemivuo *

【**Abstract**】 The aim of this article is to give an overview on rule of law and administrative procedure in Finland. In addition, there are also comparative aspects from Nordic countries, other European countries, the Council of Europe, and the European Union. The article begins with an old Nordic adage "The country must be built by law", which is still an important starting point in decision-making in the Nordic countries. The concept of rule of law has been partly changed during the last decades: nowadays it does not mean only a formal but also a real legal security in the administrative decision-making. Legal security is provided to reach a lawful decision in a concrete matter. In addition, the decision must be just and fair, too. In other words: legal security is achieved, when such a decision has been made by an administrative authority.

The Finnish Constitution of 2000 and its concept of good administration has been a model for some legal frameworks in Europe. In Finland, the Administrative Procedure Act of 2003 is a modern Law which guarantees legal security for ordinary citizens. The most important elements of the Act are as follows: guarantees of good administration, promptness in decision-making, hearing, and duty to provide grounds for decisions.

Conclusions of the article highlight the importance of legislation of a high standard, well-functioned administrative machinery, sufficiently competent civil servants, and rapid non-contentious, administrative procedures for challenging of

---

* Professor, University of Lapland (Finland) .

administrative decisions. Finally, it is absolutely necessary that judicial review is available, when an incorrect decision has been made by an administrative authority.

I. Introduction

Law is commonly regarded as a central instrument available to the State to steer the development of society. This is an old view, expressed in an ancient Nordic adage "the country must be built by law". Belief of the omnipotence of the law and its magical powers is alive in Nordic societies. It is believed that defects in society can be corrected by enacting a law or changing existing legislation.

Of course, law is not always the best way to guide development in the desired direction. In particular, in the public administration of various countries many other methods have been taken into use (e. g. , soft law, planning and consultation systems). However, the basic idea of building a society by law is still appropriate for a modern constitutional State (Rechtsstaat).

Earlier the Finnish concept of rule of law, like the German one, underlined the formal understanding of legal security and rule of law. But after the 1995 reform of basic rights and liberties and the Finnish Constitution of 2000 the substantive elements of legal security have become more and more important. Section 2 (3) and 21 of the Finnish Constitution are fundamental in this connection.

The law is essential in the relations between the administration and the individual. Growing attention has been paid to the legal security of the individual in the administration and in the judicial control of administrative decisions. What is then legal security? Generally, it could be described as security against despotism and despotic decisions. It is mainly concerned with the means and factors of maintaining and strengthening such security. Legal security is provided to reach a lawful decision in a concrete matter. In addition, the decision must be just and fair, too. In other words, legal security is achieved, when such a decision has been made by an administrative authority.

In everyday life people become involved with administrative authorities in different kinds of matter. Often these issues are important for them personally. A few examples may illustrate this: (1) a person applies for a public office and is appointed, (2) the police grant a passport to an applicant, (3) a residence permit is granted to a foreigner who has entered the country, (4) a municipal authority grants a building permit and (5) the tax authority assesses taxation and orders the over-paid amount to be refunded to the taxpayer.

When the administrative authority has made the kind of decision the person wanted, there is nothing problematic in the matter from his point of view. The situation changes completely, however,

(1) if another applicant who does not even fulfill the qualification requirements is appointed,

(2) if the passport is not granted even if the applicant does not see any reason for refusal,

(3) if the foreigner is turned back at the border without thorough proceedings,

(4) if the building permit is not granted although in corresponding cases it has always been granted, or

(5) if the tax authority imposes an additional tax even though the taxpayer considers he should get a tax refund.

The most essential question from the point of view of the applicant for the office or the passport, the foreigner, the applicant for the building permit and the taxpayer is whether he can in this concrete situation have this, in his opinion mistaken decision of the administrative authority changed. What means are available to him? From a more general viewpoint the matter is not as simple. Socially and in terms of legal policy the most important question is undoubtedly how to ensure in advance the legality and the expediency of decisions made by the administrative authorities. If and when incorrect decisions are made by administrative authorities, the other essential question is how to guarantee, at least retroactively, the legal security of the citizen.

II. Good Administration/Good Governance

Issues of good administration and good governance have during the past decades been highly prominent in a number of contexts. Some of the more significant international exercises include the Council of Europe handbook *The Administration and you* (1996) and *Recommendation on good administration* of the Council of Europe (2007). These legal documents content the principles of good administration quite thoroughly.

Also the European Union Ombudsman's *Code of Good Administrative Behavior* (1999) and *the EU Charter of Fundamental Rights* (1999) are important steps in promoting good administration. In both legal documents can be seen the Finnish influence.

Good governance has to do with politics like societal goal setting. The European Commission in its White Paper on European Governance (2001) emphasizes five principles of good governance: openness, participation, accountability, effectiveness and coherence. In particular, principles of transparency, accountability and participation are the three core concepts in good governance.

In all systems of good governance, Parliament plays very important role. At the same time, it represents and rules citizens. Lawmaking is a central task of Parliament. Of course, it does not draft legislation, but it may initiate legislation, scrutinize government bills and make amendments.

In Finland discussion on good administration has been lively since the 1995 reform of the basic rights and liberties, in which connection good administration was declared to be a basic right. The right to good administration was included almost word by word to the Finnish Constitution (2000). In addition, the Constitution contains also a provision (section 124) on the delegation of administrative tasks to others than public authorities. This provision has an effect on privatization exercises.

According to the Finnish Constitution, "the guarantees of good administration shall be laid down by an Act". The new Finnish Administrative Procedure Act (434/2003) came into force at the beginning of 2004. It repealed the Administrative Procedure Act (1982). The former Act had retained its status as the main enactment in the field of administrative law in Finland, containing the leading rules and principles governing administrative matters. The Act constituted a solid foundation for procedures before the authorities. The experiences of its application had been mainly positive.

III. Background to the Reform of the Administrative Procedure Act

Why did we reform our administrative Procedure, when the Administrative

Procedure Act of 1982 had functioned well? The main reasons were the developments in administration and society since enactment of the Administrative Procedure Act of 1982 and the new requirements caused by them. In particular, there were five specific reform needs. Firstly, the reform was necessary because of the Constitution of 2000 according to which everyone has right to good administration. Secondly, the reform was needed because of structural changes in the public sector caused by privatization and outsourcing. Thirdly, the boom in computerized services had to take into account in the development of legislation on administrative procedure. Fourthly, the European law posed new challenges to our legislation. And finally, there was a need for codification and reform of legislation on administrative procedure in general.

The reform of the administrative procedure legislation started at the Ministry of Justice at the end of 1980s by monitoring how the Administrative Procedure Act of 1982 functioned in practice. At the beginning of 1990, the Finnish Ministry of Justice also organized a discussion with its counterparts on Nordic administrative laws. All the participants at the meeting agreed that the Nordic administrative acts were effective.

In 1992, the Ministry of Justice decided to begin preparations for a new, modern administrative procedure Act. However, other urgent legislative reforms delayed establishment of a project group for the reform until 1997. In the same year, the Ministry of Justice published an overall report on the problem of the Administrative Procedure Act of 1982 and its reform objective. [1] A few years later, another expert report was published. [2] This expert report considered the relationship of the Administrative Procedure Act of 1982 to the fundamental rights provisions, to the special administrative legislation, and to European law. In addition, the report contained the results of an empirical study on application of the Administrative Procedure Act by 34 administrative authorities on the central, regional and local level. The third expert report on administrative contracts was published in 2001. [3] These three reports formed the basis for the Draft

---

[1]   Ministry of Justice, Law Drafting Department publications No. 4/1997.

[2]   Ministry of Justice, Law Drafting Department publications No. 2/2000.

[3]   Ministry of Justice, Law Drafting Department publications No. 2/2001.

Administrative Procedure Act.

In September 2001, the proposal for a new Administrative Procedure Act was finalized at the Ministry of Justice and written statements on the proposal were requested from the various authorities and other organizations. By the end of January 2002, the Ministry of Justice had received 128 written statements on its proposal. On the whole, attitudes towards the reform and detailed comments on it were very positive. Only the Ministry of Finance opposed the reform because of its financial effects. Also, the Supreme Administrative Court made several critical remarks on the proposal.

During January and February 2002, the Ministry of Justice redrafted its proposal on the Administrative Procedure Act and negotiated with the other Ministries on the new version. Later on in March and April, the new draft law was discussed by the permanent secretaries of the Ministries and was given political scrutiny by the ministerial working group on development of administration and regional policy.

In May 2002, the Bill on the Administrative Procedure Act was submitted to Parliament. The preliminary debate on the proposal in a plenary session in Parliament was positive. After the debate, the Bill was sent to the Parliamentary Committee of Administration for detailed discussion. Because of the large number of other Bills, the Parliamentary Committee was unable to begin its work until January 2003. After hearing several experts, the Parliamentary Committee prepared a report in which it proposed only a few small changes in the law text. On 17 February 2003, Parliament unanimously adopted the new administrative Procedure Act.

Finally, on 6 June 2003, the President of the Republic signed the new Act, which came into force at the beginning of 2004. So the whole legislative drafting process had lasted over ten years.

IV. The Finnish Administrative Procedure Act

The objective of the Administrative Procedure Act is to achieve and promote good administration and access to justice in administrative matters. The Act also promotes the quality and productivity of administrative services.

The Act is a general law on good administration and on the procedure applicable in administrative mattes. In some areas (e. g. , taxation and environmental issues) there are provisions which are not in line with the Administrative Procedure Act. In special administrative legislation, there can be provisions which are contrary to it only, if this is absolutely necessary. Otherwise, provisions of special legislation may only complement the Administrative Procedure Act.

The Finnish Administrative Procedure Act is not a very long document. It contains about 80 sections, which have been divided into four Parts and 12 Chapters as follows:

Part One-General Provisions

Chapter 1-Objective and scope of the Act

Chapter 2-Foundations of good administration

Chapter 3-Status and exercise of the right to be heard

Part Two-Pending Effect of an Administrative Matter and its Consideration by an Authority

Chapter 4-Delivery of documents to an authority and pending effect of an administrative matter

Chapter 5-General requirements on the consideration of a matter

Chapter 6-Clarification of matters and hearing of parties

Chapter 7-Decision in a matter

Chapter 7a-Rectification (administrative appeal)

Chapter 8-Correction of an error in a decision

Part Three-Service of Administrative Decisions and Other Documents

Chapter 9-General provisions on service

Chapter 10-Service procedure

Part Four-Miscellaneous Provisions and Entry into Force

Chapter 11-Miscellaneous provisions

Chapter 12-Entry into force and transitional provisions

The *scope of application of the Act* is very broad. The Act is applicable to all public authorities, state enterprises and associations subject to public law, and to private entities when they perform public administrative tasks.

Chapter two contains the *foundations of good administration*. *Section 6* on legal principles of administration is one of the key provisions. According to this Section, an authority shall treat clients of administration on an equal basis and exercise its competence only for purposes that are acceptable under the law. The acts of the authority shall be impartial and proportionate to their objective. They shall protect legitimate expectations based on legal system. *Section* 7 contains a provision on the service principle and *Section* 8 deals with advice. *Section* 9 requires that an authority shall use appropriate, clear and comprehensible language. Finally, *Section* 10 contains provisions on inter-authority co-operation. Chapter Two does not contain all the main principles of administration, e. g. , the principle of legality includes in our Constitution.

One of the main issues in the reform was providing time limits for decision-making by an authority. This arises mainly due to the requirement in Section 21 (1) of the Constitution according to which everyone has the right to have his or her matter considered without undue delay by a court of law or other authority. According to *Section* 23 of the Administrative Procedure Act, a matter shall be considered without undue delay. In addition, it is stated that upon request, the authority shall supply the party with an estimated time for the decision and respond to queries on the progress of the matter. Although Section 23 does not contain an expressed time limit, the regulation highlights the importance of promptness in decision-making.

Provisions on hearing a party before the matter is decided are extremely important. According to Section 34, a party shall be provided with an opportunity to express an opinion on a matter and submit an explanation on any demands and information that may have an effect on the decision. A matter can be decided without hearing the parties in only a few cases, for example if the demand is ruled inadmissible or immediately rejected as groundless or if the hearing would jeopardize the objectives of the decision or delay in consideration of the matter arising from the hearing causes a significant health hazard or danger to public safety or the environment.

The *duty to provide grounds for decisions* is also a key element in the Administrative Procedure Act. According to Section 21 of the Finnish Constitution, it is a fundamental right to receive the grounds for a decision. According to Section 45 of the Administrative Procedure Act, the grounds for a decision must be supplied. The statements of the reasons must indicate the circumstances and information that have affected the decision and the provisions that have been applied. A statement of the grounds is unnecessary in only a few cases, for example if an important public or private interest requires a decision to be issued at once, or if the decision approves a demand that does not pertain to other parties and others who do not have the standing needed to appeal against the decision.

In 2010, the new Chapter 7 a on *rectification* (administrative appeal) was included in the Administrative Procedure Act. Chapter 8 contains provisions on the *correction of an error* in a decision. These rules give to an authority and a client a flexible opportunity to correct a decision without using a judicial review of the administrative act.

V. Comparative Aspects

Legal documents of Council of Europe and the European Union are extremely important as a model in promoting good administration and good governance. Some of the documents are also binding and applicable in the Member States. European institutions, the European Court of Human Rights, the Commissioner for Human Rights and the European Ombudsman deal with issues concerning maladministration.

The European Union has not yet a general regulation on administrative procedure. However, preparation for such a legislation has already started.

All *Nordic Countries* have modern administrative Procedure Acts. These are clearly shorter than the Finnish Administrative Procedure Act. In Sweden, a new Administrative Procedure Act is under preparation on the basis of the expert proposal of the year 2010. ①

In *France*, the principles of administrative law are well developed. Because of this it is amazing that there is no general Administrative Procedure Act in France.

Germany, *Austria* and *Hungary* have very extensive and detailed administrative procedure Acts. Southern European countries like *Spain* and *Portugal* have quite modern laws on administrative procedure. It should be mentioned that the legislation of Portugal was the basis when the Council of Europe prepared the handbook "Administration and you" (1996).

VI. Conclusion

I will conclude with five remarks. To begin with, in my opinion the most

---

① Statens offentliga utredningar: En ny förvaltningslag. Betänkande av Förvaltningslagutredningen. SOU 2010: 29. Stockholm 2010.

important question is how to ensure *in advance* the legality and expediency of decisions made by administrative authorities. My primary answer is the legislation of a high standard. In particular, for an individual it is important that he gets the decision as soon as possible and it is correct and fair.

Secondly, the structure of administration must be clear and effective. In addition, it is also very important that the administrative machinery functions well. That is why there must be rules for administrative procedures.

Thirdly, good administration is not achieved mere by legal norms. A competent, motivated and sufficient body of civil servants with satisfactory working equipment is necessary. This ensures a prompt and efficient way of handling matters in the administrative machinery.

Fourthly, there are a number of valid reasons for developing the procedure of administrative correction. It is a rapid remedy. It is easy for a citizen to claim correction and it should be fairly easy for an authority to correct a faulty decision. This procedure applies well in cases which are judicially simply, such as tax cases, state grants to municipalities, social insurances and various kinds of allowances. Then again, the procedure of correction should be developed so that all the judicially difficult matters could be brought before a court as soon as possible.

Finally, it is most essential that all decisions of administrative authorities can be appealed against to an independent court of law. Whether it is an administrative court or a general court is not important. Experiences in different countries prove that both of these systems function well in practice.

法治和行政程序

马蒂·涅米渥

【摘要】本文的目的是概述芬兰的法治和行政程序,并与北欧国家、其他欧洲国家、欧洲理事会和欧洲联盟相比较。文章以北欧格言"国家必须通过法律建立"为开篇,这至今仍作为北欧国家决策的重要出发点。法治的概念在过去几十年中已部分改变,如今它意味着不仅是形式上的而且也是真正意义上的行政决策中的法律保障。法律保障用于在一个具体事项上实现一个合法的决定;同时,该决定也必须是公正和公平的。当行政机关作出这样的一个决定时，法律保障就实现了。

芬兰 2000 年宪法和其良好行政的概念在欧洲已经成为几个法律框架的典范。芬兰 2003 年行政程序法是一部保障普通公民的现代性法律。该法最重要的因素包括保障良好行政、决策的及时性、听证以及对决定说明理由的义务。

文章的结论是强调高标准立法、行政机构的良好运作、高度合格的公务员、高效的以非诉讼手段质疑行政决定的行政程序的重要性。最后强调，当行政机关已经作出一个错误决定时，司法审查机制是绝对必须的。

新中国行政复议制度的
历史变迁与发展

湛中乐[*]

【摘要】 本文回顾了中国行政复议制度的规范变迁史，并阐述了《行政复议法》颁行前后行政复议制度实施情况的变化。《行政复议法》颁行后，行政复议制度一度呈现良好的发展势头，但最近几年又遭遇回潮，其根本问题在于行政复议制度的公正性与公信力。对此，我们应当从体制和程序两方面进行改革：在体制方面，应建立相对独立的行政复议委员会制度；在程序方面，应当借鉴司法程序进行完善，并且注重发挥行政复议制度所潜在的政治功能。

【关键词】 行政复议法　行政复议委员会　行政复议程序

行政复议作为一种重要的行政法律制度，在新中国从初创至今已整整20年。[1] 改革开放以来，行政复议制度经历了从几近空白到《行政复议条例》、《中华人民共和国行政复议法》（下称《行政复议法》）再及于《中华

---

* 北京大学法学院教授。

① 这里谈的行政复议制度变迁史，系指新中国成立以来行政复议制度的变迁历史。实际上，准确地说，我国行政复议制度起源于民国时期的诉愿制度，1914 年《诉愿条例》是中国行政复议制度的最初起源。这一条例旋即为同年的《诉愿法》所取替。1930 年，当时的国民政府颁行了新的《诉愿法》，该法于 1935 年、1937 年历经两次修订，但因兵燹战乱，未得到良好实施。新中国成立后，台湾地区的诉愿制度仍以该法为基础，历经多次修订沿用至今，亦为大陆的行政复议法制建设提供了重要参考，是我国行政复议制度的重要支脉。参见翟小波《制度在历史的积累中成长——行政复议制度：中国与广州》，《博览群书》2006年第 4 期，第 4～5 页；参见戴桂洪《清末和民国时期行政程序法制的发展介评》，《学海》2008 年第 3 期，第 147 页。

人民共和国行政复议法实施条例》的发展。通过对行政复议制度的历史与发展进行检视，我们或许能从中受到有益启发，而作继往开来的努力。

一　行政复议制度的规范变迁史

1. 新中国成立后至《行政复议条例》颁布前（1949～1990年）

在1990年《行政复议条例》出台以前，我国的行政复议制度几近空白，但并非全无相关机制。新中国成立后即有部分法律、法规和规章载有"复核处理"、"复查"或"复议"的规定，例如1957年《中华人民共和国国境卫生检疫条例》（全国人大常委会通过的法律）第7条第2款规定："受处分人对所受的处分如果不服，可以在接到处分通知或者判决书后十日内，向原处分机关或者它的上级机关声请复议或者申诉，或者依法向上诉审人民法院提起上诉。"1951年《中华人民共和国城市房地产税暂行条例》（政务院发布的行政法规）第12条规定："税务机关应设置房地产税查征底册，绘制土地分级地图，根据评价委员会之评价结果及纳税义务人之申报，分别进行调查、登记、核税，并开发交款通知书，限期交库。纳税义务人对房地产评价结果，如有异议时，得一面交纳税款，一面向评价委员会申请复议。"1958年《湖南省农业税实施办法》第31条规定："纳税人认为对农业税征收有调查不实、评议不公、错算或错征的情况，可请求乡镇人民委员会复查和复议，如果纳税人对复查和复议的结果仍不同意，还可请求上一级人民委员会复查……纳税人在请求上一级人民委员会复查的同时，仍应按乡镇人民委员会复查复议的结果执行。……"至20世纪80年代，有关行政复议的规定日益丰富，在税收领域体现得尤为突出。在其他领域，例如针对商业执法检查的处理措施、违反节约用水规定的行政处罚等行为，亦有规章设置了复议规定。① 从1990年以前的诸多规定看，出台时间越晚，在规则内容方面越接近《行政复议条例》。实际上，《行政复议条例》并非凭空臆造或单纯法律移植的产物，早期这些分散于各地、各部门的复议规范及相关实践，为《行政复议条例》打下了基础。

---

① 《城市节约用水管理规定》（建设部，1988年）第20条；《商业部门执法检查工作暂行规定》（商业部，1989年）第16、17条。

2.《行政复议条例》颁行至《行政复议法》实施前（1991～1999 年）

1991 年《行政复议条例》的实施是我国行政复议制度的里程碑。《行政复议条例》全面规定了行政复议的基本原则和制度、申请复议范围、复议管辖、复议机构（和人员）、复议参加人、复议程序（申请与受理、审理与决定、期间与送达）、法律责任等内容，为行政复议法制建立了一个全面的制度架构。在这个架构之下，各地也进一步出台了一系列有关行政复议的法规、规章，例如《吉林省行政复议若干规定》（1992 年）。但《行政复议条例》存在行政复议制度定位不明、复议范围较窄、申请期限过短、管辖方式不理想（以"条条"管辖为主）等问题。针对较为突出的两处缺陷（资源确权民事纠纷的行政调处、仲裁亟须纳入复议范围；"条条"管辖过于僵化），《行政复议条例》在 1994 年经历了一次修订，其中以上一级部门管辖为主改变为可以由上一级部门或本级人民政府管辖这一点尤为重要，这一革新使得行政复议不再主要由某一行政子系统内部解决纠纷，而使行政相对人有了更宽广的选择空间。但总的来说，此时尚未有机会全面解决《条例》中存在的种种问题。

3.《行政复议法》的早期规范体系（1999～2007 年）

为全面完善行政复议制度，并提升其规范位阶和权威性，中国全国人大常委会第九次会议于 1999 年通过了《行政复议法》。《行政复议法》对《行政复议条例》的改进，主要体现在以下几个方面：①扩大了行政复议受案范围，不仅补充列举了数类具体行政行为，并排除了对具体行政行为进行复议在保底规定上的权利类型限制，[1] 而且将抽象行政行为有条件地纳入受案范围；②调整了管辖模式，从规范上明确了申请人的选择权；③复议程序便民化，例如放宽了复议期限、允许提出口头申请、缩短审查期限、建立直接受理制度等；④通过规定阅卷权、上级机关直接受理和加强法律责任等法律机制，强化了对复议机关的监督；⑤调整了决定形式，增加了确认型的复议决定，取消了补正型的决定。《行政复议法》的出台大大推动了行政复议实践，标志着我国行政复议制度发展到一个全新的阶段。[2] 但是，关于复议机关的定位、复议程序的公开与透明等关键点则仍为制度的空白地带，冀望能通过实践探索去寻求较理想的处理方式。

---

[1] 《行政复议条例》中为"认为行政机关侵犯其他人身权、财产权的"；《行政复议法》中为"认为行政机关的其他具体行政行为侵犯其合法权益的"。

[2] 湛中乐、姜岸：《论我国行政复议制度的发展与完善——兼评我国〈行政复议法〉立法之得失》，《科技与法律》1999 年第 2 期。

4. 行政复议规范体系的新近发展（2007 年至今）

为解决行政复议在实践中遇到的一系列问题，2007 年国务院颁行了《行政复议法实施条例》（以下简称《实施条例》）。《实施条例》主要在以下若干方面作了进一步细化：明确了行政复议机关应履行的具体职责；详细解答了若干情形下申请人与被申请人的认定问题；明晰了复议程序的期限计算（尤其是期限起点的认定）；规定了提交复议申请的有关细节；确立无例外则必须受理原则并明确受理要求；细化审理程序并增添有关复议中调解的规定；完善了复议的监督指导机制；补充了相关法律责任；等等。《实施条例》的突破与革新至少在规范上是值得肯定的，也取得了一定的实践效果，但尚待进一步观察才能得出较为周全的结论。

二　行政复议制度实施情况的变化

规范的变迁带来了实施情况的变化。在《行政复议条例》颁行之初，曾经出现一个行政复议热潮，各地行政复议案件数量大增，不少地方甚至超过了行政诉讼案件。但自 1993 年起各地的行政复议案件数量就开始下降，在《行政复议法》颁布以前，再未达到《行政复议条例》实施初期的水平。① 1994 年国务院对行政复议管辖体制作了调整，由此前的"条条"管辖为主改为除法律另有规定外，实行条块结合、由申请人自主选择的原则，行政复议案件有所回升，但是在《行政复议法》出台前，始终未能超过 1991～1992 年的案件数。②

《行政复议法》颁行以后，复议案件大量增加，1998 年全国已纳入统计的 24 个省、自治区、直辖市新收行政复议申请只有 23802 件；1999 年，已统计的 23 个省、自治区、直辖市新收行政复议申请即有 32170 件。③ 从 2000 年起，纳入统计的 31 个省、自治区、直辖市的行政复议申请、受理、结案的数量在 2002 年前后的短暂回流后，总体呈现增长趋势。

而维持、变更、撤销、责令履行义务、相对人撤回申请以及其他处理

---

① 刘莘：《行政复议的发展历程与未来展望》，《江苏社会科学》2008 年第 5 期，第 121 页。

② 方军：《我国行政复议制度的实施现状、问题和展望（二）》，北大法律信息网，http://article. chinalawinfo. com/Article_ Detail. asp? ArticleID = 37883&Type = mod，2009 年 8 月 12 日访问。

③ 图 1 和图 2 的数字与图表的数据源均来自方军：《我国行政复议制度的实施现状、问题和展望（二）》，以及方军《我国行政复议制度的实施现状、问题和展望（一）》，北大法律信息网，http://article. chinalawinfo. com/Article_ Detail. asp? ArticleID = 37884&Type = mod，2009 年 8 月 12 日访问。此外尚包括部分新近从国务院法制办行政复议司获得的新数据。

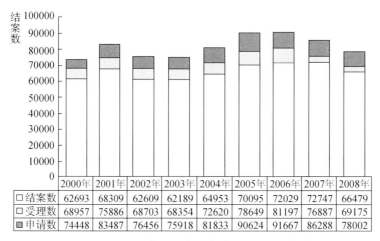

图 1　2000～2008 年行政复议申请、受理、结案情况

方式等不同案件结果亦呈现出一定的变化趋势:

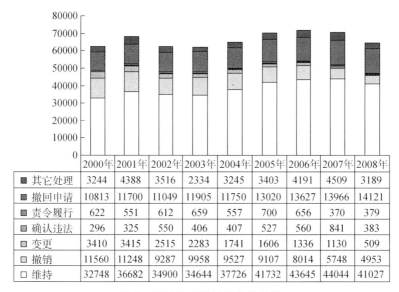

图 2　不同处理结果的变化趋势

　　在这些数据的变化背后,并不仅仅是规范的变迁,相应地,政府也采取了许多相关措施。最主要的影响上述数据的一些措施包括政府内部会议、对复议法制的宣传、对法制工作人员的培训等。这些措施对于转变政府工作人员意识、观念,提高法制运作的技术水平,起到不可忽视的作用。2002年的回潮低落也与规范变动无关,有学者指出,一些地方尤其是市、县两级政府在这次机构改革中撤并了行政复议机构，复议人员流失严重，行政复议相对独立的问题始终未得到解决，该受理而不受理或者受理后简单维持的现象又有所抬头，行政复议的质量和效率不高，是该段时期复议案件数量下降的重要原因。① 另外，值得一提的是，2007 年全国行政复议申请数量又有所下降，而同期的行政诉讼案件增长明显，信访中行政纠纷方面的案件也节节攀升，向人民法院提起行政诉讼的案件中，70% 以上是没有经过复议而直接起诉的，这也从一个侧面反映出行政复议的公正性在一定程度上是不太被公众认同的。② 近两三年行政复议申请数量的回落，进一步说明了行政复议制度在民众中的认可度不足。

从影响行政复议案件数量及处理结果的因素看，公共行政的规范化水平、案件管辖方式、政府宣传力度、复议机构的定位（是否有专门的行政复议机构和工作人员，行政复议机构的设置模式、对案件的实际处理权和处理方式、在行政机关中的实际地位和经费保障，以及复议机构的负责范围）、工作人员的业务素质、复议决定的质量、复议案件的维持率与纠错率、复议程序的便利性、复议过程的公开性与透明度等，均对行政复议制度的运行状况有影响。③ 总的来说，我们可以通过行政复议制度的历史发展，观察到影响行政复议法制运行的多种因素，在以上诸多因素中，目前纳入法律规范的因素只占一小部分，尚有许多规范外的因素在对行政复议制度在过去、当前的运行及未来的发展起着不可忽视的作用。

三　行政复议制度的历史启示与走向问题

通过分析新中国行政复议制度历史与发展，我们可以总结出影响行政复议制度历史与发展的诸多因素，而在这些因素的背后，正如学者们敏锐地指出的，是行政复议制度的公信力问题，即民众是否对行政复议制度产生足够的信任。若行政复议能有效维护民众的合法权益，则民众将更倾向于通过复议机制来解决纠纷；否则，民众将选择其他纠纷解决方式（有人

---

① 同上注。
② 刘莘：《行政复议的发展历程与未来展望》，第 121 页。
③ 总结自青锋《中国行政复议制度的发展、现状和展望》，《法治论丛》2006 年第 1 期，第 16～30 页；方军：《论中国行政复议的观念更新和制度重构》，《环球法律评论》2004 年春季号，第 41～42 页；黄红星：《对我国现行行政复议体制的两点反思》，《法学研究》2004 年第 2 期，第 149～150 页；张华民：《论提升我国行政复议公信力》，《广东行政学院学报》2008 年第 6 期，第 45～48 页。

曾借用著名的"用脚投票"一词来形容这一情形①），从而给复议制度带来变革的压力与动力。上述各种因素，都直接或间接地影响着行政复议制度的公信力。1994年《行政复议条例》的修改，1999年《行政复议法》的制定，甚至是后来《实施条例》的出台，都与行政复议制度所面对的公信力压力有关。

　　基于这一点，许多了解行政复议制度历史的学者与实务工作者对行政复议制度的未来发展发表了他们的看法。乍看之下，最主要的主张有以下三种：② 第一种可以称为"司法化路径"，认为行政复议应当向司法化靠拢，行政复议应当参考司法模式而建立中立裁判、专家主持、公开辩论（至少是听取各方意见）、合意本位的复议机制，并增进复议机构与复议人员的独立性；③ 即便未明确主张行政复议应当靠拢司法模式的学者，亦认为需要改革目前的书面审理方式，强调行政复议的争讼特征。④ 第二种可以称为"独立化路径"，认为应当确保行政复议工作由相对独立的专门机构和专职人员进行，不少学者和实务工作者主张采用独立性和专业性较为突出的行政复议委员会模式。⑤ 第三种可以称为"透明化路径"，主张加强公开透明价值，要用看得见的正义解决行政争议，减少对受理范围、申请主体、时效等方面的限制，特别要突出程序正义、审理公开。⑥

　　这些主张各有其道理。但实际上认真考究司法化路径和透明化路径的异同，它们在具体的主张上大同小异。归根结底，行政复议制度的公信力之源，不仅在于能否更有效地在更大范围上维护民众的合法权益，亦在于复议的处理过程、决定质量能否让人信服。强调司法化模式与争讼特征的

---

①　黄庆畅：《〈行政复议法〉将适时修改》，《政府法制》2009年第11期，第46页。

②　在这三种主张以外，尚有一些较为特殊的主张，例如采用行政法院模式，合并行政复议制度与行政诉讼制度，废止普通法院对行政案件的司法审查权，从而实现行政审判专业性和公正性。参见赵力《论行政复议"司法化"改革的可能和限度——从制度运行动力的视角出发》，《河南省政法管理干部学院学报》2009年第1期，第60页。

③　参见朱新力《行政复议应向司法化逼近》，《法学研究》2004年第2期，第148～149页；参见周汉华《我国行政复议制度的司法化改革思路》，《法学研究》2004年第2期，第146～147页。

④　杨小君：《对行政复议书面审查方式的异议》，《法律科学（西北政法大学学报）》2005年第4期，第92～96页。

⑤　周婉玲：《我国行政复议组织与程序的改革》，《法学研究》2004年第2期，第151～152页；方军：《论中国行政复议的观念更新和制度重构》，《环球法律评论》2004年春季号，第42～43页。

⑥　黄庆畅：《〈行政复议法〉将适时修改》，《政府法制》2009年第11期。（姜明安教授观点）

学者，志在以司法上发展较为充分的程序正义对行政复议机制进行要求；撇开"司法"的形式不论，其实质价值取向乃是充分的程序正义价值。独立化（含专业化）、透明化等路径，在程序正义的目标外，还包括对复议决定质量的价值考量，这些是由行政复议的体制和程序设计来承担的。因此，未来关键的革新之处，是建立一个相对独立而专业的复议体制，并且完善以公开、平衡、合理为目标的复议程序。相关体制和程序应当如何定位呢？

1. 行政复议委员会：未被充分认识的体制变革思路

学术界对于行政复议体制改革的最突出观点，乃是保证复议的相对独立性；唯有保证行政复议的相对独立性，其才能有效地发挥复议的最佳功能，相对中立于双方当事人的利益，采取平衡的价值立场对待和解决纠纷，达致公平、公正的复议结果。但这种独立性很难在行政系统以外去寻求。首先，其与司法审查有叠床架屋、重复建设之嫌；其次，如不充分嵌入行政系统，它也很难获得足够的实际权力去促使被复议人（或复议被申请人）接受及履行复议决定；最后，这里存在一个深层的矛盾，如果复议机构纯然来自行政系统以外，对内部信息、行政技术、影响行政决定的具体情势、行政系统内部的运作机制等了解较少，在事实认知和责任划分上就可能不是很合理，并且或许难以体谅行政主体的难处，其处理从主客观两方面都有可能难以落实。

即使我们选择在行政系统之内建构相对独立的复议制度，另一个根本的政治——行政运作逻辑我们很难忽视：中国的整个行政制度具有深刻的同化与统合趋向。造成这一点的原因很多，例如下级行政主体为防范行政处理结果被推翻的风险，采取请示上级或与其他有审查权的主体交换意见的策略；未载于明文法律规范之中，甚至仅为内部所共知的部门政策要求或地方政策目标；上下级行政组织同构、功能同构甚至人员派系与流动的一贯性；① 行政权力不轻易与社会主体分享，而仅仅遵循政治——行政本身的单一运行逻辑；等等。这就使我们不得不深入思考：如何能够在行政系统之内建构出一个相对独立而又专业化的空间？这将是对于行政复议制度未来走向最为重要的疑问。

---

① 关于上下级行政组织与功能的同构，参见徐继敏《地方行政体制变革与服务型政府建设》，《中共浙江省委党校学报》2009 年第 2 期，第 57 页；参见江海松、徐小鸥《县级机构统筹设置与大部门体制改革》，《党政干部论坛》2008 年第 3 期，第 15 页。

要回答这一重要疑问,应该首先考察中国的行政系统能在多大程度上、以什么方式容纳一种相对意义上的异质性。此处的异质性并非指政治上和行政上的异见,而是指来自不同系统的价值认知、影响力和决定权。这种异质性必须实质有助于强化复议决定的质量和可接受性,包括熟悉行政活动过程、行政主体能力的界限、实际的责任划分方式等,能够作出合理的复议决定而易为行政主体所接受。在目前的条件下,这种相对的异质性只能来自于专家,包括相关领域的业务专家和法律专家。

因此,某种容纳专家参与的复议机构成为行政复议制度改革的一个理想。相当一部分学者及实务工作者认为,行政复议委员会(由政府法制工作人员和人大代表、政协委员、业务专家、法律专家等构成)可以成为行政复议制度的未来重要突破。它承载了多种行政复议制度革新的理想:专业性、独立性、相对客观中立的地位、公开透明的程序、辩论或听取意见、说明理由等,它们对于完善复议过程、提高复议决定质量等目标无疑有着关键意义。此前的许多革新,除阅卷权、选择管辖等少数几点以外,其思路一直是考虑如何加强行政系统内部的监督与制约,而将复议决定的参与者扩展到行政系统以外,借助外界的专业技术、中立地位与社会公信力,是一种值得尝试的思路,其是否能借由一定的外力支持反过来使复议机构能从上级行政主体的意志中相对地获得抽身而出的机会,在实践探索中或可得到有益的检视。与我国制度文化相似的韩国,在行政复议方面,从行政复议机关和咨议性的诉愿委员会转向行政审判委员会制度已经取得了成功。① 我国目前不少地区也已经开展了行政复议委员会(主要是在地方政府而非行政部门中建立)的制度实践,例如在哈尔滨市,根据 2008 年发布的

---

① 韩国目前将行政复议称为"行政审判",以 1984 年制定(后经多次修订)的《行政审判法》为依据,此前使用的是 1951 年《行政诉愿法》。在《行政诉愿法》中,诉愿机关负责审查并作出决定,虽然当时也尝试在国务总理以及行政各部部长之下设置了诉愿审议会,由其对案件进行审查,但该诉愿审议会只不过是一个咨询机构,并没有从根本上改变诉愿机关独立性差的问题。《行政审判法》的主要任务之一便是提高复议机关的独立性,而且在这方面取得了很大成效。行政复议委员会的委员包括公务员、有律师资格的人士、在韩国《高等教育法》第 2 条第 1 项或者第 3 项规定的学校中担任或者曾经担任教授法律学等的副教授以上职务的人士,以及曾是行政机关 4 级以上公务员的人士,或者其他有行政复议知识和经验的人士,行政审判委员会召开会议时,必须有过半数的来自复议机关外部且符合上述三项条件之一的人士参加。参见吕艳滨《日本、韩国的行政复议制度——行政复议司法化的若干实例》,《环球法律评论》2004 年春季号,第 14～15 页。

《哈尔滨市行政复议规定》第 50 条的规定①和哈尔滨市的实际情况，在委员会组成人员中，市政府以外的法律方面的教授、学者、资深律师、人大代表、政协委员等"外部委员"约占全部委员的 93%，在一定程度上保证和促进了行政复议的民主性、公正性、科学性，体现了广泛参与的要求。② 北京市的类似改革也得到了充分肯定。③ 复议委员会制度通常与行政复议简易程序相并行、相配合，以达到分别处理复杂程度不同的纠纷的效果。当前复议委员会制度所起的作用，主要是对疑难案件和研究一般性行政问题这两点产生了重要突破。④

　　但是，也有学者指出：要使设立相对独立的复议机构的改革目标最终得以实现，必须满足至少两个前提条件，一是行政机关的高度自我约束和守法意识，二是需要强有力的外部监督，否则，单纯地增设相对独立的复议机构或是在现有机构内部增设专家，都无法保证行政复议不受到行政机关的干预而达到独立和公正的目标。其忧虑是，在一个现实的制度运行空间之内，事实上是不存在可以通过颁行新的法律、建立新的机构就能够摆脱既有体制的约束、影响甚至同化的可能性的。⑤ 这种担忧不可谓毫无道理，实际上，行政复议委员会相对较为成功的实践试点都来自大城市。大

---

① 第 50 条规定："行政复议委员会由本级人民政府聘请有关专家、学者以及其他专业人员组成，其中本级人民政府以外的委员应当占全部委员的半数以上。""行政复议委员会议决本级人民政府受理的需要政府作出行政复议决定的行政复议案件，但适用简易程序的除外。"

② 周玉华、李延超：《论行政复议制度的改革与探索——兼论〈哈尔滨市行政复议规定〉的立法特色》，《行政与法》2009 年第 10 期，第 85 页。

③ 2007 年 11 月 14 日，北京市成立了行政复议委员会，作为北京市政府负责审议行政复议案件、指导行政复议制度建设的审议机构。行政复议委员会由主任委员、常务副主任委员、副主任委员、常任委员和非常任委员组成。第一届行政复议委员会由 28 名委员组成，遴选任命了北京部分高校、研究机构和国家部委的 18 名知名专家学者为非常任委员。作为市政府处理行政复议案件的审议机构，行政复议委员会通过召开行政复议案件审理会和全体会来开展工作，对重大疑难行政复议案件进行会审、会商，并最终将审理结果上报市政府。行政复议案件审理会由 9 名委员组成，主要负责审议市政府行政复议案件。"北京模式"得到了国务院法制办的肯定，2008 年 9 月，国务院法制办发出通知，明确在北京、黑龙江、江苏、山东、河南、广东、海南和贵州 8 个省市，开展行政复议委员会试点工作。笔者有幸从 2007 年起被北京市人民政府聘为行政复议委员会委员（第一届、第二届），参加了不少行政复议案件的审理与审议。与此同时，笔者还被北京市海淀区人民政府和石景山区人民政府分别聘为行政复议委员会委员，参加该区重大复杂的行政复议案件的审理。相比之下，笔者认为北京市人民政府行政复议委员会的案件审理工作更加常态化和规范化。

④ 参见金国坤《行政复议改革北京探路》，《决策》2009 年第 5 期，第 40～41 页。

⑤ 赵力：《论行政复议"司法化"改革的可能和限度——从制度运行动力的视角出发》，《河南省政法管理干部学院学报》2009 年第 1 期，第 61～62 页。

城市有几个突出特点对行政复议委员会的独立性造成了深刻的潜在影响：第一，大城市聚集了许多社会地位不受当地政府影响的专家和"政治—行政"人员，他们在发表意见和参与决定时无须听从行政主体的意志；第二，大城市的管理模式、行政主体的任务更具复杂性和综合性，每一部门的工作对最终城市发展目标的贡献，能够被直接感知的比例相对较小，这种复杂而间接的影响使得行政部门难以依托迫切或重要的发展目标作抵触行动；① 第三，大城市相对地更具有受法理型正当性支配②的色彩，政府及其部门之间的私人关系网相对松散，而中小城市的行政人员（甚至还有将来可能参加行政复议委员会的人员）陷于紧密的私人关系网络的可能性更大一些，这种私人关系网往往突破法理上的适度权力区隔，超越机构设置的独立性，而将整个权威秩序整合得更为紧密。③ 在这种较强的私人关系网络中，委员会的讨论及决定的详细过程容易被行政部门所获知，对参与成员的打击报复或会成为一个很难防范的问题。我们必须认真负责地考虑中国基层政府的"政治—行政"现实生态，去思考行政复议委员会的推广问题。

　　正是在这一意义上，行政复议委员会是一种未被充分认识的体制变革思路。它实际上要求一定程度的几类资源和条件，包括独立专家资源、整

---

① 在中小城市尤其是小城市，对于城市领导确定的一系列重要，尤其是紧急的发展与建设目标，为保证建设的顺利进行，领导很可能对相关部门的工作进行特殊保护，从而影响行政纠纷的解决。客观地说，这种联结于重大发展与建设目标的行政事项，在大城市中也存在，但大城市发展目标的多元性、发展模式的综合性、发展手段的多样性使得它不像小城市那样往往需要聚焦于直接可见的少数重点活动（例如作为许多小城市发展瓶颈的招商引资工作），而很大程度上分散到不同部门的各种工作进程中，在这种态势下，更有利于行政复议机构独立开展工作。相比之下，小城市的行政复议机构要相对独立地解决关系到当地政府行政工作重要组成部分和迫切目标的纠纷，例如关系到招商引资重点企业的一些纠纷，难度是更大的。从另一个角度来说，也可以认为，大城市受"必需"（necessity）的压力更小、更间接，而 necessity 对合法性往往产生很大的负面影响。（关于 necessity 与合法性之间的紧张关系，参见 Richard H. Fallon, Jr., "Legitimacy and the Constitution", *Harvard Law Review*, Vol. 118, No. 6 (Apr., 2005), pp. 1845 - 1847。

② 法理型正当性支配方式是德国著名思想家马克斯·韦伯提出的三种纯粹的正当性支配方式之一，相对于传统型支配和卡里斯玛型支配而言，法理型支配靠的是人对法律规范明文条款之妥当性的信任、对于按照合理性方式制定的规则所界定的事务性的职权之妥当性的信任。近代西方典型的"国家公务员"以及在这一方面类似公务人员的权力拥有者，所运用的支配便属此型。参见〔德〕马克斯·韦伯著《学术与政治》，钱永祥等译，广西师范大学出版社，2008，第199页。

③ 大城市的行政部门和复议机构的工作人员、包括负责人之间亦存在一定的私人关系网络，但从经验上看，总体上这种私人关系网络及交往水平，其紧密程度不如中小城市，尤其是陷入熟人社会关系网更深的基层小城市。

个制度环境的人员法律素质与法律技术水平、较弱的必需之压力以及相对松散的私人关系网络等。如果我们未来意图在行政复议委员会中增加直接来自公众的代表，添加一种新的相对异质性，对制度环境的要求将更高。笔者认为，行政复议委员会作为一种融合行政系统内外不同价值认知和思维方式的审理形式，对于各复议机构的改革都是适用的；但其中充实的内容可能需根据不同地方和层级的复议机构在可用资源和条件上的巨大差异而作重要调整。复议委员会的功能是综合行政系统内外视角来加强复议结果的正当性、质量和权威。在缺少必要资源和条件的地方政府中，如果这一切不容易从专家方面取得，就应当适度转向高素质的公众，诉诸民主参与的合法性和权威。① 这一方向也必然成为整个行政复议制度的一个改革目标。

2. 司法化与政治化：未被充分讨论的程序变革思路

在行政复议程序的改革上，很多学者支持行政复议程序适当借鉴司法程序的主张，这些主张是很有道理的，行政复议借鉴司法程序与精神，确实能够对实现程序正义、保障复议结果公平起一定作用。但是，仔细考究行政复议司法化的建议，能够在里面瞥见一种程度差异：其中，一部分学者与实务工作者所主张的"司法化"或"准司法化"，仅限于确保审查独立、推进审查中立、确立行政复议决定的准司法效力等，旨在排除行政干预，确立其公信力；② 另一部分意见则推进得更远，主张建立保障当事人平等地位和争讼对抗的程序规则。这主要可以引入实行类似庭审的听证制度、案卷排他性制度、确立证据规则、确立告知权利制度、复议审理实行合议制等。③ 部分新颁行的规章体现了这一思路，例如最近发布的《国土资源行

---

① 这一举措可以通过一系列的措施来加以保障，重点解决公众代表的代表性和公众代表素质问题，使得他们能够在一定程度上代替专家的作用；并且设置匿名化的决策机制，在很大程度上，许多机制需要与大城市中已经实行试点的行政复议委员会制度作不同的安排。大城市中的参与人员筛选、专家库等机制，在基层县市中可能需要通过实行代表选举之类的创新举措，通过大众广泛、积极的认可（而非消极的无异议）来保证其合法性、代表性与权威性（并间接保证公众代表的素质）。当然，最后呈现的趋势应当是"专家"（省一级政府以及大城市政府的行政复议委员会的主要参与者）与公众（资源匮乏、条件不足的基层县市的主要参与者）的适度融合，但由于资源和条件上不可避免的差异，"适度融合"不能演化为"一刀切"的同化处理。

② 周汉华：《我国行政复议制度的司法化改革思路》，《法学研究》2004 年第 2 期，第 146～147 页；方军：《论中国行政复议的观念更新和制度重构》，《环球法律评论》2004 年春季号，第 43～44 页。

③ 胡晓玲：《行政复议司法化及其建构探讨》，《行政论坛》2008 年第 4 期，第 73 页。

政复议规定》即建立了类似庭审的听证制度，成为一种有典型代表性的尝试。①

后一种思路乍观之下，也是很有道理的。在这些程序规则的理想中，行政复议对于相对人的权利保障能够更充分，纠纷解决的结果也更有公信力。其中，听证制度（未必是类似庭审的听证制度）、告知权利制度、复议审理的合议制（简易程序除外）等也已经得到了有益的尝试和肯定。但是，在这种思路的核心主张上，有一点却是不得不认真处理的：争讼对抗的基本规则以及围绕此种基本规则构建的系列具体程序规则，是否适合于行政复议制度？

对抗方式以及与此紧密联结的平等武装（equality of arms）原则②作为审理程序的模板，在我国学界广为流行，在混合制的司法模式中，控辩对抗也受到国内学者的尊崇，缺乏对抗的纯粹纠问制方式则无人支持，可以认为对抗性是司法程序的一个关键特征，但并非所有领域都适合对抗性的处理方式。带有对抗色彩的程序机制若不实现双方当事人的平等武装，则对抗将走向一边倒的局面，效果上并不如职权主义模式的程序机制。而当事人的平等武装需要充分的资源保障，不仅需要程序内的支持，亦需要程序外的众多配套机制；前者通过程序控制权和证明责任的不同配置保障双方当事人的平等武装得以在程序中实现，后者实质性地加强当事人获得平等武装的可能性，并且消除由于审理过程中高度对抗在日后所可能产生的负面作用。目前我国均不完全具备这两种条件。在我国行政救济法制中，实现程序内的平等武装的主要机制在于有利于行政相对人的、包含了事实与法律问题的证明责任配置，但在复议实践中，证明标准实际上是模糊的，

---

① 《国土资源行政复议规定》第 21 条第 1 款规定："第二十条　重大、复杂的行政复议案件，申请人提出要求或者行政复议机构认为必要时，可以采取听证的方式审理。"第 23 条规定："听证应当按照以下程序进行：（一）核对当事人的身份，告知当事人权利和义务；（二）当事人陈述；（三）当事人质证；（四）当事人辩论；（五）当事人进行最后陈述。"这一规定应认为体现了"类似庭审的听证制度"的思路。

② 平等武装原则，最初起源于刑事审判，其中的基本观点是，如果检察官在审判中有特定的权力，那么被告方也应当具有相同的权力；它是从立法上对控辩双方之权力以及权利的配置层面而言的，它要求在立法上赋予控辩双方平等的诉讼权利和攻防手段。〔美〕弗莱彻：《"公正"的比较性思考》，《国家检察官学院学报》2009 年第 4 期，第 150 页；冀祥德：《控辩平等之现代内涵解读》，《政法论坛》2007 年第 6 期，第 90 页。后来这种程序模式推广到其他领域。关于对抗性程序与平等武装的紧密关联，参见 Jay Sterling Silver, "Equality of Arms and the Adversarial Process: A New Constitutional Right", *Wisconsin Law Review* (July, 1990) p. 1032。

如果说行政复议实际上采取了盖然性优势的证明标准，那么，这一标准实际上已经抵消了证明责任分配所带来的平等武装效果；[①] 我们也很难通过提升证明标准来改善程序内的平等武装，盖因证明标准是一种相当缺乏确定外观表现的法律机制，裁决者容易人为地作出实质性的变更（在行政复议制度中，由于复议机构与被复议人处于同一系统，较之行政诉讼更可能作出这种变更）。在程序外的方面，我们既缺乏充分的、全面的法律援助资源，又难以消除双方因高度对抗而引起的对立性，消除行政主体——行政相对人互动关系被破坏的负面后果；相对人选择行政复议的渠道，有可能是先行尝试是否能以更小的时间和金钱成本、更弱的未来负面影响为代价而解决纠纷，复议制度引入对抗程序并不适宜。即使是在有充分的政治、社会条件而引入言词辩论机制的一些国家和地区，对抗色彩也相对较弱。[②] 因此，我们谈复议制度的司法化改革，并不包括司法程序的这种关键特征。

实际上，回到前述两种具有程度差异的主张上，在讨论复议程序司法化时，更多学者实际上仍是在追求实现体制上的独立性和中立性。至于复议程序本身，它确实需要改革，更好地排除干扰，但在司法模式之外，行政复议制度需要它独特的优势和发展空间。若这一制度基本转变成司法诉讼过程的一个复版或攻防演练，对于行政复议制度的未来发展亦并无助益。我们需要追问的是，行政复议程序，除了借鉴部分必要的、适合于审查案件真相的司法程序外，还需要考虑何种合适于其特色的程序革新？

首先回到联系于行政复议委员会制度的基本程序类型。一个基本的程

---

① 如果采用盖然性优势标准，若思维方式中存在排中律的假设，实际上证明责任的分配是无关紧要的；但是，证明责任正是在中间情形（既不能证明又不能否证）的情况下起作用，从理论上说，即使采用盖然性优势标准，证明责任配置给行政主体一方，依然对行政相对人有利。但是，在面对"盖然性"的问题上，这一问题是存在复杂性的。盖然性只能适用于事实判断，但在行政复议和行政诉讼中，行政主体所负的证明责任主要是针对行政行为的合法性而言，在此处，实际上并不存在一种规范而非事实的"盖然性"，当然，合法性判断会存在模糊地带，但它在逻辑上从不合法到合法是一个连续体，并不存在概率判断那种严格意义上的中间状态。这时，行政相对人即未受到平等武装原则的实际帮助。其实行政复议和行政诉讼的证明标准问题是一个相当艰深的问题（因为合法性证明也包含了支持合法性的事实根据），与民事、刑事诉讼均存在重要区别，但学术界在这方面的努力仍然不足，复议和诉讼的现状多少也阻碍了这方面的深入努力。

② 例如台湾地区《诉愿法》第 65 条规定："受理诉愿机关应依诉愿人、参加人之申请或于必要时，得依职权通知诉愿人、参加人或其代表人、诉愿代理人、辅佐人及原行政处分机关派员于指定期日到达指定处所言词辩论。"其言词辩论的具体程序规定（第 66 条）有一定的对抗性，但与诉讼法上的对抗规则有很大差距。日本《行政不服审查法案》第 30 条用五个了项规定了口头陈述程序，但并不表现出对抗性。

序划分方式,是简易程序与进入复议委员会讨论、乃至由部分委员组成合议庭作出决定的一般程序,这里集中讨论一般程序。我们注意到,行政复议结果的正当性构成与行政诉讼结果的正当性构成是不尽一致的。行政复议结果的正当性更多地掺入了来自层级权威和专家理性的内容,但仅仅以此种正当性根基尚构不成与司法审查的正当性根基(除形式上的法律授权外,主要来自法官对法律在具体案件中的最终解释权,[①] 以及在理想情况下典型的、充分的程序正义设计)并驾齐驱的一个坚实基础,除了强调形式上的法律授权并借鉴若干反映程序正义的规则作为一种合法性补充外,行政复议制度尚需要其他的合法性来源,充实到它的程序中,使复议结果更公正,更能让各方当事人甚至公众接受。

实际上,在这里存在隐藏着的主体。结果的公正和正当,都不仅仅存在于双方当事人之间;公众作为提供公正评价和正当性判断的重要主体,在强调减少外部压力的司法诉讼中不宜出面,但在行政复议制度中却不仅可以,而且应当出场。当前的一些程序改革尝试,例如行政复议听证程序的丰富和加强,就是这种方向上的重要努力。它实际上是从带有一定政治性质的方向,而非司法化的方向来完善行政复议程序,在中国,政治与行政紧密地联结,行政复议所要解决的复杂问题(非简易程序的对象)很多情况下实际上是一个局部的政治问题,需要包括双方当事人、专家、公众、其他相关行政主体在内的各种群体共同参与去协商解决之道,不仅形成推动解决当前纠纷的合力,而且由于行政复议就在行政系统内部进行,容易迅速转化到行政主体的运作中,对未来类似的问题也能提供适当的处理。行政复议制度的发展并不拘泥于其传统功能,我们需要打开更广阔的视野去寻找它的未来定位,例如在具体的程序设计中,它可以表现为超越复议双方当事人直接对抗的听证程序,邀请更多的相关群体参与复议过程、进行讨论和商议,形成超越具体个案的解决策略,并且允许行政复议机构在复议申请人同意的前提下,适当越出其复议请求范围作灵活的决定。

因此,在行政复议的程序改革中,我们首先需要划分一般程序与简易程序。在简易程序中,我们要适度借鉴司法程序,完善受理手续、证据规则、期限规则等;而在一般程序中,我们需要重点建立一种包含广泛参与

---

① 这里说的解释权是具体案件中的解释权,并非一般地对法律条文进行解释的权力。鉴于复议终局的情形只是极少数,大部分情况下,一个案件的法律问题,法官会享有最终的解释权及决定权。此时,法官可以看作法律的一个代言(Reprasentation),从而司法审查在正当性问题上较传统的行政复议具有相当大的优势。

的听证程序，并适当地在听证程序中采用政治性的协商、讨论与决策方式协助复议结果（很多情况下可以表现为一种实现和解或调解的、包含不限于当事人复议请求的灵活安排的结果）的产生，在注重纠纷解决的同时，同样注意寻找对于此类问题更好的、一般化的解决方式。这种联结"政治—行政"的复议程序，是一种重要的制度创新，需要通过充分的试点工作来探讨其具体构建方式。最后，我们应当完善一般程序与简易程序的分流标准，防止行政复议机构滥用简易程序（很可能衔接于简单的形式合法性审查）来逃避复杂甚至棘手的复议案件，关键在于案件分流的决定权不能完全由行政复议机构自身的工作人员来进行，应当保持复议委员会对于案件分流过程的参与，或至少是监督。

总之，纵观多年的历史发展，可以说新中国行政复议制度是在艰苦探索中不断前进、不断得到完善的，虽然仍存在这样那样的问题，公正性和公信力亦有待强化，但整个制度从建立至今的发展依然值得肯定。我们所需要做的，就是在既有实践的基础上，深入反思，不懈探索，以突破性的制度创新推动行政复议制度大步前进。

Historical Development of the Administrative Reconsideration System in the People's Republic of China

Zhan Zhongyue

【**Abstract**】 This article reviews the historical development of the administrative reconsideration system in China and the situation of the implementation of the administrative reconsideration system before and after the promulgation of the Law on Administrative Reconsideration. The system of administrative reconsideration enjoyed a sound development momentum in the first years of the implementation of the Law on Administrative Reconsideration, but has suffered some setbacks in recent years, the root causes of which being the lack of fairness and public trust. In view of this fact, the author suggests that China should carry out reform on both the institution and the procedure of administrative reconsideration. With respect to the former, a system of relatively independent administrative reconsideration committees should be established; with respect to the latter, the relevant procedures should be further improved by taking judicial procedures as reference and more attentions should be paid to the potential political function of the administrative reconsideration system.

【**Key words**】 Law on Administrative Reconsideration, Administrative Reconsideration Committee, Administrative Reconsideration Procedure

The Rule of Law and Administrative Implementation in Finland

Olli Mäenpää [*]

【Abstract】 The presentation attempts to give an overview of the rule of law as applied in the Finnish administrative law. In Finnish public administration the quantitative emphasis has shifted to providing social benefits and public services. Public administration has also become more involved in administrative networks and economic activities. The administrative machinery has simultaneously grown, become more complicated, multi-layered and integrated into European administration.

The significance of the rule of law in public action has by no means diminished. However, new challenges are posed by such developments as privatization and decentralization, regulatory reform and new forms of normative regulation, transformations in the mode and methods of governance as well as the requirements posed by European law and human rights. Also new forms of the supervision of legality in administrative implementation have been developed.

Administrative authorities may act in various different roles. Public regulation and administrative supervision have traditionally formed the substance of executive activity. With the development of the welfare state, the provision of public services has become the predominant administrative activity. In addition, the administrative authorities may also enter into private law relationships when carrying out their duties.

---

[*] Professor, Faculty of Law, University of Helsinki.

Public regulation is based on strict conformity with the law. Ordinarily, this results in unilaterality of the regulatory relationships since the administrative decision is made in compliance with the law and by applying legal regulations. As a consequence, administrative law relationships are considered to be nonconsensual; the rights and duties are non-transferable and outside the scope of contractual obligations.

Public services comprise, for example, education, health care, social welfare and support to cultural activity. The economic benefits provided by the welfare state consist especially of different kinds of economic transfers. Private law relationships are used when a public authority acts in the capacity of a private law subject, e. g. as a landlord, tenant, buyer or employer. In that role, it may enter into private law relationships under the same conditions as any private subject.

I. Introduction: Three Elements of the Rule of Law

A distinction is conventionally made between rule by law and rule of law. Rule by law denotes that government and governance use only lawful means to attain their goals. This is, of course, necessary and important. Rule of law, however, sets the standard higher. Also government and governors must be subjected to law and their actions must be independently reviewable. In addition, the right to challenge rulers' decisions on legal grounds is a central guarantee of individual rights. This is why it is necessary to impose independent judicial control and review on executive actions.

The rule of law is best understood as a composite concept with multi-dimensional elements. It consists of various, qualitatively different aspects and characteristic features. First, there are the necessary formative elements of rule of law. They are of crucial significance for the rule of law to exist legitimately and therefore they form its core area. There is a fairly wide consensus of such core elements: they include legality, basic rights, division of powers including executive power under law and independent judiciary, effective judicial protection for individual rights, openness and accountability of the exercise of public power. The purpose here is not to exhaustively define the elements of rule of law-this is only an indicative list of these elements.

There is also another core area of rule of law. Making rule of law function properly is not just a formalistic exercise with abstract dimensions. Similarly, the concept cannot be reduced to merely observing the sum of its abstract elements. Instead, rule of law is also a functional concept and its effectiveness is a necessary element in determining whether rule of law is actually observed. To be sure, there is a diversity of ways to ensure the effectiveness of rule of law. They all should guarantee at least that rights are made real and obligations are implemented in a proper way. Making rights real and obligations effective and functional is therefore another central component of rule of law. This element is of special significance in administrative implementation of law.

A third dimension is formed by more substantive and value-based elements. What is the objective of rule of law? It is, of course, important to be able execute and implement laws effectively and to ensure compliance with them. This at least is what administration should attempt to accomplish. But arguably it would be a very limited and formalistic view of rule of law that would be content with only the objective of attaining effectiveness. Regard should be had to other objectives, as well. Rule of law is not an end itself although its formal core elements are indispensable and cannot be dismissed by choosing some and rejecting others. In addition, rule of law should also be understood as a tool to attain such goals as social justice, equality, proportionate use of public powers and the value of individuals. These and comparable goals or values should be counted as the superior and qualitative aspects of rule of law.

This presentation attempts to give an overview of the rule of law as applied in the Finnish administrative law. In Finnish public administration the quantitative emphasis has shifted to providing social benefits and public services. Public administration has also become more involved in administrative networks and economic activities. The administrative machinery has simultaneously grown, become more complicated, multi-layered and integrated into European administration.

The significance of the rule of law in public action has by no means diminished. However, new challenges are posed by such developments as privatization and decentralization, regulatory reform and new forms of normative regulation, transformations in the mode and methods of governance as well as the requirements posed by European law and human rights. Also new forms of the supervision of legality in administrative implementation have been developed. Although these developments cannot be analyzed in detail they form a necessary backdrop of this presentation.

II. Rules and Principles Constituting Administrative Law

Varieties of administrative activity

Administrative authorities may act in various different roles. Public regulation and administrative control have traditionally formed the substance of executive activity. With the development of the welfare state, the provision of public services has become the predominant administrative activity. In addition, the administrative authorities may also enter into private law relationships when carrying out their duties.

Public regulation is based on strict conformity with the law. Ordinarily, this results in unilaterality of the regulatory relationships since the administrative decision is made in compliance with the law and by applying legal regulations. As a consequence, administrative law relationships are considered to be non-consensual and indispositive; the rights and duties are non-transferable and outside the scope of contractual obligations.

Public services produced and provided by administrative organs of the modern state comprise, for example, education, health care, social welfare and support to cultural activity. The economic benefits provided by the welfare state, on the other hand, consist especially of different kinds of economic transfer, such as social benefits and support to business activity. Apart from providing services and benefits, the administrative machinery oversees the construction and maintenance of public roads and means of public transportation, and it also in other ways makes various performances and commodities available for use. Service relationships may take various different legal forms ranging from consensual arrangements to unilateral administrative decisions.

Private law relationships are used when a public authority acts in the capacity of a private law subject, e. g. as a landlord, tenant, buyer or employer. In that role, it may enter into private law relationships under the same conditions as any private subject. For instance, administrative authorities make contracts concerning public procurement, production and provision of public services (contracting-out), financial arrangement or research commissions. Such contractual relationships are governed by private law and the contracts are enforceable and justiciable.

Principal legal sources of administrative law

All administrative action takes places within an administrative law relationship which has two principal actors: the administrative authority vested with executive power and the private party. The contents of administrative law relationships are regulated by both general administrative law and the substantive laws to be applied and enforced by the administrative body.

The principal and most important sources of general administrative law are defined in the Constitution Act (2000). Its provisions identify the general constitutional limits of the executive as well as qualitative requirements for the activities of the administrative authorities. Of special significance are the rule of law, the right to good administration, the right of access to government documents and freedom of information, legal accountability of public officials and access to justice in administrative matters.

The principal legislative sources of administrative activity are the Administrative Procedure Act (2003), and the Act on the Openness of Government Activities (1999). The framework for judicial procedure in the administrative courts is provided by the Act on Judicial Procedure in Administrative Courts (1996). The Act contains general provisions on the right of appeal, the procedure to be followed in instituting the administrative appeal procedure and details of the review procedure in administrative courts.

In addition to normative legal regulation, a number of legal principles enjoy a prominent role in all administrative activity. The administrative law principles provide a qualitative value basis for the interpretation and application law by administrative authorities. They include the principles of objectivity, neutrality, transparency, good governance and the prohibition of abuse of power. While such principles have originally been developed in administrative law doctrine and judicial practice, many of them have gradually been assigned a more binding legal role by elevating them to constitutional entitlements or by regulating them in ordinary laws.

III. Right to Good Administration

Section 21 of the Constitution confers the right to a due process the status of a basic right. The first paragraph guarantees everyone the general right to have his or her affairs "considered appropriately and without undue delay by a lawfully competent … public authority as well as to have a decision pertaining to his/her rights or obligations reviewed by a court of law".

Section 21 (2) of the Constitution provides an express list of some of the central guarantees of *good administration*. These guarantees include:

－openness of administrative procedure

－right to be heard

－right to receive a decision with stated grounds

－right to appeal against the decision.

The catalogue is by no means exhaustive. Additional elements have also been recognised as indispensable in guaranteeing good administration. They include, among others, the right to a fair and unbiased procedure, the right to compensation for damages caused by unlawful administrative activity and the right to initiate judicial proceedings against an official infringing material or procedural norms. Also essential in this context is that the right to good administration is given a constitutional status. It will therefore also serve as an interpretative guideline for applying statutory rules and the more detailed procedural provisions in the Administrative Procedure Act.

IV. Openness and Access to Information

Right of access

The right of access to official documents is included as a fundamental right in the Constitution. Section 12 (2) lays down the principle of openness and freedom of information:

"The documents and other records in the possession of public authorities shall be public unless their publicity has been separately restricted by Act of Parliament for compelling reasons. Everyone shall have the right to obtain information from public documents and records. "

The right of access to government held information may be invoked by anyone regardless of standing or the purpose for which information is sought. As a constitutional right, access also takes precedence over lower ranking legislation. For instance, if the application of a ministerial regulation or a municipal decree would be in conflict with the right to information, the access provision in the Constitution would be given precedence in proceedings concerning that application.

Together with the guarantees of freedom of expression and freedom of information, the access right forms a vital component of an open government. An additional stimulus to functioning access legislation is found in the constitutional provision defining a positive obligation on the administrative authorities to promote openness. According to Sec. 14 (3), "It shall be the task of public authorities to promote the opportunities of the individual to participate in the activities of society and to influence decision-making affecting him. "

The right of free access to administrative documents forms one of the most significant guarantees of the transparency and openness of public administration. Detailed rules governing access to administrative documents are laid down in the Openness Act. According to the general principle stipulated in Section 1 of the Openness Act, all official documents shall be public, unless specifically otherwise provided in this Act or another Act.

The right of access is applicable to a variety of documents regardless of their external configuration and manner of storage. Since the use of the term document is not restricted to written texts or pictures only, the Act is applicable to information stored in a specific form such as electronic documents, data disks and files, tapes as well as visual presentations, maps and x-ray pictures. A recording is considered a document even if it can be comprehended only by means of technical aids. The same applies to any message that can be deciphered only by means of a computer, an audio or video recorder or some other technical device.

With respect to the organization of the administrative entities, the scope of application of the Openness Act is wide. It comprises all state, regional and municipal authorities as well as judicial bodies; e. g. ministries, administrative authorities, courts, tribunals and representative bodies. Access to Parliament documents is regulated solely in the Constitution, however.

In a rapidly transforming environment of public administration it is important that access to information is available also with regard to semi-public organizations to the extent that they perform public functions. Therefore, the application of the Openness Act extends to formally private bodies such as corporations, associations and foundations to the extent that they are authorized to exercise public authority.

The Openness Act also defines the objectives of its application. Section 3 lists as the goals promotion of openness and good practice on information management, the opportunity to monitor and influence the exercise of public authority, to possibility to observe the use of public resources, to freely form an opinion, and to protect one's rights and interest. The list is intended to serve as more than a mere declaration of good intentions. It must be taken seriously because, pursuant to Section 17, the authorities are under the duty to take the list into consideration when making any decision concerning access. The objectives of the Act, consequently, are meant to serve as a directive in all instances of its application.

Obligation to promote openness

Under the Openness Act the authorities not only have the duty to respond to requests for access, they are also under an active obligation to provide information and promote openness. There are several provisions to this effect in the Act. The authorities must actively produce and disseminate information on their activities. For this purpose, they must produce guides, statistics and other publications, as well as information materials on their services and practices and on the social conditions and developments in their field of competence (Sec. 20). The authorities must also ensure the availability of this information by making it available in libraries and on the Internet.

Good practice on information management denotes the duty to see to the appropriate availability, usability, protection, integrity and other matters of quality pertaining to documents and information management systems (Sec. 18). An element of the good practice is the obligation to arrange the documents, information management and data systems in a manner that facilitates the operation of the openness principle.

Presumption of accessibility and official secrets

Since the Openness Act is based on the presumption of openness, access to documents is the predominant rule, whereas secrecy or confidentiality is the exception that must in each case have an express legal base. Everyone is presumed to have a general right to examine the contents of an official document and obtain information contained therein, subject only to exceptions provided in law. In addition, the exceptions must be construed narrowly.

To protect such legitimate interests as personal integrity, commercial confidentiality and national security, access has been restricted with regard to information about e. g. issues falling under the core areas of foreign policy, privacy, business secrets and professional confidence. One reason for restrictions is that the personal data obtained in the course of government work need to be protected because of its sensitivity. The operations of authorities can also not be wholly public in matters dealing with national security or crime prevention. These reasons account for the majority of express secrecy or confidentiality provisions. Furthermore, rapid advances in automatic data processing set new demands on the protection of privacy, currently being met by developing data protection legislation.

The list of the criteria of secrecy in Section 24 of the Openness Act is based on the following interests. They may be protected by keeping the official documents secret:

-personal integrity and other important personal interests

-protection of private business interests

-the economic interests of the state and the municipalities

-protection of the nature

-prevention and prosecution of crime

-safeguarding judicial proceedings and data protection

-security of the state and foreign relations

-interests of defense.

In many cases it is possible that a document contains both confidential information (e. g. , health data or business secrets) and public information. Such a document is not considered completely but only partially secret, and the public information in it must be divulged on demand. When only a part of a document must be kept secret, access must be granted to the public part of the document if this is possible without disclosing the secret part (Sec. 10). The authorities are also under an obligation to manage their documents and data systems so as to guarantee access to public information without disclosing secret information. In this respect, the presumption of access extends not just to the document as a whole but also to the public information contained therein. Release of information is therefore assessed on a "contents basis".

IV. General Principles of Administrative Law

The role of administrative law principles

General principles of administrative law have gradually acquired their binding quality in the case law of the Supreme Administrative Court. At present, there are five statutory legal principles that must be observed in all executive activity and administrative decision-making. These are the principles of equality, impartiality, proportionality, prohibition of the abuse of power, and the protection of legitimate interests.

The principles have recently been codified in the Administrative Procedure Act. Pursuant to Section 6, "An authority shall treat the customers of the administration on an equal basis and exercise its competence only for purposes that are acceptable under the law. The acts of the authority shall be impartial and proportionate to their objective. They shall protect legitimate expectations as based on the legal system."

The principles function mainly as guidelines and constraints in using discretionary administrative powers. The principles may be relied on by individuals in administrative procedure, and as such they can be asserted also in judicial proceedings related to administrative decisions. Administrative decisions taken in breach of one of these principles may be annulled or revoked by administrative courts.

Any procedure or decision conflicting with general administrative principles can be challenged as involving misuse of power, especially in connection with an appeal. In judicial review, the misuse of executive power has been established as an independent legal ground, which in itself makes it possible to annul or revoke an administrative decision. The observance of these principles can also be deemed to belong to the official duties of the public servants. The establishment of legal accountability for a public act is, thus, possible as a consequence of a procedure that violates these principles.

The five central principles

The general principle of equality is connected with Section 6 (1) of the Constitution providing that "Everyone shall be equal before the law." This provision also applies to the activity of executive authorities. Similar situations shall not be treated differently, unless there is an objectively justified cause for such treatment. Discrimination or favouritism, for example, on the basis of origin, religion, sex, age, political or social view, trade union activity or for other similar reasons is prohibited. A similar procedure and a consistent approach must be complied with in similar cases although for a justified reason an authority may also change its practice if this practice will be followed consistently.

One of the more efficient ways to produce real guarantees for procedural equality is to alleviate the actual difficulties that the individuals are confronted with in administrative matters. In this sense the duty to provide appropriate procedural advice to clients can also be regarded as a way to lower the bureaucratic obstacles, taking into account the differences in individual propensity to deal with administrative matters. However, even formal equality is important, especially if a matter is subject to joint proceedings or where several parties are involved. In such cases, the authorities are under an obligation to ensure that the preparation of the decision is carried out in a way that does not prejudice the equality of the parties.

Impartiality means that only the factors objectively relevant to the case may be taken into account. The decision-making and other official activities of an authority must also otherwise be impartial and objectively justified. This principle has acquired concrete form in, for example, bias provisions emphasizing the neutrality of administrative action. According to them, an official will be disqualified if confidence in the impartiality of the official is at risk for a particular reason. The principle of impartiality is reflected also in the prohibition in the Act of State Officials to accept any benefit that could diminish the trust in the impartiality of an official or in an authority. In case law, impartiality has also been understood as decision-making based only on objective facts. Thus, a decision concerning the appointment of a social worker was annulled because it was based on party favouritism.

Objectivity and neutrality are indispensable qualitative components of a due procedure in general. Putting the requirements of public interest into effect even-handedly and without bias forms the basic object of a fair procedure even in administrative cases. Neither undue external standpoints nor the personal preferences of the officials may be allowed to influence the conduct in administrative cases. Indeed, the right to impartiality is also a basic requisite of a fair procedure. It is mainly for these reasons that procedural rules disqualify ostensibly impartial decision-makers from deciding cases whose outcome directly or substantially affects their own personal interests or the financial concerns of organizations with which they are affiliated.

The principle of *proportionality* requires that a reasonable relationship should be observed in all circumstances between the relative importance of the ends pursued and the means put into operation. Consequently, the exercise of public authority must be determined in an appropriate way in relation to the desired objectives. Such a determination can usually be made on the basis of the general interest involved and the reasonableness of the activity to attain it. For example, when using administrative coercive means or disciplinary punishments, their severity must be determined as reasonable in relation to the quality and blameworthiness of an act or a failure to act. Similarly, the benefits granted by an authority should also not be disproportionate. In legal practice, on the one hand, a fine imposed with excessively high conditions has been reduced and, on the other hand, the municipal decision to sell a plot far more cheaply than a current price has been annulled as disproportionate.

The exercise of administrative competence is allowed only for purposes that are acceptable under the law. This means that all *abuse of power* (including discretionary power) is prohibited. According to this principle, administration must not pursue a purpose other than for which the corresponding power has been conferred. If a decision is taken for purposes other than those stated, it may constitute an abuse of power, even if the decision as such stays within the powers of the authority. As, for example, offices are established to perform certain official duties of general interest, it would amount to a misuse of power to establish an office especially for a certain person. Neither must the granting of financial support be made conditional on the performance of a duty that is not related to the use of that support.

Protection of legitimate expectations is a fairly recent addition to the administrative law principles. Under this principle, administrative authorities are expected to act in a lawful and predictable manner. Administrative decisions may not have retroactive effect but for instance the revocation of a license or a benefit is possible provided that it has a legal basis. Legitimate expectations may be created by consistent administrative practice and they may also be based on information or advice supplied by an official. A person may rely on justified expectations only provided that he or she has acted in a legitimate manner, for instance, by submitting correct information.

The service principle

The public administration has a general obligation to provide service to all citizens. In this sense, one can speak of a service principle governing administrative procedure. One of the principal applications of that principle is the duty to ensure that it is actually possible for the individuals to comply with their procedural duties. The authorities and officials are also obliged to supply necessary guidance and advice concerning the formal requirements in individual cases. The Administrative Procedure Act provides that authorities shall, where necessary, advise the party and other persons as to how the proceedings are initiated and how one is to proceed in a matter pertaining to the functions of the authority. The assistance shall be given to the extent that is deemed appropriate with regard to the nature of the matter, the person's need of assistance and the activity of the authority.

There are other express enunciations of the service principle in the Administrative Procedure Act as well. For instance, when considering the case the authority is under an overall obligation to ascertain that the relevant facts are established although the duty to provide evidence may lie on either the private party of the public authority. The authority thus has a duty to see to it that a matter is investigated to the extent that its nature requires before any decision is taken.

VI. Rule of Law and Official Accountability

The principle of legality and exercise of administrative powers

According to the Constitution, all exercise of public powers shall be based on an

Act of Parliament and the law shall be strictly observed in all public activity. With respect to public administration, the rule of law thus requires that the executive powers of any administrative authority must have an express basis in law and be justified on the grounds laid down by law. The principle applies especially when an administrative authority (e. g. Ministry, agency, municipality or public official) makes decisions or other acts that directly affect the rights and obligations of a person. Rule of law, thus, is a necessary prerequisite in all exercise of administrative authority.

In practice, the rule of law entails among other things, that administrative authorities have no general competence to perform their duties. For instance, although the main duty of the police force is to keep public order and security, any intervention by the police in the sphere of private activities must possess an express legal basis in each individual case. The principle of conformity to law also denotes that the decision-making power cannot be based solely on administrative regulations, guidelines or plans. It is the duty of an authority within its sphere of competence to apply law, not internal administrative instructions. It is another matter that administrative regulations and directives can guide decision-making, provided that this kind of supervision is based on a sufficiently precise rule of competence.

Literally understood, the constitutional rule of law is a relatively formal requirement of conformity to law. According to it, the duty of authorities and officials is to strictly obey the provisions that are in force. This requirement applies to all activities of public administration. It is binding not only on the decision-maker and the drafter of an administrative decision, but also on any official responsible for providing public services.

Different hierarchical levels in the sources of administrative law must also be taken into consideration in the strict application of different provisions. Section 107 of the Constitution provides that if a provision in a decree or another statute of lower level is in conflict with the Constitution or an Act of Parliament, a court or an administrative authority shall not apply it. The duty, and at the same time, the right of an authority is not to apply provisions of a decree which are considered inconsistent with a law enacted by the Parliament.

In this connection, other regulations of lower standing are comparable with decrees. These types of regulation are primarily the regulations issued by the President, the Government or the Ministries. A similar order of precedence applies to other normative enactments by administrative authorities subordinate to the Government, normative decisions of municipal organs and various implementing provisions issued by administrative authorities. If they are inconsistent with the law, they must not be applied.

The requirement and principle of conformity to law can still be problematic in the administration of the modern state. On one hand, the law cannot be 'strictly' observed, to the extent that the applicable provisions are broad and if they entitle an authority to use discretionary power. In these kinds of situations, the administrative law principles supplement the formal liability to legal norms.

On the other hand, the requirement of strict adherence to law applies mainly to the exercise of public authority. In the provision of public services it often remains in the background. Yet, it has been considered important that also administrative activity offering rights and benefits to the citizens must be based on law. Among other things, the anticipation and binding force of administrative activity, as well as the equality between citizens, presume the ability to know in advance, for example, on which conditions a social benefit or right can be granted or denied.

Oversight of legality

The general oversight of legality in public administration is the duty of specific supervisory organs or ombudsmen, the Chancellor of Justice and the Parliamentary Ombudsman. Superior administrative organs also exercise control of legality and appropriateness within the administration. Anyone has the right to contact the overseers of legality and request, by way of administrative complaint, that the lawfulness of an administrative activity (or inactivity) be investigated. Inherent in the supervisory powers of both of the two ombudsmen as well as any superior authorities is the power to examine and decide administrative complaints.

Since it is the official duty of any superior authority to see to it that the authorities under its direction observe the law, an administrative complaint is the ordinary procedure for any individual to bring an administrative irregularity into the knowledge of the superior authority, the Chancellor of Justice, or the Parliamentary Ombudsman. The administrative complaint lacks the function of a formal judicial appeal, however, and it is incapable of initiating judicial review.

The President of the Republic appoints the Chancellor of Justice and he or she must possess "outstanding knowledge of the circumstances in the country related to justice and law." The Chancellor is formally part of the Council of State and is present at its sittings. Moreover, the Chancellor is closely connected with the work of the Government by supplying legal counsel and advisory opinions both to the President and the Cabinet on the legality of the government business.

The Chancellor also acts as a general overseer of legality in public administration, the courts, and in the performance of public duties. It is the duty of the Chancellor to observe and keep an eye on the activities of public bodies, and to see that the authorities and officials uphold the law and carry out their duties so that no person is adversely affected or suppressed in his or her lawful rights. The Chancellor has the right to be present at the meetings of all courts and public authorities.

The Parliamentary Ombudsman is elected by the Parliament for a term of four years. The activity of the Ombudsman focuses more on the general surveillance of legality in administrative matters and in the exercise of public authority. The specific duties of the Ombudsman include the supervision of legality in the defence forces, prison administration and closed institutions. In actual practice, the Ombudsman has also proven to be more accessible to ordinary citizens than the Chancellor.

Official accountability

Each civil servant is individually responsible for the lawfulness of his or her acts in office. The official accountability extends to all decisions made by an official multi-member body that he or she has supported as one of its members. Section 118 (3) of the Constitution Act plays a crucial role as a guarantee of individual access to civil and criminal procedure even in administrative cases. This section stipulates that "anyone who has suffered a loss of rights or damage due to the unlawful act or omission of an official or a person responsible for a public duty shall have the right to demand that the person be sentenced to a punishment and that the public authority or the official or the person undertaking the public duty be ordered to compensate for the damage, as provided in law."

Civil procedure can (and shall) be used whenever compensation is sought for damages caused by the activity (or failure to act, as the case may be) of an administrative authority or a public official. The administrative courts cannot award compensation for such damages. Criminal procedure is also relevant in the field of administrative action when criminal conduct or other serious irregularities are concerned. Public officials have traditionally been subject to qualified criminal responsibility, which embraces practically all their activities as officials. Under Section 118 (3) of the Constitution, it is up to each violated subject to prosecute the official, irrespective of what the public prosecutor does. While the prosecution of public servants private parties is not unheard of, the main thrust of the qualified criminal responsibility of public officials probably lies in its preventive effect.

VII. Access to Justice and Judicial Review

General access to a court

As a rule, all decisions of administrative authorities are reviewable in administrative courts. Such authorities include all state and municipal administrative authorities as well as the ecclesiastical authorities. In this respect, no distinction is made between administrative decisions and acts of the State. Decisions by the Cabinet or the ministries may thus be subject to appeal even if they were based on a very wide margin of discretion.

Access to justice in all administrative cases is defined as a constitutional right by virtue of Section 21 (2) of the Constitution:

"Everyone shall have the right to have his or her case heard appropriately and without undue delay by a court of justice or other authority competent under an Act of Parliament as well as the right to have a decision relating to his or her rights and duties reviewed by a court or other independent tribunal.

Openness of the proceedings as well as the right to be heard, to receive a decision with stated reasons and to appeal the decision as well as any other safeguards of fair trial and good government shall be secured by an Act of Parliament. "

The judiciary consists of two sectors. The *administrative courts*, with the Supreme Administrative Court in the highest instance, have jurisdiction in all administrative cases. The administrative courts are mainly concerned with administrative appeals concerning administrative decisions. Their jurisdiction also covers administrative litigation over disputes between a public authority and private actors arising, for instance, from administrative contracts.

The judicial procedure in administrative courts is regulated uniformly in the Act on Judicial Procedure in Administrative Courts. It also defines in more detail the right to appeal an administrative decision and the reviewability of administrative acts. In addition to affirming or annulling the decision subject to review an administrative court may also amend it although not to the detriment of the appellant.

The *general courts* have jurisdiction in civil and criminal cases. Due to the constitutionally guaranteed public accountability of administrative staff, civil and criminal procedure can also be used as avenues of seeking redress for administrative wrongs. However, since neither kind of procedure can result in a reversal or a modification of the administrative decision they usually serve as individual remedies complementing the judicial procedure in administrative courts. Disputes concerning private law contracts and actions fall under the jurisdiction of general courts also in cases where a public body is party to such a contract.

Judicial review of administrative decisions

An administrative appeal may be directed against any act or measure of an administrative authority whereby a matter has been resolved or dismissed. The right to appeal may be exercised by any person to whom a decision is addressed or whose right, obligation or interest is directly affected by a decision. The judicial review exercised by administrative courts is focused on whether the administration acted in a legal manner and within the powers defined by law. Therefore, policy issues are left outside of judicial review. This means that the investigation of the advisability and expediency of the decision falls outside the jurisdiction of the administrative courts-provided, of course, that the authority has used its discretion within the limits defined in law.

An appeal may be directed against any final act or measure of an administrative authority. To be ripe for appeal, the decision must contain a final and conclusive settlement of an individual case. This means that appeal is not available either against initial or tentative decisions made at the preparatory stage or against technical decisions concerning merely the implementation of a decision. Recommendations as well as decisions of a general nature, such as administrative circulars, instructions concerning implementation and project plans, also fall outside the scope of appealability. However, the legality of such acts may be reviewed if an administrative decision is based on them.

The judicial procedure may be initiated in different ways, mainly by lodging an administrative appeal or an extraordinary appeal or by submitting an application for administrative litigation. Even though the procedural features are thus regulated uniformly, the grounds of substantive review depend mainly on whether the appeal procedure has been initiated by an ordinary administrative appeal or by a municipal appeal.

Decisions made by state administrative authorities are subject to an *administrative appeal*, while decisions made by municipal authorities within the unregulated field of municipal self-government may be challenged by a *municipal appeal*. Administrative appeal is the one most frequently used since it is available against all administrative decisions taken by state administrative authorities. It is also applicable against a majority of those municipal decisions made pursuant to special legislation regulating such things as welfare benefits and health care.

Ordinary administrative appeal is characterized as a reformatory type of appeal which allows the court to be more active at the investigative stage and which also gives it wider powers in passing the judgment. The municipal appeal is cassatory in nature, which means that the appellate court is required to conduct the procedure in a more passive and adversarial manner and its powers are more limited. In general, the conduct of the procedure is more active in administrative appeals, where the court is empowered to take a more detailed stand on the contents of the case.

By and large the scope of review also depends on the nature of the appeal. The degree of judicial scrutiny is more comprehensive as regards an ordinary administrative appeal; by contrast, it is more limited and passive in cases where a municipal appeal is concerned. In both cases, the court has the power either to affirm or overrule the decision challenged by an appeal.

Fair trial in administrative matters

Guarantees of procedural fairness must apply also in judicial proceedings concerning administrative cases. These guarantees include the right to be heard, procedurally equal status of the parties and public hearing in addition to the essential right of access to a court.

In administrative decision-making the administrative authority usually has a superiority of power compared to the private party. Its superior position is based on several factors, usually including the right to exercise unilateral public power, sophisticated expertise in legal and administrative issues and broader access to government held data and information. Of significance is also the government authority's general proficiency in conducting the decision-making procedure and participating in a judicial procedure. It is rarely and perhaps only in the case of large companies or organizations that the private party is actually capable of matching the government in all these areas.

Against this backdrop, *material equality* is how the requirement of fairness is understood in the Finnish law governing administrative-judicial proceedings. To start with, the executive authority is not considered to have its own rights to defend in the proceedings. Procedurally it is a party, but it is bound to the principles of legality and objectivity as well as to the obligation to protect general interest. Its position as a procedural party neither relieves the authority of its official duties nor does it authorize partial action.

That is why the administrative authority must act in a detached and impartial manner in the judicial procedure. For instance, the authority must provide all the evidence at its disposal even if it might be compromising for the authority's case. Also the official statements submitted by the authority must be based on a neutral and objective evaluation.

The gist of the judicial control of executive action is the public hearing conducted by the court. Both the private party and the public authority have a right to be heard. Both parties (or all the parties, as the case may be) must be reserved an opportunity to comment on the demands of other parties. They are also entitled to give their opinions on all the factual evidence that may affect the resolution of the matter.

In order to exercise the right to be heard, the private party to an administrative judicial procedure enjoys considerable right of access to the case documents. The private appellant usually gains access also to classified documents if they may be or may have been of influence in the processing of the case.

The role of the administrative courts

The administrative courts are under a general obligation to actively conduct the procedure and to obtain evidence and factual information also on their own initiative. In this sense, the procedure is characterized by the *investigation principle*, according to which the court is responsible for scrutinizing the contested decision comprehensively. As a part of this responsibility, the court is required to review all evidence available and to examine the facts and considerations on which the decision is based.

The court hearing the case may also, on its own initiative, acquire the necessary supplementary information, in so far as the impartiality and fairness of the procedure and the nature of the case so require. The administrative courts are thus empowered to make their own investigation of the substantial issues of the case and to collect evidence. The courts may also take into account facts that have not been presented by the parties.

VIII. Conclusion: New Developments

While the rule of law has retained its central role in defining the core legal principles and guarantees in Finnish administrative law, its basic tenets have recently been subjected to considerable pressures, mainly domestic and European but to a certain degree also global. First, the relative autonomy of the administration especially with respect to its legislative control has been growing. This is due to several interconnected factors. Detailed legislative regulation quite simply faces limits based on knowledge, technical exigencies, the need to reach political compromises and the like. The transfer of legislative powers to the European level or the increased use of private or semi-private regulation has not alleviated these problems. All this has resulted in the strengthening of the role of the executive as the provider of practical problem-solving based on the interpretation and application of law-not in the traditional form of unilateral decision-making but more often in a negotiated, horizontal mode based on partnership and participation.

Second, one can note a clear and perhaps partly concomitant shift from executive government to public governance. It reflects a number of significant developments ranging from a change of mindset concerning the role of the "public" in public administration to a transformation of the traditional executive function into public governance based on partnership and association, hybrid forms of decision-making etc. denoting, instead of an execution of laws, problem-solving in a predominately administrative setting. Third, the emergence and strengthening of multi-level European governance based on interplay of committees, networks, European and national agencies shared governance has probably strengthened the position of national administrations while simultaneously their inter-linkages have weakened their national accountability, regulated by the Constitution. Such novel features in public governance will not necessarily undermine the rule of law but require an update of how it is understood and applied in a new administrative environment.

Selected bibliography on Finnish Administrative Law

Mäenpää, O., Local Government in Finland. Angel-Manuel Moreno, ed., Local government in the member states of the European Union: a comparative legal perspective. Madrid 2012, pp. 185 −202.

Mäenpää, O., The Administrative Procedure Act and the Guarantees of Good Administration. Helsinki, 2011.

Mäenpää, O., Rozen Noguellou & Ulrich Stelkens, eds., Comparative Law on Public Contracts. Bruylant. Bruxelles 2010, pp. 657 −673.

Mäenpää, O., Judicial Procedure in Administrative Courts. Helsinki, 2007. (in Finnish)

Mäenpää, O., Openness and Access to Information in Finland, in The World's First Freedom of Information Act. Kokkola, 2006, pp. 58-73.

Mäenpää, O., Administrative Law. Helsinki, 2004. (in Finnish)

Mäenpää, O., Comparative Analysis of Administrative Law. European Public Law Series Vol. XXIV. London, 2002, pp. 147-200.

Mäenpää, O., Towards a Unified Judicial Protection of Citizens in Europe. Spiliotopoulos, E., ed., Towards a Unified Protection of Citizens in Europe. (London, 2000), pp. 251-290.

法治和芬兰的行政执行

奥利·梅恩佩

【摘要】 本文试图给芬兰行政法治做一个概述。芬兰公共行政的重点已经转移到提供社会福利和公共服务方面。公共行政也更多地涉及行政网络和经济活动。行政机制已同步发展，变得更为复杂、多层化，并融入欧洲的行政活动中。

法治在公共行政的重要性并未减少。然而，以下发展对行政法治提出了新的挑战：包括私有化与非中央化、行政管理的改革与新形式的规范性管理、治理模式与方法的变革，以及欧盟法和人权提出的要求。当然，对行政执行的合法性进行监督的新形式也有所发展。

行政机关可以起各种不同的作用。公共管理和行政监督构成了传统行政活动的内容。随着福利国家的发展，提供公共服务成了占主导地位的行政活动。此外，行政机关还可以履行其职责时建立受到私法支配的法律关系。

公共管理是以严格遵守法律为基础的。行政决定是依据法律法规作出的，这通常会导致监管关系的单方面性。因此，行政法律关系被视为非自愿的；权利与义务具有不可转让性，并且不属于合同义务的范围。公共服务包括了例如教育、医疗卫生、社会福利和对文化活动的支持。福利国家提供的经济利益尤其包括了不同类型的经济转移。当公共权力以一个私法主体的身份行事时，诸如房东、承租人、买受人或雇主，那么就适用私法关系。此时，它可以在相同的条件下，跟其他任何私法主体一样建立私法关系。

中国行政拘禁制度的现状与改革

李洪雷[*]

【摘要】 行政拘禁，或称行政羁押，是指由国家行政机关或者法律、法规授权的组织，在实施行政管理过程中所做出的剥夺公民人身自由的行政行为或制度。中国的行政拘禁，主要包括劳动教养（含劳教戒毒）、收容教养、收容教育、强制治疗、强制戒毒、行政管束、立即拘留和行政拘留等。本文对行政拘禁的概念、范围与性质，各种行政拘禁的概念、法律依据、适用对象和权利救济等，进行了全面的考察与检讨，并对中国行政拘禁制度的未来发展提出若干设想，主要是贯彻人性尊严原则、依法行政原则、比例原则、正当程序原则和权利救济原则等。

【关键词】 行政拘禁　依法行政

一　概说

（一）行政拘禁的概念与范围

行政拘禁，或称行政羁押，是指由国家行政机关或者法律、法规授权的组织，在实施行政管理过程中所做出的剥夺公民人身自由的行政行为或制度，它不包括公安机关等为侦查犯罪的目的而做出的刑事拘留与逮捕等审前拘禁（未决拘禁或未决羁押），也不包括刑罚执行机关（监狱）对罪犯的关押和监管。

中国的行政拘禁，主要包括劳动教养（含劳教戒毒）、收容教养、收容教育、强制治疗、强制戒毒、行政管束、立即拘留和行政拘留等，实践中还存在工读学校、法制学校等在实质上剥夺人身自由的设施以及"双规"、

---

[*]　中国社会科学院法学研究所副研究员。

"双指"等实质上剥夺公民人身自由的制度。本文试图对各种行政拘禁的概念、适用对象、主管机关、实施程序、权利救济等做一较为全面的考察与检讨，并对中国行政拘禁制度的未来发展提出若干设想。

在理解行政拘禁概念时，应注意行政拘禁是对公民人身自由的剥夺而不是一般限制。对公民人身自由的剥夺与对公民人身自由的一般限制对公民权益的影响差别很大，但我国在立法语言的表述上往往对此不甚重视，例如《治安管理处罚法》第 92 条规定："对决定给予行政拘留处罚的人，在处罚前已经采取强制措施限制人身自由的时间，应当折抵。限制人身自由一日，折抵行政拘留一日。"从立法原意上来看，这里的限制人身自由显然只是指采取拘留、逮捕等剥夺人身自由的拘禁或羁押措施，而不包括虽然属于限制人身自由，但不属于剥夺人身自由的取保候审、监视居住和拘传等强制措施，但从法律文意上来看则包括在内。

行政拘禁可以从目的上区分为三类。其一是强制教育治疗性的行政拘禁。其典型是强制治疗和强制戒毒等。其二是惩罚性的行政拘禁。其典型是行政拘留。其三是即时处置性的行政拘禁。其典型是行政管束和立即拘留，是一种应对特殊情况的程序性暂时性处置，本身不构成一种实体上的终局决定。在实践当中，强制教育治疗性的行政拘禁与惩罚性的行政拘禁存在很大程度的混淆。诸如劳动教养和收容教育等，名为强制教育性的行政拘禁，实质上其惩罚性非常明显。我国行政拘禁制度未来发展的一个重要任务，是厘清这两类行政拘禁的差别，做出不同的制度设计。

（二）行政拘禁与保安处分

保安处分是西方许多国家极为重要的一项法律制度。它是指国家为了维护社会秩序、满足社会大众的安全需求，在行使刑罚权之外，对具有社会危险性的行为人，以医疗、警戒、强制工作、监禁、撤销假释许可、禁止执业、监督素行、驱逐出境等手段作出的保安措施。保安处分所使用的手段可分为剥夺人身自由与限制人身自由两大类。前者又可分为积极性的矫治医疗处分以及消极性的隔离与监禁。[①] 保安处分是以防卫社会免受危险的人的侵害为目的，因此宽泛来说，只要能认定行为人具有社会危险性即可实施。但仅仅以社会危险性作为保安处分的条件，容易导致权力的滥用，因此各国法制均要求，只有在行为人实施了为刑法所禁止的行为，并且仍

[①]　林山田：《刑罚学》，商务印书馆，1983，第 335～336 页；〔日〕大塚仁著《刑法概说（总论）》，冯军译，中国人民大学出版社，2003，第 508 页。

有将来再犯的可能性时，才能针对其危险性采取保安处分这一特别预防措施。①

保安处分本来是针对被处分者的危险性，为防卫社会而采取的措施。但在第二次世界大战以后，保安处分制度发生了很大的变化，在目的上与防卫社会相比，更注重对被处分人的治疗、改造，从而更多地从积极的治疗、改造来寻求其正当化的根据。这主要是担心在预测了危险性之后所采取的预防性措施会侵犯人权。②

我国的多数行政拘禁（不包括即时性的行政管束和惩罚性的行政拘留等）与剥夺人身自由的保安处分存在很大的相似之处，例如同样强调教育、感化、治疗，针对的是违法现象但又不属于刑事惩罚等，因此有许多论者主张参照国外的保安处分改革我国的行政拘禁，尤其是劳动教养制度。但是，我国的行政拘禁与国外剥夺人身自由的保安处分存在许多差异。①西方保安处分是针对已经实施刑法所禁止行为的行为人，而我国的劳动教养、收容教养、收容教育、强制戒毒等行政拘禁所针对的均是尚未触犯刑法的一般违法人。②西方保安处分的基础是行为人具有将来犯罪的可能性，要求其具有反复犯罪的危险性，而我国的劳动教养、收容教养、收容教育、强制戒毒等行政拘禁并不以此为基础。这个区别非常重要。③西方保安处分是出于特别预防的构想，单纯针对行为人的特别危险性而提出的防卫措施，其在本质上对于行为人并不具有惩罚性与非难性，而我国的劳动教养、收容教育等具有明显的惩罚性与非难性。这种区别也具有相对性，因为剥夺人身自由的保安处分其对人身自由的强烈干预往往并不比惩罚性措施轻，从而必须遵循法治原则和比例原则等要求。④西方保安处分需要遵循司法程序，由司法机关科处，而我国的行政拘禁则是由行政机关科处。当然这一区别不是本质性的区别，可以通过制度设计而改变，我国的行政拘禁同样可以采取由行政机关申请、司法机关裁决的程序进行，这并不影响行政拘禁的性质。

我们认为，中国的劳动教养、收容教养、收容教育等行政拘禁制度与西方国家的保安处分制度在制度功能和具体设计上均存在巨大的差别。只要认真检讨我国这些相关制度的产生与发展过程以及正视实践中的状况，

---

① 〔日〕大谷实著《刑事政策学》，黎宏译，法律出版社，2000，第151页。

② 但有论者认为，将治疗的必要性作为保安处分的要件，实际上在一定程度上偏离了作为刑事政策的保安处分的范围。保安处分正当化的根据在根本上还应当是被处分者的社会危险性。〔日〕大谷实著《刑事政策学》，黎宏译，法律出版社，2000，第151页。

而非拘泥于一些纸面上或宣传中的说法，我们就很容易得出这样的结论，即我国的这些行政拘禁制度在很大程度上是作为一种相较于刑罚为轻，而又比一般行政处罚更重的惩罚形态而存在。因为与西方国家不同，由于我国犯罪构成不仅有定性的要求而且具有定量的要求，犯罪的概念在我国范围比较狭窄，我国劳动教养等所适用的对象，很多实际上是相当于西方刑法中所规定的"轻罪"或"违警罪"。有的学者仅仅依据相关制度对劳动教养等的表述上存在"屡教不改"等字样，就认为其与西方保安处分一样是针对行为人的特别危险性。这种观点忽视了这样的问题，如果说对于仅仅是屡次一般违法甚至仅仅是违反纪律的人就因其特别危险性而需要采取劳动教养这样的"保安处分"，那么对于那些屡次犯罪从而特别危险性更高的行为人为何不使用这样的"保安处分"？有一些学者还提出了行政法上的保安处分概念，但缺乏深入的阐述和论证。我们认为，我国的这些制度只要其基本功能不做根本调整，与西方保安处分的可比性非常之小，更具可比性的是西方对"轻罪"和"违警罪"的制度和理论。

（三）行政拘禁概念与《公民权利和政治权利国际公约》

我国已经签署了《公民权利和政治权利国际公约》，正在为正式批准该公约做积极的准备工作。《公民权利和政治权利国际公约》中的相关规定，是我们检讨我国行政拘禁制度的一个重要标准。《公民权利和政治权利国际公约》中与行政拘禁关系最为密切的是第9条。该条条文为：

"一、人人享有人身自由和安全。任何人不得加以任意逮捕和拘禁。除非依照法律所确定的根据和程序，任何人不得被剥夺自由。"

"二、任何被逮捕的人，在被逮捕时应被告知逮捕他的理由，并应被迅速告知对他提出的任何指控。"

"三、任何因刑事指控被逮捕或拘禁的人，应被迅速带见审判官或其他经法律授权行使司法权力的官员，并有权在合理的时间内受审判或被释放。等候审判的人受监禁不应作为一般规则，但可规定释放时应保证在司法程序的任何其他阶段出席审判，并在必要时报到听候执行判决。"

"四、任何因逮捕或拘禁被剥夺自由的人，有资格向法庭提出起诉，以便法庭能不推延地决定他是否合法以及如果拘禁不合法时命令予以释放。"

"五、任何遭受非法逮捕或拘禁的受害者，有得到赔偿的权利。"

这里所规定的逮捕与拘禁，与剥夺自由具有同一含义，除了逮捕与拘禁，人权事务委员会不承认存在剥夺人身自由的其他形式，其中逮捕是指剥夺人身自由的行为，一般它涵盖该人被带到一个主管当局前的这段时间，而拘禁则是指剥夺人身自由的状态。第9条的规定，除了第2款中的一部分与第3款仅仅与刑事诉讼程序有关以外，其他规定均适用于包括行政拘禁在内的所有剥夺人身自由的情况，如联合国人权事务委员会所指出的："不论它涉及刑事案件或涉及诸如精神病、游荡、吸毒成瘾、为教育目的、管制移民等其他情况。"从而一个国家的行政拘禁制度，必须符合以下要求：①行政拘禁，必须要有法律所确定的根据，并遵循法律所规定的程序，并且不得任意进行。一般认为，这里的"法律"是指严格意义上的、一般抽象的、议会或立法机关制定的成文法或是同等的、非成文的普通法规范。这些法律都必须能被处于有关管辖权之下的所有人知晓。因此行政规章是不够的。一项行政行为对人身自由的限制，只有当其是在执行某一足够清晰地规定了这种干预以及这种干预所应遵循的程序的法律时，才是可允许的。并且，仅仅由法律规定剥夺自由仍然是不充分的，法律本身也不能具有任意性，并在某一具体情况中对法律的实施也不能任意进行。这里的任意性或专断，包含了非正义、不可预见性、不合理性、反复无常性和不成比例性的因素。此外，应当注意，不能侵犯平等保护，不能利用行政拘禁不当干预公民的迁徙自由（第12条）、思想、良心、宗教和信仰自由（第18条），意见、表达和信息自由（第19条），集会自由（第21条），结社和工会自由（22条）。②被行政拘禁的人，应当有被告知原因的权利。任何被逮捕的人，不仅仅是因刑事指控而被逮捕的人，必须被告知原因，即对其进行逮捕的法律与事实依据。③被行政拘禁的人，有获得人身保护令的权利。其应当有资格向法庭提出起诉，以便法庭能不推延地拘禁他是否合法以及不合法时命令给予释放。如果拘禁不合法，则法庭必须下令立即释放被拘禁的人，该裁决必须"不拖延地"作出，即一般是在几个星期之内。但是具体地限制要根据被剥夺自由的类型以及所涉及案件的具体情况而定。④任何遭受非法逮捕或拘禁的受害者，有得到赔偿的权利。⑤被拘禁人有保持身体和精神完整性的权利，并应获得人道及尊重其固有的人格尊严的待遇。①

二　中国行政拘禁制度的现状

（一）劳动教养

1. 概念

劳动教养，简称劳教，即劳动、教育和培养，这里的劳动是强制劳动，

---

① 〔奥〕诺瓦克著《民权公约评注——联合国〈公民权利和政治权利国际公约〉（上）》，毕小青等译，三联书店，2003，第158页。

组织他们"劳动生产，替国家做工，自食其力"；教育，即教育改造，"对他们进行政治、思想改造工作"；培养，使他们"逐渐成为国家的真正有用的人"。劳动教养制度是中国行政拘禁制度中一个核心的并且具有典范意义的制度。但由于其对象、性质与职能等经历了复杂的发展过程，因此很难对劳动教养的概念作出准确的界定。大略而言，劳动教养是对部分具有轻微违法犯罪行为的人所进行的强制性教育改革的一种行政措施。

劳动教养最初并未规定明确期限。1979 年《国务院关于劳动教养问题的补充决定》将期限确定为 1～3 年，必要时得延长 1 年。但公安部和司法部 1984 年发布的《关于劳动教养和注销劳教人员城市户口问题的通知》将期限规定为 2～3 年。

2. 法律依据

1956 年 1 月 10 日中共中央发布《关于各省、市应立即筹办劳动教养机构的指示》，对劳动教养的性质、任务、组织机构、方针政策和审批管理等问题作了原则规定。此后劳动教养机构开始在全国各省、市建立。1957 年 8 月 1 日，经全国人大常委会批准，国务院于 8 月 3 日公布了《关于劳动教养问题的决定》。1979 年 11 月 29 日经全国人大常委会批准，国务院 12 月 5 日公布了《关于劳动教养问题的补充规定》，并重新公布了《关于劳动教养问题的决定》。1982 年 1 月 21 日，经国务院批准，公安部发布了《劳动教养试行办法》。全国人大常委会在 1986 年通过的《中华人民共和国治安管理处罚条例》、1990 年通过的《关于禁毒的决定》、1991 年通过的《关于严禁卖淫嫖娼的决定》等法律中对劳动教养的对象作了扩大。此外，一些行政法规、司法解释甚至地方的相关规范性文件也对劳动教养的对象和程序等作了补充规定，如 1989 年国务院发布的《铁路运输安全保护条例》，最高人民法院、最高人民检察院、公安部、司法部《关于处理反动会道门工作有关问题的通知》等。

对于国务院经全国人大常委会批准公布的《关于劳动教养问题的决定》和《关于劳动教养问题的补充规定》，在法律层级上属于狭义的"法律"还是行政法规，理论界有不同的看法。这个问题在《立法法》通过以后显得特别重要，因为《立法法》规定，限制人身自由的处罚或强制处罚只能由法律规定。一种折中的观点认为，这两个决定属于"准法律"。

各地根据当地治安形势的需要，也制订了诸多与劳动教养工作有关的地方性法规、规章与规范性文件。其中一般是对中央规定的细化，但也不乏扩张性的规定，包括对劳动教养对象范围的扩大。

3. 法律性质

劳动教养到底是行政处罚还是行政强制措施,对于劳动教养制度设计具有重大影响。但在这个问题上存在很大的争议。1957 年《国务院关于劳动教养问题的决定》规定,劳动教养是对被劳动教养的人实行强制性教育改造的一种措施,也是对其安置就业的方法。1982 年《劳动教养试行办法》规定:劳动教养,是对被劳动教养的人实行强制性教育改造的行政措施,是处理人民内部矛盾的一种方法。不再将其作为安置就业的一种办法。根据这些规定,我们难以明确劳动教养的性质:单纯从文义上看,可以将其界定为一种行政强制措施。但根据《行政强制法》第 2 条的规定,行政强制措施是指行政机关在行政管理过程中,为制止违法行为、防止证据损毁、避免危害发生、控制危险扩大等情形,依法对公民的人身自由实施暂时性限制,或者对公民、法人或者其他组织的财物实施暂时性控制的行为。劳动教养不符合这种"暂时性"的特点,其本身即是一种终局性的决定。当然,也可以将行政强制措施的概念区分为广义与狭义两种,狭义的行政强制措施是指《行政强制法》中所规定的暂时性措施,而广义的行政强制措施是除此之外,还包括强制性的教育改造和矫正措施。

另一种观点是将劳动教养界定为行政处罚。这种观点认为,从劳动教养对被教养人的实际影响来看,将其界定为行政处罚是符合实际的。处罚与教育改造并不矛盾,正如对犯罪的人进行劳动"改造"并不影响其刑事处罚的性质一样。1991 年国务院发布的《中国人权状况》白皮书指出,劳动教养不是刑事处罚,而是行政处罚。1995 年国务院发布的《关于进一步加强监狱管理和劳动教养工作的通知》指出:劳动教养所是国家治安行政处罚的执行机关,将劳动教养定位于"治安行政处罚"。1997 年的《行政处罚法》对于行政处罚的设定与实施规定了一系列规范、严格的制度,劳动教养的现行做法与其相比存在很大的差距,如果将其定性为行政处罚,这意味着有关劳动教养的很多规定必须废止,劳动教养制度必须进行重大改革,可能是由于官方认为劳动教养的改革时机尚不成熟,在 1997 年以后,官方也不再坚持劳动教养的行政处罚特性,而是强调其属于行政强制性教育措施。但随着 2000 年《立法法》和 2011 年《行政强制法》的通过,行政强制措施的设定和实施均已受到严格规范,企图通过将劳动教养定性为行政强制措施而不是行政处罚来逃遁法律严格规制已经不再可能。

我们认为,不能以劳动教养(包括收容教养、收容教育)等的教育矫正目的而否定其惩罚的性质。在国外的某些保安处分中,例如对犯罪精神病人的强制治疗，因为精神病人不具有刑事责任能力，这属于单纯的矫治性质而非惩罚性质。但对于我国的劳动教养等行政拘禁制度，其所针对的是具有责任能力的公民。实际上，所有的行政处罚甚至包括刑罚都必须遵循惩罚与教育相结合的原则，我们不能因为一种惩罚措施需要考虑教育矫治的目的而否定其惩罚的性质，若然，则除了死刑以外，在现代社会还能否找到所谓的国家惩罚呢？

4. 决定与执行

《国务院关于劳动教养问题的决定》、国务院《关于劳动教养的补充规定》和公安部《劳动教养试行办法》规定劳动教养的审查批准由省、自治区、直辖市和大中城市人民政府成立的劳动教养管理委员会行使，但是1984年由公安部和司法部联合对劳动教养问题所作的通知中规定：劳动教养审批机构设在公安机关，受劳动教养管理委员会的委托，审查批准需要劳动教养的人。这样，劳动教养的审批权实际上转由公安机关独家行使。目前，劳动教养的审批机构设在公安机关，具体由公安机关的法制部门负责。长期以来，劳动教养的决定程序比较粗疏，不仅说明理由、听取意见、公开等公正程序的基本要求都没有得到贯彻，而且也缺乏起码的规范性。2002年公安部颁发的《公安机关办理劳动教养案件规定》在这方面有所进步。按照这一规定劳动教养的决定程序分为三个阶段，即审查复核、聆询以及决定和案件处理。

负责执行劳动教养的管理机构称为劳动教养所，是国家司法行政机构，其中的人民警察是国家公务员。劳动教养所分为省属劳教所和地市管理的劳教所，其经费分别由省财政和地市财政负担。

（二）收容教育

1. 概念

收容教育，是指对卖淫、嫖娼人员集中进行法律教育和道德教育、组织参加生产劳动以及进行性病检查、治疗的行政强制教育措施。收容教育期限为六个月至二年。

2. 法律依据和性质

《全国人民代表大会常务委员会关于严惩卖淫嫖娼的决定》（1991年）是收容教养最为主要的规定，该决定第4条规定："卖淫、嫖娼的，依照治安管理处罚条例第三十条的规定处罚。对卖淫、嫖娼的，可以由公安机关会同有关部门强制集中进行法律、道德教育和生产劳动，使之改掉恶习。

期限为六个月至二年。具体办法由国务院规定。"① 1991 年 11 月 23 日，公安部发布了《关于认真贯彻执行全国人大常委会〈关于严禁卖淫嫖娼的决定〉的通知》。国务院于 1993 年通过了《卖淫嫖娼人员收容教育办法》。② 这三个文件成为收容教育的主要规范基础。

对于上述文件能否作为对卖淫嫖娼人员进行收容教育的规范依据，理论界存在不同的看法。有人认为，尽管 1991 年全国人大常委会《关于严禁卖淫嫖娼的决定》中规定了收容教育，但是 1994 年全国人大常委会修正的《治安管理处罚条例》中第 30 条 1 款明确规定："严厉禁止卖淫、嫖宿暗娼以及介绍或者容留卖淫、嫖宿暗娼，违者处十五日以下拘留、警告、责令具结悔过或者依照规定实行劳动教养，可以并处五千元以下罚款；构成犯罪，依法追究刑事责任。"其中对于卖淫、嫖娼并没有规定收容教育，按照后法优于前法的基本法理，可以得出下列结论：对卖淫、嫖娼人员的处理，应该依照《治安管理处罚条例》的规定来处理，即进行拘留、警告、责令具结悔过、劳动教养或罚款。2005 年《治安管理处罚法》第 66 条也没有规定收容教育（和劳动教养）。③ 该法第 76 条有关强制性教育措施的规定，④ 针对的是该法第 67 条、第 68 条和第 70 条的行为，这些行为并不包括卖淫嫖娼。⑤

国务院的《卖淫嫖娼人员收容教育办法》是根据《全国人民代表大会常务委员会关于严惩卖淫嫖娼的决定》（1991 年）的授权制定的。但依照 2000 年颁布的《立法法》第 8 条，限制人身自由的强制措施和处罚，必须制定法律，而法律的制定权属于全国人大及其常委会，并且根据该法第 9 条

---

① 1994 年经过全国人大常委会修正的《治安管理处罚条例》第 30 条 1 款规定："严厉禁止卖淫、嫖宿暗娼以及介绍或者容留卖淫、嫖宿暗娼，违者处十五日以下拘留、警告、责令具结悔过或者依照规定实行劳动教养，可以并处五千元以下罚款；构成犯罪的，依法追究刑事责任。"

② 1993 年 9 月 4 日通过并实施。

③ 《治安管理处罚法》第 66 条规定："卖淫、嫖娼的，处十日以上十五日以下拘留，可以并处五千元以下罚款；情节较轻的，处五日以下拘留或者五百元以下罚款。在公共场所拉客招嫖的，处五日以下拘留或者五百元以下罚款。"

④ 《治安管理处罚法》第 76 条规定："有本法第六十七条、第六十八条、第七十条的行为，屡教不改的，可以按照国家规定采取强制性教育措施。"

⑤ 2009 年 11 月 27 日，浙江省第十一届人大常委第 14 次会议表决通过废止《浙江省严禁卖淫嫖娼活动的规定》，对于卖淫、嫖娼按照《刑法》和《治安管理处罚法》的规定办理，从而在浙江不再存在对卖淫、嫖娼人员的收容教育（和劳动教养）。《浙江人大官员解释废止严禁卖淫嫖娼规定原因》，2009 年 11 月 27 日法制网。

的规定，"本法第八条规定的事项尚未制定法律的，全国人民代表大会及其常务委员会有权作出决定，授权国务院可以根据实际需要，对其中的部分事项先制定行政法规，但是有关犯罪和刑罚、对公民政治权利的剥夺和限制人身自由的强制措施和处罚、司法制度等事项除外"。可见，对剥夺公民人身自由的收容教育，全国人大及其常委会不得授权国务院在未有法律之前先制定行政法规。因此，有学者认为《关于严禁卖淫嫖娼的决定》中对国务院的授权违反了《立法法》的规定，应当无效。

对于收容教育的法律性质，与前述劳动教养同样存在着属于行政强制教育措施还是行政处罚的争论。我们认为，其与收容教养一样，应当属于行政处罚。

3. 决定与执行

收容教育工作由公安机关主管。对卖淫、嫖娼人员实行收容教育，由县级公安机关决定。

收容教育所是负责收容教育执行工作的机构。对被收容教育人员，应当按照性别和有无性病实行分别管理。对被收容教育人员应当进行法律教育和道德教育，并组织他们参加生产劳动，学习生产技能，增强劳动观念。被收容教育人员参加生产劳动所获得的劳动收入，用于改善被收容教育人员的生活和收容教育所的建设。对参加生产劳动的被收容教育人员，可以按照规定支付一定的劳动报酬。

（三）收容教养[①]

1. 概念

收容教养是对因不满 16 周岁不予刑事处罚的未成年人而采取的强制性教育改造措施。收容教养的期限一般为 1～3 年。如果收容教养人员在收容教养期间有新的犯罪行为，由公安机关对新的犯罪行为作出收容教养的决定，并与原收容教养的剩余期限合并执行，但实际执行期限不得超过 4 年。

2. 法律依据

1979 年《刑法》第 14 条第 2 款规定，对于不满十六岁的人犯罪又不需要追究刑事责任的，在必要的时候，可以由政府收容教养。1991 年《未成年人保护法》第 39 条规定："已满十四周岁的未成年人犯罪，因不满十六周

---

① 对我国收容教养制度的全面介绍，详见陈泽宪《收容教养制度及其改革》，载陈斯喜主编《中国人身权的法律保护及其改革》，社会科学文献出版社，2007；郭建安、郑霞泽主编《限制对人身自由的限制——中国行政性限制人身自由法律处分的法治建设》，法律出版社，2005，第 471 页。

岁不予刑事处罚的，责令其家长或者其他监护人加以管教，必要时，也可以由政府收容教养。"1993 年公安部《关于对不满十四岁的少年犯罪人员收容教养问题的通知》明确地将收容教养的对象扩大至不满十四岁的犯罪少年。该通知明确规定，对未满十四岁的人犯有杀人、重伤、抢劫、放火、惯窃罪或者其他严重破坏社会秩序罪的，应当依照原《刑法》第 14 条的规定办理，即在必要的时候，可以收容教养。《刑法》第 17 条规定，对于因不满十六岁不予刑事处罚的，在必要的时候，可以由政府收容教养。《刑法》和《未成年人保护法》是我国收容教养制度的主要法律依据，但其规定得过于原则，与《立法法》规定的法律保留原则并不完全符合，而同时又缺乏配套的法规、规章的系统规定，导致收容教养的规范化存在较大缺陷，执法机关的裁量权过大。另外，根据联合国《儿童权利公约》第 37 条的规定，"不得非法或任意剥夺任何儿童的自由。对儿童的逮捕、挽留或监禁应符合法律规定并仅应作为最后手段，期限应为最短的适当时间"。我国目前对收容教养制度存在使用过宽过滥的问题。

3. 法律性质

对于收容教养的法律性质，存在不同的观点。有人着眼其矫治性和社会救济性，认为是一种强制性的教育改造和救济措施，有人则着眼其对当事人影响的严重性，认为是一种行政处罚。之所以存在这种认识的分歧，主要是因为收容教养制度的理想和现实之间存在的差距，收容教养制度的最初目的是通过收容这一方式，教育犯罪少年，使其成为守法的自食其力的公民，因此教育矫治性应当是其主要性质，但其实践中的运作，实际上具有强烈的惩戒性。

4. 决定与执行

1956 年 2 月 7 日最高人民检察院、最高人民法院、内务部、司法部、公安部《对少年犯收押界限、捕押手续和清理等问题的联合通知》中规定，"由民政部门负责收容教养"，"对刑期已满的少年犯……应介绍到社会救济机关予以收容教养"。但是在 1982 年，公安部《关于少年犯管教所收押、收容范围的通知》中明确规定，"对于确有必要由政府收容教养的犯罪少年，应当由地区行政公署公安处或者省辖市公安局审批，遇有犯罪少年不满十四岁等特殊情况，须报请省、市、自治区公安厅、局审批"。从此，收容教养的审批权归于公安机关。收容教养制度针对的是实施犯罪的未成年人，由公安机关决定收容教养实际上就意味着其具有对公民定罪的权力，这不符合法治原则的要求。

在 1996 年之前，执行收容教养的场所不一，各地差异很大，有工读学校、收容所、少年犯管教所和劳动教养场所等。1996 年 1 月 22 日司法部《关于将政府收容教养的犯罪少年移至劳动教养场所收容教养的通知》规定，收容教养人员要由劳教所负责管理，但应和成年劳教人员分别关押。目前在实践中，将少年收容教养人员与成年劳动教养人员混合关押的情况仍在一定范围内存在，这容易使少年收教人员感染某些成年劳教人员的恶习，不利于对犯罪少年的教育改造。

（四）　强制性戒毒[①]

1. 概念

强制性戒毒是指行政机关通过一定的行政措施强制毒品成瘾人员戒除毒瘾，包括强制戒毒和劳教戒毒两种类型。其中强制戒毒是指在一定时期内通过行政措施对吸食、注射毒品成瘾人员强制进行药物治疗、心理治疗和法制、道德教育，使其戒除毒瘾（《强制戒毒办法》第 2 条）。强制戒毒期限为 3 ~ 6 个月，对强制戒毒期满仍未戒除毒瘾的戒毒人员，强制戒毒所可以提出意见，报原作出决定的公安机关批准，延长强制戒毒期限；但是，实际执行的强制戒毒期限连续计算不超过 1 年。

劳教戒毒就是通过劳动教养对毒品成瘾人员戒除毒瘾。根据 1996 年 5 月 30 日公安部《关于贯彻执行〈强制戒毒办法〉有关问题的通知》的要求，"强制戒毒后又吸食、注射毒品的，要依法送劳动教养"。劳教戒毒的期限为 1 ~ 3 年，必要时可延长 1 年。

2. 法律依据

我国的强制性戒毒制度最早规定在《全国人民代表大会常务委员会关于禁毒的决定》中，其中第 8 条规定："吸食、注射毒品的，由公安机关处十五日以下拘留，可以单处或者并处二千元以下罚款，并没收毒品和吸食、注射器具。吸食、注射毒品成瘾的，除依照前款规定处罚外，予以强制戒除，进行治疗、教育。强制戒除后又吸食、注射毒品的，可以实行劳动教养，并在劳动教养中强制戒除。"其具体制度则见于中央的行政法规、部门规章以及地方性的法规和规章。目前，强制戒毒方面的行政法规有《强制戒毒办法》（1995 年 1 月 12 日国务院颁布），部门规章主要是《强制戒毒所

---

① 对我国强制性戒毒制度的全面讨论，参见陈泽宪《强制性戒毒制度及其改革》，载陈斯喜主编《中国人身权的法律保护及其改革》，社会科学文献出版社，2007；郭建安、郑霞泽主编《限制对人身自由的限制——中国行政性限制人身自由法律处分的法治建设》，法律出版社，2005，第 367 页。

管理办法》（2000 年 1 月 17 日公安部颁发）。地方上的一些戒毒办法中也规定了强制戒毒制度。关于劳教戒毒，1999 年 12 月司法部劳教局颁发了《劳动教养戒毒工作管理办法（试行）》，这是我国第一个全国性的关于劳教戒毒的部门规章。2003 年 8 月 1 日司法部《劳动教养戒毒工作规定》正式施行。根据《立法法》的规定，限制人身自由的处罚和强制措施，只能由全国人大及其常委会的法律来规定，我国现行的强制戒毒制度所依据的除了行政法规和规章外，只有全国人大常委会禁毒决定中的一条规定，与《立法法》的规定并不符合。

3. 性质

对于强制戒毒，目前普遍定性为强制性的行政措施。而对于劳教戒毒，基于对劳动教养的不同认识，而有不同的定性。根据《劳动教养戒毒工作规定》，劳教戒毒包括对吸毒人员的"管理、治疗和教育工作"，但实践中对劳教戒毒人员的惩戒和管理是工作的重点。

4. 决定与执行

强制戒毒工作由公安机关主管。对需要送入强制戒毒所的吸食、注射毒品成瘾人员实施强制戒毒，由县级人民政府公安机关决定。强制戒毒决定书应当于戒毒人员入所前交给本人。强制戒毒决定应当自作出决定之日起三日内通知戒毒人员的家属、所在单位和户口所在地公安派出所。

劳教戒毒与其他劳动教养一样，决定权在公安机关，而执行则由司法行政机关下属的劳动教养管理机构负责，其形式有戒毒劳动教养管理所和劳动教养管理所戒毒大（中）队两种。

（五）对精神病人的强制治疗

1. 概念

对精神病人的强制治疗，是指将特定精神病人收容于一定场所，以保护其本人或社会安全。

2. 法律依据

关于精神病人的强制治疗，在中央层面上我国目前尚缺乏完整、全面的法律规范。[①] 1997 年修订的《刑法》第 18 条规定，"精神病人在不能辨认或者不能控制自己行为的时候造成危害结果，经法定程度鉴定确认的，

---

① 2011 年 9 月 19 日国务院常务会议讨论并原则通过《中华人民共和国精神卫生法（草案）》，在经进一步修改后交由国务院提请全国人大常委会审议。2011 年 10 月十一届全国人大常委会第二十三次会议初次审议了《中华人民共和国精神卫生法（草案）》。

不负刑事责任，但是应当责令他的家属或者监护人严加看管和治疗；在必要的时候，由政府强制医疗"。① 但现实中有很多精神病人尽管没有触犯国家刑事法律、造成严重后果，但触犯了国家的治安管理行政法规，造成一般的社会危害后果；或者尽管还没有造成危害社会的后果，但具有极大的危险性；或者自身的生命健康处在危险之中；等等。这些情况应当如何处理，均不明确。

目前在一些地方，如上海市、广东省、黑龙江省、石家庄市、大连市、青岛市、沈阳市都均出台了关于精神病人问题的地方性法规和地方性规章。总体而言，现有的地方规定，不同程度的存在程序简陋粗疏、对被收治人权利保护不足等问题，而且各地的规定相互之间也存在很大的差别，影响了法律的统一性。

3. 法律性质

强制医疗包括对触犯刑法的精神病人的强制治疗和未触犯刑法的精神病人的强制治疗。对于后者，学者一般认为属于行政法上的措施，目前对强制治疗性质的讨论主要集中于前者。争论的焦点是其属于刑事法性的处分还是行政法性的处分。有人认为，强制医疗是刑法中所规定的，有别于在行政法中规定的强制措施，因此属于刑事措施。有人认为，无刑事责任能力精神病人的危害行为，虽然在刑法上不是犯罪，不能处以刑罚制裁，但其认定、防治毕竟是刑法、刑事诉讼法和其他刑事法律以及刑事司法需要处理的问题，人为地将其排除在刑事法律和刑事司法领域以外，不利于防止精神病人实施危害行为，也不利于保障精神病人的合法权益，应当肯定并且维护强制医疗的刑事法性质。还有人认为，强制医疗虽然规定在刑法中，但实际上是行政法性的。

4. 决定与执行

《刑法》第18条规定，对触犯刑律的精神病人在必要的时候，由政府强制治疗。首先，是指由政府决定还是由法院决定、政府执行不是很明确。其次，由政府哪一部门负责也不清楚。公安部门与民政部门经常存在扯皮的现象。除了设置有安康病院的地方，实践中常出现公安机关转交民政部门，而民政部门一般又只管退役的军人。公安机关出于种种考虑，往往长

---

① 应当注意的是，《人民警察法》第14条规定："公安机关的人民警察对严重危害公共安全或者他人人身安全的精神病人，可以采取保护性约束措施。需要送往指定的单位、场所加以监护的，应当报请县级以上人民政府公安机关批准，并及时通知其监护人。"这一规定虽然也与精神病人有关，但属于一种临时性的约束措施，与强制治疗仍有所不同。

期将触犯刑律的危险性精神病人留置在看守所里来缓解社会矛盾。

对于未触犯刑法但对社会治安具有危险性的病人，实践中也非常混乱。在传统和习惯上，强制精神病人住院是由家属或者单位决定的。一方面，家属（他们多数都没有成为法定的监护人）甚至单位自行决定将精神病人强制住院的事情经常发生；另一方面，国家对有危险性的精神病人很少实行强制住院治疗，只有等到精神病人犯罪，才能启动刑法上的强制住院治疗程序，使得需要予以强制医疗的人流散在社会上，对他们本人的人身安全，特别是社会上其他人的人身安全造成危害。另一方面，在重大节日或重大活动期间，又往往将强制医疗的范围随意扩大，等这一时期一过就因经济压力而放人。

安康医院是由公安机关设立的专门收治严重肇事肇祸、病情较严重的精神病人的医疗机构。1998 年 11 月，公安部决定将安康医院的业务工作由公安机关治安部门划归监管部门统一归口管理和指导，在监管部门专门成立了安康医院业务指导机构，并根据全国各地安康医院的现状，由公安部监管局牵头，陆续出台了《安康医院管理办法》、《安康医院装备标准》、《收治危害社会治安精神病人的规定》等一系列部门规章。

（六）强制隔离

1．概念

强制隔离是指为了防止传染病传播与扩散，对严重的传染病人或者对有罹患严重传染病之虞的人员，由有关部门将其收留在指定的场所并予以观察或治疗的行政行为。在实践中，强制隔离在两种意义上加以运用，第一种意义是指有关部门做出的要求有关人员接受隔离的决定本身，因为这种决定的内容不是由相对人自己决定的，并且相对人有义务履行这一决定而没有自由选择的权利，而被称为强制隔离。强制隔离的另一种意义则是指当相对人自己不自愿履行隔离决定（拒绝隔离决定或者隔离期未满擅自离开隔离场所）时，由有关部门依法采取的强制执行措施，这是隔离决定强制性的物理实现。这两种意义上的强制隔离在性质与程序上具有密切的内在关联。

2．法律依据

《传染病防治法》（1989 年通过，2004 年 8 月修订）第 39 条、第 40 条对传染病人的隔离治疗措施作了原则性的规定。《国境卫生检疫法》第 12 条规定了对国境卫生检疫机关发现的传染病人染疫人的强制隔离。国务院《突发公共卫生事件应急条例》（2003 年 5 月）对在传染病暴发、流行时可以采取的应急措施做了规定。有关部门和地方也制定了一些相关的部门规章、地方性法规和规章以及其他行政规范性文件。

3. 法律性质

前述第一种意义上的强制隔离在性质上属于一种具有法律拘束力的、强制性的行政决定（具体行政行为），当相对人不依法履行其内容时有关部门可以依法采取强制执行措施。医疗机构尽管不是国家行政机关，但在其做出强制性的隔离决定时，是被法律授权的行政主体，是实质意义上的行政机关。第二种意义上的强制隔离是行政强制执行措施。

4. 决定与执行

根据《传染病防治法》的规定，"医疗机构发现甲类传染病时，应当及时采取下列措施：（一）对病人、病原携带者，予以隔离治疗，隔离期限根据医学检查结果确定；（二）对疑似病人，确诊前在指定场所单独隔离治疗；（三）对医疗机构内的病人、病原携带者、疑似病人的密切接触者，在指定场所进行医学观察和采取其他必要的预防措施。拒绝隔离治疗或者隔离期未满擅自脱离隔离治疗的，可以由公安机关协助医疗机构采取强制隔离治疗措施"。"对已经发生甲类传染病病例的场所或者该场所内的特定区域的人员，所在地的县级以上地方人民政府可以实施隔离措施，并同时向上一级人民政府报告；接到报告的上级人民政府应当即时作出是否批准的决定。上级人民政府作出不予批准决定的，实施隔离措施的人民政府应当立即解除隔离措施。在隔离期间，实施隔离措施的人民政府应当对被隔离人员提供生活保障；被隔离人员有工作单位的，所在单位不得停止支付其隔离期间的工作报酬。隔离措施的解除，由原决定机关决定并宣布。"

《突发公共卫生事件应急条例》规定，在传染病暴发、流行区域，根据传染病疫情控制和突发事件应急处理的需要，突发事件应急指挥部和县级以上政府及其卫生行政主管部门，必要时有权对人员进行疏散或采取隔离措施。在突发事件中需要接受隔离治疗、医学观察措施的病人、疑似病人和传染病病人密切接触者在卫生行政主管部门或者有关机构采取医学措施时应当予以配合；拒绝配合的，由公安机关依法协助强制执行。有关单位和人员不配合或拒绝接受在突发事件应急处理中采取的隔离措施，对有关责任人员依法给予行政处分或者纪律处分；触犯《治安管理处罚条例》，构成违反治安管理行为的，由公安机关依法予以处罚；构成犯罪的，依法追究刑事责任。

《国境卫生检疫法》规定，国境卫生检疫机关对检疫传染病染疫人必须立即将其隔离,隔离期限根据医学检查结果确定;对检疫传染病染疫嫌疑人应当将其留验,留验期限根据该传染病的潜伏期确定。

强制隔离的地点一般是在医疗机构,但也可能是其他指定场所。根据《传染病防治法》的规定,在隔离期间,实施隔离措施的人民政府应当为被隔离人员提供生活保障;被隔离人员有工作单位的,所在单位不得停止支付隔离期间的工作报酬。疾病预防控制机构、医疗机构不得泄露涉及个人隐私的有关信息、资料。

(七) 行政管束

行政管束是指违反公民的意愿或未经其同意,暂时全面的剥夺其行动自由。

1. 保护性管束

保护性管束是为保护公民的人身安全而采取的管束措施。当公民因为故意或者意志丧失而可能导致严重自伤或自杀行为时适用保护性管束。《治安管理处罚法》第15条第2款规定:"醉酒的人在醉酒状态中,对本人有危险或者对他人的人身、财产或者公共安全有威胁的,应当对其采取保护性措施约束至酒醒。"这里所规定的"保护性措施"就是保护性管束,但因对他人的人身、财产或者公共安全有威胁而采取的管束措施,不应属于保护性管束措施。

2. 安全性管束,

这是为维护社会治安秩序和公共安全而对具有一定人身危险性的被管束人进行的管束。《人民警察法》第14条规定:"公安机关的人民警察对严重危害公共安全或者他人人身安全的精神病人,可以采取保护性约束措施。需要送往指定的单位、场所加以监护的,应当报请县级以上人民政府公安机关批准,并及时通知其监护人。"这里的保护性约束措施实际上应为安全性管束,《治安管理处罚法》第15条第2款规定的因对他人的人身、财产或者公共安全有威胁而采取的管束措施,也应属于安全性管束措施。

我国目前对行政管束的程序、期限等缺乏具体规定。全国人大常委会于2011年6月30日通过,自2012年1月1日起开始施行的《行政强制法》对行政强制措施的实施程序作了详细规定,这些规定可以适用于行政管束。

(八) 留置盘问

1. 概念

留置盘问是指公安机关为维护社会治安秩序,在一定时间内剥夺公民的人身自由,并对其进行盘问的一种治安行政措施。

2. 法律依据

《人民警察法》对留置盘问做了原则性规定。公安部的行政规章《公安机关适用继续盘问规定》（2004 年 6 月）做了细化规定。

3. 法律性质

实践中对于留置盘问是行政强制措施还是刑事强制措施存在争论，最高人民法院行政庭曾于 1997 年 10 月 29 日作出（1997）法行字第 21 号《关于对当事人不服公安机关采取的留置措施提起诉讼法院能否作为行政案件受理的答复》，认为留置是公安机关行政管理职权的一种行政强制措施，属于《行政诉讼法》第 11 条第 1 款第 2 项规定的人民法院行政诉讼受案范围。

留置盘问虽然不属于刑事诉讼强制措施，但在刑事侦查实践中，却被大量地运用。与拘传相比，留置盘问更具有强制力、条件更低、运用更加灵活。为了方便，许多刑事警察明明知道嫌疑人的行为已经构成刑事犯罪，仍弃正规的刑事诉讼强制措施的拘传不用，而采用留置盘问这种行政措施来查处刑事案件，导致在司法实践中留置盘问在一定程度上被滥用。

4. 决定与执行

根据《人民警察法》第 9 条，"为维护社会治安秩序，公安机关的人民警察对有违法犯罪嫌疑的人员，经出示相应证件，可以当场盘问、检查；经盘问、检查，有下列情形之一的，可以将其带至公安机关，经该公安机关批准，对其继续盘问：（一）被指控有犯罪行为的；（二）有现场作案嫌疑的；（三）有作案嫌疑身份不明的；（四）携带的物品有可能是赃物的。对被盘问人的留置时间自带至公安机关之时起不超过二十四小时，在特殊情况下，经县级以上公安机关批准，可以延长至四十八小时，并应当留有盘问记录。对于批准继续盘问的，应当立即通知其家属或者其所在单位。对于不批准继续盘问的，应当立即释放被盘问人。经继续盘问，公安机关认为对被盘问人需要依法采取拘留或者其他强制措施的，应当在前款规定的期间作出决定；在前款规定的期间不能作出上述决定的，应当立即释放被盘问人"。

《人民警察法》对等候继续盘问的专门场所没有规定。各地公安机关设置"留置室"作为等候继续盘问的专门场所，但一些地方设置"留置室"不规范和"留置室"不能保障被盘问人基本人权等问题突出，甚至发生被盘问人在"留置室"自杀的事故。为解决这些问题，《公安机关适用继续盘问规定》规定："县、市、旗公安局或者城市公安分局经报请设区的市级以上公安机关批准，可以在符合下列条件的公安派出所设置候问室：（一）确有维护社会治安秩序的工作需要；（二）警力配置上能够保证在使用候问室时由人民警察值班、看管和巡查。县、市、旗公安局或者城市公安分局以上公安机关及其内设机构，不得设置候问室"。候问室必须经过设区的市级以上公安机关验收合格后，才能投入使用。

（九）行政拘留与立即拘留

根据《治安管理处罚法》（原《治安管理处罚条例》）、《中国公民出境入境管理法》、《外国人入境出境管理法》、《集会游行示威法》、《枪支管理法》、《居民身份证法》、《消防法》、《道路交通安全法》等法律的规定，我国的公安机关和国家安全机关有权按照行政程序拘留违反行政管理秩序的公民，这被称为行政拘留。

此处应讨论的一个问题是，立即拘留与行政拘留的关系。所谓立即拘留，是指人民警察和有关人员在处置突发事件时，依据《集会游行示威法》和《戒严法》等法律，对实施严重危害社会治安秩序行为，并且不服从命令的人员在现场宣布剥夺其人身自由的强制性措施。立即拘留是什么性质？有人认为，立即拘留是一种特殊性质的行政拘留。而有人则认为，立即拘留与行政拘留在所依照的法律、适用条件、适用程序、立法意图上都有不同，因此构成一种与刑事拘留、行政拘留并列的拘留类型。我们认为，立即拘留是一种行政强制措施，与作为行政处罚的一般所谓的行政拘留具有不同的性质。立即拘留本身不是惩罚，它是人民警察在严重危害社会治安秩序的突发事件的当场采取的措施，以控制、平息事态为目的，它不是对被拘留人员的最后处理，在实行立即拘留之后，对被拘留的人还必须根据具体情况作出行政拘留或刑事拘留的决定。根据《集会游行示威法实施条例》等法律法规的规定，对于被立即拘留的人员，公安机关应当在二十四小时以内进行讯问。根据其情节轻重作出相应的处理：对情节轻微的人予以释放；对情节较重的人依照《治安处罚条例》予以拘留；对情节严重构成犯罪的追究其刑事责任。

（十）其他相关措施

1. "双规"与"双指"

"双指"的法律依据是《行政监察法》第 20 条的规定："监察机关在调查违反行政纪律行为时，可以根据实际情况和需要采取下列措施……（三）责令有违反行政纪律嫌疑的人员在指定的时间、地点就调查事项涉及的问题作出解释和说明，但是不得对其实行拘禁或者变相拘禁……""双规"的依据是《中国共产党纪律检查机关案件检查工作条例》第 28 条的规定，党的纪律检查机关组织的违纪案件调查组有权按照规定程序，"要求有关人员在规定的时间、地点就案件所涉及的问题作出说明"。

从《行政监察法》和《检查工作条例》的规定本身来看，并没有将"双规"与"双指"作为强制性剥夺公民人身自由的措施，行政监察法还特别强调"不得对其实行拘禁或变相拘禁"。但由于条文规定得比较模糊，在条文中既没有规定在什么时间，多长时间，也没有规定在什么地点。纪检监察机关为了办案需要而无限扩充其内涵，导致在实践中这两项措施演变为强制性剥夺人身自由措施，甚至作为一种刑事强制措施，针对有明确犯罪嫌疑的人。纪检监察机关往往将被调查人由办案人员带至纪检监察机关自己的办案点或自办的宾馆、招待所的房间，由纪检监察机关抽调的人员二十四小时轮班"陪同"（实际上是看守），并不得与外界任何人接触，也不得与家人见面或通信、通电话。同时将其随身携带的物品和财物强行扣留和检查。这一措施的执行时间长短则由办案人员视办案情况而定，多的甚至有 1～2 年。"双规"、"双指"的决定程序也比较简单，有的地方是纪委书记办公会研究决定，有的是纪委常委研究决定，有的是办案人员直接请示分管书记批准即可，有的根据"双规"人员的级别和管理权限分别决定，等等。在通知被"双规"人员时，有的通过所在党委通知，有的直接通知本人，有的有书面决定，有的就直接电话通知，也没有统一的规范。

2. 工读学校

工读学校教育是对品德行为偏常及有违法或轻微犯罪行为的未成年学生进行教育和挽救的一种特殊的教育形式。《未成年人保护法》（第18条）、《预防未成年人犯罪法》（第35条、36条）对工读学校做了规定。

工读学校起源于苏联卫国战争时期。我国第一所工读学校于 1955 年在北京市海淀区开办。我国曾经有 180 所工读学校，但近年来工读学校数量每年以 3%～4% 的速度下降，截至 2005 年 6 月份，全国仅存工读学校 68 所，且其中 4 所没有学生。同时工读学校的分布和发展也很不平衡，主要集中在北京、上海、重庆等 20 多个大中城市，而包括河北、山东等人口大省在内的 8 个省区尚未建立工读学校。据中国青少年研究中心的调查数据显示，40% 的工读学校得不到当地政府重视；近 50% 的工读学校所在地政府自从1987 年后没有出台工读教育的地方政策、法规和文件；65% 的工读学校办学经费不足；一半以上的学校教学设施简陋，无法与当地普通学校相比；60% 的学校教师待遇低。

目前各地的工读学校按照入学是自愿性质还是强制性质可分为自愿性

与强制型两种，但以自愿性为主。①自愿型。例如郑州市工读学校始建于1980年。在1988年以前，工读学校由公安和教育联合办学，招收十三至十七岁有违法和轻微犯罪行为及有严重不良行为、不适宜留在原学校继续学习，但又不够劳动教养、少年收容教养或刑事处罚的中学生；学校曾入驻3名民警，协助"问题"学生的教育转化工作。对这些"问题"学生送到工读学校可以采取强制措施。1986年《治安管理处罚条例》颁布实施后，郑州市建起了少管所。从那时起，工读学校遵循三同意（家长、学生和学校）的原则，招生方向有所改变，现在变为挽救、教育、矫治具有不良心理、不良行为青少年的教育场所，不良行为具体表现为经常打架、旷课、逃学、小偷小摸、常与同学发生纠纷等行为。再如北京工读学校招生实行的也是"三自愿"原则，即孩子进入工读学校必须经过原学校、学生本人及家长三方同意。但实践中做到三方同意很困难。学生往往宁肯在社会上无所事事地游荡，也不愿进入工读学校受约束。而在不少家长的眼中，工读学校是"坏孩子的集中营"，他们担心孩子在里面会受到交叉感染，同时也有一部分家长认为孩子在工读学校就读有失面子，因此不愿送孩子进去。②强制型。目前有些地方的工读学校是强制型的，例如浦东新区工读学校。它的教育对象是年满十三周岁，有违法或轻微犯罪行为的青少年学生，经学校和有关部门教育不改的，报教育、公安机构批准送工读学校。其办理程序是：原学校提名，经工读学校初审，再由原学校、工读学校、地区派出所、社会发展局教育处、新区公安局五单位共同审核盖章，批准后通知学生本人和家长。

3. 法制学校教育

法制教育学校是目前一种性质特殊的剥夺公民人身自由的场所。它既非工读学校，也不是少管所，却同样能限制甚至剥夺公民的人身自由。这种法制教育学校在全国范围内普遍存在，前一阶段在感化"法轮功"练习人员的工作中发挥了一定的积极作用。但目前我国有关的法律法规中并没有设立法制教育这类性质学校的明确规定，这一能够剥夺人身自由的法制教育学校的设立于法无据，缺乏任何的程序规定，也没有有效的救济渠道，其合法性与正当性均有不足。

三　我国行政拘禁制度的改革

（一）人性尊严原则与行政拘禁

人性尊严要求以个人本身为目的，保障个人享有自治与自决，摆脱拥有统治权的国家运用其权力毫无节制地过度主宰与控制，禁止国家凭借其统治权任意干预个人的人性尊严，将个人视为国家权力运作的单纯客体，恣意行使各种足以损害个人在身体或精神方面的同一性或完整性的统治手段。① 我国《宪法》第38条规定："中华人民共和国公民的人格尊严不受侵犯。禁止用任何方法对公民进行侮辱、诽谤和诬告陷害。"这是我国现行宪法总结了"文化大革命"中大量发生的侵犯和践踏人格尊严事件的惨痛历史教训，并参考国外宪政实践的经验作出的一项重要规定。② 这一关于人格尊严的规定，从立宪原意上考虑，固然主要是着眼于人的自尊心和自爱心，指向诸如姓名权、肖像权、名誉权和人身权等具体的权利。但并非不可以通过宪法解释的技术，将其解释为对于中国宪法价值秩序的一种宣示，"建构或诠释我国宪法权利规范的核心原理"，③ 而不仅仅是指向具体的宪法基本权利。

根据人性尊严的要求，有关机关在作出行政拘禁决定之前，应当遵循正当程序的要求，不得对违法嫌疑人实施刑讯逼供；被拘禁人有保持身体和精神完整性的权利，并应获得人道及尊重其固有的人格尊严的待遇。《公民权利和政治权利国际公约》和《禁止酷刑和其他残忍、不人道或有辱人格的待遇或处罚公约》（以下简称《禁止酷刑公约》）等国际公约的相关规定，集中体现了人性尊严原则对拘禁制度的具体要求。

被拘禁人免受酷刑或残忍的、不人道的或侮辱性的待遇或惩罚，即保持身体和精神完整性的权利，在国际人权法中具有特殊的地位，它是一项不可克减、应当不受任何限制的得到保障的权利。《公民权利和政治权利国际公约》第7条规定："任何人均不得加以酷刑或施以残忍的、不人道的或侮辱性的待遇或刑罚。特别是对任何人均不得未经其自由同意而施以医药或科学试验。"根据联合国《禁止酷刑公约》，"酷刑"系指为了向某人或第三者取得情报或供状，为了他或第三者所作或被怀疑所作的行为对他加以处罚，或为了恐吓或威胁他或第三者，或为了基于任何一种歧视的任何理由，蓄意使某人

---

① 许志雄等编《现代宪法论》，台湾元照出版公司，1999，第52页。
② 许崇德主编《中国宪法》，中国人民大学出版社，1996，第418页。
③ 林来梵：《从宪法规范到规范宪法——规范宪法学的一种前言》，法律出版社，2001，第175页。

在肉体或精神上遭受剧烈疼痛或痛苦的任何行为，而这种疼痛或痛苦又是在公职人员或以官方身份行使职权的其他人所造成或在其唆使、同意或默许下造成的。纯因法律制裁而引起或法律制裁所固有或随附的疼痛或痛苦则不包括在内。第 2 条规定，每一缔约国应采取有效的立法、行政、司法或其他措施，防止在其管辖的任何领土内出现施行酷刑的行为。任何意外情况，如战争状态、战争威胁、国内政局不稳定或任何其他社会紧急状态，均不得作为施行酷刑之理由。上级官员或政府当局之命令不得作为施行酷刑之理由。第 10 条规定，每一缔约国应保证，在对可能参与拘留、审讯或处理遭到任何形式的逮捕、扣押或监禁的人的民事或军事执法人员、医务人员、公职人员及其他人员的训练中，要充分进行关于禁止酷刑的教育和宣传。每一缔约国应将禁止酷刑列入就此类人员职责发出的规则或指示之中。第 11 条规定，每一缔约国应经常审查对在其管辖的领土内遭到任何形式的逮捕、扣押或监禁的人的拘留和处理的审讯规则、指示、方法、作法和安排，以避免发生任何酷刑事件。第 12 条规定，每一缔约国应确保在有理由认为在其管辖的领土内有施用酷刑的行为时，其主管当局应立即对此进行公正的调查。第 13 条规定，每一缔约国应确保任何声称在其管辖的领土内遭到酷刑的个人有权向该国主管当局申诉，其案件应得到该主管当局迅速而公正的审查。应采取步骤确保申诉人和证人不因提出申诉或提供证据而遭受苛待或恐吓。第 14 条规定，每一缔约国应在其法律体制内确保酷刑受害者得到补偿，并享有获得公平和足够赔偿（包括尽可能使其完全复原的费用）的可强行权利。如果受害者因受酷刑死亡，其受抚养人应享有获得赔偿的权利。

　　与《公民权利和政治权利国际公约》第 7 条主要针对人身和人格完整性、具体的、通常是暴力的攻击不同，公约第 10 条更多关注的是拘禁场所或其他不公开机构的一般状况以及拘禁的具体条件。根据联合国人权事务委员会的意见，第 7 条主要是被拘禁人一项消极的权利主张，即国家机关不应作出某些行为（禁止不良待遇），而第 10 条还包括国家保证采取某些行动的积极义务：不管经济如何困难，国家必须确定人道的拘禁条件的最低标准（人道待遇的要求）。因此，国家必须向被拘禁人提供最起码的条件以满足他们的基本需要（食物、衣服、医疗、卫生设施、通讯、光线、活动的机会和隐私等）。①

---

① 〔奥〕诺瓦克：《民权公约评注——联合国〈公民权利和政治权利国际公约〉（上）》，毕小青等译，三联书店，2003，第 182 页。

根据《公民权利和政治权利国际公约》第 8 条的规定，任何人不得使为奴役，任何人不应被强迫役使，这里的"役使"可适用于所有被想像到的一些人对另一些人的主宰或贬低的形式。公约也要求，任何人不应被要求从事强迫或强制劳动，除非一国把苦役监禁作为一种对犯罪的惩罚。这里应注意的是以下几点：[①]①这一例外仅仅适用于苦役监禁，即传统意义上的在工场或劳动营进行强迫劳动的形式，判处较轻劳动不在此列。②这一惩罚只能针对犯罪，也即严重违法行为。③作为惩罚的苦役只能由合格法庭根据明确规定该惩罚的法律所作出的刑事判决来规定。④在这种例外情况中，从事强迫或强制性劳动仍然受到一定的限制。这方面，最主要的是国际劳工组织关于废除强迫劳动的公约，包括 1930 年《强迫劳动公约》（第 29 号公约）和 1957 年《废除强迫劳动公约》（第 105 号公约）。根据相关规定，仅年龄在 18 岁与 45 岁之间，身体健全的男子才可被要求从事强迫或强制性劳动；一年中强迫或强制性劳动的最长期限累积不应超过 60 天，并且工时应与自愿工作情形下的普遍工时相对应。公约还规定了有关强迫或强制性劳动的报酬以及在事故、疾病、伤残或死亡时一定的最低社会福利请求。公约禁止将强制劳动用作政治要挟、经济发展或劳动纪律惩罚或歧视的手段。我国是国际劳工组织的成员国，尽管目前尚未加入这两个公约，但由于这两个公约属于国际劳工组织的八大"基本劳动公约"，我国应该积极创造条件，争取尽早达到国际标准。[②]

从相关国际公约的规定来看，我国目前的劳动教养等制度，将强制劳动适用于不构成犯罪的行为，直接构成了对国际公约的违反。这项制度如果仍旧保留，则从制度名称和内容设计上必须做出重要变革。被拘禁人的待遇也亟待提高，需要采取有力措施强化被拘禁人在拘禁场所的人权保护水平，提高生活福利待遇。

（二）依法行政原则

依法行政原则包括法律保留与法律优位两个方面。

1. 法律保留原则

根据法律优位原则，只要某一行政领域存在相关法律规范时，行政机关就必须予以正确执行，但其并未解决在法律规定缺位，即某一领域中不

---

① 〔奥〕诺瓦克：《民权公约评注——联合国〈公民权利和政治权利国际公约〉（上）》，毕小青等译，三联书店，2003，第 143 页。

② 周长征：《WTO 的"社会条款"之争与中国的劳动标准》，中国劳动法律网（www. zgldfl. com/nnews. asp？id=2045）2005 年 12 月 28 日。

存在相关法律规范对行政机关的授权时，行政机关是否可以进行行政活动这一问题。法律保留原则要求，在某些领域中，行政机关必须有法律的授权才能采取行政措施。

根据我国 1997 年《行政处罚法》和 2000 年《立法法》所确立的法律保留原则，对于限制人身自由的强制措施和处罚，必须有法律的依据，并且法律不得授权其他主体制定规定。但从我国目前实践情况来看，许多剥夺人身自由的行政拘禁措施都没有法律的依据，有些所依据的是全国人大常委会的批转，是否符合《立法法》中规定的"法律"的含义，也具有很大的争议。

2. 法律优位原则

法律优位原则，或称法律优先原则，要求行政必须受法律的拘束，一切行政活动（权力性行政活动与非权力性行政活动，加负担行为、授益行为以及事实行为等）均不得与法律相抵触。在某一行政领域，只要存在现行有效的法律，行政机关就必须予以适用（适用之强制），且应正确适用而不能有所偏离（偏离之禁止）。法律优位原则的功能在于防止行政活动违背法律，为了实现这一功能必须满足两项前提条件:[1] 一是确认法律规范的位阶性。行政机关制定的法规也不得与法律相抵触。二是法律必须有具体而明确的内容，一旦违反就将有制裁的效果出现。如果法律的规定空泛而无实质内容，也没有制裁的效果，则所谓法律优位原则将没有任何意义。明确性原则来自依法治国原则的要求。依法治国原则包括法安定性原则、权力分立原则、依法行政原则和保障基本权等内涵，从其中均可以导出明确性原则，其中特别是法安定性原则。在专制国家中由于法律的不确定性，统治者可以任意决定何时与如何干预私人的权利自由，而在法治国家，法律规定的构成要件与法律后果应当明确，以方便私人预知国家对自己行为的态度，并从而在此基础上安排自己的生活、处置自己的财产。

从法律优位原则来看我国的行政拘禁规定，我们可以发现存在以下问题:一是模糊性。一些规范的条文极度模糊，为有权机关恣意执法留下了空间。二是零散性。有关各类行政拘禁的规定，多是一事一定，缺乏通盘和整体考虑。三是混乱性。不同时期、不同部门颁布的规范之间缺乏协调，甚至相互冲突、矛盾，许多下位阶的规范突破了上位阶的规范。

---

[1]　吴庚:《行政法之理论与实用》，中国人民大学出版社，2005，第 53 页。

（三）比例原则、平等原则与行政拘禁制度

1. 比例原则

比例原则要求国家机关在行使裁量权时，应在其所追求的目的和为追求该目的所采取的手段给私人的权利、自由与利益所造成的损害之间进行适当的平衡。目前，诸多法治发达国家与地区均已承认比例原则为控制行政权与立法权的重要行政法原则与宪法原则，使公共利益和私人权益达到了一种协调、均衡状态，对私人利益保护发挥了极大的作用。比例原则包括三个下位阶的子原则，即适当性原则、必要性原则以及狭义比例原则。①适当性原则。这是指国家权力的设定与行使必须适合于实现公益目的。②必要性原则。必要性原则又可称为最小侵害原则，指国家权力对私人权益的影响不得超越实现公益目的的必要程度，也即有多种可能的手段均能达到公益目的，但各自对公民权利造成的侵害程度不一时，必须以必要性为标准进行审查衡量。③衡量性原则。衡量性原则或狭义比例原则，是指在所有可以达到某一公益目的的手段中，给私人权益造成损害（不利益）最小的手段，其所造成的损害仍然超过该手段所能实现的公益时，则这个公益目的就不值得追求，应该放弃。

从比例原则的角度考察我国行政拘禁制度与实施，我们可以发现，我国现行的行政拘禁制度在立法与执法环节都与比例原则的要求存在一定的距离。在立法环节，我国行政拘禁制度的主要目的是维护公共秩序，这一目的本身是正当的，但我们还要考虑所采取的行政拘禁措施能否有效地实现目的，例如强制戒毒的实施效果就值得深入研究。另外，在确定具体采取何种内容的行政拘禁时，也需要根据公民的违法行为的性质、人身危险性的大小等综合加以判断，在能达到公益目的的情形下选择对公民权利侵害最小的手段，并且所采取的手段应与其能够实现的目的相均衡，如果在现阶段不能找到一种能够有效实现某一行政目的的手段，则该目的在现阶段就可能需要被放弃。在执法过程中，除了在必要性原则和衡量性原则方面存在问题外，在适当性原则方面也存在问题。一些行政机关出于一些非法不当的目的，例如为机关创收等来实施行政拘禁。

2. 平等原则

平等原则是指同等情况同等对待，不同情况不同对待。它首先要求立法机关在制定法律时必须保证同等情况同等对待，只有在具有合理依据、能够得到客观证明时才可以作出区别对待。而对于解释、适用和执行法律的主体来说，即使其根据法律拥有一定的判断余地或裁量空间，也不能作

出恣意的决定，他们必须保证法律的统一适用，在作出差别对待时应当具有合理的依据。

我国行政拘禁的制度与实践在诸多方面与平等原则的要求尚存在很大差距。首先在制度层面，最典型的是劳动教养。作为处置罪行轻微和不够刑事处罚的行为人的一种行政措施，其实际的严厉性却大大超过了刑罚中的管制、拘役和短期自由刑，与短期自由刑的区别也不明显。在实践中，多年来一直将"两劳"（劳动改造、劳动教养）并称，这显然是违背平等原则的要求。对卖淫、嫖娼人员的收容教育存在同样的问题。而在行政拘禁执法实践中，因为权力、金钱、关系（人情）影响平等、公正执法的现象极为普遍，法律的普适性没有得到贯彻，恣意执法司空见惯。我国实践中经常采取的"搞运动"（或者所谓的"专项整治"）和"抓典型"等执法方式，严格说来都不符合平等原则的要求，带有很强的随意性。

（四）正当程序与行政拘禁制度

程序是指进行活动的方式、步骤、时限与顺序等。合理的程序设置一方面对于实体目标的实现具有工具价值，另一方面也具有自身的内在价值，例如对私人法律主体性的尊重等。我国法制建设中长期以来存在"重实体、轻程序"的倾向，对行政程序法不够重视，欠缺基本的程序规定，在各种部门行政法律规范中所规定的程序往往是基于限制公民自由的目的而不是控制和制约行政机关的权力，因此特别需要利用正当程序原则作为行政执法活动所应遵守的最低限度程序义务。这在行政拘禁领域也体现得非常明显。

行政拘禁的程序设计，应当贯彻正当程序等法律原则的要求，重视对公民权利的保障。首先应当明确，行政拘禁作为剥夺公民人身自由、严重侵害公民基本权利的措施和制度，必须要纳入司法程序，由人民法院决定。将剥夺人身自由的处分纳入司法程序是各国通例，例如德国《基本法》第104条规定："只有法官才能对准许和继续剥夺自由作出裁决。如果不依据法官命令作出剥夺自由时，应该立即获得司法裁决。"荷兰《宪法》第113条规定："剥夺自由的判决只能由司法机关作出。"我国已经签署的《公民权利和政治权利国际公约》第9条对此也作了规定。当然对出于紧急情况的特殊情形，可以设定例外，由行政执法人员当场立即作出决定并制定，但事后也必须立即将案件移交法院。我国《宪法》第37条规定："中华人民共和国公民的人身自由不受侵犯。任何公民，非经人民检察院批准或者决定或者人民法院决定，并由公安机关执行，不受逮捕。禁止非法拘禁和以其他方法非法剥夺或者限制公民的人身自由，禁止非法搜查公民的身体。"对这一规定中的"逮捕"存在两种解释。一种观点认为，这里的逮捕仅指刑事诉讼法中对犯罪嫌疑人采取的强制措施，从而对行政性强制措施不需要经过这样的程序。另一种观点对逮捕作广义的理解，认为逮捕是采用强制方式使相关人员到案的一种措施，每一种剥夺人身自由的措施都包括逮捕与将被逮捕人拘禁于一定场所这两个阶段，从而行政机关限制公民人身自由必须经过司法机关（法院、检察院）的决定或者批准，否则就是非法拘禁。从法治国家和尊重与保障人权的原则出发，我们倾向于对其加以扩大解释。

这里存在的一个概念上的问题，在现有的行政拘禁改由法院而非行政机关决定后，还能否称作"行政"拘禁？我们认为结论应当是肯定的。理由是：其一，这种行为的目的是出于行政目的，这一制度是国家行政管理制度的一环；其二，在程序上它是由行政机关向法院提出申请，而非由私人或者检察机关提出申请；其三，行政强制执行这一概念中即包括行政机关申请人民法院强制执行，可见即使冠以"行政"二字并不意味着必须由行政机关作出决定。

其次，行政拘禁程序的制度设计上，应贯彻以下原则：①公开原则。除非涉及国家秘密、个人隐私和未成年人等案件以外，应一律公开审理。②尊重公民的程序主体地位，保障公民的陈述权、质证权和辩护权。公民有权对行政机关提出的事实和证据进行反驳或者提出证据，证明不应对自己适用行政拘禁。作为裁判依据的证据、事实和适用法律的意见，必须经过控辩双方的当庭质证和辩论。公民有权请律师为自己辩护。③在诉讼资料的收集上，应采取职权探知原则。这是考虑到在我国行政机关拥有强大的行政权，并且常以保密等各种理由拒绝公民获得证据，公民调查事实、收集证据以及对法律掌握的能力都无法与行政机关相抗衡，而且由于大多数行政诉讼的代理费用较少，并且阻力和压力大，不能吸引更多的律师（特别是优秀律师）作为代理人参与诉讼；因此，如果实行辩论主义，必将严重影响行政审判的实体公正，不利于对相对人权益的保护。以职权探知主义为基础应当体现在下列方面：法院的决定不以行政机关所主张的事实为限，而应当从行政拘禁的合法要件出发对其进行全面审查；法院对于有助于查明行政拘禁申请合法性的证据，应当依职权进行积极全面的调查；公民当事人的自认对于法院没有拘束力，法院仍应当调查必要的证据。④实行二审终审，保障公民的上诉权。⑤及时性原则。"迟来的正义为非正义"，根据有关国际公约的规定，任何人都享有其诉讼案件在合理期限内得到审理的权利。行政拘禁由于涉及公民人身自由的剥夺，其决定对公民具有重大影响，而且实践中往往还进行先行羁押，因此其程序应当及时、迅速进行，使案件在必要且合理的期限内得到解决。

最后，行政拘禁程序应体现出与刑事诉讼程序的不同。可以借鉴美国民事收容程序，由有关机关（包括公安机关、医疗机构、教育机构等）直接向人民法院提出申请，由人民法院作出裁决。如果在司法改革中能够设立行政法院，则由行政法院负责对行政拘禁申请的受理和裁决。

（五）权利救济与行政拘禁

"有权利必有救济，有损害必有赔偿。"公法权利救济制度的完善程度是评价一国法制发展水平的重要标准。我国自从 1989 年制定《行政诉讼法》以来，在公法权利救济制度建设方面有了长足进展。行政诉讼、行政复议、信访以及行政赔偿和补偿等权利救济方式逐步完善，为因合法权益受到违法或不当行政行为侵犯的公民或组织提供了较为多样和有效的救济途径。但是，我国权利救济制度也面临着重大的挑战，在行政拘禁领域尤其如此，这突出表现在现有救济途径的公正性与实效性存在很大的不足，一些重要的救济途径也有待建立。

1. 完善司法审查制度，增强司法救济的实效性

法治国家在一定程度上意味着是司法国家，司法权对制约行政权的滥用、保障公民的权利和自由具有重要作用。我国《行政诉讼法》确立了法院对具体行政行为的合法性进行审查的基本原则，系统的、完整的司法审查制度随着《行政诉讼法》的颁布而得以确立。司法审查在维护法制统一、保障公民权利、确保依法行政、化解社会矛盾等方面具有重要价值。但我国的《行政诉讼法》对行政诉讼受案范围的限制过于严格，应加以扩充。①设立行政法院，切实保证行政审判的独立性。行政审判独立的功能在于排除行政审判活动中的法外干涉，我国作为一个行政权长期占据优势、司法权威一直未能确立的国家，更需要采取切实有效的措施保证行政审判的独立。在造成目前行政审判难的诸多因素中，由于司法不独立而造成的执法不公正是最核心也是最棘手的一环。我们认为，为了保障我国行政审判的独立性，可以设立相对独立的行政法院，各级行政法院的活动经费由中央财政直接拨付，行政法院的人、财、物权由最高人民法院集中掌握，不受行政机关的控制，设在地方的行政法院不向地方人大负责和报告工作。同时提高行政法官的素质，以精英化、专业化为指导思想建设行政法官队

伍，确立和实行统一、严格的法官任用和考核标准。②扩大司法审查的范围。第一，应当逐步确立对部分抽象行政行为的司法审查权。根据我国《行政诉讼法》的规定，法院只能对行政机关的具体行政行为进行审查。但目前行政机关对行政拘禁制定的一些行政规范性文件存在很多问题，例如越权现象严重，制定程序随意性较大，其内容很多不符合宪法规定的法治国家和人权保障原则的要求，与上位法抵触等。对其给公民权利造成的损害应当予以救济。应当将那些直接干预公民自由权利的抽象行政行为纳入司法审查范围。第二，关于特别权力关系的救济。特别权力关系理论通行于第二次世界大战前的德国和日本等国家。所谓特别权力关系，是指在特定的行政领域内个人对国家具有较强紧密性和附属性的关系。如公务员或军人与国家的关系，公立学校的学生与学校的关系，监狱服刑人与监狱的关系等。特别权力关系理论因为不利于对人权的保障，第二次世界大战后已经被逐步加以废除。我国虽然没有明确采纳特别权力关系的理论，但法制实践受到特别权力关系理论影响。应当允许对传统的特别权力关系领域的争议提起行政诉讼，这对于行政拘禁领域特别重要。目前发生在行政拘留执行场所的违法现象很多，但却缺乏有效的救济，使得执行场所成为正义不及的领域，这种现象亟待改变。③严格司法审查的标准。在现代社会，行政机关拥有较大的裁量权，但是行政裁量权绝不是任意裁量权，行政机关在进行裁量时虽然没有法律的明确规定，但仍然需要遵守一些法律的基本原则，如平等原则、比例原则、诚实信用原则和正当法律程序原则等，而不能恣意行事。依法行政中的"法"不仅包括国家的成文法，那些作为法律价值载体的基本法律原则同样也是法，如果行政机关的行为严重违反了这些原则，也属于违法行政，法院就可以撤销这样的行政行为。在行政拘留领域给公民合法权益造成侵害的许多行为，从形式上看并没有违反法律的明确规定，但却属于违反比例原则等法律原则的行为，对此法院必须予以救济。

2. 设立公安（警察）行政复议委员会，增强行政复议的公正性

我国目前行政复议的制度设计，一律采取行政化和反司法化的思路，强调复议组织对行政首长的依附性和程序的简便高效，而没有考虑到不同行政领域的特殊性。我们认为，由于行政拘禁所属的领域属于专业性、敏感性的领域，外部监督受到很大的限制，而对人权保障又具有很大的威胁，因此对此领域中行政复议制度的设计，应遵循司法化的改革思路，着眼于行政复议的权利救济功能，要求强化复议组织的独立性和程序的正式性。

目前可在公安系统设立独立的行政复议委员会，其人员配备和职权行使具有独立性，以保障决定的中立性与公正性；增设回避制度和禁止单方面接触制度；保障当事人陈述意见的机会；完善行政复议机构口头听取意见程序；增设言词辩论的正式听证程序；对行政复议机关增设说明理由的义务。

　　3. 建立中国的督察专员制度，创新监督和救济手段

　　督察专员是一种对国家行政和司法活动进行监督的特别机构，世界上第一位督察专员是 1809 年在瑞典设立的，他是由瑞典议会选任的高级官员，负责调查和建议解决公民对司法机关和行政机关不良行为的申诉。最初这个制度影响了瑞典的邻邦——挪威和芬兰。第二次世界大战后先是丹麦仿效，并开始引起其他国家的注意。到目前，全世界有八十多个国家设立了督察专员制度，包括新西兰、英国、澳大利亚、法国、意大利、加拿大（一些州）和美国（部分州）等。督察专员有的设立在议会，也有设立在政府行政部门的，前者称为议会督察专员，后者则一般专业性比较强，如卫生行政督察专员、消费者督察专员等。督察专员不仅监督违法的行政行为，而且对于各种行政管理不良的行为（不良行政），例如行政机关的官僚作风，拖拉推诿恶习，不负责任的言行等，同样可以采取一定的措施。督察专员容易接近，效率高，办事比其他管理机构快捷，而且不收费。通过视察、调查和审理控诉案件，对于确有违法或不当行为的行政官员，督察专员可以根据情节轻重，给予忠告，或公开批评，或要求有关当局予以停职或撤职等纪律处分，或对其直接提出追诉，追究其法律责任。督察专员对官吏作出的处理决定以及每年向议会作的书面报告，报刊上经常给予详细登载，这对于行政机关及其工作人员的违法不良行为，具有一定的抑制作用。

　　借鉴议会督察专员制度，建立中国的人大督察专员制度，对于保障我国公民的合法权益、控制不良行政具有现实意义，也具有可行性。人民代表大会制度是我国的根本政治制度，各级人民政府都由人大产生，并向人大负责。由于在实践中，行政机关的违法行政和不良行政的现象比较严重，近年来人大制度建设的一个重要方向就是加强对行政机关的监督，通过建立监督专员制度，由人大选任或聘请通晓行政和法律专业知识的人士作为监督专员，受理相对人的控诉，对行政机关进行监督，符合我国人大的性质以及人大制度的发展方向。为了对实践中问题较为突出的行政领域，包括行政拘禁领域，消除民众与社会的不满，在行政机关内部也同样可以设立专业性的监督专员。

4. 扩大对违法受到行政拘禁的公民的国家赔偿范围

（1）关于国家负责赔偿的行政侵权行为范围。第一，应将违法的抽象行政行为造成的损害纳入赔偿范围。第二，对于具体行政行为的违法性应作扩大解释。具体行政行为的违法不仅包括行政机关违反了成文法的明确规定，例如法定的权限和程序等，还包括行政机关违反一般法律原则滥用行政裁量权。

（2）关于国家负责赔偿的侵权损害范围。我国目前国家赔偿的计算标准采慰抚性原则，称为"生存权保障原则"，也即对受害者所受财产损失只赔偿直接损失而不赔偿间接损失；人身权所受损害只赔偿身体所受损害及直接损失而不赔偿精神痛苦及间接损失，且有最高额限制。与民事侵权法赔偿实际损失相比，国家赔偿的计算标准更低。我们认为对赔偿的计算标准可改采补偿性原则，提高国家赔偿的计算标准，与民事赔偿标准达到基本一致。第一，对人身自由权的赔偿额应当提高到一个适当的幅度。第二，造成身体健康权伤害的，应当参照《民法通则》的规定对受害人的实际损失予以赔偿。第三，造成财产权损害的，不仅应赔偿直接损失，还应赔偿间接损失。第四，应当扩大对精神损害的财产赔偿（抚慰金）。考虑到我国经济发展的现状，对精神损害予以赔偿应当有所限制，一般可限于生命权、身体权以及健康权遭受损害的情形，若人身自由遭受侵犯有其他严重情节的，也应给予赔偿。

The Current Situation and the Reform of the System of Administrative Detention in China

Li Honglei

【 **Abstract** 】 Administrative detention refers to the system whereby state administrative organs or other organizations authorized by law or administrative regulations take the administrative act of depriving citizens of their personal freedom in the process of public administration. Administrative detention in China mainly takes the forms of reeducation through labor (including drug rehabilitation through labor) (laodong jiaoyang), detention for education (shourong jiaoyang or shourong jiaoyu), coercive treatment (qiangzhi zhiliao), coercive drug rehabilitation (qiangzhi jiedu), administrative control (xingzheng guanshu), immediate detention (liji juliu) and administrative attachment (xingzheng juliu). This article carries out a comprehensive examination of the concept, scope and nature of administrative detention, as well as the concept, legal basis, applicable objects of, and remedies for, various forms of administrative detention, and puts forward suggestions on the future development of the administrative detention system in China, including implementing the principles of respecting human dignity, administration by law, proportionality, due procedure and remedies for rights.

【Key words】 Administrative Detention, Adminis Tration by Law

第三部分

刑事法治与经济社会管理法治

The Ethics of Criminal Justice[*]

Kimmo Nuotio[**]

[Abstract] In this article the author discusses the way in which one should understand criminal justice in the context of a democratic Rechtsstaat. The point is that in a democratic Rechtsstaat the entire thinking about criminal justice should be informed about certain specific view which sets the individual into the center. Even the offender must be seen as a member of the same community from which the law so defining originates, Breach of the rules by someone does not justify exclusion or simply instrumental approach to the matter. In a democratic Rechtsstaat, the role of criminal law and criminal justice should be generally minimized. An ethics of criminal justice committed to the non-utilitarian questions, the issues of what are good rules for separating legally right from wrong, and what forms of action in the last resort should be offences, that would build on mutual recognition and mutual respect, that would let these ideas penetrate all the levels of criminal justice, would mark a good polity. It would preserve the moral contents of criminal justice without turning it into moralism. It would address people as members of their community, but would leave the legal and moral responsibility for actions to individual people.

"Of all the features of social organization, criminal justice has proved the most resistant to the effect of reasoned deliberation and discussion about the nature of the

---

  * Originally a paper presented at the Democratic Criminal Justice conference, Law Faculty, University of Warsaw, Poland, 14 – 15 October 2006.

  ** Professor, Faculty of Law, University of Helsinki.

good society and the good polity. " -Philip Pettit①

I. Introduction

The saying is that criminal procedure is a "seismograph" or "barometer" of the constitution of a state. ② This is true indeed. When the former socialist countries joined the Council of Europe during the 1990s, criminal procedure broadly understood was a key issue meriting a lot of attention and work. The socialist legal practices did not satisfactorily guarantee the procedural rights of the accused. Many deficiencies were related to problematic institutional arrangements, such as the extensive powers of the investigating authorities, the lack of independence of many of the key actors in the state machinery, and deficient organization of defence. All these features made the necessary reforms rather deep-going. For many years this was a central issue for European Covention on Human Rights as well. The West quite literally learned that the human rights law had implications for the constitutional design of a state, not merely for minor details of procedural arrangements.

By starting with the problems of transition from socialist criminal justice to a western human-rights inspired and constitutionally anchored conception, I wish to draw attention to the fact that criminal justice is indeed an important defining factor when we look at certain general characteristics of polities and how individuals and groups are being treated in them. The legally guaranteed freedom of the citizens of these socialist countries was very different from what we expect in a country that supposedly offers its citizens full protection vis-á-vis the state itself. Measured by socialist yardsticks, the human rights situation was perhaps not all that detrimental, because the underlying understanding of individual rights was different. The interests of society generally counted for more than the rights of the individual. Law was more a matter of needs than of rights. As long as the state was regarded as good by definition, there was no need to worry about legal safeguards. The "goodness" of a polity thus depends on the yardsticks chosen. Since the collapse of socialist law, the western view of what a good polity should look like has fewer alternatives, but we should keep in mind that the yardsticks are not fixed

---

① Philip Pettit, "Is Criminal Justice Politically Feasible?", 5 Buff. Criminal Law Review 427, p. 427.

② Claus Roxin, Strafverfahrensrecht. 20. Auflage. C. H. Beck: München 1987, p. 9.

beforehand. We need to look at the issue of yardsticks as part of our exercise.

If we look at substantive criminal laws instead of criminal procedure, the differences between socialist laws and western laws were probably less eye-catching. Surely the socialist criminal laws had characteristics of their own, including a different understanding of what was actually wrong with criminal offences. The emphasis on "social dangerousness" or "social harmfulness" of the act led to offences such as hooliganism being regarded as severe. The rating of the severity of offences was different. The attitudes of the offenders counted for more than in the liberal west. Such features certainly had some impact on the exercise of rights under such circumstances.

I do not wish to turn this presentation into a general comparison of various kinds of actual criminal justice systems and their implications for the rights of the citizens. Instead, I wish to say something about how the legitimacy of criminal justice builds on democracy and respect for human rights. I also wish to say a few words on why democracy and human rights are perhaps not enough in themselves, when we discuss the premises of good criminal justice. The missing pieces I will try to abstract out of something that could be called social and historical experience concerning criminal justice. The rise and fall of *Rechtsstaat* has recently been depicted by Vagn Greve among others. [1] I believe that problems related to repressive law are very useful when we wish to understand general issues related to polities, citizenship, etc. . We might learn important things as regards normative political theory by bringing these historically more limited criminal justice issues onto the table of political thinking.

II. Reconstructing a Democratic *Rechtsstaat*

In a Hobbesian world, it would be enough for the people that they were able to predict the actions of the authorities sufficiently to plan their lives. Legislation needs to be put in place, and it is the duty of the sovereign to do what is needed.

It is true that this stage already means a significant step forward from conditions of anarchy. In a Hobbesian Leviathan, the institutionalisation of rights of the

---

[1] "Sheep or Wolves", *European Journal of Crime, Criminal Law and Criminal Justice.* Vol. 13/4 (2005): 515–532.

individual is only partial. An individual would have no say as far as the content of laws is concerned. According to this model, political rights of the citizens are not part of the social contract.

The philosophy of enlightenment introduced views that built on a stronger position for citizens vis-à-vis the sovereign power. In a democratic *Rechtsstaat*, it was thought, people could achieve a new level of legality, that of the legislation being " self-legislation ". The *Rechtsstaat* of sovereign people was to be characterized by the fact that the political legitimacy of criminal justice and the corresponding penal practices flow from the general legitimacy of laws under such conditions.

The concept of a democratic *Rechtsstaat* has been discussed by Jürgen Habermas. [①] The analysis in that book builds heavily on Kantian premises. The idea is that the public reason will be made operative in the structures of a state when the communicative flows from the society to the political and legal system have been secured by institutionalizing the fundamental rights and democratic principles in the constitution, the core of the legal system. In a democratic *Rechtsstaat*, the citizenship grows to its full potential, enabling a balanced exercise of rights for the individuals in both roles, the private and the public. People can make use of their liberties in social life as they participate in political decision-making.

The normative reconstruction that Habermas has carried out is useful in itself, showing how the legitimacy of modern law is based on a complex falling together of various pieces, enabling us to understand both the permanent challenges and conditions of the legitimacy of modern law as well as the " positive " nature of modern law in the changeability of its contents. The procedural aspects of modern law account for the fact that we cannot define substantially the contents of law by referring to reason or rationality, since these substantial issues have to be debated, and political decisions have to be taken.

The formal aspects of the legal system also enable legal progress in terms of

---

① *Between facts and norms: contributions to a discourse theory of law and democracy*, translated by William Rehg. Polity Press, Cambridge 1996; *Faktizität und Geltung. Beiträge zur Diskurstheorie des Rechts und des demokratischen Rechtsstaats.* Suhrkamp, Frankfurt a. M. 1992.

further institutionalization of new types of civil rights. In human rights terminology, we usually speak of various generations of human rights and fundamental rights. The rights to freedom and the political rights have been supplemented by new types of social and cultural rights, not to mention environmental rights or rights of those of the next generations. As such changes happen, the social contract, the project of living under a constitution, is in fact being renegotiated.

For Habermas, the actual legal order represents a system of rights that has been manifested in the legislation and court practice. This order is constantly developing as decisions are being taken that define legal rights and obligations in practice.

Understood this way, the *Rechtsstaat* and the social welfare state are not in opposition, but are different stages of development of a state and the legal order. The formal structures of the *Rechtsstaat* have opened the way to a development towards a social welfare state as new types of rights and laws have been introduced. At the same time, however, the social welfare state which adopts new types of functions and policies still needs to accommodate its formal constitutional structures. The legitimacy of the legal system continues to build on the original structures. The welfare state also needs to be a *Rechtsstaat*.

III. Criminal Justice as Part of a Normative Reconstruction of a Democratic *Rechtsstaat*

Some words now need to be said about how criminal justice fits into this picture. Is criminal law a legitimate part of general laws? Is it alright that the public decides to fight criminality by resorting to criminal justice? And what about the move from a minimalist *Rechtsstaat* towards an interventionist welfare state? Is criminal law part of the original liberal *Rechtsstaat*, or is the criminal law of a social welfare state different? Is there something specific about criminal law and how does "*Rechtsstaatlichkeit*" connect with it?

I think that criminal justice presents a problem for the general Habermasian approach to begin with. The defence of the voice of the people, and ultimately of the communicative reason, is so dominant in that theory that it seems to entail the risk of legitimating too much of positive law. Criminal justice could be just the area in which this might easily be the case being almost by definition based on positive law. This positiveness does not guarantee much internal quality. Additional substantial requirements need to be put in place, which is where we get started.

I believe that there is indeed a sense in which criminal law needs to preserve more of its *Rechtsstaatlichkeit* than do other branches of law. The core values and principles of criminal law continue to be limiting and protective, because we are dealing with repressive law. The principle of legality with its various dimensions, the principle of culpability, and the *ultima ratio* principle are all part of the *Rechtsstaat* tradition, and all have a close connection with the constitution since they all represent constitutional values in some sense. A strictly and legally limited system of criminal law is actually a condition for effective protection of fundamental rights. Without strict legality, many of our rights could be endangered. *Rechtsstaatlichkeit* is a matter of culture, a matter of doing things.

Criminal justice also has its aims and policies, and needs to justify itself by the promise of some functionality. Criminal law needs to deliver goods; it needs to grant protection to various rights and interests. It needs to be socially relevant. The German key word is *Rechtsgüterschutz*, protection of legal interests. The defensive aspects of *Rechtsstaatlichkeit* are related to some sort of offensive goal. Criminal law needs to satisfy expectations both as regards its substantive content as well as its form.

The tension between the form and substance, between defensive and offensive also manifests itself in the two aspects of criminal law norms as rules of behavior. Criminal law norms on setting some forms of conduct under the threat of punishment can be regarded either as intervention on the part of legislature, or as expressions of certain fundamental values. Quite often, both of these understandings are possible. Having provisions on theft or murder in the penal code can be regarded as an expression of shared values in the community. Since it is very unlikely that practices such as theft and murder could be publicly defended politically, we do not take such regulations to be of interventionist nature. It is really not a matter of communicating censure. Rather, the polity can be seen as defining itself by deciding on questions of right and wrong. No sharp distinction between these two types of law is possible, being more a matter of degree, and a matter of perspective.

In multicultural societies, different groups could look at the criminalisations differently. One group might regard the issue as already settled, whereas another might wish to contest the views adopted. The criminalization of the use of drugs would hit the community of the Indians deep, if they were longer entitled to smoke their peyote-pipes during ritual ceremonies.

The adoption of a rights perspective might also raise new issues and conflicts. Many practices that have not been regarded as legally relevant, such as the circumcision of boys, might suddenly appear as topics to be discussed. The rights perspective forces us to rethink traditional practices which, according to the new perspective, might become problematic. It is clear that the fact of multiculturalism presents new kinds of challenges from the point of view of reaching political agreements on how to deal with various kinds of issues. [1] It might often be best not to enter the field at all with criminal justice. [2]

IV. From *Rechtsstaat* to *Rechtsstaatlichkeit*

The tradition-boundness of criminal justice suggests that there is something specific about criminal law that merits attention. Our way of thinking about criminal law and issues of legitimate punishment always needs to be brought back to this *Rechtsstaat* context. We cannot adopt fully instrumentalist positions as regards criminal justice, because this would in some important sense be contrary to our presuppositions about the nature of our mutual relationships as members of the political and legal community.

As participants and members of the polity, we are all political people basically possessing the ability to participate. The concept of citizenship summarizes these presuppositions. As members of the legal community, we are legal persons who share the ability to possess rights and have duties. As legal persons we are the addressees of legal norms, and we can be held accountable for our failures to act

---

[1] Some of these I have discussed in the paper "Between Denial and Recognition: Criminal Law and Cultural Sensitivity", presented at the workshop "Criminal Law and Cultural Diversity", University of Columbia, N. Y., March 10 – 12, 2006. To be published in *Retfaerd* 1/2008 (forthcoming).

[2] Duncan Ivison, "Communication and punishment just do not sit comfortably together", in his "Justifying Punishment in Intercultural Contexts", in Matravers, *Punishment and Political Theory*. (Hart Publishing, Oxford, 1999), p. 106.

according to them. In fact, the criminal justice presupposes that issues of guilt and responsibility can be dealt with adequately within this context of legal personhood. It cannot be doubted that this double back-up of criminal justice is absolutely fundamental, because theorizing about issues such as civil disobedience requires that we be able to distinguish between these two person-roles, but simultaneously bring them into contact with each other. For political reasons, sometimes we have to understand civilly disobedient behavior, which at the surface level looks like ordinary law-breaking. Both of these roles imply that we as persons are rational, that is, that we can be moved by reasons. Both of these roles imply certain ability to deliberate, to give reasons, and to get involved in arguments. [1]

This ability to reason and to give reasons is indeed needed, when issues of criminal justice are on the agenda. *Rechtsstaatlichkeit* generally summarizes certain ethical principles, and this applies specifically in a criminal justice context. Nils Jareborg, for instance, mentions that the *ultima ratio* principle, the idea of resorting to criminal justice only when no other alternative is at hand, is an important principle of legislative ethics rather than a constitutional principle. [2] I believe that we could read into such principles of legislative ethics a view of constitutionality which is crucial for our topic. The polity which takes the principle of *ultima ratio* seriously is at the same time one which respects certain specific ethical requirements for criminal justice.

The discussion of a good polity needs, in my view, to start by recognizing that criminal justice is different, that criminal justice is in need of good reasons, and that it is a matter of an ethical discussion in general. The ethical context is also indicated by the internal links between the criminal justice and the moral and ethical as well as political reasoning.

Some abolitionists might take this ethical requirement so seriously that they would not accept the use of criminal justice at all. I think this makes sense. A good polity might be one which manages to do without criminal law and punishment in

---

[1] On the issue of the two roles of the deliberative person, see Klaus Günther, *Schuld und kommunikative Freiheit. Studien zur personalen Zurechnung strafbaren Unrechts im demokratischen Rechtsstaat.* Vittorio Klostermann, Frankfurt am Main 2005, p. 248.

[2] Nils Jareborg, "Criminalization as Last Resort (Ultima Ratio)", 2 *Ohio St. J. Crim. L.* 2005, p. 521.

the first place. A community which could arrange its internal affairs without repressive law would be ideal in some sense. As long as there are other alternatives, criminal justice is unethical, says the principle. Panu Minkkinen's view is not much less radical. He speaks in favor of a reversal of the logic of argumentation: the last resort principle, understood as a binding legal principle, forces all criminal law argument to be critical. The justification of a sentence is always conditional, because it requires the satisfaction of this very demanding principle. [1]

We might also continue the search for the ethical path further, and ask whether we really need the enforcement of punishment in order to achieve the goals we have set for criminal justice. Why is it not enough that we carry out the procedure and pass a guilty verdict on those who deserve it? It would certainly be easier to justify the use of criminal justice if this did not have to include infliction of pain. A criminal procedure would be able to perform most of the tasks that are necessary also without formal enforcement of sanctions, and without sentencing. It would allocate responsibilities and draw lines between right and wrong, it would communicate blameworthiness, give the victims of crime an opportunity to present their views and be heard, restitution could be ordered, etc.. The question of "why punish" should be dealt with sophistically enough, and it clearly has consequences as concerns the issue of a good polity. In fact, Klaus Günther has proceeded in this direction, questioning the legitimacy of inflicting punishment and defending the sufficiency of attribution of responsibility. [2] Certainly, in a good polity, the attribution of responsibility is the main task of criminal justice, not the enforcement of punishment entailing hard treatment.

We might here also refer to the experiences that have been gathered from court proceedings for international war crimes and crimes against humanity. Many traditional legal principles lose their meaning when we shift to dealing with massive human disasters. It is almost macabre to try to meet out sentences for genocide

---

[1]　Panu Minkkinen, " 'If Taken in Earnest' . Criminal Law Doctrine and the Last Resort", 45 *Howard J. of Crim. J.* 5 (2006), pp. 521 – 536.

[2]　Klaus Günther, "Responsibility and Punishment" . Draft paper presented at the 21st IVR Congress 2003, Lund, Sweden; Special Workshop on Criminal Responsibility. See also his *Schuld und kommunikative Freiheit. Studien zur personalen Zurechnung strafbaren Unrechts im demokratischen Rechtsstaat.* Vittorio Klostermann Verlag, Frankfurt am Main 2005.

according to just desert principles. In such proceedings, the aims must be something quite else. It must be necessary to go through the process, and the main point is to clarify what has happened and who can be regarded to be responsible for it. Once again, the attribution of responsibility is the crucial point, not the punishment aspects of the sentencing.

There is also something important in the fact that the historical experience, the surrounding insecurity and the weaknesses in the legitimacy of criminal justice have probably raised the significance of the protective ethical principles as an issue specifically related to crime and punishment. I would like to maintain that this ethos is very important if we wish to read further consequences as to the nature of the polity into criminal justice context. In a good polity, criminal justice would be kept with ethical limits. This might entail a general warning and caution about resorting to criminal justice measures. We need to elaborate a bit on what this might mean.

It is an important aspect of a *Rechtsstaat* that, before entering on particular legal and political issues, people recognize each other's specific roles as subjects. First, we need to regard each other as persons capable of at least some extent rational action, action arising from understandable internal reasons, and responsible for the actions taken. This recognition establishes some sort of a community between us in which we start seeing ourselves as members of the same association. At the next step, we can say that we recognize each other as holders of rights. It would be helpful to elaborate more on this stepwise foundation of a polity to see all the nuances that being part of the same polity implies and presupposes. Of course this is not a new topic: much of the history of political thinking consists of efforts to present some sort of reconstruction of the terms for a legitimate political and legal rule.

The mutual recognition as persons and as holders of rights which is part of the normative reconstruction of a *Rechtsstaat* has important implications for the ideology of criminal justice. It entails a particular picture of human agency in moral terms. In some sense it implies, at a normative level, the presupposition that people are willing to be bound by commonly agreed laws, that people are in some sense committed to the polity they are part of. It is for this reason that so-called positive general prevention is a legitimate goal for criminal justice, but not necessarily general deterrence. The former addresses citizens as responsible people instead of sources of trouble. In a *Rechtsstaat*, we should not normatively take a position that our fellow citizens need to be deterred, at least before we get some evidence that this is indeed the fact.

The theory of positive general prevention actually has several interesting aspects: it forces the we-perspective on the system, including the political system, and shifts the emphasis from punishment to the attribution of responsibility. [1] It at least indirectly disconnects criminal politics from the mechanical dynamics of raising stakes and raising punitiveness that seems to go along with the deterrence approach, according to which every crime is a proof of failed deterrence. Positive general prevention theory brings to the fore the issues of self-definition through political decision-making, seeing criminal laws more from the point of view of their symbolic-normative content than as means of combating criminality. The theory of positive criminal prevention has a different kind of approach towards what it is to abide by the law, compared with its competitor (s).

This approach has a counterpart in rehabilitation as a goal of punishment, since it re-establishes full belonging to the community when the sentence has been served. A prison sentence without such, without regaining full membership of the community, would risk being inhumane and unethical. In a good polity, prisoners continue to be members of their communities, continuing to participate in public elections, etc. , even during the time of servitude.

V. The Ethics of Criminal Justice

It should be clear by now that if we wish to look at what a good polity would have to be like, in some normative sense, and what we could expect of a good criminal justice of such a polity, democracy and human rights (or fundamental rights) are an elementary and necessary part of the conception. Still, in my view, democracy and human rights need to be placed in a wider context of a *rechtsstaatlich* ideology and culture, in order to give a full account of such a view.

Democracy without human rights runs the obvious risk of the tyranny of the

---

[1] *Positive Generalprävention. Kritische Analysen im deutsch-englischen Dialog.* Uppsala-Symposium 1996. eds. Schünemann, von Hirsch und Jareborg. C. F. Müller Verlag. Heidelberg 1996.

majority, whereas human rights without democracy runs against the presupposition that the law is ours. I think we could say that both of these requirements count nowadays as some sort of minimum requirement for an ethically defensible criminal justice. But as mentioned earlier, this does not amount to full proof of the legitimacy of criminal justice. It would be valuable to go beyond them, and see if there are other relevant ethical points of view which need to be added. These additional requirements stem in one way or another from the quality of criminal justice as repressive.

The ethical principles for the use of criminal law must be normative and idealistic in nature, because it is self-evident that actual criminal justice often fails to satisfy such high ethical criteria. The *ultima ratio* principle, for instance, has been widely neglected. The death sentence is still in use in many countries, even those that have committed themselves to human rights and democracy. It would be very difficult to present a coherent philosophy of criminal justice that would fit the current systems.

The issues concerning the qualities of a good polity are probably an optimal context for deliberations concerning what a good criminal justice should be like. It is self-evident that the history of criminal justice, the brutality of which very few of us surely wish to doubt, has a lot to offer to such a normatively ethical scrutiny.

Philip Pettit has noticed the fact that not do only undemocratic societies do badly by criminal justice, but even democracies have problems. There seems to be something like a general difficulty in legislating properly on issues relating to criminal justice, which could be seen as a weak point of democracy. Why so? Pettit claims that the answer is that criminal policy is so difficult to carry out. There is a kind of an outrage dynamic which favors offensive solutions above defensive, high penalties above low ones. In the minds of the people criminal justice promises security and freedom for the good citizens, and the more we have of it the better. The paradox of humanness is that the more sensitive we become to cruelty and violence, the more harshly we wish to react to it. The vicious circle acts by the force of a kind of psychological law. The problem with democracy is that it cannot ameliorate anything. For that reason, Pettit proposes specific institutional arrangements that could leave more room for truly informed politics. ①

---

① Philip Pettit, "Is Criminal Justice Politically Feasible?", 5 *Buff. Crim. L. Rev*; 427.

I think we could relate this finding to the general ethical mentality that I have been speaking about as *Rechtsstaatlichkeit*, since the outrage logic builds on the polarization between us and them. It is not citizens who commit crime, but "the other" . Criminal justice is there to protect us against them. In a polity that takes our perspective seriously, the criminal political talk could not adopt such a polarized perspective. Criminal politics would rather be about defining our relationships with each other. Under such conditions criminal justice would amount to a self-definition of the community.

An ethics of criminal justice committed to the non-utilitarian questions, the issues of what are good rules for separating legally right from wrong, and what forms of action in the last resort should be offences, that would build on mutual recognition and mutual respect, that would let these ideas penetrate all the levels of criminal justice, would mark a good polity. It would preserve the moral contents of criminal justice without turning it into moralism. It would address people as members of their community, but would leave the legal and moral responsibility for actions to individual people.

This sounds idealistic, certainly. We should therefore say something to the critics who will immediately raise their voices. What about crimes of violence, what about habitual criminals that do not feel at all committed to the polity? Should we really neglect the interests of the society when framing the issues of good criminal justice of a good polity?

To my mind, the crucial ideological division is whether we really commit ourselves to the we-perspective and try to design criminal justice so that it respects as far as possible the fact that the offender also is part of the community, and continues to be so despite having done something wrong. For people who are, as indicated by their criminal history, really not capable of being motivated by good moral reasons, another type of system may apply. But this is not the topic here: I wish to discuss the quality of a polity in terms of how it views the ordinary issues of justice related to crime.

Human rights are universal by nature. They are also idealistic in the sense that they are not always respected. And, as we saw before, the content of human rights may develop. Human rights represent idealism is some sense. If we wish to elaborate the sources of a criminal justice ethics we could try to point out commonalities behind such an ethics and the ethics of human rights.

I think we can clearly point out such commonalities. Both of these types of law base their rationale on some factual premises. H. L. A. Hart once spoke about the minimum content of natural law. [1] Law matters because we are all vulnerable and we need law to arrange our social life. As individuals we are not perfect; we are neither angels nor devils.

I think that the ethics needed at least partly stands on the footing of the awareness that life is full of risks, and that not even the law can guarantee full safety. We will all die anyway.

Such a basic understanding of human life adds something to the ethics of criminal justice. Even though we all possess particular capabilities, we are different in many ways. We do good things and we do bad. Some of us as are more vulnerable than others, and some of us might be more tempted to commit crime than others. My proposal is that when we reconstruct the democratic *Rechtsstaat* we should add something about this to the underlying mutual recognition structure. We should recognize certain facts of life, and not simply the rights of others. By introducing this mutual recognition of the vulnerability of life we come to understand better why repressive law faces specific challenges. Establishing an order by means of criminal justice cannot change this fundamental human condition. It cannot prevent evil from existing. Evil is part of human life irrespective of the polity in question.

This factual premise might also be phrased in terms of some sort of solidarity. Belonging to the same polity has its rationale in that our all being equal before of the challenges of life, equal in spite of our being different. Our politics need to take such relevant differences into account.

Another point in making this realistic amendment is that we will also see the facts of punishment more realistically. We should keep in mind that many forms of hard treatment, such as long-term imprisonment, have an impact on the prisoners' lives and existence that almost certainly goes much beyond what has been the original purpose of ordering such punishment. We humans are weak and vulnerable not only as offenders and victims of crime, but as objects of enforcement of sanctions as

---

[1] H. L. A. Hart, *The Concept of Law*. Second Edition. (Clarendon Press, Oxford, 1994), Ch. IX.

well. The criminal justice of a good polity takes all these matters into account. In general, I believe that in a good polity the public policy is reluctant to react to criminality with harsh punishment. A realistic approach does not tend towards increased punitiveness, but recognizes the somehow fundamental character of criminal justice. Repressive law thus needs to be dealt with as something special, as not quite ordinary law. The ethical context limits the possibility of seeing criminal justice in purely utilitarian terms. Criminal justice has to be measured by ethical yardsticks.

This ethical context of course causes tensions when criminal justice should be adapted to interventionist functions. A modern welfare state adopts by construing new types of offence, and liability structures need to follow. The culpability requirement may sometimes be dropped, and legal entities punished for crimes. The modernization of law has not left criminal justice untouched. My claim is, however, that bringing issues such as safety at work or environmental pollution into the core of criminal justice changes the ethical context. This has many consequences. Criminal justice always needs to be built according to models that respect the specifics of this branch of law. I would say that even market phenomena become ethical when we look at them in terms of criminal justice. We are forcing the market players to adopt a common we-perspective, which may be difficult for them. But, if we do not wish to impose an ethical context on actors "who act" on entirely other grounds, then we should resort to another way of managing the issue. In fact, I do not believe that companies, for instance, are incapable understanding issues of blameworthiness, social responsibility, and the like. They may calculate the costs and benefits of their decisions, and they may not be able to fully understand the moral communications of criminal justice, but as long as human actions are necessarily involved, the criminal justice may succeed in bringing the ethical aspects to the front.

If the picture that I have been painting is correct, the pressures that a polity faces when designing and operating criminal justice are not really easy to handle. The defensive, ethically contextualized model that I have presented can rather clearly be contrasted with other models. My claim is that a good polity should see the legitimacy of its criminal justice in this light, and that a criminal justice built on such premises would probably deserve to be called good at least in some sense.

Without a doubt, the approach remains at the level of a very general reconstruction. The difficulty is that the polity should, even after choosing some fundamentals of a criminal justice ideology, still have to turn these ethical building blocks into actual legal norms and institutions. In my understanding, the law's positivity also needs to be taken into account. This positivity will, however, be limited in many ways. The imagination of the legislature should be restricted by forcing it to regard issues of criminal justice as ethical issues that cannot be dealt with politically on the basis of interest representation only. They require political handling as ethical issues.

Put in another way, democracy and human rights thus require balancing. The most important thing is that criminal justice issues always need to put in the context of human rights, and cannot be separated from them. The connection with human rights guarantees that the context is right.

Some reflections need to follow now concerning the issue of feasibility of this normative program. I believe that we need to look at parliamentary decision-making. From my point of view, criminal law issues require deliberative forms of democracy. [1] The parliament needs to be able to discuss issues concerning the limits of criminalisation and other details of the legislation with due diligence. Issues concerning participation would merit much more attention than has been the case in this paper. We should have to include in such discussions topics such as lay participation, the specific legal culture of lawyers, the legal arguments in legal application and how they can be understood by the larger legal community, etc. . The legal cultures probably have significant differences in the practices adopted. How popular participation should be arranged and taken into account in the design of the system may also vary.

If we think specifically about the parliamentary level of participation, we see that this political level is also tight controlled by legal reason in a "good" polity. The enacted laws and norms need to be adapted to the existing body of law. An effective human rights or fundamental rights discourse might be valuable in this context, because it imposes a specific burden of argument on the side of those who

---

[1]　Cf. the various essays included in James Bohman and William Rehg, eds. , *Deliberative Democracy. Essays on Reason and Politics.* (The MIT Press, Cambridge, 1997) .

require resort to criminal justice. In the Finnish context the issues of legitimate criminalizations are today viewed in terms of constitutional principles in that a doctrine has been developed that sets limits to enactment of new criminalisations on the basis of fundamental rights.

Not only does the work of legislature need to be controlled legally, but the work of the judiciary as well. In my view, the natural way is to let the fundamental rights and other relevant pieces of law have an impact on the application of criminal laws. This is natural because the fundamental rights will be manifested as an effect of legal application in any case. Freedom of speech will be partly defined when the courts decide on the limits of what is regarded as punishable as insult. Why should we not let the general legal principles and the fundamental rights guide the application of penal laws?

Another thing is that we probably also need some sort of republicanist amendments to our theory. An ombudsman, for instance, might be an important additional actor ensuring that the courts and the officials stick to their roles, and that the judges and the officials also continue to take responsibilities for their actions. Even legal science has a role to play, in building bridges between different levels. It needs to elaborate on the premises of various doctrines and principles, and to assess normatively systemic premises of criminal justice. At the deepest level, criminal law theory needs to consider the roots of legitimacy of criminal justice in the more general context of a democratic *Rechtsstaat* and in the political thinking rendering the law of such a polity legitimate. Under such scrutiny, I suggest, criminal justice being of repressive character is a relevant fact.

VI. Repressive Justice?

If criminal law and criminal procedure can be regarded as good indicators of the current stage of the *Rechtsstaat*, we could also say that the criminal justice cannot do much better than the overall legal order and the constitution. The erosion of the *Rechtsstaatlichkeit* of criminal justice could, as we readily apprehend, mean the erosion of the *Rechtsstaat* itself.

There is one aspect left which is especially interesting and which affects all possible efforts to "tame" the ultimate expression of a state's authority, that is, the execution of a punishment by building ethical or constitutional limits to its use.

This relates to the fact that the right to punish, the ultimate original source of the right of the state to punish, has never really made its way into the written constitutions. [①] It is difficult to tame something which is of constitutional nature but which creeps into the state's powers without ever really being put on the table. Probably for this reason the repressive law normatively presupposes the right to punish is different and raises issues that go far beyond ordinary ones.

刑事司法的伦理学

基默·诺迪欧

【摘要】 在本文中，作者探讨的是在一个民主法治国家的框架下，应该以何种方式去理解刑事正义。作者的观点是，在一个民主法治国家中，对刑事正义的全部构想应当认识到以个人为中心的一些特定观念。尽管一个罪犯必须被看作社会的一员，且该社会的法律定义了罪犯，但是某些人对规则的违反并不能够将罪犯排除在社会之外，或使得简单的工具主义方法获得正当性。在一个民主法治国家中，刑法和刑事正义的角色总体上应当被最小化。刑事正义的伦理学致力于非功利性问题，什么是区分法律上是与非的好规则，以及在不得已的情况下何种行为构成犯罪。这些问题的研究将建立在互相承认和尊重的基础上，将渗透刑事正义的各个层次，这也是一个好的政体的标志。刑事正义的伦理学既保留刑事正义中的道德成分又不致陷于道德主义。它将人作为社会成员来处理，但同时将行动的法律责任和道德责任保留给个人。

---

① This I have discussed in "Criminal law of a transnational polity", in Müller-Dietz et al, eds. , *Festschrift für Heike Jung.* (Nomos, Baden-Baden, 2007): 685 – 698.

The Rule of Law and Criminal Law: The Constitutionalization of Criminal Law in Finland

Sakari Melander [*]

【Abstract】 Constitutionalization is without doubt one of the most significant changes in Finnish criminal law. Traditionally criminal law and constitutional law have been separated in legal science and in practice. There are, however, certain features and developments that inevitably move them closer to each other and even connect them in a manner that does not respect the traditional boundaries of these legal domains. The constitutionalization of criminal law is not uniquely a Finnish phenomenon but has also a wider scope that is related, inter alia, to the Europeanization of criminal law. The purpose of this article is to explore the constitutionalization of Finnish criminal law that has mainly taken place after the reform of the fundamental rights provisions of the Finnish Constitution in the mid-1990s. The purpose of the article is, thus, to explore the meaning and the scope of the rule of law within criminal law with first providing a brief overview on the general meaning of the rule of law. Secondly, the general trend or development of constitutionalization of Finnish criminal law is examined. Thirdly, perhaps the most significant and universal manifestation of rule of law within criminal law, principle of legality, is discussed.

* LL. D., Senior Lecturer, University of Helsinki.

Introduction

"The rule of law" might be called a truly universal value that shapes the political and legal culture of a polity profoundly. Various political and legal cultures identify and recognise the rule of law as a political ideal or a value on which the system at least ought to be constructed. It or some form of it is common to European, American, Asian and African political and legal cultures. [1] The fact that the rule of law is recognized in various political and legal cultures, however, tells us very little about the substance of those cultures. At least it tells us that rule of law as a value or at least the same phrase is recognised in various parts of the world.

It has been stated that while there seems to be unanimous and at least nearly universal understanding on the existence of "the rule of law" its exact meaning seems to be somewhat unclear. As *Brian Z. Tamanaha* has stated, "Notwithstanding its quick and remarkable ascendance as a global ideal, however, the rule of law is an exceedingly elusive notion. "[2] This means that we have no unanimous definition. The rule of law could be used in various connections with varying content. In the following, I will offer a brief overview of the connection between the rule of law and criminal law in Finland.

Firstly, I will concentrate on the character of the criminal justice system that illustrates the role given to the rule of law. If we adopt the approach to criminal law manifested by "the rule of law", the character and functions of the criminal justice system are far removed from the system manifested by this approach. Secondly, I will concentrate on the general constitutionalization of criminal law in Finland – a major trend in Finnish criminal law literature and criminal legislation since the 1990s. Thirdly, I will elaborate the principle of legality that is perhaps the most significant principle in Finnish as well as European criminal law and which also has a central role in international criminal law. The principle of legality symbolizes the connection between the rule of law and criminal law and the criminal justice system.

---

[1]　Brian Z. Tamanaha, *On the Rule of Law* (Cambridge University Press, 2004), pp. 1 – 4.
[2]　*Ibid.*, p. 3.

The Rule of Law or Rule by Law?[1]

The role of the "rule of law" state was basically regarded as a factor defining the character of classical criminal law. The main task of the criminal justice system was to defend and protect individual fundamental interests that, according the social contract, belonged to equal and free individuals who acted as rational agents. The task of the criminal justice system and criminal law was thus rather to protect individuals and impose certain limits on individual and state action than to impose orders and obligations on individuals. Criminal law functioned in a "ad hoc" way and the criminal justice system was in a state of stability which ensured that individuals would enjoy a certain minimum ethical level, while the criminal justice system would only begin to function in cases of individual infringements of rights. [2]

The Swedish criminal law scholar *Nils Jareborg* has used the term defensive criminal law policy to describe the "classical" position for criminal law introduced above. In defensive criminal law or criminal justice policy, the criminal justice system protects individuals against arbitrary use and misuse of power. The criminal justice system operates in these situations only when interests that are explicitly protected in (penal) legislation are actually infringed or threatened. The limitations on the use of state punishment and the legal protection of individuals impose constraints upon the use of the criminal law and on the criminal justice system generally. [3]

Within its classical position, the criminal law system mainly concentrates on criminalizing the so-called core crimes: murder, manslaughter, robbery, arson, assault, etc. In other words, acts or omissions that are criminalized mainly protect

---

[1] This section is partly based on Chapter III ("Differentiation in Expanding and Deepening Criminal Law") of the article written by the author in 2007. Sakari Melander, "The Differentiated Structure of Contemporary Criminal Law", in Kimmo Nuotio, eds., *Festschrift in Honour of Raimo Lahti* (Forum Iuris, Helsinki, 2007), pp. 189 – 206.

[2] Winfried Hassemer, "Symbolisches Strafrecht und Rechtsgüterschutz", *Neue Zeitschrift für Strafrecht* 1989, p. 553.

[3] Nils Jareborg, "What Kind of Criminal Law Do We Want?: On Defensive and Offensive Criminal Law Policy", in Annika Snare, eds., *Beware of Punishment: On the Utility and Futility of Criminal Law* (Scandinavian Studies in Criminology vol. 14, Oslo, 1995), pp. 17 – 36.

traditional civil rights or traditionally protected interests (die traditionellen Rechtsgüter). [1]

However, criminal law has in recent decades begun to cover more diverse interests, especially those that are no longer directly associated with individuals. Instead of being used sparingly to protect individuals, the state now believes that criminal law and criminal justice system in general is a good option where solutions to particular societal problems are needed. At the same time, criminal law has begun to protect new areas such as the economy, the stock market, and the environment. On the other hand, the operative action of the criminal law system no longer requires that certain interests be directly infringed. Criminal law also protects some interests that are "only" endangered. [2] Nils Jareborg has also noted this development in the nature and character of criminal law, introducing the concept of offensive criminal law policy as an alternative to traditional defensive criminal law or criminal justice policy. Among the crucial features of offensive criminal law policy are the use of the criminal justice system in solving societal problems, the goal-oriented use of the criminal justice system, the system's rapid intervention in phenomena that the state considers to be harmful, and the increase in endangerment offences in criminal codes as well as crimes that protect not only the individual but also the public interest. [3] In other words, one could also speak, like Raimo Lahti, of the dynamic evolution of the criminal law. [4]

The dynamics of the evolution or development of the criminal law has not, however, ceased in recent years. The Norwegian criminal law scholar *Erling Johannes Husabø* has recently used the term "proactive criminal law" to describe the current developments in criminal law, especially relating to the fight against terrorism and more generally against organised crime. Husabø's point is that criminal law has traditionally been reactive, which is illustrated by the fact that pre-

---

[1] Raimo Lahti, " Die Gesamtreform des Finnischen Strafrechts: Zielsetzung und Stand der Reformarbeit bis 1991 — inbesondere im Blick auf die erste Phase der Gesamtreform", in Raimo Lahti and Kimmo Nuotio, eds., *Criminal Law Theory in Transition: Finnish and Comparative Perspective—Strafrechtstheorie im Umbruch: Finnische und vergleichende Perspektiven* (Helsinki 1992), p. 33 (27 – 52).

[2] E. g., Hassemer 1989.

[3] Jareborg 1995.

[4] Lahti 1992, p. 36.

trial investigation usually takes place before the trial and the fact that criminal law has normally criminalised acts that imply doing something by nature. [1] The contemporary criminal law is by contrast characterised by proactive operation. The criminal justice system seeks to intervene in criminal behaviour before the result of the criminal act appears. This has inter alia meant that a greater number of preparative offences and attempts are criminalised. [2]

The development of criminal law and criminal justice policy from defensive model to offensive or even proactive model illustrates the role of the rule of law in criminal law and the criminal justice system. While the point of departure has been the strict commitment to the principles and demands of the rule of law, the dynamic development of the criminal justice system along with the general social development has led to a situation in which criminal law sometimes or perhaps more often is seen as a means of achieving something, a means to an end. Although criminal law at least formally is committed to the rule of law, the dynamic development illustrated by the offensive and proactive model of criminal law represents rule by law rather than the rule of law. The political will to use the criminal justice system and criminal law in serving the manifold needs or ends established by governments and legislators creates the need to limit the scope of criminal law and strengthen the role of the rule of law in a system that may otherwise be in danger of representing rule by law rather than the rule of law. Certain limits and principles setting these limits are needed to avoid the use of criminal law as a mere tool for such ends as a government suppressing its citizens in a legalistic manner. These limits could serve the true rule of law.

The Constitutionalization of Criminal Law

Perhaps the most significant change in Finnish criminal law is its constitutionalization-alongside its Europeanization. Criminal law and constitutional law have traditionally been separated and of course these two branches of law still are autonomous and independent. There are, however, certain features and developments that inevitably move them closer to each other and even connect

---

[1]   Erling Johannes Husabø, "Pre-aktiv strafferett", *Tidskrift for strafferett* 1/2003, p. 98.

[2]   Husabø 2003, pp. 98 – 99.

them in a manner that does not respect the traditional boundaries of these legal domains.

The first sign of the constitutionalization of criminal law appeared when a full reform of the Finnish Penal Code was launched in the early 1970s. At that time, the committee preparing the guidelines for the reform (The Criminal Law Committee established by the Ministry of Justice) briefly elaborated the connection between criminal law and fundamental rights. This committee published its report in 1976. [1] One fundamental aspect of the committee was that when the grounds for criminalization were discussed and deliberated on fundamental rights must be taken into account as protected interests. More generally, the relation between conceivable criminalization and fundamental rights needed to be deliberated on according to the Committee.

During the 1970s and 1980s, the relation between constitutional law and criminal law was hardly ever discussed in Finnish criminal law literature—or the discussion was almost unsubstantial. The question was also almost nonexistent in parliamentary proceedings since criminal legislation was considered to be quite independent from constitutional law issues. Criminal law was in a sense considered to be a domain where the legislator had " a free hand " in deciding what was criminalized and to what extent. However, after the Finnish reform of provisions on fundamental rights and freedoms in 1995, [2] criminal law literature became interested in the effects of constitutional law in general, in particular on the relation between fundamental rights and criminal law. It could be even claimed that since the late 1990s it has pretty much obligatory to broaden the perspective to cover issues relating to constitutional law as well when examining criminal law. [3] It must be noted that Finnish legal science and law in general have undergone a development in constitutionalization from the mid-1990s, and criminal law may

---

[1]   Rikosoikeuskomitean mietintö, KM 1976: 72 (*The Report of the Criminal Law Committee, Committee Report* 1976: 72, Ministry of Justice, Finland, published in 1976).

[2]   See Government Bill 309/1993.

[3]   Among the first contributions to the relation was the dissertation of Ari-Matti Nuutila, *Rikosoikeudellinen huolimattomuus* (Fahslässigkeit als Verhaltensform und als Schuldform-Negligence in Criminal Law) (Helsinki 1996). See also Ari-Matti Nuutila, " Crime, Punishment and Fundamental Rights", *Turku Law Journal* 2000, pp. 1 – 18.

have been an area where the development of constitutionalization was most marked and rapid and where the effects of constitutionalization may have been far-reaching.

Beside legal science, criminal law has been associated with fundamental rights in criminal legislation, parliamentary proceedings and court decisions as well. First and foremost, this connection became evident when the provisions on fundamental rights were amended in Finland in 1995. At the time, the Finnish Constitution saw its first explicit provision on the principle of legality-although it must be mentioned that Finnish criminal law was of course committed to the principle even before the explicit provision-this provision was, however, symbolically important; criminal law was in a sense accorded its own fundamental right. ①

The constitutionalization of criminal law was almost immediately apparent in the parliamentary proceedings in the late 1990s in Finland. Immediately after the fundamental rights reform in 1995, the Constitutional Law Committee of the Parliament issued a statement on a criminal law bill that dealt with such matters as sexual offences, offences against public order, etc. ② In the statement published in 1997 the Constitutional Law Committee formulated its opinion on the relation between criminal law and fundamental rights in a manner that since then has become established in Finland. ③ The Committee's statement formulated the general principles or general doctrines of fundamental rights, which aptly describe the crucial role of the statement and the Committee's opinion on the relation between constitutional law and criminal law. ④

The Committee stated, for example, that the criminalizations that restrict the use of a certain fundamental right must be judged similarly to restrictions on fundamental rights in general. This means that criminal law and criminal legislation has no special position in the fundamental rights system—and that fundamental rights must always be taken into account when criminalizations are drafted. The

---

① See Sakari Melander, *Kriminalisointiteoria: rangaistavaksi säätämisen oikeudelliset rajoitukset* (A Theory of Criminalization: Legal Constraints to Criminal Legislation) (Helsinki 2008), pp. 16 – 27, pp. 193 – 200.

② Government Bill 6/1997.

③ The Statement of the Constitutional Law Committee of the Finnish Parliament 23/1997.

④ The unpublished presentation of Professor of Constitutional Law *Veli-Pekka Viljanen* (University of Turku) in Turku, Finland, 6 November 2007.

Committee also stated that fundamental rights are always relevant in drafting criminalizations since imprisonment is an infringement of the right to liberty and a fine or pecuniary penalty is an infringement of protection of property. This means that at least criminal sanctions are always significant with regard to fundamental rights and that legal argumentation related to fundamental rights is or at least should be highly relevant when criminal law is amended or when new criminalizations are drafted. Moreover, the Committee proportioned the restriction criteria for fundamental rights it had formulated in its previous practice to criminal legislation. The basic idea is that if legislation in some way restricts fundamental rights and freedoms guaranteed by the constitution the legislation must fulfil certain criteria. The legislation must for example be precise enough, the restriction of a fundamental right must be based on an acceptable societal need, be acceptable with regard to the system of fundamental rights, and not be disproportionate to the aim pursued. [1] With regard to criminal legislation especially, the preciseness and the proportionality of proposed legislation have become important requirements for acceptable and legitimate criminal legislation in Finland. [2]

Since the 1997 statement, the Constitutional Law Committee has strengthened its considerations on the relation between criminal law and fundamental rights in several further statements. It is worth noting that it is now quite normal for governmental bills containing amendments to the Penal Code are discussed in the Constitutional Law Committee as well as the Law Committee of the Parliament. The bills proposing amendments to the Penal Code also quite often contain considerations on the relation between the proposed amendment or new criminalization and fundamental rights. The practice of the Committee-and its general influence on legislative proceedings in criminal law-is so stable that the constitutionalization of criminal law or, more precisely, the constitutional effects on criminal legislation in the sense of fundamental rights oriented interpretation could be said to belong to the general part of criminal law in contemporary Finnish legal science. While the Committee's view on the connection between criminal law and fundamental rights has also been considered to belong to the general part of

---

[1]　The Statement of the Constitutional Law Committee of the Finnish Parliament 23/1997, p. 2.
[2]　Melander 2008, pp. 117 – 132.

fundamental rights law or to its general doctrines, criminal law and constitutional law have inevitably been connected and interdependent.

The constitutionalization of criminal has not restricted its impact merely legislatively. The effect has also touched the judiciary. The Supreme Court of Finland has in some cases, such as case 1999: 46 of the Finnish Supreme Court, rejected charges when the criminal legislation has been so imprecise that the accused has not been able to determine what is criminalized and what is not. The impreciseness of criminal legislation-when the preciceness of such legislation is a strong requirement for criminal legislation set by the Constitution and various international human rights treaties-may thus lead directly to rejection of charges and mean that the constitutionalization of criminal law has direct effects on case law as well. Despite the developments in the judiciary, this is conceivably the area that has to improve most of all with regard to the constitutionalization of criminal law. The Supreme Court in Finland has in some cases identified the connection and analysed the constitutional dimensions in criminal cases but there is still work to be done, especially in lower courts of justice.

The Principle of Legality

The principle of legality clearly illustrates the practical effects of the constitutionalization of criminal law, a trend that started in the mid-1990s and intensified in the 2000s. As already mentioned, the principle of legality is defined as an explicit fundamental right in the Finnish Constitution (Section 8). The explicit provision on this principle was added to the Constitution in 1995, when the provisions on fundamental rights generally were reformed in Finland. In addition, another explicit provision on the principle of legality was added to the Finnish Penal Code when the provisions on its general part were reformed in 2004 (Chapter 3, Section 1). This means that the principle of legality is a principle of both constitutional law and criminal law. The ideal formulation and interpretation of the principle would thus combine both aspects of constitutional law and criminal law, which inevitably creates a close connection between these two legal domains. The legal practice, which has mainly taken place in parliamentary proceedings but in some court decisions as well, on the principle has shown that the interpretation of the principle in practice has also connected aspects of constitutional law and criminal law.

The principle of legality demands that both the definition of a criminal offence and the criminal sanction must be defined in an act of parliament. The exact wording of section 8 of the Finnish Constitution is: "No one shall be found guilty of a criminal offence or be sentenced to a punishment on the basis of a deed, which has not been determined punishable by an Act at the time of its commission. The penalty imposed for an offence shall not be more severe than that provided by an Act at the time of commission of the offence. "[1]

It could firstly be noted that the principle demands that criminal offences and sanctions must be defined in an Act of Parliament. This means that criminalization of an act simply by decree or at another "lower" level regulation is not possible. From the viewpoint of the courts, this means that a criminalization simply in a decree or at a lower regulative level is ineffective and must not be applied. The purpose is to ensure that criminal offences and sanctions are basically defined by the parliament and thus that criminal legislation is defined in a democratic setting.

Another highly relevant dimension of the principle of legality is that of accuracy or the precision of the criminal legislation. The Constitutional Law Committee of the Finnish Parliament has strongly highlighted this dimension, and the requirement for sufficient precision in criminal legislation has become a very important requirement in the practice of the Constitutional Law Committee. The formulation often repeated by the Committee is that everyone should be able to foresee if a certain act or omission is punishable from the wording of the criminal offence. [2] This in a sense accentuates the role of the citizen in relation to the criminal justice system and thus places the role of equality in defining and interpreting criminal statues in a strong position. [3]

---

[1] Unofficial translation of the Finnish Constitution, Ministry of Justice, Finland (http: // www. finlex. fi/fi/laki/kaannokset/1999/en19990731).

[2] See the following statements of the Constitutional Law Committee of the Finnish Parliament: Statement 10/2000 vp, p. 2, Statement 22/2001, p. 3, Statement 29/2001, p. 3, Statement 41/ 2001, p. 2, Statement 26/2002, p. 2, Statement 40/2002, p. 7, Statement 48/2002, p. 2, Statement 26/2004, p. 3, Statement 7/2005, p. 3, Statement 17/2006, p. 3, Statement 18/2007, p. 5 and Statement 68/2010, p. 4.

[3] Sakari Melander, "Yhdenvertaisuus rikosoikeudessa" ("Equality in Criminal Law"), *Oikeus* 2011, pp. 173 – 196.

The formulation of the Committee could be considered to contain extremely important requirements in more detail. The first requirement is that the addressee of criminal legislation should be a citizen. In other words, criminal legislation should be designed for everyone—bearing in mind that every one of us is a potential offender who should be able to foresee what is punishable by reading the legislative text and prearrange her acts in order to refrain from the punishable act. This formulation has a close relation to the requirement of equality. It could also be noted that this basic assumption, which affects the design of criminal legislation, every one being a potential offender, also contains the requirement for a humane criminal justice system, which is illustrated in Nordic criminal justice policy, often described as rational and humane. The idea is to design the system bearing in mind that one could in some situation be the subject of the system—in other words, the idea is to refrain the separation between "us" and "them" . ① Thus, the idea of humanness of the criminal justice system also highlights the role of the citizen in designing the system and therefore illustrates the powerful role of the rule of law in criminal law thinking in Finland.

The second dimension of the requirement of adequate precision imposes high standards for the language used in criminal legislation. Everyone should be able to foresee if an act or omission is criminalized or not by the wording of the criminal offence. When this is related to the first dimension, which sets up the citizen as the main subject of the criminal legislation, the requirement for the wording of the provision requires that the language used be first and foremost standard language. Of course this is not always possible, and legal language or more technical language must sometimes be used. In any case, the intelligibility and the use of standard language is a basis for drafting criminal legislation. The main reason is foreseeability. If criminal legislation is not foreseeable, the use of the criminal justice system could in the worse case be arbitrary, which would be contrary to the principles of legality and equality. Thus the demands for legal protection or due process of law, which are also main elements of the rule of law principle, require

---

① See Sakari Melander, "Nordic Criminal Justice Policy: Single Path or Separate Ways?", in Jaakko Husa, Heikki Pihlajamäki, Kimmo Nuotio, eds., *Nordic Law: Between Tradition and Dynamism* (Intersentia, 2007), pp 119 – 120.

the foreseeability of criminal legislation.

Of course it could be mentioned that there are criminal offences that are mostly designed for certain groups, such as entrepreneurs etc. With regard to the case law from the European Court of Human Rights such criminal provisions might not be under such a strict scrutiny of preciseness. It might even be demanded in actual cases that members of such groups, e. g. entrepreneurs, have knowledge or seek information on legislation that affects their businesses and activities. [1]

Conclusion

The brief and tentative discussion in this paper could be summarised in the following notion. The recent developments in criminal law have led to a situation in which criminal law and criminal legislation has been understood in a dynamic way that could allow the use of criminal law as a mean to an end. This represents the "rule by law" approach to criminal justice system rather than the "rule of law" approach. It has been necessary to create certain counterforces to this dynamic development. One such force is the constitutionalization of criminal law and its most active manifestation, the principle of legality. The requirements set by the principle and constitutionalization of criminal law in general work to secure the rule of law in the dynamic evolution of criminal law. The rule of law thus operates as an active and powerful counterforce to the dynamic evolution of criminal law. The rule of law, constitutionalization and principle of legality, the criminal justice system allows us even today to understand the traditional and crucially important character of the criminal justice system, which is basically repressive. By creating counterforces, the fundamentally repressive nature of criminal justice system could be counteracted.

法治和刑法： 芬兰的刑法宪法化

萨卡里·梅兰德

【摘要】 宪法化无疑是芬兰刑法最显著的变化之一。传统意义上，刑

---

[1] *Cantoni v. France*, 15. 11. 1996, Reports 1996-V, paragraph 29 and *Groppera Radio SG v. Other v. Switzerland*, 28 March 1990, 173-A, paragraph 68.

法和宪法在法律科学和实践领域是完全独立的。但是，有一些特征和发展不可避免地使它们彼此变得更加紧密，甚至以不尊重这些法律领域传统分界的方式将它们互相联结。刑法的宪法化并不是芬兰所特有的现象，在一个更大的层面上与刑法的欧洲化有关。本文旨在探究在 20 世纪 90 年代中期，芬兰宪法中的基本权利条款改革以后所发生的芬兰刑法的宪法化。因此，本文的目的首先是对法治的一般意义作出一个简要概述，而后探究刑法中法治的含义与范畴，对法治的一般意义作出一个简要概述。其次，检验芬兰刑法宪法化的大致发展趋势。最后，探讨刑法法治中或许是最重要、最普遍的罪刑法定原则。

中国死刑改革的回顾与展望

刘仁文[*]

刘仁文 *

【摘要】 近年来，中国的死刑削减取得了很大的进步，主要表现在：一是以 2007 年 1 月 1 日最高人民法院收回死刑核准权为标志的从司法上慎用死刑；二是以 2011 年 2 月 25 日全国人大常委会通过的《刑法修正案（八）》为标志的取消 13 个非暴力犯罪的死刑。中国还应该继续从司法上和立法上做出努力，进一步压缩死刑。目前死刑还不能彻底废除，未来中国的死刑制度改革还应包括：把死刑复核程序改造成为第三审程序，至少是控、辩、审三方都在场的公开听证程序；废止枪决，统一用注射来执行死刑；把死刑的执行主体与宣判主体相分离；建立死刑案件的特赦制度。

【关键词】 死刑 改革 展望

2007 年 1 月 1 日，中国最高人民法院收回了死刑核准权，这被视为中国从司法上严格限制死刑的一个重要举措；2011 年 2 月 25 日，中国立法机关通过《刑法修正案（八）》，取消了 13 个非暴力犯罪的死刑，这是中国首次从立法上减少死刑罪名，对下一步继续减少死刑具有重要的意义。短短几年，中国在减少死刑方面取得了重大进展。本文旨在对这一进展作一回顾和分析，并对下一步中国的死刑改革作些展望和建议。

一 司法上慎用死刑

1997 年中国颁布新刑法时，刑法学界普遍认为死刑太多，呼吁减少死刑，立法机关认为，这种意见虽然值得重视，"但考虑到目前社会治安的形

---

* 中国社会科学院法学研究所研究员。

势严峻，经济犯罪的情况严重，还不具备减少死刑的条件"，①因此决定对死刑"原则上不减少也不增加"。在这种思想指导下，1997 年刑法将当时所有单行刑法中的死刑罪名都吸收进来，使死刑罪名达到 68 个。当然，1997年刑法也在限制死刑方面取得了某些进步，如将未满 18 周岁的未成年人犯罪的最高刑由可以判处死刑缓期两年执行改为无期徒刑，②将盗窃罪的死刑仅保留盗窃金融机构、数额特别巨大和盗窃珍贵文物情节严重这两种情形，而取消了实践中发案率很高的普通盗窃罪的死刑。

1998 年，中国政府签署了《公民权利和政治权利国际公约》，该公约第 6 条明确规定："在未废除死刑的国家，判处死刑只能是作为对最严重的罪行的惩罚。"根据联合国人权事务委员会的解释，这里的"最严重的罪行"应当严格限定，"死刑应当只是一种非常例外的刑罚方式"。中国正在准备批准《公民权利和政治权利国际公约》，需要从立法和司法上对死刑作进一步的限制。③

司法上对死刑进行严格限制，突出表现在 2007 年 1 月 1 日最高人民法院在中央政府的支持下，④收回死刑核准权。1979 年刑法本来规定死刑核准权由最高人民法院行使，但自 20 世纪 80 年代初，随着社会治安形势的严峻，最高人民法院陆续将一些犯罪的死刑核准权下放到省一级的高级法院，致使死刑二审和死刑核准均由高级人民法院来行使，这对保证死刑案件质量、从严控制死刑、统一死刑案件的量刑标准都造成了很大的负面影响。在学界的长期呼吁下，最高人民法院终于在 2007 年 1 月 1 日收回了死刑核准权，并为此新成立了三个刑事审判庭。

为了配合收回死刑核准权，最高人民法院在 2005 年 12 月发出《关于进

---

① 时任全国人大常委会副委员长的王汉斌在全国人民代表大会上所作的《关于〈中华人民共和国刑法（修订草案）〉的说明》中如是说。

② 在中国刑法中，死刑缓期两年执行属于死刑的一种执行方法。如果在死刑缓期两年执行期间没有故意犯罪，就减为无期徒刑。

③ 最初，中国对《公民权利和政治权利国际公约》关于死刑的态度研究还不够透彻，如中国 1997 年修订刑法时只是把刑法总则中的一句话改了一下，由原来的"死刑只适用于罪大恶极的犯罪分子"改为"死刑只适用于罪行极其严重的犯罪"，以为这样就和公约接轨了。现在回过头来看，这个认识是欠科学的。在分则中有 68 个死刑罪名，且其中有大量的非暴力犯罪的情况下，应当承认，这与公约对死刑适用范围的要求显然还是有很大的差距的。

④ 最高人民法院为了收回死刑核准权，增加了几百个法官的编制，从而使中国的最高人民法院成为世界上最大的最高法院。

一步做好死刑第二审案件开庭审理工作的通知》,要求各高级人民法院做好准备,自 2006 年 1 月 1 日起先对案件重要事实和证据问题提出上诉的死刑二审案件落实开庭审理,然后自该年 7 月 1 日起对所有死刑二审案件一律实行开庭审理,以提高二审质量,进而为最高人民法院的死刑核准打下良好的基础。①

死刑核准权的收回,直接或间接引起了死刑判决和执行的下降。2008 年全国人民代表大会开会期间,当时的最高人民法院院长肖扬曾向人大代表透露:判处死缓的人数首次超过了判处死刑立即执行的人数,死刑执行减少了,由于运用多种形式打击刑事犯罪,依然能保障社会稳定,甚至 2007 年的爆炸、杀人、放火等恶性案件比 2006 年还有明显下降。另据当时的最高人民法院新闻发言人倪寿明在解读最高人民法院的工作报告时指出:最高人民法院统一行使死刑核准权后,促进了一、二审质量的提高,即使在这种情况下,2007 年最高人民法院因原判事实不清、证据不足、量刑不当、程序违法等原因不核准的死刑案件仍然占到总数的 15% 左右。实际上死刑下降远不止 15%,因为最高人民法院收回死刑核准权这一举动本身带给各地法院的一个信息就是要严格控制死刑,所以在一、二审时能不判死刑的就不判死刑,有的法院反映说:过去一有严重犯罪发生,首先想到的就是要判处犯罪人死刑,现在则首先要考虑有没有从宽的因素可以不判其死刑。来自检察机关的信息也表明,近年来针对死缓案件提起抗诉、要求判处死刑立即执行的比率明显下降,这也是检察机关配合国家减少死刑的刑事政策的结果。据估计,2007 年收回死刑核准权后,中国的死刑执行数至少减少了二分之一,甚至三分之二。②

对死刑的司法控制还在进行之中,包括进一步完善死刑核准程序、规范死刑案件的证据审查判断标准等。如 2010 年 6 月最高人民法院等部门又印发了《关于办理死刑案件审查判断证据若干问题的规定》和《关于办理刑事案件排除非法证据若干问题的规定》的通知,针对办案实际中存在的证据收集、审查、判断和非法证据排除尚有不尽规范、不尽严格、不尽统一的问题,对司法机关办理刑事案件特别是死刑案件提出了更高的标准。此外,针对死刑复核过程中律师如何介入、检察机关如何介入、如何确保死刑复核

---

① 在此前,二审大多为书面审。

② 中国的死刑执行数至今不公开,这遭到了包括国内学者在内的批评。参见陈光中《公布死刑人数利弊考》,《南方周末》2009 年 12 月 16 日。

的公正、防止死刑复核过程中可能发生的腐败，也正在完善之中。①

二　立法上削减死刑

从司法上慎用死刑到立法上削减死刑，这是一个质的飞跃。2011年初通过的《刑法修正案（八）》谨慎地取消了13个非暴力犯罪的死刑，包括4个走私类罪、5个金融类犯罪、2个妨害文物管理类罪，以及盗窃罪和传授犯罪方法罪。此外，还增加规定："审判的时候已满七十五周岁的人，不适用死刑，但以特别残忍手段致人死亡的除外。"②

立法之所以在减少死刑方面迈出较大的步伐，主要有以下背景和原因：

一是国际背景。当前，废除死刑已成为国际趋势。根据联合国秘书长2008年发布的有关暂停适用死刑的报告，截至2008年7月1日，在世界范围内，已有141个国家和地区从法律上或在实践中废除了死刑，只有56个国家和地区还保留并执行死刑。就是在还保留并执行死刑的国家和地区，也越来越多地将死刑作为一种带有象征性的刑罚来适用，而不是常规性地适用。像中国的邻国韩国已经连续10年没有执行过一例死刑，另一个邻国俄罗斯从2011年1月1日起，已经正式由宪法法院裁定不再执行死刑。在这些废除死刑和很少适用死刑的国家里，没有证据显示社会治安变得更加严峻，也没有证据显示死刑的废除与犯罪率的升降有什么必然联系。这些信息越来越多地为全社会和国家领导人所知晓。特别是近年来中国成功举办北京奥运会、上海世博会等许多大型国际活动，进一步拉近了中国与世界的距离。

二是国内的经济发展和经济领域管理经验的丰富。一方面，经济发展必然带来对人的生命的尊重，当一个社会物质不再贫乏时，自然就会认同生命无价，再多的金钱也不能和生命相比。另一方面，较20世纪80年代改革开放之初，我们在经济领域进一步建立健全了各种经济、行政监管措施，而这是预防经济犯罪的关键，远比带有"马后炮"性质的刑罚要管用。事实上，这次取消的13个死刑罪名，大多是在20世纪80年代经济发展过程中，因旧的一套管理制度失效、新的一套又没有完全建立起来，致使经济

---

① 最高人民检察院自2007年就设立了死刑复核检察工作办公室的内部机构，现在已经得到中央的正式批准，下一步可能也要较大幅度地增加这方面的检察官编制，从而推动死刑复核检察监督工作的规范化。包括笔者在内的不少学者都希望，死刑复核能从最高人民法院内部审查走向包括检察官和律师在内的公开听证。

② 过去对老年人犯罪没有这类"优惠"措施。

犯罪猖獗而刑法被迫作出严厉反应，因而陆续增设这些罪的死刑。现在，这些领域的犯罪得到了较好遏制，相应的民愤也就降下来，而这又为减少死刑创造了条件。据立法机关事先所做的调查，这13个罪近年来已经很少适用死刑，相当一部分是"留而不用"。因此，从这些罪名入手来减少死刑，既不会给社会带来危害，也不会遭遇民意的抵触。

三是我国立法和司法的实证经验为进一步减少死刑提供了支持。1997年我国废除了普通盗窃罪的死刑，只保留对盗窃国家金融机构和珍贵文物两种特殊盗窃的死刑，当时社会上曾有一种担心，担心普通盗窃罪这种与广大人民群众联系密切的犯罪会增多，但10多年来的实践表明，普通盗窃罪的发案率并没有上升，这说明犯罪与死刑并不是想象中的那种简单联系，影响犯罪的原因是复杂的。死刑核准权收回4年多来，死刑执行大幅度减少，非但没有带来犯罪率的上升，反而在某些领域由于改善了社会管理，还使犯罪率有所下降。这有力地说明了国家通过改善治理手段和方法，完全可以减少死刑而不使社会稳定受到威胁。

四是通过调整刑罚结构，消除民众的担忧。社会上有一种担忧，担心某些严重暴力犯罪分子如果不判处死刑，就会钻法律的空子，很快放出来，威胁到社会的安全。针对这种担忧，为配合减少死刑，《刑法修正案（八）》贯彻落实宽严相济的刑事政策，对有关配套制度进行了设计，如严格限制对某些被判处死缓的罪行严重的罪犯的减刑，延长其实际服刑期（如对判处死刑缓期执行的，如果确有重大立功表现，二年期满以后，原来规定减为十五年以上二十年以下有期徒刑，现在规定减为二十五年有期徒刑），还规定"对被判处死刑缓期执行的累犯以及因故意杀人、强奸、抢劫、绑架、放火、爆炸、投放危险物质或者有组织的暴力性犯罪被判处死刑缓期执行的犯罪分子，人民法院根据犯罪情节等情况可以同时决定对其限制减刑"。

五是公众的观念得到正确引导。中国已将"国家尊重和保障人权"写进《宪法》，近年来在刑事立法和刑事司法领域又大力提倡以人为本，这些对营造一种宽容、人道的社会心理无疑起到了积极作用。在死刑还不能彻底废除的情况下，我们对死刑执行进行了改革，如推广注射执行死刑、逐步废止枪决执行死刑、允许死刑犯临刑前会见亲属等，也有利于社会树立尊重生命的概念。加上新闻媒体对佘祥林、赵作海、聂树斌等冤假错案的广泛报道和深入剖析，使公众更加理解和支持国家慎用死刑、为把死刑案件办成铁案而采取的一系列措施。

六是在选择削减死刑的罪名时，充分注意到公众的关切。尽管这次一下取消 13 个死刑罪名，但我国刑法中仍然保留有 55 个死刑罪名，毋庸讳言，死刑罪名还有很大的压缩空间。对此，立法机关采取了循序渐进的步骤，如对贪污、受贿等贪腐犯罪，考虑到目前这类犯罪还很严重，群众对这类犯罪反应强烈，故立法者认为事关执政党的执政根基，因而尽管其也属于非暴力犯罪，尽管有学者论证也应当属于废除死刑之列，① 但立法者并没有贸然取消这些罪的死刑。

三　死刑的进一步压缩

《刑法修正案（八）》取消 13 个死刑罪名后，中国刑法仍然有 55 个死刑罪名，其中还包括大量的非暴力犯罪，如前所述，这与《公民权利和政治权利国际公约》关于"判处死刑只能是作为对最严重的罪行的惩罚"的规定还是有很大距离的。我国正在准备批准 1998 年就已经签署的《公民权利和政治权利国际公约》，一旦批准，就将向联合国人权事务委员会提交有关包括死刑问题在内的公民权利和政治权利的报告。如果到时我们仍保留多达 55 个死刑罪名，从人权事务委员会以往的工作情况来看，肯定是不行的。目前国际社会对于何为可予判处死刑的"最严重的罪行"达成的共识是：非暴力犯罪肯定不属于这一范畴，例如，联合国经济及社会理事会在 1984 年通过的《保护面对死刑者权利的保障措施》中提出"最严重的罪行"应理解为"其范围不应超出带有致命或其他极端严重后果的蓄意犯罪行为"。虽然该决议提到的"带有其他极端严重后果的蓄意犯罪行为"使得广义解释成为可能，但联合国秘书长其后在《死刑和关于保护死刑犯权利的保障措施的执行情况》的报告中进一步指出，蓄意犯罪以及具有致命或其他极端严重后果意味着罪行应该是危及生命的，即危及生命是罪行很可能发生的后果，由此，任何不危及生命的犯罪，无论其后果从其他角度来看多么严重，都不属于可对之适用死刑的"最严重罪行"。

因此，我国要继续从立法上加大削减死刑的力度。现在还保留的 55 个死刑罪名中，还有一多半是非暴力犯罪，比如还保留有金融类的集资诈骗罪，还有贪污罪、受贿罪等。要废除这些条款，还必须创造条件，使得这些犯罪的发案率大幅下降。像贪污罪、受贿罪，当这类犯罪发案率很严重

---

① 参见刘仁文《创造条件取消贪腐犯罪死刑》，《经济参考报》2010 年 9 月 21 日。由于此文发表时间正好在《刑法修正案（八）》讨论过程中，立法机关为了回应民意，还专门召开了新闻发布会，特意指出此次刑法修正从没有考虑过要废除贪腐犯罪的死刑。

时，要取消死刑是很难的，会遇到巨大的社会阻力。对于这类犯罪，要最终达到废除死刑的目标，必须在反腐败的制度建设方面取得实际成效，如通过颁行《公职人员财产申报法》、强化新闻媒体对公权力的监督等。只有当某一类犯罪不是那么大范围地发生、对国家和社会造成的危害不是那么普遍时，民意对这类犯罪的愤怒才会降低，那时再取消这类犯罪就不会遇到民意的强烈反弹。① 从这个意义上来说，解决贪腐犯罪的死刑问题功夫在刑法之外。

　　未来一段时间，只要中国的国内外局势继续保持平稳，中国就会朝着继续压缩死刑的方向前进。因此，一个和平、稳定的中国对于中国废除死刑来说也是至关重要的。在此前提下，笔者愿意对中国废除死刑的路线图作如下描述：先把非暴力犯罪的死刑罪拿掉，最后再来废除暴力犯罪的死刑。而非暴力犯罪的死刑，又可以先考虑取消"集资诈骗"这类经济犯罪，再考虑"贪污、受贿"等腐败犯罪。至于暴力犯罪的死刑，又可以把"严重的有预谋杀人"这类犯罪放到最后，因为中国的文化中的确存在根深蒂固的"杀人偿命"观念，所以把它作为废除死刑道路上的最后一个堡垒来攻克，比较务实。在立法上暂时还不能废除某个罪的死刑时，我们要通过司法政策来引导司法实践，使司法中判处死刑的人数不断减少，这反过来也有利于最终废除该罪的死刑，因为当某一个死刑罪名已经近乎"死亡条款"时，要拿掉它的死刑也就容易得多。

四　死刑改革中的几项具体制度

（一）关于死刑复核中的检察监督

　　按照中国宪法，中国的检察机关不仅是公诉机关，还是国家法律监督机关。据此，最高人民检察院在 2007 年最高人民法院收回死刑核准权后，设立了死刑复核检察工作办公室，现在该机构已经得到中央编制委员会的正式批准。在这一现实下，死刑复核中的检察监督如何运作？笔者的初步意见是：

---

① 尽管死刑的废除主要不是一个民意问题，而是一个原则问题，但任何政治家在废除死刑时都不可能不考虑民意。巴丹戴尔先生在他的《为废除死刑而战》一书中披露，早在德斯坦总统时期，总统本人就已经认为死刑应当被废除，但由于当时法国整个社会支持死刑的民意占绝对多数，因此他不敢公开表示要废除死刑。到后来密特朗当选总统时，虽然法国民意支持死刑的还是占多数，但已经下降了，在这种情况下，他才有可能基于自己的政治信仰，成功推动了法国废除死刑。

1. 最高人民法院收回死刑核准权的一个重要目的就是贯彻落实少杀、慎杀的死刑政策，因此，检察机关对死刑复核活动实行法律监督，也应体现死刑复核制度的这一价值追求，将严格限制和减少死刑适用作为重要目的。对于被告人不应被判处死刑而被判处或核准死刑的，要及时提出不应核准死刑的法律监督意见或者依法提出抗诉，推动最高人民法院依法撤销不当的死刑裁判。

2. 作为死刑复核程序中的法律监督者，最高人民检察院还负有维护公平和社会公共利益的责任。对于法官因收受贿赂、徇私枉法或者不严格依照法定程序办案而作出不核准死刑裁定的，或者不核准死刑既没有法律依据又缺乏事实根据而明显不公的，检察机关应当依法提出抗诉，并对涉嫌职务犯罪的法官依法立案侦查，维护死刑复核活动的严肃性和公正性。

3. 最高人民法院在进行死刑复核时，不论是否开庭审理，都不仅应当听取被告人及其辩护人提出的辩护意见，还应当听取检察机关提出的法律监督意见。这是保证兼听则明、防止偏信则暗的必然要求，也是遵循司法规律办事的题中之意。最好是在《刑事诉讼法》中明确把死刑复核程序定位为第三审程序，至少是三方都在场的公开听证。

（二）关于统一死刑执行方式

从1996年修改《刑事诉讼法》，增设注射执行死刑的方式，到1997年昆明市在全国实施第一例注射执行死刑，再到现在的部分省市全面推行注射执行死刑，这一历程反映了中国在死刑执行方式上的人道化进展。

联合国经济及社会理事会在1984年通过的《保护面临死刑者权利的保障措施》中要求，对于那些尚未废除死刑的国家，执行死刑"应以尽量减轻痛苦的方式执行"。我国过去对执行死刑的方式只规定了枪决一种，但1996年刑事诉讼法修改时，基于对注射执行死刑比枪决更能减轻死刑犯痛苦的认识，以及考虑到注射执行死刑能够更好地保全死刑犯的尸体、防止出现枪决所导致的脑浆迸裂的残忍场面等因素，规定"死刑采用枪决或者注射等方法执行"。之所以仍然保留枪决执行死刑的方法，是因为注射执行死刑的药物研制、场所建设、人员培训等都还需要一个过程。

经过10多年的摸索和试点，笔者认为现在到了废止枪决、统一用注射来执行死刑的时候了。现在死刑执行方式两者并用，到底谁用注射，谁用枪决，标准是什么均不明确，以致社会上发出"为什么贪官多用注射来执行死刑"的质疑，不利于树立法律面前人人平等的信仰。至于实践中有些法院以犯罪分子的民愤大小来决定采用何种方式执行死刑，也是不符合立法原意的。立法原意是要推进死刑执行的人道化,只不过在注射执行死刑条件还不成熟的时候,将枪决作为一种过渡措施。在历史上,死刑执行方法曾经分为"剥夺人的生命"和"在剥夺人的生命的同时使被处决者备受痛苦和煎熬"两类方法,后者包括了凌迟、枭首、戮尸等,清末沈家本主持修律时,就力主死刑执行方式统一,废除凌迟、枭首、戮尸等"使被处决者备受痛苦和煎熬"的方法,并最后得到清廷的允准。今天我们的死刑执行方式当然不能跟封建社会的酷刑同日而语,但沈氏关于统一死刑执行方式的主张却值得我们借鉴。毕竟当今世界废除和严格限制死刑已成趋势,我们即使暂时还保留死刑,也不能在已经解决了更加人道化的死刑执行方式后,仍然去选择性使用一种使死刑犯更加痛苦的执行方式。

为了改变各地注射执行死刑发展的不平衡,也为了更好地规范注射执行死刑,现在亟须改变各地各自为政的局面,从中央层面统一规划,落实废止枪决、统一用注射来执行死刑的日程表。现在广大农村地区还欠缺专门的注射执行死刑场所和器材,由于建这样的场所投入较大,客观上限制了这些地方推广注射执行死刑,应当由国家统筹解决。此外,对于注射执行死刑的司法警察和专职法医应当在全国法院系统内统一配置和接受必要的培训。建议最高人民法院尽快出台规范注射执行死刑的文件,进一步完善程序保障,以确保死刑执行方式人道化的改革能在每一个个案中得到体现。同时,要及时跟踪和总结实践中暴露出来的问题,最大限度地克服美国等国家在注射执行死刑中所出现的"拙劣表演"等造成死刑犯痛苦的现象。

(三) 关于死刑执行主体与宣判主体的分离

讨论死刑的执行主体与宣判主体相分离,在当前严格控制死刑的语境下具有特别的意义,因为如果死刑的宣判是一回事,执行是另一回事,那就可以改变我国目前凡是被判处死刑立即执行的就一律将在短期内被执行死刑的局面,① 这对减少死刑实际执行数是有好处的。

事实上,刑罚判决和刑罚执行本来就是两码事,前者属司法权,后者属行政权,我国的有期徒刑、无期徒刑都是在经法院宣判后,交由司法行政部门去执行的,具体而言就是监狱等服刑机构。但对死刑,我们长期以

---

① 根据中国刑事诉讼法的规定,最高人民法院判处和核准的死刑立即执行的判决,应当由最高人民法院院长签发执行死刑的命令。下级人民法院接到最高人民法院执行死刑的命令后,应当在七日内交付执行。

来似乎已经习惯了由法院自己判决自己执行的体制，这种体制导致死刑在一经确定后就立即无拖延地被执行，它与其他一些死刑保留国的做法显著不同，后者往往在法院宣判死刑后，由司法部长（法务部长）来签署死刑执行令，只要该命令没有下发，死刑就不得执行，所以我们常常看到这样的报道，说某某国家某一年度判处了多少人的死刑，实际执行了多少人的死刑，两者是不一致的，实际执行的比判处的要少。

以日本为例，虽然现在它还没有废除死刑，但死刑已经成为一种名副其实的"象征性刑罚"，每年执行的死刑人数也就一至二人，有时一年一个都没有。促成这种局面的一个重要原因就是日本将死刑执行权赋予了法务部长，从而使死刑宣判和死刑执行分离开来。日本现在的死囚牢里大概关有 100 个虽然已经被判处死刑但仍然没有被执行死刑的人，之所以如此，原因是：

首先，按照日本法律，即使法院最后宣判某人死刑，他还拥有申请再审、特别上告、申请赦免等一系列救济措施。任何死刑犯，只要他提出此类权利主张，法务部长就得暂停死刑执行令的签发。

其次，法务部长在签发死刑执行令之前，他还有一个内部审查程序，该审查程序先由一个小组负责对某个死刑案子进行把关，然后汇报到上一级，再次把关后认为没有问题才报到法务部长那里，此程序常常持续很长时间。

再次，如果一个案子是共同犯罪，或者某个被告与其他被告的案子有牵连，则在其他被告的审判结束前，法务部长不能签发死刑执行令。

最后，有的法务部长基于信仰等原因，就是不签发死刑执行令。如海部内阁时期的佐藤惠在 1990～1991 的年任法务部长期间以及小泉内阁时期的杉浦正健在 2005～2006 年任法务部长期间，均没有签发过一件死刑执行令，其中的一个重要原因是这两人都是佛教徒，他们虽然没有明说，但许多人相信他们的佛教信仰对他们作出的选择起了作用。

特别值得一提的是，根据日本《刑事诉讼法》第 475 条的规定，法务部长应当在法院作出生效的死刑判决后 6 个月内签发死刑执行令，但随着对死刑犯人权保障的日益重视，如今该条款已经名存实亡，实践中几乎不存在在如此短的时间内完成签发死刑执行令的有关审查工作。因此，在 1998 年的一个著名判决中，当一个死囚犯状告政府不在 6 个月内执行他的死刑时，法院能动地将这条解释为"在可能的情况下应在 6 个月内签发死刑执行令"，但现在证明 6 个月属"不可能"，据此驳回了原告的主张。

（四）关于建立死刑案件的特赦制度

《公民权利和政治权利国际公约》第 6 条第 4 项规定："任何被判处死

刑的人应有权要求赦免或减刑。对一切判处死刑的案件，均得给予大赦、特赦或减刑的机会。"我国已经签署该公约，并正在为批准该公约做准备。鉴于我国短期内不可能废除死刑，因此需要在死刑案件中增设申请特别赦免程序，以满足公约在这方面的人权标准。①

增设申请特别赦免程序也是完善办理死刑案件刑事诉讼制度的需要。我国 1997 年《刑事诉讼法》第 211 条规定："下级人民法院收到最高人民法院执行死刑的命令后，应当在七日以内交付执行。但是发现有下列情形之一的，应当停止执行，并且立即报告最高人民法院，由最高人民法院作出裁定：（一）在执行前发现判决可能有错误的；（二）在执行前罪犯揭发重大犯罪事实或者有其他重大立功表现，可能需要改判的；（三）罪犯正在怀孕。"最高人民法院在 1999 年《关于对在执行死刑前发现重大情况需要改判的案件如何适用程序问题的批复》中指出：对上述需要改判的案件，由有死刑核准权的人民法院适用审判监督程序依法改判或者指令下级人民法院再审。但问题是，根据我国 1997 年《刑事诉讼法》第 204 条和第 205条的规定，刑事案件再审的理由是原生效判决"确有错误"，而《刑事诉讼法》第 211 条规定的第二种情形，即死刑犯在死刑执行前揭发重大犯罪事实或者有其他重大立功表现的，这种改判理由并不是因为原判决在认定事实和适用法律上有错误；第 211 条规定的第三种情形，改判理由也不一定是原判决在认定事实和适用法律上有错误，因为该妇女可能不是"审判时正在怀孕的"，而是在审判后才受孕，甚至是判决生效后才受孕，② 对在审判后才受孕的女死刑犯进行改判，是基于人道主义和避免株连另一无辜生命的考虑，也是《公民权利和政治权利国际公约》第 6 条第 5 项规定的"怀胎妇女被判死刑，不得执行其刑"的要求。因此，笔者同意对此两种情形构建一个新的程序即死刑赦免程序的设想。③

---

① 可以说，死刑犯申请特赦或减刑已经成为一项国际公认的权利，其他如联合国经济及社会理事会《保护面临死刑者权利的保障措施》第 7 条规定：任何被判死刑的人"有权寻求赦免或减刑"；《美洲人权公约》第 4 条规定：任何一个被处死刑者"都有权请求赦免、特赦或者减刑"。

② 有人可能会说，审判后或判决生效后犯人被关在看守所里，怎么可能怀孕呢？这种可能性是完全存在的，例如，《江南时报》2000 年 7 月 15 日以"谁令死刑无法执行"为题，报道了一名"血债累累、罪大恶极"的女囚，在看守所内被看守所所长等人多次强奸而怀孕，本应处以死刑的她被改判无期徒刑。

③ 参见竹怀军《论我国死刑赦免制度的构建》，《湖南师范大学社会科学学报》2004 年第 5期。

或许有人会说，我国的死刑案件已经有了一套普通刑事案件所没有的复核程序，已经体现了对死刑案件的特别重视，该复核程序可充当前述特别赦免程序的功能。对此，笔者的意见是否定的。首先，死刑复核程序是一套司法程序，而特别赦免程序是独立于司法机关之外的另一套程序。在死刑核准之前，死刑判决仍然是未生效的判决，但特别赦免程序则是在判决已经生效的情况下才提起。其次，死刑复核并不能代行特别赦免的功能，如对被判死刑后患精神病或绝症的罪犯，可以赦免，但复核就不一定能从法律上找到免死的依据。最后，在一审、二审和复核之外再加一套特别赦免程序，一点都不算多。许多教训表明，经过三级司法审查后仍然不能发现死刑案件的全部错误。即便像美国这样死刑案件诉讼程序近乎漫长的国家，近年来仍不断爆出无辜者被错误定罪，而且许多差点被错误执行死刑的消息。[①]

在死刑特别赦免程序的设计中，有以下问题需要注意：

死刑特别赦免机关。有论者认为，赦免死刑的机关应是最高人民法院。[②] 这种意见值得商榷，因为在死刑核准权统一收回后，最高人民法院目前已经行使死刑核准权了，再将赦免权赋予它，在实际工作中核准权和赦免权就将由同一机构来行使，这样可能会带来机制上的不顺，导致效果不佳，例如，最高人民法院先核准死刑，再赦免死刑，即使是由不同的部门决定，也难免对最高人民法院决定的严肃性产生一定的冲击。因此，对于死刑案件的特别赦免程序，可以考虑个案的特别赦免由国家主席直接决定并颁发特别赦免令，多案的特别赦免则在由全国人大常委会决定后再由国家主席以特别赦免令的形式颁行。

死刑特别赦免类型。死刑犯申请的特别赦免类型以减刑为妥，不宜特赦和复权。特赦，即免除死刑犯的刑罚，走得太远，社会公众难以接受。相应地，由于赦免性复权以刑罚执行终了或刑罚执行免除为前提，而死刑案件还没有达到这一步，所以也不存在赦免性复权。而且这里的赦免性减刑也应有

---

① 需要指出的是，国内媒体报道美国有许多无辜者被处死（参见王菊芳《二十七年全美近百人蒙冤而死 伊州死刑大赦引起强烈反响》，《检察日报》2003年1月14日），但在一次国际会议上，美国学者告诉笔者，这个消息是不准确的，正确的说法应当是："不可能确切知道，但也许有无辜者被执行了死刑。"（参见 DPIC 网站，DPIC 是 Death Peanalty Information Center 的简称，即"死刑信息中心"）根据这个信息，我们至少可以看出，美国尚无明确被证明是杀错了人的报道，这说明它的死刑案件诉讼程序近乎漫长还是比较有效地防止了死刑案件中的冤杀。

② 参见竹怀军《论我国死刑赦免制度的构建》，《湖南师范大学社会科学学报》2004年第5期。

所限制，即不应无限制地减刑，减刑为死刑缓期两年执行即可。因为毕竟经过了前面的一审和二审以及复核程序，所以到这一关不宜步子迈得太大。

死刑特别赦免对象。主要包括：一是前面所说的 1997 年《刑事诉讼法》第 211 条规定的有关情形，即死刑犯在死刑执行前揭发重大犯罪事实或者有其他重大立功表现的，以及死刑犯在审判后怀孕的；二是出于外交等因素考虑的，如我国 2009 年判处英国毒贩阿克毛死刑并随后处决，不仅在英国，甚至在欧盟都引起强烈"地震"，因为包括英国在内的欧盟早已废除死刑，但依据我国法律，似乎不判其死刑又没有法律根据，类似案件如果有特别赦免程序，则可先由法院判处其死刑，然后再借助特别赦免这一渠道，将其减刑；三是对被判死刑后患精神病或绝症的罪犯，应准予减刑；四是对于年老或刚满十八周岁的罪犯，[①] 以及弱智罪犯，[②] 还有新生婴儿母亲等，如果被判处死刑，应当尽量考虑通过赦免途径来减轻其刑罚。

死刑执行期限。与死刑特别赦免制度相关的一个问题是，按照目前我国刑事诉讼法的规定，死刑一旦核准，就将在七天内执行死刑，这一间隔早已被学界批评为太短，若从构建死刑特别赦免制度而言，则必须延长死刑执行的期限，否则可能还没来得及启动特别赦免程序，死刑就已经执行了。

Reform of the Death Penalty System in China: Retrospect and Prospect

Liu Renwen

【Abstract】 In recent years China has made significant progress in the reduction of the death penalty, which is mainly manifested in the following two measures: first, the implementation of the policy of prudent application of the death penalty in

---

① 《刑法修正案（八）》增加规定了对审判的时候已满七十五周岁的人一般不适用死刑，这固然是一大进步，但它一是留了个尾巴，即"以特别残忍手段致人死亡的除外"，二是把年龄定为 75 周岁有过高之嫌，因此这方面仍然有视个案通过特别赦免来减刑之必要。

② 美国最高法院认为：处决弱智罪犯违反了美国宪法第 8 条规定的"不得施加残忍的和异常的惩罚"，因而不得对弱智犯执行死刑。参见刘仁文《弱智罪犯不执行死刑之启示》，《检察日报》2003 年 1 月 17 日。

judicial practice, marked by the taking back of the power to approve death sentences by the Supreme Court on January 1, 2007; and second, the abolition of the death penalty for 13 different kinds of non-violent crimes, marked by the adoption of the Eighth Amendment to the Criminal Law by the Standing Committee of the National People's Congress on February 25, 2011. In the future, China should make continuous legislative and judicial efforts to further reduce the application of death penalty. Before complete abolition of the death penalty, China should carry out the following reforms on the death penalty system: to transform the procedure for the review of death sentences into a procedure of the third instance, or at least a public hearing procedure participated by the prosecution, the defense and the judge; to abolish shooting as the method of execution of death sentence and to replace it with the uniform method of execution by injection; to separate the body responsible for the execution of the death penalty from the body responsible for the imposition of death sentence; and to establish a system of amnesty for death penalty cases.

【Key words】 Death Penalty, Reform, Prospect

A Design for Criminal Law

—the General Principles of the Total Reform of the Finnish Penal Code

Sakari Melander[*]

【Abstract】 Finland has undergone a total reform of its Penal Code since the beginning of the 1970s. The reform first started with the work of the Criminal Law Committee, which carefully pondered the foundations of the reform and the basic principles and commitments that were to form the basis of the actual reform. The reform work continued with the work of the Criminal Law Project, the task of which was to continue the work of the Criminal Law Committee and actually draft the new provisions forming the future Penal Code of Finland. The reform was officially completed in 1999, but actually it is, however, not complete even today. Criminal Law Committee and Criminal Law Project based the total reform of the Finnish Penal Code on certain principles. These principles illustrate the very design of Finnish criminal law and criminal justice policy. These principles also illustrate that the total reform of the Finnish Penal Code has not been carried out without a vision on the functions and objectives of criminal law and criminal justice policy. Instead, quite of an amount of time has been consumed in formulating these principles. This has, however, perhaps led to a situation where single substantive penal provisions have not been so carefully designed. The main purpose of the article is to carefully elaborate these principles that formed the foundation of the total reform of the Finnish Penal Code and the function of each principle. In

* LL. D. , Docent in Criminal Law, University of Helsinki.

addition, a wider perspective is also adopted. The principles formulated illustrate also the close connection of criminal justice policy and criminal legislation in Finland while the principles are explicitly affiliated with the objectives of the Finnish criminal justice policy. Also constitutional connections of the principles, such as connections to legal certainty, are examined.

I. Introduction

When we speak of design, we usually think of fashion or stylish furniture. Design could be, inter alia, defined to mean a preliminary sketch or outline showing the main features of something to be executed. [1] We could, for example, introduce a design for the new stadium that is to be built in the future. However, we are also familiar with the concept of institutional design. In social sciences, theories of institutional design aim to improve the public sphere[2]. Institutional design is also important with regard to business entities. The structure of the companies needs to be designed in order to obtain the ideal stage of efficiency and productivity. Also the states need to design different areas of their infrastructures. Institutional design is needed, for example, when telecommunication markets are constructed. The states need a plan according to which the future networks and the role of the operators, among others, are designed.

Legislation is a vital tool in institutional design. According to some American legal realists, legislation and lawyers had an irreplaceable role in developing the society. Roscoe Pound famously characterized lawyers as social engineers whose most important calling was to "make a social process or activity achieve its purpose with a minimum of friction and waste" . [3] According to Pound, law is also the most highly developed form of social control. [4] This means that the role of legislation is

---

[1] Merriam-Webster online (http: //www. merriam-webster. com/dictionary/design? show = 1&t = 1314092720).

[2] See, e. g. , Archon Fung, "Survey Article: Recipes for Public Spheres: Eight Institutional Design Choices and Their Consequences", 11 *Journal of Political Philofophy* (2003): pp. 338 – 367.

[3] Roscoe Pound, "The Lawyer as a Social Engineer", 3 *Journal of Public Law* (1954): p. 292 (292 – 303).

[4] *Ibid.*

crucial with regard to institutional design of a society. With the means with the help of legislation society can be developed in general, resources can be distributed equally and in a just manner, and societal problems or phenomena that entail harm or risk to can be taken under consideration and conceivably take necessary actions in minimizing the harmful incidents.

Criminal law as such is among the most crucial branches of law. Although criminal law had perhaps not in the history of law and legal science always been among the subjects of the most intellectual innovations and development[1], criminal law appears to offer the most coercive tools and means for state authorities that may be directed to-or against-the citizens. With the means of criminal law and penal legislation criminal liability may be directed toward individuals, and criminal liability is the strongest formal condemnation of the society. [2] In addition, criminal punishment when directed toward an individual offender directly breaches interests generally protected by the state. Imprisonment as a criminal punishment directly breaches the right to liberty protected by several international human rights instruments and pecuniary punishment directly affects the constitutional protection of property, which is likewise protected in various international human rights instruments. [3] When criminal punishment is always relevant relative to human rights and fundamental rights the presupposition should be that criminal law and criminal legislation should be carefully designed. And with criminal liability being the strongest and most coercive form of social condemnation used by the state we should presuppose that the institutional design of criminal law should be very carefully deliberated and constructed.

---

[1]　Roscoe Pound, for example, has stated that "Criminal law, whether in Roman law or in English law, never attained the systematic perfection that marks the civil side of the law". Roman criminal law, according to Pound, rather was "crude and unscientific to the last". Roscoe Pound, "The Future of Criminal Law", 21 *Columbia Law Review* (1921), p. 2 (1 – 16).

[2]　Andrew Ashworth, *Principles of Criminal Law* (Sixth Edition), (Oxford University Press, 2009), p. 1.

[3]　It could be noted that the Constitutional Law Committee of the Finnish Parliament has explicitly stated that criminal punishment is always relevant with regard to fundamental rights protected by Constitution since imprisonment invariably affects liberty and pecuniary punishment property. See Statement of the Constitutional Law Committee of the Finnish Parliament 23/1997, p. 2.

H. L. A. Hart famously stated that the general rationale behind making certain offences punishable, i. e. criminalizing certain acts or omissions, is to announce to society that these actions are not to be done and to secure that fewer of them are done. [1] In other words with the means of criminal legislation society is actually condemning certain acts and omissions on a general level. This general condemnation made by the legislative machinery of the state is not a minor aspect what it comes down to the legitimacy of criminal justice system. By criminalizing various acts and making them offences the state is using its ultimate power toward the citizens. Certain acts and omissions conceivably done by at least some citizens are announced as forbidden acts or omissions. If anything whatever and however could be criminalized, the state would be oppressing its citizens and drastically limiting the freedoms of the citizens. [2] By declaring various acts criminal the state is-if we adopt the view of the objectives of criminal law introduced by H. L. A. Hart-actually defining the minimum level of societal morality in a state. The state is declaring what acts are desirable and what acts are blameworthy.

Even if not proclaiming oneself a retributivist, one might admit that a theory of legislation is a moral theory[3] since with the means of-penal-legislation society is condemning certain acts on a general level. The general justifying aim of criminal law has traditionally-in the Nordic Countries-been general prevention but at the same time it has been accentuated that communication of generally acknowledged common values with the means of penal legislation and criminal justice system is a vital aspect belonging to the general justifying aim. [4] This means that the Nordic criminal law has a slight communitarian or-what comes to punishment theories-

---

[1] H. L. A. Hart, *Punishment and Responsibility*, Essays in the Philosophy of Law (Clarendon Press, Oxford, 1968) p. 6.

[2] As *Henry M. Hart* has stated: "What sense does it make to insist upon procedural safeguards in criminal prosecutions if anything whatever can be made a crime in the first place?" See Henry M. Hart, Jr., "The Aims of the Criminal Law", 23 *Law & Contemporary Problems* (1958), p. 431 (401 – 441).

[3] Michael S. Moore, *Placing Blame. A Theory of Criminal Law* (Clarendon Press, Oxford, 1997), p. 640.

[4] Nils Jareborg, "What Kind of Criminal Law Do We Want? On Defensive and Offensive Criminal Law Policy", in Nils Jareborg, *Scraps of Penal Theory* (Iustus Förlag, Uppsala, 2002), p. 90 (89 – 106).

communicative shade. [1] By stressing the general condemnation of certain acts and making it a vital requirement of a criminalization the moral aspects of criminal law and criminal legislation are at the same time highlighted. Criminal law, ultimately, is a normative system that seeks to maintain and support its explicit demands, i. e. criminalizations. It has been stated that it is logically impossible to enforce a normative system that gives or tries to give effect to its normative requirements but that at the same time is not giving expression to disapproval. [2] If we adopt this view, criminal law is always communicating condemnation, either at the level of legislation or by imputing criminal liability in single criminal cases. When this strong-or basically the strongest-form of official condemnation is connected to actual and explicit potential to limit the freedoms of the citizens with the help of criminal justice system the immediate need to carefully design criminal law becomes evident. What we need is a careful and thorough institutional design of criminal law that is based on a profound understanding of the reality criminal law is facing today.

The aim of this paper is to explore the design of Finnish criminal law with a view to criminal justice policy as well. Finland has undergone a total reform of criminal law since the 1970s. The Criminal Law Committee and Criminal Law Project, which has realized the reform work, have formulated some principles and objectives that illustrate the design of the Finnish criminal law. These principles and objectives show that the total reform has not been carried out without vision on the functions and objectives of the criminal law and criminal justice policy. Instead, quite amount of time has been consumed in formulating the principles in accordance of which the total reform is realized. However, this has perhaps led to a situation where single substantive provisions have not been so carefully designed. In any case the elaboration of the Finnish total reform of the Penal Code illustrates that in order to comprehensively reform (criminal) legislation the design of the reform needs to be carefully deliberated. Legislation always has societal impacts and also conceivable

---

① Sakari Melander, "Nordic Criminal Justice Policy—Single Path or Separate Ways?", in Jaakko Husa, Heikki Pihlajamäki, Kimmo Nuotio, eds., *Nordic Law—Between Tradition and Dynamism* (Intersentia, Antwerp, Oxford, 2007), p. 115 – 120 (109 – 125).

② Alf Ross, *On Guilt, Responsibility and Punishment* (University of California Press, Berkeley and Los Angeles, 1975), p. 36.

negative consequences that accentuate the role of lawyers and legislator as social engineers.

II. The Foundations of Criminal Justice Policy in Finland

The traditional view on criminal justice policy has accentuated that crime and criminality needs to be fought against. This view could be called as "fight against crime" -approach. When adopting this view the ultimate goal in criminal justice policy is fight against crime. This, among others, implicates that crime is something worth fighting against and that in the end the battle could be won. The traditional view also easily implicates that offenders are to not be regarded as fellow citizens. They are "they" and we are "us" and we need to be separated. The separation of "us" and "them" within criminal law is traditionally connected to "Feindstrafrecht" ("Enemy Criminal Law"), which treats offenders as second class citizens and guarantees no due process of law etc.

The Finnish view on criminal justice policy has adopted a different view from the 1960s and 1970s. This view-it must be mentioned-is still valid and relevant in Finland although considerable and relevant aspects foremost resulting from the Europeanization of criminal law have at least partly challenged the Finnish view. According to the Finnish view the fundamental aims or objectives of criminal justice policy are the following:

(1) to regulate/minimize the sum total of the social costs (including human suffering) caused by crime and by society's response to crime, and

(2) to distribute these social costs fairly among the involved parties, i. e. offenders, crime victims, tax payers etc. [1]

These objectives differ significantly from the traditional "fight against crime" -approach. Firstly these objectives presuppose that fight against crime-if one wants to use such rhetoric-can't be won. The Finnish view admits that there will always be a certain level of criminality in the society that is not desirable but that somehow

---

[1] See Patrik Törnudd, "In Defense of General Prevention", in Facts, Values and Visions. Essays in Crminology and Crime Policy (Helsinki, 1996), p. 15.

needs to be tolerated. Instead of fighting crime and criminality, which actually presupposes that this fight somehow and sometime really can be won, the sum total of the social costs caused by criminality should be minimized. In addition the sum total of the costs created by society's response to crime also needs to be minimized.

Secondly the Finnish objectives admit that crime and criminality should not be fought with any cost. The society must adopt an approach that contains cost awareness in its response to crime. This, quite naturally, is partly linked with the above-described view on the impossibility to totally abolish criminality from the society. If one were of the opinion that crime indeed could be fought against, one would perhaps have to do this with considerable amount of resources.

This could be illustrated by an example relating to public safety in city parks. Increasing the amount of policemen and security guards would to certain extent diminish the number of violent acts, robberies, and pick pocketing in the parks. However it could be estimated that a slight increase on the amount of policemen and security guards only would have a slight effect on criminality in park areas. In order to totally abolish criminal activity in park areas the number of policemen and security guards in park areas would have to be very high. Even if this were done, there would still be a chance for some criminal activity in park areas. In addition, a very high number of policemen and security guards may also create a feeling of insecurity among citizens.

The second objective in Finnish criminal justice policy highlights the role of the just distribution of the costs caused by criminality and the costs caused by society's response to crime and criminality. The aim behind this objective is that no one should alone bear these costs or that no one should be left alone in taking responsibility over reactions on criminal activity. Of course the role of the state in bearing the costs is evident. State should always take the primary responsibility in taking actions against crime and criminality. According to the Section 22 of the Finnish Constitution the public authorities shall guarantee the observance of basic rights and liberties and human rights. The state is therefore obliged to criminalize certain acts and see that the rights and interests that these criminalizations protect also in practice are protected-by police, prosecutors and by the court system.

The offender needs to bear his/her part of the costs, but this is mainly done with the burden affected by criminal sentence to the offender. The burden affected by criminal sanction is a heavy one. The Nordic view on criminal justice policy has traditionally emphasized that if-and the traditional answer to this if-question has been affirmative-we need to have a criminal justice system that uses criminal sanctions the system must be as humane as possible. Humanity is evident in the Nordic criminal justice system since the basic idea is to design the system bearing in mind that everyone-including the person who drafted the law-is a potential offender. It must be kept in mind that the fact that we ourselves could end up as a subject of a criminal justice system is at least conceivable. ① This is related-albeit the view on humaneness was adopted already in the 1970s-to the notion made by Constitutional Law Committee of the Finnish Parliament in 1997. The Committee stated that criminal sanction always interferes fundamental rights of a person; imprisonment infringes the right to a liberty and fine or a pecuniary punishment infringes a right to a property. ② By admitting that criminal penalties always infringe fundamental rights and taking the strong role of fundamental rights in Finnish legal science as a starting point, it is more likely appraise the role of humanity in criminal justice system when it may be connected to the system of fundamental rights and freedoms.

Considering the role of humanity within criminal justice system, an interesting comparison with the Chinese system may be done. *Guo Jian'an* wrote on his article "Implementation and Influence of a Criminal Policy Featured by Tempering Justice with Mercy" on the role of mercy and leniency in the traditional Chinese criminal law. According to Guo Juan'an criminal policy of this kind was quite recently officially introduced in the 16th Central Committee of the Communist Party of China (CPC) and the policy is related to the delivery of the VIII Amendment of the Chinese Penal Code. ③ Mercy or leniency could according to Juan'an in this context mean decriminalization, the use of non-judicial punishment (e. g. means of restorative justice) and mitigation of punishment. Juan'an also points that mercy

---

① See Sakari Melander, "Nordic Criminal Justice Policy—Single Path or Separate Ways?", in Jaakko Husa, Heikki Pihlajamäki and Kimmo Nuotio (eds.), *Nordic Law—Between Tradition and Dynamism* (Intersentia, 2007), pp. 119 – 120.

② The Statement of the Constitutional Law Committee of the Finnish Parliament 23/1997, p. 2.

③ Guo Jian'an, "Implementation and Influence of a Criminal Policy Featured by Tempering Justice with Mercy", *China Law* 3/2011, p. 82.

or leniency in criminal policy would enhance the objective of constructing the harmo nious society. [1] This objective of moving toward leniency and its connection with the construction of harmonious society seems to be in connection with the Nordic notion on the role of humanity in designing criminal justice system. Adopting the general societal point of view, the welfare of a society assessed as a whole is more efficiently promoted when the most repressive system of the state-i. e. criminal justice system-in general is as lenient and humane as possible. This does not mean that serious crime is judged with leniency. Instead, serious crime needs to be judged with severe means and severe enough sanctions. However, what humanity calls is that the overall level of repression caused by criminal justice system must be kept at the level that is as lenient and humane as possible.

Also the victim has his/her part with regard to the costs-although the participation of a victim needs to be kept on a moderate and reasonable level. It is however thinkable that the possible victims in certain situations prepare oneself with insurance or take necessary other actions, e. g. keep their possessions behind locked doors or use security systems in cars (immobilizers etc.). These actions do not basically affect the criminal liability of the offender in conceivable criminal cases but illustrate that also victims could take precautionary measures that minimize the sum total of the costs caused by crime and criminality.

The objectives described above also illustrate why Finnish-and Nordic, although the Finnish objectives of criminal justice policy are not explicitly shared by the other Nordic Countries-view on criminal justice policy is often described as rational and humane. Rationality is embodied in the objective of minimizing the costs. Humanity, however, is evident in the objective demanding the just distribution of the costs-although humanity has been appraised also to be a general principle of Finnish criminal justice policy.

---

[1] Guo Jian'an, "Implementation and Influence of a Criminal Pohily Featured by Tempering Justice with Mercy", China Law 31 2011, p. 83.

III. The Total Reform of the Finnish Penal Code (1972— 1999—?)

The total reform of the Finnish Penal Code was launched in the early 1970s. At the time Finnish Penal Code was from 1889-formally it actually still is since the total reform of the code has not been completed-and the code was severely out of date. Naturally several chapters of the code hade been revised but when assessed as a whole the code anyhow was a criminal code that was not able to answer the societal development that had undergone in the 1900s and the social situation of the 1960s and 1970s. Especially provisions on economic crime were seriously outdated or defective-the legislation at the time was not in accord with the rapid changes of the Finnish society and especially economical changes that took place in the 1960's and 1970's.

The launch of the total reform was the appointment of the Criminal Law Committee in 1972. The task of the committee was to prepare a comprehensive reform of the Finnish Penal Code. However, the Committee spent four years in defining the general principles and guidelines on how the penal code should be reformed. In other words the Criminal Law Committee only succeeded in formulating general principles and views on the general objectives and frameworks of the reform.

Four years after that the actual work of the total reform of the Finnish Penal Code was launched. The Criminal Law Project was appointed in 1980. The task of the project was to continue the work of the Criminal Law Committee and thus to actually propose explicit new criminal provisions forming the future Penal Code. It was also explicitly stated that the basis of this work was the report of the Criminal Law Committee. This means that there was a logical continuation between the Committee and the Project.

The Criminal Law Project realized that the Penal Code was so broad and extensive that the reform of the code as a whole in a single reform was impossible. Instead it decided to carry out the total reform in form of various partial reforms. The partial reforms were designed to encompass appropriate and functional composites of the chapters of the code. The work of the Criminal Law Project came into an end in 1999 when the Project was officially disbanded. It is anyhow worth noticing that at that time the total reform was not complete. In fact the work in order to complete the total reform continued right after and at the time of the disbandment of the Project. The total reform is not completed even today, some chapters of the Penal Code still are in their original form (from 1889, although these provisions are practically not applied).

IV. The Substantive Design of Finnish Criminal Law

The criminal law committee's views on criminalization and on the objectives of the criminal justice system that affect the design of criminal law could be divided into substantive and formal views. The substantive view deals mainly with the objectives of the criminal law while the formal view is concentrating on the formulation of various principles on how penal legislation should be drafted. While the formal view may seem to contain solely technical requirements on the formation of penal legislation it, however, contains important substantive dimensions on the use and objectives of criminal law.

The task of the Criminal Law Project was to adjust the penal legislation to meet new needs and requirements created by transition that had taken place in the Finnish society. In carrying out its adjusting task the Project still, however, needed to bear in mind that the settled legal expectations of the citizens and their sense of justice simultaneously were reasonably paid attention to. In addition in its total assessment of the scope of punishable behaviour the Project was encouraged to seek such legal solutions that as widely as possible could be accepted within different groups of the society. ① The main objective of the total revision of the Finnish Penal Code was, thus, to consider and evaluate the objectives, interests and values that could be promoted with the help of criminal justice system. In doing this, the Project was encouraged to weight the central values protected by criminal law and to completely reassess the scope of punishable behaviour. At the bottom these objectives could be said to illustrate the connection between criminal justice or

① Grönqvist, 1982, p. 146.

penal legislation and social justice. The idea is that criminal legislation needs to be accepted as widely as possible within society. Criminal justice system would otherwise not have the general preventive effect it is striving for.

Criminal Law Project also adopted certain tangible and general notions on criminalizations. Like mentioned above, the Project was of the opinion that the question on the contents of criminalizations at the same time is a question on social justice. When provisions on offences are drafted the interests of various societal groups need to be taken into account. In addition, criminal provisions deed to be drafted in a manner that provides more legal security. It seems like the Criminal Law Project has emphasized the requirement for maintaining the criminal justice system as just as possible. This is extremely evident in setting the various interests of the different groups of the society into central role in the legislative reform. The requirement on legal certainty, in turn, accentuates the repressive nature of the criminal justice system. If and when legal security is highlighted the conceivable problems on legal certainty caused by the utilitarian objectives of the system, particularly objectives relating to general prevention, are hopefully diminished. ①

V. The Formal Criteria on the Design of Finnish Criminal Law

Like mentioned above, the Criminal Law Project adopted also some formal criteria on how criminal provisions on the special part of the Penal Code should be formulated. Regardless of the characterization of these criteria in this paper, which solely accentuates the formal nature of the criteria, these criteria contain also important substantive requirements that have deeper objectives than the formal design of the provisions of the special part. In the law drafting materials of the Project the principles were named as the principles of total reform. In the following these principles are briefly elaborated since they illustrate the design of Finnish criminal law. It could be briefly mentioned that in the official documents (mostly on the document from the Finnish Ministry of Justice) these principles have been said to enjoy a status of established principle of legislation, which practically means

① Lahti, 1991, p. 263.

that the legislator is more or less bound to these principles. The principles need to be followed unless there are serious reasons that justify the deviation from these principles.

1. *The Principle of Centralization.* The principle of centralization seeks to centralize all essential criminal provisions, i. e. , criminalizations, with a possibility to a prison sentence into Penal Code. In practice this meant that during the Criminal Law Project relevant offences that located in legislation outside the Penal Code-like provisions on drug offences and provisions on traffic offences-were gathered into the Penal Code. At the same time the principle of centralization meant that the Chapters of the Penal Code were designed to be as consistent and coherent as possible. The aim was to create a consistent and coherent Penal Code by gathering offences that breached similar interests under the same Chapter-e. g. , offences against privacy, public peace and personal reputation (Chapter 24) or offences against personal liberty (Chapter 25) -or by gathering offences relating to the same area of living under the same Chapter-e. g. , traffic offences (Chapter 23) , employment offences (Chapter 47).

The practice has shown that principle of centralization has proven to be an important principle of the total reform. The Finnish parliament, for instance, has in some occasions highly advocated the principle and stressed the importance of it. ① It must, however, be noted that the principle of centralization does not in all situations provide that the preconditions of the punishable acts are exhaustively defined in the Penal Code. In some situations, for instance, the legislation that defines the limits of the punishable act is so technical and extensive that it would be impossible and impractical if the regulation of this kind would be located into the Penal Code. In these situations the provisions on the Penal Code criminalize various acts that are in more detail defined in a decree. The legislative design of this kind is, however, a bit problematic with regard to the principle of legality.

The practical background and basis of the principle of centralization is to be located on the fact that before the total reform of the Penal Code provisions on

---

① Report of the Law Committee of the Finnish Parliament 22/1994, p. 6; Report of the Law Committee of the Finnish Parliament 12/2006, p. 4 and Report of the Law Committee of the Finnish Parliament 27/2006, p. 1 – 2.

offences outspreaded throughout legislation. There was, therefore, a strong practical need to gather the most important offences under one Penal Code. On a deeper substantive level the principle is relevant from the perspective of the principles of legality and legal certainty. Firstly, the principle of legality provides that everyone should be able to foresee if a certain act or omission is punishable from the wording of the criminal offence. [1] This information should be easily available for everyone since otherwise they would perhaps not feel that the criminal justice system operates in a legitimate matter. Also the functioning mechanism of general prevention necessitates that citizens are actually aware on the contents of the penal legislation. Defined to encompass this, the principle of centralization also works to strengthen the internalization of legal rules, which is one of the main hypothesis of the Nordic view on general prevention. Secondly principle of centralization promotes legal certainty since it makes the recognition of limits of the punishable easier with regard to the citizen and also with regard to the criminal process.

2. *The Principle of Standardization.* The principles of standardization or the principle on the standardized formulation of penal provisions provides that criminal provisions are drafted by respecting uniform design. In practice the principles has meant that the provisions on the special part of the Penal Code had been drafted in a similar matter. All provisions on the special part of the Penal Code could be divided into three parts:

1) A name of the provisions [e. g. , Assault (Chapter 21, Section 5)],

2) A description on the essential elements of the crime (e. g. , "A person who employs physical violence on another or, without such violence, injures the health of another, causes pain to another or renders another unconscious or into a comparable condition"), and

---

[1]　See the following statements of the Constitutional Law Committee of the Finnish Parliament: Statement 10/2000 vp, p. 2, Statement 22/2001, p. 3, Statement 29/2001, p. 3, Statement 41/ 2001, p. 2, Statement 26/2002, p. 2, Statement 40/2002, p. 7, Statement 48/2002, p. 2, Statement 26/2004, p. 3, Statement 7/2005, p. 3, Statement 17/2006, p. 3, Statement 18/2007, p. 5 and Statement 68/2010, p. 4. The formulation is also often referred by the European Court of Human Rights.

3) Penalty scale (e. g. , shall be sentenced for assault to a fine or to imprisonment for at most two years).

At the same time the compliance with the principle has meant that the penal provisions had become more generally defined. This may be in contradiction with the principle of legality, which requires that penal provisions are accurate enough. However, one objective of the total reform was to avoid criminal provisions that are too casuistic, since the rapid development of the society easily makes casuistic provisions outdated. Because of the principle of legality, principle of standardization does not allow too general provisions while in any case demanding a certain level of generality. [1] The principle demands that the legislator needs to walk a tightrope between the principle of legality and principle of standardization-where principle of legality naturally gains more weight during this tricky journey.

3. *Principle of established penalty scales.* The Criminal Law Project strived for the realization of the inner proportionality of the Penal Code with adopting a somewhat similar view on the abstract seriousness of the offences than the Criminal Law Committee had adopted. The project introduced a variety of model penalty scales that were intended to be used in the provisions of the special part. The penalty scales most typically used were-and still are, unless the Penal Code naturally recognises other penalty scales as well-the following:

Fine;

Fine-imprisonment for at most 6 months;

Fine-imprisonment for at most 1 year;

Fine-imprisonment for at most 1 year and 6 months;

Fine-imprisonment for at most 2 years;

Imprisonment for at least 4 months and at most 4 years;

Imprisonment for at least 1 year and at most 10 years; and

Imprisonment for at least 2 years and at most 10 years.

With the adoption of these model penalty scales the intention was firstly to affect the total level of penalties. The idea was to make the criminal justice system more lenient and the adoption of these model penalty scales was one move to that direction. Secondly, by adopting a variety of model penalty scales the intention

---

[1] Grönqvist, 1982, p. 150.

was to refrain from enacting too vague penalty scales, which could lead to inaccuracy and unforeseeability. This intention aims at the uniformity of sentencing practice, which is highly relevant with regard to equality. If we are having too broad and vague penalty scales penalties on a different level could actually be imposed more easily in similar cases. If the penalty scales, whereas, are restricted a little, possibilities that courts will deliver unequal penalties are at the same time diminished.

It has been stated that the model penalty scales adopted within the total reform of the Finnish Penal code are a vital part of consistent and coherent criminal justice policy carried out in Finland and that these model penalty scales indicate that legislative reforms have had a strong effect on practice-that is: sentencing practices. [1] On my opinion, the model penalty scales also indicate that the criminal justice system was within the total reform reviewed as a whole-it was seen to encompass an entity that needed to be constructed by taking different parts into account and by realizing the effects that a certain legislative act has on other parts of the system. At least the model penalty scales show that the question on criminalization inevitably is related to sentencing.

The model penalty scales have been challenged with especially the Europeanization of criminal law. The national implementation of the criminal law framework decisions and directives of the European Union has forced the Finnish legislator to adopt new penalty scales that are not consistent with regard to the model penalty scales adopted in the total reform. The maximum of 8 years of imprisonment, for instance, has been adopted in the Penal Code since it has been required by some framework decisions of the Union. It has been stated that these "new" penalty scales have disturbed the supposed inner proportionality of the Penal Code.

4. *Principle on the formulation of petty and aggravated offences.* This principle is strongly connected to model penalty scales described above. In addition to the penalty scales almost consistently used in the Finnish Penal Code, offences are usually divided in three categories with regard to the blameworthiness or seriousness of the-abstract-act. An offence in the Finnish Penal Code is usually divided into a

① Lahti, 2004, pp. 416 – 417.

"normal" offence, a petty offence and an aggravated offence. The model penalty scales are normally used in these offences. It could be stated that a "normal" penalty scale used in many aggravated forms of offences is imprisonment for at least 4 months and at most 4 years (e. g. , aggravated deprivation of personal liberty (Chapter 25 , Section 2), aggravated theft (Chapter 28 , Section 2), aggravated embezzlement (Chapter 25 , Section 5), and aggravates subsidy fraud (Chapter 29 , Section 6).

The most visible form of the principle is that aggravated offences need to be formulated in a manner that leaves no room for inaccuracy. The grounds under which an offence may be considered as aggravating need to be exhaustively listed in a provisions on aggravated offence in question. The main reason for this is the principle of legality, which does not-according to the Finnish understanding of the principle-allow that provisions on aggravated offences contain an open clause with the basis of which an offence could be considered as aggravating, e. g. , "under similar situations". Besides that at least the demands set in one explicitly formulated situation where the offence may be considered aggravated need to be fulfilled, an offence always ought to be aggravated when assessed as a whole- this so called total assessment clause is included in every aggravated offence, except on a provisions on causing a serious traffic hazard (Chapter 23 , Section 2). The aim of the total assessment clause is to limit the use of the aggravated provisions and to force the courts to assess the provisions and the criminal act in question completely- as a whole, taking all things into consideration and by setting an extra threshold on aggravated offences. The requirements on the explicit formulation on aggravating grounds and the total assessment clause as such signify the rational and humane criminal justice policy traditionally emphasized in Finland, since they strive for the limited use of the aggravated offences. In addition, legal certainty is being increased with more explicit formulations on aggravated offences that may result to harsh penalties.

An example of an aggravated offence in the Finnish Penal Code could be as follows:

Chapter 28

Section 2-*Aggravated theft* (769/1990)

(1) If in the theft

(1) the object of the appropriation is very valuable,

(2) the appropriation causes particularly significant loss to the victim of the offence, in view of the victim's circumstances,

(3) the offender takes advantage of the helplessness or distress of the victim of the offence,

(4) in order to carry out the act, the offender or a participant equips himself or herself with a firearm, explosives or another similar dangerous instrument, or

(5) the offender breaks into an occupied residence,

and the theft is aggravated also when assessed as a whole, the offender shall be sentenced for *aggravated theft* to imprisonment for at least four months and at most four years.

(2) An attempt is punishable.

A significant problem in legal practice is that the total assessment clause has practically gained no substantive content in court action. Basically an offence is assessed as aggravated with reference to one ground under which an offence may be considered as aggravating. The courts in Finland usually merely state after stating that one aggravating ground set in the provision has been fulfilled that the "act is also aggravated when assessed as a whole". This means that there usually is no reasoning with regard to the total assessment clause. This is very problematic relative to principle of legality and legal certainty. Perhaps the better solution would be the abolition of the clause since it has no practical meaning or the practical meaning of the clause is highly limited.

5. *Principle on the grounds of imputability.* This principle also manifests the aims or objectives of rational and humane criminal justice policy. In addition, the principle could, however, be connected to the Constitution of Finland which explicitly states that the constitution shall guarantee the inviolability of human dignity (Section 1, Subsection 2 of the Finnish Constitution). However, when the Finnish criminal justice system has been widely connected to the Finnish constitution and to Finnish provisions on fundamental rights, it has also been essential to detect the basic value behind the system of fundamental rights, human dignity. Therefore the connection between criminal justice system and the inviolability of human dignity has been considered to be essential. The principle for example forbids strict liability in criminal law as the principle foremost concentrates

on guaranteeing the autonomy of individual[①].

A basic foundation adopted in the total reform of the Finnish Penal Code is that imputability always presupposes either intent or negligence. This is currently explicitly stated in the general part of the Penal Code (Chapter 3, Section 5, Subsection 1: "Intent or negligence are prerequisites for criminal liability"). In order to mainly advocate intent as a primary form of imputability, if negligent forms of act or omissions need to be criminalized-for, e. g. , reasons relating to general prevention-, this always needs to be done explicitly in a criminal provision on the special part (Chapter 3, Section 5, Subsection 2: "Unless otherwise provided, an act referred to in this Code is punishable only as an intentional act"). This means that intent is regarded as the basic form of imputability. However, there are numerous offences where negligent behavior also has been criminalized. In any case the requirement for explicit criminalization of the negligence calls the legislator to consider if this kind of widening of criminalized behavior is necessary.

The most important dimension of this principle is the prohibition of strict liability offences. This is absolutely important also with regard to the constitutionalization of Finnish Criminal Law.

VI. Conclusion

The substantive and formal-that contain important substantive dimensions-principles and the Finnish objectives on criminal justice policy implicate that there is actually is a quite well-considered design behind the Finnish Penal Code. Within this design the principle of legality and legal certainty have a central role, not to forget the important dimensions of equality that the principles contain. Equality is especially evident on the substantive view on the use of criminal law the Criminal Law Project formulated. The formal principles, in turn, mainly illustrate legality and legal certainty, although equality has its position also within these formal principles.

The design of the Finnish Criminal Law could be said to be very carefully and

---

① See generally Melander 2008, pp. 261 - 325.

thoroughly considered. The Criminal Law Committee, which operated from 1972 to 1976, mainly concentrated on general issues, on principles on how to reform and design criminal legislation. The Criminal Law Project, in turn, took the actual law drafting that was designated to result a wholly new Penal Code. First of all the work of the Criminal Law Project took a considerably long time-the project was launched in 1980, it was officially abolished in 1999, but several partial reforms belonging to the total reform have been carried out after 1999. In addition, the total reform is not complete even today. However, despite of the thorough and long-lasting pondering on principles and objectives, especially provisions on the special part could be criticized since they do not on a best possible way to meet the demands of the actual cases. This is perhaps due to the principle standardization that required a certain level of generality of penal provisions.

The most significant lack of the total reform is that many aspects relating to the total reform and, besides, various provisions amended at the time of the total reform already are-and some aspects and provisions already at the time of the total reform were-out of date. The Penal Code contains, for instance, no explicit chapter on computer and Internet crimes. The work of the total reform was mainly carried out in the 1980s when computers, networks, mobile phones had on a considerably smaller role in the everyday life of the citizens than today. It could be stated that the Finnish criminal law with regard to computer and Internet crimes is highly underdeveloped.

Another considerable deficit is the relation of the total reform to the Europeanization and internalization of criminal law, which have been the main trends in criminal law since the 1990s. These developments do not in any way become visible on the reports and bills prepared in connection with the total reform. It could, therefore, be questioned, if the objectives and principles are of any importance. On my opinion they are, but the traditional view adopted in Finland inevitably needs to be adjusted to meet the new situation. In some cases the adjustment of the objectives and principles may result to the partial alteration of the objectives and principles.

刑法的设计

—— 芬兰刑法典全面改革的一般原则

萨卡里·梅兰德

【摘要】 自 20 世纪 70 年代初以来，芬兰对其刑法典进行了全面的改革。改革始于刑法委员会的工作，它仔细地考察了改革的基础、基本原则和目标，这些工作构成了实际改革的基石。改革工作由刑法项目（Criminal Law Project）开展，该项目的主要任务是继续刑法委员会的工作，并实际起草最终成为芬兰未来刑法典的新条文。官方层面上来说，改革是在 1999 年就完成了，然而实际上至今仍尚未完成。刑法委员会和刑法项目将芬兰刑法典的总体改革构建在某些原则上，这些原则体现了芬兰刑法典和刑事司法政策的设计。这些原则还说明了芬兰刑法典的总体改革并非是在对刑法和刑事司法政策的功能和目标缺乏展望的基础上展开的。相反，制定这些原则耗费了相当多的时间。恰恰这也许导致了对个别实体性的刑法条款未能谨慎设计的情况。本文的主要目的在于详细阐明构成芬兰刑法典全面改革的基础的那些原则以及每个原则的功能。另外，从更为开阔的视角来看，这些原则表明了在芬兰刑事司法政策和刑事立法之间的密切关系，这些原则是明确服务于芬兰刑事司法政策的目标。同时，本文还将检验这些原则与宪法的联系，例如与法律确定性的联系。

毒品控制与毒品刑法

樊　文[*]

【摘要】 毒品消费引发的毒品问题是毒品滥用而成瘾癖。毒品刑法保护的法益是免于陷入毒品依赖的不自由状态的危险。但是，不同于毒品消费引发的毒品问题，毒品的刑法控制，也会形成新的毒品问题。因为把刑法用作毒品控制的第一手段，不能减少毒品市场的供给和需求，也不能遏制毒品犯罪的持续增长，反而引发毒品犯罪的有组织化发展趋势。因此，现行刑法上的重刑对于毒品控制是过剩的手段。禁毒造成黑市，黑市的垄断造成对毒品消费者的勒索和剥削；同时，黑市也驱动犯罪，应对的措施应是在降低刑法严厉性的同时，通过国家监控下的海洛因处方制度来瓦解毒品黑市。尽管对于毒品及其药理效果的错误认知以及对毒品零忍耐的历史文化观念，是借鉴成功的海洛因处方制度的障碍，但是，为尽量避免毒品消费者生存条件和人权状况因严厉禁毒的负面后果而继续恶化，由此产生的针对毒品需求方的"损害最小化"设想和实践，是每个人都不会反对的、符合实际的毒品控制方向。

【关键词】 毒品控制　毒品刑法

　　毒品消费是一种极为复杂的现象，我们没有什么奇妙的办法能有朝一日把毒品滥用的现象彻底根绝。各种形式的毒品消费将会像历史上曾经出现过的那样，一直存在下去，这是无法回避的事实。因此，把毒品政策的总目标定位在实现一个根本没有毒品的社会，[①] 是与现实不符的乌托邦。[②]减

---

*　中国社会科学院法学所副研究员。

①　2000 年 6 月，中国国务院新闻办公室发表的《中国的禁毒》白皮书的前言中写道："中国政府坚持严厉禁毒的立场，采取一切必要措施，尽最大努力禁绝毒品，造福人民。"

②　随着放弃无毒品社会和全面禁戒的目标要求，欧洲国家毒品政策的措辞已经发生了变化（即便是在不愿放弃这个目标的瑞典，如今也认为无毒品社会的目标只是个梦想），欧洲行动计划和国家毒品项目中突出的措辞是希望减少非法毒品和合法毒品的消费。

少所有形式的毒品消费，倒是每个人都不会反对的毒品控制的重要共识。通常来说，减少毒品消费的共识下可以衍生出控制、预防和干预三种理念和五种模式。模式具体是：经济模式，通过提高价格来减少需求；垄断/许可经营模式，通过限制经营资格，限制供货，来减少供给；少年保护模式，宣传毒品危害，教育涉毒少年，严格限制少年接触毒品的机会，比如严禁出售毒品给青少年；医疗模式，通过医生的处方义务来限制接触毒品的渠道，以此来减少供给，通过治疗成瘾癖者，来减少需求；刑法的禁止模式，着力于通过禁止和镇压手段，比如刑罚、强制戒毒措施来实现减少供给和需求的目的。

尽管世界上大多数国家包括我国，对于毒品实行的是刑法禁止模式主导的绝对的全面禁止制度，[①] 但是如果想用刑法手段实现政策定位错误的无毒品社会，那是不人道的，也是不自量力的。为实现这样的乌托邦，更有甚者有些国家如今把对毒品的治理已经升级为"针对毒品的战争"，[②] 而这种"战争"形式的镇压，本质上就意味着法治国家原则下法律层面的治理多多少少已经不甚重要。

如果国家想用刑法手段对已经成年、健康的公民规定他们应该吃什么和喝什么，那就是一种地地道道的国家监护。宪法对公民人格自由发展的构想，[③] 把是否享用或摄取以及在什么程度（剂量）上享用或摄取什么样的生活品，完全交给了公民个人自己去决定。因此，尽管我们不希望看到享乐主义的吸毒盛行的社会，但是，应该努力去阻止这种刑法禁止、干预范式，即利用刑法手段把一些本应自主决定的东西强加给少数人。因此，当今毒品政策争论的关键问题就是：人们是否希望实现一个没有毒品的社会以及采用什么样的手段来实现这样一个目标。

刑法是国家进行社会控制的最为严厉的手段，只能作为可以考虑的最后手段予以适用。但是，在毒品政策上，刑法常常被用作对待毒品问题的第一手段。这是一种后果很严重的决策，因为解决毒品问题把刑法作为第一手段，首先是不适合的，其次是具有反作用效果的。

尽管刑法资源的投入在不断加大（增加罪名、提高刑罚幅度、投入新

---

① 从《中华人民共和国刑法》第 357 条关于毒品的定义中就可以看出这一点。

② 比如，投入军事武装力量来打击武装毒品走私或贩卖。在南美洲、亚洲的许多国家都会发现这种针对毒品的战争状态。

③ 参见《中华人民共和国宪法》第 5 条第 1 款，第 33 条第 3 款，第 38 条第 1 句，第 43 条第 1 款。

的侦查措施①等），但是，每年新加入吸毒行列的人数仍在增长，比如，俄罗斯的吸毒人数每年新增约有 7.5 万人，② 我国近年来的增幅更大。③ 吸毒导致死亡的人数也在大幅增长。数据显示，20 世纪 70 年代初，德国每年吸毒死亡的是 200 人以下。到了 80 年代，吸食鸦片而导致死亡的每年平均有 500 人。1989 年，与吸食鸦片有关的死亡数增长到近 1000 起。1990 年因吸毒死亡的人数达到了 1491 起，1991 年达到峰值 2125 起，从 1991 年到 2002 年，每年因吸毒死亡的人数徘徊在 1500 人至 2100 人之间。④ 从其他西方工业国家也都可以观察到类似情况。俄罗斯每年因吸毒死亡的人数高达 3 万人。⑤ 中国禁毒年度报告称，2004 年因吸毒造成的死亡人数累计达到了 33975 名。尽管刑法的毒品控制日趋严厉，为获取毒品而实施的犯罪也在持续增长。⑥

---

① 中国的缉毒机构在重大毒品犯罪案件中广泛运用着诱惑侦查、控制下交付、监控侦查、特情侦查和卧底侦查五种主动且秘密型侦查方式以及搭梯子、金融调查这两种侦查策略。这些在实务中运用了很长时期的措施，以增加"技术侦查"专节的方式在近来讨论的《刑事诉讼法修正草案》中建议予以立法承认。

② 参阅中国日报网消息，http：//www.chinadaily.com.cn/hqgj/2010 - 03/11/content_ 9574652.htm。

③ 中国的年度在册吸毒人数：2000 年 86 万，2001 年 90 万，2002 年 100 万，2003 年 105 万，2004 年 114 万，2005 年 116 万，参见《中国刑事法杂志》2004 年第 1 期，第 106 页。《中国禁毒年度报告》称，2007 年 12 月底，全国吸毒人员数据库中的人员达到 95.7 万。到 2008 年 12 月底，全国网上入库的吸毒人数是 112.67 万，其中滥用海洛因等阿片类毒品的 90 万人。根据国家禁毒委办公室发布的数据，截至 2009 年底，全国现有登记在册吸毒人数达 133.5 万，比 2008 年增加 209158 人，其中男性占 84.6%，女性占 15.4%。从年龄结构看，35 岁以下人员占 58.1%，与往年相比继续呈下降趋势。从滥用种类看，滥用海洛因人员 97.8 万人，所占比例下降到 73.2%。滥用冰毒、氯胺酮合成毒品人员 36 万人，所占比例上升到 27%。其中滥用冰毒人数上升较快，2009 年各地公安机关在执法活动中共发现吸食冰毒人员 75505 名，占该年新登记吸毒人员总数的 37.9%。（参见新京报电子报 2010 年 2 月 3 日星期三，中国新闻 - 综合 A17，http：//epaper.bjnews.com.cn/html/2010 - 02/03/content_ 62650.htm？div = -1，记者李静睿）。《2011 年中国禁毒报告》称，2010 年新发现 21.4 万吸毒人员，截至 2010 年底，全国共发现登记吸毒人员总数达到 154.5 万（其中海洛因成瘾人数 106.5 万，占 69%。滥用合成毒品问题更加突出，仅查获登记的就有 43.2 万名，其中新查获 11.94 万名，多数是 25 岁以下青少年）。有专家估计，实际的吸毒人数可能是公布数据的 4 倍以上。

④ Vgl. von Danwitz, Examens-Repetitorium Kriminologie, C. F. Mueller, 2004, S. 120；PKS 2002, S. 227.

⑤ 参阅中国日报网消息，http：//www.chinadaily.com.cn/hqgj/2010 - 03/11/content_ 9574652.htm。

⑥ 俄罗斯联邦毒品监督局 2010 年 3 月 10 日发布一份声明称，在俄罗斯记录在册的吸毒者就有 55 万人，而全俄预计有多达 250 万人吸毒，占到俄罗斯总人口的 2%。而且吸毒者遍布全俄各地。声明还指出，在过去的 10 年，吸毒者的数量迅速增加，随之增加的是由毒品引发的各类犯罪。

如果用经济学的视角观察这个问题，就会发现，刑法对毒品的供给和需求的影响从来就不曾成功过。首先，通过刑法手段全面控制毒品市场的供给是不可能的。比如，德国评估数据显示，德国警方没收的非法毒品仅占市场上流通的5%～10%。① 这就是说，一次成功起获毒品的记录同时也是总体上控制失败的一次记录。还可以观察到的有趣的事实是，警方在哪里成功起获并没收了毒品，那里的毒品价格很快就会上涨，② 那里获取毒品型的犯罪发生率也几乎同时走高。③ 这种价格的变化只是暂时的，因为毒品市场上其他地方的毒品会很快补充过来。即使投入刑事追诉的新手段，比如卧底侦探、电讯监控、窃听技术，这种企图以刑法控制供给的状况并不曾得到明显的改善。④ 此外还要注意到，采取刑法手段控制毒品而引起的毒品市场的结构性变化，会引发更多的伴随市场"重新洗牌"的暴力冲突；在卖方市场的条件下，缴获毒品而导致的毒品成本的增加，最终会转嫁给始终受剥削的毒品消费者。

其次，用刑法也很难控制毒品消费者的需求。虽然立法者尊重公民"自我伤害的权利"，不用刑罚处罚毒品消费行为，但这并不能说对毒品消费者就是实际的恩惠，因为消费毒品的前提是消费者必须提前获得或者持有毒品。而这种获得和持有的行为是受刑罚处罚的。⑤ 把持有毒品规定为犯罪在法律上就很难把毒品消费和毒品犯罪清楚地区分开来。从形式上看，毒品消费是不受刑罚处罚的，但是，事实上是受刑罚处罚的。研究表明，刑罚处罚（更不用说加大力度的刑罚处罚），对于毒品消费行为都没有产生过任何影响。⑥

一般而言，刑法的主导思想是：行为必须侵害了他人的法益，才能给

① *Albrecht*, *H. -J. /A. v. Kalmthout*, Drug Policies in Western Europe, 1989, S. 437.

② 由于浙江警方打击严厉，导致浙江地下毒品市场价格水涨船高，特别是合成毒品，价格越来越离谱，如一粒高纯度的麻古（冰毒片剂）达180多元，而一克纯度高的冰毒竟要1000多元。http://news. ifeng. com/gundong/detail_ 2011_ 06/24/7221942_ 0. shtml.

③ *Neskovic*, W. , vom Elend der prohibitiven Drogenpolitik, in: Goessner, R. （Hrsg.）, Mythos Sicherheit, Nomos, 1995, S. 359.

④ Vgl. Frankfurter Rundshau vom 01. 09. 1992, "Senat legt Horrorzahlen ueber gescheiterte Drogenpolitik vor".

⑤ 《中华人民共和国刑法》第347条，第348条。

⑥ *Neskovic*, W. , vom Elend der prohibitiven Drogenpolitik, in: Goessner, R. （Hrsg.）, Mythos Sicherheit, Nomos, 1995, S. 356.

予刑法上的处罚。但是，毒品犯罪没有明显的被害人；行为人和被害人有时甚至是同一个人。这种特征会导致，比如，为了自己消费而持有毒品的犯罪行为人被置于国家监护之下，他们不接受立法者把他们和强奸犯、杀人犯或者抢劫犯放在同一个犯罪层次上予以对待。如果说刑法应该赎抵的是对于他人法益的侵害，那么，这里的问题是，非法持有毒品罪究竟应该赎抵的是什么样的不法？[①]

当下依靠刑法希望对供给和需求产生影响，这样的毒品政策本身不仅是不合适的，要达到刑罚威慑的目的也是不可能的，而且还会起反作用。最成问题的是毒品刑法中对走私、贩卖、运输和制造毒品犯罪设置的死刑。[②]

《2010 年联合国死刑状况报告》显示，全世界有 32 个司法区域（包括国家和地区）[③]的立法对毒品犯罪规定了死刑。除了法律上有死刑规定、但实际上至少有 10 年没有执行过死刑的 5 个国家[④]以及很少仅仅因为毒品犯罪而执行死刑的 4 个国家[⑤]，规定并执行毒品犯罪死刑的国家和地区就剩下了 23 个。中国便是这个 23 个国家和地区中的一员。超过一半的亚洲国家对毒品犯罪规定了死刑，2008 年到 2010 年，仍有 8 个国家[⑥]对毒品犯罪执行死刑。[⑦] 中国属于八分之一。

1979 年中国刑法对于毒品犯罪只设立了 1 个条文（第 171 条），规定的犯罪是制造、贩卖、运输毒品罪，基本刑罚是：处五年以下有期徒刑或者拘役，可以并处罚金。对于一贯或者大量制造、贩卖、运输毒品的，处五

---

① 有学者认为，如果根据查获的证据，不能认定非法持有较大数量毒品是为了进行走私、贩卖、运输或者窝藏毒品犯罪的，就可以认定为非法持有毒品罪。从这个观点中，可以看到，非法持有毒品罪是前面几种犯罪的兜底犯罪构成。但是，这里立法上的问题在于非法持有这种行为损害的是哪个被害人的什么法益。如果没有损害他人的法益，那么动用刑法来处罚这种行为，就是刑法的滥用。

② 《中华人民共和国刑法》第 347 条第 2 款。

③ 包括：中国、伊朗、沙特阿拉伯、越南、新加坡、马来西亚、印度尼西亚、科威特、泰国、巴基斯坦、埃及、叙利亚、也门、孟加拉、古巴、阿曼、阿拉伯联合酋长国、巴林、印度、卡塔尔、美国、朝鲜、伊拉克、苏丹、利比亚、斯里兰卡、老挝、缅甸、韩国、文莱－达鲁萨兰国共 30 个国家。另外还有 2 个地区：中国台湾和加沙地区（原巴勒斯坦领土）。

④ 斯里兰卡、老挝、缅甸、韩国、文莱－达鲁萨兰国。

⑤ 阿拉伯联合酋长国、巴林、印度、美国。

⑥ 朝鲜、印度尼西亚、马来西亚、巴基斯坦、泰国、中国、新加坡和越南。

⑦ Global State of Harm Reduction 2010, Key issues for broadening the response, ihra, S. 17.

年以上有期徒刑，可以并处没收财产。1982 年 3 月 8 日全国人大常委会通过的《关于严惩严重破坏经济的罪犯的决定》第 1 条第 1 款对该罪情节特别严重的毒品犯罪第一次规定了死刑。① 1990 年 12 月 28 日全国人大常务会通过的《关于禁毒的决定》第 2 条把"特别严重"的情节具体为五种情节，具备其一可以适用死刑。② 直到现在这种毒品犯罪的死刑规定一直没有改变。死刑范围扩大到毒品犯罪与围绕人权和死刑适用而出现的国际规范是冲突的。负责监督《公民权利和政治权利国际公约》的联合国人权委员会在很多场合多次表示，即便是贩毒也"不能算是最严重的罪行"③；联合国条约机构和人权监督系统④发表的许多国际人权法的报告和解释，批评对毒品犯罪使用死刑是对国际人权法的侵犯，明确反对将死刑应用于毒品犯罪⑤。近年来，中国的法律专家和司法、立法机构也开始积极讨论毒品犯罪的死刑问题，尤其是与走私、制造毒品的危害性比较，质疑贩卖毒品和运输毒品犯罪的死刑是否存在必要性。⑥ 2010 年中国的最高人民法院在《刑法修正案（八）》的修正意见中建议废除运输毒品罪的死刑，但遗憾的是全国人大常委会的审议中没有通过。

　　立法上的动向是减少毒品犯罪的死刑罪名，司法上也有积极的表现。2007 年最高人民法院、最高人民检察院、公安部联合发布《办理毒品犯罪案件适用法律若干问题的意见》，要求可能判处死刑的毒品犯罪案件，必须

---

① 该款规定是"处十年以上有期徒刑、无期徒刑或者死刑，可以并处没收财产"。把原来的最低刑提高到了 10 年，增加了无期徒刑和死刑。

② 走私、贩卖、运输、制造毒品罪可以适用死刑的五种情节是：量大（鸦片 1000 克，海洛因 50 克）；集团首要分子；武装掩护的；以暴力抗拒检查、拘留、逮捕，情节严重的；参与有组织的国际贩毒活动的。法定最低刑为确定的 15 年有期徒刑，可选的其他两个刑种是无期徒刑和死刑。把 1982 年决定的"可以并处没收财产"改为"并处没收财产"。1991 年 6 月在国际反对毒品滥用和非法贩运日四周年之际召开了毒品控制大会，中国政府公开宣布开展"禁毒人民战争"。

③ Schabas：《毒品犯罪的死刑问题》，中国—欧盟人权对话：人权与禁毒、人权与科技研讨会论文，2011 年 9 月 6~7 日，第 54 页。

④ 包括联合国人权事务高级专员，联合国酷刑问题特别报告员，联合国法外处决、即决处决或任意处决问题特别报告员，联合国毒品和犯罪问题办公室等。

⑤ Schabas：《毒品犯罪的死刑问题》，中国—欧盟人权对话：人权与禁毒、人权与科技研讨会论文，2011 年 9 月 6~7 日，第 54、55 页。

⑥ 2010 年 8 月 26 日南方周末记者对清华大学周光权教授的访谈，http：//nf. nfdaily. cn/epaper/nfzm/content/20100826/ArticelA05002FM. htm，访问日期：2011 年 9 月 17 日。

进行毒品含量鉴定，毒品鉴定结论中应有含量鉴定的结论;① 2009 年最高人民法院总结毒品犯罪案件的审判经验，统一了死刑裁判的标准，把可判处死刑立即执行的情形具体限定为 5 种,② 要求下级人民法院进一步严把毒品犯罪死刑案件的事实关、证据关、程序关和法律适用关，确保毒品犯罪死刑案件的审判质量。尽管如此，各级法院仍然必须坚持最高人民法院 2010 年《关于贯彻宽严相济刑事政策的若干意见》提出的依法严惩走私、贩卖、运输、制造毒品犯罪的方针,③ 司法上不可避免地出现了特别令人担忧的毒品犯罪重刑化实践（见表 1）。根据 2011 年 6 月 26 日最高人民法院新闻发布会的信息，2011 年 1 月至 5 月全国法院共新收毒品犯罪案件 25986 件，审

① 1997 年制定新刑法时，有的部门提出，搞毒品含量鉴定要求比较高，基层公安机关无论是财力、物力、人力都达不到。所以 1997 年《刑法》第 357 条第 2 款规定："毒品的数量以查证属实的走私、贩卖、运输、制造、非法持有毒品的数量计算，不以纯度折算。"从那之后，公安机关不再做纯度鉴定，起诉到法院的案件也只鉴定定性。如果不做含量鉴定，法院只按照数量量刑，会出现严重的量刑不公。因为，1994 年，最高人民法院针对全国人大常委会《关于禁毒的决定》出台了一个司法解释，对含量鉴定提出要求，以含量为 25% 的海洛因视为刑法中规定的海洛因。此后，最高人民法院一直要求对死刑毒品案件不仅要做定性分析，而且要做定量分析，即含量鉴定。因为那时候发现有些涉案毒品大量掺假，含量很低。比如 1000 克海洛因，含量是 1%，仅相当于含量为 25% 的海洛因 40 克。而国际上通行标准是含量达到 25% 的海洛因才视为纯品，所以最高人民法院当时规定按 25% 折算。如果不做含量鉴定，同样贩卖毒品 500 克，可能一个就会判处死刑，含量较低的就可能不处以死刑。该意见明确要求死刑案件毒品含量鉴定问题，有利于进一步严格死刑标准，解决了实践当中的一个问题。

② 这 5 种情形分别是：①具有毒品犯罪集团首要分子、武装掩护毒品犯罪、暴力抗拒检查、拘留或者逮捕、参与有组织的国际贩毒活动等严重情节的；②毒品数量达到实际掌握的死刑数量标准，并具有毒品再犯、累犯，利用、教唆未成年人走私、贩卖、运输、制造毒品，或者向未成年人出售毒品等法定从重处罚情节的；③毒品数量达到实际掌握的死刑数量标准，并具有多次走私、贩卖、运输、制造毒品，向多人贩毒，在毒品犯罪中诱使、容留多人吸毒，在戒毒监管场所贩毒，国家工作人员利用职务便利实施毒品犯罪，或者职业犯、惯犯、主犯等情节的；④毒品数量达到实际掌握的死刑数量标准，并具有其他从重处罚情节的；⑤毒品数量超过实际掌握的死刑数量标准，且没有法定、酌定从轻处罚情节的。

③ 最高人民法院于 2010 年印发的《关于贯彻宽严相济刑事政策的若干意见》（以下简称《意见》）提出，必须毫不动摇地坚持依法严惩严重刑事犯罪的方针，对于走私、贩卖、运输、制造毒品等毒害人民健康的犯罪，要作为严惩的重点，依法从重处罚；要依法从严惩处累犯和毒品再犯，凡是依法构成累犯和毒品再犯的，即使犯罪情节较轻，也要体现从严惩处的精神。各级人民法院认真贯彻《意见》精神，突出打击重点，依法严惩严重毒品犯罪和毒枭、职业毒犯、累犯、毒品再犯等主观恶性深、人身危险性大、危害严重的毒品犯罪分子，以及具有将毒品走私入境，多次、大量或者向多人贩卖毒品，武装掩护、暴力抗拒查缉、参与有组织国际毒品犯罪等情节的毒品犯罪分子。参阅 http://www.scio.gov.cn/xwfbh/qyxwfbh/201107/t952747.htm，最后访问日期：2011 年 9 月 17 日。

结 22633 件；判决发生法律效力的犯罪分子 24815 人，其中被判处五年以上有期徒刑、无期徒刑至死刑的 6667 人，重刑率为 26.86%，高出同期全部刑事案件重刑率 12.06 个百分点。①

表 1　2008 年②和 2010 年③全国法院审理
毒品案件适用刑罚的重刑化趋势

年份	年度毒品案件审结总数（件）	同比增长（%）	判决发生法律效力的罪犯（人）	其中判处五年以上有期徒刑、无期徒刑至死刑（人）	同比增长（%）	重刑率（%）	高出同期全部刑事案件重刑率百分点（个）
2008	43726	31.4	50307	16053	23.7	31.9	16.13
2010	59234	14.9	66298	18961	8.6	28.6	12.8

如果某些人甘愿冒死去贩卖毒品，那么，认为通过提高制裁威胁的确定性或者严重性（比如说判处死刑）就可以让他们不去贩毒，就只能是毫无意义的假说。因为他们本来就不指望着活着承受刑罚的处罚，那么，被判死刑或者被判无期徒刑在他们的盘算中究竟还有什么区别？恰恰相反，越是确定而没有回旋余地的死刑威慑，越是可能坚定他们鱼死网破、同归于尽的犯罪动机，甚至促使他们选择有组织武装对抗的犯罪方式。④ 毒品刑法中的死刑和重刑实务，几乎彻底动摇了刑罚威慑理论的根基。

前面提到，毒品犯罪是没有被害人的犯罪，不可能像其他犯罪一样有建立在被害人举报基础上的统计数据。因此，对于刑法对毒品犯罪控制效果和发展变化的趋势性观察，只能借助于反映控制工作力度的统计数据。根据 1992 年到 2011 年的《中国禁毒报告》和相关年度的《最高人民法院工作报告》提供的数据以及根据报告提到的比例推算的数据，可以看到 20 年来毒品违法犯罪和毒品犯罪在破案起数、抓获的犯罪嫌疑人、逮捕人数

---

① http：//www.scio.gov.cn/xwfbh/qyxwfbh/201107/t952747.htm，最后访问日期：2011 年 9 月 17 日。

② http：//www.gov.cn/jrzg/2009－06/26/content_ 1350715.htm，最后访问日期：2011 年 9 月 17 日。

③ http：//www.scio.gov.cn/xwfbh/qyxwfbh/201107/t952747.htm，最后访问日期：2011 年 9 月 17 日。

④ 武装走私、贩卖毒品和武装运输毒品这种犯罪现象，就是由于这类犯罪中规定了死刑以及国家动用军事力量控制毒品而出现的。在废除了死刑的国家很少出现武装走私、贩卖、运输毒品的情况。

和判刑人数上的发展变化。

图 1 显示，1991 年到 1998 年的统计标准是毒品违法犯罪，包括毒品违法行为和毒品犯罪行为两类。尽管破案起数和抓获嫌疑人数增幅特别大，[①]但是逮捕和判刑的人数自 1991 年到 1995 年从趋势上看增幅不大，1995 年到 1998 年的增长比较明显。1998 年起，统计标准发生了变化，统计数据反映的仅仅是毒品犯罪，不再包括毒品违法。尽管 1995 年到 2010 年破案起数和抓获嫌疑人数有比较大的起伏，但是直到 2010 年逮捕和判刑的人数都有稳定而显著的增长。显然，毒品犯罪尤其是从 1995 年以来一直保持着显著增长的势头。特别值得注意的是，从 2005 年起抓获的嫌疑人数超过了破案起数，这说明多人参与毒品犯罪的团伙特征或者有组织特征在统计意义上突出起来了。

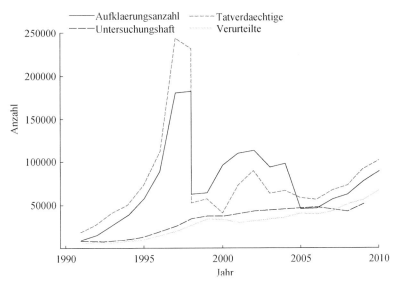

图 1　1991 年至 1998 年毒品违法犯罪和 1998 年至 2010 年毒品犯罪在
控制层面的发展变化（**Aufklaerungsanzahl**：破案数；**Tatverdaechtige**：
抓获的嫌疑人数；**Untersuchungshaft**：逮捕人数；**Verurteilte**：
判刑人数；**Anzahl**：数目；**Jahr**：年度）

把毒品成瘾者监管起来，他们更容易学到毒品犯罪的知识和技术，也更容易向他人交流和学习新型毒品的知识。这样，不仅可能把恶习和经验

---

① 这种急剧增长与 1991 年 6 月中国政府在国际禁毒日四周年之际召开毒品控制大会、宣布开展"禁毒人民战争"以及 1996 年 4 月起开展的"严打"运动有关。

传授给他人，而且也可能引起成瘾者对新型毒品的尝试动机。

毒品刑法对毒品犯罪行为在再犯[1]速度上所造成的、比较快的"旋转门效应"[2]，也是很明显的。2006 年对我国毒品犯罪的再犯研究发现，[3] 毒品犯罪的再犯间隔时间[4]（或者再犯速度）是平均 30 个月，与抢劫、勒索（35 个月）、伤害（36 个月）、盗窃（46 个月）、诈骗（45 个月）等的平均再犯速度相比，毒品犯罪的再犯是最快的（表 2）。

表 2　犯罪的专业化和毒品犯罪的刑度

	绝对数	%	N
初犯：			
第一次被判的他罪 + 毒品犯罪	85	13%	644
—其中仅仅因毒品罪而判刑的	73		85
再犯：			
第一次被判的他罪 + 毒品犯罪	102	19%	528
—其中只因毒品罪被判刑的	101		102
第二次被判的他罪 + 毒品犯罪	141	27 ± 2%	529
—其中只因毒品罪而判刑的	138		141
专业化的毒品犯罪	89	87 ± 3%	102
第一次判决科处的平均刑期	33 个月		
对专业化再犯科处的平均刑期	105 个月		
第一次服刑的实际平均时间	29 个月		
再犯的平均间隔时间	30 个月		

　　从与其他犯罪类型的持续专业化系数（FSC）[5] 的比较（表 3）中，也

---

① 中国刑法对于毒品犯罪的再犯在第 356 条规定了特别的没有再犯时效的从重处罚制度：因走私、贩卖、运输、制造、非法持有毒品罪被判过刑，又犯第七节规定之罪的，从重处罚。《刑法》第 65 条第 1 款对其他犯罪规定的 5 年再犯时效，不适用于毒品犯罪。

② 是指行为人陷入犯罪、监禁、释放、再犯罪、再监禁、再释放的不断循环往复之中。

③ *Fan*，W.，Kriminelle Karrieren. Straftaten, Sanktionen und Rueckfall. Duncker & Humblot，2009，S. 200.

④ 再犯间隔时间是指从监狱释放之后到再次实施犯罪之间的时间跨度。

⑤ 持续专业化系数反映的是不断实施该种犯罪的趋势。持续专业化系数值越高，说明再次实施这种犯罪的倾向越强或者说可能性越大。它的计算公式是：FSC =（O-E）/（R-E）；参阅 *Fan*，W.，Kriminelle Karrieren. Straftaten, Sanktionen und Rueckfall. Duncker & Humblot，2009，S. 201。

可以看到，毒品犯罪的系数值达到了 0.84，在所有七种犯罪类型中是最高的。而且也证明了这样的假设：具体实施的犯罪行为之间的时间间隔越短，持续专业化系数越高。毒品刑法对于毒品犯罪的再犯并没有能够起到所期待的有效预防作用。

表 3　不同罪群的持续专业化系数（司法记录）

	持续专业化系数*	这种犯罪在第一次判决中出现的比率**
杀人罪	- 0.01	0.4
强奸罪	0.27	3.2
抢劫或者勒索罪	0.40	17
伤害罪	0.44	7.2
一般的暴力犯罪	0.62	29
盗窃罪	0.25	40
诈骗罪	0.70	10
毒品罪	0.84	19
一般的盈利犯罪	0.33	75

* Forward Specialization Coefficient；

** Vorkommen dieses Delikts in der 1. Verurteilung［％］（Mehrfachnennungen möglich）.

　　毒品犯罪最快的再犯速度和最高的专业化系数至少说明这样的事实：和其他常见的犯罪相比较，毒品刑法在预防涉毒再犯上的效果是最差的，差到了几乎是引起或者促进毒品犯罪再次发生的程度。这个事实也得到了国际上大多数国家可比实证证据相近程度上的确认。[1]

　　最后，作为医疗卫生政策的手段，刑法是没有效率的，甚至是起反作用的，而且另一方面是不人道的。如果说毒品成瘾者是病了，那么，国家政策必须关心的是给他治病，或者至少是为他缓解病痛创造条件[2]。对于吸毒成瘾的病人作犯罪化处理，并不是着眼于保障和促进健康的医疗卫生政策的手段和做法；判处病人刑罚或者让他在狱中服刑，不是治疗病人，而是惩罚病人。

---

[1]　*Blumstein*，*Cohen*，*Das*，*Moitra*，Specialization and Seriousness during Adult Criminal Careers. *Journal of Quantitative Criminology* 4（1988），S. 341f.；*Kyvsgaard*，B.，The criminal career. The Danish longitudinal Study. Cambridge u. a 2003，S. 242.

[2]　参见《中华人民共和国宪法》第 45 条。

基于前面的分析，在彻底转变观念的前提下可以设想并归纳出不同形式的备选毒品政策。这些政策原则上并不是相互排斥的，而是可以综合考虑的：

1. 毒品消费的全面除罪化①

主要是为自己消费毒品而进行准备的行为，比如购买、持有或者获赠毒品，以及容留他人吸食毒品的行为，将来不再作为犯罪予以处罚。

2. 废除毒品刑法中的死刑制度②和没有再犯时效的从重处罚制度③

3. 软毒品的合法化

对于有较低瘾癖危险的毒品和没有瘾癖危险的精神药品，在严格的限制下予以合法化。可以设定这样的限制：严格规定禁止出售给青少年。此外，禁止对于这类毒品任何形式的广告。还有，这种软毒品只允许在药店出售。在出售时，在纯度和出售的量上要严格执行国家控制的标准。最后，就像药物一样，在包装上明示吸食的危险并在说明书中给出合成成分。

4. 国家控制下的硬毒品配售

在其他替代供给不能有效治疗海洛因消费的情况下，可以尝试海洛因国家控制下的供给模式。不过，这种理念的尝试，必须伴随同步的实证评估谨慎进行。

类似于国家对于烟酒的控制，这种做法实质上是特定限制条件下的非法毒品的完全合法化。这种限制表现在如下几个方面：

（1）禁止对于毒品，包括烈酒和香烟的所有毒品的广告。

（2）设立国家机构，其任务是对原料的输入进行检测，对于原料原产地的种植实施质量监督，对于生产终端产品颁发制药学上的许可证。而且负责终端产品的质量监督，负责防御性的低价销售，负责发布成分合成、剂量、对身体的危害、形成瘾癖的潜力以及副作用方面的信息。

（3）建立有条件的许可证制度或者处方制度，这种制度能够保证消费

---

① 这个问题在欧盟国家比较突出，大部分成员国把毒品消费和为自我消费而持有毒品规定为犯罪（在西班牙和意大利，为自己消费而持有毒品不是犯罪）。不过，近年来除罪化的立法动议已经越来越多了。比如在瑞士，伯尔尼政府就给瑞士联邦立法机构提交过非犯罪化的建议。该建议提议把吸食鸦片和为消费而获得毒品的行为（比如购买、持有等）除罪化。并且，建议彻底把软毒品（比如印度大麻、大麻制剂）除罪化。德国的绿党也给德国联邦议会多次提出过类似的建议。

② 否则，毒品犯罪在不同国家的刑罚差异就特别大。比如，在德国贩卖毒品 3～5 千克，只判了 8 年自由刑，但在中国就会被判死刑。

③ 比如中国刑法第 356 条的规定。

硬毒品瘾癖深重的群体有获得毒品的合法途径。同时这种制度还应该严防没有染上毒瘾的人获得毒品消费的机会。

在国家控制下由药店根据处方配售毒品有如下好处：①会自然而然地取缔有组织贩毒。②对居民安全构成威胁的、为获取购买毒品的钱而实施的犯罪会因此而大幅减少。③对于消费者来说，他明确知道出现在市场上的是药理学上无瑕疵的纯正毒品。而绝大多数吸食毒品死亡的事件都是由于根本不知道毒品的纯度而过量吸食或者由于其中的致命物质而导致的。药店售卖可以大幅减少因过量吸食毒品而致死的人数。④还可以把许多不曾发现的毒品成瘾人员纳入控制，为毒瘾的替代性治疗（比如美沙酮疗法）创造条件。

5. 根据实务经验和专业人士的说法，有一部分长年吸食硬毒品的消费者，普通的镇压措施和预防手段对于这部分人基本上不可能再起什么作用。为了避免其健康和经济状况的恶化，也为了打破瘾癖和犯罪之间的恶性循环，就必须尝试新的控制理念：设立定点消费空间，在该空间内成瘾者可以获得帮助和咨询。

尽管这种毒品控制策略并不能从根本上解决毒品问题，但是，它有助于缓解毒品消费引起的连锁问题。另外，值得注意的是，合法化的毒品控制模式在法律上还有许多障碍，一方面是在国内法上的实施空间很小，另一方面，国家在打击毒品犯罪领域承担着许多国际法上刑事追究和保障毒品消费者人权的义务。因此，毒品控制新理念的具体落实，急需扫清立法层面上的障碍。

Drug Control and Drug-related Criminal Law

Fan Wen

【**Abstract**】Problems caused by the consumption of narcotic drugs include the abuse of and addiction to drugs. The legal interest protected by drug-related criminal law is the right to be free from the danger of getting into non-free condition resulting from dependence on drugs. However, the criminal law control of drugs may create new problems because using the criminal law as the primary means of controlling drugs will neither reduce the demand or supply in the drug market, nor stop the continuous growth of drug-related crimes, but will instead encourage the organized development of drug-related crimes. Therefore, the severe punishments of drug-related crimes under the current Criminal Law are excess drug-control measures. The prohibition of drugs leads to black drug market, and the monopoly of the black market leads to the extortion and exploitation of drug-users. Meanwhile, the black drug market also causes many other crimes. To solve this problem, China needs to reduce the severity of the punishments against drug-related crimes and use the heroin prescription under the state supervision to breakdown the black drug market. While the misunderstanding of narcotic drugs and their pharmacological effects and the traditional idea of zero-tolerance of drugs pose obstacles to China's adoption of the heroin prescription system, the idea and practice of "minimizing the harms to the drug-users" and preventing their life and human rights conditions from worsening as a result of the negative effects of severe laws against drug are opposed by nobody and indicate the actual direction of development of drug control policy.

【Key words】 Drug Control, Drug-related Criminal Law

Regulating the Prison Populations in Finland

Tapio Lappi-Seppälä [*]

【Abstract】 First part of the article gives an overview of major changes in Finnish penal policy. The period from the civil war 1918 till the end of war with Soviet Union (1945) is characterized by recurring political, social and economic crisis and high incarceration rates. This period was followed by a criminal justice reform from the 1960s onwards. New criminal political ideology stressed legal safeguards against the overuse of imprisonment. The use of imprisonment was reduced by systematic law reform: by expanding the use of fines and conditional sentences, by lowering penalties for property offenses and by expanding the system of early release. In the 1990s new alternatives for imprisonment were introduced and com-munity service orders replaced a large part of short term prison sentences.

As a result, Finland managed to reduce its imprisonment rates from over 150 per 100000 population, which was the highest in all Western in the 1960s, to around 60 being the lowest in the European Union in the mid-1990s. When crime trends in Finland and in the other Nordic countries are compared, one finds that this dramatic reduction in the use of imprisonment had no visible effect on our crime rates. The Finnish crime rates developed in an identical manner with the crime rates of those Nordic countries, which had kept the prisoner rates almost stable (and even with those European countries, which had increased the use of

---

[*] Director-General, National Research Institute of Legal Policy, Finland; Docent in Criminal Law, Faculty of Law, university of Helsinki.

imprisonment). This, once again, support the general criminological conclusion that crime and incarceration rates are fairly independent of one another; each rises and falls accor ding to its own laws and dynamics.

The latter parts of the article discusses of the major features of the Finnish sanction system. The Finnish constitution forbids the use of death penalty-as well as any degrading and inhuman punishments. The principal punishments are fines, conditional imprisonment, community service, electronically monitored supervision order, juvenile punishment (for offenders between 15 – 17 years of age) and unconditional imprisonment. A clear majority of all sanctions imposed by courts consists of fines, with community sanctions to follow. About one out of ten offenders is sentenced to a prison term and more than half of the prison sentences are less than 6 months.

I. Introduction

Finland is a small Nordic country with a population of 5. 3 million. The Finnish juridical system is manifestly rooted in western, continental legal culture with strong influence from neighbouring Nordic Countries. Today Finland profiles itself-together with the other Nordic countries Denmark, Iceland, Norway and Sweden-as a county with internationally high level of social security and equality, higher levels of social trust and political legitimacy, and lower levels of penal repression. [①] However, this has not always been the cases. During the last century, Finland has experienced three wars (the 1918 Civil War and the two wars against Soviet Union between 1939 and 1944). These crises have left their marks also in the Finnish society and its criminal policy. The trends in prison rates have been more turbulent than presumably in any other Western European country.

The harsh history of Finland can be read from its prison statistics (figure III. 1). Figure I. 1. displays the trends in prison rates (relative to 100000 population) throughout the last century. The role of political and social and economic crises is highlighted by dividing prisoners in three categories：(1) prisoners serving their sentences for ordinary crimes, (2) prisoners placed in prisons for political crimes

---

[①] The central social and political characteristics of the Nordic countries and their relevance on national penal policies are discussed in more detail in Lappi-Seppälä & Tonry 2011 and Lappi-Seppälä 2007 and 2008 a.

(treason like activities) or those sentenced by the martial courts during the war-times, and (3) prisoners placed in prisons for unpaid fines (fine defaulters).

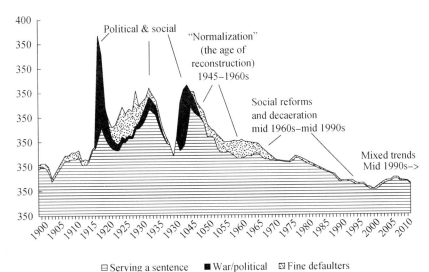

Figure I. 1   **Prisoner rates in Finland 1900 – 2010 (annual averages).**

Source: National Statistics

Three main phases may be detected. The period from the civil war 1918 till the end of war with Soviet Union is characterized by recurring political, social and economic crisis-and a hugely varying incarceration rates. From the early 1950s started a period of normalization (known as the "age of reconstruction"). Finland was recovering from the damages of war and paying the war compensations; thus establishing also the industrial infrastructures which formed the foundations of forthcoming welfare state.

The dire economic circumstances were reflected also in the prison administration. In general terms, the criminal justice system of Finland in the 1950s and still in the 1960s was less resourceful, less flexible and more repressive than that of its Nordic neighbours. This all was about to change during the third phase of social reform the 1960s onwards, which form also the starting point of the following presentation. ①

---

① For a broader view of penal changes in Finland see Anttila 1971, Lahti 2000 and Lappi-Seppälä 2008 and 2011b.

II. The Decline of Imprisonment in Finland

A. The reform-ideology of the 1960s and the 1970s

Against coercive care

In the 1960s, the Nordic countries experienced heated social debate on the results and justifications of involuntary treatment in institutions, both penal and otherwise (such as in health care and in the treatment of alcoholics). In Finland the criticism of the treatment ideology was merged with another reform ideology that was directed against the overly severe Criminal Code and the excessive use of custodial sentences. The resulting criminal political ideology was labeled as "humane neo-classicism". It stressed both legal safeguards against coercive care and the goal of less repressive measures in general. In sentencing the principles of proportionality and predictability became the central values. Individualized sentencing, as well as sentencing for general preventive reasons or perceived dangerousness was put in the background (see in more detail Anttila 1971, Lahti 2000, Lappi-Seppälä 2007 and Törnudd 1996).

Broadening the aims and means of criminal policy

Behind the shift in the strategies in criminal policy were more profound changes in the way the entire problem of crime was conceived. The theoretical criminal political framework and the conceptualization of the aims and means of criminal policy underwent a change, as the social sciences and planning strategies merged with the criminal political analysis. The aims of criminal policy were defined in par with the overall aims of general social policy. Cost-benefit analysis was introduced into criminal political thinking. The result of all this was that the arsenal of the possible means of criminal policy expanded to cover also general social welfare interventions, environmental planning and situational crime prevention. This new ideology was crystallised in slogans such as "criminal policy is an inseparable part of general social development policy" and "good social development policy is the best criminal policy". The role of punishment came to be seen as relative. Once regarded as the primary means of criminal policy, it came to be regarded as only one option among many.

The function of criminal justice: *Indirect general prevention*

After the fall of the rehabilitative ideal, also the aim and the justification of punishment was subjected to re-evaluation. The shift was once again towards general prevention. However, this concept was now understood in a different manner. It was assumed that this effect could be reached not through fear (deterrence), but through the moral creating and value shaping effect of punishment. According to this idea, the disapproval expressed in punishment is assumed to influence the values and moral views of individuals. As a result of this process, the norms of criminal law and the values they reflect are internalized; people refrain from illegal behaviour not because such behaviour would be followed by unpleasant punishment, but because the behaviour itself is regarded as morally blameworthy (see Andenaes 1974 and Lappi-Seppälä 1995). This, too, had a number of policy implications. Indirect prevention is best served by a system of sanctions which maintains a moral character and demonstrates the blameworthiness of the act and follows procedures perceived as fair and just by all parties. Instrumental compliance based on fear and sentence severity was reserved but a marginal role.

Sentencing: *humane neo-classicism*

In sentencing this all was condensed in a new sentencing ideology, "humane neo-classicism". The classical element in this theory was the revival of the old principle of proportionality. The humane elements were to be found in systematic efforts towards leniency. Minimisation of the suffering caused by the crime control system was among the generally accepted crime policy goals. The role and functions of the principle of proportionality were also seen in this spirit: It had its roots in the rule of law and the guarantees against the excessive use of force. The main function of the proportionality principle in Finland was to impose the upper limit which the punishment may not exceed. It is much less restrictive (but still relevant) when considering the possibilities of imposing sentences that are less severe than the offender's act would prima facie have deserved (see closer Lappi-Seppälä 2001).

B. Legislative reforms and sentencing practices

Systematic legislative reforms started during the mid-1960s, and continued until the mid 1990s. They dealt both the general sanction system as well as specific offenses.

The major law reforms affecting the number of prisoners are summarized and commented briefly below.

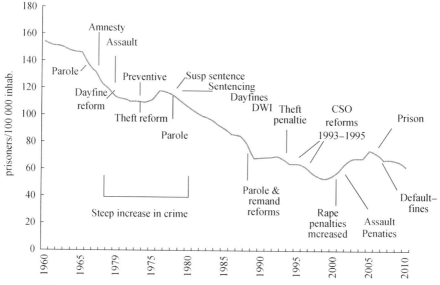

Figure II. 1　Prison rates and policy reforms in Finland 1960 – 2010

General structure of sanctions in 1950 – 1990

The general structure of sanctions system remained untouched in 1950 – 1990s consisting of fines, conditional sentence and imprisonment. The decrease of prisoner rates in 1950 – 1980 was technically a result of the general decline in the length of prison sentences and the expansion in the use of fines and conditional sentences. In 1950 the average length of all sentences of imprisonment imposed for theft was 12 months, in 1971 it was 7 months and in 1991 it was 3 months. Similar changes occurred also in other major crimes, such as robbery, assaults and drunken driving. In 1950 – 1970 this reductions was court-initiated, from the 1970s onwards the trend was supported also by legislative reforms.

From the late 1960s onwards all major offenses started to increase, but the number of prison sentences remained more or less stable. The increased number of property and violent offenses were punished either by conditional prison sentences or fines. The use of fines was expanded in order to substitute to short-term imprisonment in 1977 by raising the monetary value of day-fines (and thus making fines more severe). The scope of *conditional imprisonment* (suspended sentence) was

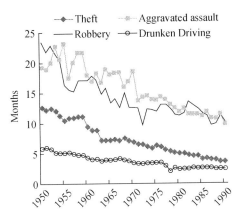

Figure II. 2   The average length of sentences of imprisonment for four different offense from 1950 to 1990.

Source: Statistics Finland.

extended by relaxing the prerequisites for the use of this sanction. The number of annually imposed conditional sentences rose from 4000 (in 1960) to 18000 (in 1990). *Sentencing reform* in 1976 restricted the role of prior record in sentencing by replacing old mechanical provisions with a regulation which allowed aggravation only when recidivism implies increased act-oriented culpability. This reduced the length of prison sentences especially among chronic property offenders.

The expansion of petty traffic and property offenses increased the use of fines. This expansion also forced the legislator to adopt different forms of summary proceedings (see table III. 1. section A). The number of prosecutors fines expanded from 80000 in 1950 to over 300000 in the 1990s. To ease these pressures an even more simplified fixed police fine was introduced in the 1980s. Today both the police and the prosecutor impose about half of million of small fines, mainly for traffic and small property offenses.

The adoption of summary proceedings has kept the annual number of court-imposed penalties on a fairly stable level (50000 −80000). The absolute number of imposed prison sentences is today on the same level as over 50 years ago, and on a much lower than some 30 years ago (see section B). The increased number of medium rank offenses have been sentenced either to fines or other community sanctions. Comparison between other court-ordered sanctions than fines, show how the relative share of prison has reduced from 70% to 25% in 2008 (section C below).

**Table II. 1   The use of different sentencing alternatives
and processes from 1950 to 2008**

	A. Summary fines N		B. Courts: all sanctions N					C. Courts: other than fines%			
	Prosecutor	Police	Prison	CSO	Conditional	Fines	All	Prison%	Condit. %	CSO%	All N
1950	80000		6741		2812	39027	48580	70. 6	29. 4		9553
1960	148000		6900		3686	40812	51398	65. 2	34. 8		10586
1970	150000		10212		5215	42248	57675	66. 2	33. 8		15427
1980	250000		10326		14556	47401	72283	41. 5	58. 5		24882
1990	312000	70000	11657		17428	52542	81627	40. 1	59. 9		29085
2000	196000	104000	8147	3413	13974	37504	63038	31. 9	54. 7	13. 4	25534
2008	255000	202000	6872	3222	15998	37615	63707	26. 3	61. 3	12. 3	26092

Source: Statistics Finland

Reducing the penalty-scales for specific offenses

In 1977 the law on drunken driving was changed in order to replace unconditional prison sentences with conditional sentences and fines. In a short period of time the proportion of prison sentences dropped from 90% to 20%. The introduction of community service in the mid-1990s brought another drop in the use of imprisonment till around 10%.

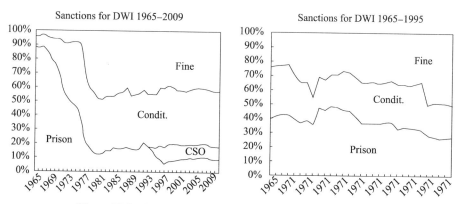

**Figure II. 3   The use of different sentencing alternatives for
drunk driving and theft.**

Source: Statistics Finland.

Besides drunk drivers, Finnish prisons in the 1950 −1970s were crowded also by property offenders, especially theft. Penalties for theft were reduced both in 1972 and 1991. These reforms decreased the share of unconditional imprisonment from

50% to 25% , while the share of fines increased from 20% to 50% (Fig. II. 3)

This de-penalisation of drunk-driving and property offenses was reflected also on prison statistics. In the mid-1970s two out three prisoners were sentenced either for drunk-driving of theft. Today the relative share of these offenses has dropped into about one third. In 1975 there were 1800 prisoners serving a sentence for theft, today their number is around 450. For drunk driving the corresponding figures are 1000 and 300.

Specific offender-groups

Targeted actions were taken to reduce the size of prison populations in three groups of inmates.

The use of *default imprisonment for unpaid fines* was approaching the all time record levels in the 1960s (almost 1800 fine-defaulters at any given day). In 1969 the use of default imprisonment was restricted and the major source for these fines was removed by decriminalizing public drunkenness. The daily number of fine-defaulters fell from over 1000 to less than 50 (fig. III. 5, for subsequent changes see below IV).

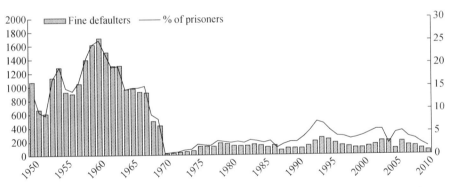

Figure II. 4   The number of fine defaulters 1950 – 2010 (absolute figures and as percentages of all prisoners).

Source: Criminal Justice Agency.

In the course of the 1960s the use of *preventive (secure) detention* for repeat offenders had expanded to cover also large number of property offenders. This lifted the number of prisoners held in prolonged custody to over 400 (5% of overall prisoner rate). In 1971 the use of preventive detention was restricted only to serious violent recidivists, and the number of people held in preventive detention fell overnight from 250 to less than 10 (for subsequent changes, see below IV).

During the 1970s the use on imprisonment for *young offenders* started to raise increasing critics. This was reflected also on the courts sentencing practices, as the

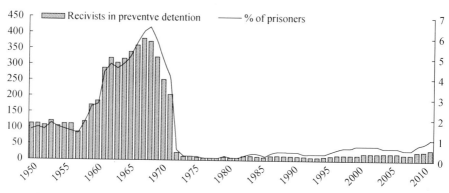

Figure II. 5　The number of recidivist in preventive detention 1950 – 2005
（absolute figures and as percentages of all prisoners）.

Source：Criminal Justice Agency.

number of prison sentences imposed for juveniles started to decrease. Two law reforms contributed to this change in the shift of the 1990s. The Conditional Sentence Act was amended in 1989 by including a provision which allows the use of unconditional sentence for young offenders only if there are extraordinary reasons calling for this. Also the reduction of minimum penalties for car-thefts（joy-riding）in 1991 had impact on younger age groups as this offense is typically committed by young offenders（one third of prison sentences in the age group of 15 −17 were imposed for this offense）.

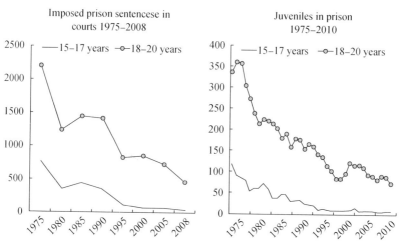

Figure II. 6　Imposed prison sentences and the number of juvenile prisoners
1975 – 2010（annual averages, absolute figures, remand included）.

Sources：Statistics Finland, Criminal Sanctions Agency.

In 1975 the courts imposed over 2000 prison sentences for young adults (18 – 20 years) and more than 700 sentences for juveniles (15 – 17 years). In 2010 the corresponding figures were 500 and 50. In 2010 there were about 70 prisoners between the ages of 18 and 20 and in the 15 to 17 age group. In the mid-1970s the numbers were five to ten times higher. [1]

Community service

The next major sanction reform was the introduction of community service in the mid-1990s. In order to ensure that community service will really be used in lieu of unconditional sentences of imprisonment (and not instead of other more lenient penalties) , a specific two-step procedure was adopted. First the court is supposed to make its sentencing decision without considering the possibility of community service. If the result is unconditional imprisonment, then the court may commute the sentence into community service under certain conditions prescribed in the law. The duration of community service varies between 20 and 200 hours. In commuting imprisonment into community service, one day in prison equals one hour of community service.

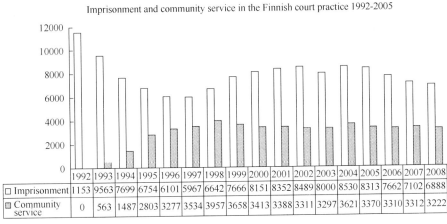

Imprisonment and community service in the Finnish court practice 1992-2005

	1992	1993	1994	1995	1996	1997	1998	1999	2000	2001	2002	2003	2004	2005	2006	2007	2008
Imprisonment	11539	9563	7699	6754	6101	5967	6642	7666	8151	8352	8489	8000	8530	8313	7662	7102	6888
Community service	0	563	1487	2803	3277	3534	3957	3658	3413	3388	3311	3297	3621	3370	3310	3312	3222

**Figure II. 7   Imprisonment and community service in Finland
1992 – 2008 (court statistics).**

Source: Statistics Finland.

---

[1]   One needs to remember that in the age-group 15 – 17 child welfare bears the basic responsibility for rehabilitative actions including institutional care when necessary. Finnish juvenile justice system is discussed in more detail in Lappi-Seppälä 2011a.

The number of prison sentences fell together with the increase in the number of community service orders in 1992-1997. Within a short period of time, community service proved to be an important alternative to imprisonment. Today community service replaces around 35% of short term (max 8 months) prison sentences.

Parole

The system of parole and early release has also proven to be a very powerful tool in controlling prisoner rates. In Finland practically all prisoners are released on parole on a routine basis. The minimum time to be served before the prisoner is eligible for parole is 14 days. A series of Reforms have brought it down to this. During the mid-1960s this period was shortened from six to four months, during the mid-1970s from four to three months, and finally in the late 1980s from three months to 14 days. Also the criteria for early release were relaxed and the conditions for the revocations of parole were made more strict. All this had a substantial effect on the overall scope of parole and early release. In the early 1960s less 40% of annually released prisoners were released on parole. In the late 1960s their share has increased into 50% and during the 1970s already to 75%. After the 1989 parole reform practically all prisoners are released on parole (see in more detail Lappi-Seppälä 2011b).

III. Causes and Consequences

A. Explaining penal liberalization

The long list of law reforms supports the conclusion that the decrease in the Finnish prison population was a result of a conscious, long term and systematic criminal policy. In order to explain what made it possible to carry out these reforms during these years, we will begin with certain features specific to Finnish society and the composition of Finnish political culture and proceed from there to more general social, structural and cultural factors.

Political culture

Part of the answer can be found in the structure of our political culture. The Finnish criminologist Patrik *Törnudd* has stressed the importance of the *political will and consensus* to bring the prison rate down. As he summarizes, "those experts who were in charge of planning the reforms and research shared an almost unanimous conviction that Finland's comparatively high prison rate was a disgrace and that it would be possible to significantly reduce the amount and length of prison sentences without serious repercussions on the crime situation. " (Törnudd 1993, p. 12). This conviction was shared by the civil servants, the judiciary, the prison authorities and, as was equally important, by the politicians. [1]

Another and closely related way for characterizing the Finnish criminal policy would be to describe it as *exceptionally expert-oriented*: Reforms have been prepared and conducted by a relatively small group of experts whose thinking on criminal policy, at least in the basic points, has followed similar lines. The impact of these professionals was, furthermore, reinforced by *close personal and professional contacts* with senior politicians and with academic research. [2] Consequently, crime control has never been a central political issue in election campaigns in Finland, unlike in many other countries. At least the "heavyweight" politicians have not relied on populist policies, such as "three strikes" or "truth in sentencing" .

Media

This takes us to another element in the Finnish criminal policy composition-*media-market and the role of the media*. In Finland the media have retained a quite sober and reasonable attitude towards issues of criminal policy. The Finns have largely been saved from low-level populism. There is a striking difference between British and Finnish crime-reports in the media. The tone in the Finnish reports is less emotional, and reports-also when dealing with singular events-are usually accompanied with commented research based data on the development of the crime situation.

In fact, the whole structure of the Finnish media market looks a bit peculiar. For one, according to the information given by the World Association of Newspapers (World Press Trends 2004), the most busy newspaper-readers in Europe are to be founded in Finland and Sweden (90% of the population read

---

[1]   At least to the extent that they did not oppose the reform proposals prepared by the Ministry of Justice.

[2]   Several of our Ministers of Justice during the 1970s and 1980s have had direct contact with research work; indeed, one of them, Inkeri Anttila, was a professor of criminal law and the director of the National Research Institute of Legal Policy at the time of her appointment as Minister.

newspaper every day, while in France, Italy and the UK the figures are 44%, 41% and 33%). Secondly, the clear market leader can be classified as a quality-paper; tabloids have a far less prominent role in Finland than in many other countries (including the UK). Thirdly, only small fraction (12%) of newspapers-distribution is based on selling single copies. Almost 90% of the newspapers are sold on the basis of subscription, which means that the papers do not have to rely on dramatic events in order to draw the reader's attention each day. In short, in Finland the newspapers reach a large segment of the population, the market leaders are quality papers which do not have to sell themselves every day, since distribution is based on subscriptions. This all may have an effect both on the ways crime is reported, and the way people think about these matters.

Nordic co-operation

The early 1960s was a period of intensifying Nordic co-operation in legal matters. Crime and criminal justice were among the key issues in this agenda. In 1960 The Scandinavian Research Council was established with the support of the ministries of justice. This Council became a central forum for the exchange of information between the Nordic countries. Interest in criminological research expanded and the status and resources of criminology were strengthened in the Nordic countries. The reform-work of the 1960s and 1970s in Finland was heavily influenced by this exchange of ideas, as well as by the legislative models offered by our Scandinavian neighbors (especially Sweden). In many instances liberal reforms could be defended with reference to positive experiences gained from other Nordic countries and the need for Inter-Nordic harmonization. This "Nordic identity" was strengthened in Finland also by the fact that Finland was in the 1960s quickly reaching other Scandinavian partners in economic and welfare resources.

A specific feature of this co-operation was that it was not founded on conventions but on non-binding agreements between the nations. [1] It was not led by politicians and governments, but by Ministries of Justice and their experts. It proved to be very effective and less bureaucratic. The results of this co-operation were manifested in

---

[1] The foundation for the co-operation is based on the Helsinki Treaty (1962). The treaty obliged the contracting parties to "strive to create uniform provisions concerning crime and sanctions of crime". A general overview is to be found in Lahti 2000.

legislative acts that have been adopted separately in each Nordic country, but with identical contents. These acts concern, for example, extradition from one Nordic country to another as well as the enforcement of sentences within these countries.

Judicial culture and sentencing structures

Also micro-level institutional arrangements and specific professional practices have contributed to this change. Co-operation with the judicial authorities-the judges and the prosecutors-and their "attitudinal readiness" for liberal criminal policies have been of great importance in Finland. In many cases, legislators have been strongly supported by the judiciary and especially by the courts of first instance. Quite often the courts had changed their practice even before legislators had changed the law.

Also the fact that judges and prosecutors are trained career officials with training in criminology and criminal policy in the law schools, contribute to this explanation. In addition, different courses and seminars arranged for judges (and prosecutors) on a regular basis by judicial authorities-in co-operation with the universities-have also had an impact on sentencing and prosecutorial practices.

The Finnish sentencing structure, which treats sentencing as an area of normal judicial decision making, guided by valid sources of sentencing law, may also function as a shield against political pressures. Finland (and Sweden) has a highly structured system with detailed written provision on the general principles and specific sentencing criteria to be taken into account in deciding both on the type and on the amount of punishment. Arguments that affect sentencing must be presented in a form that fits the accepted rules and standards. The specific structure of the decision-making process, as outlined in the general sentencing provisions (the "notion of normal punishments") stress the importance of uniformity in sentencing (i. e. avoiding unwarranted disparities). This places the existing sentencing patterns in a central position as starting points in sentencing. And this, in turn, gives sentencing strong inertia: rapid changes are unlikely to occur, unless these changes have not been channeled through the valid sources of sentencing law (see in general Lappi-Seppälä 2001).

Socio-economic and political factors

All factors mentioned above, are more or less obvious for anyone familiar with Finnish society in general. However, a full account of the factors behind the humanization of the Finns should be able to explain it more fully: In the first place, it should explain the timing, why this process started when it did and why the liberal policies have (more or less) prevailed ever since. Second, these explanations should be able to cover also the patterns to be found among different countries. This applies particularly to the other Scandinavian countries, as the policies adopted in Finland were strongly influenced by similar policies in the other Nordic countries. In short, the explanations for the Finnish exceptionalism should be able to cover also the more general Scandinavian exceptionalism.

This search for a more substantial explanation should start from the Nordic Welfare Model and the underlying social, political and cultural factors. Introducing these Social and economical factors in the analyses (and the respective changes within them) helps to explain both the timing and the prevailing regional patterns. Liberal penal policies are associated with a strong welfare state. The years of penal liberation in Finland were also a period of radical social, economic and structural changes. From 1950 to 1970 the gross domestic product of Finland increased by 125% , while the growth in OECD was in average 75% , and in the UK and the US 55% . Between 1960 and 1998 the total public social expenditure as a percentage of GDP increased in Finland by 18 percentage points, in OECD countries by 13, in the UK by 11 and in the US by 7. Between 1966 and 1990 the income differences, measured by the GINI-index, was reduced in Finland by 8. 3 points (from 33. 4-> 25. 1). In short, Finland was joining the Scandinavian welfare family in terms of the level of economic prosperity, welfare provisions and income-equality, and this change was also reflected in our penal policies. Just the same way, as the prison expansion in the Anglo-Saxon world coincides with the concomitant general scaling down of welfare states (see Garland 2001).

Nordic Countries still represent a regional unity both in terms of their liberal penal model and their universalistic welfare model. This welfare model, in turn, has its own background, which also should be included in the analyses. Thus, giving a more complete explanation for those changes that occurred in Finland since the 1960s would require a wider perspective which encompasses also general social, economic, political and cultural factors. [1]

---

[1] The role of macro-sociological factors in explaining penal differences is analysed in more detail in Lappi-Seppälä 2008 a.

B. Imprisonment rates and crime rates

A profound change in the use of imprisonment naturally raises questions about its effects on crime rates. There are several well known methodological difficulties in measuring causal relations between crime rates and prison rates. However, the possibility of comparing the Nordic countries with strong social and structural similarities but with very different penal histories provides an unusual opportunity to see how drastic changes in penal practices in one country have been reflected in the crime rates, compared with countries which have kept their penal systems more or less stable. Figure III. 9 shows incarceration and reported crime rates in Finland, Sweden, Denmark and Norway, from 1950 to 2010.

Figure III. 1   Prison rates and crime rates 1950 – 2009

Sources: Falck et al 2003 and Kristofferssen 2010 updated.

There is a striking difference in the use of imprisonment (left), and a striking similarity in the trends in recorded criminality (right). That Finland has substantially reduced its incarceration rate has not disturbed the symmetry of Nordic the crime rates. These figures, once again, support the general criminological conclusion that crime and incarceration rates are fairly independent of one another; each rises and falls according to its own laws and dynamics.

IV. Mixed Trends

The downward trend in prison population rates continued with only short-term interruptions till late 1990s. The rates hit the bottom in 1999 with the annual average of 2743 prisoners (53/pop, the top figure in the 1970s was 118/pop). After that followed a sharp period of increase in 1999 −2005 from 53 to 74/pop (= +40%). Then the figures again took a downward trend, and by 2010 the rates are on the same level as in the mid-1990s (61/pop). The following discusses briefly of the diverse trends behind these fluctuations.

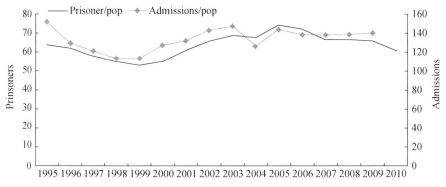

Figure IV. 1   Prisoner rates and admission rates 1995 −2010

Source: Criminal Sanctions Agency

A. The punitive turn of the late 1990s

Legislative changes in violent and sexual offenses

The period of toughening penal policy started with a reform in 1995 which placed domestic violence (and other assault offenses committed in private locations) under public prosecution. This had immediate effects on crime reporting and house calls doubled in a short period of time. Also the number of court-imposed penalties increased. Prosecutorial rules of domestic violence were further reformed in 2004 as the scope of non-prosecution was restricted in these cases. The next major reform increased penalties for rape in 1999. This took place by dividing rape offenses in three categories of gravity and by increasing the minimum penalty for the basic form of rape from 6 months to one year. As a result, the length of prison sentences increased on average by 6 months.

In 2001 the minimum penalty for aggravated assault was doubled from 6 months to one year. In a short period of time the average length of prison terms for aggravated assault increased by 6 months. Prosecutorial rules for domestic violence were reformed again in 2004 in order to restrict the use of non-prosecution in assault cases. In 2004 also penalties for human trafficking, procuring and child-pornography were increased. In 2006 prohibition for purchasing prostitution services entered into force. In 2010 the government passed another bill to increase penalties for domestic violence. In 2011 the definition of rape was expanded to cover also sexual intercourse with unconscious (or sleeping) victims. All changes were explicitly motivated by Nordic (mostly Swedish) examples.

Explaining the post 1990s punitive turn

There were visible advocates for these penal aggravation, including the newly appointed Prosecutor General and the former Minister of Justice. But in explaining this shift we may need go behind these individuals, to changes in the media culture, public sentiments, and social and economic circumstances.

The 1990s was a decade of increased subjective insecurity and fears. National victim surveys report a steady increase of fears of violence from 1988 to 1997, despite the fact that actual victimization rates remained either stable or were in decline. There is a lot speaking for the conclusion that the growth of fear in Finland was associated with more fundamental socio-economic changes including a deep recession and the associated social and economic insecurities. Finland experienced a deep recession in the early 1990s with substantial welfare cuts and increasing income differences. This all was accentuated by the opening of the Eastern border, the fears of the Russian mafia invading Finland (soon to disappear before the end of the 1990s), an increase in the foreign population, and also Finland joining the EU in 1995.

Changes in media reporting on crime need to be added to the list as well. Crime reporting in tabloids (but not on TV-news) underwent substantial growth during the 1990s. There is also a remarkable convergence between trends in fears and the visibility of front-page violence: as the amount of tabloid reports on violent crime grew by 50% , fears increased by one third while the overall victimization remained constant (see Kivivuori et al. 2002). On a cross-national level, fears and feelings of insecurity, in turn, go together with penal severity.

As a conclusion: what the punitive critics really did, was just to give an expression to these anxieties, frustrations and fears following the deep recession, the opening of the borders and the growing social distances among people, as the income differences had also grown as a result of taxation reforms after the recession (see in more detail Lappi-Seppälä 2008b).

B. Reforming the sanction systems in the 2000s

Sanction reforms as "safety valves"

Specific offenses offer the politicians a visible platform for showing their "firmness" in face of the threat of crime. The sanction system, with all its diverse dimensions, offers the safety-valve to ease the pressures created by politically oriented sentence aggravations for the enforcement agencies. Once compared, there emerges a clear pattern between aggravating and mitigating reforms: the former deal with specific offenses, while mitigating reforms more often deal with the sanction system. This division of labor is clearly visible in four Scandinavian countries from the late 1960s onwards (see Lappi-Seppälä 2007, p. 258 – 259). Also the reforms in Finland since the mid-1990s confirm these findings. The aggravating reforms dealt with visible specific offenses (sexual and violent offenses), to be followed by "balancing reforms" within the sanction system. As a reaction for the rapidly increased prison rates the Ministry of Justice declared the "control of prison rates" as one of the key strategic aims in its policy plan for the years of 2007 – 2011. Focal points in this plan included intensified local crime-prevention work, a more nuanced and socially equal sanction system, expansion of community sanctions as replacements for short-term prison sentences, integration of substance abuse programs and social support with criminal sanctions, enhancement of victim support services and increased investment and use of criminological research in political decision making. [1] Concrete reforms emanating from this plan include restrictions for the use of default imprisonment and the adoption of electronically monitored supervision.

Reducing the number of fine defaulters

Fine-defaulters have been a recurrent problem for the Finnish prison administration. Several reforms have been conducted to cut down the from time to

---

[1]   See Criminal policy in Welfare State: Ministry of Justice Policy Plan for 2007 – 2011.

time increasing number of fine defaulters, but with only temporary success. In the early 2000s the number of default prisoners reached level of 200 prisoners. [1] In order to bring these figures down the Ministry of Justice conducted s series of reforms in 2006 and 2007. The conversion rate between day-fines and imprisonment was changed from one half to one third (three day-fines equals one day in prison) and the maximum duration of default imprisonment was reduced from 90 days to 60 days. More importantly, all smaller fines (prosecutor fines and court-ordered fines under 20 day-fines) were excluded from the default system. The estimated overall effect on prison rates is a reduction of 170 − 210 prisoners, which would reduce the use of default imprisonment to one tenth of its earlier scope.

Prison reform 2006

In 2006 Finland carried out the total reform of prison law. The decisive impulse came from constitutional reform in 1995 and 2000, which obliged the legislator to enact in much more detail (and in the level of parliamentary law) of all restrictions to the fundamental rights of prisoners. New prison law enhances the protection of constitutional rights of prisoners. Also the enforcement process is organized in more systematic manner with individual enforcement plans for all prisoners. The general principles of enforcement is defined more clearly [including the requirements of minimum intervention, the general aim of rehabilitation, and the principle of normality principle and harm-minimization (see in more detail Lappi-Seppälä 2009)].

There were also changes that effect also on the extent of the use of imprisonment. These included the adoption of a *new early release program* (supervised probationary period), designed for long-term prisoners, who needed more support and more intensive program-work. Probationary liberty may be available at the earliest six months prior to normal conditional release. Today, some 100 prisoners are under this programs (and supervised by GSM-mobile phones), contributed to a 3 −4% decrease in the daily prison population. Prior to 2006 the prison authorities had the

---

[1]   To these figures we must add those prisoners who serve combination sentences of both ordinary prison terms and default fines. This increases the annual prison rates by about 100 − 150 prisoners, meaning that 6 7% of prison resources arc used as a back up system for fines.

theoretical possibility of keeping dangerous recidivists in prison also after they had served their original sentence in full. None had been kept in prisons longer than their original sentence would justify since the 1960s, still this option (preventive detention) was problematic for principal reasons.

In 2006 *preventive detention was abolished* and replaced by a system that enables the courts to order serious violent offenders to serve their sentence "in full" (without parole). Today about 30 prisoners are serving their sentence in this manner.

The third change concerns *the recall of parole.* Courts were given more detailed guidance in deciding how to deal with the remaining sentence once an that has been released on parole commits a new offense during the probation. As a rule parole can be revoked only due to offences which would lead to an unconditional prison sentence of at least three months. Shorter remaining sentences (under three months) are usually not revoked even in these cases. Should the court choose to enforce the remaining sentence, it must form a joint sentence of imprisonment for the remaining sentence and the sentence imposed for the new offence. In practice the courts add a fraction, on average around a quarter or a fifth of the remaining sentence, into the new joint punishment. As a result of these new rules, the number of parole revocations has declined from the level of 1500 annually to around 600 −700.

Electronic monitoring

Last amendment in the Finnish sanction system took place in 2010 when the parliament passed a bill on new supervision order. This sanction is tailored for those offenders who do not qualify for community service due to their alcohol or other social problems. The order will replace prison sentences up to 6 months. Supervision will be carried out through electronic monitoring. In addition, the order will contain other program-elements, aimed to enhance the offender's social abilities to live a crime-free life. Estimated reduction of the prison population is around 130 prisoners (at any given day). The enforcement day has not yet been set, due to technical arrangements.

C. Measuring the effects of the policy reforms 1998 − 2010

The effects of these reforms can be traced both from sentencing and prison statistics (see table IV. 1).

Penal aggravations 1999–2005

The total *number or prisoners* increased by 42% (see sections C and D). The number of prisoners serving a sentence increased in all offense categories (+34%) with the steepest increase in violence (+48%) and drug offenses (+42%). This change was much a result of *increased sentence severity* for violent crimes and an increased number of drug offenders. The average length of unconditional prison sentences for aggravated assault increased from 17 to 22 months from 1998 to 2005 (section A). This change was accompanied by increased penalties also for lethal violence. All in all, the *total volume of annually imposed prison years* (counted as average length in years multiplied by the number of imposed prison sentences) increased by 52% from 1998 to 2005 (section B). For violent offenses this increase was 112% and for sexual offenses 69%. As regards to other groups of prisoners, fine defaulters increased by 75% and foreigners 104% (from 138 to 282, note that in 1976 their number was 24).

Table IV. 1   Court imposed prison sentences for selected offenses 1998/99 – 2009/10

I. COURT STATISTICS	Sep. 1998	2005	Oct. 2009	Change 1998 – 2005	Change 2005 – 2009
A. The length of unconditional prison term imposed for...	Months	Months	Months	%	%
– aggravated assault	17. 1	22. 3	24. 8	30%	11%
– sexual offenses (all offenses)	21. 7	25. 4	29. 9	17%	18%
– aggravated drug offenses	36. 5	42. 2	42. 4	16%	0%
B. Total volume of prison years imposed for...	Years	Years	Years	%	%
– all offenses	4135	6076	5548	+52%	–10%
– violence (all violent offenses)	1456	2207	1982	+112%	+44%
– sexual offenses (all offenses)	107	226	326	+69%	–8%
– drugs (all offenses)	653	1105	1016	+47%	–9%
II. PRISON STATISTICS					
C. Prisoners by prisoner group (annual average)	N	N	N	%	%
– total	2743	3888	3291	+42%	–15%
– serving a sentence	2287	3190	2635	+39%	–17%
– remand	354	519	599	+47%	+15%
– fine defaulters	102	179	57	+75%	–68%
– foreigners (included in above)	138	282	394	+104%	+40%

Continued

I. COURT STATISTICS	Sep. 98	2005	Oct. 09	Change 1998 – 2005	Change 2005 – 2009
D. Prisoners by the type of offense (1.5.)					
– violence	794	1172	1167	+48%	+0%
– drugs	360	512	424	+42%	–19%
– property	552	667	453	+21%	–32%
– drunk driving	312	409	316	+31%	–23%

Sources: Courts: Compiled from Statistics Finland. Life sentences excluded.

Prisoners: Compiled from Criminal sanctions Agency

Penal mitigations 2005 – 2010

The total number or prisoners fell by 15% and the number of prisoners serving a sentence by 17%. The latter decline is caused mainly by property offenses (−32%), drink driving (−23%) and drug-offenses (−19%). In 2005 −2009 penalties for aggravated assault still increased by two months. However the total number of imposed prison years decreased (mainly due to the decline of homicide cases). Penalties for sexual offenses continued to increase by almost 5 months. This increase was reflected also in the total number of imposed prison years (+44%, but as sexual offenses cover only 6% of all imposed prison-years, this is not reflected in the overall figures). In 2005 −2010 penalties and imposed prison years for drug offenses remained stable. As regards to other groups of prisoners, fine defaulters decreased by 68%, but foreigners increased by 40%.

All in all, the *increase* of prison rates in Finland during 1999 − 2005 (+1145 prisoners and 42%) was a summary effect of an increase in the number of foreign prisoners (+144, mainly from Russia and the Baltic countries), an increase in drug trafficking (+152, often linked to the former groups), an increase in the number of fine defaulters (+77) and prisoners on remand (+165), and an increase in violent offenders (+378). The post-2005 *decrease* (597 prisoners and 15%) is explainable by a decrease in drug, drunk-driving and property offenders (−395), as well as in fine defaulters (−122). The categories remaining stable or increasing during 2005 − 2010 were foreigners, pre-trial detainees, and violent offenders.

V. Criminal Sanctions Today

The Finnish constitution forbids the use of death penalty-as well as any degrading and inhuman punishments. The principal punishments are petty fine, fine, conditional imprisonment, community service, electronically monitored supervision order, juvenile punishment (for offenders between 15 – 17 years of age) and unconditional imprisonment.

Fines

Fines are imposed as dayfines. This system was adopted in Finland in 1921. The main objective of the dayfine-system, is to ensure equal severity of the fine for offenders of differint income and wealth. In this system the *number* of day-fines is determined on the basis of the seriousness of the offence while the *amount* of a dayfine depends on the financial situation of the offender. The amount of the dayfine equals roughly half of the offender's daily income after taxes. The number of day-fines varies between 1 and 120. If the fine is not paid it may be converted into imprisonment (default imprisonment) through separate proceedings. A fine may be imposed either in an ordinary trial or, in the case of certain petty offences, through simplified summary penal proceedings (penalty orders given by the prosecutor, or by fixed ticket fines by the police). Majority (around 60%) of case tried by the courts are dealt by fines.

Imprisonment

Imprisonment may be imposed either for a determinate period (at least fourteen days and at most twelve years for a single offence and fifteen years for several offences) or for life. [1] The applicable penal latitude for each offense is defined separately in the law.

Sentences of imprisonment are enforced either in closed prisons or in open institutions. Open institutions hold around 25% of the current prison population. Open institutions are in practice prisons without walls: the prisoner is obliged to stay in the prison area, but there are no guards or fences. There are 18 open prisons and 13 closed prisons. All prisons are state funded and run by the state

---

[1] A life sentence may be imposed for a very restricted number of offences-in practice only for murder. Those serving life sentence actually spend approximately 12 to 14 years in prison.

officials. There are no private prisons in Finland, neither are there any plans on that direction. Private prisons would not meet the demands of the Finnish constitution paragraph 124, stating that any "task involving significant exercise of public powers can only be delegated to public authorities."

Prisons are fairly small in their size. The largest closed units carry over 300 prisoners, while the smallest have a size of 40 - 50 prisoners. The system of early release is used on a routine basis. In Finland, practically all prisoners are released on parole after either 1/2 or 2/3 of their sentence. Parole revocations occur generally only due to a new offense punishable by unconditional prison terms and committed during the parole period.

Conditional imprisonment

Sentences of imprisonment of at most two years may be imposed conditionally, provided that "the seriousness of the offence, the culpability of the offender manifested in the offence, or previous convictions of the offender do not require an unconditional imprisonment". Young offenders under the age of 18 years may be sentenced to unconditional imprisonment only if special reasons call for this option. If a conditional imprisonment alone is not considered to be a sufficient sanction for the offence, an *unconditional fine* may be imposed on the offender as well. If the length of the sentence is between one to two years, *short community service* order (20 - 90 hours) may be sentenced alongside conditional imprisonment. Young offenders under the age of 21 years (at the time of the offence) may be placed under *supervision* if this is considered "justified in view of the promotion of the social adjustment of the offender and of the prevention of new offences". Imposing the sentence conditionally means that the enforcement will be suspended for a probation period of at least one year and at most three years. A person who has been sentenced to conditional imprisonment can be ordered to serve his or her sentence in prison if he or she commits a new offence during the probation period for which the court imposes a sentence of imprisonment. Thus, a behavioural infraction alone is not enough for enforcement of a conditional imprisonment. The courts impose annually some 15000 conditional sentences. Each year around 700 - 800 sentences are revoked (enforced).

Community service

Community service is imposed only instead of unconditional imprisonment. The duration of community service may vary between 20 and 200 hours. The prerequisites for sentencing the offender to community service are: (a) that the convicted person consents to this, (b) that the sentence does not exceed eight months, and (c) that the offender is deemed capable of carrying out the community service order. Also (d) prior convictions may in some case prevent the use of this option. The offender's ability to carry out the work is evaluated on the basis of a specific *suitability report*. This report may be requested by any one of the parties, the prosecutor or the court. The suitability report is prepared by the Probation Service. If the conditions of the community service order are violated, the court normally imposes a new sentence of unconditional imprisonment.

Youth justice

The age of criminal responsibility is 15 years old. All offenders under the age of 15 are dealt with only by the child welfare authorities. Young offenders aged 15 to 17 are dealt with both by the child welfare system and the system of criminal justice. All offenders below 18 receive a reduction for their sentence. There are further restrictions against the use of imprisonment for young offenders. Prison can be sentenced for offenders between 15 − 17 only for exceptional reasons (for more detail, see Hinkkanen & Lappi-Seppälä 2011).

Sentencing principles

In individual cases the type and amount of criminal punishment is determined by the penal latitude, general sentencing rules and the principles defined in Penal Code chapter 6. The leading principle in sentencing is proportionality. As the FPC 6 : 4 states: "The sentence shall be determined so that it is in just proportion to the harmfulness and dangerousness of the offence, the motives for the act and the other culpability of the offender manifested in the offence. " Chapter 6 on sentencing defines further the general criteria provisions for aggravation and mitigation, as well as for the implementation of specific types of sanctions. [1]

Finnish authorities impose around 550000 sanctions each year. Half of these (270000) are police fines and 40% prosecutors fines. Courts impose 65000 sentences. Over 40% (27000) of these are for traffic offenses, mostly by drunken

---

[1]　The Finnish sanction structure, sentencing principles and practice are discussed in more detail in Lappi-Seppälä 2001 and Hinkkanen & Lappi-Seppälä 2011.

driving (20000). This leaves around 39000 court imposed sentences for non-traffic offenses. All in all, 6 − 7% of all penalties are imposed by the courts for non-traffic offenses. As many countries exclude traffic-offenses, as well as minor fines from their sentencing statistics, the Finnish conviction figures must be used with great care in international comparisons. In 2009 prison sentences (in 6657) cover 10% of all court imposed sanctions and 1.2% of all penalties imposed either by the police, prosecutor of the courts.

Sentencing practice

The overall use of different sentencing options by offense-type is displayed in table in appendix. (Only cases dealt by the courts are included). Imprisonment covers around 10% of all penalties imposed by the courts. Median length of prisons term is 4 months and mean 10 months (the difference is explainable by shape of the distribution and the effect of long prison sentence imposed for serious offenses). Community service is used in 5% and conditional imprisonment in 25% of cases. Fines cover 60% of all court dispositions.

Distribution of penalties in different offense categories looks like the following (see in more detail the appendix).

- Completed homicide is punished by a little below 10 year prison term (in addition some 10 − 15 murder cases receive a life sentence).
- Basic form of rape is punished with about 2 years prison term (around 60%) and aggravated rape by 4 − 5 years prison term.
- Basic assault leads to fines in around 65% cases, while aggravated assault is punished either by two years unconditional prisons (little below 60%) or by 1 − 2 years conditional prison.
- Basic theft is punished by fines (little over 50%) or 2 − 3 months unconditional or conditional prison term. Aggravated theft leads to around one years unconditional (50%) prison term or to a little shorter conditional prison term (40%). One out of ten offender are sentenced to community service.
- Penalties for basic robbery are very much on the same level with aggravated theft. Aggravated robbery, in turn, leads to unconditional (90%) prison term of around 2 − 3 years.
- Drunk drivers receive fines when their BAC is below 1.2 o/oo. In the level

of alcohol in ones blood exceed 1.2 o/oo the penalty is either conditional prison term (15−45 days), or, for repeat offenders, community service or unconditional prison term (2−4 months).

- The consumption of drugs in punished in Finland by a fine (20 dayfines, same as for petty theft). Distributing and trafficking smaller amounts is punished either by fines (66%) or short conditional (20%) or 2−6 months unconditional prison term. Larger quantities are sanctioned as aggravated drug offenses with unconditional prison terms starting from 2 up to 10 years (mean 3.5 years and 50% of cases falling between 22 and 60 months).

VI. The Role of Resterative Justice-mediation

Mediation has gained a substantial role in the handling of criminal cases in Finland, however, this has taken place outside the criminal law. [1] Mediation does not constitute a part of the criminal justice system but it has frequent interrelations with that system as far as referral of cases and their further processing is concerned. The criminal code mentions an agreement or settlement between the offender and the victim as a possible grounds for waiving of charges by the prosecutor, or waiving of punishment by the court and as a grounds of mitigating the sentence.

The first mediation experiment in Finland started in 1983 (see closer Grönfors 1989 and Iivari 2000). As was the case with other countries, the idea was to provide an alternative to the official criminal justice system. By the early 2000s mediation services were available to about 80 percent of the population. In order to secure equality before the law and to expand the application of mediation schemes- mediation was extended to cover the whole country in 2006 by passing a national law on mediation. Provincial governments are obliged to arrange mediation service in their region, either in co-operation with municipal authorities or with other public or private partners. The overall organizational responsibility and supervision lies within the ministry of social affairs. Mediators have no formal requirements,

---

[1] Other elements of restorative justice in the Finnish criminal justice system are discussed in more detail in Lappi-Seppälä 1996.

but they must have proper "skills and experience". General preconditions for mediation include voluntariness and ability of the parties to understand the content and meaning of mediation. The parties have also always the right to withdraw from the process.

The 2006 legislation did not change this basic character of mediation, but gives closer instructions on how to handle mediation cases where minors are involved. Furthermore, there are general guidelines for the selection of cases suitable for mediation. In other respects, the law is quite flexible and much less formal that the corresponding Norwegian law, to take one example. In this context mediation was also given an official definition in the law, referring to " (...) a non-chargeable service in which a crime suspect and the victim of that crime are provided the opportunity to meet confidentially through an independent conciliator, to discuss the mental and material harm caused to the victim by the crime and, on their own initiative, to agree on measures to redress the harm." (Law on Mediation, Chapter 1, section 1).

The process

Mediation can start at any time between the commission of the offence and execution of the sentence and by any of the possible parties. Once a case has been referred to the mediation office, the office contacts the parties in order to query their willingness to participate in mediation. Where this is successful, a first meeting is arranged.

The mediation programme is managed by the municipal social welfare office. The initiative for submitting cases to mediation comes, as a rule, from the police or from the prosecutor. However, the consent of all parties is required before going into reconciliation. The sessions are often held in the evening, participants are addressed on first-name terms and the flow of discussion is relatively free. The mediator's principal role is only to mediate and act on a neutral basis. Once the process has started it normally leads to a written contract that contains the subject (what sort of offence), the content of a settlement (how the offender has consented to repair the damages), the place and date of the restitution as well as consequences for a breach of the contract.

What happens after a successful mediation depends largely on the category and seriousness of the offence. In complainant offences, successful mediation automatically means that the prosecutor drops the case. In non-complainant offences it is under the discretion of the prosecutor whether he/she is willing to drop the charge. This would be possible according to the law if prosecution seemed "either unreasonable or pointless" due to successful reconciliation, and if non-prosecution did not violate "an important public or private interest". In mediation cases non-prosecution is, thus, always discretionary. Unlike in some other countries, mediation does not automatically divert the case from the criminal justice system. This may narrow its diversionary effect, but on the other hand, it also prevents mediation from becoming restricted to trivial cases.

Aims and achievements

The roots of Finnish mediation initiatives locate in the abolitionistic writings of Thomas Mathiesen and Nils Christie in Norway and Louk Hulsman in the Netherlands in the 1970s, as well as in the practices and experiments in New Zealand and North America (see Grönfors 1989). The elements of informality, voluntariness, and community involvement were crucial from the very beginning. The forerunners of the mediation movement were careful not to integrate the system too closely into the criminal justice. There were healthy suspicions against "institutionalization". Mediation had been presented as form of diversion and as an alternative to criminal justice. And this "informal appeal" may partly explain its initial success and fast spreading in Finland. There were plenty of voluntary workers who wished to join a project that promised to do things differently and aimed to deliver services that the official criminal justice system was unable to deliver. In this point respect mediation has retained its original line: It has remained as a genuine informal alternative.

Having said this, it is equally clear that its diversionary function is restricted only to minor offenses, not to those punishable by imprisonment (at least in Finland). The diversionary role of mediation can be seen especially in the expansion in the use of non-prosecution among juveniles. It is equally clear that for a substantial part of victims, mediation has provided a means to receive at least some compensation from the offender. One of the main goals of mediation is also to interrupt the criminal career of young offenders. The hope has been that the mediation process would enhance the offender's ability to realise the meaning of his/her offence and thereby enable a fuller accountability for the crime. Some studies, indeed, indicate that reoffending is more common in control group than among those young offenders that have undergone the mediation process. ①

Most heated debates have concerned the use of mediation in cases of domestic violence. During the enactment of the mediation act, feminist organisations expressed strong doubts of the suitability of mediation in these cases. Consequently, the parliament, when approving the bill, added extra limitations for the use of mediation in these cases. According to the law domestic violence may be submitted to mediation only by the initiative of the police or prosecutor. Also the governmental program for the year 2011 - 2015 obliges the authorities to evaluate the existing mediation practices in cases of intimate and domestic violence.

A recent evaluation study on mediation takes a critical view on some of these restrictions. According to Iivari 2010, interviews with police and prosecuting officials suggest that the heads of mediation offices and municipal social workers should have more discretion to decide which cases are referred. In overall, the key objectives of mediation-expertise, objectivity, confidentiality and justice-were met in the majority of cases. Clients who had been involved in mediation of domestic had the most positive experiences of the objectivity, confidentiality and voluntary nature of mediation. On the other hand, in domestic violence mediation had not generally furthered the treatment of mental harm caused to the victim. The results suggest that mediation in domestic violence involves true challenges and careful preparation. There is also a risk of disappointment. There was a striking differences between the experience between those who had reached an agreement and those who had not. The latter group expressed deep disappointment over the mediation. All in all one out of three of those that answered the free-form questions (and 5% of all respondents) reported having had very negative experiences with mediation, for example in terms of the quality of the services. According to the author of report, this warrants "further intensive training for and supervision of mediators. It also warrants considering the introduction of a requirement of certification for voluntary mediators" (Iivari 2010).

---

① See Mielityinen 1999. Reoffending was examined in a quasi-experimental setting, which still leaves open the question whether control group and mediation group were similar enough. For broader discussions on the experiences on mediation in Finland see Elonheimo 2010, Grönfors 1989, Iivari 2000 and 2010 and Lappi-Seppälä 1996, all with references.

Practice

In numbers mediation plays a substantial role in the Finnish justice system. After the introduction of mediation in the early 1980s, the total annual number of mediation cases had exceeded 5000 by the mid-1990s. The enactment of the Mediation Act in 2006 extended mediation across the entire country and the latest statistics indicate that over 10000 referrals to mediation in 2010. This almost double the number of annually imposed unconditional prison sentences. Detailed statistics for 2007 show the following profile.

The clear majority of cases involve either minor property offences or minor forms of assault and battery (around 40% in both cases).

Table VI. 1   Statistics on mediation by type of offence in 2007

	N	%
All offences	9054	100
Minor assault	623	6. 9
Assault	2965	32. 7
Aggravated assault	60	0. 7
Robbery	27	0. 3
Theft	889	9. 8
Fraud/embezzlement	493	5. 4
Damage to property	1983	21. 9
Car theft	96	1. 1
Disturbance of domestic peace	421	4. 6
Unlawful threat	408	4. 5
Defamation	353	3. 9
Other	736	8. 1

Source: Stakes, Ministry of Social and Welfare Affairs.

Most cases are sent to mediation by the police (72%) or by the prosecutor (24%). Only a small number of cases come directly from either the parties or the social welfare authorities (two percent each).

Table VI. 2   Statistics on mediation in criminal offence cases according to the initiator, 2007

	N	%
In criminal cases, mediation was initiated by:	8315	100
Police	5977	71.9
Prosecutor	1943	23.4
The parties	140	1.7
The victim	65	–
The offender	66	–
Social welfare authorities	153	1.8
Parents	22	0.3
Other	80	1.0

Source: Stakes, Ministry of Social and Welfare Affairs.

In around half of the cases in 2007 the offender was under the age of 21. 14% of the cases involved children below the age of criminal responsibility, and one fifth were attributable to the age group from 15 to 17. The majority of the victims were aged 30 and older.

Table VI. 3   Mediation according to the age of the parties, 2007

	N	%
The age of the offender/perpetrator (at the time of the offence/event)	10198	100
< 15 y.	1422	13.9
15 – 17 y.	2092	20.5
18 – 20 y.	1499	14.7
21 – 29 y.	2121	20.8
30 – 64 y.	2928	28.7
65 – y.	136	1.3
The age of the victim/plaintiff	7375	100
< 15 y.	564	7.6
15 – 17 y.	674	9.1
18 – 20 y.	814	11.0
21 – 29 y.	1709	23.2
30 – 64 y.	3377	45.8
65 + y.	237	3.2

Source: Stakes, Ministry of Social and Welfare Affairs.

Just over 60% of all referrals ended in an agreement, and on average 90% of the resulting contracts were fulfilled. The majority of the contracts contained monetary compensation, but may also have included compensation through work, an apology or a promise not to repeat the behaviour.

Table VI. 4   The number and content of mediation agreements, 2007

Agreements	N	%
In criminal cases during the year	5540	62. 9
In civil cases during the year	86	46. 2
No agreement	1321	15. 0
The contents of the agreements		
Monetary compensation-N	3271	
Monetary compensation-total	1573099	
Work compensation-N	376	
Work compensation-value in	102832	
Property returned-N	48	
Behavioural agreements-N	343	
Apologies-N	1969	
No demands (withdrawal from demand) -N	855	

Source: Stakes, Ministry of Social and Welfare Affairs.

VII. Conclusions

Today, Finnish penal policy can be seen as an example of a pragmatic and non-moralistic Nordic approach, with a clear social policy orientation. It reflects the values of the Nordic welfare-state ideal and emphasizes that measures against social marginalization and equality work also as measures against crime. Factors to all this were discussed in chapters II and III. As became evident, the 30 year period of de-carceration would not have been possible without political consensus and agreements on principles. This was reached and upheld partly thanks to an active and influential group of penal reformers, working actively both in political life, civil service, judiciary, universities and research institutes. The political system, in general, showed little interest in crime policy. Also the media retained a fairly reasonable attitude on these issues, at least in comparison to many other countries. For Finland, the intensified Nordic co-operation in legal matters and the strengthening sense of a Common Nordic Identity provided extra elements in our effort to humanize the Finnish criminal justice system in the 1960s and 1970s. Further developments were sustained and supported also by the effective spreading of criminological insight and knowledge among the criminal justice practitioners, often in co-operation with the Ministry of Justice, judiciary and universities.

A full account of the factors behind the humanization of the Finnish penal system should, however, explain more. It should be able to address the question of timing: why did this all start when it did? The explanation should also be general enough to cover patterns across countries and possibly even across regions. As the policies adopted in Finland were highly influenced by similar policies in the other Nordic countries, the explanations for the "Finnish exceptionalism" should be able to cover also the more general "Scandinavian exceptionalism". [1]

The old slogan, "Good Social Policy is the Best Criminal Policy" tells the essential: societies do better by investing more money in schools, social work and families than in prisons. Historical and comparative analyses confirm that liberal penal policies are associated with strong welfare states. [2] The years of penal liberalization in Finland were also the period when Finland was joining the Scandinavian welfare family in terms of economic prosperity, welfare provision and income equality. That change was reflected also in our penal policies, in the same way as the prison expansion in the Anglo-Saxon world coincides with the concomitant general dismantling of welfare states.

But also the Nordic Welfare states-and Finland perhaps harder than the others-have suffered of the economic crisis during the last 20 years. Nordic Welfare States were not saved from the cutbacks in the public sector and the general scaling down of welfare provisions, increases in income differences and growing social distances. And also the Nordic criminal justice systems have received their share of

---

[1] On the other end of the scale we would find the "American exceptionalism" and the expansion of penal culture in the US and many Anglo-Saxon countries (see Garland 2001 and Tonry 2004 and 2009).

[2] On the relationships between macro-sociological factors and penal practices, see Lappi-Seppälä 2007 and 2008.

the global "punitive turn". These changes may not be comparable in type and magnitude to those that have taken place elsewhere in Europe and overseas, but they are still real for the Nordics (see for the discussions Tham 2001 and Balvig 2005).

The question whether Finland will also face similar growth in the prison population as is found in so many other countries would probably receive different answer from different observers. An optimist would point out that very few of the social, political, economic and cultural background conditions which explain the rise of mass imprisonment in the United States apply to Finland. The social and economic security granted by the Nordic welfare state model may still function as a social backup system for a tolerant criminal policy. Political culture still encourages negotiations and appreciates expert opinions. Social security, equality, trust and legitimacy granted by an affluent, universalistic welfare state will dampen public fears, punitive projections and reactive populist posturing. And the fact that Finland managed to reverse the steep increase in imprisonment rates in the shift of the millennium into a almost as steep decrease from 2005 onwards, does give some support for this assertion.

For a pessimist, neo-liberalism has gained a firm footing in Finland already from the early 1990s onward and will tighten its grip also in the coming years. Punitive and populist trends-more visible in Sweden and Denmark-will invade also Finland. An optimist might argue that the tone, still, is different compared to similar changes in many other countries. The Nordic Welfare Model may be under threat, but it certainly has not been abnegated or rejected. On the contrary, it has become a part of the Common Nordic Identity and is widely supported across the whole political field, at least on the level of political rhetoric. Uncontested as this model is, it may well prove to be one of the cornerstones for the argument for a more social and human penal policy?

References

Andenaes, J. (1974), *Punishment and Deterrence*. Ann Arbor: University of Michigan Press.

Anttila, I. (1971), "Conservative and Radical Criminal Policy in the Nordic Countries," *Scandinavian Studies in Criminology*, *Vol.* 3. Oslo (1967), pp. 9 −21.

Balvig, F. (2004), "When Law and Order returned to Denmark", *Journal of Scandinavian Studies in Criminology* Vol 5 (2005), pp. 167 –187.

Criminal policy in Welfare State: Ministry of Justice Policy Plan for 2007 –2011, Ministry of Justice, Helsinki 2006.

Elonheimo, H. (2010), *Nuorisorikollisuuden esiintyvyys, taustatekijät ja sovittelu*, Turun Yliopiston julkaisuja 2999/2010, Turku.

Falck, S. von Hofer, H. and Storgaard; A. (2003), Nordic Criminal Statistics 1950 – 2000, Department of Criminology, Stockholm University, Report 2003: 3.

Garland, D. (2001), *The Culture of Control—Crime and Social Order in Contemporary Society*. The University of Chicago Press.

Grönfors, M. (1989), "Ideals and reality in community mediation." In Martin Wright & Burt Galaway, eds., *Mediation and Criminal Justice*. London, 1989, pp. 140 –151.

Iivari, J. (2000), "Victim-offender mediation in Finland", In *Victim-Offender Mediation in Europe, Making Restorative Justice Work*, Leuven University Press.

Iivari, J. (2010), Oikeutta oikeuden varjossa. Rikossovittelulain täytäntöönpanon arviointitutkimus [Justice in the Shadow of Justice], An Evaluation Study of the Implementation of the Act on Mediation in Criminal Cases, National Institute for Health and Welfare (THL), Report 5/2010. 193 pages. Helsinki 2010. ISBN 978 –952 –245 –227 –6 (printed), ISBN 978 –952 –245 –228 –3 (pdf).

Kivivuori, J. and Lehti M, "Homicide in the Nordic Area: Finland and Sweden Compared." In Tonry & Lappi-Seppälä 2011.

Kivivuori, J. & Kemppi, S. and Smolej, M. (2002), *Front-Page Violence, Violence Reporting on the Front Pages of the Finnish Tabloid Press* 1980 –2000. National Research Institute of Legal Policy. Publication No. 196/2000.

Kristofferssen, R. (2010), *Correctional Statistics of Denmark, Finland, Iceland, Norway and Sweden* 2004 –2008. Correctional Service of Norway Staff Academy 1/2010. Oslo 2010.

Lahti, R. (2000), "Towards a Rational and Humane Criminal Policy (Trends in Scandinavian Penal Thinking." *Journal of Scandinavian Studies and Crime Prevention*. Vol 1/2000, pp. 141 –155.

Lappi-Seppälä, T. (1995), "General Prevention-Hypotheses and empirical evidence". In *Ideologi og Empiri i Kriminologien*. Scandinavian Research Council for Criminology. Reykjavik 1995.

Lappi-Seppälä, T. (1996), "Reparation in Criminal Law –Finnish National Report. " In Albin Eser & Susanne Walther eds. *Wiedergutmachung im Strafrecht*. Max-Planck-Institut, Freiburg im. Br. 1996. p. 317 –420.

Lappi-Seppälä, T. (2001), "Sentencing and Punishment in Finland: The Decline of the

Repressive Ideal". In *Punishment and Penal Systems in Western Countries*, edited by M. Tonry and R. Frase. , New York, Oxford University Press, p. 92 −150.

Lappi-Seppälä, T. (2007), "Penal Policy in Scandinavia. " In *Crime, Punishment, and Politics in Comparative Perspective*, edited by Michael Tonry. Vol. 36 of *Crime and Justice: A Review of Research*, edited by Michael Tonry (Chicago, University of Chicago Press) .

Lappi-Seppälä, T. (2008a), "Trust, Welfare, and Political Culture: Explaining Differences in National Penal Policies. " In *Crime and Justice: A Review of Research*, vol. 37, edited by Michael Tonry (Chicago, University of Chicago Press) .

Lappi-Seppälä, T. (2008b), "Politics or Policy-Fluctuations in the Finnish Penal Policy", In *Ikke kun straf... Festskrift til Vagn Greve*. Juris-og Ökonomiforbundets Forlag. Köbenhavn 2008: 333 −357.

Lappi-Seppälä, T. (2011a), "Nordic Youth Justice: Juvenile Sanctions in Four Nordic Countries. " In Tonry & Lappi-Seppälä 2011.

Lappi-Seppälä, T. (2011b), "Changes in Penal Policy in Finland" . In Helmuth Kury & Evelyn Shea, eds. , *Punitivity. International developments. Vol. 1, Punitiveness-global Phenomenon?* Universitätäverlag Dr. N. Brockmeyer. Bochum/Germany, 2011.

Lappi-Seppälä, T. & Tonry M. (2011), "Crime, Criminal Justice, and Criminology in the Nordic Countries", In *Crime and Justice: A Review of Research*, Vol. 40, edited by Michael Tonry & Tapio Lappi-Seppälä (Chicago, University of Chicago Press) .

Mielityinen, I. (1999), *Rikos ja sovittelu*. National Research Institute of legal Policy 167/ 1999. Helsinki.

Tham, H. (2001), "Law and order as a leftist project?" Punishment & Society. The International Journal of Penology, Vol. 3. , No. 3. Sage Publications, pp. 409 −426.

Tonry, M & Lappi-Seppälä T. (2011), *Crime and Justice: A Review of Research*, Vol. 40, edited by Michael Tonry & Tapio Lappi-Seppälä (Chicago, University of Chicago Press) .

Törnudd P. (1993), *Fifteen Years of Decreasing Prison Rates in Finland*. National Research Institute of Legal Policy. Research Communication 8.

Törnudd, P. (1996), *Facts, Values and Visions*. Essays in Criminology and Crime Policy, edited by Inkeri Anttila, Kauko Aromaa, Risto Jaakkola, Tapio Lappi-Seppälä & Hannu Takala. National Research Institute of Legal Policy Publication No. 138. Helsinki, 1996.

芬兰监狱人口的规制

塔皮奥·拉匹·塞佩莱

【摘要】本文的第一部分概述了芬兰刑事政策的主要变化，从 1918 年内战到 1945 年与苏联战争结束这段时期，呈现出了反复的政治、社会和经济危机和高监禁率的特征。从 20 世纪 60 年代起，刑事司法的改革拉开帷幕。新的刑事政策理念强调法律的保障措施，从而防止监禁的过度滥用。通过扩大使用罚款和有条件惩罚，减轻对财产型犯罪的处罚和扩大提前释放制度的范围，系统的法律改革减少了监禁的使用。1990 年监禁的替代方案出台，社区服务令取代了很大一部分的短期徒刑。

因此，芬兰设法将原先 20 世纪 60 年代的超过 0.15% 的监禁率降至 20世纪 90 年代中期的 0.06%。前者是当时欧洲国家中最高的，而欧盟国家中最低的。将芬兰和其他北欧国家的犯罪趋势作比较，我们会发现：监禁使用率的急剧下降对其犯罪率并没有显著的影响。芬兰的犯罪率同北欧国家一样，都保持着一个较为稳定的发展（甚至与那些增加使用监禁的欧洲国家一样）。这再一次印证了一个一般刑的犯罪学结论：犯罪和监禁率是两相对独立的，各自的增长和降低都依据其自身的法律和动态。

文章的后一部分讨论了芬兰刑罚制度的主要特点。芬兰的宪法禁止使用死刑，以及任何有辱人格或不人道的惩罚。主要的刑罚措施包括罚款、有条件的监禁、社区服务、以电子方式监测的监管令、少年刑罚（对年龄在 15～17 岁之间的罪犯）和无条件监禁。法院适用最多的是罚款，其次是社区服务。大约每十个犯罪人中有一人会被判处有期徒刑，其中超过一半的刑期低于 6 个月。

Efficiency and Justice in Procedural Reforms: the Rise and Fall of the Oral Hearing

Johanna Niemi [*]

【Abstract】 The purpose of this article is to examine the (potentially) conflicting claims of fair trial and efficiency of justice. The contemporary discussions on the reform and the development of procedural laws are dominated by two conflicting discourses, the pursuit for human rights, especially the right to a fair trial, and the constraints of insufficient resources. The conflicting trends are first explored in the activities of the Council of Europe, placing emphasis on the development of the justice systems of the member states. The second part of the paper uses Finland as a case study on procedural reform. In Finland the procedural laws were modernized in the 1990s with the ambitious aim to implement the principles of modern procedural law. These reforms implemented the principles of orality, immediacy and concentration of the main hearing into the civil and criminal proceedings. The reform was quite successful in the first instance courts but met with difficulties in the appeal courts. After the turn of the century the tide has changed. The principle of an oral main hearing is in decline and several reforms have reduced its application. The present reform proposals are driven by the need to increase efficiency of court proceedings and to press down the costs of justice. The purpose of the article is to stimulate discussion on fair trial and efficiency in court reform. Can the claims to due process and efficiency be adjusted?

[*] Professor, Faculty of Law, University of Helsinki.

Introduction[①]

The contemporary discussions on the reform and the development of procedural laws are usually dominated by two conflicting discourses, the pursuit for human rights, especially the right to a fair trial, and the constraints of insufficient resources. These aims seem to be in constant conflict with each other and their advocates seem to have little understanding for the argument of the other side. On the one side, human rights advocates have a legitimate claim for just procedures and show little concern for the limited resources.[②] On the other side, the civil justice systems of most countries seem to be in a constant state of crisis. The backlog of cases accumulates, the trials are delayed, the costs of litigation are on a rise, the recruitment of competent judges and other personal is difficult and the parties express dissatisfaction with the handling of their cases by the courts.[③] The civil justice administrations streamline the procedures and seek for cuts in costs with little regard for the implications for due process-or so the human rights advocates argue.

The purpose of this article is to examine the (potentially) conflicting claims of fair trial and efficiency of justice. The starting point of the article is the right to a fair trial as one of the fundamental human rights and a cornerstone of democratic government. It is also acknowledged that the crisis of civil litigation is real in many countries and that limited resources need efficient allocation. The conflicting trends are first explored in the activities of the Council of Europe, which has traditionally played a major role in the development of human rights in Europe and which has after the collapse of the iron curtain even taken an active role in the reforms of the court systems of the former East European countries. The second part of the paper

---

① This article is an updated version of an article published in C. H. van Rhee and A. Uzelac, eds., Civil Justice between Efficiency and Quality: From Ius Commune to the CEPEJ (Intersentia, Antwerp 2008), pp. 29 – 45.

② A whole branch of literature analyses the human rights in criminal procedure. One of the early works is Andrews 1982. See also Trechsel 2005; Stavros 1993; Aall 1996. There is far less literature on the human rights aspects of civil procedure. See, however, Jacob 2007.

③ The crisis is reflected in the titles of contemporary analyses of the civil justice system. See, for example, Zuckermann 1999.

uses Finland as a case study on procedural reform. In Finland the procedural laws were modernized in the 1990s with the ambitious aim to implement the principles of modern procedural law. The project may have been too ambitious and costly and new reforms are drafted with the efficiency arguments in the foreground.

The purpose of the article is to stimulate discussion on fair trial and efficiency in court reform. Can the claims to due process and efficiency be adjusted? Can we afford a fair trial? In the end, I also wish to facilitate discussion on what the adherence to the right to a fair trial means for a democratic government.

I. The Council of Europe and the Law of Procedure

Human Rights

Human rights have always been the cornerstone of the activities of the Council of Europe. Founded in 1949 after the horrors of the war, the purpose of the Council has been to maintain and promote peace in Europe, based on democratic values, justice, individual freedom, political liberty and the rule of law. [1] The Council of Europe has today 47 member states covering in addition to all the European Union member states also the countries of the former Soviet Union and Yugoslavia. Reaching a large number of countries with different backgrounds, the Council of Europe has become a major contributor to the legal reform in Europe. One of its most important institutions is the European Convention on Human Rights. [2]

The Convention and the Court of Human Rights have played a crucial role in the upholding of human rights in Europe. As a model for the UN conventions on human rights and regional conventions, it has had a wide and lasting impact all over the world on the respect of individual rights. Still today the European Court of Human Rights, with its jurisdiction over individual complaints and the high

---

[1] Statute of the Council of Europe, 5 May. 1949, ETS 001, preamble.

[2] Convention for the Protection of Human Rights and Fundamental Freedoms, CETS No. 5, Rome, 4 Nov. 1950.

respect

for its decisions in all Member States, has a leading role in the development of human rights.

Paradoxically, development in the Court of Human Rights itself is an apt illustration of the difficulty to satisfy simultaneously the requirements of a fair trial and efficiency. The Court is at the moment struggling with a mounting case load. [1] The most common finding of the Court, when examining the applications from the member states, seems to be a violation against the procedural rights and, most specifically, against the right to a fair trial. An integral part of the concept of fair trial is the reasonable time requirement according to which everyone has a right to a fair trial within a reasonable time (Art. 6 (1)). The Court has frequently found that the member states have not fulfilled this obligation. [2] Sometimes a case has been pending in the Court of Human Rights far longer than in the domestic courts. The need of reform of the procedures of the Court of Human Rights has been acknowledged, but it has turned out to be quite difficult to achieve a satisfactory reform plan. The paradoxical situation in the Court of Human Rights illustrates how important it is to accommodate the standards of fair trial and due process and procedural efficiency.

Recommendations

Besides the activities of the Court, the Council of Europe is active in other arenas. In particular, the Council of Europe promotes a greater unity among its members through common action, agreements and discussions in economic, social, cultural, scientific, legal and administrative matters. [3] In the field of justice and legal procedures the Committee of Ministers has since the beginning of 1980s adopted several recommendations to promote human rights and to facilitate the

---

[1]　European Court of Human Rights, Annual Report 2010, p. 4, reports that the amount of pending cases has increased every year, mounting to nearly 140000 by the end of 2010.

[2]　At the time of writing this paper I have in front of a judgement from April 2007, in which the Court found a violation against fair trial that had taken place in 1996 and in which the domestic procedures were completed in 2000. *V* v. *Finland*, judgment 24, April 2007, Appl. 40412/98. The case is one of several, in which Finland has been found guilty of exceeding the reasonable time in its procedures.

[3]　Statute of the Council of Europe, 5 May 1949, Art. 15 (b).

reform of court procedures. ①

The recommendations are based on the deliberations of legal experts and processed through the political bodies to the member states. Some of the recommendations are quite concrete and detailed: the Recommendation on civil procedure from 1984 as a prime example. ② No doubt a lot of work and expertise had been put into the preparation of this Recommendation. The intention seems to have been to convince the Member States through good arguments. The Appendix to the Recommendation, "Principles of civil procedure designed to improve the functioning of justice", could be the first step towards a model law. The tone of the recommendations is benevolent and encouraging, always starting with an emphasis of human rights and reference to Article 6 of the ECHR.

Both the case law of the Court and the activity of the Committee of Ministers have changed the nature of procedural law from predominantly domestic law to an area of international concern. ③

Besides Council of Europe also European Union has become active in the field of procedural law. European Union has traditionally been interested in the effective enforcement of judgements in commercial disputes. ④ Even more far-reaching

---

① Recommendation (84) 5 of the Committee of Ministers to Member States on the principles to improve the functioning of justice. Recommendation (2005) 9E of the Committee of Ministers to the Member States on the protection of witnesses and collaborators of justice (2003); Recommendation (2003) 17E of the Committee of Ministers to the Member States on enforcement; Recommendation (97) 13E concerning intimidation of witnesses and the rights of the defence.

② Recommendation R (84) 5 of the Committee of Ministers to the Member States on the principles to improve the functioning of justice.

③ As Storme rightly points out, procedural law is not any more the most nationally based field of law. See Storme 2007, p. 15. It has to be noted that within European Union even more far-reaching integration of procedural law, especially concerning procedural issues that have cross-border effects, has been initiated. This has become possible since the reform of the European Union Treaty (Lisbon Treaty) that entered into force 1 Dec. 2009, bringing international procedural issues within the normal decision making procedures and competences of the Union (Avt. 81 and 82 of the FTEU).

④ Brussels Convention on Jurisdiction and the Enforcement of Judgments in Civil and Commercial Matters 1968 and within the EEA countries through the Lugano Convention on jurisdiction and the enforcement of judgments in civil and commercial matters 1988, and subsequently through Council Regulation (EC) No. 44/2001 of 22 December 2000 on jurisdiction and the recognition and enforcement of judgments in civil and commercial matters and through European Enforcement Order Regulation No. 805/2004 (EEO).

integration of procedural law, especially concerning procedural issues that have cross-border effects, has been initiated. ① This has become possible since the reform of the European Union Treaty (Lisbon Treaty) that entered into force 1 Dec, 2009, bringing international procedural issues within the normal decision making procedures and competences of the Union. ②

In this article the focus is on the developments in the Council of Europe with its emphasis on human rights. Covering a far wider network of countries than the European Union, the Council of Europe offers a view to general principles that have been accepted by countries with varying cultural and legal backgrounds.

Procedural Reform

Procedural reform has become part of the activities of the Council of Europe in the development programs for the new Member States since the upheaval of the Eastern European countries in 1990. Many East European court systems were in the need of reform and their judges had to be educated in for example issues of human rights. Council of Europe has been one of the central actors in the development programs and co-operation in the field of legal and judicial reform.

The cooperation has been intensified in the beginning of the 21 st century with the establishment of the CEPEJ, the European Commission on Efficiency of Justice. CEPEJ is a new body, working under the auspices of the Council of Europe and consisting of experts on the administration of justice from each member state. The Resolution establishing the CEPEJ and confirming its Statute has become the foundation of a new way of working with procedural issues in the Council of Europe. ③ With the establishment of the CEPEJ in 2002 the work on reform of court systems and procedures has become more organized, permanent and systematic.

---

① The latest development in the efficiency of enforcement in the EU is to harmonize summary proceedings to recover debts. Regulation (EC) No. 861/2007 of July 2007 establishing a European Small Claims Procedure and Regulation (EC) No. 1896/2006 of the European parliament and of the Council of 12 December 2006 creating a European order for payment procedure. Act on the European Small Claims Procedure 753/2008 and Act on the European Payment Order Procedure 754/2008.

② Treaty on the Functioning of the European Union (FTEU), 9 May, 2008, Art. 81 and 82.

③ Council of Europe Committee of Ministers Resolution Res. (December 2002) establishing the European Commission on Efficiency of Justice (CEPEJ), preamble.

The change in the work on procedural reform can also be seen as the emergence of a new approach to the management of the courts, related to new public management (NPM). New public management is the term used in the social sciences for the new culture of leadership, management and organization of public sector services that has emerged during the 1990s and 2000s. [1] New public management can be seen in the context of the reorganization of the public services when the public financing of the European welfare states has become more difficult. In the era of decreasing public funding and pressures to privatization, the possibility for the preservation of public services is seen in the more efficient organization of the services. [2]

New public management is sometimes described as the introduction of the managerial principles of the private sector in public governance. This characterization is an oversimplification, if not directly misleading, in the context of procedural reform. Even if NPM has taken model from management in the private sector, there is no doubt that the court system cannot be compared to private enterprises; the goals are simply too different. [3] However, the emphasis on the functioning of organizational units (in this case courts) and their efficiency as well as a shift from a bureaucratic administration model towards a client/producer model can also be seen in the approaches to court reform. Key characteristics of NPM are economic efficiency, the use of contracts as the principle of organization[4] (instead of administration), the emphasis on the results (instead of input and activity) and the development of leadership and management (instead of expertise and experience).

Already in the resolution establishing the CEPEJ the influence of new public management is apparent. The efficiency of the judicial systems becomes the key concept of the work. Human rights are still a point of reference but the emphasis is

---

[1]   The term new public government probably originates from Osborne & Gaebler 1992. On NPM as an international trend, see Barzelay 2001. New public management has become a slogan for reform of the public sector along the models of the private sector since the 1980s. An enthusiastic introduction can be found in Sanjeev Reddy 2006, pp. ix-xxi.

[2]   Clarke, Gewertz & McLaughlin, 2001.

[3]   The relationship between NPM and the "imperatives of justice" is explored in Fabri & Langbroek 2000. The term imperatives of justice is from Drewry 2000.

[4]   On contractualism as the leading principle of NPM, see Lane 2000.

now clearly on efficiency and the functioning of the judicial systems. An important part of the NPM approach is the measurement of results and the evaluation of performance that, at least in theory, also lead to reallocation of resources. The results of the judicial systems are mentioned in the establishment Resolution of the CEPEJ[1] and the Statute defines the examination of the results of the judicial systems as a task of the CEPEJ. The examination of results, which is typical to the new managerial culture, requires quantifiable measures. [2] The economy and concern for the costs of justice are present in these two documents. Further attention is paid to administration, management and the use of information and communication technologies.

In the work of the CEPEJ this new approach has taken concrete forms. The CEPEJ has carried out a major project collecting data on the functioning of the legal systems in the Member States[3] and it has commissioned several other studies on specific issues. The focus of this work is on the collection of quantifiable data from the justice systems of the Member States and the development of criteria for evaluation. [4]

Obviously, economic factors and measurements on the personnel and other resources are collected and compared. Another important measure for the functioning of the justice system is time, which coincides with one of the important human rights, right to trial within a reasonable time. A number of studies to analyse the practice of ECHR on this issue have been published. [5] A whole program to analyse the processing time and delays in the national courts has

---

[1] Council of Europe Committee of Ministers Resolution Res. (December 2002) establishing the European Commission for the Efficiency of Justice (CEPEJ), preamble.

[2] They are also mentioned in the Statute of the European Commission for the Efficiency of Justice, Art. 2 (1) a.

[3] European Judicial Systems. CEPEJ 2006.

[4] On quality evaluation of court work see Ng 2007. Critically about the measurement criteria for criminal justice systems: Loveday 2000, pp. 167 – 186.

[5] The length of court proceedings in the Member States of the Council of Europe based on the case-law of the European Court of Human Rights. CEPEJ (2006). See also Edel 2007. There are a number of doctoral theses in Member States that approach this issue as well. For a Finnish example, see Spolander 2007.

been set up,[1] measuring
criteria are developed and best practices identified.

Concluding on Reform Policy

Behind the shift in policy from recommendations to monitoring and evaluating the national justice systems seems to be the need for more active facilitation of reform in the member states. The modernization of the procedures in the member states that have joined Council of Europe after 1990 is still underway but also many of the old member states struggle with growing case loads and pressure to cut the costs of the justice system. The benevolent tone of the recommendations and the human right policy, which may at times be insensitive to resource shortages, have not been sufficient to promote needed reforms.

Good policy reasons can be presented for the support of both human rights and cost management approaches. There has obviously been, and still is, a need for more cost and time conscious management of the courts. But there is also need for further discussions and reflection on the relationship between the requirements of fair trial and efficiency. Can we maintain a good quality of procedures in the face of the pressures of a declining funding of the courts?

II. Case Study: Finland

To facilitate such discussions I will present the Finnish court reform as a case study. Finland is a particularly interesting case because its out-dated procedural laws of 1734 were completely reformed in the 1990s according to modern procedural principles. The reforms have covered civil and criminal procedure in first instance courts and in appeal courts. The slogan of these reforms was orality, immediacy and concentration of the main hearing. The reform was quite successful in the first instance courts. After the turn of the century the tide has changed. The principle of an oral main hearing is in decline and several reforms have reduced its application. The present reform proposals are driven by the need to increase

---

[1]   A new objective for judicial systems: the processing of each case within an optimum and foreseeable timeframe. Framework Programme CEPEJ (2004). European Commission for the Efficiency of Justice (CEPEJ). See also Johnsen and Smolej 2006.

efficiency of court proceedings and to press down the costs of justice. ①

The Background of the Reform

The reform of civil procedure in 1993 was an interesting experiment as it brought an antiquated Code of Procedure from 1734 to modernity almost overnight. ②

The Finnish Code of Procedure dates from the Swedish Codex of 1734. The structures of the trial had remained almost intact since then. Some partial reforms had been made during two and a half centuries, most remarkably the reform of the rules of evidence in 1948,③ the introduction of legal aid from the 1950s onwards and the reform of procedures in the Supreme Court in 1978, but they had not touched the main structures of the trial.

A number of earlier reform efforts had laid down the main principles for the reform. The first reform proposal was presented already in 1903 by Professor R. W. Wrede, who was well acquainted with the procedural laws of other countries; Bosnia Herzegovina and Bulgaria in particular were among the examples he referred to. Many of his ideas saw the light of day in the reforms of the 1990s. Before that history took its course and delayed all legal reform in Finland until independence in 1917. Some of the later proposals were delayed because of the World Wars. In the 1970s, the position and recruitment of judges became an object of heated political controversy that effectively delayed the reform plans for more than a decade.

Therefore, the pre-reform procedure (until 1993) was out-dated and did not generally respect the modern principles of fair trial. Trials in the first instance were "semi-oral", that is, they consisted of a sequence of unstructured hearings. The intervals between the hearings were usually one or two months. Many trials, however, needed only one hearing because a number of simple cases were

---

① More on Finnish civil procedure, see Niemi 2010. Generally about the Finnish law of procedure, see Jokela 2002, pp. 357 – 402.

② The reform introduced a new Chapter 2 on Quorum, Chapter 5 on Preparation of the Trial and Chapter 6 on the Main Hearing (Law 1052/1991). Several other amendments were made at the same time. The reform entered into force on 1 December 1993. An English translation of the Code can be found at http: //www. finlex. fi. The translation is not, however, updated.

③ Ervo 1997, p. 295 – 299. Pihlajamäki 1997.

processed in the same way. The hearings of witnesses could be spread out over several hearings. Since the trials could take a long time, it was possible that the same judge did not preside over the whole trial and sometimes the judge who wrote and gave the judgment had not himself heard the witnesses. Therefore, what was said during the hearings was recorded and the transcriptions were often the basis of the judgement and the proceedings on appeal.

The Reform of Civil Procedure

The reform of 1993 was based on modern procedural principles. The aim of the reform was, not surprisingly, to improve legal certainty. [1] More specifically, the aim was to improve the possibilities of courts to handle cases in a thorough manner and to write a well reasoned judgement. [2]

To achieve these aims, the structure of the trial was changed. A clear distinction between the preparatory stage and the main hearing was made. To allocate resources optimally, simple cases need to be decided during the preparatory stage. The main hearing should be organized according to the principles of orality, immediacy and concentration. These three principles-orality, immediacy and concentration-soon became the slogan of the reform.

To achieve these aims and to realize these principles, two structural reforms were made. First, the procedure has to be flexible and be fitted to the demands of the nature of the individual case. Secondly, the process would be the structured into two phases, the preparatory phase and the main hearing. The main hearing is uninterrupted (concentration) and oral and the same judge has to preside over the whole trial (immediacy).

In the preparation of the 1993 Reform, a funnel metaphor was frequently used to illustrate the flow of cases through the civil procedure. All cases would enter the procedure in the same way, simple cases would be decided in a written procedure, a number of cases would be decided after a preparatory hearing and only the most demanding cases would proceed to the main hearing. Thus, the flow of cases

---

[1] Government Proposal for the reform of civil procedure in district courts HE 15/1990 p. 5. On the reform, see Ervo 1995, pp. 56 – 64.

[2] Legal Affairs Committee of the Parliament LaVM 16/1990.

became narrower with each step in the procedure and an illustration of the procedure looked like a funnel.

Several institutions of civil procedure were changed in order to facilitate these aims and principles.

Flexible process forms were developed. A separate process for the collection of undisputed monetary claims (*maksamismääräys*; payment order) was abolished. These kinds of collection claims are now decided in civil procedure on the basis of a summary action. The decisions are usually made without a hearing during the preparatory stage of the trial. [1] The transfer of cases from these summary proceedings to an ordinary civil proceeding, when the claim is disputed, is smooth. A separate procedure for family matters and *jurisdictio voluntaria* remained[2] but the differences between application matters and ordinary proceedings diminished.

The flexibility of proceedings also means that the judge can make a final decision or judgement at different stages of the proceedings, depending on the nature of the claim. The courts were given powers to judge on undisputed claims, for example when the defendant admits the claim, and on manifestly unfounded claims, on the documents during the preparatory stage. A default judgement can be given during the preparation if the defendant declines to respond to the summons or, at a later stage, if a party fails to respond to a request to deliver a statement or to appear in the court.

During and after the reform, most discussions have focused on the introduction of rather inflexible preclusion rules. [3] The object of the trial should be defined clearly already at an early stage of the trial. Both the application for the summons and the defendant's response are regulated in detail by law. The claims, grounds and evidence should be given in detail. In the response, the defendant must make all procedural objections, state whether she contests or admits the claim or part of

---

① Ervo 2001, pp. 121 – 129.

② Application as a form of action was first regulated in 1987 by the Law on application proceedings (306/1986). The regulation of applications was transferred to Chapter 8 (" Procedure in Application Matters") of the Code of Procedure in 2002 (768/2002).

③ A doctoral thesis that had a strong focus on preclusion rules was published a few years after the reform. See Leppänen 1998.

the claim, state the grounds for contesting and identify evidence. The preparatory stage proceedings are also regulated in detail. The parties are only allowed to file one written statement after a defined request and only one preparatory hearing should be held. The amendment of claims or their grounds and the introduction of new evidence is restricted to the preparatory stage and all but denied during the main hearing (preclusion).

If the reception of the preclusion rules has been ambivalent, the tendency to favour mediation has been generally applauded. As a matter of fact, the drafters of the reform could probably not anticipate how popular this part of the reform would become. According to the new paragraph on court mediation,[1] the court shall discuss the possibilities of conciliation between the parties and, if appropriate, promote and propose a settlement. The court can confirm a settlement and such a confirmation has the same legal effect as a judgement. [2] The district court judges took this part of the reform to their hearts and started to encourage settlements.

The heart of the reform was the oral, immediate and concentrated main hearing (the trial). The main hearing was clearly structured around the presentation of the claim and the response, the opening statements, the presentation of evidence and the closing arguments. According to the principle of concentration, the main hearing may not be interrupted and it can be adjourned only under strict conditions. In case of interruptions, a new main hearing has to be held.

According to the principle of immediacy, the material presented at the main hearing is the basis of the judgement. Thus, even though the claims and grounds are clarified and documentary evidence collected during the preparation, they have to be presented at the main hearing. [3] Another aspect of the principle of immediacy is that the same judges hear the case from the beginning to the end. If a judge has an impediment to attend the trial to the end, a new main hearing must be held with a new judge. [4]

The presentation of the case and the closing arguments are not documented, taped or recorded in stenography. The oral evidence is taped and the tape is stored

---

[1]   Code of Procedure OK 5: 26.

[2]   See Ervasti 2007, pp. 185 – 200.

[3]   For exceptions, see Code of Procedure OK 17: 8a-e.

[4]   Code of Procedure OK 6: 1.

until a final judgement in the case is reached and, in any case, for at least a six-month period. The tape is usually not transcribed; this occurs only if the court decides to do so. ①

The rules on compensation of legal costs were changed. The main rule has consistently been that the losing party shall compensate the costs of the winning party. To discourage "unnecessary" law suits, a rule that each party shall bear its own costs if the legal issues at trial are so uncertain and unclear that there is a reasonable ground for the trial, was repealed in the 1993 reform. ②

The overall assessment of the reform has been quite positive. On most criteria, it has been very successful. The flexible structure of the trial has been utilized and simple cases are processed fast. Since 2004, about 96% of civil actions have decided on documents. The majority of those were undisputed money collection claims. Hearings were held in 5,500 cases in district courts in 2008. About 40% of those were decided after a preparatory hearing and less than two-thirds after a main hearing. The number of oral hearings in civil cases declined after the 1993 reform from over 10,000 in 1995 to its present level 5,500 during the latter half of the 1990s. Also, in a long perspective the number of civil cases seems to be low. ③

The hearings have generally been structured as intended. The reform has enhanced good legal culture and the self-respect of the judges has increased.

Shortcomings of the Reform

Even though the overall assessment is positive, not everything turned out as expected. The structural distinction between the preparatory hearing and the main hearing has been adopted in practice. In some ways, however, the boundary between the preparation and the main hearing became blurred. The court could hold a main hearing immediately after the preparatory hearing, in practice on the same day or within 14 days. Such main hearings became very common, almost the rule, and in practice they could be viewed as a continuation of the preparatory

---

① Code of Procedure OK 22：6, 22：9 and 22：10.
② Government Proposal for the reform of compensation for legal costs HE 191/1993, p. 3. As will be explained later, the regulation has already been changed.
③ Ervasti 2005, p. 19 and Ervasti 2004, pp. 57 – 58.

meeting.

The quality of judgements has no doubt improved. But the judgements tend to be long and detailed. This is partly due to the fact that witness and party testimonies are not transcribed and the judges feel obliged to make detailed references to the evidence in the grounds of the judgement.

The preparatory stage has become more extended than anticipated. The law mentions only one session for the preparatory hearing. In practice, however, the preparatory hearing is sometimes adjourned and continued after some other preparatory measures, such as obtaining documentation, settlement negotiations or the exchange of briefs, have been carried out. The preparation of a case can also be differentiated so that separable parts of the case are each prepared separately (OK 5 : 23). These provisions give the court a flexible tool for an appropriate preparation of large lawsuits but they also allow the preparatory stage to linger on. Finland has been very seriously reprehended by the European Court of Human right for not fulfilling the right to a fair trial within reasonable time. The Court has found a delay in the proceedings both in criminal and civil cases. ①

The most critical part of the reform assessment has been the increase in costs. According to the recent statistics the legal costs have doubled since 1995. Costs may have a prohibitive effect on the middle class disputants. Even if legal aid or insurance may cover the costs of the party in some civil cases, the losing party is liable to compensate the costs of the winning party and these costs are not covered by any compensation scheme. The threshold for going to court is deemed too high at the moment. ②

Subsequent Developments

Some of these concerns were addressed by the review of the legislation in 2002. ③ The border line between the preparatory stage and the main hearing was made clearer. The specific provisions for the main hearing immediately after the preparatory meeting were abolished. Thus, the main hearing will be conducted

---

① The trial was exceeded what was acceptable in civil cases in, for example, Raita v. Finland, 16 Feb. 2010; Ragndell v. Finland, 19 Jan. 2010; Horsti v. Finland, 10 Nov. 2009.

② Ervasti 2004, p. 60.

③ Law /68/2002 (entered into force on 1 January 2003).

always according to the same rules. The main hearing should be more efficient and start with a summary by the court of the events in the preparatory stage, instead of the party dispositions. The court should ask whether the summary correctly presents the opinions of the parties.

Before the reform in 2002, a judgement on the merits in a disputed civil case was only given after the main hearing. After the 2002 reform the case can be decided on the documents submitted during the preparatory stage if the facts are not disputed or the only evidence put forward is documentary evidence. [1] Such a decision requires that both parties have consented not to have a hearing. It has to be noted that after a preliminary hearing, a judgement cannot be given according to OK 5: 27a but the case goes to the main hearing. The preparatory hearing became more flexible as it can be hold as a telephone conference or by other communicative link when appropriate (OK 5: 15d).

A new cost rule allows the court to decide that each party is partly or totally liable for its own costs when the losing party had reasonable legal grounds for the litigation or because litigation was otherwise reasonable. [2]

An additional reform that promotes the processing of complex matters is the introduction a class actions in 2007. [3] A class action can be raised in consumer law cases, the consumer ombudsman acting as the plaintiff.

A new Act on Mediation in Civil Procedure[4] came into force in the beginning of 2006. The Act provides a mediation procedure in the district court that can be initiated either before a case has been filed with the court or during civil litigation. In this procedure, the district court judges act as mediators. [5]

The proceedings have become more efficient through successive reforms in which the electronic processing has been taken into use. Summary payment claims are today to a great degree processed electronically. Big institutional claimants, such as banks and credit collection agencies can send their claims in electronic form and the court grants summons in electronic format. The summons are usually

---

[1] Code of Procedure OK 5: 27a, Government Proposal HE 32/2001, 54.

[2] OK 21: 8a (368/1999). In case law KKO 2002: 89, KKO 2005: 15.

[3] Act on Class Actions 444/2007.

[4] Act on Mediation in Civil Procedure 663/2005.

[5] See Laukkanen 2007, p. 72 – 82 and Ervasti 2007, p. 194

served personally by a bailiff. In a summary proceedings, summons can now also be served by phone (OK 11: 3b; 362/2010).

Criminal Procedure

Criminal procedure was reformed in 1997 according to the same principles as civil procedure four years earlier. ① Since criminal procedure starts with the investigation of the crime, there was no need for a reparatory stage of the trial. Most trials go directly to the main hearing. The main hearing in criminal procedure tends to be well structured and conducted in a disciplinary manner. This is partly due to the training programs for prosecutors.

The problem, however, has been the low percentage of accused, and occasionally also of witnesses, that are present at the main hearing. Because the main hearing has to be cancelled when it cannot be held uninterruptedly, cancellations became common. The remedy for this in the 2006 Reform has been somewhat drastic; a criminal judgement can now be given on the basis of documents only. The conditions are: 1) the defendant and the victim must agree to the procedure on the documents, 2) the maximum legal punishment for the crime is at most a two years' prison sentence, 3) the concrete punishment may not exceed a six months' prison sentence and 4) the accused confesses the crime. Interestingly, the law does not require that the accused is informed of the sentence and agrees to it, nor should he or she agree to claims for damages. At the same time, a law on mediation in criminal cases was passed. Mediation is carried out by lay persons and organized by the municipalities. ②

Appeal

The procedure in the appeal courts was reformed in 1998. ③ The essence of the reform was the introduction of oral hearings where the procedure had previously been mostly based on documents. The reform of 1998 was absolutely necessary since the procedure on the basis of documents alone did not fulfil the requirements

---

① Criminal Procedure Act (Laki oikeudenkäynnistä rikosasioissa 689/1997).
② Act on Conciliation in Criminal and Certain Civil Cases (1015/2005).
③ Reform of the Code of Procedure, Chapters 25 and 26, Law 615/1998.

of a fair trial. Therefore Finland had to make a reservation to the ECHR on this point; the reservation was removed after the reform.

The reform has been the object of heated controversy ever since. ① It also turned out to be extremely difficult to enforce and in 2003 the appeal court procedure was changed again, this time to curtail full hearings of cases that were obviously correctly decided by the district courts. In 2009 the government presented again new Bill to the Parliament on the reform of the access to the appeal court and the reform became effective in 2011. Now any appeal on a civil suit that has at appeal a disputed value of less than 10, 000 is subject to leave. The leave is not needed in a suit concerning the alimony of a child or in an application matter. A leave is granted if there is reason to suspect that the judgment of the district court is not correct, or if it cannot be assessed on the documents, the decision would have prejudicial value or there are other weighty reasons. The appeal court grants the leave.

The main hearing in appeal courts for the re-evaluation of oral testimony is experienced as a problem. The appeal court may not change the judgement on the basis of a re-evaluation of the oral testimony if it does not hear the testimony itself. ② This general principle of procedure, which has been confirmed in the practice of the ECHR, has turned out to be extremely problematic because the law does not stipulate what triggers the need to re-evaluate the testimony. The practice of the Supreme Court indicated, before the 2010 amendments, that when a party has challenged the evaluation of testimony by the district court, the appeal court must, as a main rule, hear the testimony again-without prejudice to the outcome of the re-evaluation. The 2010 reform finally gives to the courts of appeal more discretion in the issue when to hold an oral hearing.

Remedies for excessive length of the trial

Several measures have been taken to speed up the trials and while the average length of the trial is quite reasonable, the excessively long trials have brought Finland to the European Court of Human Rights many times. In 2009, a new law

---

① About the concerns and the discussion, see Nylund 2006.

② The same applies to a site visit by the court.

(362/2009) that entered into force 17 May 2011, stipulates on monetary compensation for excessively long trials. The basic principle of the law is that when a trial would be too long according to the case law of the European Court of Human Rights, the party has a right to compensation of 1, 500 per year and at most 10, 000. This compensation does not prejudice the possibility that a delay in the trial can diminish the criminal sanction. The claim for compensation has to be made during the trial that is claimed to be excessively long. It remains to be seen whether this regulation will end the cases from going up to the Court of Human Rights.

Court Structure

Simultaneously with the reform of civil procedure the structure of the district courts was changed. The historical difference between city and rural courts was abolished. Today, there are 27 district courts (*käräjäoikeus*). [1] The chief judge of the district court who has the historical title *laamanni* has a managerial responsibility for the court. The district court judges (*käräjätuomari*) are independent in their judicial discretion. In criminal matters also lay judges participate in the decisions.

In civil cases, the basic quorum according to the law is three judges. The full quorum of three judges is only used in about four per cent of the cases. If the full quorum is not necessary because of the nature of the case and neither party requests it, the main hearing can be held before a court consisting of only one judge. Almost all civil cases are adjudged by a sole judge.

A judge does not necessarily handle default judgements based on a summary investigation of the matter. Young lawyers who take their court training (clerkship) in the district court and other personnel of the court, who obtained the necessary education, can also render default judgements.

A quorum of one judge and three laymen is used in major criminal cases. A sole judge presides over cases in which the scale allows a sentence of two years in prison at most.

---

[1]   According to the reform plans many district court will be merged so the final number of them would be 27. The reform plan presented by the Minister of Justice, Tuija Brax, 13 March 2008.

Conclusion

In the reform processes on procedural law we can distinguish a shift from emphasis on procedural and human rights towards a managerial style of designing reform. This was evident in the way Council of Europe has promoted procedural reform since the 1980s. From the recommendations based on procedural principles in 1980s, the emphasis in the 1990s has been on monitoring reform and measuring costs and case flows.

In the development of Finnish procedural law parallels with the development in the policies of the Council of Europe can be distinguished. The comprehensive reforms of procedural law in the 1990s were based on an ambitious application of principles of fair and good trial. Actually, many recommendations of the Council of Europe on civil procedure were implemented. An overall assessment of the reforms has been quite positive. The unstructured procedures in the first instance were transformed into a modern, professionally led trial with a focus on the main hearing.

The success was probably partly due to certain over-emphasis of some reform principles, such as restrictions on amendments of claims and actions. As an educational matter this was probably necessary and today we can say that the main principles of the reforms have been well adopted into the court practice. The Finnish reform is an example of that a major procedural reform is possible and new principles of due process can be introduced.

A major reform produces often unintended consequences. The main problems have been the accelerating costs, excessively long trials and the difficulties introducing the oral hearings in the appeal courts. Especially the reform of appeal procedures has been difficult to realize, and has led to several amendments later on. It is difficult to say whether the problem with long trials has been a consequence of the reforms. Complex cases used to take a long time in the district courts also before the reform. The new structure and better tools for the judge to conduct the trial should have made it possible to conduct a trial in a reasonable time. There have been several efforts to identify the bottlenecks and as a latest measure, the courts have been given powers to grant compensation for slow proceedings.

Among the measures to facilitate the case flow and to allocate resources to complex cases has been the facilitation of summary and simple cases. These measures have included more efficient use of electronic processing, making processing on documents possible and reducing the quorum to a single judge alone.

Both the developments in the Council of Europe and the case study of Finland raise the question what is the content of the human right to a fair trial. The right to a fair hearing is an important part of the right to a fair trial. There seems to be a risk that when a hearing is made optional, those claimants and defendants who have not strong capabilities to claim their rights are in the danger of losing their right to a hearing. It seems, however, that the tension between efficient administration of justice and a fair trial may be overstated. A hearing may be an efficient way of processing a case, especially when the facts are disputed. Often a hearing with the parties may clarify the facts, notwithstanding any other evidence.

The European Court of Human Rights has taken a broad view of fair trial requirements, evaluating the procedures as a whole and leaving the details of procedural law to the discretion of the member states. It is important the states evaluate their procedural systems continuously, both from the perspective of efficiency and of a fair trial.

Bibliography

Aall 1996

Aall, J. , *Rettergang og menneskerettigheter: den europeiske menneskerettighetskonventions artikkel 6 og norsk straffeprocess* (Bergen: Universitetsforlaget, 1996) .

Andrews 1982

Andrews, J. A. (ed.), *Human Rights in Criminal Procedure: A Comparative Study* (The Hague: Martinus Nijhoff, 1982) .

Barzelay 2001

Barzelay M. , *The New Public Management: Improving Research and Policy Dialogue* (Berkley: University of California Press, 2001) .

Clarke, Gewertz & McLaughlin 2001

Clarke, J. , Gewertz, S. & McLaughlin, E. (eds.), *New Managerialism, New Welfare?* (London: Sage Publications, 2001) .

Drewry 2000

Drewry, G. R. , "Public Management Reform: A Challenge to Judicial Independence?", in Fabri, M. & Langbroek, P. M. , eds. , *The Challenge of Change for Judicial Systems: Developing a Public Administration Perspective*, Amsterdam etc. (IOS Press, 2000), p. 93 −110.

Edel. F. , The length of civil and criminal proceedings in the case-law of the European Court of Human Rights. Council of European Publishing 2nd ed. 2007

Ervasti 2005

Ervasti K. , "Riidat käräjäoikeuksissa. Empiirinen tutkimus riita-asioista ja oikeudenkäyntikuluista" (217 *Oikeuspoliittinen tutkimuslaitos*, 2005).

Ervasti 2007

Ervasti K. , "Conflicts Before the Courts and Court-annexed Mediation in Finland", in Wahlgren. P. , ed. , *Procedural Law-Court Administrations:* Scandinavian Studies in Law, Vol. 51, (Stockholm: Almqvist & Wiksell, 2007), p. 185 −200.

Ervasti Kaijus, Riita-asiat tuomioistuimissa. In Lasola Marjukka, ed. , Oikeusolot 2009. Oikeuspoliittisen tutkimuslaitoksen julkaisuja 244/2009, s. 43 −64.

Ervo 1995

Ervo L. , "The Reform of Civil Procedure in Finland", *Civil Justice Quarterly*, (1995), p. 56 −64.

Ervo 1997

Ervo, L. , "The Principle of the Free Reception of Evidence in Finland", in Nijboer J. F. & Reijntjes J. M. , eds. , *Proceedings of the First World Conference on New Trends in Criminal Investigation and Evidence* (Open University of the Netherlands, 1997), pp. 295 −299.

Ervo 2001

Ervo L. , "Order for Payment in Finland", in Rechenberger, W. H. & Kodek Georg, E. eds. , *Orders for Payment in the European Union* (The Hague: Kluwer, 2001), p. 121 −129.

European Court of Human Rights, Analysis of Statistics 2010, http: //www. echr. coe. int/NR/ rdonlyres/0A35997B-B907 −4A38 −85F4 −A93113A78F10/0/Analysis_ of_ statistics_ 2010. pdf

Fabri & Langbroek 2000

Fabri, M. & Langbroek, P. M. , eds. , *The Challenge of Change for Judicial Systems: Developing a Public Administration Perspective*, Amsterdam etc. (IOS Press, 2000).

Jacob 2006

Jacob, J. , *Civil Justice in the Age of Human Rights* (Ashgate: Darthmouth, 2006).

Johnsen & Smolej 2006

Johnsen, J. & Smolej, M. , "Time management of justice systems: a Northern Europe study". Taskforce of Timeframes for Proceedings, CEPEJ (2006) 14. https: //wcd. coe. int.

Jokela 2002

Jokela, J. , "Legal Procedure", in Pöyhönen, J. , ed. , *An introduction to Finnish Law*

(Helsinki: Finnish Lawyer's Publishing, 2002) , pp. 357 −402.

Laukkanen 2007

Laukkanen, S. , "Last Trends in the Finnish Civil Procedure and Judicial Administration", in Vebraite, V. , ed. , *The Recent Tendencies of Development in Civil Procedure Law: Between East and West. International Conference to Celebrate the* 100th *Anniversary of the Birth of Professor Jonas Žeruolis* (Vilnus: Justitia, 2007) , p. 72 −82.

Lane 2000

Lane, J-E. , *New Public Management* (London: Routledge, 2000) .

Leppänen 1998

Leppänen, T. , *Riita-asian valmistelu todistusaineiston osalta* (Helsinki: Finnish Lawyers' Association, 1998) . (Civil Pre-Trial Procedure concerning evidence, with an English summary).

Loveday 2000

Loveday, B. , "Measuring Performance in Criminal Justice: An Initial Evaluation of the Application of the New Public Management to Criminal Justice Agencies in England and Wales", in Fabri, M. & Langbroek, P. M. , eds. , *The Challenge of Change for Judicial Systems: Developing a Public Administration Perspective*, Amsterdam etc. (IOS Press, 2000) , p. 167 −186.

Ng 2007

Ng, G. Y. , *Quality of Judicial Organisation and Checks and Balances* (Antwerpen: Intersentia, 2007) .

Niemi 2010

Niem, J. , "Finland, Civil Procedure", in Taelman P. , ed. , *International Encyclopaedia of Laws: Civil Procedure* (The Hague: Kluwer Law International, 2010) .

Nylund 2006

Nylund, A. , " *Tillgången till den andra instansen i tvistemål*" . Finnish Lawyers' Association, 2006.

Osborne & Gaebler 1992

Osborne, R. & Gaebler, T. , *Reinventing Government: How Entrepreneurial Spirit is Transforming the Public Sector* (MA: Addison-Welsley, Reading, 1992) .

Pihlajamäki 1997

Pihlajamäki, H. , *Evidence, Crime, and the Legal Profession: the Emergence of Free Evaluation of Evidence in the Finnish Nineteenth Century Criminal Procedure* (Lund: Institutet för rättshistorisk forskning, 1997) .

Sanjeev Reddy 2006

P. L. Sanjeev Reddy, "Foreword", in Bakore, M. & Shah, P. J. , eds. , Handbook on New Public Government (*New Delhi: Center for Civil Society*, 2006) , pp. ix-xxi.

Spolander 2007

Spolander, M. M. , *Menettelyn joutuisuus oikeudenmukaisen oikeudenkäynnin osatekijänä erityisesti Euroopan ihmisoikeustuomioistuimen ratkaisukäytännön valossa* (*Reasonable length of proceedings as part of a fair trial, particularly in the light of the case law of the European Court of Human Rights*), Finnish Lawyers' Association, 2007.

Stavros 1993

Stavros, S. , *The Guarantees for Accused Persons under Article 6 of the European Convention on Human Rights: An Analysis of the Application of the Convention and a Comparison with other Instruments* (Dordrecht: Martinus Nijhoff, 1993) .

Storme 2007

Storme M. , "Tomorrow's Civil Trial", in Verbraite, V. , eds. , *The Recent Tendencies of Development in Civil Procedure Law-Between East and West. International Conference to Celebrate the 100th Anniversary of the Birth of Professor Jonas Žeruolis* (Vilnius: Justitia, 2007) , pp. 14 −25.

Trechsel 2005

Trechsel, S. , *Human Rights in Criminal Proceedings* (Oxford: Oxford University Press, 2005) .

Zuckermann 1999

Zuckermann A. S. , ed. , *Civil Justice in Crisis: Comparative Perspectives of Civil Procedure* (Oxford; New York: Oxford University Press, 1999) .

程序改革中的效率和正义:
口头听证的起伏

约翰娜·涅米

【摘要】这篇文章的目的是检验关于公正审判和司法效率的（潜在的）冲突性主张。当前关于程序法改革和发展的讨论是由两个互相冲突的话语主导的，一方面是追求人权，特别是公正审判的权利，另一个方面是资源不足的制约。冲突的趋势在欧洲理事会的一些活动中已初现端倪，强调成员国司法系统的发展。本文的第二部分将芬兰作为一个案例来研究程序改革。在实施现代程序法基本原则的宏伟目标下，芬兰的程序法于20世纪90年代进行了现代化改革。这些改革把主要听证会中的口头化、迅即性和集中性原则运用到民事和刑事诉讼中。这项改革在初审法院相当成功，但在上诉法院的实施中遇到了困难。世纪之交之后，这种改革浪潮发生了变化。举行一个主要口头听证会的原则在衰落并且多项改革措施也已减少实施。提高法院诉讼程序的效率和降低司法成本的需要驱动着当前的改革建议。本文的目的是激发关于在法庭改革中对公正审判和提高效率的讨论。正当程序和效率的主张可以加以协调吗？

社会管理创新的法治框架与人文环境

王越飞 *

【摘要】 温家宝总理在政府工作报告中强调，推进依法行政和社会管理创新，理顺政府、公民和社会组织的关系，建设服务、责任、法治、廉洁政府。在依法治国的背景下，社会管理创新，本质上是在法律框架内的社会自我完善，妥善处理党委、政府、市场与社会之间的互动关系，充分发挥政府、社会和公民等多元主体的作用，促进秩序优化和社会和谐。同时，和谐社会并不是一个没有矛盾和冲突的社会，而是有一套完善的预防和化解矛盾的机制，在法治框架下建造一种良好的人文环境。现代社会，法律已不再单纯作为一种解决纠纷的手段，而日益成为一种创造新型社会的工具、组织和改革社会的手段。本文中，笔者将主要围绕社会管理的价值定位和模式选择、社会管理过程中的权力配置、社会治理方式的变革以及社会关系均衡等内容进行阐述，并提出个人观点。

【关键词】 社会管理创新　社会治理　法治

社会管理创新，作为 21 世纪的重要课题——不论是东方人还是西方人——都给予超乎寻常的关注和热情期盼，尤其是法治与人文因素。周永康同志强调：要把化解社会矛盾作为加强社会管理的重要基础性工作，建立健全社会稳定风险评估机制……要把以人为本、服务为先贯穿于社会管理工作中，更新管理理念和管理方式，实现由防范、控制型管理向服务型管理的转变。要把社会管理和公共服务延伸到新经济组织和新社会组织，促进健康发展，发挥好积极作用。……要把基层基础建设作为整个社会管理的根基，进一步建好基层组织、壮大基层力量、整合基层资源、夯实基

---

* 河北省廊坊市中级人民法院院长。

础工作。要把继承和创新群众工作作为加强社会管理的重要法宝，紧紧依靠广大人民群众搞好社会管理。……要把依法治国基本方略落实到社会管理的各领域、全过程，更加注重用法律手段管理社会，在全社会形成学法知法守法、依法理性表达诉求和维护权益的良好氛围。① 社会管理或公共治理是一项系统工程，应当发挥国家与民间作用，坚持新旧治理方式相结合，重视与研究人性发展，调动各个组织的积极因素，在法治框架下循序渐进改革与创新。

一 社会管理的基本问题——价值定位与模式选择

社会管理应当与所在历史发展阶段的社会基本情况相匹配，既不能超前，也不能落后，恰当反映社会结构的内在需求，从而有效选择社会管理的模式。

1. 定义。社会管理的定义有广义和狭义之分，广义的社会管理是指管理主体对于政治、经济、文化、社会整个社会系统的管理。而狭义的社会管理则指除政治、经济、文化系统外，仅限于与之相并列的社会系统的管理。关于社会管理的定义，理论界存在不同争议：一种观点认为，社会管理主要是政府和社会组织为促进社会系统协调运转，对社会系统的组成部分、社会生活的不同领域以及社会发展的各个环节进行组织、协调、服务、监督和控制的过程；② 另一种观点认为，社会管理是指在一定共同价值基础上，人们处理社会事务和提供社会公共服务的过程，社会管理的目标是实现社会公平、公正以及社会效率，社会管理的对象是社会事业、社会事务和社会价值，社会管理的主体是社会组织和政府，它们通过综合决策建立社会管理模式。③ 笔者认为，社会管理是指党委、政府和社会组织等管理主体通过计划、组织、服务、领导和控制，合理配置社会资源，协调公共利益与社会发展，有效实现公平与正义目标的社会活动。

2. 主体。社会管理的主体，在传统社会里，政府是主要的主体，在管理的方法上多呈现为人治，它们包揽一切事务，对社会实施组织化管理，从而削弱了其他管理主体的作用，致使管理效能低下，寻租现象严重，出现了畸形社会发展的不良态势。随着社会的发展与进步，出现了许多新型

---

① 摘自 2010 年 6 月 19 日周永康在全国社会治安综合治理工作会议上的讲话。

② 参见郑杭生主编《中国人民大学中国社会发展研究报告 2006——走向更讲治理的社会：社会建设与社会管理》，中国人民大学出版社，2006。

③ 参见丁元竹《中国社会管理的理论建构》，《学术月刊》2008 年 2 月号。

的管理主体，它们与政府协同治理社会，从而不断推动社会进步。正如治理理论创始人罗西瑙所言："与统治不同，治理指的是一种由共同的目标支持的活动，这些管理活动的主体未必是政府，也无须依靠国家的强制力量来实现。"① 笔者认为，社会管理的主体：一是各级党委，作为执政党，党委对社会管理具有领导作用，是社会主义建设事业的坚强核心。二是各级政府，政府作为社会管理的主体发挥了主导作用，它与党委一样，能够有效调动不同社会资源，协调社会利益关系，对社会稳定与发展所起的作用不可代替。三是社会组织，社会组织作为新型社会管理主体，其产生和发展打破了政府治理的唯一模式。一般而言，政府治理具有强制性，而社会组织的治理具有非强制性，因此，面对纷杂的社会状况，社会组织治理较政府治理而言有其优势。但是，我国的社会组织起步时间不长，尚不发达，故其对社会治理的功效有待于进一步发挥。据统计，截至 2010 年底，我国依法登记的社会组织已经超过 43.9 万个。每万人拥有社会组织的数量，法国达到 110 个，日本达到 97 个，美国达到 52 个，阿根廷达到 25 个，新加坡达到 14.5 个，巴西达到 13 个，而我国仅为 3.37 个。② 四是公民，公民既是社会管理的对象，也是社会管理的主体，如果仅仅将其作为被管理者，那就大错特错。社会管理的任务就是要动员和教育公民，将其纳入管理主体的范围，自我服务，自我教育，自我管理，进一步发挥自治功能，才能实现有序社会目标。需要说明的是，当前有一种怪论，即崇拜西方的社会组织治理和公民自治，而忽视与排斥政府治理的作用，这是极其错误的，尤其是在社会主义初级阶段，党委和政府治理社会的责任只能加强，不能削弱。现在有一种观点叫"小政府、大社会"，相对于传统的政府治理模式而言，或许是一种进步，但过分迷信或夸大社会组织的作用——有意或无意的削弱政府职权——很有可能使社会管理误入歧途。意大利学者普特南提出"强社会、强国家"的政府与社会合作的模式，得到北欧很多国家的青睐。③ 普特南的观点具有代表性，笔者认为，应对我国的社会管理理论与实践有所启发，政府、社会组织及公民对社会治理的作用同等重要，不能孰轻孰重。笔者也深深地感受到，研究社会管理如果忽视了党委和政府的推动力量，必然导致类似东欧剧变等乱象，所以，社会管理不单纯是一个

---

① 参见〔美〕詹姆斯 N. 罗西瑙《没有政府的治理》，江西人民出版社，2001。
② 参见中央党校社会学教授向春玲有关社会管理论述。消息来源：http://www.gmw.cn，人民网理论频道 2011 年 3 月 7 日消息。
③ 参见〔意〕普特南《使民主运转起来》，江西人民出版社，2001。

法律和社会问题，而且关乎国家的政治前途。正如陆文荣所言："我们不得不承认一点，那就是作为强有力的中国政府的推动作用，所以我们在研究中国公民社会相关问题的时候，始终不要忘记政府这只重要推手，不管怎么样，现实状况是，政府现在仍然掌握着重要的资源，仍然具有强大的动员能力。"①

3. 价值。社会管理具有自然属性和社会属性。在自然属性上，通过管理活动对社会的人、财、物合理配置资源，有效协调产、供、销等市场要素，实现生产力科学组织与发展；在社会属性上，有效协调不同群体之间的利益分配，促进人与人之间和善的社会关系，使生产关系与社会制度协调发展。社会管理的价值与目标归根结底是为了公众利益，实现社会的公平与正义，使社会发展有序、健康和高效运转。正如张康之在《社会治理中的价值》一文中认为，对于一切社会治理体系而言，秩序、公平与效率、服务等，都是基本的价值。但是，这些基本价值在社会治理体系中的构成方式是不同的。在传统型社会治理模式中，秩序是核心价值；在管理型社会治理模式中，公平与效率是它的核心价值；服务性社会治理模式是指一种新型的社会治理模式，把服务作为自己的核心价值，让其他一些价值都从属于和服务于这种价值。② 社会管理反映了能动与被动、自发与强制，以及服务与管理的有机结合，是秩序、规范与人性的综合反映，其价值的实现需要调动方方面面的积极因素，有效发挥社会庞大系统工程的功能与作用，重要的是，建立健全利益协调和社会平衡的调节机制，遏制、减少与消除反社会的行为，实现人与自然、人与社会的和睦相处与全面发展。

4. 任务。当前既是可以大有作为的战略机遇期，也是矛盾凸显期，社会管理面临许多新情况和新问题。我们要使经济社会发展既充满活力，又和谐稳定，就必须着力加强社会管理。要牢固树立"以人为本、服务为先"的理念，坚持一切从维护人民群众利益出发，在建设好各项民生工程的同时，研究加强社会管理和创新的体制机制，健全和完善各项法规制度，加强城市社区和农村基层的社会管理，做好矛盾纠纷排查调处工作。要坚持树立群众观点，走群众路线，办事情、做决策都要更多地倾听群众意见、尊重群众意愿。当前，社会管理方面存在很多问题：既有宏观上的问题，

---

① 参见陆文荣《社会管理：概念界定和中国经验》，来源：中国社会学网 2011 年 3 月 2 日消息。

② 参见张康之《社会治理中的价值》，《国家行政学院学报》2003 年第 5 期。

也有微观上的问题；既有管理主体与范围上的问题，也有功能与机制上的问题。朱勇同志将其总结为"七重七轻"：重经济建设、轻民生保障；重物质丰富、轻思想道德；重静态管理、轻动态管理；重各自为政、轻通力协作；重普遍管理、轻特殊管理；重管理管控、轻服务尊重；重实体管理、轻虚拟管理。[①] 围绕上述问题与差距，笔者认为，社会管理的任务包括：一是增强管理主体对社会管理重要性、必要性和适时性的认识，有效调动参与社会管理及其创新的主动性、积极性和创造性；二是遵循社会管理及其创新的基本原则，立足中国现实，放眼世界变化，继承和发展传统治理方式，吸收国际文明发展成果，使其符合人类社会发展的普遍规律；三是建立健全社会管理体系，加强社会管理主体工作协同，实现社会管理的制度化、法治化、人性化和科学化。

5. 模式。社会管理，有人称之为社会治理，也有人称之为公共治理，甚至有人认为三者系三种社会治理模式，往往在理论和实践上产生误导和模糊认识。笔者认为，三者虽然表述不同，但在性质上具有同一属性，基本含义也大体一致。首先，目的相同，均是发挥政府、社会和公民等多元治理主体之作用，促进秩序优化和社会和谐；其次，主体相同，即政府、市场主体、社会组织和公民等多元和混合的管理主体；最后，方法相同，即均采用柔性与刚性相结合的手段与方法对社会进行治理。当然，三者的不同表述也表明了治理策略与重点上的不同差异：社会管理侧重于党委和政府在社会治理中的责任，强调其主导性价值；社会治理侧重于多元治理主体的共同责任承担，强调其共同性价值；而公共治理更关注公共政策、公共关系和公共产品，强调其公众性价值。

向春玲教授认为，社会管理的模式主要有政府主导型模式、市场管理型模式和社会自治管理型模式，认为按照"党委领导、政府负责、社会协同、公众参与"的社会管理格局应当归属于政府主导加上社会自治的管理模式。[②] 张康之则认为："现在已经倾向于把公共管理看作为一种新型的社会治理模式，是建立在服务精神和服务原则基础上的服务型社会治理模式，它的治理体系有明显的'德治'特征。就人类的社会治理而言，是一个从'权治'到'法治'再到'德治'的历史演进过程，'权治'是农业社会的

---

① 摘自法制网 2011 年 3 月 4 日消息。

② 参见中央党校社会学教授向春玲有关社会管理论述。消息来源：http：//www.gmw.cn，人民网理论频道 2011 年 3 月 7 日消息。

基本治理模式，用权力去治理社会，从属于统治型的社会治理；'法治'是工业社会的基本治理模式，人用法律治理社会，从属于管理型的社会治理；到了后工业社会，以公共管理为形式的服务型社会治理属于'德治'的社会治理，人们用道德治理。也就是说，权治、法治和德治代表了三种不同的社会治理行为模式，在统治型社会治理模式中，以权治为主，法治和德治只是辅助手段；在管理型社会治理模式中，是以法治为主，在法制的规范下，也有着权治的内容，而德治是受到排斥的；服务型社会治理是德治的治理体系，它把法治与德治统一起来。当然，在公共管理中也会包含权治的内容，但权治是受到严格限制的，仅仅存在于一些特定的领域，是作为一种极其边缘化的治理手段而存在的。"① 不论对治理方式如何表述，但相对于传统模式而言，在主体上范围进一步扩大，在方式方法上内容更加丰富，在治理功效上效果更加明显，正如孙晓莉所言："社会治理模式的变迁是对传统社会管理方式的一次重大变革，即由行政集权式向民主式、参与型转变。"② 不仅如此，在目标追求上，"治理是一种新的政治型模式，实现治理的关键是建立现代宪政制度或实现宪政制度创新"。③

　　6. 路径。社会治理的核心问题是恰当处理政府与非政府组织以及各类社会主体之间的各种利益关系，倡导社会的共同精神，即坚持政治平等，鼓励团结与合作，提倡信任和宽容，强调权利和义务的一致性，建立起政府—社会—市场良性互动的社会管理新格局。关于社会管理的路径，陆文荣认为关键在两个方面：一是引导规范各种社会组织的发展，培育时代新公民；二是重构政府和社会的关系，利用既有组织资源，重点在于刺激集体行动的发生。并且进一步认为，村民自治与居民自治这两种社区治理模式，作为人民群众的伟大实践具有重要意义，应当继续发挥其功能以适应社会管理的实践需求。④ 杨党校认为，社会是一个由低级到高级，由简单到复杂的发展过程，相应的，人类社会治理也应从统治型到管理型，再到服务型治理方式演变，在路径与对策上应从以下四个方面着手：①转变政府职能，确立服务型政府的新定位；②扩大参与型基层民主，提高社会治理的能力；③根据转型时期社会利益结构的变化，在社会治理方式上进行多

---

① 参见张康之《作为新型社会治理模式的公共管理》，《中国政法大学学报》2008 年第 6 期。

② 参见孙晓莉《社会治理模式的变迁》，《学习时报》第 288 页。

③ 参见蒋永甫《治理·宪政·财产》，《湖北行政学院学报》2005 年第 5 期。

④ 参见陆文荣《社会管理：概念界定和中国经验》，来源：中国社会学网 2011 年 3 月 2 日消息。

元治理；④倡导公共精神，加强道德立法，在社会治理中实行德法同构。①

当前，社会管理路径选择上的难题：一是社会组织正在孕育和发展之中，其功效发挥随着社会主义市场经济体制的建立，有一个不断健全与完善的过程；二是村民自治与居民自治，包括商会、行业自治尚不成熟，与传统的文化格格不入，很多地区自治功效徒有虚名，一盘散沙，加重了政府治理的负担与责任；三是政府治理滞后，应当更新观念，创新模式，强化职能，尤其是在当前社会转型、利益格局变动的新形势、新任务下，应当建立应急管理机制和社会风险评估机制，提升管理能力，有效预防和妥善处理群体性事件与突发性事件，打造社会和谐，促进经济繁荣。

二　公权与私权结合——权力配置再审视

公共权力配置至关重要。笔者认为，当前应当重视私权，限制并优化公权，促进二者的有机结合。作为和解与调解的"东方经验"，恰当地融合了公权与私权的形式，在当今世界不失为一剂治理社会问题的良方。范愉教授强调："调解在中国绝不仅是一种纠纷解决的技术或方法，而是社会治理的一种制度性或体制性存在，因此，研究调解决不能仅仅着眼于程序的层面，而必须将其视为社会治理机制中的一环，结合社会转型的背景展开。"② 我国司法调解与行政调解无时无刻不在体现着公权力行使的特征，司法调解的基础是国家的审判权，而行政调解的基础是国家的行政权，两者都是以国家公权力作保障，这既是矛盾纠纷解决所借助的强力资源，又是社会管理的动力之所在。人民调解虽然没有直接以国家公权力作保障，但是来源于当事人私权的法理支撑，同时体现了群众性自治的宪政要求。《人民调解法》的颁布，赋予了人民调解协议寻求国家公权力救济的途径，经过人民法院司法确认后，当事人如果不履行，对方可以申请法院强制执行，实际上，人民调解直接或间接地获得了国家公权力的支持。河北创设并推行的"三位一体"调解体系反映了公权与私权的恰当结合，一方面，使当事人的意思自治原则得到有效落实，当事人可以根据自己的意思表示，自主自愿地享受权利与承担义务，从而缔造出人与人之间的和谐价值，使社会更加公平有序；另一方面，大量矛盾纠纷的妥善化解，减轻了公共治

---

① 参见杨党校《论服务型社会治理模式的构建》，《中共伊犁州委党校学报》2008 年第 1 期。

② 参见范愉《调解的重构——以法院调解的改革为重点》，《法制与社会发展》2004 年第 3期。

理的压力，促进了社会管理水平的提高，毫无疑问对于政府执政方式嬗变具有重要作用。

三　国家责任与社会责任分担——社会治理方式变革

江平教授认为，改革开放以来，我国法治有四条主线：一是人治和法治，二是国家与社会，三是公权和私权，四是从法制到法治。难能可贵的是从法学的视角实事求是分析了中国社会存在的问题，抓住了要害与症结，展望了社会主义国家法治的进步。江平教授在解读国家与社会问题时说道：以前国家干预过多，经济完全由国家计划，甚至老百姓的生活、教育、婚姻、生育等一切都是国家来干预。改革开放一个很大的变化是给予社会更多自治的地位。社会要讲自治，没有国家干预的时候，社会也有自己的职能，比如社会有经济发展的职能、家庭婚姻的职能。所以，我们可以看到，改革开放以来经济方面一个非常重要的做法就是给企业松绑，给企业放权让利，给企业更多的自主权。这个自主权是指不是国家再来干预一切。其他方面也在给社会更大的自主权，包括教育、医疗等。我们可以看到国家和社会是改革开放非常重要的基础，强调国家就是强调专政的力量，国家靠强制力；强调社会就是更多强调社会公平。某种意义上说这也是法律理念的转变：过去法律就是国家强制的工具，现在法律是社会公平的工具。到底是强调国家强制还是强调社会公平，这是一个法律理念上的巨大转变。①

由于东西方在文化背景、社会基础等方面存在差异，所以在社会治理方式上存在明显的不同，正如马小红所言："中国社会的治理以人情为核心，以道德为基础，社会治理以由里及表为主，西方社会则以理性为中心，以制度为基础，社会治理以由表及里为主。"② 长期以来，我国社会治埋的方式建立在党委、政府管理社会"一统天下"的基础之上，半个多世纪以来，特定条件下的这种模式的确发挥了重要作用，然而，随着市场经济体制的建立，社会的治理面临诸多挑战，因此，必须打破传统的管理模式，建立起政府治理为主导，社会各个部门与群体共同参与，民众自我管理与约束的协调联动的多元社会治理结构，即着力打造"党委领导、政府负责、

① 资料来源：《财经》杂志2010年第21期。
② 参见马小红《礼与法》，经济管理出版社，1997，第230页。

社会协同、公众参与"的社会管理新格局，① 正如河北省委常委、政法委书记张越同志所言："同频同步、共振共鸣、应时应变、自省自觉"，② 从而促进社会秩序的根本好转。孙晓莉提出了多元社会治理的观点，认为其基本内涵包括：①社会治理的主体是多元的，既包括在社会管理中一直承担重要甚至主导角色的政府，也包括这些年逐渐凸现出来的作为政府重要补充力量的社会非营利组织、市场化的组织、公民社会，等等。②社会治理的手段是复合的，既有政府通过行政或者市场手段提供公共产品和公共服务，也有市场化组织通过市场化手段提供公共产品和公共服务，还有非营利组织通过市场化手段或者社会动员手段提供公共产品和公共服务。多元社会治理模式的特点包括：多元社会治理模式的运行以法治为基础；多元社会治理是一种互动的过程，以协商、参与机制为基础；多元社会治理主体之间是相互协作的关系，追求公共责任的实现等。③

四　人的相互包容与合作——社会关系均衡

马克思指出："无论在什么情况下，每个人都会从自身出发考虑问题。但是每一个人的欲望、本性以及满足欲望的方式相互之间是连在一起的，因此个人与个人间便不得不结成各种各样的关系。"④ 一切社会关系均都以人作为中心，没有人的存在，社会关系就无从谈起，人常常以自己为原点，不断扩展着社会关系，从而实现自我价值，正如费孝通先生所言："我们的格局不是一捆一捆扎清楚的柴，而好像是把一块石头丢在水面上所发生的一圈圈推出去的波纹。每个人都是他社会影响所推出去的圈子的中心。被圈子的波纹所推及的就发生联系。每个人在某一时间某一地点所动用的圈子是不一定相同的。"⑤ 人作为社会主体有亲有疏，这种亲疏关系不但具有社会学意义，而且反映了法的价值与作用，美国法社会学家唐纳德·布莱克研究发现，如果将社会横向关系和分工、亲密度、团结性等人员分布状况的普遍变量看成关系距离，那么关系距离与法的变化之间存在曲线相关：在关系较亲密的社会群体中，诉诸法律和诉讼会尽量被避免。而随着关系的疏远，法的作用会相应增大，但关系距离增大到人们完全相互隔绝的状

---

① 摘录《人民日报》2011 年 2 月 20 日第 1 版消息。
② 摘录 2010 年 8 月张越同志在河北省公安机关社会管理创新工作座谈会上的讲话。
③ 参见孙晓莉《多元社会治理模式探析》，《理论导刊》2005 年第 5 期。
④ 参见汪培伦编译《马克思箴言》，中国长安出版社，2010，第 27 页。
⑤ 参见费孝通《差序格局》，《乡土中国》，三联书店，1948。

态时，法律又开始减少。社会主体之间的关系距离决定着他们对法律和诉讼的使用频繁度。①

综上所述，我们可以看出，人具有自然属性与社会属性，往往以相互间的联系为纽带，大大丰富了社会关系之内涵。法治社会与和谐社会之理念，建立在人性基础之上，既坚持规则与秩序，又倡导包容与合作，旨在营建人与人之间良好的社会关系，从而极力消除仇恨、凶杀、报复、破坏等恶念，以公平、正义为使命，最大程度地增加和谐因素，最大程度地减少不和谐因素，努力在法治框架下建造一种良好的人文环境和均衡的社会形态。

The Legal Framework and Cultural Environment of Innovation in Social Management

Wang Yuefei

【**Abstract**】 Premier Wen Jiabao stressed in a government work report that China would implement the system of administration by law and innovative social management, rationalize the relationships between the government, citizens and mass organizations, and build a service-oriented, responsible, law-based, clean and honest government. Against the background of administration by law, innovative social management is in essence self-improvement of society within the framework of law, proper handling of the interactive relationships between Party committees, the government, the market and society, giving full play to the roles of the government, society and citizens, and promoting the optimization of social order and realization of social harmony. Meanwhile, a harmonious society means not a society without contradictions and conflicts, but a set of well-functioning mechanisms for preventing and resolving conflicts and a good cultural environment created under the framework of the rule of law. In modern society, law is no

---

① 参见〔美〕唐纳德·布莱克《法律的运作行为》，唐越、苏力译，中国政法大学出版社，1994，第47～56页。

longer mere a means for confliction resolution, but also increasingly becomes a tool for creating new types of society and for organizing and reforming society. In this article, the author puts forward opinions and suggestions on such issues as the value orientation and choice of mode of social management, allocation of power in the process of social management, the reform of the method of social management, and balancing of social relationships in social management.

【**Key words**】Innovative Social Management, Social Management, Rule of Law

The Finnish Limited Liability Companies Act from the Perspective of Small and Medium-Sized Enterprises

Ville Pönkä *

【Abstract】 The limited liability company is by far the most commonly used form of company in Finland. At the moment there are over 270000 companies in total and over 220000 of them are registered as limited liability companies. This is an enormous number considering the size of the population of Finland. In Finland, however, the legislation recognizes only one limited liability company form. These companies can be either private or public, but there are no separate laws for them. In other words the Finnish Limited Liability Companies Act ("Companies Act") governs all limited liability company forms, and there is no hybrid company structure that combines some attributes of partnerships and corporations.

In this article I will raise some questions concerning the current status of Finnish company legislation from the perspective of small and medium-sized enterprises ("SMEs"). This is a very important topic, because it seems that the special legislative needs of these kinds of companies have not been adequately taken into account by Finnish legislators. The main research questions of this study are: is one limited liability company form enough and how could the Companies Act be developed to suit the needs of SMEs? Before going into these questions, the other company forms recognized by Finnish legislation will be briefly introduced. As for

* Post-doctoral Researcher, Faculty of Law, University of Helsinki.

the first research question the answer is yes, there is definitely a need to expand the menu of company forms especially on behalf of SMEs. The best option for Finland would be to provide a company structure combining some attributes of limited liability companies and partnerships. As for the second research question, I will point out that the Companies Act has, in fact, improved in many ways even from the perspective of SMEs. In spite of these improvements, there are still many ways in which it could be made more suitable for SMEs.

I. Introduction

The limited liability company (or the company limited by shares) is by far the most commonly used form of company in Finland. At the moment there are over 270000 companies in total and over 220000 of them are registered as limited liability companies. This is an enormous number considering the size of the population of Finland. Of course many of these companies are not in actual use, but still there are tens of thousands of active companies making profits, paying taxes and securing employment in different branches of business. This is why it is justified to say that when considering the national economy of Finland, the significance of the limited liability company cannot be exaggerated.

The limited liability company is governed by the Limited Liability Companies Act (624/2006, later referred to as the "Companies Act"), which came into effect in 2006. [1] By global comparison the law is very modern and compared to its predecessor it has adopted a new ideological approach. While the former Companies Act (734/1978, later referred to as the "1978 Companies Act") was, ideologically, based strictly on Swedish-German doctrine, the current law is founded on the Anglo-American *law and economics* perspective of the company. [2] According to this perspective, the purpose of the company is to provide an economically efficient vehicle for business operations. The function of the Companies Act is to support this purpose and this always has to be kept in mind

---

① The Ministry of Justice provided an unofficial English translation of the Act on 1 Jan. 2010 and it is available at http://www.finlex.fi/fi/laki/kaannokset/2006/en20060624.

② See, for example, Governmental Bill 109/2005 pp. 17 – 19 and Jukka Mähönen-Seppo Villa, *Osakeyhtiö I-Yleiset opit* (WSOYpro, Helsinki, 2006), pp. 44 – 49.

when applying the law in practice. In addition it has also been said that the liberal-"corporate friendly" -legislation of the State of Delaware (U. S.) has had a great impact on the Finnish Companies Act. [1] This is actually quite easy to believe. If one looks at the general principles set out in the first chapter of the Companies Act one can see much resemblance between the Finnish Companies Act and the Delaware General Corporation Law. [2]

On a global level the limited liability company is an unclear concept. In many countries it is considered an enterprise that combines attributes of partnerships and corporations. It is often-but of course not always-considered suitable mainly for small and medium-sized enterprises (later referred to as " SMEs ") while the *corporation* is the company form meant for large public and listed companies. Although this is a very rough simplification it constitutes the general conception of the limited liability company.

In Finland, however, the legislation recognizes only one limited liability company form. These companies can be either *private* ("closed") or *public*, but there are no separate laws for them. In other words, Companies Act governs all limited liability company forms, and there is no hybrid company structure that combines some attributes of partnerships and corporations. This is a common feature in Scandinavia, excluding Norway, which has separate laws for private and public limited liability companies. It is also worth mentioning that from the legal point of view the differences between private and public companies are very small. [3] In practice, however, a small private company and a large public company are very different in nature.

Besides private and public limited liability companies there are also listed companies. This means that a public company is not automatically a listed company and in order to be listed a public company has to fulfil the qualifications and abide by the procedural requirements stated in the Companies Act, the Securities Market

---

[1] See, for example, *Osakeyhtiölain uudistaminen-Tavoitteena kilpailukykyisempi yhtiöoikeus* (Official memorandum concerning the need for a new limited liability companies act presented by Manne Airaksinen and Jyrki Jauhiainen 7 July. 2000), p. 7.

[2] For example, the Finnish business judgement rule has been adopted with only minor variations from the United States.

[3] The most important difference between the company forms is that the shares of a private company cannot be listed.

Act (495/1989) and the Rules of the Stock Exchange. ① At the moment only 205 Finnish limited liability companies are registered as public companies and just over half of them have securities listed on the NASDAQ OMX Helsinki stock exchange. Even though the number of limited liability companies has been increasing rapidly, the number of public and listed companies has been decreasing for many years.

In this article I will raise some questions concerning the current status of Finnish company legislation from the perspective of SMEs. ② This is a very important topic, because it seems that the special legislative needs of these kinds of companies have not been adequately taken into account by Finnish legislators. ③ The main research questions of this study are: is one limited liability company form enough? (*chapter* 3) *and* how could the Companies Act be developed to suit the needs of SMEs? (chapter 4). Before going into these questions, the other company forms recognized by Finnish legislation will be briefly introduced (chapter 2).

II. Other Finnish Company Forms in General

Finnish legislation recognizes altogether four different company forms: the limited liability company, the partnership, the co-operative company and the European Company. Each company form is governed by a separate law. ④

---

① http://nasdaqomx. com/listingcenter/nordicmarket/rulesandregulations/.

② There is no universally accepted definition for SMEs although within the European Union the European Commission's definition for micro, small and medium-sized enterprises is generally accepted. See Commission staff working document on the implementation of the Commission's Recommendation of 6 May 2003 concerning the definition of a micro, small and medium-sized enterprise. In this article SMEs refer to small and medium-sized limited liability companies.

③ The Swedish Companies Act (2005: 551), passed in 2005, has also been criticised for not focusing on the special needs of SMEs. See, for example, Daniel Stattin, *Company Law Reform och Aktiebolagskommitén-Bolagsrättsliga reformer i Storbritannien och Sverige* (Svensk Juristtidning, 2002), pp. 123 – 128. In Scandinavian academic discussion, SMEs have, however, recently received quite a lot of attention. See in particular Mette Neville-Karsten Engsig Sørensen, eds., *Company Law and SMEs* (Thompson Reuters, Copenhagen, 2010).

④ In some jurisdictions only the limited liability company is considered a *company* (*or a business company*). See, for example, Paul L. Davies, *Principles of Modern Company Law* (Sweet & Maxwell, London, 2008), p. 4. In Finland the term company is, however, used as a general concept that also includes partnerships and co-operative companies. See, for example, Heikki Toiviainen, *Introduction to Finnish Business Law* (Edita, Helsinki, 2008), pp. 244 – 245.

The Finnish Partnership Act (389/1988) was passed in 1988 and it is based firmly on the freedom of contract. In a partnership, co-operation is based on a *partnership agreement*, which can be designed very freely by the business partners. ①
This means that the Partnership Act consist mainly of non-mandatory provisions that are applied only if not stated otherwise in the partnership agreement.

The main principles of the Partnership Act differ essentially from the principles governing the limited liability company form. In fact, on a general level, these company forms share only two similarities: they both possess a legal personality and they both aim to create profits for the business partners / shareholders. Otherwise their differences are substantial. Unlike the shareholders of a limited liability company, the business partners are jointly responsible for the undertakings of the company and they can distribute the assets of the firm whenever they want. A partnership also has no separate administrative organs and its proportions ("shares") cannot be freely transferred. There are also many other differences between the two company forms, but they are somewhat trivial and thus not discussed here.

The co-operative company is governed by the Finnish Co-operative Companies Act (1488/2001), which came into effect in 2001. Unlike the partnership, the co-operative company and the limited liability company share many attributes. ②
Actually the Co-operative Companies Act is in several ways very similar to the Companies Act. For example, the rules governing the administrative organs and changes in company structure are practically identical for both company forms. On a general level the major difference between the limited liability company and the co-operative company is, however, very fundamental. While the purpose of the former is to create profits (that are usually distributed as dividends) for the

---

① The minimum contents of a partnership agreement is not defined in the Partnership Act, but according to the practice of the National Board of Patents and Registration of Finland at least the name, the location and the branch of business of the company have to be mentioned. Naturally, the names and signatures of the business partners also have to be included in the agreement.

② For example, professor Henry Hansmann in his famous book *The Ownership of Enterprise* (Harvard University Press, Cambridge, Massachusetts-London, England, 1996, pp. 12 – 16) considered the "business corporation" as a special form of "cooperative". Even though this view has not been widely adopted in academic discussion, it illustrates incisively the similarities between the two company forms.

shareholders, the co-operative company is a community that provides goods and/or services for its members as cheaply as possible. Unlike the limited liability company, the co-operative company may not distribute its profits to its members for example in the form of dividends. ① This is the main reason why the limited liability company and the co-operative company are not usually considered as alternatives when deciding which company form to choose.

The European Company (or the "Societas Europaea", "SE") is based on a regulation (The Council Regulation on the Statute for a European Company 2157/2001) adopted by the European Council in 2001. The regulation was implemented in Finland three years later by the European Companies Act (742/2004).

The European Companies Act provides a company structure for multinational business groups. Its main function is to allow companies incorporated in different European Union countries to merge or form holding companies or joint subsidiaries, while avoiding the legal and practical constraints that arise from the existence of different legal systems. ② Finnish entrepreneurs have not yet taken advantage of the European Company form, ③ but in several other European Union countries (especially in the Czech Republic) it has had more significance. At the moment there are altogether a little over 700 registered European Companies. ④

III. Is One Limited Liability Company Form Enough?

Before the 2006 Companies Act, Finland had only two laws governing the limited liability company form. The first law (22/1895) was enacted in 1895 and, excluding provisions concerning incorporation and asset distribution, it was based

---

① In the articles of association, it is possible to amend the purpose of a limited liability company so that it is able to provide goods or services for its shareholders on a cost basis instead of giving out dividends. In other words the limited liability company can be used in practice as a co-operative company.

② http://europa. eu/legislation_ summaries/employment_ and_ social_ policy/social_ dialogue/l26016_ en. htm.

③ Actually, at least at the moment no European Company headquarters are situated in Finland.

④ http://ecdb. worker-participation. eu/.

firmly on the principal of contractual freedom. For example, the internal affairs of the company were left almost completely unregulated. [1] The 1978 Companies Act (the predecessor of the 2006 Companies Act) had a more interventionist approach on company matters. Compared to the first law, it had for example very specific provisions concerning the protection of minority shareholders and creditors. [2] In this sense, the 1978 Companies Act was obviously a product of its era-an era during which contractual freedom was rather explicitly limited by legislation. For example, the first and only Finnish Consumer Protection Act (38/1978) was enacted in the same year as the 1978 Companies Act.

When looking at the legislative drafts of the above-mentioned laws, one can notice that the question as to whether one limited liability company form is enough has never been considered thoroughly. Actually the topic has been discussed officially only once in a committee report "Small enterprises and company legislation" drawn up by the Ministry of Justice in 1998. In this report the need for a separate law for SMEs (i. e. the need for another limited liability company form) was rejected for several reasons. First, it was thought that the preparation of a totally new law would be a tremendously difficult task and would not provide real benefits for SMEs. Second, the committee thought that having separate laws for SMEs and larger companies would increase the amount of regulation and thus make company legislation more challenging for legal practitioners to handle. Third, it was pointed out that a new law would be internally incoherent, because it would include many references to the "primary" law (i. e. to the Companies Act). Also the fact that the use of an SME company form could make it harder for shareholders to expand their business operations in the future was mentioned. [3]

These arguments, however, overlook the fact that the legislative needs of SMEs and large private, public and listed companies are in practice very different. Small-scale business operations in particular demand a very formidable legal framework. The law governing this framework should be as non-mandatory as possible so that entrepreneurs

---

[1]   Jukka Mähönen, "Tulo ja pääoma-Kirjanpidon merkitys osakeyhtiön sääntelyssä" (Edita, Helsinki 2001), p. 349.

[2]   See Governmental Bill 27/1978, p. 9.

[3]   See Pienyhtiöt ja yhtiölainsäädäntö. Committee report 1/1998 drawn up by the Ministry of Justice, p. 20.

have the opportunity to modify it to suit their personal needs. Denying this freedom would only lead to a loss of efficiency because legislators cannot provide a law (or "standard contract") that would be perfect for all firms. This so-called "standard contract theory" has been widely accepted in law and economics,[1] and has exceptional significance when considering the legislative needs of SMEs.

Stating this fact does not, however, explain why SMEs require different rules to those governing large private, public and listed companies. On a general level, this question can be briefly answered by examining the fundamental legal characteristics of a business company, because the Companies Act is designed to support these attributes.[2] According to the famous analysis by professors *John Armour*, *Henry Hansmann* and *Reiner Kraakman*, all modern market economies recognise at least one company form that possesses the following characteristics: 1. a legal personality, 2. limited liability, 3. transferable shares, 4. delegated management under a board structure and 5. investor ownership (i. e. the right to control the firm, and the right to receive the firm's net earnings).[3]

Especially when compared to public and listed companies, it is evident that (excluding legal personality and investor ownership[4]) SMEs work on totally different principles. For example, limited liability does not provide substantial protection for shareholders of SMEs, because these companies are usually unable to acquire external financing without shareholders giving personal debt securities. Furthermore the shares of SMEs are typically *de facto* non-transferable due to the lack of potential buyers (i. e. there are no markets for shares of SMEs). Also the transferability of the shares is nearly always, in one way or another, restricted in the articles of association and/or in a shareholders' agreement. Finally, because the shareholders of SMEs are normally also the directors of the company, there is no

---

① See, for example, Timo Kaisanlahti, *Sidosryhmät ja riski pörssiyhtiössä* (Edita, Helsinki 1999), p. 64.

② These legal characteristics are stated in the first chapter of the Companies Act.

③ John Armour-Henry Hansmann-Reiner Kraakman, "What is Corporate Law?" in Reiner Kraakman et. al. , eds. , *The Anatomy of Corporate Law-A Comparative and Functional Approach* (Oxford University Press, New York, 2009): pp. 1 – 16.

④ Actually legal personality is not a distinctive characteristic for the limited liability company form, because also all other Finnish company forms (see Chapter 2) are legal persons. It can be said that they are actually the other attributes (such as limited liability and investor ownership) that give legal personality its distinctive substance.

real delegation of management in the same sense as in larger business companies.

There is also one more important aspect that separates SMEs from large private, public and listed companies. It is the fact that all the shareholders of SMEs are usually also employees of the company,[1] whilst the shareholders of public and listed companies in particular are considered for the most part only as investors. In other words a shareholder of an SME is not actually an investor, but rather an entrepreneur whose financial wellbeing depends on the success of the company. In this sense the economic bond between the shareholders and the company is usually much stronger in SMEs than it is in larger companies.

When considering the above-mentioned characteristics of SMEs it is obvious that they have a lot in common with partnerships. Owing to this fact one should ask why entrepreneurs still choose the limited liability company form instead of the partnership? At least for small-scale business operations, wouldn't it be more adequate to choose the simpler company structure? The answer to these questions is usually *no*, for two important reasons. First, even though limited liability does not typically protect shareholders of SMEs from *known creditors* (such as banks, employees and suppliers of goods), it does still provide them with protection against *extra-contractual liabilities*.[2] This protection is often considered very important and especially when operating in branches of business where the risk of these kinds of liabilities is high. The second and perhaps even more important reason is taxation. The taxation of limited liability companies (and its shareholders) is often considered more favourable than the taxation of partnerships and this, of course, makes the first mentioned company form more attractive for entrepreneurs aiming to maximize their personal gain.

As mentioned in the first chapter, Finnish legislators have chosen the "one set of rules fits all limited liability companies" strategy. However, as also mentioned earlier, from the transaction cost point of view this strategy is not very efficient. Because shareholders of SMEs often consider provisions of the Companies Act unsuitable for their personal needs, many important company matters have to be

---

[1]   In fact in Finnish legal literature shareholders of SMEs are often called "employee shareholders". See e. g. Ville Pönkä, *Osakassopimuksen suhde työlainsäädäntöön ja erityisesti työsopimuslaissa tarkoitettuun kilpailukieltosopimukseen* (Lakimies 1/2011), pp. 65 – 66.

[2]   Seppo Villa, *Velkojan asema osakeyhtiössä* (Talentum, Helsinki 2003), p. 14.

agreed upon in shareholders' agreements. This causes *ex ante* contracting costs, which could be minimized with more adequate legislation. Shareholders' agreements also frequently promote *ex post* transaction costs in the form of shareholder disputes. The major reason for these disputes is that shareholders' agreements are not always drafted as carefully as they should be. It is also an unfortunate fact that many lawyers dealing with these agreements are not fully aware of their complex legal effects.

The "one set of rules fits all limited liability companies" strategy should also be rejected as numerous European Union company law directives regulate public and/ or listed companies. If the rules for both private and public companies are kept as similar as possible, the directives would also have a *de facto* effect on private company legislation. This is naturally a major drawback considering the development possibilities of SME legislation.

In sum, the answer to the question "is one limited liability company form enough" is clearly no. On a general level, there are at least three ways in which the present legislative situation could be improved. The first option would be to abandon the present legislative strategy and instead lay down in the same act different provisions-or even different chapters-for different types of companies. Most rules would naturally be identical for all company types, but the provisions governing shareholder relations for example could be designed so that they would more adequately take into account the special needs of SMEs.

This "same act-different rules" strategy is to a certain degree already in use in Finland. For example, with regard to companies' general meetings the fifth chapter of the Companies Act has many separate procedural rules for private and public/ listed or private/public and listed companies. [①] The Swedish Companies Act can also be mentioned as a good example of such a legislative strategy. Because the act has many separate provisions for different types of limited liability companies, it now consists of over 800 sections, being almost three times as long as its Finnish counterpart. This emphasises incisively why providing different rules for different limited liability company types in the same law is-at least when used on a larger

---

① This was caused by the implementation of the European Union directive on the exercise of certain rights of shareholders in listed companies (2007/36/EC).

scale-not a good option: it makes the law confusing and hard to manage even for legal professionals.

The second option would be to choose the "Norway model" and provide separate laws for both private and public companies. This strategy would have several benefits, but also at least two notable weaknesses. First, separate acts for private and public companies might mean in practice that some large private companies would be left without suitable legislation especially if the private companies act was designed particularly to please the needs of SMEs. The second reason for rejecting the separation of private and public company legislation is that this might be problematic from the perspective of already existing private companies. If the new private companies act was to differ essentially from the present Companies Act, it would naturally mean that the rules of existing companies would also have to be changed.

The third and best option would be to introduce a totally new law that would combine certain attributes of limited liability companies and partnerships. In other words, the best option for Finland would be to expand the menu of limited liability company forms and in this manner please the legislative needs of SMEs. Excluding the Scandinavian countries, this has actually been a modern trend in several European and Anglo-American jurisdictions. For example, the universally well-known company legislation of the State of Delaware (U. S.) has during the past 25 years introduced altogether four new limited liability forms: the limited liability company, the limited liability partnership, the limited liability limited partnership and the statutory business trust. [1]

IV. How could the Companies Act be Developed to Suit the Needs of SMEs?

When considering the legislative needs of SMEs it should be noted that legislators have not totally ignored this issue when drafting the present Companies Act. [2] In fact on a general level Finnish company legislation has in many ways been improved

---

[1] See, for example, Henry Hansmann, *Corporation and Contract* (ECGI Law Working Paper No. 66/ 2006), p. 3.

[2] See, for example, Governmental Bill 109/2005, p. 1, and Sakari Helminen, *Osakeyhtiölaki pienyhtiön näkökulmasta* (Defensor Legis No. 4/2007), p. 503.

even from the SME perspective: The Companies Act is based on the idea of contractual freedom, it is relatively compact and clear and many mandatory formalities of the 1978 Companies Act have been either removed or eased. [1] For example, the process of incorporation has been made simpler and the rules governing interest group relations (i. e. the relations between shareholders, directors and creditors) have been rationalised especially in terms of protecting creditors. Despite these improvements, there are still many ways in which the Companies Act could be made more suitable for SMEs.

On a general level, the most important question concerns the binding force of company legislation. As mentioned in the previous section, SMEs require legal provisions that are as non-mandatory as possible. If the law imposes unreasonable mandatory obligations or restrictions, entrepreneurs will draft shareholders' agreements and agree upon company matters and upon their mutual relations in a different manner. Even though a shareholders' agreement has no direct legal effect on the company level (e. g. a shareholder may not object to a decision by the company's general meeting simply by claiming that the decision is not in accordance with the provisions of the shareholders' agreement), it binds the contracting parties on a contractual level. [2] Especially when enhancing the binding force of the shareholders' agreement with special contractual sanctions, it is possible, in practice, to evade at least such mandatory provisions that concern shareholder relations. Of course this is not a desirable phenomenon and that is an important reason why rules governing SMEs should be at least initially non-mandatory. [3]

When it comes to SMEs, company legislation should provide a wide menu of non-mandatory provisions, which would make it possible for the shareholders to use the articles of association as the primary contracting platform. When drafting these menu provisions, one should of course see what other countries have done and learn from their mistakes. It would also be helpful to see what kinds of

---

①　See Governmental Bill 109/2005, pp. 16 – 33.

②　Ville Pönkä, *Osakassopimuksen tavoitteet ja voimassaolon hallinta* (Edita, Helsinki 2008), pp. 270 – 340 (see summary in English, pp. 485 – 495).

③　Of course there are always legal provisions that cannot be non-mandatory. Such provisions concern, for example, the legal structure of the company.

provisions shareholders' agreements typically consist of. Actually, when examining these agreements on a general level it is easy to notice that they are often very much alike regardless of the branch of business in which the company is operating. For example, a shareholders' agreement nearly always includes a pre-emption clause that establishes that a contracting party has an obligation to offer his/her shares to other contracting parties when he/she is about to leave the company. Shareholders' agreements also quite often have special exit-rules that on the one hand give the shareholding majority the right to get rid of a contracting party that is making co-operation impossible and give an individual shareholder the possibility of exiting the company on fair conditions, on the other hand.

In this article it is not possible, or appropriate, to discuss in more detail the specific measures that should be taken to improve legislation on behalf of SMEs. As a final thought it should be mentioned that there are also several ways in which the Companies Act could be made better for *all types* of limited liability companies. First, there is still some friction between the Companies Act and other acts concerning company matters. In other words the Companies Act is not fully compatible for example with tax laws[1] or with the Finnish Bookkeeping Act (1336/1997). [2] Second, the Companies Act still has some "traces" of the 1978 Companies Act that are no longer necessary. For example, the share capital requirements of both private and public companies are irrelevant as is the division between un-distributable and distributable equity because the so-called solvency test stated in § 13. 2 of the Companies Act[3] nowadays applies to all kinds of asset distribution and thus provides sufficient protection for creditors on its own. [4]

---

[1] For example, the Companies Act allows some changes in company structure (such as the so-called triangular merger) that are not recognized by tax laws.

[2] For example, the Companies Act and the Bookkeeping Act have conflicting norms concerning the distribution of interval dividends. See in particular Manne Airaksinen-Pekka Pulkkinen-Vesa Rasinaho, *Osakeyhtiölaki II* (Talentum, Helsinki, 2010), pp. 50 – 52 and Jukka Mähönen-Seppo Villa, *Osakeyhtiö II-Pääomarakenne ja rahoitus* (WSOYpro, Helsinki, 2006), pp. 303 – 306.

[3] "Assets shall not be distributed, if it is known or should be known at the time of the distribution decision that the company is insolvent or that the distribution will cause the insolvency of the company. "

[4] In Finland this issue has been widely discussed by professor Seppo Villa. See in particular Seppo Villa "Mihin sidottua omaa pääomaa enää tarvitaan?" in Ilari Kallio-Taina Pihlajarinne, eds. , *Business Law Forum* 2010 (Lakimiesliiton kustannus, Helsinki, 2010).

V. Conclusions

Finland-like the other Scandinavian countries-has very few company forms. In fact, Finnish legislation recognises only four different company forms, of which three are in actual use. The main company forms for normal profit aiming business activities are partnerships and (private and public) limited liability companies. Because the law governing the latter has been designed mainly to please the legislative needs of large private, public and listed companies, there is no limited liability company form that is specially designed or intended for SMEs.

In this article I have assessed the need for new company forms (Chapter 3) and also the question of how the existing Companies Act could be developed to suit the needs of SMEs (Chapter 4). As for the first research question the answer is *yes*, there is definitely a need to expand the menu of company forms especially on behalf of SMEs. The best option for Finland would be to provide a company structure combining some attributes of limited liability companies and partnerships.

As for the second research question, I have pointed out that the Companies Act has, in fact, improved in many ways even from the perspective of SMEs. In spite of these improvements, there are still many ways in which it could be made more suitable for SMEs.

On a general level, the most important aspect is that the law should be as non-mandatory as possible. It should also include a wide menu of non-mandatory provisions to reduce the contracting costs of SMEs (i. e. the need to use shareholders' agreements). When drafting these provisions, one important option would be to examine which kinds of clauses are typically used in shareholders' agreements. For example, the scale of different kinds of exit-rights could be expanded.

中小型企业视角下的芬兰有限责任公司法

威乐·蓬卡

【摘要】 在芬兰，有限责任公司是目前为止最为普遍的公司形式。目前，芬兰有超过 270000 家公司，其中超过 220000 家注册为有限责任公司。

考虑到芬兰的人口规模，这是一个巨大的数量。然而，芬兰立法只承认一种有限责任公司形式。这些公司可以是私营的，也可以是国有的，在法律适用上并无差别。换句话说，芬兰的有限责任公司法适用于所有的有限责任公司形式。结合了合伙和企业的某些属性的混合公司结构是不存在的。

本文将从中小型企业的视角，对芬兰公司立法的现状问题提出几个问题。这是一个十分重要的问题，因为芬兰的立法者似乎还没有充分地考虑到此类公司的特殊立法需求。主要研究问题包括：有限责任公司的单一形式是否充分？怎样发展公司法以便适应中小型企业的需求？在探究这些问题之前，本文还将简单介绍一下芬兰立法所承认的其他公司形式。对第一个问题的回答是肯定的，从中小型企业的角度出发，确有必要扩大公司形式的选择范围。对于芬兰来说，最佳的选择是提供一个结合了有限责任和伙伴关系属性的公司结构。对于第二个问题，笔者将指出，即便从中小企业的角度来看，芬兰的有限责任公司法在事实上已经在很多方面做了改进。虽然如此，仍然还有可以改进的方面，以便使它更适用于中小型企业。

Consumer Law: A Short Introduction to the Development and Main Principles of Finnish Consumer Law

Klaus Viitanen [*]

【Abstract】 The purpose of this article is to give a short overview of the main structure of Finnish consumer law, and at the same time also provide a picture of the Nordic model of consumer protection. The article covers the questions concerning regulation of marketing, consumer contract law and the settlement of consumer disputes.

The development of Finnish consumer law may be divided into two different periods. The first period covers the years 1978 − 1994 when Finland had not yet joined to the European Union (EU). The second period covers years after Finland's accession to the EU at the beginning of 1995.

The most typical feature for the Nordic model of consumer protection in the area of substantive law is the regulation of marketing and unfair contract terms by general clauses. These clauses have a very wide scope of application, and can also be used to adjust unfair contract terms-including the core terms such as the price of the good or service-in already concluded contracts. That is why case law forms one central part of the Nordic consumer law.

In the area of enforcement perhaps the most typical and best known feature of the Nordic consumer protection system is the establishment of special state

---

* LL. D., Docent in Commercial Law, University of Helsinki.

authorities, Consumer Ombudsmen, who supervise marketing and unfair contract terms. They strongly stress preventive actions in their supervisory work: they provide guidelines for different branches of business and negotiate with the business organisations in order to agree standard contract terms which are used in consumer contracts.

The Nordic countries were the first countries in Europe where group action for compensation was adopted. However, so far this legal instrument, which has its origin in common law countries, has been used rather seldom. The main reason has probably been the fear of high legal costs.

I. Introduction

1. The Nordic model of consumer protection

The weak position of consumers in the market started to create attention in many Western countries in the beginning of the 1960s. This led to the drafting of laws also in the Nordic countries, namely in Denmark, Finland, Iceland, Norway and Sweden. In Finland this drafting led to the adoption of the Consumer Protection Act in 1978. The original act regulated marketing (Ch. 2), unfair contract terms (Ch. 3 -4), sale of consumer goods (Ch. 5) and doorstep and distance selling (Ch. 6). In the other Nordic countries consumer protection issues were regulated by several distinct acts. There are, for example, separate acts for the regulation of marketing and for consumer contracts. However, there are a many similarities between the Nordic countries in the ways in which legislative consumer protection systems have been built. These common features justify one in speaking of the Nordic model of consumer protection. The most typical features for the Nordic model of consumer protection in the area of substantive law are the regulation of marketing and unfair contract terms by general clauses. These general clauses have a very wide application, and can be used to adjust unfair contract terms-including core terms such as the price of goods or services-in already concluded contracts.

In the area of enforcement perhaps the most typical and best-known feature of the Nordic consumer protection system is the establishment of special state authorities, Consumer Ombudsmen, who supervise marketing and unfair contract terms. Such ombudsmen strongly stress preventive actions in their supervisory work: they provide guidelines for different branches of business and negotiate with business organisations in order to agree on standard contract terms which are used in consumer contracts. Special courts-often called the Market Court or Council-are used in cases where preventive actions have proved to be ineffective. Consumer organisations have always had a rather limited role in practice, especially in enforcement. The obvious reason is the establishment and functioning of state authorities, especially Consumer Ombudsmen, who have made consumer organisations in this field unnecessary.

Public out-of-court bodies are widely used instead of private bodies in the settlement of individual consumer disputes. The out-of-court system for the settlement of individual consumer disputes in most Nordic countries is based on a two-stage model. In Finland, Norway and Sweden consumer advisers or centres exist at the district level. Their competence is limited to advice and mediation. Besides that, the Nordic countries have a special centralised body-often called the Consumer Complaint or Dispute Board-with a general jurisdiction to settle all kinds of individual consumer disputes. Their decisions are, however, at this moment only recommendations, except in Norway.

Small claims procedures in ordinary courts are typical in common law countries. However, the new Norwegian Act on Civil Procedure, which came into force in 2007, established a special small claims procedure for disputes where the monetary interest does not exceed a certain sum of money. In Denmark, where a major reform of the Danish court system and procedural rules was adopted in the summer of 2006, a small claims procedure in minor disputes has been available from the beginning of 2008. Also in Sweden a separate small claims procedure was available between 1973 and 1987.

The Nordic countries were the first countries in Europe where group action for compensation was adopted. The Swedish Group Action Act came into force in 2003. In Norway, group action for compensation has been possible from the beginning of 2007. The Finnish Group Action Act was adopted in 2007 and in Denmark the act entered into force in 2008. One typical feature for the Nordic model is also the minimal role of criminal law in enforcement. In spite of the fact that it is possible to impose criminal sanctions on those persons who have intentionally or by negligence infringed the rules concerning marketing, these sanctions are in practice very seldom used in most Nordic countries.

The purpose of this chapter is to briefly describe the development, main structure and main principles of the Finnish consumer protection system. Due to the similarities between the Nordic countries, it will at the same time also provide an overview of the Nordic model of consumer protection.

2. The influence of European Union consumer law

The development of Finnish consumer law may be divided into two periods. The first period covers the years 1978-1994 when Finland had not yet joined the European Union (EU). During those years Finland could decide independently how to legislate consumer issues. The second and still ongoing period covers the years after Finland's accession to the EU in the beginning of 1995. The EU already had its own consumer legislation-mainly in the form of directives-which set frames for the national consumer policy of the member states. However, the first directives were mainly minimum directives which obliged the member states to ensure only a certain minimum level of protection, but did not prevent them from providing a better level of protection where they wished to do so. For this reason, the effect of EU consumer directives on Finnish consumer legislation was rather small during the first years after accession.

However, EU consumer policy took a totally new direction at the beginning of this millennium when the EU started to adopt maximum directives, which also set the upper level of protection. The initial second-generation EU consumer law directive was the Unfair Commercial Practices Directive (2005/29/EC) in 2005. The second effort was the proposal of the Consumer Rights Directive in 2008. However, this proposal met with widespread and not altogether unjustified criticism, especially from the Nordic countries, who clearly saw the dangers which this directive might well have caused to their existing consumer contract law. This heavy resistance led finally to a new, firmly stripped-down directive (2011/83/EU) in 2011. It covers mainly only doorstep and distance selling.

II. Regulation of Marketing

1. The general structure

The regulation of marketing in Finland and in the other Nordic countries has two main aims. Firstly, to prohibit unfair marketing practices, including false or misleading advertising and, secondly, to ensure that traders provide consumers with certain basic information during the marketing. Different legal methods are stressed here depending on the main aim of regulation.

In the prohibition of unfair marketing practices all Nordic countries rely on general clauses. The general clause prohibits the use of all kinds of unfair marketing practices without giving any further information what kinds of marketing practices may be regarded as unfair. Some information may be found in the preliminary works, which are quite important legal sources in these countries. However, the main decision-making power whether a marketing practice is infringing the law or not, has been left to special courts, which are often called Market Courts. Over the years these special courts have created quite a comprehensive case law in the field of marketing practices. In fact, this case law forms a central part of Nordic consumer law, and consists of several leading principles which should be taken into account when assessing whether a marketing practice is infringing the law or not.

A general clause is a flexible way of regulating unfair new marketing practices, which are developing all the time. That is why there is a clear difference between legal systems which are based on general clauses, and between systems which are based only on detailed, exhaustive rules. In the latter alternative, all marketing practices which should be prohibited must be defined by specific legislative rules. Detailed rules make it much easier for advertisers to predict what kinds of marketing practices may be regarded as illegal. On the other hand, where new marketing practices are regarded as unfair, legislative changes have to be made. In the Nordic countries the combination of general clauses and more detailed rules have been used in prohibiting unfair marketing practices.

On the contrary, when the aim of regulation is to provide basic information to consumers, very detailed rules which clearly define the mandatory information have been shown to be much more effective than general clauses. General clauses which only set an obligation to provide consumers with "all necessary information", simply do not work in practice.

2. The supervision of marketing

The supervision of marketing is taken care of in Finland, as in the other Nordic countries, by a special state authority called the Consumer Ombudsman. The Ombudsman's task is not only to supervise marketing practices and the use of standard contract terms, but also to promote consumer interests in general. Where infringements of law are observed, the Consumer Ombudsman has an obligation to persuade the trader in question to abandon unfair marketing practices voluntarily. The trader is asked to sign a written engagement in which he promises not to continue illegal marketing practice.

The use of soft law methods have been shown to be rather effective over the years. The great majority of clear infringements of law are solved in this way without the need to use any sanctions. Even in more serious cases traders often prefer to change their marketing practices instead of letting the Consumer Ombudsman take the case to court. Should persuasion fail, the Consumer Ombudsman is entitled to impose an injunction order together with conditional fines in cases of minor importance. However, if the trader resists, the injunction becomes void. The Ombudsman may also impose a temporary injunction order in urgent cases, which is valid until the court begins to try the case.

A very typical feature of the Finnish system is the use of preventive action in the supervision of marketing. The same phenomenon is also found in the other Nordic countries. These preventive actions are not based on law, but have been created in practice over the years. The Finnish Consumer Ombudsman has issued marketing guidelines in different sectors of business. These guidelines are based on existing case law and their purpose is to inform traders what kinds of marketing practices infringe the law. In 2004, for example, the Consumer Ombudsman issued three new guidelines: Marketing error situations; Minors, marketing and purchases and Changes in contract terms. In addition, the Consumer Agency and the National Board of Education prepared principles concerning marketing and sponsorship in schools.

The Finnish Market Court is a special court whose jurisdiction is limited to the following areas of law: consumer law, unfair competition and competition law. In the main hearing the Court normally consists of three professional judges and from one to three expert members, with everybody having an individual right to vote. In consumer matters a court procedure in the Market Court is initiated by a petition of the Consumer Ombudsman. In cases where the Market Court regards a marketing practice to be unfair, it will impose an injunction order together with conditional fines. It may also order the trader to carry out corrective advertising. It is important to note that market disruption fees, which are imposed by the Market Court, are not found in Finland as they are in Sweden. Criminal sanctions are in principle possible in Finland, but they may only be imposed by general courts, and are in practice very seldom used. Neither does the Market Court have jurisdiction to order compensation for damages. In consumer law cases the no-cost rule is applied in the Market Court. This means that both parties have to bear their own legal expenses irrespective of the outcome of the case. Since 2002 parties have had the right to appeal to the Supreme Court provided that the Supreme Courts grants them leave to appeal.

3. Case law

Over the years the Finnish Market Court has created quite a comprehensive case law in the field of marketing practices. In fact this case law forms a central part of Finnish consumer law. Several leading marketing law principles may be drawn on the basis of case law, and they should be taken into account when assessing whether a marketing practice infringes the law or not. These principles are virtually identical in the other Nordic countries.

The first leading principle is the principle of identification of marketing. According to this principle, consumers should always be able to make a difference between commercial and non-commercial material. Since 2002 this principle has also been based on a special article in the Consumer Protection Act. The principle of general impression is an important one whereby the lawfulness of marketing is evaluated on the basis of what kind of general impression consumers get after a reasonably short acquaintance with an advertisement. This means, for instance, that relevant information may not be hidden in small print at the end of an advertisement.

The claims presented in the marketing may not be false or misleading. In addition, the principle of the burden of proof means that a trader must always be able to prove that the facts he presents in his marketing are true. Relevant in this context is the difference between facts and matters of taste. "The cheapest in town" is a fact which must be proven, but "the best service in town" is a matter of taste which cannot be proven. As consumers have started to pay increasing attention to the environmental friendliness of the products they buy, claims concerning the environmental friendliness of the marketed product have become more usual. The principles of true information and the burden of proof also concern these claims. Test results are often used in comparative advertising, where their presentation plays a central role. The use of test results in marketing is accepted in cases where certain conditions are fulfilled, e. g. , the test itself has been made by an objective third party and only relevant features have been tested and compared.

Many cases are concerned with the principle of sufficient and exact price information. This means that the price should always be mentioned in an advertisement where a certain product or service is identified. The price mentioned should always be the total price, including all taxes and service charges. The promised discount should always be real, which means that the price should not be announced as being reduced more than it actually has been.

The use of the word guarantee in marketing has often caused confusion. According to case law, a guarantee should always mean that a consumer receives a certain benefit compared to his legal rights. The use of benefits based on chance (e. g. lotteries) and additional benefits (e. g. regular customer cards) are accepted, but they should not play a dominant role in the marketing. The focus in marketing should always be on the product or service itself. In many cases the Market Court has dealt with marketing targeted at minors. Marketing to them is in principle allowed, but it must comply with much stricter rules than marketing to adults.

Case law in Finland and in other Nordic countries has also given protection to so-called social values in marketing. In several cases the Market Court has stopped marketing for reasons which are not connected with the truthfulness of marketing, but with the protection of different social values. In these cases it has often been question of using unnecessary violence in marketing or discrimination based on sex.

4. The new full harmonisation directive

The Unfair Commercial Practices Directive (2005/29/EC) was adopted in May 2005. Unlike most former directives in the field of consumer protection, the new directive aims at maximum harmonisation. This means that the member states are no longer entitled to give better protection to their citizens through national legislation than is provided by the directive. It is interesting to note, however, that the new directive is heavily based on general clause, which is a familiar legal instrument in Nordic consumer law.

According to the new general clause, commercial practice is regarded as unfair if it is contrary to the requirements of professional diligence, e. g. , by being false or misleading, and it at the same time materially distorts or is likely to distort the economic behaviour of the average consumer. It will be interesting to see what effect this new general clause will have on the previously mentioned leading principles which have been created by case law in the Nordic countries.

The main questions will be the interpretation of the concept of the average consumer and the requirement of material distortion to consumers' economic behaviour. Does the average consumer mean a normal consumer or are the requirements higher as the former case law of the European Court of Justice seems to suggest, i. e. , the average consumer should be reasonably well informed and reasonably observant and circumspect. Should a single false marketing practice distort the average consumer's economic behaviour in a way which causes him to take a transactional decision that he would not have taken otherwise or should we also take into account other factors which usually have significance in a consumer's decision-making procedure? The answers to these fundamental questions will decide in which direction the supervision of marketing rules will go in the future, not only in the Nordic countries but also in other European countries.

A positive element in the new directive is, however, that it clearly gives protection to so-called vulnerable consumers, including minors. Commercial practices which are likely to materially distort the economic behaviour of a group of vulnerable consumers, e. g. , minors, shall be assessed from the perspective of the average member of that group. It is thus obvious that the new directive recognises the special needs of minors in the regulation of marketing practices. From the Nordic viewpoint, it will, however, be interesting to see whether the protection given by the new directive differs from the earlier protection provided by case law.

III. Consumer Contract Law

1. General

The traditional view of how contracts are concluded is based on a presumption that the contracting parties are in an equal position. The leading principle of general contract law, pacta sund servanda (a contract binds both parties according to its terms) is based on this presumption. However, the reality at least in consumer contracts is totally different. The contracting parties, consumers and traders, are in most cases unequal. Firstly, the problem is the lack of information. Consumers do not in most cases have enough comparative information concerning quality, prices, and other central questions which are essential in order to conclude a good contract. The second problem is an imbalance in negotiation power: even if they are well informed, consumers do not have as much influence on the content of contract terms as their counterpart. The wide use of standard contract terms-written by the trader party only-offers a good example here and shows clearly that the presumption of equal parties does not correspond with reality. Thus, in practice consumers need protection in their contractual relations with traders.

There are several contract law methods available to provide protection to consumers when they conclude contracts with traders: (1) cooling-off periods, (2) mandatory contract law provisions, (3) prohibition of using unfair contract terms, (4) the possibility of adjusting unfair contracts terms and (5) the transparency requirement and interpretation rules.

2. Cooling-off periods

What is meant by a cooling-off period is the consumer's right to withdraw from a contract within a certain time, normally from 7 to 14 days, without penalty and without having to give a reason. Cooling-off periods based on law are normally provided in those types of contracts where it is typical that consumers do not have an opportunity to compare the price and quality of the marketed product with other similar products before making their decision (doorstep selling), or consumers do not have an opportunity to check the product before the contract is made (distance selling), or aggressive methods of marketing are often used (timeshare contracts) or there is a risk of consumer's excessive indebtedness (consumer credits).

The cooling-off periods are based on EU directives and the length of the cooling-off period depends on whether or not the trader has fulfilled his obligation to provide a consumer with certain information referred to in the directives. Cooling-off periods based on law should not be confused with cooling-off periods based on an individual contract. In Finland, cooling-off periods based on a contract are usual in, for example, big department stores.

3. Mandatory provisions of consumer contract law

General contract law provisions, e. g. , concerning the sale of goods, are typically non-mandatory, which means that the contracting parties are free to agree otherwise. However, in consumer contracts there is a serious threat that a trader may use his stronger negotiation power. That is why contract law provisions which are applicable in consumer contracts are mandatory. This means that parties are not entitled to conclude individual contracts imposing worse terms regarding the weaker party than the terms provided by the mandatory provisions of consumer contract law.

Especially in the sale of goods essential questions on consumer contracts have been regulated by mandatory provisions of law. These questions are, e. g. , the goods' conformity with the contract and the burden of proof in cases where a lack of conformity is said to exist. On the basis of the Sale of Consumer Goods Directive (1999/44/EC) the Finnish law also provides a legal guarantee in consumer contracts. This means that any lack of conformity which becomes apparent within six months of delivery is presumed to have existed at the time of delivery, unless proved otherwise.

Mandatory provisions also exist concerning the consumer's right to remedy in cases where there is a lack of conformity. In the first place, repair free of charge or replacement of the product should take place. If that is not possible or if it is not carried out, the consumer has a right to a reduction in price or the right to have the contract rescinded. The latter remedy is available only when the lack of conformity is not minor. The consumer must inform the seller within a reasonable time, which is always at least two months from the date when he detected the lack of conformity. The minimum time limit for liability is at least two years from the delivery of the goods. In Finland there is no maximum time for the seller's liability. However, the consumer has the burden of proof whether, e. g. , the product that was bought three years ago was already defective at the time of delivery. In practice, it may be extremely difficult to prove the existence of a hidden defect.

4. Prohibition to use unfair contract terms in consumer contracts

It is not possible or even sensible to regulate all potential contract terms by mandatory provisions. A wide range of different kinds of questions have always be left to the parties to agree. That is why there is also a need for different ways of balancing the contractual relationship between parties. One method is to prevent the use of unfair terms in consumer contracts. At the EU level these questions have been regulated by the Unfair Contract Terms Directive (93/13/EEC). It is, however, a minimum directive, and does not prevent the member states from providing better protection to their citizens. An unfair contract term is a contractual term which causes a significant imbalance in the parties' contractual rights and obligations. Finnish legislation on unfair contracts terms also covers individually negotiated contract terms, and not only standard contract terms. In addition, it covers the so-called core terms, e. g. , price terms.

In the Nordic countries the system of preventing the use of unfair contract terms is rather similar than in marketing. The fairness of contract terms is regulated by general clauses, which means that case law is in practice the most important legal source. The Consumer Ombudsman tries to prevent the use of unfair contract terms mainly by using persuasion. Where persuasion fails, he may issue a permanent (in cases where the trader does not resist) or a temporary (in urgent cases) injunction order. If necessary, the Ombudsman is entitled to take legal action against the trader in the Market Court.

Typically unfair contract terms have often been connected to the following items: (1) the trader has had the right to make changes to the contract terms including the price without the consumer's approval, (2) the trader has excluded or limited his legal liability in cases where he has breached the contract, (3) sanctions which are available concerning the consumer's breach of contract have been very hard and (4) the contract has contained an arbitration clause which excludes the consumer's access to a court.

There is an interesting preventive method used by the Nordic Consumer Ombudsmen. It is not based on law, but has been created in practice over the years. Standard contract terms have been negotiated between the Ombudsman and trade organisations in several branches of business. A good example of these negotiated standard contract terms in Finland are the Package Travel Contract Terms, which are used by almost all Finnish Travel Agencies. Negotiations do not mean that the Ombudsman approves all the contract terms used in the negotiated standard contract terms, but he approves most of them. There are many benefits connected to these negotiations. From the trader's point of view the probability that the Ombudsman would take actions against negotiated contract terms is in practice quite minimal. From the consumer's point of view consumer law only prohibits the use of unfair contract terms. By these negotiations it is possible to add new terms to the standard contracts which improve the consumer's contractual position compared to the standard contract terms used earlier. In Finland the consumer's right to withdraw from a package travel contract with small expenses provides a good example here.

5. Voidness and adjustment of unfair contract terms

The possibility of declaring unfair contract terms void or of adjusting them supplements the system which aims to protect consumers against unfair contracts terms. It is a repressive control method, and is available when a consumer has already concluded a contract which contains unfair contract terms. The weakness of this method is that in disputed cases the consumer has to take the case to court or another dispute settlement body, which will then consider the unfairness of a contract term. The consumer has to be active and sometimes wealthy enough to take the case to a dispute settlement body. Secondly, the action or complaint has legal effect in the disputed case alone. Other similar unfair terms in contracts made by other consumers, who remain passive, still remain valid.

A typical feature in Nordic contract law is the possibility of adjusting unfair contract terms instead of declaring them void. Adjustment of a contract term means that a court or an alternative dispute resolution body changes the content of an individual contract term. Even individually negotiated contract terms and the so-called core terms, e. g. , the price of the product or service, may be adjusted in the Nordic countries.

6. Transparency and interpretation of contract terms

The protection given to consumers by contract law also contains a regulation concerning transparency and the interpretation of unfair contract terms. Contract terms must always be drafted in plain and intelligible language. In cases where there is any doubt about the meaning of a standard contract term, the interpretation which is most favourable to the consumer prevails. The latter is simply the ancient in dubio contra stipulatorem rule, which is based on Roman civil law.

7. The future of consumer contract law

The review of consumer protection rules, the so-called consumer acquis, is a topical issue in the EU at this moment. Most of the existing contract law directives are based on minimum clauses. However, the review of the consumer acquis is based on the idea of full harmonisation. This means that minimum clauses will no longer be used, and those member states who have used their rights to provide better protection to their citizens-especially the Nordic countries-are afraid that new directives will mean weaker consumer protection in the future.

These fears proved to be real when the proposal for the directive of consumers' rights was published in October 2008 (COM (2008) 614 final). Its aim was to replace four former minimum directives which had been adopted between 1985 and 1999. The main problem in the proposal from the viewpoint of consumer protection was the fact that the proposal was heavily based on the former minimum directives with no larger changes suggested. The minimum level of protection had suddenly become the maximum level of protection. Those countries which had used the earlier opportunity to provide better protection to their citizens would have been forced to essentially lower their former level of protection. Not surprisingly, the proposal met with a great deal of resistance among those member states which were expected to lower their level of protection. When the consumers' rights directive was finally adopted in October 2011, its scope of application was only limited to doorstep and distance selling.

There are many problems in fully harmonising EU consumer law. Firstly, so far the quality of law drafting has been very poor. Proposals and even finally adopted directives have contained many unclear and even conflicting definitions, which are interpreted differently in the member states. Secondly, the new full harmonisation directives often leave many important questions totally unregulated. Thirdly, there are numerous differences between the member states in their legal traditions, social values, etc. These differences mean that even full harmonisation directives are implemented and interpreted in a way which fits best to individual legal systems, corresponding to their social values, and enforced in a way that suits their legal traditions. The result will not be a uniform legal system.

IV. The Settlement of Consumer Disputes

1. The out-of-court settlement

One typical feature in the Nordic countries is the possibility of receiving consumer advice and sometimes even mediation help at the local level. In Finland there are 30 regional offices where consumer advisers can provide legal advice, and in some cases they can also mediate between quarrelling parties. A successful mediation from the consumer's point of view has been the outcome in approximately 65 per cent of the cases. This may be considered quite a good result, especially when taking into account the fact that the outcome is generally based on only a few telephone calls between the adviser and the trader.

The basic idea is that consumer advisers would first deal with disputes and only those in which advice or mediation proves to be unsuccessful would be sent to the Consumer Dispute Board. The board is a centralised, state body and situated in Helsinki and was established in 1978. The board has a general jurisdiction to settle all kinds of individual consumer disputes concerning either the quality of consumer goods or services, or a trader's performance in other respects. The main purpose of the board is to give recommendations how these individual disputes between a consumer and a trader should be solved. The board receives more than 4000 written complaints every year. In practice traders comply with on average 70 per cent of the recommendations which are in favour of the consumers. There are considerable differences between the branches of business how well the recommendations are complied with. In some branches the compliance rate is clearly under 50 per cent. This problem could be easily solved by changing the legal nature of the board's decision from a recommendation to a legally binding and enforceable decree.

2. The court procedure

In Finland there are no small claims procedures in the courts or other kinds of alternative judicial procedures for the settlement of individual consumer disputes. Earlier there was a special, simplified procedure in the ten largest cities for the settlement of landlord-tenant disputes, but this procedure was abolished in 2003. Only the no-cost rule remained, which is still applied when landlord-tenant disputes are dealt with in a normal civil procedure. In other cases, including consumer disputes, the loser pays all expenses rule is applied. The main problem here is that there is no ceiling limit on the liability to pay the expenses of the other party. That is why the party who has lost his case, has to pay, e. g. , all the attorney fees of the winner in cases this is considered necessary. The expenses in consumer disputes may easily exceed 20000 Euros. This means that the normal procedure in Finland is at present largely inapplicable for the settlement of individual consumer disputes, where the monetary interest is in the majority of cases less than 1000 Euros. Here it might be advisable to follow the examples of Denmark and Norway. These two countries adopted small claims procedures during 2007 − 2008. In small claims procedures, which are available for most disputes where the monetary interest does not exceed a certain limit, the no-cost rule is applied. The use of attorneys is also discouraged by making the role of the judge more active than it is in a normal civil procedure.

3. Group action for compensation

In the Nordic countries there has been an attempt to improve the applicability of ordinary civil procedures for the settlement of mass consumer disputes by introducing a new type of action: group action for compensation. By using this action it is possible to claim monetary compensation for damages which a certain group of person has suffered due to the infringement of their individual rights. Group action for compensation may be non-representative or representative. In a non-representative group action for compensation all persons who have suffered damage have to be parties in the trial in order to receive compensation. These kinds of non-representative actions have traditionally been possible in Finnish courts on the basis of joint actions and consolidation of actions. In addition, test and pilot cases are also possible in the Finnish courts, although they are not given any kind of special treatment in Finnish procedural legislation.

After fifteen years of discussions and hard debate the Finnish Group Action Act (444/2007) was finally adopted in February 2007 and it came into force in October 2007. This act, which is only applicable in mass consumer disputes, provided for the first time a possibility for a representative group action for compensation. According to this act, the Finnish Consumer Ombudsman may in a mass consumer dispute take a legal action in a general court and represent a specified group of consumers without an express permission of group members, and this result in a judgment that is binding both for and against all the members of the group.

This act has, however, not been used once during the first four and a half year of its existence. The main reason is probably the fear of high legal costs. The loser pays all rule is also applied in group actions of compensation. Should the case be lost the members of the group will not be liable and the costs will be covered by the Consumer Ombudsman. The risk of hundreds of thousands of Euros in legal expenses makes the Ombudsman extremely careful and selective when choosing whether to take a mass consumer dispute to court or not.

Since 1978 the Finnish Consumer Ombudsman has also had a right to assist individual consumers in ordinary courts. Assistance is given in two to six cases every year. However, these are not mass consumer disputes, but disputes which have a principal significance, e. g. , when it is question of the interpretation of consumer contract law. In a recent case, where the Ombudsman assisted a consumer in court, the Finnish Supreme court decided that the VISA credit card company was liable, on the grounds of connected lender liability for the non-delivery of goods which a consumer had bought from the USA by using his credit card via the internet. So, it is not question of a collective redress scheme, but of assisting individual consumers in principally interesting cases in order to create case law which could help to apply consumer law in the future.

V. Conclusions

The Finnish Consumer Protection Act is now under revision. There are several questions where one might carefully consider the need to update the present regulation. The first question concerns the scope of application. Should the scope of application in the future be limited only to consumer protection, or should it be enlarged towards a wider concept of customer protection? This latter alternative has already been adopted in transport issues, where protection is given to all customers irrespective of whether they have bought the trip for private use or for business purposes.

The second question is related to enforcement and sanctions when the regulation of marketing has been infringed. The present system, where the prohibition on continuing illegal activities is the strongest sanction, is rather toothless. Most traders are willing to make changes to their marketing practices in a voluntarily way, but there is an urgent need for stricter sanctions to deal with unscrupulous traders. The market disruption fee, which is already available in Sweden, could provide a useful weapon here. There is also a clear need to improve the legal status of the decisions made by the Consumer Dispute Board. One could simply make these decisions enforceable as court judgments. This solution was adopted in Norway several decades ago, and it works well.

New digital products provide challenges for existing consumer sales laws. Many digital products may be not regarded as goods so that consumer sales provisions at this moment are not applicable. In many cases it is not even a question of the sale of movable property, but a rental agreement. That is why it is necessary to update consumer contract law to cover different kinds of digital products. Otherwise only general contract law principles would be available in the settlement of these modern disputes.

Literature

Alessi, Dario, "Unfair Contractual Advantage in Finnish and Italian Law: A Comparative Analysis", *Turku Law Journal* (2003): pp. 3 −33.

Bärlund, Johan, "The Concept of Business Undertaking in Finnish and European Consumer Law: A Critical Review of a Finnish Supreme Court Case", *Scandinavian Studies in Law* 57 (not yet published).

Viitanen, Klaus, "Implementation of the EC Directive on Product Liability in Finland". In The Implementation Process of EU-directives on Product Safety, Product Liability and Unfair Contract Terms, edited by Francoise Maniet and Beata Dunaj. Proceedings of a conference held in Riga on 13 −14 October 1994, European Union, EFTA, pp. 165 −177.

Viitanen, Klaus, "The Scandinavian Public Complaint Boards: the Aims, Present Situation and the Future" *Consumer Law Journal* 4, (1996) pp. 118 −126.

Viitanen, Klaus, "The Unfair Commercial Practices Directive and Marketing Targeted at Minors". in Private Law and the Many Cultures of Europe, edited by Thomas Wilhelmsson, Elina Paunio and Annika Pohjolainen, Alphen aan den Rijn 2007, pp. 283 −303.

Viitanen, Klaus, "Enforcement of Consumers' Collective Interests by Regulatory Agencies in the Nordic Countries", in Collective Enforcement of Consumer Law. Securing Compliance in Europe through Private Group Action and Public Authority Intervention, edited by Willem van Boom and Marco Loos, Groningen 2007, pp. 81 −103.

Viitanen, Klaus, "Nordic Experiences on Group Action for Compensation", in Auf dem Weg zu einer europäichen Sammelklage? edited by Mathias Casper, Andre Janssen, Petra Pohlmann ja Reiner Schulze, Munich 2009, pp. 219 −241.

Wilhemsson, Thomas, Twelwe Essays on Consumer Law and Policy. Publications of the Department of Private Law No. 51. University of Helsinki. Edited by Tuuli Junkkari. Helsinki, 1996.

Wilhemsson, Thomas, "The Implementation of the EC directive on Unfair Contract Terms in Finland", *European Review of Private Law* (1997), pp. 151 −156.

消费者法：　芬兰消费者法的发展及主要原则概述

克劳斯·维塔宁

【摘要】本文旨在给芬兰消费者法的主体结构做一个简要的概述，同时，为消费者保护的北欧模式构建一个蓝图。文章介绍了有关市场调节、消费者合同法，以及解决消费纠纷的问题。

芬兰消费者法的发展可以分为两个不同的阶段。第一阶段是 1978 年到 1994 年间，此时，芬兰还没有加入欧洲联盟。第二阶段则是 1995 年芬兰加入欧洲联盟之后。

实体法中，北欧消费者保护模式的最典型特征是通过一般规则来监管市场行为和不公平合同条款。这些规则的应用十分宽泛，它们可以用于变更已订立合同之不公平合同条款，包括一些核心条款，例如合同中的商品或服务的价格。这就是为什么判例法构成北欧消费者法的核心部分。

在执法领域，北欧消费者保护系统最典型、最广为人知的特征就是建立专门国家机关——消费者监察专员（Consumer Ombudsmen）——来监管市场行为和不公平合同条款。在监督工作中，专员们特别强调预防行为，他们向不同的商业部门提供行为指南，就消费者合同中的标准合同条款与商业组织进行谈判。

北欧国家是欧洲率先采用集团诉讼求偿机制的国家。然而，迄今为止，这一源于普通法国家的法律工具极少被应用，其主要原因可能是出于对高昂法律成本的畏惧。

社会管理创新的法制化路径

刘洪岩[*]

【摘要】 中国步入社会转型期以来，社会问题日趋复杂，社会诉求不断增多。现实中，传统文化缺失和社会失范则更是引发了诸多的社会风险。社会问题的日趋复杂昭示着必须改变传统的以管控为主的社会管理模式，探索一条结合中国社会实际，以服务社会和民众、维护公平正义为价值取向，同时应遵循公开化和法治化的社会管理实践路径。在社会管理创新的整个制度设计中，政府职能的转变、市民社会的培养、合理公正的法治化环境和诚信社会的构建是社会管理创新的基本前提和保障。

【关键词】 社会管理　创新　法制化　政府职能

改革开放以来，伴随着大量社会财富迅速积累和人民生活水平的提高，新旧社会矛盾也日益凸显并有积聚爆发的趋势，经济社会的发展和变迁给中国社会管理带来了许多新的问题与挑战，中国开始步入社会风险高发阶段。在此背景下，2004 年党的十六届四中全会提出要"加强社会建设和管理，推进社会管理体制创新"。2007 年党的十七大报告提出要"建立健全党委领导、政府负责、社会协同、公众参与的社会管理格局"。加强社会管理、推进管理模式创新已成为构建中国社会主义和谐社会的主要任务。

一　中国的社会管理中存在的问题

社会管理的概念在理论上有狭义和广义两种内涵，狭义的观点仅将社会管理作为政府的一项职能；而广义的观点在管理主体中还包括了具有一定公共管理职能的社会组织。从社会管理的国际实践来看，广义的内涵更

---

*　中国社会科学院法学研究所副研究员。

符合实际情况，即社会管理是指政府和社会组织为促进社会系统协调运转，对社会系统的组成部分、社会生活的不同领域以及社会发展的各个环节（如社会结构、社会制度、社会事业和社会观念等）进行组织、协调、服务、监督和控制的过程。① 社会管理的基本目标在于协调社会关系、规范社会行为、解决社会问题、化解社会矛盾、促进社会公正、应对社会风险以及保持社会稳定。对中国而言，社会管理的目的还在于寻找国家利益与人民利益一致的契合点，谋求国家发展、社会稳定与公民权益保障之间的良性互动与平衡。

近些年来，伴随着市场经济的进一步发展和社会变革的深化，中国的社会管理在取得诸多成效的同时，也凸显了许多新的问题。主要体现在以下方面：

1. 社会管理理念滞后。当今时代社会急剧发展，客观上要求政府必须积极回应社会需求和公民诉求。与此相适应，政府的职能也应逐步地实现以社会管控为主到以公共服务为主的转变，由管理型政府走向服务型政府，进而实现向服务型社会的转变。但是在现实中，中国过分重视经济建设，轻视社会管理；重视强势群体权利，轻视弱势群体权利；管控思想严重，服务意识淡薄。② 这些问题的存在折射出中国社会管理观念严重落后的状况。

2. 社会管理主体严重缺位。社会管理主体多元化是社会管理成功的主要表现之一。当前中国社会管理主体很单一，目前中国政府还是社会管理的唯一主体，社会组织数量少且缺乏独立性，公众很少参与社会管理，社会自治、公民自治更是难以实现。

3. 社会管理方式单一。在社会管理方面，目前中国刚性的行政管理手段运用较多，欠缺柔性的管理手段；公民参与社会管理不够，缺乏有效的平台和途径；社会管理缺乏制度常态化；社会管理的信息和资源不够公开透明。以上原因直接导致了公民利益表达机制不完善和社会矛盾纠纷解决机制不畅通问题。

4. 社会管理法律体系不健全。社会管理缺乏完善的法律法规体系是当前中国面临的突出问题，一些涉及"民生"、推动市民社会发展、有效解决

---

① 参见孙立平《断裂：20 世纪 90 年代以来的中国社会》，社会科学文献出版社，2003，第 67 页。

② 仲伟金：《浅谈社会管理存在的问题及解决对策》，载《中国法学会行政法学研究会 2010 年年会论文集》。

社会纠纷以及规范行政程序的法律应当成为今后立法完善的重点。

当前，中国处于社会转型期，正从单一社会结构向以市场经济为基础的多元社会结构过渡。在此剧烈变革的时期，历史上长期积累起来的深层次社会问题在凸显的同时，一些新的社会问题和不确定因素也随之出现，如：社会结构、利益结构的变化，社会阶层分化，以维权为目的的社会诉求增多，价值真空引发的社会失范，等等。诸多社会问题相互交织在一起，加大了社会系统性的风险，或者说加剧了社会的脆弱性，隐含潜在的发展风险。[①] 在当前的复杂形势下旧有的社会管理体制已难以适应社会发展的需要，而前述中国社会管理中存在的问题也亟待得到有效的弥补，在此情况下实行社会管理创新已成为保障中国稳定与发展的迫切之需。

二　中国社会管理创新的价值取向及基本路径

社会管理创新，是指在现有的社会资源和管理经验的基础上，引入新的社会管理理念、知识和方法，对传统的社会管理模式及管理方法进行完善，从而建构新的社会管理机制，更好地实现社会管理目标的活动[②]。对中国而言，社会管理创新即是完善社会管理手段，实现由单一的行政手段向综合运用法律、政策、经济、行政、教育等手段转变。无论是社会管理，还是社会管理创新，都必须有相应的法律规范作为支撑和制度性保障，国家管理的运作不能脱离法制的架构，以服务社会和人权保障为主体的价值指引应当成为中国社会管理创新的基本价值目标，具体体现在以下几个方面：

（一）坚持以人为本

在社会管理中坚持以人为本，就是以满足人的需求作为发展目的，切实保障各类发展主体的经济、政治和文化权益，保障各类社会主体平等地享受社会发展成果，就是要尊重人的主体地位，充分发挥人的主动性、能动性、创新性。[③] 因此，政府及其公务人员要转变旧有的管理意识，在立法、社会政策的制定、执行，社会事务的处理等方面重视市民社会的诉求，为各种社会主体平等地参与社会事务管理创造条件、营造良好的环境。

（二）贯彻服务为民原则

"权利本位"和"社会本位"是当今时代社会管理的发展趋向，为公民

---

① 李学举：《加强社会建设和管理促进社会和谐与发展》，《求是》2005 年第 6 期。

② 应松年：《社会管理创新引论》，《法学论坛》2010 年第 6 期。

③ 鞠正江：《我国社会管理体制的历史变迁与改革》，《攀登》2009 年第 1 期。

与社会服务成为当今政府的主要责任之一。政府应该从民众的利益和社会实际需要出发，尽快实现从管制行政向服务行政的职能转型。为实现此目的，首先应对政府进行必要的限权和分权，培育多元治理主体，使市民社会的民众有可能参与社会管理和监督公权力运行；其次，应当通过立法建立一系列保障制度和正当程序，保证执政为民的理念在实践中得到真正的贯彻执行。

（三） 实现社会管理的公平正义

完善社会管理应当坚持公平优先的原则。社会管理创新的目的是解决市场经济发展中出现的一系列问题，其中包括为公民和社会团体追求各自的私人利益、群体利益提供均等的机会，以此调节利益冲突，保障公民权利和维护社会公益。贫富分化是中国存在的现实问题，政府在社会管理的立法与政策制定中要特别兼顾弱势群体的权益，通过社会保障制度实现分配正义。公平还应当体现在对公民及社会的权利保障方面，社会管理体制的创新应当以保障和增进公民权利为导向，避免因公权力扩张而限制公民权利现象的发生。

（四） 践行法律至上原则

法治作为现代文明社会的主要标志，是中国既定的社会发展方向。在法治社会里，公共权力既受法律保护，又受法律的制约，政府管理社会的行为也必须在法治的轨道内进行。在创新社会管理过程中，应当以法治思想作为基本指导原则，确立法律在社会管理中的权威性、至上性，以法律的约束力、强制力和教育作用规范政府行为，保障公民权利，实现国家与社会、公权力与私权利的良性互动与和谐统一。

（五） 实现社会管理上的公开透明

在社会管理创新中保持公开透明是创建服务政府、法治政府的必然要求，市民社会只有在及时获得政府信息的情况下才能高效的参与社会管理、维护权利和监督公权力运行。公开透明原则要求政府信息公开、服务透明，直接涉及立法、执法等与公民利益密切相关的所有事项，这能够有效减少和防止政府管理中存在的信息不畅、暗箱操作、服务水平差的顽疾。

基于对上述社会管理中基本价值的把握，在社会管理创新的发展架构及方向上，应从以下三方面问题入手：

第一，社会管理理念革新。以人为本是中国政府既定的国家治理和政府管理的价值目标，在此目标下，引发了人们对民生问题和社会公平正义的持续关注。中国几千年的官本位思想是当前社会管理创新的最大阻却和障碍。实践中，政府或其工作人员所固持的某些体制和做法对于提升人民生活质量没有作用甚至产生了反作用，僵化陈旧甚至"左"的思想仍然被一些政府主政者和理论工作者坚持着，这种不思变革的状态必然对社会管理的创新造成一系列障碍和矛盾。① 当前，政府及其工作人员进行思维转变是国家实现善治的一种必然需要。从另一个角度看，在当今时代，伴随着市民社会的兴起，公民完全成为被动受管理者的状况已成为历史，而政府常常处于被动也必然会使国家陷入危机。因此，培育和塑造社会管理新理念已成为中国政府完善社会管理、实现创新的最基本途径和保障，这些新理念包括：服务政府理念、政务公开理念、有限政府理念及公民参与理念，等等。如何将现有的政府机构从"社会管理的衙门"到"社会服务窗口"的转变体现着创建善治政府的价值追求，代表着当今时代最进步和最具人权特色的公共治理思维模式。

第二，转变政府职能与变革社会管理体制。政府的作用在于服务而非管制，这是 21 世纪公共行政的主旨精神和基本价值所在。中国的社会管理的趋向应当立足将政府从管制型政府向服务型政府职能的转变。政府职能的转变应以凸显政府的公共服务职能、建立有限政府、保障社会公平正义和维护民生为主要目标。在此基础上所进行的管理体制变革也应坚持还政于民的理念，如：明确政府的权利与义务、减少行政审批、实行政务透明、增强社会自治功能、建立利益诉求表达和协调机制、建立完善、公平的分配与社会保障机制，等等。总之，保证政府行为的民本性、公开性、有限性与规范性应成为中国完善与创新社会管理的基本目标取向。②

第三，推动市民社会发展与鼓励公民参与。既有的社会管理经验告诉我们，加快市民社会培育是创新社会管理的有效手段和重要目标。只有实现社会自治，才能真正达到社会管理的目的。市民社会组织可以在缓解国家与公民矛盾、协调利益关系、弥补政府公共服务不足等方面发挥积极的作用。③ 但是，目前中国的市民社会尚不成熟，社会组织弱小且缺乏独立性，社会协同、公众参与的社会管理格局远未形成。当前，中国政府应为推动市民社会发展和社会组织发挥作用创造良好的外部环境，保证社会组织的独立性，将其纳入合作治理的框架，充分挖掘和发挥市民社会在社会

---

① 马庆钰：《全面认识当前社会管理中的十五个矛盾》，《学习时报》2005 年第 16 期。
② 孟繁华、宫立杰：《创新政府社会管理与公共服务体制》，载《中国行政管理学会 2008 年哲学学年会论文集》。
③ 苏咏喜：《公民社会视角下的社会管理创新研究》，《四川行政学院学报》2011 年第 4 期。

管理方面的功能，形成国家与社会良性互动的关系。

三　中国社会管理创新的法制化方向

在实践中，中国的社会管理创新必须坚持以人为本、公平、透明、法治、服务等若干原则，[①] 其中法治原则是实现社会管理规范和有序进行的基本保障。西方国家的实践证明，法治秩序是一种较为稳定的社会秩序，政治国家与公民社会能够在法治框架下各司其职、各行其是，法治的社会管理能确保公民权利、公共利益，促进良善、和谐的社会管理状态的实现。[②] 推进社会管理创新的过程，只有以法治理念为指导，以法制体系、法治程序和规范为支撑，才能真正实现最佳的政治、经济和社会效益。

（一）服务型法治政府构建

从社会发展来看，中国政府要实现由防范型管理向平等型、服务型、无偿型管理转变，必须要将"国家尊重和保障人权"的宪法原则及时、充分且准确地转化为各类法律规范和制度，转化为国家机关及其工作人员切实确立和竭力践行的基本价值追求，转化为各类社会管理主体进行价值取舍和决策判断的基本行为准则。[③] 为实现这一目的，必须通过一系列法律规范予以保障。

首先，要通过完善立法实现政府行为的法定化与规范化，即建立法治政府。政府行为有法可依能够有效地防止权力交叉、公权力滥用，利于公众监督、追究行政主体责任和保障公民权益。目前而言，完善中国行政管理法律制度已刻不容缓，重点是要在以下九个方面实现法定化：政府的职能范围、机构设置、内部管理、投资行为、招标采购、工作程序、行政审批、行政收费、行政执法。[④] 其中政府职能的法制化使政府拥有的权力和权威更加科学合理，更加清晰、明确，有利于强化对政府行使公共权力的约束，扩大对普通公民参与社会管理的范围和途径。

其次，应当进一步完善程序立法。社会实践证明，程序缺失必然影响社会管理的运作，而程序公正有利于保障社会稳定。要从规范行政权运作

---

① 胡淑晶：《我国政府社会管理模式创新》，载《"构建和谐社会与深化行政管理体制改革"研讨会暨中国行政管理学会 2007 年年会论文集》。

② 付子堂：《论建构法治型社会管理模式》，《法学论坛》2011 年第 2 期。

③ 杨建顺：《优良的行政文化凝聚民心》，《观察与思考》2009 年第 10 期。

④ 孟繁华、宫立杰：《创新政府社会管理与公共服务体制》，载《中国行政管理学会 2008 年哲学年会论文集》。

和促进公众参与的角度，制定完善的行政程序法体系。

最后，适应建设服务型政府的要求，还必须进一步健全有关规范政府责任的法律法规体系，要在完善《行政诉讼法》、《行政监察法》、《行政复议法》、《政府采购法》、《公务员法》、《行政许可法》、《行政处罚法》、《国家赔偿法》等已有法律的基础上，尽快出台《行政问责法》和《行政执法责任追究条例》等法律法规。

（二） 社会管理体制创新的法制化保障

健全与优化社会管理体制，西方国家的社会管理经验启示我们，必须建立公民广泛参与、社会自治、政府协调的社会管理体制，才能真正实现现代社会保障人权和促进国家与社会协调发展的社会管理目标，其实质是建立一个社会参与管理的有限政府。其中关键在于明确政府和社会的职责，即明确公民个人、社会组织以及政府的责任。在此管理体制下，政府的规模、职能、权力和行为方式都受到社会的有效制约，在实践中应当建立健全的基本制度包括以下方面：社会管理的领导与工作、社会保障、社会服务、社会治安及应急、社团管理、社区管理等。其中最重要的是确立对社会主体的救济制度、保障决策民主与透明的法律制度，以此防止公权力滥用和维护公民权利。只有建立上述制度，市民社会的价值，即现代意义上的人权、社会生活的多元化、公民对国家的多方参与、公共领域的法治原则和公民社会自身的独立性、自主性才能得到真正的实现。[①]

为实现向服务政府的转变，在社会立法层面，还应当完善社会保障和民生领域的立法，以此强化政府的服务职能。民生问题直接关系社会稳定和政权巩固，因而成为社会管理创新的重要内容，而社会管理的核心也同样在于寻求国家与公民利益协同一致的契合点与交汇点，寻找最适合社会发展的动力机制。实践证明，民生问题的解决在于建立有效的利益协调机制、诉求表达机制、矛盾调处机制以及权益保障机制，重点应健全社会分配、社会保障、教育及就业等方面的法律法规，特别要加强涉及生存权和平等发展权等基本人权方面的立法。

此外，实行明确的分权化管理，中央与地方、政府与民选机构各司其职协同完成国家管理任务；实施社区化的社会管理，将公共组织的决策、资源和任务等实质性控制权转移给社区组织，让社区居民普遍地参与社区

---

① 吕宏强：《政府社会管理的前提及面临的问题》，《长安大学学报（社会科学版）》2005 年第 1 期。

管理，如：兴办公益事业、组织邻里互助、街道联防，以及改进社会服务等。① 但从根本上来看，能否迅速而有效地实现社会管理创新，还在于国家与政府能否真正地放权和将社会利益放在首位。

（三）　社会管理的司法协助

从宏观角度看，司法机关同样是社会管理的主体，但是其发挥作用的方式与政府机关不同，主要体现为一种事后救济。面对社会转型时期复杂的社会管理，司法机关一方面在解决纠纷中发挥着积极的作用，另一方面又在审查权力、保障权利方面发挥政治功用。

在社会管理中，行政权应受到司法权的审查和监督。司法问责具有重要的价值与作用，在司法为民的政策指引下通过司法的治理可以保障并实现政府管理方式上的转型。例如，在实践中经法院审查行政规章可以作为司法审判的依据，因此根据现实需要，可以将政府制定行政法规、行政规章的抽象行政行为纳入可诉范围，这是中国行政诉讼制度发展的必然趋势；此外，也可以先在少数部门、小范围内试行对管理者的司法监督和审查制度，将这些部门制定的政策纳入司法审查的范围，允许公众、企业和利益团体等就政府管理向法院提出诉讼；还可以设立专门的政策督察专员，处理与管理问题有关的投诉，强化管理者的行政解释责任。②

（四）　市民社会培育与社会自治的法律及制度构建

社会管理创新最主要的是实现多元主体的协调运作，培育社会组织管理主体，尊重社会自治，助推社会自律，确认并保障社会多元主体的多元价值和利益诉求③。在西方发达国家，市民社会组织始终是国家进行社会管理的基本主体，这正是中国所欠缺的。市民社会的不成熟直接影响了中国社会管理创新的进程。目前而言，培育市民社会应成为中国政府社会管理工作的主要目标和职责。当前，中国的社会空间狭小，非政府组织的发展尚处在起步阶段。在这样的状态下，市民社会的自治不能单纯依赖本身的自我发展、自我构建，急需政府的大力推动。

从立法维度看，中国立法机关应加快对社会组织的专门立法，促进社会组织更好地发挥社会功能。迄今为止，中国仅出台了《社会团体登记管理条例》、《基金会管理条例》、《民办非企业单位登记管理暂行条例》等几

---

① 岳世平：《西方社会管理的成功经验》，《党政论坛》2011年第1期。
② 王伟：《公众参与在社会管理中的实践及在社会稳定中的作用》，载《第19届中国社会学年会社会稳定与社会管理机制研究论文集》（2009年）。
③ 参见杨建顺《行政规制与权利保障》，中国人民大学出版社，2007，第171页。

部管理条例，最基本的法律，如社团法、商会法、行业协会法、公共服务组织法等都尚未出台，这显然已不能适应国家实施社会管理创新的现实需要。此外，在研究制定社会组织管理方面法律法规时，应当整合村民委员会、居民委员会、社区等社会管理基层组织的法律属性、职能和权限，为村民自治、社区自治奠定法律基础。

培育市民社会和推动社会自治的一个主要途径是建立公民参与的法律制度，从国内外社会管理的经验来看，公众参与社会管理已成为时代发展的必然要求。

首先，行政立法和作出公共决策应当允许公众参与，政府要完善立法听证、广泛听取社会意见制度（如社情民意反映制度、专家咨询制度等等），尤其是立法的内容涉及限制公民的权利或牵涉利益的情况。

其次，要健全行政执法中公民参与的保障制度，如：申辩与质证制度、说明理由制度、资讯公开制度等，尽快出台《公民参与程序法》以保障公民参与权的实现。

最后，应当完善行政监督救济制度，可以尝试建构起规范化的行政怨情处理制度和人大监督专员制度①。在现有的"两会"组织不能够充分反映民意的情况下，可以借鉴俄罗斯的做法，在"两会"组织机构之外成立一个类似社会院的组织机构，囊括各领域的民意代表，为社会管理的政策制定与立法提供建议和反馈，以此实现国家意志与社会意志的二元互动。

此外，还可通过建立与完善一系列的信息立法，如：《电子签名法》、《电子投票法》、《电子网络监督法》、《个人信息保护法》、《互联网信息服务管理办法》和《信息网络传播权保护条例》等法律、法规，建立社会管理的网络参与制度。通过网络平台公民可以足不出户参与下列的社会管理活动：在政策的起草阶段在网上表达观点和发表建议；及时地监督政策执行情况并反馈意见；在网上投票评价社会管理政策的绩效。网络信息平台能够极大地降低管理成本，使更多的公民及社会组织参与到政府社会管理活动中来，进而促进决策的科学化与民主化。

在上述社会管理创新制度法制化设计过程中应致力于解决三方面问题：

第一，社会管理理念滞后问题。如：政府可以在行政系统内通过制定转变管理理念的宣传教育政策和规划提升公务人员的服务意识；通过严格

---

① 莫于川、郭庆珠：《论现代服务行政与服务行政法——以我国服务行政法律体系建构为重点》，《法学杂志》2007 年第 2 期。

责任追究制强化执法者的责任意识。

第二，社会管理主体缺位问题。在社会管理立法中密切关注社会力量介入制度的设计，使公民个体、社会组织、社区及村民自治组织有参与社会管理、监督法制运行和维护权利的合法依据。

第三，社会管理方式单一问题。在行政手段之外，立法中国家应充分发挥社会政策、经济杠杆、宣传教育在社会管理方面的作用。如：可以实行市场化的社会管理，通过立法和招标鼓励民间组织或企业履行管理职能；还可通过全民教育规划培育公民的权利维护和参与管理意识。

社会管理是个极其复杂的系统性工程，不可能一蹴而就，中国的社会管理创新依然任重而道远。从中国目前的情况来看，社会管理创新的实践要达到应有的绩效显然还存在诸多的困难。市民社会的欠发达和落后的管理体制的变革都需要一个过程，公民权利意识、参与意识的增强以及政府服务意识的转变在短期内也难以实现，传统习惯与势力对社会管理改革产生阻碍作用亦不容忽视。我们必须结合中国国情和实际，稳步推进社会管理法制化的进程，逐步推进社会管理主体、管理方式、管理体制方面的变革，逐步完成从一元到多元、从管制到服务、从人治到法治、从集权到分权的过渡和转换。

The Rule-of-Law Approach to Innovation in Social Management

Liu Hongyan

【**Abstract**】Since entering into a period of social transition, China has been met with more and more social demands and numerous social risks caused by social anomie and the absence of traditional culture. Increasingly complicated social problems indicate that China must abandon the traditional mode of social management characterized mainly by control and explore a new social management mode that is based on the reality in China, takes servicing society and the people as its value orientation, and adheres to the principle of transparency and the rule of law. In the institutional design, the transformation of government function, the cultivation of civil society, and the construction of an equitable and reasonable environment for the rule of law and an honest society should be the basic precondition and safeguard of innovation in social management.

【**Key words**】 Social Management, Innovation, Construction of the Rule of Law, Transformation of Government Function

法治视野下社会管理的路径分析

罗斌飞[*]

【摘要】"法治"是一个开放的概念,有着丰富的内涵,而社会管理是随着社会的发展和人们法律意识的不断增强、法治实践经验的不断丰富,而"与时俱进"地发展变化。两者之间存在相辅相成、相互制约、相互包含的逻辑关系。当前社会管理存在职能的迟缓性、权威的弱化性、手段的滞后性、利益的局限性等突出问题。要形成一种长效的社会管理模式,就必须实现社会管理的法治化,即社会管理的主体以法治理念为基点、社会管理的措施以法治手段为依据、社会管理的职能以法治原则为界限、社会管理的过程以法治程序为始终、社会管理的责任以法治监督为保障、社会管理的成效以法治价值为评估。

【关键词】法治　社会管理

法治对于人类社会来说既是一个现实,也是一个理想。当今世界存在许许多多的"法治国家"或"法治社会",都努力在国家和社会管理中贯彻法治原则和精神。但是,任何一个国家都不能说它已经建成法治国家或法治社会,因为,法治理想的许多方面都还没有成为现实,都还需要我们一代又一代人前赴后继地努力,以便最终能够真正使每一个人的基本权利和自由都能得到切实的保障和最大限度的实现。

一　法治与社会管理

(一)法治与社会管理的基本内涵

所谓法治,即法律的统治,又称契约之治。法治思想起源于西方社会,

＊　江西警察学院副教授。

发端于亚里士多德《政治学》中的名言："已成立的法律获得普遍的遵从，普遍遵从的法律本身应该是制定得良好的法律。"从法治理论形成和制度发展的角度上理解，注重的是法治在保护人权和防止权力滥用方面的作用；但如果将法治作为一种治国方略去探究，则是注重法治在实现国家秩序或社会治安方面的作用。在实现法治的过程中，观念的更新就成为不容忽视的问题。尤其在建设中国特色社会主义市场经济体制过程中，必须明确地倡导法治并排除人治的影响。如果否定了法律至上，而是突出了立法者或执法者的至上性，则是对法治全面的曲解，对市场经济体制的改革也必然起到巨大的阻碍作用。狭义的社会管理，指政府和社会组织为促进社会系统协调运转，对社会系统的组成部分、社会生活的不同领域以及社会发展的各个环节进行组织、协调、监督和控制的过程。广义的社会管理，是指由社会成员组成专门机构对社会的经济、政治和文化事务进行的统筹管理。

本文所讲的社会管理，是中国特色社会主义经济建设、政治建设、文化建设、社会建设四位一体总体格局中的社会建设的一个重要组成部分，它是指以维系社会秩序为核心，通过政府主导、多方参与、规范社会行为、协调社会关系、促进社会认同、秉持社会公正、解决社会问题、化解社会矛盾、维护社会治安、应对社会风险，为人类社会生存和发展创造既有秩序又有活力的基础运行条件和社会环境，促进社会和谐的活动。

（二）法治与社会管理的逻辑关系

法治与社会管理是一种相辅相成的关系，如果没有法治赋予社会管理的具体内容，社会管理就缺乏合法性；如果没有法治指导社会管理的基本原则，社会管理就缺乏公平性。但是，法治没有社会管理的内容和人们遵守的自觉性，也将缺乏孕育的土壤。一个现代的法治理念通常可以形成长效的社会管理制度和模式。反之，社会管理可能会带有极大的随意性，缺乏法律的形式也可能发挥效用，但会丧失社会管理所具有的稳定性、规范性、权威性和可预测性等。只要两者相辅相成，才能增进"法治国家"的进度。

法治与社会管理是一种相互制约的关系，法治既要求依法办事，又要求所依之法必须为良法，并且该良法能得到普遍遵循，这样既体现法律的至上性，也体现法律的正义性和公平性。而社会管理依据的法律可以是良法，也可以是恶法，其实质是要求国家机关和公民对已颁布的法律，无论良法或恶法，均应服从。社会管理仅在形式上确立了法律的至上性，却不顾及法律的来源及法律是否符合正义原则，是否能够得到人们的普遍遵从。

只有两者相互制约，才能共同体现法律的至上性与正义性。

法治与社会管理是一种相互包含的关系，法治既要求社会管理合乎形式的正义，又要求社会管理合乎实质的正义。形式正义只是指社会管理能够得到公正和一贯的执行，而不管其价值内核是否合乎正义原则；实质正义则是要求支撑社会管理制度本身所依据的原则合乎正义标准。当然，社会管理也只有合乎形式正义且合乎实质正义，才称得上是长效的管理模式。但是，人们对正义的定义与理解是不尽一致的，且通常包括对人们自身的安全、平等、自由和效率的需要，故在通常情况下，社会管理应能够充分发挥保障安全、维护平等、促进自由、增进效率的功能。正是因为法治对社会管理的要求，使两者存在相互包含的关系。

二　当前社会管理面临的突出问题

1. 社会管理职能的迟缓性

一些地方和部门管理体制机制老化，机构运作迟钝和麻木，职能转变和职责内容更新迟缓，社会管理方法陈旧，负有执行法律和政令责任的机关单位治理能力退化。不仅对于社会矛盾和冲突不能有效疏导，甚至连正常的社会管理职能和协调职能都难以发挥。一些部门对社会违法现象不闻不问或出于地方或部门利益的动机，对违法现象保驾护航，成为利益集团的工具，甚至黑恶势力的保护伞。近年来披露的黑煤窑非法经营、黑砖窑奴工事件等，均不同程度地反映出一些地方的社会管理危机及其严重程度。

2. 社会管理权威的弱化性

一些地方和部门的管理体系作为国家公权力的权威性和公信力急剧弱化。公共管理的权威被削弱后，社会管理领域出现权威空白，给一些社会势力乘势获利提供了机会，形成非正式的管理力量。这些势力违法乱纪，甚至以种种手段攫取一些社会群体维权的主导权，向法律公开挑战。而政府机构公信力弱化，更是对社会管理有效性的瓦解。公信力不足意味着社会公众对政府的信任度降低，不仅直接影响党和政府的号召力，更导致政府机构在社会管理过程中管理绩效的降低和解决社会问题困难的增大。

3. 社会管理手段的滞后性

体制转型中新旧体制过渡的磨合以及公共管理体制改革与法律推进的不完全同步，对社会管理产生负面影响。转型期的社会管理承担着推进自身变革与发挥保障社会秩序作用的双重任务，新旧体制机制的过渡交替，不可避免地产生一些社会管理上的空当和摩擦，从而降低社会管理能力。

在体制变革和法律变革的关系上,经常出现的是,一方面新的法律不断制定和通过,法律文件越来越多,表面上给人以法制不断健全的印象,但另一方面由于管理体制机制的改革通常滞后于法律文件的更新,特别是政府职能转变是一个极为复杂的过程,更多地受到既定体制、利益结构以及公务员素质的影响和支配,很难与法律变革保持完全同步,因而必然出现社会管理现实与新的法律理念的落差。进而更提出了加快社会管理体制机制创新的迫切性和必要性。

4. 社会管理利益的局限性

某些社会管理单位利用体制改革不到位的漏洞成为利益实体,而利益实体必然追求部门的利益,部门利益往往最终演变为私人利益,将公权变私利,出现权力性质的蜕变。这种现象势必影响社会管理过程中社会公正的实现,成为影响社会管理的最大制约因素。现实中,一些部门利益本身就是社会问题产生和蔓延的病灶和源头,因而更加突出了社会管理体制机制改革的重要性。

三 法治视野下社会管理的路径分析

加强和创新社会管理的关键环节是着力改革和创新社会管理的有关体制机制。只有在法治视野下建立社会管理体制机制,才能形成一种长效的社会管理模式。社会管理体制是国家和人们为了维护社会秩序而用以规范和协调社会组织、社会事务和社会生活的一系列制度和机制,包括规范社会管理主体、厘清社会管理措施、创新社会管理内容、完善社会管理过程、追究社会管理责任、评估社会管理成效等。通过对社会管理的法治化,可以最大限度地实现社会管理的根本目的,使人民群众的合法权益得到最大限度的维护,使人人都享受和谐状态。

(一) 以法治理念为基点,实现社会管理主体的多元性

法治理念是治理国家的一种理念,是指在社会管理中依照相关良性法律进行治理。而社会管理的目的是依法实现保障公民的权益,即社会公权力如何为社会服务。下面从社会管理的几个主体进行分析:首先,政府官员作为社会管理活动的主要主体,其法治理念的强弱,直接决定着其依法管理、依法行政的水平。政府官员弘扬法治观念,对于完善社会管理格局,提高社会管理水平具有重要作用。比如,我国有些官员在权力运行时存在暗箱化和不规范化现象,往往觉察不到法律的存在,有的甚至以为法律就是自己治理社会的工具,对自己有利时,就搬出来用一下,对自己不利时,

就搁在一边。长此以往，必然造成某些官员法律意识、法治理念的淡薄和缺失。为此，政府官员要自觉弘扬法治精神，在社会管理中坚持依法管理、科学管理，切切实实地把人民放在首要位置，坚持以人为本。其次是社会组织，根据我国社会组织管理的现行法规，可以将我国的社会组织分为三大类，即社会团体、基金会和民办非企业单位。社会组织所具有的民间性、公益性、自发性、自愿性、自律性等特点，使社会组织在政府和社会、政府和企业、企业和社会之间，以及在党、政府与公众、企业与公众、各种不同公众之间，搭建了一个沟通、合作的桥梁。这些特点和功能赋予了社会组织独特的协同优势。充分发挥各类社会组织，尤其是人民团体、行业协会、社会中介组织提供服务、反映诉求、规范行为等方面的作用，是健全社会管理体制，有效配置社会资源，优化公共服务，满足社会多方需求的必要途径，也是增强社会自治，促进社会和谐的有效措施。最后是公众，公众参与社会管理又包括以社会组织成员的身份参与和以单个公民身份参与这两种方式。社会组织具有共同的利益和目标，组织化程度较高。一般来说，以社会组织方式参与比以个体方式参与，社会影响力更大，提出的意见更加集中、理性，也更具代表性，更易于得到政府回应，因此参与实效也就更强，公众参与应更加重视这种方式。以个体方式参加社会管理主要通过以下几种渠道：听证会、论证会、座谈会、咨询会、慈善事业、公益活动、社会公示、意见征求、问卷调查、信访、报刊、互联网等。

（二）以法治手段为依据，实现社会管理措施的规范性

社会管理的措施包括运用政策、法律、经济、行政等手段，采用教育、协商、调解、司法等方法。但在现实当中，社会管理的目的表现为发展，法治只是发展的手段之一。为了发展，法治手段好用和有效，就用法治手段，法治手段"不好用"、"不奏效"，就弃法治而用其他手段。由于这一认识误区，一些地方的官员在推动所在地区经济、社会发展的过程中，特别是在推动经济发展的过程中，往往以法治手段"不好用"、"不奏效"为由，漠视法治乃至践踏法治。[①] 比如，2011 年年初，国务院颁布的《国有土地上房屋征收与补偿条例》，明令禁止采取暴力、威胁或违法断水、断热、断气、断电、断路等非法方式强制拆迁，但一些地方官员为了确保项目进展，仍违法强拆、暴力强拆，严重侵害了被拆迁人的合法权益。当然，法治也并非是社会管理的唯一模式，法治手段并非十全十美，也有其固有的缺陷。

---

① 姜明安：《发展、改革、创新与法治》，《中共中央党校学报》2011 年第 8 期。

但是，与其他的管理手段相比，法治手段是透明度最高、社会成本最低、最容易让人接受的方式。① 只有通过法治手段的社会管理，社会管理措施的法治化，才能确保公民权利的实现与公共利益的和谐，才能形成社会管理的长效机制。为此，社会管理的措施应建立法治手段的主导作用。

（三）以法治原则为界限，实现社会管理职能的目的性

法治意味着社会管理的职能都必须遵循法律规则，并且给人们的行为提供有效的指引。社会管理的职能主要体现在以下几方面，即规范社会行为、协调社会关系、促进社会认同、秉持社会公正、解决社会问题、化解社会矛盾、维护社会治安、应对社会风险等。然而社会管理的职能失去了法治原则也将失去管理的权威和效果，因为没有法治原则的社会管理只是代表少数人的阶级利益，是一种形式的正义，不是形式和实质正义的统一体。比如规范社会行为，如果没有法治原则的界限，这种社会管理只能是对管理对象的管理，而对社会管理的主体将会偏袒和庇护，失去社会管理的正义，最终社会管理将走向"人治"。因此，社会管理职能在法治原则下，首先，应体现法律面前人人平等，即相同的情形，应以相同的方法处理，除非法律另有规定，否则不应在司法过程中因为种族、肤色、宗教、信仰、财富、地位或势力等原因而歧视或偏袒任何人。要求所有公民都同样享有获得律师服务的权利，使他们在法律上的权益得到充分的保障。其次，人们最基本的权利和自由得到保障和维护，人权和自由不受侵犯，并且通过积极的努力来促进人的基本权利和自由的实现。最后，要求刑法必须"罪刑法定"和"无罪推定"。

（四）以法治程序为始终，实现社会管理过程的正义性

法治程序意味着程序正义。程序正义对一个法治社会来说，是一个必不可少的法律原则。社会管理程序上的保障对维护法律的尊严和权威是非常重要的，它的目的是使政府机关及其工作人员的办事程序和办事方法更加合乎公平、正义的要求。比如，法治社会的一个重要的程序原则，就是政府不应毫无预兆地做出一个不利于某个公民的决定，去剥夺他的人身自由或其他权益，除非它预先通知这个公民，告诉他政府准备做出这个决定，并给他机会去替自己辩护，提出反对这个决定的理由。社会管理的法治程序主要体现在社会管理的立法、执法和司法过程中。社会管理过程的立法是法治的一个首要环节，制定完备和良善的法律是进行法治建设的前提和

---

① 付子堂:《构建法治型社会管理模式》,《检察风云》2011 年第 10 期。

基础。如果没有经过严格立法程序出台的社会管理方面的法律或规范性法律文件，将不能作为社会管理过程中的法律依据，否则实施的社会管理行为是违法的。社会管理过程的执法是法治的中间环节，不仅体现出国家的权威性和强制性，还体现出执法的主动性和单一方面性。在社会管理的执法过程中，如果没有程序上的公平、公正，将会使人们的基本权利和自由受到不法伤害，诸如生命和财产等权利的非法侵犯和破坏。社会管理过程的司法是法治的重要环节，不仅体现出司法的合法与平等，还要体现出司法的独立与责任。如果社会管理的司法缺乏法治程序，将会使"法秩序"失衡，人为使社会发生骚乱，"法秩序"必然要受到损害。

（五）以法治监督为保障，实现社会管理责任的制度性

法治监督是指对国家机关及其工作人员是否合法正确地行使职权所进行的监督与控制。法治监督意味着"以权力制约权力"，目的就是要对社会管理的权力进行有效的监督和制约，使各种社会管理权力既相对独立又相互制衡，防止社会管理权力的异化。这样既能充分地利用社会管理的权力促进和保障公民权利，又能防止社会管理的权力滥用和腐败，保证国家机关和工作人员正确行使权力，把人民赋予的权力真正用来为人民谋利益。如果没有法治来规制社会管理中应承担的责任，就有可能滥用权力，产生腐败。要防止权力滥用和保证权力正确行使的基本措施就是建立结构合理、配置科学、程序严密、制约有效、监督有力的权力运行机制，把决策、执行等环节的权力全部纳入监督制约机制之中，保证权力沿着制度化、法律化的轨道运行。加强对权力的监督和制约的方法和途径是多样的，最重要的是保证各个监督系统的整体协调和依法进行，必须实现监督工作的法制化，健全监督法制。要树立权力接受监督制约的观念，必须全面贯彻分工负责、互相配合、互相制约的宪法原则，反对重配合、轻制约的做法，反对排斥监督的专横主义。对于一个法治社会来说，仅有一套完美的法律是不够的。如果负责解释和适用法律的司法机关和人员不能独立于行政机关，偏袒政府或某一种势力，或依照他们的指示判案，或者不遵守司法工作的职业道德标准，那么用法治来规范社会管理权力、限制社会管理权力的理想就无法实现。

（六）以法治价值为评估，实现社会管理成效的明显性

法治价值是指在作为客体的法律与作为主体的人的关系中，法律对一定主体需要的满足状况以及由此所产生的人对法律性状、属性和作用的评价。然而在社会管理中，法治价值主要体现为两种，即法律的形式价值

和法律的目的价值。形式价值是指法律自身所具有的价值因素，应当值得肯定的、好的品质。目的价值是指法律所追求的社会目的和社会理想。为此，社会管理的成效要以上述两种价值为评估标准，确保所有人的价值和尊严的实现。社会管理应该确立一种信念，即相信一切良性法治的基础；应该实践一种目的，即每一个人都应该得到尊重和关怀，无论他或她是谁，无论他或她做过些什么，不分种族、肤色、宗教、性别、收入、阶级、地位、职业或其他特点；应该实现一种理想，即创造和维持一套原则、规则、程序和机构，以保障每个人的权益，防止它受到政府或其他人的侵犯，使每个人都有机会过一种合乎人权尊严的生活；应该实现一种转变，即在社会管理中应以公民为本位，树立服务和责任意识，完成"权力本位"向"责任本位"的转变，以规范公权力运行来保障公民基本权利的实现，社会管理的价值取向是要将维持社会秩序的理念，转变到更深层次地以维护人民群众利益作为社会管理的核心价值。

参考文献

1. 《中共中央总书记、国家主席、中央军委主席胡锦涛在省部级主要领导干部社会管理及其创新专题研讨班开班式的重要讲话》。
2. 姜明安：《发展、改革、创新与法治》，《中共中央党校学报》2011 年第 8 期。
3. 中共天津市委党校第 81 期进修一班"民生与社会建设"课题组：《当前社会管理体制创新的意义、内容及实践》，2011 年 6 月。
4. 付子堂：《构建法治型社会管理模式》，《检察风云》2011 年第 10 期。
5. 陆敏菊：《法治内涵再探讨》。

Approaches to Social Management: an Analysis from the Perspective of the Rule of Law

Luo Binfei

【**Abstract**】 The rule of law is an open concept with a rich connotation whereas social management evolves with the development of society, the continuous enhancement of people's legal consciousness and the enrichment of people's experience of the rule of law. The two form a logical relationship of being supplementary to each other, checking and balancing each other, and encompassing each other. Currently the most prominent problems in social management include the tardiness in the performance of functions, the weakening of authority, the backwardness of methods, and the localization of interest. In order to development an effective and lasting social management mode, it is necessary to bring social management into the orbit of the rule of law. Namely, subjects of social management must take the idea of the rule of law as their base point, measures of social management must take legal methods as its basis, functions of social management must take legal principles as their boundary, processes of social management must take legal procedures as their starting and end points, responsibilities of social management must take legal supervision as the safeguards, and assessment of social management must take legal values as its criteria.

【**Key words**】 the Rule of Law, Social Management

后　　记

对大部分国人而言，芬兰是一个既陌生又熟悉的国度。芬兰被誉为"千湖之国"，人口五百余万，有四分之一的国土处在北极圈内，是一个"遥远"的北欧国家；但是，闻名遐迩的圣诞老人村、几乎尽人皆知的芬兰桑拿浴、伟大的音乐家西贝柳斯以及其独特的历史文化传统，又使国人对芬兰这个千湖之国有种似曾相识的感觉。

芬兰虽然地处北欧，人口和国土面积与中国不可同日而语，但芬兰独特的历史文化、社会结构和法律制度，使得芬兰成为经济发达、社会和谐、政治昌明、法治完善的国家。特别是其不同于一般西方国家的政治体制和法律理念，为中芬的法学交流提供了得天独厚的背景和基础。

"志合者，不以山海为远。"对法治文明的共同追求，使我们走到一起。2009年，在双方努力下，中国社会科学院和芬兰科学院在北京共同举办了第一届中芬比较法研讨会，开启了中国和芬兰法学界的大规模学术交流。自那时起，在双方科学院的大力支持下，中国社会科学院法学研究所和芬兰赫尔辛基大学法学院等芬方机构在相互平等、彼此尊重的基础上密切合作，每年轮流在中芬举办比较法研讨会，共同研讨法治问题，至今已举办了四届，取得了丰硕成果。

现在呈现给读者的是2010年、2011年分别在赫尔辛基和北京举办的第二、三届研讨会的优秀成果。两次研讨会均围绕法治的理论和实践问题展开研讨，具体议题既有法治的重要理论问题，如法治价值、法治模式、法治变迁等，也有重要的法治实践课题，如宪法实施、社会管理、行政法治、刑事司法等。通过交流研讨，中芬学者分享了彼此法治建设的经验，加深了对彼此法治道路的理解，提升了对彼此法治发展的信心。

在论文集即将出版之际，首先要感谢中国社会科学院和芬兰科学院对中芬比较法项目的支持，没有当年项目的启动就不会有今天中芬法学交流的成果。感谢芬兰赫尔辛基大学法学院、拉普兰大学法学院、图尔库大学法学院的支持和参与，特别是赫尔辛基大学法学院院长 Kimmo Nuotio 教授的大力支持和努力，他也为本书写了深刻而生动的序言。在本书编辑出版过程中，中国社会科学院国际法研究所李西霞女士、芬兰赫尔辛基大学法学院陈一峰博士做了许多联络和编辑工作；社会科学文献出版社刘骁军编辑为本书的出版做了许多努力，对他们的贡献谨致谢忱。要特别感谢本书的作者和译者，没有他们的智识和参与，本书的出版是不可能的。

最后想说明的是，尽管我们做了很大努力，由于本书成果时间跨度较大，作者分布广泛，本书编辑过程中内容和技术上定有疏漏和错误，敬请读者不吝指正。

李　林　谢增毅

2013 年 4 月于北京沙滩北街

Postscript

To most Chinese people, Finland is a both strange and familiar country: on the one hand, it is a far away Nordic country known as "the land of thousands of lakes", with a population of only a little more than 5 million and with one fourth of its territory located inside the Arctic Circle; but on the other hand, the Santa Claus Village, the Finnish Sauna, the great musician Jean Sibelius, and the unique historical and cultural tradition of Finland are all well known in China.

Although Finland is a Nordic country very different from China in terms of size and population, its unique historical culture, social structure and legal system have made it a country with advanced economy, harmonious society, and democratic political system based on the rule of law. Especially the Finnish political system and legal ideas, which are different from those of other western countries, provide a unique background and basis for the legal exchange between China and Finland.

As an ancient Chinese saying goes: "Nothing can separate people with common goals and ideals, not even mountains and seas", the pursuit of the common goal of the rule of law has brought together the legal scholars from China and Finland. In 2009, as a result of the concerted efforts of the Chinese Academy of Social Sciences (CASS) and the Academy of Finland, the first Sino-Finnish Seminar on Comparative Law was held in Beijing, marking the beginning of a large-scale cooperation between the Chinese and Finnish law circles. From then on, with the strong support from the two academies and on the basis of the principles of equality and mutual respect, the Institute of Law and the Law Faculty of Helsinki University have carried out close cooperation in academic exchange by taking turns to host annual Sino-Finnish Seminar on Comparative Law, held in China and in Finland alternately, to discuss various issues of the rule of law. Up to now, they have already organized four such seminars, which have produced fruitful results.

This book presents the results of the second and the third Sino-Finnish seminars on comparative law, in both of which Chinese and Finnish legal scholars had carried out discussions on important theoretical and practical issues of the rule of law, including the value, the mode and the evolution of the rule of law, the implementation of the constitution, social management, the rule of administrative law and criminal justice. Through these seminars, Chinese and Finnish scholars have shared their experiences of construction of the rule of law, deepened their understanding of the different approaches to the rule of law, and increased their confidence in the development of the rule of law, in each other's countries.

On the occasion of the publication of this collection of papers, we would like to express our sincere thanks to the following organizations and individuals: CASS and the Academy of Finland, their support to this project have been crucial to the achievements we have made in the academic exchange between Chinese and Finnish law circles; the Faculty of Law of University of Helsinki, the Law School of University of Lapland and the Law School of University of Turku, which have energetically supported and actively participated in the project, and especially Professor Kimmo Nuotio, Dean of the Faculty of Law of University of Helsinki, who has written an eloquent and thought-provoking preface for this book; Ms. Li Xixia from Institute of Law, CASS and Dr. Chen Yifeng from the Law Faculty of the University of Helsinki, who have undertaken a large amount of liaison and editing work for this book; Mr. Liu Xiaojun, an editor from Social Sciences Academic Press, who has made great efforts for the publication of this book; and, last but not least, the authors and translators of the papers in this book, without whose wisdoms and participation the publication of this book would not be possible.

Finally we would like to point out that, due to the large time span covered by the book and the wide distribution of its authors, omissions and errors, both in terms of content and in terms of technique, are inevitable in our editing work, despite the tremendous efforts we have made, and readers are sincerely invited to help us correct any such omissions and errors.

Li Lin, Xie Zengyi
Shatan Beijie, Beijing
April 2013

图书在版编目（CIP）数据

法治发展与法治模式：中国与芬兰的比较/李林主编.
— 北京：社会科学文献出版社，2013.6
（中国法治论坛）
ISBN 978 - 7 - 5097 - 4600 - 4

Ⅰ.①法…　Ⅱ.①李…　Ⅲ.①法制 - 对比研究 -
中国、芬兰　Ⅳ.①D920.0②D953.1

中国版本图书馆 CIP 数据核字（2013）第 097764 号

·中国法治论坛·

法治发展与法治模式：中国与芬兰的比较

主　　编／李　林
副 主 编／谢增毅

出 版 人／谢寿光
出 版 者／社会科学文献出版社
地　　址／北京市西城区北三环中路甲 29 号院 3 号楼华龙大厦
邮政编码／100029

责任部门／社会政法分社　（010）59367156　　　责任编辑／张慧强　关晶焱
电子信箱／shekebu@ ssap. cn　　　　　　　　责任校对／岳爱华
项目统筹／刘骁军　　　　　　　　　　　　　　责任印制／岳　阳
经　　销／社会科学文献出版社市场营销中心　（010）59367081　59367089
读者服务／读者服务中心　（010）59367028

印　　装／北京季蜂印刷有限公司
开　　本／787mm×1092mm　1/16　　　　　　印　　张／40
版　　次／2013 年 6 月第 1 版　　　　　　　　字　　数／691 千字
印　　次／2013 年 6 月第 1 次印刷
书　　号／ISBN 978 - 7 - 5097 - 4600 - 4
定　　价／148.00 元

本书如有破损、缺页、装订错误，请与本社读者服务中心联系更换
△ 版权所有　翻印必究